Boer Invasion of Natal ...uiuiana

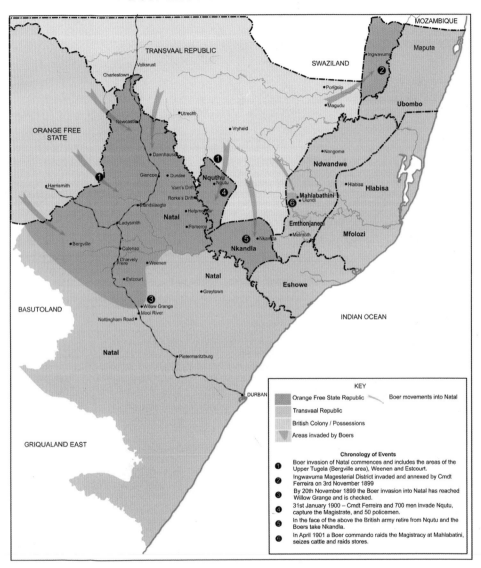

KEY

Orange Free State Republic	Boer movements into Natal
Transvaal Republic	
British Colony / Possessions	
Areas invaded by Boers	

Chronology of Events

1. Boer invasion of Natal commences and includes the areas of the Upper Tugela (Bergville area), Weenen and Estcourt.
2. Ingwavuma Magesterial District invaded and annexed by Cmdt Ferreira on 3rd November 1899
3. By 20th November 1899 the Boer invasion into Natal has reached Willow Grange and is checked.
4. 31st January 1900 – Cmdt Ferreira and 700 men invade Nqutu, capture the Magistrate, and 50 policemen.
5. In the face of the above the British army retire from Nqutu and the Boers take Nkandla.
6. In April 1901 a Boer commando raids the Magistracy at Mahlabatini, seizes cattle and raids stores.

The High-Water Mark of the Boer Invasions, 1899

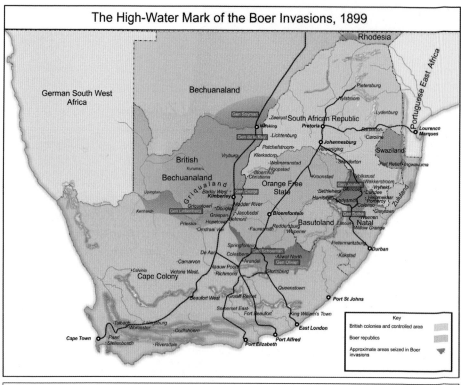

Significant Battles, 1899–1901

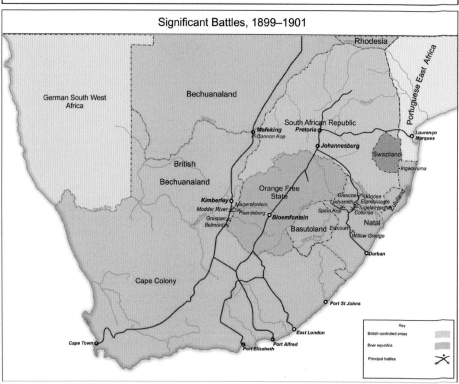

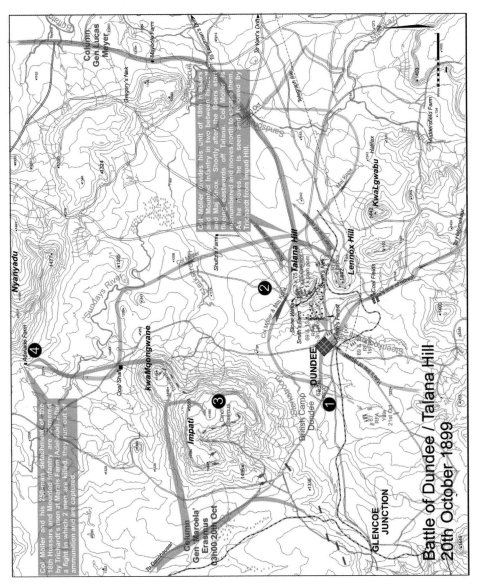

Battle of Dundee / Talana Hill
20th October 1899

See key and blown-up view overleaf

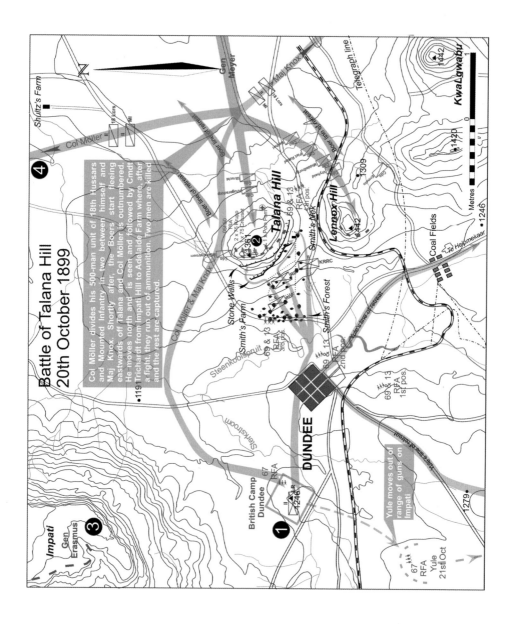

Battle of Talana Hill
20th October 1899

Col Möller divides his 500-man unit of 18th Hussars and Mounted Infantry in two between himself and Maj Knox. Shortly after, the Boers start fleeing eastwards off Talana and Col Möller is outnumbered. He moves north and is seen and followed by Cmdt Trichardt from Impati Hill to Adelaide Farm where, after a fight, they run out of ammunition. Two men are killed and the rest are captured.

Yule moves out of range of guns on Impati

iv

Battle of Dundee / Talana Hill

1 At first light on the 20th October, the British garrison at Dundee comes under fire from a Boer commando which has occupied positions on Talana Hill, just outside the town. Royal Artillery batteries quickly respond, flaying the Boer positions and causing hundreds of the republicans to flee in panic.

2 Despite coming under heavy rifle fire, the Tommies of the 8th Infantry Brigade storm the Boer positions, fighting their way forward, capturing the hill and sending the republicans fleeing eastwards.

3 The Boer commando on Impati Hill makes no effort to intervene.

4 However, an attempt by British mounted troops under Colonel Möller to cut off the retreating republicans, sees Möller's small force isolated by this commando and forced to surrender.

KEY

British Forces

Overall Command: Lt-Gen Penn Symons
Brig-Gen Yule

KRRC	King's Royal Rifle Corps
RDF	Royal Dublin Fusiliers
RIF	Royal Irish Fusiliers
LR	Leicestershire Regiment
18th Hus	18th Hussars
RDFMI	Royal Dublin Fusiliers Mounted Infantry

Boer Forces

Overall Command: Gen Meyer
Gen Erasmus

Bethel	Bethel Commando
Ermelo	Ermelo Commando
Krugersdorp	Krugersdorp Commando
Middelburg	Middelburg Commando
Piet Retief	Piet Retief Commando
Utrecht	Utrecht Commando
Vryheid	Vryheid Commando
Wakkerstroom	Wakkerstroom Commando

Artillery

Royal Field Artillery
69 and 13 Batteries
67 Battery

British movements
British defensive positions

Transvaal State Artillery

Boer movements
Boer defensive positions
Boer Hospital

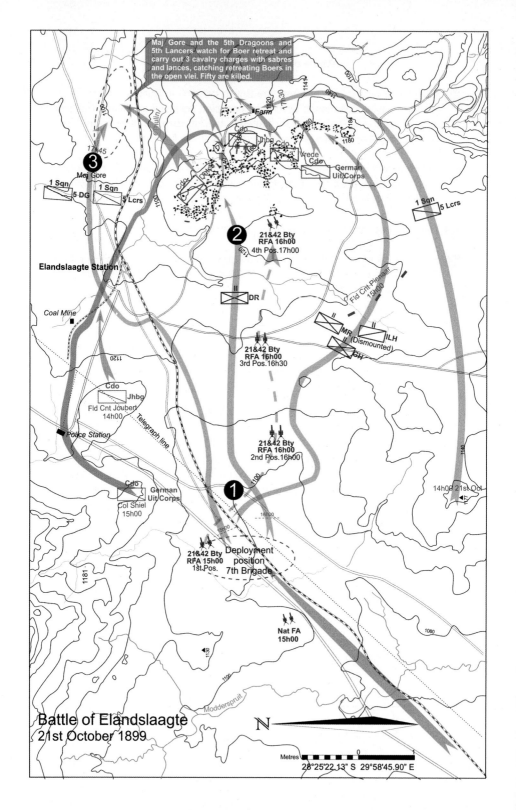

Maj Gore and the 5th Dragoons and 5th Lancers watch for Boer retreat and carry out 3 cavalry charges with sabres and lances, catching retreating Boers in the open vlei. Fifty are killed.

❸

Maj Gore

1 Sqn | 1 Sqn
5 DG | 5 Lcrs

Farm

Cdo
Jhbg Cdo
Vrede
Cdo
German Uit Corps

1 Sqn | 5 Lcrs

❷ 21&42 Bty RFA 16h00
4th Pos. 17h00

Elandslaagte Station

DR

Fld Cnt Pienaar 15h00

MR (Dismounted)
ILH
CH

Coal Mine

21&42 Bty RFA 16h00
3rd Pos. 16h30

Cdo
Jhbg
Fld Cnt Joubert 14h00

Telegraph line

Police Station

21&42 Bty RFA 16h00
2nd Pos. 16h00

Cdo
German Uit Corps
Col Shiel 15h00

❶

14h00 21st Oct

Deployment position 7th Brigade

21&42 Bty RFA 15h00
1st Pos.

Nat FA 15h00

Battle of Elandslaagte
21st October 1899

N

Modderspruit

Metres
0

28°25'22.13" S   29°58'45.90" E

Battle of Elandslaagte

1 The Tommies of the 7th Infantry Brigade commence their attack at 1530 hours on the 21st October with the Devons mounting a frontal assault, and the Gordons, Manchesters and Imperial Light Horse attacking from the flank. Two RA batteries provide support.

2 The Devons are forced to ground about 800 yards short of the Boer positions, but the flank attack pushes home, seizing the hill.

3 As the republicans stream away in disorganized retreat, a squadron each of the 5th Lancers and 5th Dragoons charge into them, killing and injuring dozens.

Key

British Forces	Boer Forces
Overall Command: Gen French **Gen Hamilton**	**Overall Command: General Kock**

7th Brigade – Gen Hamilton

	British Forces		Boer Forces
⊠ DR	Devonshire Regiment	Cdo German Uit Corps	German Uitlander Corps (Vol)
⊠ MR	Manchester Regiment	Cdo Jhbg	Johannesburg Commando
⊠ GH	Gordon Highlanders	Cdo Dutch Vol	Dutch Volunteer Commando
		Cdo Fordsburg	Fordsburg Commando (F. Pienaar)
ILH (Dismounted)	Imperial Light Horse	Cdo Vrede	Vrede Commando (Cmdt Lombaard)
1 Sqn 5 DG	5th Dragoon Guards (Maj Gore)	Cdo ZARPS	Zuit Afrikaansche Republiek Polisie Commando
1 Sqn 5 Lcrs	5th Lancers		

Artillery

♦♦♦ Natal Field Artillery

Royal Field Artillery

♦♦♦ 21 and 24 Batteries

Artillery

♥♥♥ Staats Artillerie

⟋ British movements

r—ᴗ Boer defensive positions

⟋ Boer movements

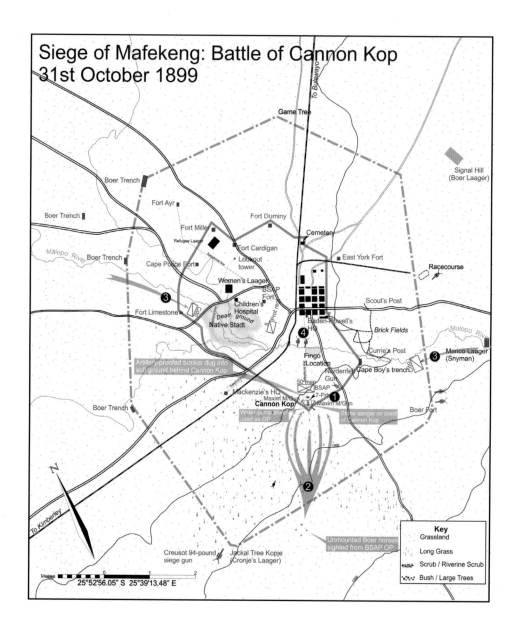

Siege of Mafekeng: Battle of Cannon Kop
31st October 1899

To Bulawayo

Game Tree

Signal Hill
(Boer Laager)

Boer Trench

Fort Ayr

Boer Trench

Fort Miller

Fort Duminy

Malopo River   Boer Trench

Refugee Laager

Fort Cardigan

Cemetery

East York Fort

Racecourse

Cape Police Fort

Lookout
tower

Women's Laager

BSAP
Fort

Scout's Post

Fort Limestone

Children's
Hospital

Dead ground

Native Stadt

Baden-Powell's
HQ

Brick Fields

Malopo River

Currie's Post

Marico Laager
(Snyman)

Fingo
Location

Artillery-proofed bunker dug into
soft ground behind Cannon Kop

Nordenfelt
Gun

Cape Boy's trench

Mackenzie's HQ

50 men

Maxim M/Gun

BSAP
7-Pdr

Maxim M/Gun

Boer Trench

Cannon Kop

Winter-pump tower
used as OP

Stone sangar on crest
of Cannon Kop

Boer Fort

To Kimberley

N

Creusot 94-pound
siege gun

Jackal Tree Kopje
(Cronje's Laager)

Unmounted Boer horses
sighted from BSAP OP

Key

Grassland

Long Grass

Scrub / Riverine Scrub

Bush / Large Trees

Metres 0   1   2

25°52'56.05" S 25°39'13,48" E

Siege of Mafekeng: Battle of Cannon Kop

1 Starting at 0430 hours, Boer guns commence bombardment of the BSAP position at Cannon Kop on the 31st October 1899.

2 At around 0500 hours, approximately 1,000 Boers advance on the isolated outpost. The BSAP wait until the attackers are within 200 yards before opening fire and breaking up the attack in short order.

3 Simultaneously, two groups of mounted Boers (each approximately 500 men) are seen approaching from the west and east along the Malopo River. Walford warns Baden-Powell by telephone. This move is blocked by the mounted squadron of the Protectorate regiment.

4 A pair of 7-pounders is rushed into position to support the BSAP at Cannon Kop. These guns quickly find the range and after a few shells, the Boers on all sides break and rapidly retreat, leaving at least 100 dead and wounded on the battlefield.

British Forces	**Boer Forces**
Overall Command: Col R. Baden-Powell	Overall Command: Gen Cronjé
Col Walford (BSAP)	Cmdt Snyman

BSAP — British South Africa Police (Rhodesia)

Prot regt — Protectorate regiment (Mtd Sqn) (Bechuanaland)

.303 Maxim machine gun

7-pounders

British movements

Limits of British defensive positions

British defensive positions

Boer movements

Limits of Boer investment

Boer positions

Boer heavy artillery

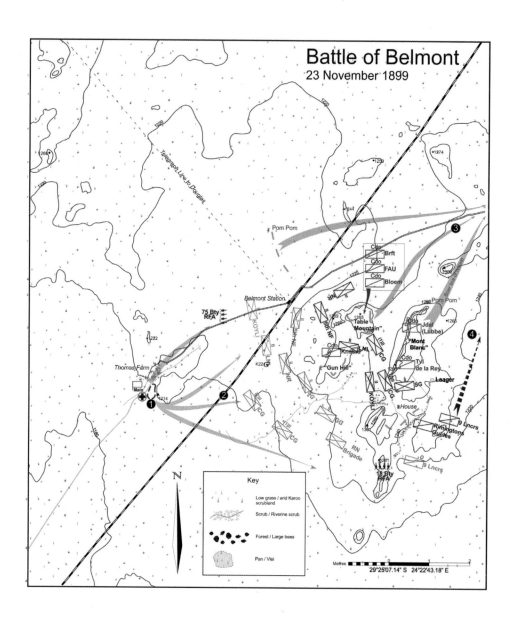

Battle of Belmont
23 November 1899

Battle of Belmont

(1) In the early hours of the 23rd November, imperial forces approach the Boer position at Belmont, though they do not reach their planned start line by dawn. The republicans open fire, prompting the British infantry to commence their assault before the supporting artillery is in position.

(2) With the 9th Infantry Brigade on the left, and the Guards Brigade on the right, the British troops storm up the slopes, driving the republicans back at bayonet point. Pursued by the Tommies, the Boers retreat farther up into the hills.

(3) The Boers are forced back and are soon driven off these hilltops. No attempt is made to defend the third peak and the beaten republicans begin streaming away, retreating in a north-easterly direction.

(4) Methuen's lack of mounted troops means that only the 9th Lancers is available to ride down the retreating Boers. An attempt is made, but achieves little.

KEY

British Forces	Boer Forces
Overall Command: Lt-Gen Lord Methuen	**Overall Command: Gen Cronjé, Cmdt Prinsloo**

British Forces		Boer Forces	
CG	Coldstream Guards	Brft	Brandfort Commando
GG	Grenadier Guards	FAU	Faure Commando
SG	Scots Guards	Bloem	Bloemfontein Commando
5th NF	5th Northumberland Fusiliers	Knstad	Kroonstad Commando
KOYLI	King's Own Yorkshire Light Infantry	Tvl De la Rey	Transvaal Commandos Gen de la Rey
LNL	Loyal North Lancashire Regiment	Jdal (Lubbe)	Jacobsdal Commando (Cmdt Lubbe)
NR	Northamptonshire Regiment	Pom Pom	Boer 37-mm QF Pom Pom'
9 Lncrs	9th Lancers		Boer defensive positions
R G	Rimington's Guides		Boer lines of retreat
RN Brigade	Royal Naval Brigade (Art and Royal Marines Light Infantry)		
18 Bty RFA / 75 Bty RFA	Royal Field Artillery		
	Bivouac and HQ area. Start of night march to start line		
✚	British Field Hospital		
	Direction of attempted pursuit by 9th Lancers and Mounted Infantry		
	British movements		

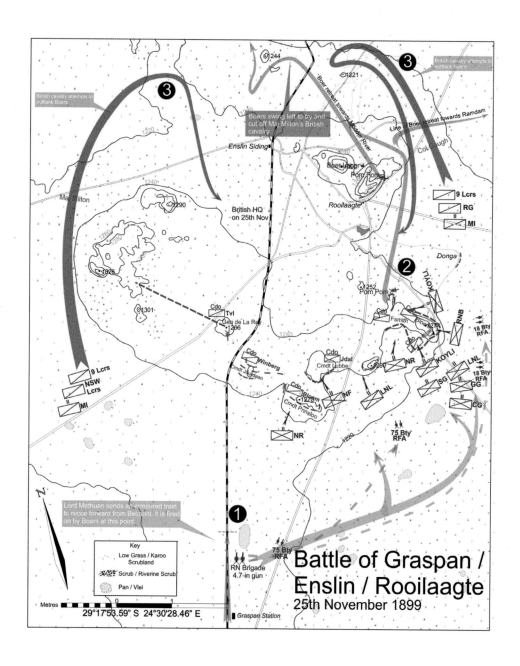

**Battle of Graspan /
Enslin / Rooilaagte**
25th November 1899

Battle of Graspan / Enslin / Rooilaagte

1 After several hours of artillery bombardment, the 9th Infantry Brigade (with attached Naval Brigade) launches its attack at 0900 hours on the 25th November.

2 Despite taking significant losses, the Blue Jackets and infantry quickly storm the position and the republicans retreat northwards.

3 The imperial mounted troops, operating on the flanks, make an attempt to get around the rear to cut off the Boer retreat. As at Belmont two days earlier, this is unsuccessful and the republicans withdraw without hindrance.

BRITISH FORCES

Overall Command: Lt-Gen Lord Methuen

9th Brigade

- NR — Northamptonshire Regiment
- LNL — Loyal North Lancashire Regiment
- KOYLI — King's Own Yorkshire Light Infantry
- NF — 5th Northumberland Fusiliers

Guards Brigade

- CG — Coldstream Guards
- SG — Scots Guards
- GG — Grenadier Guards

Artillery

- 18 Bty RFA — 18th Battery Royal Field Artillery
- 75 Bty RFA — 75th Battery Royal Field Artillery

Royal Naval Brigade

- RNB — Royal Naval Brigade (Arty, Royal Marines Light Infantry and RN ship crews)

Cavalry / Mounted Infantry

- 9 Lcrs — 9th Lancers
- RG — Rimington's Guides
- NSW Lcrs — New South Wales Lancers (Aus)
- MI — Mounted Infantry Brigade (Aus)
- ➤ British cavalry flanking movements

BOER FORCES

Overall Command: Gen Prinsloo / Gen de la Rey

- Tvl — Transvaal Commando (Gen de la Rey)
- Bloem — Bloemfontein Commando (Cmdt Prinsloo)
- Jdal — Jacobsdal Commando (Cmdt Lubbe)
- Winberg — Winberg Commando (Cmdt Jourdaan)
- Hstad — Hoopstad Commando (Cmdt Fourie)
- Fsmith — Fauriesmith Commando (Cmdt van der Venter)

- ➤— Free State Artillery 3 x Krupp – Maj Albrecht
- ·–·–· Boer defensive positions
- ➤ Boer lines of retreat

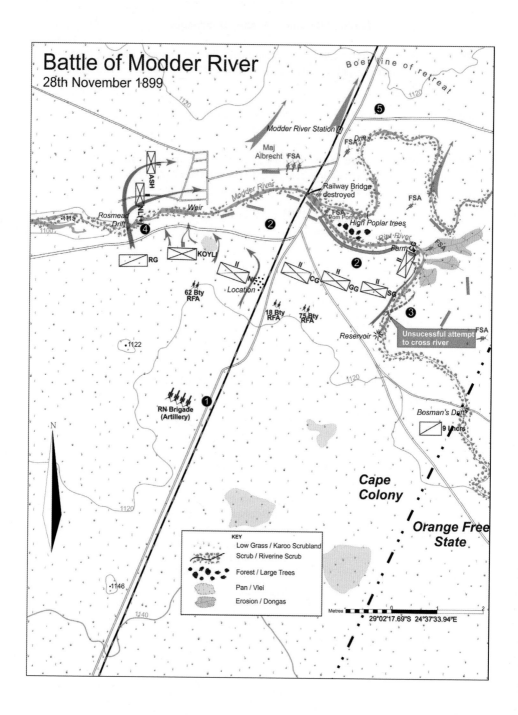

Battle of Modder River
28th November 1899

Boer line of retreat

Modder River Station

Maj Albrecht **FSA**

FSA Drift

FSA

Railway Bridge destroyed

ASH

NL

Rosmead Drift

Weir

Modder River

FSA Pom Pom

High Poplar trees

Riet River

Farm

FSA

RG

KOYLI

NL Location

62 Bty RFA

CG

GG

SG

18 Bty RFA

75 Bty RFA

Reservoir

Unsucessful attempt to cross river

FSA

N

RN Brigade (Artillery)

Bosman's Drift

9 Lncrs

Cape Colony

Orange Free State

KEY
Low Grass / Karoo Scrubland
Scrub / Riverine Scrub
Forest / Large Trees
Pan / Vlei
Erosion / Dongas

Metres 0   1   2

29°02'17.69"S 24°37'33.94"E

Battle of Modder River

1 With two RA batteries (a third arrived in the midst of the action) and naval guns in support, Methuen deploys the 9th Brigade under Major-General Pole-Carew on the left of the railway line, with the Guards Brigade, under Major-General Colville, deployed on the right.

2 The advancing Tommies come under heavy fire at about 800 yards as the republicans spring their ambush too early.

3 An attempt by the Guards to push round to the right through the Riet River is unsuccessful.

4 At midday, on the left, although under heavy fire, elements of the 9th Brigade are able to fight their way across Rosmead Drift, and establish themselves on the far side of the river.

5 With their flank turned, and the rest of the 9th Brigade crossing the river, some of the Boers give up and begin retreating on their own accord. This becomes a general withdrawal and the position is abandoned.

KEY

British Forces

Overall Command: Lt-Gen Lord Methuen

9th Brigade – Maj-Gen R. Pole-Carew

NF	Northumberland Fusiliers
KOYLI	King's Own Yorkshire Light Infantry
LNL	Loyal North Lancashire Regiment
ASH	Argyll & Sutherland Highlanders
RG	Rimington's Guides
9 Lncrs	9th Lancers

Royal Field Artillery

75 Bty RFA	75th Battery RFA
18 Bty RFA	18th Battery RFA
62 Bty RFA	62nd Battery RFA
RN Brigade (Artillery)	Royal Naval Brigade (Arty)
	British movements

Guards Brigade – Maj-Gen H. Colville

CG	Coldstream Guards
GG	Grenadier Guards
SG	Scots Guards

Boer Forces

Overall Command: Gen de la Rey, Gen Cronjé

Boer defensive positions

Orange Free State Artillery

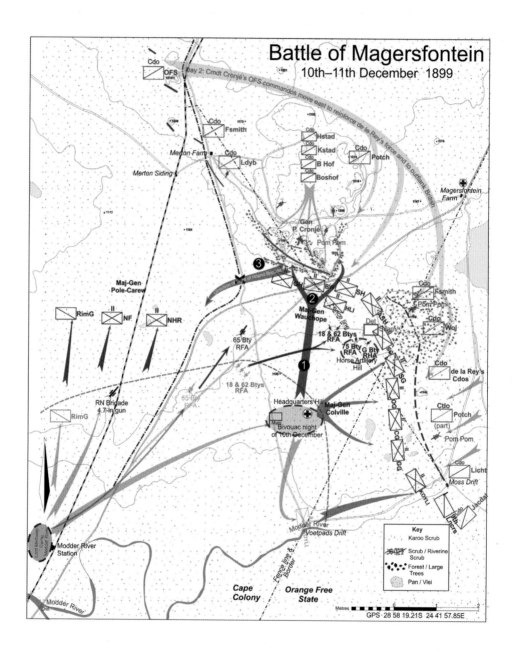

Battle of Magersfontein
10th–11th December 1899

Day 2: Cmdt Cronjé's OFS commandos move east to reinforce de la Rey's force and to outflank British

Cdo OFS

Cdo Fsmith

Merton Farm

Cdo Ldyb

Merton Siding

Cdo Hstad
Cdo Kstad
Cdo B Hof
Cdo Boshof

Cdo Potch

Magersfontein Farm

Gen P. Cronjé

Pom Pom

③ Direction of Night of Hiland Brigade

Maj-Gen Pole-Carew

RimG NF NHR

65 Bty RFA

② Maj-Gen Wauchope

GH II BW SH
II HLI
II
II Del
75 Bty RFA G Bty RFA RHA
18 & 62 Btys RFA
Horse Artillery Hill

SH
ASH II

Cdo Fsmith
Pom Pom

Cdo Wol

Fence line

SG
II

T
II
Og

Cdo de la Rey's Cdos

Ctlo Potch (part)

Pom Pom

18 & 62 Btys RFA

65 Bty RFA

①

Headquarters Hill

Maj-Gen Colville

Og
II

Og
II

Map Bivouac night of 10th December

GG
II

GG

Cdo Licht
Moss Drift

RN Brigade 4.7-in gun

RimG

Koffu
II
Btn Ldrs

Cdo
Btn

Jackal

Modder River
Voetpads Drift

Lord Methuen Camp Modder River
Modder River Station

Modder River Drift

Fence line & Border
TRACK

Cape Colony

Orange Free State

Key
Karoo Scrub
Scrub / Riverine Scrub
Forest / Large Trees
Pan / Vlei

Metres 0 2
GPS 28 58 19.21S 24 41 57.85E

Battle of Magersfontein

1 The newly arrived Highland Brigade approaches the Boer positions under the cover of darkness, marching in column to maintain order.

2 The Highlanders are caught, still in close order, as dawn breaks and come under intense fire at 400 yards, causing heavy casualties. Attempts are made to storm the republican trenches but these are all shattered and the whole brigade is pinned down.

3 After many hours of this, a Boer attempt to outflank the pinned Highlanders leads to confusion and a general rout. General Wauchope, commanding the Highland Brigade, is killed in the action.

KEY

British Forces

Overall Command: Lt-Gen Lord Methuen

3rd Highland Brigade – Maj-Gen Wauchope

BW	Black Watch
HLI	Highland Light Infantry
SH	Seaforth Highlanders
ASH	Argyll & Sutherland Highlanders

9th Brigade – Maj-Gen Pole-Carew

NF	Northumberland Fusiliers
NR	Northamptonshire Regiment
LNLR	Loyal North Lancashire Regiment
KOYLI	King's Own Yorkshire Light Infantry

Guards Brigade – Maj-Gen Colville

CG	1st Battalion Coldstream Guards
CG	2nd Battalion Coldstream Guards
GG	Grenadier Guards
SG	Scots Guards

Divisional troops

GH	Gordon Highlanders
9th Lncrs	9th Lancers
12th Lncrs	12th Lancers
RimG	Rimington's Guides

British Artillery

65, 75, 18 & 62 Batteries RFA
'G' Battery RHA

1 x 4.7-in Naval Brigade

Field Hospital

Brigade Boundary
British movements

Boer Forces

Overall Command: Gen Cronjé (OVSR)

Gen de la Rey (TR)

B Hof	Bloemhof Commando
Boshof	Boshoff Commando
Fsmith	Fauresmith Commando
Ldyb	Ladybrand Commando
Hstad	Hoopstad Commando
Jacdal	Jacobsdal Commando
Kstad	Kroonstad Commando
Licht	Lichtenburg Commando
Potch	Potchefstroom Commando
Wol	Wolmaranstad Commando
ScanV	Scandinavian Volunteers

Boer movements and
defensive positions

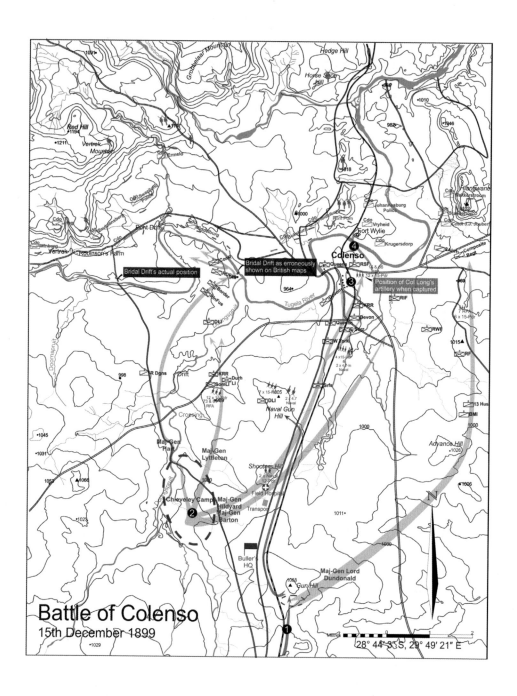

Battle of Colenso
15th December 1899

28° 44' 33 S, 29° 49' 21" E

Battle of Colenso

1 The British attack commences with Hart's 5th (Irish) Brigade on the left, Hildyard's 2nd Infantry Brigade in the centre, and the small Mounted Brigade on the right, but things quickly begin to go wrong.

2 Hart's Brigade cannot find a way across the Tugela and is caught in a loop of the river. Under fire from three sides, it suffers heavy casualties.

3 Two RA batteries under Colonel Long have been deployed too far forward and come under rifle fire from the Boer trenches.

4 Though Hildyard's men occupy the village of Colenso, they can achieve nothing more and Buller withdraws his force, leaving behind ten 15-pounders to be captured that night by the jubilant Boers.

KEY

British Forces
Overall Command: General Buller

5th Irish Brigade – Maj-Gen Hart
- ConR — Connaught Rangers
- RDFus — Royal Dublin Fusiliers
- RInFus — Inniskilling Fusiliers
- Border — Border Regiment

4th Brigade – Maj-Gen Lyttleton
- S Rfs — Scottish Rifles
- Durh LI — Durham Light Infantry
- KRR — King's Royal Rifles
- SomLI — Somersetshire Light Infantry

2nd (Infantry) Brigade – Maj-Gen Hildyard
- Queens — Queen's West Surrey Regiment
- E Surr — East Surrey Regiment
- W York — West Yorkshire Regiment
- Devon — Devonshire Regiment

6th Brigade – Maj-Gen Barton
- RWF — Royal Welsh Fusiliers
- RF — Royal Fusiliers
- RSF — Royal Scots Fusiliers
- GH — Gordon Highlanders
- DLI — Durban Light Infantry

Mounted Brigade – Maj-Gen Lord Dundonald
- R Dgns — Royal Dragoon Guards
- 13th Hus — 13th Hussars
- Composite Regt — Composite Regiment MI
- Beth MI — Bethune's Mounted Infantry
- TMI — Thorneycroft's Mounted Infantry
- SALH — South African Light Horse
- ILH — Imperial Light Horse
- Ncarb — Natal Carbineers

British Artillery
- 7 RFA / 6 x 15-Pdr — 7th Field Battery RFA (15-pdr)
- 14 & 66 RFA / 12 x 15-Pdr — 14th & 66th Field Batteries RFA (15-pdr)
- 53 & 64 RFA / 12 x 15-Pdr — 53rd & 64th Field Batteries RFA
- 2 x 4.7inch Naval — Royal Naval Brigade (Artillery) (4.7-in)
- 2 x Naval 12-Pdr — Royal Naval Brigade (Artillery) (12-pdr)
- British movements

Boer Forces
Overall Command: Gen Louis Both

- Winberg — Winberg Commando
- Jhbg — Johannesburg Commando
- Zoutpansberg — Zoutpansberg Commando
- Middelberg — Middelburg Commando
- Swaziland — Swaziland Commando
- Ermelo — Ermelo Commando
- Standerton — Standerton Commando
- Boksburg — Boksburg Commando
- Heidelberg — Heidelberg Commando
- Krugersdorp — Krugersdorp Commando
- Vryheid — Vryheid Commando
- Johannesburg Police — Johannesburg Police Commando

Artillery
- Boer pom pom (QF) gun
- Boer heavy artillery (Krupp 75s)
- Boer defensive positions

Lead-up to the Battle of Spion Kop, 17th–24th January 1900

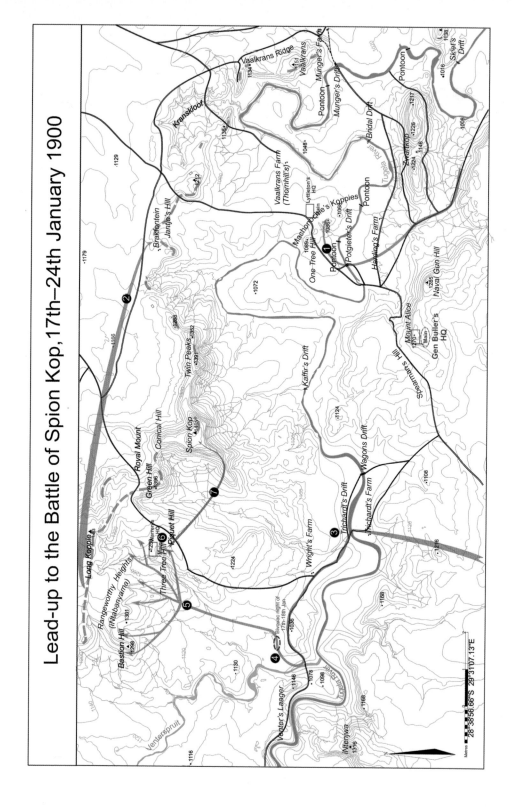

Lead-up to the Battle of Spion Kop

1 On the night of 16th January 1900, British troops and artillery under Major-General Lyttleton cross the Tugela at Potgieter's Drift and occupy 'Machonohie Kopjes'.

2 The Boers, believing that their positions at Brakfontein are threatened by the British, move forces immediately from the area around iNtabanyama, to reinforce Brakfontein, so denuding that area of troops.

3 On the 17th January, Lieutenant-General Warren, with 15,000 men and 36 field guns, crosses the Tugela at Trichardt's Drift, upstream of his position, with the task of outflanking the Boers at iNtabanyama and Brakfontein.

4 Warren's base camp on night of 17th January.

5 Warren then moves his force north where it splits and attacks iNtabanyama over the period 20th / 21st January.

6 Warren establishes a base camp at Three Tree Hill on the 23rd January. His multi-pronged attacks make no headway.

7 Warren dispatches a force under Major-General Woodgate at 23h00 hours to attack Spion Kop at first light on the 24th January.

KEY

British Forces	Boer Forces
Overall Command: Gen Buller	**Overall Command: Gen Louis Botha**
Lt-Gen Sir Charles Warren	Gen S.W. Burger
Lt-Gen Lyttleton	Cmdt H. Prinsloo
Maj-Gen Woodgate	
Lt-Col Thorneycroft	

 British movements

 Boer movements and defensive positions

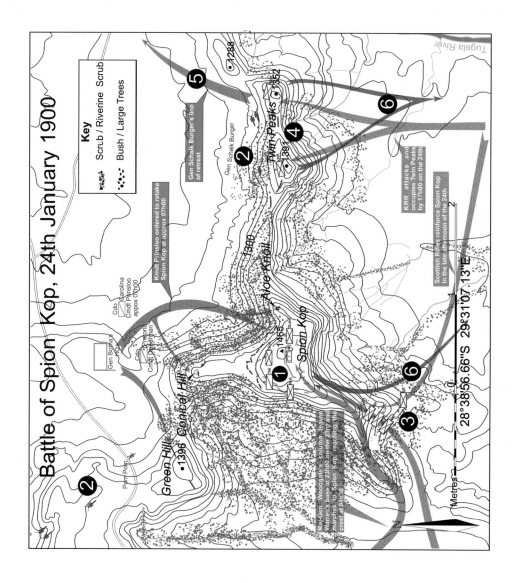

Battle of Spion Kop, 24th January 1900

Key

- ⠿ Scrub / Riverine Scrub
- ⠿ Bush / Large Trees

Cdo
Carolina
Cmdt Prinsloo
approx 0h00

Cdo Pretoria
Cmdt Opperman

Gen Botha's HQ

Kmdt Prinsloo ordered to retake
Spion Kop at approx 07h00

Gen Schalk Burger's line
of retreat

Gen Schalk Burger

•1288

Tugela River

•1352

Twin Peaks

▲1391

KRR attacks and
occupies Twin Peaks
by 17h00 on the 24th

Scottish Rifles reinforce Spion Kop
in the late afternoon of the 24th

1500

1500

Aloe Knoll

Spion Kop

▲1465

Maj-Gen Woodgate's column leaves
Warren's base at 23h00 on the 23rd and
marches to Spion Kop, reaching the
crest at 04h30

•1396 Conical Hill

Green Hill

Pom Pom

N

Metres

28°38'56.66"S 29°31'07.13"E

Battle of Spion Kop

1 After a night march, British units under Major-General Woodgate capture Spion Kop in the early hours of the 24th January.

2 At first light, this position comes under intense artillery fire from Boer guns on the nearby hills.

3 Imperial reinforcements are moved up the hill throughout the battle.

4 In an effort to relieve the pressure on the defenders of Spion Kop, the KRRC is ordered to capture the neighbouring heights of Twin Peaks. This is duly done.

5 Many Boers, thinking the battle is lost, start retreating. However, in the confusion the KRRC is ordered to withdraw.

6 As night falls, and even as reinforcements and artillery are being brought up Spion Kop, the decision is taken to abandon the hill.

KEY

British Forces	Boer Forces
Overall Command: Gen Buller	**Overall Command:** Gen Louis Botha
Maj-Gen Woodgate	Cmdt H. Prinsloo
Lt-Col Thornycroft	Cmdt Opperman
Lt-Gen Warren	

RLR — Royal Lancashire Regiment

LFus — Lancashire Fusiliers

SLanc — South Lancashire Regiment

TMI — Thorneycroft's Mounted Infantry

RE — Royal Engineers

MR — Middlesex Regiment

ILI — Imperial Light Infantry

SR — Scottish Rifles (Cameronians)

DR — Dorsetshire Regiment

KRR — King's Royal Rifles

— British movements

╷╶╶╲╴ British defensive positions

Cdo Carolina (Cmdt Prinsloo) — Carolina Commando (Prinsloo)

Cdo Pretoria (Cmdt Opperman) — Pretoria Commando (Opperman)

Boer 37mm pom pom (QF) gun

Boer heavy artillery (Krupp 75s)

— Boer movements

╷╶╶╲╴ Boer defensive positions

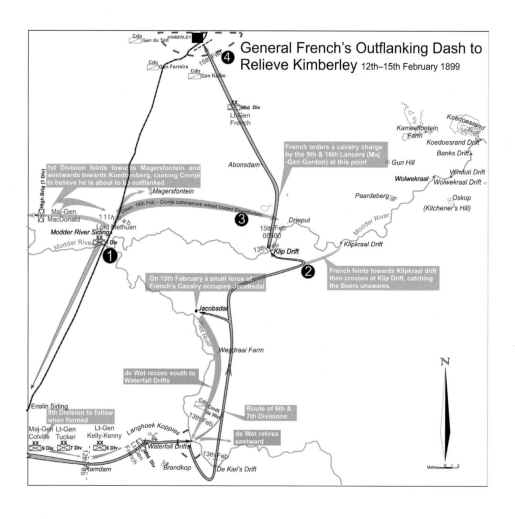

General French's Outflanking Dash to Relieve Kimberley 12th–15th February 1899

KIMBERLEY

Cdo Gen du Toit

Cdo Gen Ferreira

Cdo Gen Kolbe

XX Mtd Div
Lt-Gen French

Koedoesrand

Kameelfontein Farm

Koedoesrand Drift

Banks Drift

French orders a cavalry charge by the 9th & 16th Lancers (Maj-Gen Gordon) at this point

Gun Hill

Abonsdam

Venduti Drift

Wolwekraal Wolwekraal Drift

1st Division feints towards Magersfontein and westwards towards Koedoesberg, causing Cronjé to believe he is about to be outflanked

Magersfontein

Paardeberg

Oskop (Kitchener's Hill)

16th Feb: - Cronjé commences retreat toward Bloemfontein

High Brig (1 Div)

Maj-Gen MacDonald

11th Feb

Lord Methuen

Modder River Siding

1 Div

Modder River

Drieput

15th Feb 09h00

13th Feb

Klip Drift

Modder River

Klipkraal Drift

French feints towards Klipkraal drift then crosses at Klip Drift, catching the Boers unawares.

On 13th February a small force of French's Cavalry occupies Jacobsdal

Jacobsdal

Riet River

Wegdraai Farm

de Wet recces south to Waterfall Drifts

N

Enslin Siding

9th Division to follow when formed

Maj-Gen Colville

Lt-Gen Tucker

Lt-Gen Kelly-Kenny

Langhoek Koppies

Cdo Cmdt de Wet

13th Feb

Route of 6th & 7th Divisions

de Wet retires eastward

XX 9 Div

XX 7 Div

XX 6 Div

12th Feb

Riet River

Mtd Div

Waterfall Drifts

13th Feb

Ramdam

Brandkop

De Kiel's Drift

Metres 0 1 2

General French's Outflanking Dash to Relieve Kimberley

1 At the head of his Cavalry Division, French sets off on his wide flanking move on the 11th February 1900. He moves east from Graspan, heading initially for Ramdam and thereafter towards Waterfall Drift, where he intends to cross the Riet River before swinging north.

2 With the Infantry Division trudging behind, the cavalry feints towards Klipdraal Drift, wrong-footing the Boers and thus crossing at Klip Drift without incident.

3 After pausing to rest horses and allow the infantry to catch up, on the morning of the 15th, French's cavalry charges through the hills to the north of the river.

4 Kimberley is relieved on the evening of the 15th.

British Forces

Overall Command: Field Marshal Lord Roberts

Cavalry Division – Brig-Gen French

1st Brigade – Brig-Gen Broadwood
Household Cavalry Regiment
10th Hussars
9th &16th Lancers
Dragoons

1st Division – Lt-Gen Lord Methuen
6th Division – Lt-Gen Kelly-Kenny

13th Brigade – Maj-Gen Knox
2nd East Kents
2nd Gloucesters
1st West Riding Regiment
1st Oxfordshire Light Infantry

18th Brigade – Maj-Gen Stevenson
2nd Royal Warwickshire
1st Yorkshire
1st Welsh
1st Essex

RFA: 76th, 81st and 82nd Batteries
RE: 38th Company

7th Division – Lt-Gen Tucker

14th Brigade – Brig-Gen Chermside
2nd Norfolk Regiment
2nd Lincolnshire
1 King's Own Scottish Borderers
2nd Hampshires

9th Division – Maj-Gen Colville

3rd Highland Brigade – Maj-Gen McDonald
2nd Black Watch
1st Highland Light Infantry
2nd Seaforth Highlanders
1st Argyll & Sutherland Highlanders

19 (Inf) Brigade – Maj-Gen Smith-Dorrien

Maj-Gen French's route

Other British division and brigade movements

Boer Forces

Overall Command: Cmdt-Gen P Cronjé

Gen Cronjé
Cmdt de Wet

Boer movements

Boer defensive position

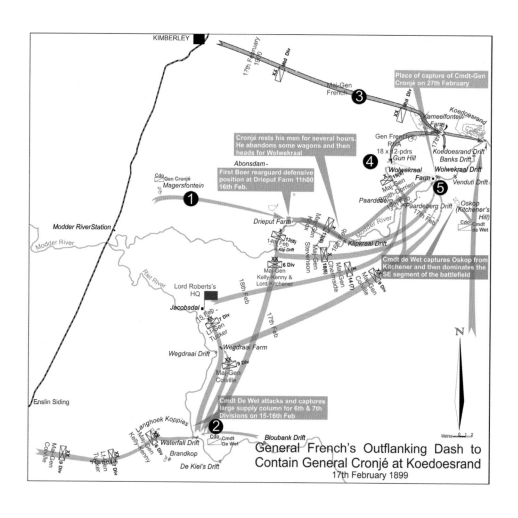

General French's Outflanking Dash to Contain General Cronjé at Koedoesrand
17th February 1899

General French's Outflanking Dash to Contain General Cronjé at Koedoesrand

1 At dawn on the 16th February, General Cronjé belatedly begins falling back from his positions at Magersfontein.

2 De Wet attacks a supply column at Waterfall Drifts, but does not halt the imperial advance.

3 Despite the exhaustion of this men and horses, French, who is in Kimberley, is ordered to cut off the retreating Boers at Koedoesrand Drift, covering the distance in good time and preventing Cronjé's escape.

4 French brings his RHA batteries into action, shelling Cronjé's column as they try to cross at Vendutie Drift.

5 Despite outnumbering French's blocking force, Cronjé's inexplicable reaction is to dig in, thus sealing his fate and that of his entire command.

British Forces
Overall Command: Field Marshal Lord Roberts

Cavalry Division – Brig-Gen French

    1st Brigade – Brig-Gen Broadwood
    Household Cavalry Regiment
    10th Hussars
    9th &16th Lancers
    Dragoons

    1st Division – Lt-Gen Lord Methuen
6th Division – Lt-Gen Kelly-Kenny

13th Brigade – Maj-Gen Knox
2nd East Kents
2nd Gloucesters
1st West Riding Regiment
1st Oxfordshire Light Infantry

18th Brigade – Maj-Gen Stevenson
2nd Royal Warwickshire
1st Yorkshire
1st Welsh
1st Essex

RFA: 76th, 81st and 82nd Batteries
RE: 38th Company

7th Division – Lt-Gen Tucker

14th Brigade – Brig-Gen Chermside
2nd Norfolk Regiment
2nd Lincolnshire
1st King's Own Scottish Borderers
2nd Hampshires

9th Division – Maj-Gen Colville

3rd Highland Brigade – Maj-Gen McDonald
2nd Black Watch
1st Highland Light Infantry
2nd Seaforth Highlanders
1st Argyll & Sutherland Highlanders

19 (Inf) Brigade – Maj-Gen Smith-Dorrien

➤ Maj-Gen French's route

➤ Other British division and brigade movements

Boer Forces
Overall Command: Cmdt Gen P. Cronjé

Gen Cronjé

Cmdt de Wet

➤ Boer movements

Boer defensive position

Battle of Paardeberg

1 With Cronjé's command cut off by French's cavalry, the Boers dig in near Wolweskraal Drift.

2 Kitchener orders Cronjé's position to be stormed by the recently arrived British infantry, but this attack is driven off and ends in costly failure.

3 In an attempt to break through to Cronjé, de Wet captures Oskop but this is recaptured by French's cavalry on the 22nd February.

4 Artillery continues to pound Cronjé into submission while imperial infantry tighten the noose over the following days.

5 At first light on the 27th February, as the imperial forces are poised to make a final assault on the Boer position, Cronjé surrenders.

British Forces
Overall Command: Lord Kitchener / Lord Roberts

19th Brigade – Maj-Gen Smith-Dorrien

KOSLI King's Own Shropshire Light Infantry

DCLI Duke of Cornwall's Light Infantry

GH Gordon Highlanders

RCR Royal Canadian Regiment

18th Brigade – Maj-Gen Stephenson

RWR Royal Warwickshire Regiment

York Yorkshire Regiment

Welsh Welsh Regiment

Essex Essex Regiment

3rd Highland Brigade – Maj-Gen McDonald

BW Black Watch

HLI Highland Light Infantry

SH Seaforth Highlanders

A&SH Argyll & Sutherland Highlanders

R Eng Royal Engineers

British movements

British defensive positions

13th Brigade – Maj-Gen Knox

EKR East Kent Regiment (Buffs)

Gloster Gloucestershire Regiment

WRI West Riding Regiment

OxfLI Oxfordshire Light Infantry

76 & 81 Btys 82 Bty
RFA RFA

Naval Brigade Artillery

Boer Forces
Overall Command: Gen Cronjé

South African Republic Commandos: Gen Cronjé

Orange Free State Commandos: Gen Botha / Cmdt C. de Wet

Boer movements and defensive positions

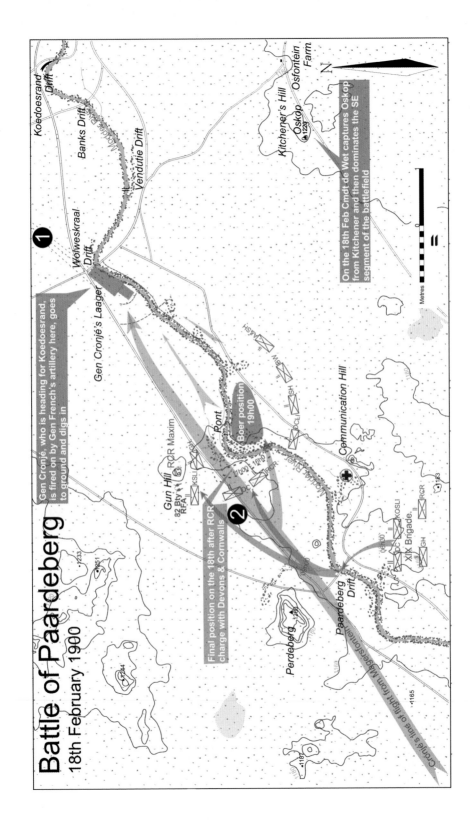

Battle of Paardeberg
18th February 1900

Gen Cronjé, who is heading for Koedoesrand, is fired on by Gen French's artillery here, goes to ground and digs in

On the 18th Feb Cmdt de Wet captures Oskop from Kitchener and then dominates the SE segment of the battlefield

Final position on the 18th after RCR charge with Devons & Cornwalls

Koedoesrand Drift

Banks Drift

Vendutie Drift

Osfontein Farm

Kitchener's Hill

Oskop
▲1220

Wolweskraal Drift

Gen Cronjé's Laager

Pont

Boer position 19h00

Gun Hill

RCR Maxim

82 Bty RFA

Communication Hill

Perdeberg

Paardeberg Drift

Cronjé's line of flight from Magersfontein

Metres

xxix

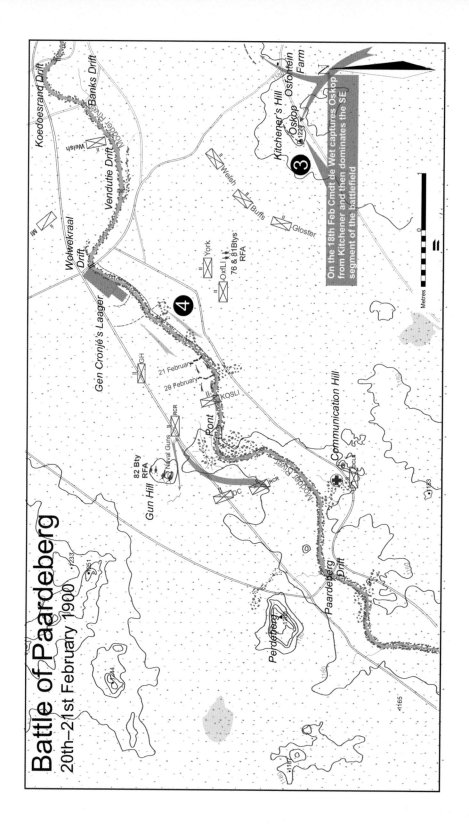

Battle of Paardeberg
20th–21st February 1900

Koedoesrand Drift

Banks Drift

Modder River

Welsh

Vendutie Drift

MI

Wolwekraal Drift

Gen Cronjé's Lager

Welsh

Buffs

Gloster

Kitchener's Hill

Oskop
1220

③

On the 18th Feb Cmdt de Wet captures Oskop from Kitchener and then dominates the SE segment of the battlefield

Osfontein Farm

N

0

Metres

York

OxLI

76 & 81Btys RFA

④

GH

21 February

20 February

KOSLI

Pont

RCR

82 Bty RFA

Naval Guns

Gun Hill

DC

RCR

Communication Hill

1180

1180

Modder River

1183

Perdeberg
1290

Paardeberg Drift

1190

1180

1165

1233

1251

1244

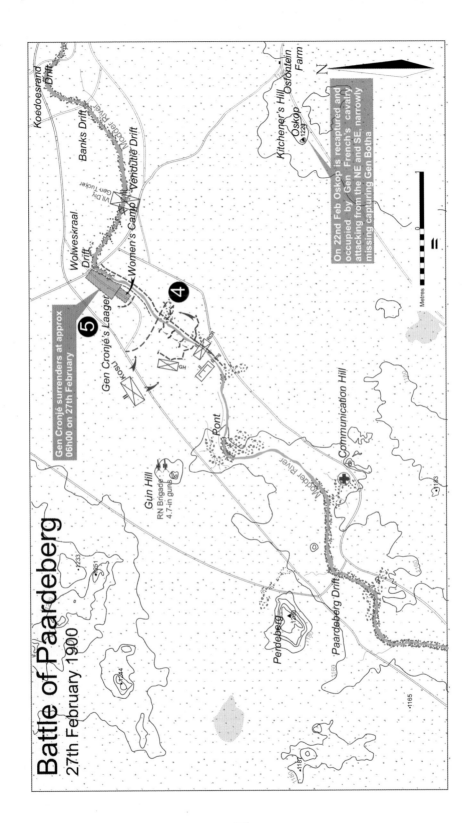

Battle of Paardeberg
27th February 1900

Gen Cronjé surrenders at approx 06h00 on 27th February

On 22nd Feb Oskop is recaptured and occupied by Gen French's cavalry attacking from the NE and SE, narrowly missing capturing Gen Botha

Koedoesrand Drift

Banks Drift

Vendutie Drift

Modder RIVER

Gen Tucker

VII Div

Wolweskraal Drift

Women's Camp

Gen Cronjé's Laager

Nkosili

5

4

GH

Pont

Gun Hill

RN Brigade
4.7-in guns

Modder River

Communication Hill

Pont

Pendeberg

Paardeberg Drift

Kitchener's Hill

Oskop
1229

Ostfontein Farm

N

Metres

.1233

.1251

.1244

.1165

.1183

.1180

.1160

.1160

.1150

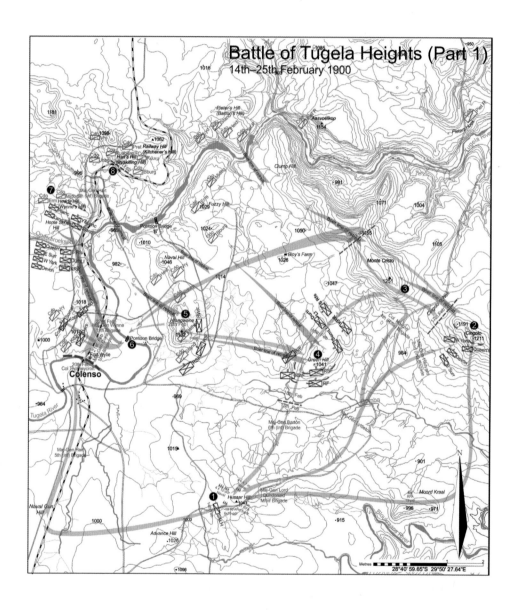

Battle of Tugela Heights (Part 1)
14th–25th February 1900

Battle of Tugela Heights (Part 1)

1 On the 14th February 1900, Dundonald's Mounted Brigade seizes Hussar Hill and guns are dragged up it.

2 After a two-day bombardment, Hildyard's 2nd Brigade storms and captures Cingolo Hill on the 17th.

3 At first light on the 18th, Hildyard's men push forward to assault and capture Monte Cristo.

4 Also on the 18th February, the 4th and 6th Brigades storm and seize Green Hill. By nightfall of the 18th, naval guns have been dragged up both captured peaks.

5 Hlangwane is captured on the 20th, with the Boer defenders fleeing across the Tugela.

6 A pontoon bridge is built and, on the 21st February, British troops begin to cross the Tugela.

7 An assault on Wynne's Hill on the 22nd February by the 11th Brigade fails to break through.

8 Hart's 5th (Irish) Brigade pushes forward to the right of Wynne's Hill and attacks Hart's Hill, but—despite several attempts—also cannot break through.

British Forces
Overall Command: Gen Buller

5th (Irish) Brigade – Maj-Gen Hart

ConR	Connaught Rangers
RDFus	Royal Dublin Fusiliers
RInFus	Inniskilling Fusiliers
Border	Border Regiment

4th (Rifle) Brigade – Maj-Gen Lyttleton
Maj-Gen Norcott

S Rfs	Scottish Rifles
Durh LI	Durham Light Infantry
KRR	King's Royal Rifles
SomLI	Somersetshire Light Infantry

2nd (Inf) Brigade – Maj-Gen Hildyard

Queens	Queen's West Surrey Regiment
E Surr	East Surrey Regiment
W York	West Yorkshire Regiment
Devon	Devonshire Regiment

6th Brigade – Maj-Gen Barton

RWF	Royal Welsh Fusiliers
RIF	Royal Irish Fusiliers
RSF	Royal Scots Fusiliers
GH	Gordon Highlanders
DLI	Durban Light Infantry

10th Brigade – Maj-Gen Coke

Midd	Middlesex Regiment
Dors	Dorsetshire Regiment
Somer	Somerset Regiment

11th Brigade – Maj-Gen Wynne
Brig-Gen Kitchener

RLanc	Royal Lancaster Regiment
Y&Lanc	York and Lancaster Regiment
Lanc Fus	Lancashire Fusiliers
SLanc	South Lancashire Regiment

Mounted Brigade – Maj-Gen Lord Dundonald

13 th Hus	13th Hussars
Composite Regt	Composite Regiment MI
Beth MI	Bethune's Mounted Infantry
TMI	Thorneycroft's Mounted Infantry
SALH	South African Light Horse
ILH	Imperial Light Horse
Ncarb	Natal Carbineers

Artillery

RFA (15-pdr)
2x4.7-in Naval	Royal Naval Brigade (Artillery) (4.7-in)
2 x Naval 12-pdr	Royal Naval Brigade (Artillery) (12-pdr)
→	British movements

Boer Forces
Overall Command: Gen Louis Botha / Gen Lukas Meyer

Bethel	Bethel Commando
Boksburg	Boksburg Commando
Ermelo	Ermelo Commando
Heidelberg	Heidelberg Commando
Jhbg	Johannesburg Commando
Johannesburg Police	Johannesburg Police Commando
Krugersdorp	Krugersdorp Commando
Lydenburg	Lydenburg Commando

Middelburg	Middelburg Commando
Piet Retief	Piet Retief Commando
Rustenburg	Rustenburg Commando
Standerton	Standerton Commando
Swaziland	Swaziland Commando
Vryheid	Vryheid Commando
Winberg	Winberg Commando
Zoutpansberg	Zoutpansberg Commando

Boer defensive positions
→	Boer movements

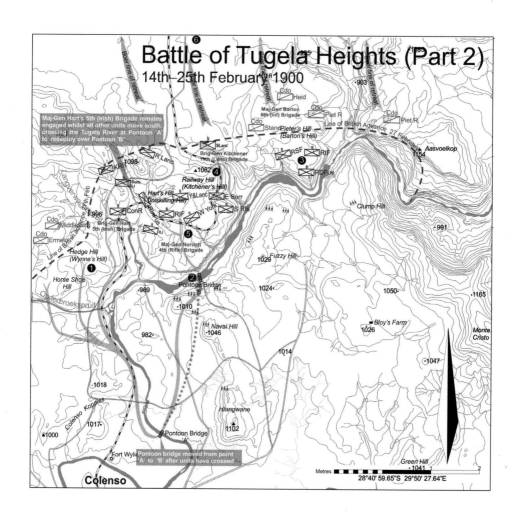

Battle of Tugela Heights (Part 2)
14th–25th February 1900

Battle of Tugela Heights (Part 2)

1 Leaving Hart's Irishmen to hold their positions, Buller changes his axis of attack.

2 On the 27th February, under cover of an artillery barrage from over 68 guns, the infantry cross the pontoon and move under cover of the high banks east along the river until opposite their objectives. The order to attack is given and the brigades move forward under a creeping artillery barrage.

3 Barton's 6th Brigade storms up and seizes Pieter's Hill on the extreme right of the line.

4 Meanwhile, the 11th Brigade assaults and captures Railway Hill.

5 With the Boers now streaming north in retreat, Norcott's 4th (Rifle) Brigade is flung into action to capture Hart's Hill.

6 By the evening of the 27th February, all three objectives are in British hands, with the Boers in full retreat. Ladysmith is relieved the following day.

British Forces
Overall Command: Gen Buller

5th (Irish) Brigade – Maj-Gen Hart

ConR	Connaught Rangers
RDFus	Royal Dublin Fusiliers
RInFus	Inniskilling Fusiliers
Border	Border Regiment

4th (Rifle) Brigade – Maj-Gen Lyttleton
Maj-Gen Norcott

S Rfs	Scottish Rifles
Durh LI	Durham Light Infantry
KRR	King's Royal Rifles
SomLI	Somersetshire Light Infantry

2nd (Inf) Brigade – Maj-Gen Hildyard

Queens	Queen's West Surrey Regiment
E Surr	East Surrey Regiment
W York	West Yorkshire Regiment
Devon	Devonshire Regiment

6th Brigade – Maj-Gen Barton

RWF	Royal Welsh Fusiliers
RIF	Royal Irish Fusiliers
RSF	Royal Scots Fusiliers
GH	Gordon Highlanders
DLI	Durban Light Infantry

10th Brigade – Maj-Gen Coke

Midd	Middlesex Regiment
Dors	Dorsetshire Regiment
Somer	Somerset Regiment

11th Brigade – Maj-Gen Wynne / Brig-Gen Kitchener

RLanc	Royal Lancaster Regiment
Y&Lanc	York and Lancaster Regiment
Lanc Fus	Lancashire Fusiliers
SLanc	South Lancashire Regiment

Mounted Brigade – Maj-Gen Lord Dundonald

13 th Hus	13th Hussars
Composite Regt	Composite Regiment MI
Beth MI	Bethune's Mounted Infantry
TMI	Thorneycroft's Mounted Infantry
SALH	South African Light Horse
ILH	Imperial Light Horse
Ncarb	Natal Carbineers

Artillery

	RFA (15-pdr)
4.7-in Naval	Royal Naval Brigade (Artillery) (4.7-in)
12-pdr Naval	Royal Naval Brigade (Artillery) (12-pdr)

British movements

Boer Forces
Overall Command: Gen Louis Botha / Gen Lukas Meyer

Bethel	Bethel Commando
Boksburg	Boksburg Commando
Ermelo	Ermelo Commando
Heidelberg	Heidelberg Commando
Jhbg	Johannesburg Commando
Johannesburg Police	Johannesburg Police Commando
Krugersdorp	Krugersdorp Commando
Lydenburg	Lydenburg Commando

Middelburg	Middelburg Commando
Piet Retief	Piet Retief Commando
Rustenburg	Rustenburg Commando
Standerton	Standerton Commando
Swaziland	Swaziland Commando
Vryheid	Vryheid Commando
Winberg	Winberg Commando
Zoutpansberg	Zoutpansberg Commando

Boer defensive positions
Boer movements

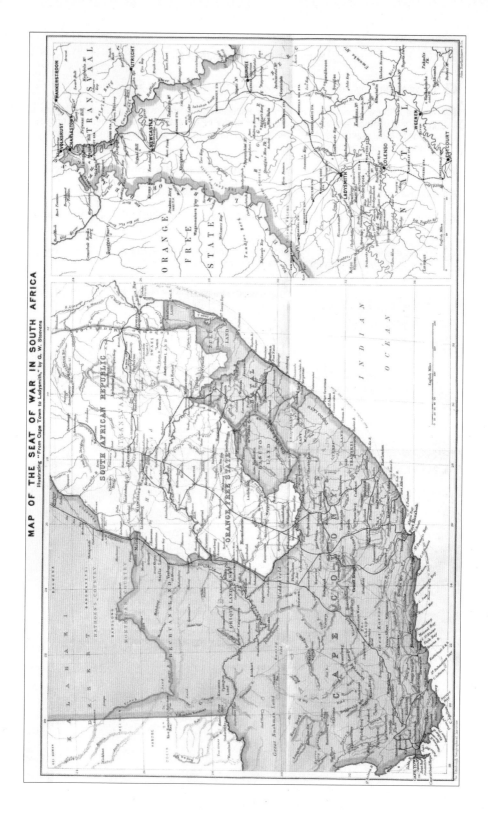

MAP OF THE SEAT OF WAR IN SOUTH AFRICA

Illustrating "From Cape Town to Ladysmith," by G. W. Steevens

KRUGER, KOMMANDOS & KAK

KRUGER
KOMMANDOS
& KAK

Debunking the myths of the Boer War

CHRIS ASH

Also by Chris Ash:
The If Man: Dr Leander Starr Jameson, The Inspiration for Kipling's Masterpiece (2012)

Published in 2014 by:
30° South Publishers (Pty) Ltd
16 Ivy Road
Pinetown 3610
South Africa
info@30degreessouth.co.za
www.30degreessouth.co.za

ISBN 978-1-920143-99-2
ebook 978-1-928211-22-8

Designed & typeset by SA Publishing Services, South Africa (kerrincocks@gmail.com)
Cover design by Kerrin Cocks
Printed by Pinetown Printers, Durban, South Africa

Names used in the text and maps are contemporaneous. Many place names have changed in recent years and, indeed, are still being changed, sometimes more than once.

For the officers and men of the Imperial Light Horse who fought and died
pro imperium et libertas

Contents

"I hate rebels, I hate traitors, I hate tyranny come from where it will.
I have seen much of the world, and I have learnt from experience
to hate and detest republics."
—Admiral Lord Nelson

Illustrations

"We admit that the British soldiers are the best in the world"—imperial infantry find what cover they can.

"and your regimental officers the bravest"—some rather dapper-looking imperial officers ready to have a go.

Tommies skirmish up a rocky hillside with fixed bayonets—almost all such photographs were staged for the benefit of the press corps.

"dashing, fiery, brilliant"—the Jocks of the Highland regiments were some of the finest troops in the British army.

"Jolly pig-sticking"—many Boers proved to be utterly terrified of the sabres and lances of imperial cavalry.

The sort of image of a clean-cut, gallant bitter-einder favoured by post-war propagandists—in reality, many were little more than murdering bandits.

One of the famous Boer 94-pounder Creusot guns, or 'Long Toms'. The Transvaal had another twelve such guns and a further eighty-two 75mm pieces on order when Kruger launched his invasions.

The victor of Stormberg, General Olivier, was later sent to what appears a very comfortable exile in Ceylon (Sir Lanka) after his somewhat shameless offer to switch sides and join the British was rejected.

'Hairy Mary', a rather Heath-Robinson attempt at an early armoured train, using heavy ship's rope to render the locomotive bullet-proof.

A more formidable-looking armoured train and her crew.

Another impressive-looking armoured train. Though badly handled at first, imperial forces learned the optimum use of these assets, which later proved their worth in protecting supply lines.

Armoured trains could not be everywhere and railway bridges were a favourite target of the Boers. Such attacks impacted on getting supplies to imperial troops, but also to the residents of the concentration camps.

Despite the post-war spin, many bitter-einder attacks against trains were arbitrary acts of terrorism and banditry. Note the female civilian on the right.

Despite the modern-day perceptions, the British army was quick to embrace the latest innovations. Here, an observation balloon—'the scaly, brown-coloured monster'—is readied for use.

Exotically-named 'aeronauts' were sent up in such balloons to direct artillery
fire by field telephone.

"They leisurely descend into spruits, roll across, and wheel up stiff, long
climbs, like flies climbing a wall"—imperial forces were also quick to
make use of new-fangled traction engines.

Searchlights were commonly used to flash signals to and from the besieged
towns in the early stages of the war.

This train is equipped with one of the signalling lamps developed the
remarkable Captain Percy Scott RN.

Cecil Rhodes offers the townspeople of Kimberley the chance to shelter in
the De Beers mines to escape the Boer shelling.

Imperial pontoon bridge unit. Caught completely by surprise, the British
army of 1899 was in no state to fight a major war, and only had eighty
yards' worth of such bridges.

"Slogging over Africa"—dauntless, but long-suffering imperial infantry
cross a similar pontoon bridge and push on.

Though imperial troops benefited greatly from the latest medical advances,
almost twice as many died of disease than from enemy action—something
often overlooked in the stampede to blame the British for all the civilian
deaths of the conflict.

Despite the modern-day myths, professional nurses were recruited from all
over the Empire to serve in the concentration camp hospitals.

Concentration camp medical staff were well paid and helped train large
numbers of Afrikaans girls as nurses.

A happy, healthy and very well-dressed group of camp residents.

Not quite so happy, but equally well-dressed and healthy camp residents
pose for the camera. Hundreds of such photos are ignored by most
latter-day histories of the conflict, presumably as they do not support the
popular notion that the camps were all unspeakable hellholes.

Though often dismissed today as a white elephant, Kitchener's great chains
of blockhouses helped to hem in the remaining bands of bitter-einders.
Thousands were being hunted down and captured every month by
imperial flying columns…

Maps

Timeline

1899
September
27th   Transvaal mobilizes her forces
29th   Transvaal military takes control of the nation's railways

October
3rd   Orange Free State mobilizes her forces
7th   British army begins to mobilize the reserves
10th   Boer ultimatum delivered
11th   War commences
12th   Boers invade Natal and Griqualand West; armoured train captured at Kraaipan
14th   General Buller departs Southampton; Boer attack on Mafeking driven off
15th   Martial law declared in northern Natal after Boer invasion
16th   Kimberley invested
20th   Battle of Talana (Natal front) ends in British victory
21st   Battle of Elandslaagte (Natal front) ends in British victory
22nd   Yule commences retreats from Dundee to Ladysmith
25th   Assault on Mafeking driven off
30th   Battle of Nicholson's Nek (Natal front) ends in Boer victory
31st   General Buller arrives in Cape Town

November
1st   Boers cross Orange River to invade Cape Colony, breaking Steyn's promise
2nd   Siege of Ladysmith begins
9th   First major assault on Ladysmith driven off with heavy loss
12th   Lord Methuen takes over command (western front)
13th   Boer attack on Kuruman fought off; Aliwal North captured by Boers
15th   Armoured train incident at Chieveley Siding (Natal front); Winston Churchill
        captured
16th   General Gatacre arrives at East London
21st   Lord Methuen commences his advance on Kimberley (western front)
22nd   General Buller leaves Cape Town for Natal
23rd   Battle of Belmont (western front) ends in British victory; battle of Willow
        Grange (Natal front) ends in Boer victory but also Boer retreat
25th   Battle of Graspan (western front) ends in British victory; successful attack on
        Boer laager at Deerdepoort (Rhodesian front)
28th   Battle of Modder River (western front) ends in British victory
29th   First Canadian contingent arrives in Cape Town

December
4th   Boers entrench at the Magersfontein hills
7th   Successful night raid on Boer guns at Ladysmith; Prinsloo attacks Enslin
        (western front) but is driven off
10th   Battle of Stormberg (central front) ends in Boer victory; second successful
        night raid on Boer guns at Ladysmith
11th   Battle of Magersfontein (western front) ends in Boer victory

13th   Boer attack near Arundel (central front) driven off
15th   Battle of Colenso (Natal front) ends in Boer victory
18th   Lord Roberts appointed Commander-in-Chief, Kitchener as his Chief of Staff
29th   Boers invade Upington district of Cape Colony

1900
January
1st   General French attacks Colesberg; Colonel Pilcher captures laager at
          Sunnyside; Kuruman surrenders after seven weeks of siege
3rd   Boer attack on Cpyhergat driven off
6th   Battle of Wagon Hill (Natal front) ends in British victory
10th   Lords Roberts and Kitchener arrive in Cape Town
14th   Colonel Plumer occupies Gaberones
24th   Battle of Spion Kop (Natal front) ends in Boer victory
25th   General Buller retreats back across the Tugela River

February
5th   General Buller captures Vaalkranz (Natal front)
7th   Vaalkranz evacuated
10th   General Buller's force returns to Chieveley
11th   Lord Roberts commences his great flank march
14th   Buller seizes Hussar Hill, starting the battle of the Tugela Heights (Natal front)
15th   Kimberley relieved
16th   Cronjé evacuates from Magersfontein (western front)
17th   Cronjé surrounded at Paardeberg (western front); Cingolo Hill captured (Natal)
18th   Monte Cristo captured (Natal front)
19th   Hlangwane Hill captured (Natal front)
20th   De Wet's attempt to relieve Cronjé driven off (western front)
23rd   Further Boer attempts to relieve Cronjé driven off (western front)
27th   Cronjé surrenders with over 4,000 men, ending the battle of Paardeberg
28th   Ladysmith relieved; Colesberg reoccupied by imperial troops

March
4th   Labuschagnes's Nek captured by Brabant's Colonial Division
7th   Battle of Poplar Grove (western front) ends in British victory; Colonel Plumer
          captures Boer laager at Gopani
10th   Battle of Driefontein ends in British victory
13th   Bloemfontein captured
14th   Gatacre and Clements cross the Orange River at Bethulie and Norval's Pont
          respectively
27th   General Joubert dies
28th   Wepener occupied by units of Brabant's Colonial Division
31st   Battle of Sannah's Post ends in Boer victory

April
3rd   Royal Irish surrounded by de Wet's commando at Reddersburg (central front)
9th   Wepener bombarded by de Wet's commando
10th   De Wet begins his attacks against Wepener—all are driven off with heavy loss
23rd   Sannah's Post waterworks recaptured by Ian Hamilton's men

24th   Explosion at the Begbie armanents factory in Johannesburg; foul play
        suspected
25th   Siege of Wepener raised; de Wet retreats in the face of a relief column
30th   Remaining British subjects expelled from the Transvaal

May
1st   Boers driven from Houtnek by Ian Hamilton
3rd   Lord Roberts occupies Brandfort
4th   Ian Hamilton drivers the Boers from Babiaansberg
5th   Action at Rooidam ends in British victory
9th   Mafeking relief column under Colonel Mahon reaches Vryburg (western front)
10th   Lord Roberts forces a crossing over the Zand River
12th   British occupy Kroonstad; Boer attack on Mafeking defeated and Commandant
        Eloff captured
13th   Colonel Mahon's column beats off an attack at Koedoesrand
14th   General Buller drives the Boers from the Biggarsberg (Natal front)
15th   Dundee and Glencoe liberated by Buller (Natal front)
16th   De la Rey defeated at Israel's Farm by Mahon and Plumer (western front)
17th   Mafeking relieved
18th   Newcastle liberated by Buller (Natal front)
20th   Bethune's Mounted Infantry defeated at Scheeper's Nek, near Vryheid
22nd   Roberts's main force moves out from Kroonstad
24th   Annexation of the Orange Free State announced; French crosses the Vaal River,
        near Parys
27th   Roberts's main force crosses the Vaal River, near Vereeniging
29th   Main army captures Germiston; battle of Doornkop ends in British victory
30th   Kruger flees Pretoria for Machadodorp
31st   Johannesburg captured by the British; 500 Irish Yeomanry surrender at Lindley

June
5th   Pretoria captured
6th   British PoWs liberated at Waterval
7th   4th Derbyshires overwhelmed by de Wet at Rhenoster River
11th   Battle of Alleman's Nek ends in British victory
12th   Battle of Diamond Hill ends in British victory
14th   Boer attack on Zand River Post repulsed
22nd   Boer attack on Katbosch Post driven off
23rd   Heidelberg captured by Ian Hamilton

July
4th   Roberts and Buller join hands at Vlakfontein
7th   De Wet driven out of Bethlehem by General Clements
11th   General French drives the Boers from Tigerfontein Ridge
21st   Boer attack on Zuikerbosch Post repulsed
26th   British capture Naauwpoort Nek
27th   Middleburg occupied by the British
28th   British capture Slaapkranz Nek
30th   General Prinsloo surrenders with over 4,000 men in the Brandwater Basin

August
4th   Siege of Elands River begins
5th   Carrington's attempt to raise the siege of Elands River driven off
7th   General Buller occupies Amersfoort
12th   Lord Methuen captures de Wet's wagons
16th   Lord Kitchener raises the siege of Elands River
24th   Belfast occupied by the British
27th   Battle of Bergendal (also known as Belfast) ends in British victory
30th   British capture Nooitgedacht and release over 2,700 half-starved prisoners

September
1st   Annexation of the Transvaal proclaimed
5th   Boer attack on the Canadians at Pan Station repulsed
6th   Buller occupies Lydenburg; French occupies Carolina
8th   Buller drives Botha from positions at Paardeplaats
11th   Kruger flees to Lourcenço Marques
13th   Lord Roberts issues proclamation calling on Boers to surrender
25th   British occupy Komati Poort

October
8th   Lord Milner appointed administrator of the two new colonies
9th   De Wet driven across the Vaal
16th   Boer attack on Jagersfontein repulsed
17th   Lord Methuen defeats Tollie de Beer near Schweizer Reneke
19th   Kruger flees Lourcenço Marques on a steamer to Marseille
20th   French occupies Bethal; de Wet invests Barton at Frederikstad
24th   Lord Methuen defeats Lemmer at Kruisrivier
25th   De Wet's investment of Frederikstad ends in failure
26th   Boer attack on Koffyfontein repulsed
27th   De Wet's guns and wagons captured at Rensburg Drift

November
6th   De Wet defeated at Bothaville
19th   Boer attacks on stations at Balmoral and Wilge River defeated
22nd   Kruger arrives in Marseille
23rd   De Wet captures Dewetsdorp
29th   Lord Kitchener replaces Lord Roberts as Commander-in-Chief

December
3rd   De La Rey captures convoy at Buffelspoort
5th   De Wet forced to abandon his raid into the Cape Colony
7th   De Wet's attack on Highland Light Infantry post at Commissie Bridge driven off
11th   Lord Roberts sails from Cape Town
12th   Boer attack on Vryheid repulsed
19th   Hertzog captures Philipstown

1901

January
4th   Commander-in-Chief's bodyguard ambushed and captured at Kromspruit
5th   Colonel Grey drives de la Rey from positions at Cyferfontein
7th   Boer attacks on Belfast and other stations on the Delagoa railway line all repulsed
10th   Boer peace emissary, Morgendaal, murdered by de Wet's men near Kroonstad
17th   Martial law extended to all of the Cape Colony except ports and native territories
18th   De la Rey defeated near Ventersburg
31st   Smuts captures Modderfontein

February
2nd   Cunningham's attack on Smuts at Modderfontein driven off
7th   Additional 30,000 mounted troops ordered to South Africa
10th   De Wet crosses the Orange River at Sand Drift in another attempt to invade the Cape Colony
12th   Colonel Plumer in touch with de Wet's invasion force
13th   Lord Kitchener approaches Louis Botha to discuss peace terms
18th   Lord Methuen defeats de La Rey at Haartebeestefontein
19th   De Wet abandons his disastrous invasion of the Cape
23rd   De Wet's guns captured
28th   Peace talks between Botha and Kitchener at Middelburg

March
3rd   De La Rey's attack on Lichtenburg driven off
7th   Botha formally rejects Kitchener's peace proposals, as discussed at the Middelburg Conference
15th   Park captures Boer laager at Kruger's Post
24th   De La Rey defeated by Babington at Wildfontein

April
1st   Colonel Plumer occupies Nylstroom
6th   Scheepers captures a small detachment at Zeekoegat, near Craddock
8th   Colonel Plumer occupies Pietersburg
14th   Rawlinson and Babington capture a Boer laager and two guns at Goedvooruitzicht
16th   Viljoen and Muller defeated at Palmietfontein

May
10th   Boer council of war meets near Ermelo
29th   De La Rey attacks Vlakfontein and is driven off

June
2nd   Jamestown captured by Kritzinger
6th   De La Rey and de Wet attack Major Sladen near Reitz and are driven off
12th   Victorian Mounted Rifles overrun at Wilmansrust
21st   Kritzinger captures detachment of Midlands Mounted Rifles near Maraisburg

July

5th	Kruger telegraphs Botha to continue fighting
11th	Broadwood captures Orange Free State government and Steyn escapes
14th	French drives Scheepers out of the Camdeboo Mountains; Myburg defeated and his laager captured
21st	Lategan's commando broken up by Cape Colony drive
30th	Viljoen defeated at Crocodile Drift, near Middelburg

August

1st	Smuts surprised and attacked at Grootvlei
6th	British parliament votes £6,500,000 grant to the Transvaal and Orange River Colony
8th	Commandant de Villiers captured at Warmbaths
12th	Kritzinger driven out of the Cape Colony
13th	Kritzinger's commando routed near Steynsburg
16th	19th Hussars ambushed by Muller at Vrieskraal
17th	South African Constabulary capture laager near Middelburg

September

3rd	Smuts invades the Cape Colony at Klaarwater Drift
5th	Lotter and his commando captured by Scobell near Craddock
7th	Botha commences his invasion of Natal
10th	Scheepers's commando routed near Laingsburg
17th	Botha cuts up Gough at Blood River Poort; Smuts surprises detachment of 17th Lancers at Modderfontein
19th	200 mounted infantry and South African Constabulary captured at Slangfontein
20th	Detachment of the Lovat Scouts surprised and cut up at Quaggafontein
26th	Botha's attacks on Fort Prospect and Itala driven off with heavy loss
30th	De La Rey's night attack on British positions at Moedwil driven off

October

9th	Martial law extended to the Cape ports
11th	Commandant Lotter executed; Commandant Scheepers captured near Blood River Station
20th	Three Boer laagers captured near Nylstroom
22nd	Benson surprises Boer laager at Klippoortje
29th	Maritz captures British convoy between Lambert's Bay and Clanwilliam
30th	Botha overruns Benson's rearguard at Bakenlaagte

November

1st	Colonel Kekewich captures van Albert's laager
11th	Du Toit's laager captured at Doornhoek
20th	Commandant Buys captured near Villiersdorp
26th	Commandant Joubert captured
29th	De Wet attacks Rimington at Spytfontein; confused action ends with Rimington's retreat

December

4th	Botha surprised by Bruce Hamilton at Osheok, near Ermelo

6th	Colonel Plumer engages Botha at Kalkoenskraal
7th	National Scouts formed from surrendered Transvaal Boers
10th	Bethal Commando surprised by Bruce Hamilton at Trigaardtsfontein
12th	Viljoen's laager captured by Bruce Hamilton
15th	Commandant Badenhorst captured by Colonel Colenbrander
16th	Kritzinger captured near Hanover Road
18th	De Wet's attack on the ILH under Colonel Dartnell at Tigerkloof Spruit driven off
19th	14th Mounted Infantry ambushed by Britz near Ermelo; Boer attack on Elandspruit repulsed
20th	Wessels surprises a small force under Colonel Damant at Tafel Kop
25th	De Wet captures camp at Tweefontein
29th	General Erasmus captured near Ermelo

1902
January

10th	Bruce Hamilton captures Major Wolmaran's laager near Ermelo
17th	Scheepers executed at Graaff-Reinet
25th	General Ben Viljoen captured near Lydenburg

February

3rd	Colonel Garratt defeats Commandant Mears at Roodekraal
4th	Commandant Albert and 130 of his men captured near Lichtenburg
5th	British convoy captured by Malan near Beaufort West
17th	Judge Kock captured in the Cape Colony
20th	Commandant Muller surprised by Colonel Park
22nd	Grobler's commando captured near Lake Chrissie
24th	Convoy captured by de la Rey at Yzer Spruit
26th	End of drive in eastern Free State, with Meyer and 600 prisoners taken

March

7th	Battle of Tweefontein ends in Boer victory, with Lord Methuen taken prisoner
15th	Bruce Hamilton captures General Emmett near Vryheid
26th	Cecil Rhodes dies

April

1st	Maritz captures Springbok
4th	Smuts invests Okiep
8th	Colonel Colenbrander defeats Beyers near Pietersburg
11th	Kemp's horsemen charge Colonel Kekewich at Roodewal and are driven off with heavy losses
12th	Lord Kitchener meets Boer peace delegation in Pretoria; Smuts attacks Okiep
18th	Peace delegation leaves Pretoria to consult with the commandos

May

3rd	Siege of Okiep raised
15th	Opening of Vereeniging conference
27th	Commandant Malan captured near Jansenville
31st	Boer surrender signed

Author's note

Ever since I watched Edward Woodward in *Breaker Morant* as a youngster, I have been fascinated by the Boer War, or 'Anglo-Boer War' as it seems fashionable to call it these days.* I have spent virtually all my adult life in southern Africa, and the war has long been something close to an obsession for me: I buy any book or piece of memorabilia I can find on the subject, and over many years have spent countless weekends walking battlefields, visiting museums and arguing with people in pubs all over the sub-continent.

One such argument took place in a backpacker lodge in Zambia when I was a very young chap. The owner was a burly Afrikaner who immediately launched into a tirade about the wickedness of the British in the Boer War. On and on he went, becoming more volatile and more knowledgeable with every double brandy that he tipped down his neck. Seeing this was going to end in a brawl, I endeavoured to change the subject and asked him if he had served in the South African army. He proudly stood up as straight as twenty double brandies would permit, and announced he had served in the "best regiment in the army—the Natal Carbineers". My knowledge of the war was fairly limited back then, but even I knew that the Natal Carbineers was an imperial regiment, raised in the most 'British' of Her Majesty's colonies, and had served with great distinction *against* the Boers in the war. When I pointed this out to him, he flew into something of a rage; I have never forgotten the sheer ignorance of the fellow—keen as mustard to argue about the war but knowing absolutely nothing about it. It has been a scenario which has been repeated on countless occasions over the years.

A few days later I found myself in the bar of Lusaka's Holiday Inn and got chatting to a BA captain who was reading Pakenham's *The Boer War*, supposedly the definitive account of the war. Inspired by my recent argument, I bought myself a copy the next day. As time went on, however, I came to realize that Pakenham's account was outrageously one-sided and, disappointingly, so were many other modern accounts of the conflict.

Worse still, on speaking to people about the conflict over the years,

---

* Indeed, one South African website postulates, "The South African War ... is a subjective term used by the British" and therefore "not acceptable". It then goes on to bizarrely claim that the long-used "Boer War ... is also not acceptable, the British was [*sic*] the aggressor and, following this line of argument, it should be called "the English War". This mindless rant concludes that "Anglo-Boer War" is the "only acceptable term". This nonsense is reason enough, I feel, to stick with the established name of 'the Boer War' and I shall do so throughout this book.

it became obvious that the war has been filed in the same pigeon hole as the First World War, i.e. everyone thinks they 'know' about it, but in the vast majority of cases, their 'knowledge' is utterly flawed, simplistic, cock-eyed and biased. It would not be an exaggeration to say that the commonly held view is that the British were the baddies, intent only on stealing gold and murdering women and children, while the Boers were the goodies, noble, innocent people desperate just to be left in peace. This book seeks to challenge this rubbish. I do not pretend that it is an exhaustive, comprehensive account of the conflict, but what it will hopefully do is torpedo a few of the more commonly held misconceptions of the war and, better yet, cause a few readers to re-evaluate their view of the conflict. Whether authors admit it or not, every book is written from a certain stand point, and I freely admit that my sympathies and loyalties are to the British Empire, rather than to Kruger's corrupt clique. This book is the product of many years of research, and while my opinions and the facts herein are copiously referenced, in many cases, they remain just that—opinions. There are two sides to every argument and this book will show the fair-minded reader that there was more to the war than apartheid-era propaganda and pro-Kruger writers like Pakenham will have you believe. If people new to the subject find their interest in the conflict piqued by this book, then I heartily recommend they read some of the many other accounts which are available, so as to enable them to make up their own minds.

I have no doubt that there will be those of every stripe who prefer not to challenge their current 'understanding' of the war and who will scream and stamp their feet at my efforts to prick the bubble of their cosy fantasy. Such closed-minded types are never interested in listening to reason, and so I don't suppose for a moment that my book will appeal to them. And though it will assuredly be painted by some morons as such, what this book is most certainly not intended to be is an attack on the *Boerevolk*. Though there were many guilty parties on both sides, I firmly believe—and my evidence supports this—that Kruger and his gaggle were primarily responsible for the war. But while I admit to a hearty dislike for Kruger and Krugerism, that by no means equates to a dislike for Afrikanerdom in general. Indeed, the majority of my friends are Afrikaans (at least, they were before this book was published) and I am lucky enough to be married to a lovely Afrikaans girl who is, incidentally, the great-great-grandniece of F.W. Reitz. To say that criticism of Krugerism is criticism of Afrikaners as a whole would be as brainless as saying that someone disapproving of Hitler's regime and ambitions must hate all Germans.

As we will explore, it is also a misconception to assume that the federal forces of the Transvaal and Orange Free State were, in any case, all Afrikaners, or that those tens of thousands of South Africans who fought for the Empire were all of British extraction. Many thousands of Afrikaners fought against Kruger's clique while the polyglot ranks of the federal armies contained large numbers of Englishmen, Scots, Irish and a whole potpourri of other international idealists, adventurers and troublemakers.

Unfortunately, however, such is the victim mentality of some South Africans, who are still fighting the war in their minds, that they see evil everywhere they look. You only have to read a few of the more deranged websites to realize just how utterly deluded some of these people are, and that the Boer War remains highly emotive. With tedious predictability, virtually everything is seized upon by such people as an 'insult'. Recently, for example, a novel about the Great Trek, *Canvas under the Sky*, attracted the attention of extremist Afrikaner groups because it featured the trekkers enjoying some giggly-weed and having the odd dalliance with dusky maidens. The outrage that this caused led to these fellows—the *Herstigte Nasionale Party* to be precise—burning copies of the novel, and I have little doubt this book will be received by some in the same fashion. But if anyone finds this book offensive, please feel free to buy up all the copies you can and have a bonfire.

Of course, in these enlightened times we all have to tiptoe about trying not to offend extremists of every colour and creed, but strangely one can say absolutely anything one likes about the British army, and the British Empire in general. For some reason, those who served on the imperial side during the Boer War are considered to be fair game for unsubstantiated accusations, wild theories and insane insults. It is my hope that this book might go a little way to standing up for these men, the vast majority of whom were brave, honourable, decent fellows, ordered to South Africa to fight a war started by Kruger and his gang.

॰ॐ

I have been helped by a great many people over the years it has taken to write this book, though it is only fair to say that not all share all my conclusions. My long-suffering sounding board, and favourite pro-Boer, Mr Rob Milne, author of *Anecdotes of the Anglo-Boer War*, has taken the time to debate dozens of points and swap hundreds of emails as well as always being happy to lend me books from his exhaustive collection. In countless discussions he valiantly fought the Boer corner and always sought to balance my opinions. Though our views often differed, Rob's deep understanding of the conflict and infectious enthusiasm were a constant source of inspiration.

Helpful as ever was the peerless Ken Gillings, the font of knowledge on all things pertaining to the Boer War. Patient, helpful and ever generous of his time, Ken assisted with various aspects of my research, though again, this book cannot be taken to represent his views on the subject. Captain Mick Holtby, curator of the The Queen's Royal Lancers & Nottinghamshire Yeomanry Museum, kindly assisted in the details of the action fought by the 17th Lancers at Modderfontein.

Crystal Warren of the National English Literary Museum at Rhodes University went above and beyond the call of duty to assist me with scans from their rare-book collection. Likewise, cartographer extraordinaire Phil Wright was equally brilliant to work with, despite our usually being in different countries throughout the whole affair. In a reminder that there are still some gentlemen around, when I asked Phil if he wanted any money up front before starting on the maps, he replied, "No, no need for that—you're from Shetland, and that's good enough for me." Chris Cocks of 30° South Publishers also deserves a special mention: without him none of this would have happened.

Last, but most importantly, I'd like to thank my darling wife Stefanie. On the rare occasions we have been in the same time zone over the last three years, our evenings together have generally been spent with me tapping furiously away at my laptop, and her waiting patiently—and sometimes not so patiently—for me to finish writing for the night and actually talk to her.

Introduction

We shall never know if he was simply swept up with a bit of World Cup fever, or had been maddened by the unending, mindless blasting of vuvuzelas, but on the 26th June 2010, the chief sports editor of the *Daily Telegraph* decided to try his hand at bit of historical writing.[1] Despite cheerfully admitting his complete and utter ignorance of events, Mr Paul Kelso didn't seem to think that this should in any way prevent him from giving his readers a potted history of the Boer War. Quickly confirming his self-confessed ignorance, Kelso sagaciously assured his readers that the "the spark for conflict was, typically, financial". Evidently warming to his newly adopted field of expertise, Kelso airily went on to claim that Great Britain—"led by Lord Kitchener", apparently—had been happy to leave the Boer republics of the Orange Free State and the Transvaal in peace, but then started the war when "diamonds were discovered in the former and gold in the latter". Contradicting himself, Kelso also claimed that the Free State was "a region that has its origins in a long battle for independence from Britain that, in 1899, culminated in the three-year Anglo-Boer War". This absolute rubbish serves as a good example of why a sports writer should not dabble in history,* though perhaps Mr Kelso's complete and utter ignorance of the Boer War is understandable if not forgivable.

While I have never heard anyone (other than the extraordinary Mr Kelso) claim that the British started the war to grab the diamond fields,† most people will assure you that the dastardly British government attacked the harmless, peaceful Transvaal to steal their gold. Perhaps the only conflict that comes close to the Boer War in terms of general misunderstanding is the First World War, and that thanks largely to the doggerel of a couple of pacifist poets, the tireless propaganda of the left-leaning British educational establishment of the 1960s and the BBC comedy series, *Blackadder Goes Forth*.

Like the First World War, the Boer War is generally regarded as a 'bad war', something the British should be frightfully ashamed of and which was fought for all the wrong reasons. Even as the war was being fought, one Mr J. A. Hobson, a British newspaper reporter and hardline leftie who dabbled with

---

* Though one expects to read such mindless tripe in a low-brow rag like *The Guardian*, one generally expects better from the *Daily Telegraph*.

† South Africa's diamonds fields, both then and now, are overwhelmingly in the area around Kimberley, a town which was in the British Cape Colony in 1899 and which, indeed, the Boers endeavoured to capture.

Marxism, was passionately declaring it to be all the fault of capitalists, Jews and bankers. Such was his passion that he did not feel the need to provide any evidence but, nonetheless, his conspiracy theory was eagerly lapped up by many. Indeed, the Boer War has been gleefully held up as the epitome of British imperial arrogance and capitalist greed ever since, and the commonly held view of the war is a gift from above for modern-day critics of Britain's colonial past. Their bizarre version of the conflict has everything they could ask for: greedy, scheming capitalists,* humiliating defeats of Her Majesty's armies, bumbling, incompetent upper-class generals, massively outnumbered yet courageous and honourable Boers and, of course—best of all—the concentration camps. No argument about the Boer War is complete without someone sagely declaring, "Well, you probably don't know this, but it wasn't the Nazis who invented the concentration camp [pause for dramatic effect], it was the British." This tediously predictable and wholly inaccurate statement is used as the Joker, the card that will trump all others and which, it is hoped, will deflect them from having to actually answer any of the questions you've posed. When I told a close friend and fellow enthusiast of the period that I was writing this book, his first response was, "I hope you're not going to mention the concentration camps?" as though they were in some way off-limits for rational discussion and investigation, which, indeed, they generally have been.

While all this nonsense was first popularized by Hobson, plenty of others have carried on the job since then. Decades of apartheid-era propaganda, lies and exaggerations have taken their toll in South Africa, to the extent that many South Africans seem to believe the war was actually fought between Great Britain and South Africa, despite the fact that the latter didn't actually exist at the time. The 'new' South African government, for example, named one of their controversial new corvettes *Spion Kop* after a Boer victory in the war. Indeed, such is the level of misunderstanding about the war in southern Africa that most people I have spoken to over the years are utterly convinced that Britain attacked the Transvaal, rather than the other way round.

Chatting at a braai one afternoon, I was informed by one fellow that the British 'lost' because they advanced toward the Boers wearing red jackets with white cross-belts and the clever old Boers used these as an aiming point. When I pointed out that he might be thinking of the first Boer War, not the second,

---

* Contemporary Liberal opponents of the war often referred to these as 'Jewish Capitalists', presumably to further illustrate just how evil they must be. This unpleasant practice has fortunately fallen out of favour, in public at least.

I was waved away and assured he was correct. Worse still, when on a tour of Spion Kop, our guide assured me that the British wore red jackets at Talana Hill and, once again, my disagreement was ignored. The same guide went on to claim that the Boers invented the concept of sniping, so obviously this genius had not heard of the American War of Independence, Rogers' Rangers in the French and Indian Wars, the Pathans of the North West Frontier or the British 95th Rifles of the Napoleonic Wars. More ridiculously still, I have even had heated arguments with English-speaking South Africans and white Zimbabweans about the conflict, the thrust of their argument usually being something like: "We taught you Pommies a lesson, but then you cheated." When it is pointed out to such people that, assuming their great-grandfathers fought in the war, it is far more likely that they would have fought for the Crown than against it, this gets them even hotter under the collar.

After a recent battlefield tour, an English-speaking South African accosted me in the bar that evening, and opened our conversation by declaring: "We really fucked you Brits up in the war." When I pointed out that the British won the war, he retorted that this was because we had killed women and children in concentration camps which, by his perverse logic, is presumably the same as the British being "really fucked up in the war". When I explained that the British did not kill these people, that they mainly died of measles, the imbecile triumphantly declared, "They didn't die of measles; they died of disease."

Farther afield, the 'definitive' modern history of the conflict, *The Boer War* by eccentric anti-establishment leftist, Thomas Pakenham, must also bear some of the blame for this widespread ignorance. First published in 1979, it is an incredibly biased and staunchly pro-Kruger* tome, gleefully heaping all the blame onto the British while glossing over anything which might in any way tarnish the reputation of the Boers. The mass murder of hundreds of black Africans by Boer commandos is, for example, covered in a couple of lines before Pakenham returns to the important business of bashing the wicked British officer class. Following in the wake of Pakenham's offering, many books have been written in recent years by a rogues' gallery of authors, all falling over themselves to blame everything on the wicked British Empire.

---

* At first glance, being both leftist and pro-Boer might seem like something of a contradiction, but it is, in fact, a very common combination. Unpatriotic British lefties have a long and unpleasant history of automatically taking the side of absolutely anyone—and I mean absolutely *anyone*, e.g. Galtieri, Saddam Hussein, Paul Kruger, Gerry Adams, Osama bin Laden—who endeavours to twist the Lion's tail.

One of the most amusing of these—for all the wrong reasons—is a work called *Why the Boers Lost the War*, written by a Professor Leopold Scholtz in 2005. Wasting no time to commence his propaganda offensive, Professor Scholtz tells us on page 1 that "on 11 October 1899 the British government explained its aggression with the argument that the British foreign nationals (*Uitlanders*) in the Transvaal were being treated unfairly … it is accepted nowadays that this was a political pretext to manipulate public opinion in Britain".[2]

Accepted quite by whom Scholtz does not deign to tell us: indeed, he offers absolutely nothing whatsoever to support his sweeping statement, which is somewhat telling in itself. Presumably Scholtz feels that the Transvaal's denial of the franchise to tens of thousands of uitlanders was completely acceptable, so one is left to assume he also defends South Africa's less restricted franchise laws of the apartheid era? At least the good professor makes a bit of an attempt to support his outlandish claim that the war was sparked by British 'aggression' rather than, as in reality, by a Boer invasion of British territory. Scholtz bases his claim on a most remarkable statement, attributed to none other than his dad, G. D. Scholtz: "the place on the globe where they saw the best opportunity to display British power was South Africa. Here the destruction of the two small Afrikaans republics had to demonstrate to the world how big Britain's power was. It had to reconfirm its position as one of the world's leading powers."[3] This is such complete and utter fantasy that, at first glance, one can be forgiven for assuming that Scholtz & Scholtz were joking; yet, incredibly, it would seem they are serious. When faced with such a surreal and baseless claim, it is difficult to know where to begin, but for a start, Scholtz the elder's wild statement unthinkingly lumps the Orange Free State in with the Transvaal, glibly ignoring the fact that Britain had absolutely no quarrel with the former and, unlike the Transvaal, had actually enjoyed very good relations with her for a generation.* As to the main claim—perhaps difficult for a twenty-first-century mind to grasp—in spite of a recently united Germany beginning to challenge her position, the Great Britain of 1899 was still the world's most pre-eminent power, both militarily and financially: though small by Continental standards, her armies had just completed the re-conquest of the Sudan, and had forced the French to back

---

* Far from being desperate to get their hands on the Orange Free State, Great Britain had forced independence on that nation in 1854. The Transvaal, in stark contrast, had tried to invade the Orange Free State in 1857.

down over the Fashoda incident. The British Empire covered a quarter of the globe, the Royal Navy ruled the waves* and London was the financial powerhouse the world.

Quite why Messrs Scholtz & Scholtz would have us believe Britain suddenly felt in any way compelled to "reconfirm its position as one of the world's leading powers" is anyone's guess, as regretfully they do not feel the need to explain such a ridiculous contention. Nor does either Scholtz explain why, just a year after forcing France to back down over her ambitions in the Sudan, that winning a war against two miniscule states would reconfirm anything to anyone. If even mighty France had shuddered and taken a step back when the Lion roared, surely that would appear 'reconfirmation' enough? Though neither Scholtz sees fit to justify his claims, somewhat amusingly and just a few pages later, Scholtz the younger momentarily forgets the party line and, in what might be the only accurate statement in his book, admits that "in 1899 Britain was still by far the strongest world power ... there was no international power who was able or willing to challenge the British economic and maritime supremacy".[4] So quite what led Scholtz & Son to declare that Great Britain had something to prove to anyone in 1899 remains a mystery.

Pakenham also seizes on a dubious quote as the basis of his theory on British intentions. Ignoring the reality that the British army had virtually no troops in theatre and trusting implicitly the notes of the Boer commando leader (and later mass murderer),[5] Jan Smuts, Pakenham claims that the British were planning an attack as early as December 1898, at a time when Boer commandos outnumbered imperial troops in southern Africa by about ten to one. This somewhat wild assertion is based entirely on a conversation which Smuts claimed to have taken place between him and the acting British agent in Pretoria, Mr Edmund Fraser, during discussions on the mistreatment of Cape Coloured† workers in the Transvaal. Rather conveniently, there don't appear to have been any witnesses, but the remarkably loose-lipped Fraser allegedly told Smuts: "We've got to show you who's the boss in South Africa ... England's fed up with the maladministration in this country, and especially with the ill-treatment of British subjects. This is the point on which England

---

* In 1889 the Royal Navy adopted the 'Two Power Standard': having more battleships than the next two largest navies combined.

† The Cape Coloureds have long been a distinct ethnic grouping, of primarily Khoikhoi, Malay and Dutch descent, and whose language is generally Afrikaans; not to be confused with the generic western term 'coloured', meaning black or non-white.

will take action. I know perfectly well that England won't go to war over abstract subjects like suzerainty—that means nothing to the man in the street. She'll go to war about things that everyone can understand."[6] Unfortunately, Pakenham doesn't trouble himself to explain why Smuts didn't go public on this outrageous utterance at the time, or think to question why on earth Mr Fraser would reveal such a startling plan to the enemy. It is also interesting that Smuts revealed this supposed conversation in a letter he wrote to Jan Hofmeyr six months later: was there a reason why, in May 1899, he suddenly felt the need to reveal this pusillanimous plot to the leader of the Afrikaner Bond in the Cape? Of course we shall never know if this conversation really took place, but it seems so far-fetched that it is sensible to take it with a pinch of salt, rather than eagerly accepting it as gospel à la Pakenham.

But of all the nonsense written by those desperate to pin the blame for the war on the scheming British, the perverse and, as usual, unsubstantiated claims by modern writers that poor old, misunderstood Kruger "never gazed beyond his own borders"[7] and that "the South African Republic asked only to be left alone"[8] are perhaps the most telling. These sorts of statements illustrate perfectly the myth that has been carefully cultivated around the origins of the conflict: the fantasy that the Transvaal Boers were a quiet, peaceful, innocent and simple people who were happy with their little corner of Africa and wanted nothing but to be left to their own devices. Apparently this harmonious and halcyon—nay—idyllic existence was suddenly shattered by the clatter of hobnailed boots as hundreds of thousands of pernicious, red-faced Tommies poured into their little corner of heaven, bayoneting babies and violating their womenfolk. That professors of history should seek to perpetuate this chimera is either amusing or alarming or perhaps both.

The Boers of Kruger's Transvaal wanted many things—mainly things belonging to other people, usually black—but the one thing in which they never showed any interest was being content with their lot. Their country had only recently been built by violent conquest in the first place, and was constantly expanding in all directions, annexing land from its neighbours. Invasions, raids, slave trading, civil war and bloodshed by the bucket were the norm. Other than during a very brief period of British rule, the Transvaal had never been stable, peace-loving or well run. Despite the chimeric delusions of modern commentators, it had most definitely never been a good neighbour, and Kruger, as we shall soon see, had constantly "gazed beyond his borders".

CHAPTER ONE

Making of the Transvaal

"The Transvaal rising was not dictated, as was believed in England, by a love of freedom and preference for a republic rather than a limited monarchy. It was inspired by men who were planning a policy which would banish the English language and English influence from South Africa. Their action was a blow directly dealt against freedom, progress, and union of Europeans in South Africa."
—Reverend John Mackenzie, writing about the war of 1881[1]

"So long as there were native cattle to be stolen and native lands worth appropriating, the absorbing process would be repeated. Tribe after tribe would be pushed back and back upon other tribes, or would perish in the process, until an inhabitable desert, or the sea, were reached as the ultimate boundary of the state."
—Sir Hercules Robinson, writing about the Transvaal's expansion into Bechuanaland[2]

"The policy of the Transvaal was to push out bands of freebooters, and to get them in quarrels with the natives. They wished to push their border over the land westwards, and realize the dream of President Pretorius, which was that the Transvaal should stretch from the Indian Ocean to the Atlantic. The result was robbery, rapine and murder."
—arch-liberal John X. Merriman, Grahamstown, 1885[3]

"the Boers were quite unable to properly control, utilize, and administer their own immense territory, but 'land hunger' is theirs as a birth curse. The individual cannot bear to see the smoke of his neighbour's chimney; he will not cultivate 50 acres, but wants 50,000; the 'nation' wants Africa—no less."
—leading uitlander and later author of *Jock of the Bushveld*, Percy Fitzpatrick, 1900

"the Boer Government had reached the zenith of incapacity; in this respect it was the worst government in the world, and I, an Austrian, say it …
Corruption battened in Pretoria as nowhere else in the world."
—illustrious Austrian traveller, Count Sternberg, 1901

To understand the true origins of the Boer War, one must first understand the volatile and aggressively expansionist Boer republic of the Transvaal, so before we return to the immediate causes of the conflict, we need to examine how the Transvaal came into being. Mr Kelso and Professor Scholtz, I hope you are both paying attention.

When the British acquired the Cape from the Dutch in the Napoleonic Wars, their subsequent banning of slavery did not go down well with some of the Dutch-speaking inhabitants, also known as Afrikaners, Boers or—less pleasantly these days—'Dutchmen'. In the 1830s thousands of these hardliners* trekked inland to escape British rule. Some established the republic of the Orange Free State (OFS), others set up the short-lived republic of Natalia (which soon became the staunchly pro-British Natal), but the most critical group was that which crossed the Vaal River and clashed with the Ndebele, an offshoot of the famous Zulus and the dominant tribe in the region. In a series of battles these settlers steadily drove the Ndebele from the area and, indeed, by 1838, had chased them out altogether, the Ndebele fleeing north into what is today Zimbabwe. In their place the new arrivals established a haphazard mish-mash of mini-republics. Though the newcomers had been ably assisted in their battles against the Ndebele by some of the other tribes in the region, they quickly forgot this, according these people no political rights and instituting a system of 'apprenticeships' which was nothing other than slavery by another name.[4]

But for all the modern-day fantasies of their apologists, the scattered settlements of the Transvaal† area could by no means be considered a functioning nation-state. Never people to settle for a small patch of land, the men among the 40,000 Boer settlers of the Transvaal each considered it his God-given right to own a 6,000-acre farm, which explains why they had spread themselves over an area larger than Great Britain.[5] Fiercely independent, poorly educated in the main and loath to pay taxes, the new arrivals in the Transvaal had little interest in law and order and were keener to resolve disputes with violence. Seemingly blessed with more chiefs than Indians, the perennially fractious settlers splintered into tiny entities, with miniscule 'capital cities' established in insignificant hamlets like Lydenburg,

---

* including a young Paul Kruger, the man who would later play the dominant role in fomenting the Boer War of 1899–1902

† literally 'beyond the Vaal'

Potchefstroom and Zoutpansberg. To complicate matters still further, they also gazed with covetous eyes on the republic of the Orange Free State (established to their south by their brother Boers) and harboured the belief that they had been cheated out of Natal by the scheming Englishmen.

But far from the venal British wishing to deny the Transvaal Boers their right to self-rule as some commentators claim, the imperial authorities duly signed the Sand River Convention in 1852. While expressly prohibiting the practice of slavery, this agreement recognized the independence of the Transvaal. Yet even this convention caused the Transvaalers to again start squabbling among themselves, as the other mini-republics refused to recognize the right of Andries Pretorius* (commandant of the Potchefstroom-based Zuid-Afrikaansche Republiek, the ZAR, or the South African Republic) to sign on behalf of all the various mini-republics.† With the death of Pretorius in 1853, his son, Marthinus,‡ a man equally given to war-lordism as his father, assumed command of the Zuid-Afrikaansche Republiek. A truly Machiavellian power struggle soon ensued as he endeavoured to gain control of, not only all the other Transvaal republics, but also the Orange Free State.[6]

Pretorius the younger brazenly declared the rival republics to be rebels and, between 1856 and 1864, the patchwork of various micro-states which would ultimately become the Transvaal fought a series of on-again-off-again wars, either with one another or with themselves. The one constant of these spluttering, chaotic civil wars was a certain Paul Kruger,§ "sometimes on the side of Pretorius, and sometimes against him, but always exceedingly ready to take up arms".[7] Kruger flitted "across the scene generally as a stormy petrel. We find him on the side of certain Boer revolutionaries or reformers, upholding them in their action and protesting against their being saddled with fine when their action failed. On two separate occasions we find him marching on Pretoria to drive out the head of a rival party. We even find him joining in a kind of raid across the border of the friendly [Orange] Free State and issuing a twenty-four hours' ultimatum to its Government".[8]

This attack on the Orange Free State was nothing less than a blatant

---

*   Andries Wilhelmus Jacobus Pretorius (1798–1853)

†   a similar convention was also signed by the British two years later, recognizing the independence of the Orange Free State

‡   Marthinus Wessel Pretorius (1819–1901)

§   Stephanus Johannes Paulus Kruger (10 October 1825–14 July 1904)

invasion after ZAR political attempts to force union on its neighbour had been rebuffed. Pretorius and Kruger were outmanoeuvred and forced to slink back to the ZAR with their tails between their legs. Such was their determination to invade the Orange Free State that agents of the ZAR were even sent to Basutoland* to persuade King Moshesh to join their attack,[9] this at a time when using black warriors against fellow whites was viewed as the ultimate act of dishonour. Though the Transvaalers were unsuccessful in this particular plot, they did later manage to snatch a chunk of the Orange Free State: in direct contravention of the Sand River Convention, ZAR forces simply occupied the Wakkerstroom district.

Though understandably opposed to being ruled by their crackpot neighbours to the north, and despite the nonsense written by *The Telegraph*'s Mr Kelso, the leaders of the newly independent Orange Free State were actually very keen to re-enter the British sphere of influence. Perhaps hopeful that this would provide stability and protection from yet another invasion attempt by the ZAR, the leaders of the OFS approached the British high commissioner of the Cape Colony, Sir George Grey, after a vote in their volksraad approved "a Union or alliance with the Cape Colony".[10] Alas, and despite Grey's enthusiasm for the union, London displayed no interest in being saddled with more colonies and the plan was shelved by the incoming Liberal government. This short-sighted decision by the Little Englanders of the Liberal Party had far-reaching consequences. Had the relatively stable, well-run and moderate Orange Free State become part of British South Africa in the 1860s, surely not even Kruger would have been insane enough to start a war.

As it was, the Zuid-Afrikaansche Republiek continued to expand and endeavoured to dominate all around it. Kruger remained a driving force in all the fighting, routing a rival faction out of Pretoria and then blasting another out of Potchefstroom with his artillery.[11] When Kruger's men marched into Potchefstroom, the inhabitants were warned that anyone who resisted would be shot.[12] The mini-republics of Lydenburg and Zoutpansberg were finally incorporated into the ZAR in 1860,† though in truth, it was really only a union on paper,[13] with the Zoutpansbergers being especially suspicious. Pretorius was named president of the vastly enlarged state and the new capital of Pretoria was established and named in honour of his late father. Still not

---

* modern-day Lesotho

† the tiny republic of Utrecht had already united with Lydenburg in 1858

content with his empire-building—an empire-building strangely overlooked today—Pretorius fancied another crack at gaining control of the Orange Free State. His agents in the OFS helped in his election as president of that state too, a feat which must be fairly unique in modern history. Not surprisingly, his latest attempt to railroad the OFS into political union did not go down well, sparking a fresh uprising in the ZAR. The Transvaal volksraad demanded Pretorius choose one state or the other, and when he chose the OFS this prompted yet further anarchy and civil war in the Transvaal. This state of utter chaos lasted until 1864, dividing the Boers, pitting brother against brother and neighbour against neighbour.[14] A semblance of order was restored only when Pretorius was finally persuaded to give up the presidency of the OFS before he—the consummate political survivor—amazingly returned to the premiership of the Transvaal. One is left astounded that there was no candidate more suitable.

As far as states go, the ZAR of the 1860s would be unrecognizable as such to modern eyes or, indeed, even by the standards of the day. The government's authority over Zoutpansberg remained no more than nominal,[15] the state coffers were generally empty and bankruptcy was never far off. "There were no schools, education being in the hands of itinerant teachers, no newspapers or libraries, nor indeed any recognizable towns."[16] There was no real law and order as such, and when a native uprising in the Zoutpansberg area sent settlers fleeing into laagers, there was nothing the central Transvaal government could do to assist. With no standing army, the ZAR relied on the auxiliary commando system to suppress the ever-troublesome natives they lived among and who vastly outnumbered them. However, the pious Boers refused to ride to the assistance of the Zoutspanberg's wild, hedonistic frontier village of Schoemansdal and it was subsequently burned to the ground. Indeed, the area remained in the hands of native rebels for several years.

One thing that the quarrelsome Transvaalers were able to agree upon, however, was the line in their 1860 constitution which confirmed, "The people are not prepared to allow any equality of the non-white with the white inhabitants, either in Church or State."[17] While the Boer constitution expressly declared that they had no interest in extending the franchise to non-whites, incoming whites could gain citizenship and the right to vote after one year's residence. This would it later be changed to a five-year qualification period, and then changed again, and again and again as the ruling clique of the Transvaal embarked on a desperate and dangerous bid to retain absolute power at all costs.

When the Transvaal Boers were not fighting each other or trying to invade the Orange Free State, they endeavoured to expand their territorial influence in every direction, dominating and marauding as they saw fit. Commandos regularly raided neighbouring tribes, killing, looting and seizing children to be brought back to serve as their 'apprentices'.[18] There was a thriving trade in slaves, with 'Slim' Piet Joubert,* the God-fearing commandant-general of the Transvaal, being known as a particularly good source of these. The *Joubert Papers* contain many letters written on the subject, with this one sent to his wife being typical: "Please ask the General to let me have a little Malaboch kaffir, as of course there are some whose father and mother have been killed. I don't mind if it's a boy or a girl. I want one about seven years old, or any one that the General will give me."[19] During these unending conflicts, the behaviour of the ZAR forces was utterly reprehensible and, in a foretaste of what the British would experience during the Boer War, the accepted rules of war were often completely disregarded by the Transvaalers. In 1868 the ubiquitous Paul Kruger led a commando in an attack on native tribes in the troubled Zoutpansberg area. After negotiating a five-day armistice with his foe, Kruger simply unleashed his men in a surprise attack the following morning.[20] On this occasion Kruger's underhand tactics failed to pay off and the sneak attack was an abject failure—poetic justice, perhaps. In another, particularly horrific, episode, a 400-man commando, including Kruger once again, was assembled to avenge the murder of a party of Boers. The tribe involved sought refuge in a vast cave reckoned to be about 2,000 feet long and 400 wide, which was then pitilessly besieged by the commando.[21] The Boers claimed to have shot down around 900 blacks who had desperately tried to get to water outside the cave. When the Boers entered the cavern after twenty-five days of siege, the bodies of twice that number of blacks were found inside, the poor buggers having died of thirst.[22] One must allow for a degree of exaggeration in such reports, but even if the reality was only a quarter as bad, it was still dreadful.

A similar event happened in the Zoutpansberg war of 1865. After large numbers of blacks had taken refuge in a system of caves, the Transvaalers decided to smoke them out. Witnesses described a truly ghastly scene: "The

---

* Petrus Jacobus Joubert (1834–1900)—*slim* is Afrikaans for 'clever' or 'cunning'

roof of the cave was black with smoke; the remains of the logs which were burnt lay at the entrance. The floor was strewn with hundreds of skulls and skeletons." Some put the death toll as high as twenty thousands.[23] While this enormous number seems outrageously improbable, there can be little doubt that, at the very least, several hundreds perished in this sickening manner.

Those who dared criticize the Transvaal's callous and inhumane treatment of blacks could expect trouble. Dr David Livingstone,* the Afrophile[24] and an outspoken, passionate opponent of the slave trade, was regarded as an especially dangerous enemy by the Transvaal Boers.[25] In a somewhat ironic foretaste of the style of raids imperial units would later make on Boer farms, and which would prompt so much controversy, Transvaal forces crossed the border into Bechuanaland to attack, loot and trash Livingstone's mission station at Kolobeng. Luckily, the churchman had unexpectedly been called away, but the Boers satisfied themselves by smashing up and thoroughly ransacking the station. Displaying impressive forward planning, the raiders had brought four empty wagons with them which they gleefully loaded with pillage. Worse still, the marauders also fell upon the natives who lived around Livingstone's mission: 300 women and children were dragged away as spoils of war, these poor wretches being divided up among the members of the commando as 'apprentices'.[26] Despite their superior weapons and the much-vaunted fighting prowess of the Boer, not all the Transvaal's attempts to snatch land or slaves from their neighbours were successful. Paul Kruger personally led a commando against the Venda in 1867 but was repulsed with heavy losses.[27] Similarly, the Pedi of what became the Eastern Transvaal were able to defy the empire-builders of the Transvaal for many years. No less a man than David Livingstone would later remark: "The Boers have generally manifested a marked antipathy to anything but 'long shot' warfare, and sidling away in their emigrations towards the more effeminate Bechuanas, have left their quarrels with the Kaffirs to be settled by the English, and their wars to be paid for by English gold."[28] The fragmented Tswana people who occupied part of Bechuanaland to the west of the Transvaal indeed proved less troublesome to the land-grabbing Boers, as the Transvaalers steadily encroached onto their territory, insidiously expanding the borders of the ZAR.[29]

---

* Dr David Livingstone (19 March 1813–1 May 1873). Born in Blantyre, Scotland, Livingstone worked in a cotton mill before becoming a Congregationalist missionary, scourge of the slave trade and intrepid explorer, discovering and naming Victoria Falls before dying in his search for the source of the Nile.

There was no attempt at subtlety, however, when the discovery of gold deposits in 1868 at Tati led President Pretorius to simply announce the extension of his borders to the north and west so as to secure these.[30] It is rather droll to compare this action to the hand-wringing indignation of Boer apologists who talk about British attempts to 'steal their gold'. Pretorius later tried to do exactly the same again when diamonds were discovered in Griqualand.[31] As we shall see later, this coup attempt was less successful, however, and his invasion force was driven off by a mob of angry prospectors.

෴

Though this is to perhaps damn with faint praise, in comparison to the near-anarchic ZAR, the Orange Free State was a fairly stable and well-run state. However, the Boers of the Orange Free State still shared their northern brethren's penchant for violently expanding their borders. In 1858, after the British made it clear they had no interest in the region, Orange Free State commandos immediately invaded Basutoland, seizing cattle and razing villages as they went.[32] Again, the fighting qualities of the Boer commandos did not live up to the reputation bestowed on them in modern times, as the Sotho rallied and managed to drive them off. The Orange Free State had another crack at grabbing Basutoland a few years later, invading for a second time in 1865. This time the Boers relentlessly destroyed so much property, livestock and farmland that the Sotho had no choice but to surrender much of their territory to the OFS. The irony of this scorched-earth policy is self-evident. However, even this was not enough as the Orange Free State commandos drove relentlessly on, determined to seize Basutoland in its entirety. This, together with the savage nature of the invasion, was a step too far for the British and they finally reacted. Moving to save the Sotho people from the tender mercies of the OFS, the governor of the Cape Colony, Sir Philip Wodehouse, annexed Basutoland in March 1868. With no interest in risking trouble with Great Britain, the Orange Free State had little choice but to begrudgingly accept this as a *fait accompli*. That they got to keep a large amount of the land they had already invaded surely sweetened the pill.[33]

Indeed, far from the British grasping at this as some dastardly excuse to expand their empire, the appeals of the Sotho king, Moshoeshoe, for a British protectorate had been ignored for several years.[34] Despite the wily king's determination, the annexation of the territory—as a new British colony formally called Basutoland—was the last thing the British had wanted, given that it would mean yet further expenditure and trouble. Such was the enthusiasm of London to be rid of her newly acquired responsibility that Basutoland was transferred to the Cape Colony in 1871. Only after the authorities of the Cape Colony proved ill-suited to governing it, did the British reluctantly re-assume direct responsibility for Basutoland in 1884.[35]

Though regarded by its modern-day critics as an empire ever eager to set her bounds "wider still, and wider", the common theme that runs through the history of the British Empire in southern Africa, at least, is that it was reluctantly dragged into matters, finding itself saddled with for responsibility for territories in which it really had no interest. What is even more telling is that this was usually the result of demands from English-speaking settlers for protection, or to counter the endlessly rapacious Boer expansion into black tribal territories.

The rewriting of the ZAR borders to incorporate the Tati gold fields meant that Pretorius had cheerfully snatched another chunk of Bechuanaland from the long-suffering, but hopelessly divided Tswana people. Indeed, Bechuanaland was largely viewed by the Transvaal Boers as theirs to do with as they chose and various attempts were made to forcibly collect tax from the Barolong, one of the principal tribes in the area. These were without success and when the ZAR sent a commando against the Barolong in 1868, it was driven off.

This constant Boer aggression led to Montsioa Toane, chief of the Barolong, to request that Great Britain take his people under imperial protection, just as the Sotho king had. In a letter flamboyantly addressed to "His Excellency Her Britannic Majesty's High Commissioner, Sir P. Wodehouse, KCB", the chief requested "refuge under your protecting wings from the injustice of the Transvaal Republic, whose Government have lately, by proclamation, included our country within the possessions of the said republic". He goes on to explain that "without the least provocation on our side, though the Boers have from time to time murdered some of my people and enslaved several Balala villages, the Transvaal Republic deprives us, by said proclamation, of our land and our liberty, against which we would protest in the strongest terms, and entreat your Excellency, as Her Britannic Majesty's High Commissioner, to protect us".[36] True to form, however, the British were not interested in acquiring yet more responsibility; the ZAR was not to give up so easily, continuing to encroach and raid their neighbours in Bechuanaland. At Buhrmansdrift in 1870, Barolong chiefs met a delegation from the ZAR, including Pretorius and Kruger, to try to and establish a boundary.[37] When no agreement was reached, the matter was referred to a neutral party, Governor Keate of Natal, but the Transvaal Boers, unenamoured with his equitable suggestion, simply ignored it and continued their schemes of expansion regardless.

In 1876 King Khama, chief of the Bamangwato people from northern Bechuanaland, joined the appeal, writing to Sir Henry Barkly to plead for a British protectorate. The letter contained the following significant passage: "I write to you, Sir Henry, in order that your queen may preserve for me my country, it being in her hands. The Boers are coming into it, and I do not like them. Their actions are cruel among us black people. We are like money, they sell us and our children. I ask Her Majesty to defend me, as she defends all her people. There are three things which distress me very much: war, selling people, and drink. All these things I shall find in the Boers, and it is these things which destroy people to make an end of them in the country. The custom of the Boers has always been to cause people to be sold, and to-day they are still selling people."[38]

Khama's statements were supported by the testimony of missionaries, including the great David Livingstone.[39] Even a Dutch clergyman, writing in 1869, described the system of 'apprenticeships' as being slavery in the fullest sense of the word. When the ZAR was later annexed by the British, one local newspaper, *The Argus*, reported: "As slavery without a doubt is still carried on in the Transvaal contrary to [the Sand River Convention], this may be the reason for the annexation."[40]

Again, and despite the reputation of the British Empire being some sort of grasping, land-hungry behemoth, desperately seeking any excuse to snatch new territory, the pleas of the Barolong and Bamangwato—like those of the Sotho—went unanswered for several years. It was only in 1878 that the British finally bowed to pressure and sent troops under Colonel (later General Sir) Charles Warren to occupy southern Bechuanaland.

By then another of the ZAR's attempts to dominate their black neighbours had backfired spectacularly. Since 1872, the president of the ZAR had been the relatively liberal and forward-looking Thomas Burgers,[41] while the distinctly illiberal and backward-looking Paul Kruger had risen to the position of vice-president. Burgers, with his modern ways and the gaggle of civil servants he had imported *en masse* from the Netherlands, had quickly become highly unpopular with many Transvaal burghers. The ultra-conservative Dopper Party announced that they had had more than enough of this progress malarkey and proposed the reassuringly blinkered Kruger as their presidential candidate.[42]

But for all his much-derided attempts at modernization, what Burgers* presided over was still less of a functioning nation-state and more of a chaotic and virtually bankrupt collection of lawless individuals scattered thinly across the veldt. Potchefstroom, Lydenburg and Pretoria were still little more than villages, there were only four state schools in the whole country, as late as 1877 total annual expenditure was less than £5,000[43] and there was by then quite simply no money to pay government workers. Though most went without any sort of salary at all, the state-surveyor took his pay in land, while the postmaster-general had a slightly less attractive deal, being forced to take his in stamps.[44] Dr Jorrissen, later one of President Kruger's chief agents, says in his reminiscences: "there was no such thing in 1876 as Transvaal patriotism, the whole country was in a state of chaos."[45]

Despite this precarious situation, the leaders of the ZAR jauntily embarked on yet another military adventure, this time against the mountain strongholds of the troublesome Pedi to the north of the Transvaal. The 1,400-strong commando was supported by an especially savage contingent of Swazi allies who were given *carte blanche* to butcher any women and children they came across.[46] Despite this, the Transvaalers came off worse and were quickly routed, scurrying in panic back to Pretoria.[47] With the flaws of the commando system exposed so starkly, and the Pedi poised to follow up the rout, the Boers had no choice but to enlist a corps of foreign mercenaries under a Prussian adventurer called von Schlieckmann.[48] Paying for these dogs of war put yet more strain on the ZAR treasury, but von Schlieckmann's hired thugs managed to temporarily stabilize the situation. The 'singular

---

* The 1905 *New International Encyclopædia* described Burger's premiership as having been "characterized by brilliant but impracticable schemes, aiming chiefly at territorial expansion".

barbarity' employed by von Schlieckmann's force was enough to revolt even his own men: "About daylight we came across four kaffirs. Saw them first, and charged in front of them to cut off their retreat. Saw they were women, and called out not to fire. In spite of that, one of the poor things got her head blown off (a damned shame) … I never heard such a cowardly bit of business in my life. No good will come of it … [von Schlieckmann] says he will cut all the women and children's throats he catches. Told him distinctly he was a damned coward."[49]

Schlieckmann's thugs killed "two women and a child at Steelport" and then, in another attack on a nearby kraal, 'he ordered his men to cut the throats of all the wounded". Field-Cornet Erasmus was another nasty piece of work, whose men killed "forty or fifty friendly natives, men and women, and carried off the children".[50]

This brutal savagery saw the Pedi just about contained, but to the south, the far more powerful and martial Zulus were mustering their forces. It looked for all the world as if the ZAR would be wiped off the map after just twenty-five years of unruly existence. Writing in 1896, William Fisher summed up a situation which many feared would spark a terrible and widespread war: "The Boers, penniless and demoralized, were under the shadow of a black cloud that seemed as if its bursting might involve half of South Africa."[51]

The Zulu king, Cetawayo, would later send a most remarkable communiqué to the British special commissioner. In this, Cetawayo admitted that he had been ready for war because "the Dutch have tired me out and I intended to fight them … you see my Impis are gathered. It was to fight the Dutch I called them together; now I will send them back to their homes … In the reign of my father, Umpanda, the Boers were constantly moving their boundary further into my country. Since his death the same thing has been done. I had therefore determined to end it once and for all".[52]

Though the Transvaalers later claimed they would have defeated any invading Zulu army, this was baseless bravado. Their commandos had just been routed by the far less fearsome Pedi and there is little doubt that the Zulus impis would have swept across the Transvaal, wiping out their hated foe. Indeed, and quite understandably fearing for their lives, the Lydenburg Boers shamelessly requested British protection. Seeing the writing on the wall, President Burgers made a remarkable speech to the volksraad: "I would rather be a policeman under a strong government than a President of such a

State. It is you—you members of the Raad and the Boers—who have ruined the country, who have sold your independence for a drink. You have ill-treated the natives, you have shot them down, you have sold them into slavery, and now you have to pay the penalty."[53]

And thus without a shot being fired—though the ungrateful Kruger greeted their saviours with a volley of vitriol—the Transvaal was annexed by Great Britain on the 12th April 1877. The British 'invasion force' was a troop of just twenty-five mounted police and there can be little doubt that the majority of the ZAR's inhabitants welcomed their arrival, breathing a very deep sigh of relief at what they represented. None other than Henry Rider Haggard[*] read the proclamation announcing the annexation, a proclamation which rightly declared the ZAR to have been facing "anarchy and bloodshed". Incidentally, and to highlight how well received the annexation was, this proclamation was printed on the presses of the government-approved newspaper of the ZAR.[54] For all his huffing and puffing, Kruger continued to work under the new British administration and draw a salary for so doing; indeed, the only member of the pre-annexation republican government to refuse to work with the British was the man who was to be Kruger's rival for the next twenty years, 'Slim' Piet Joubert. So utterly shameless was Kruger, that he even demanded a pay rise.[55]

Critics of the annexation have tended to focus on its impact on the Boers, ignoring the fact that they formed a tiny minority of the inhabitants of the Transvaal. As Henry Rider Haggard put it: "It never seems to have occurred to those who have raised so much outcry on behalf of forty thousand Boers, to inquire what was thought of the matter by the million natives."[56] Though one has to allow for a touch of exaggeration, Haggard goes on to describe how, with the exception of the Pedi who continued their war even after the annexation, "the advent of our rule was hailed with joy by every native in the Transvaal … During our period of rule in the Transvaal the natives have had, as they foresaw, more peace than at any time since the white man set foot in the land. They have paid their taxes gladly, and there has been no fighting between themselves".

Haggard stayed on as part of the British team tasked with trying to instil some sort of order into the affairs of the territory with which the Empire was

---

[*] Sir Henry Rider Haggard KBE (22 June 1856–14 May 1925). Born in England, Haggard moved to southern Africa in 1875 and would later write such classics as *She* and *King Solomon's Mines*.

now burdened. As we have learned, this task was a formidable one: according to Haggard, the treasury of the ZAR contained just "a single threepenny bit" upon annexation.[57] Others put the total at an only slightly more respectable 12s 6d. Just three years of British stewardship achieved what twenty-five years of self-rule had not. The basket-case finances of the ZAR were addressed with an injection of British money[58] and, while the Boer commandos had been sent packing by the Pedi, the British army succeeded in bringing them into line in short order.[59] Talking of the campaign at a banquet in Pretoria afterwards, the high commissioner for the Transvaal, Sir Garnet Wolseley, was heard to say: "I could not help feeling that the battle we were engaged in was essentially a Boer's battle; but there were no Boers there. There were 2,000 English soldiers, and volunteers of Africander* and European origin raised in this country, and I asked myself, In whose cause is this battle being fought? Why is it fought? Why are we left to fight it out by ourselves when these ignorant men, led by a few designing fellows, are talking nonsense and spouting sedition on the High Veldt?"[60]

When, in 1879, the British army then broke the power of Cetawayo's Zulus, the two biggest external threats to very existence of the ZAR had been removed. Indeed, Wolseley was somewhat understandably of the opinion that Britain's title to the Transvaal had been gained by defeating both the Pedi and the Zulus, either of whom might well have exterminated the Transvaal Boers had the ZAR not been annexed. It is hard to disagree.

But despite fixing the finances of the Transvaal and defeating their enemies for them, such remarks—and the annoying habit their new overlords had of collecting taxes—served to unite the previously fragmented Boers into something approaching a national identity—even if it was one mainly based on an ungrateful hatred of all things British rather than on something a little more positive. And with their enemies now vanquished and their finances on an even keel for once, Kruger and his gang fancied having another crack at running the country.

---

* A little confusingly, Sir Garnet seems to have been referring to the Colonial Dutch here, who had long since become British subjects in either the Cape Colony or Natal, as opposed to the 'real Boers' of the republics.

The rebellion of 1880–81, which later became known as the first Boer War,* was quite possibly the nadir of the British colonial period. The new imperial administrators of the Transvaal had taken an understandably dim view of the traditional attitude that the Boers had toward the payment of tax, and the prosecution of one such non-payer served as the catalyst for the uprising. Matters were not helped in that the officer in charge of collecting taxes, Colonel Sir Owen Lanyon, was "a dark-complexioned man, and service in the West Indies and in other hot climates had considerably bronzed his face; on this evidence the Boers came to the conclusion that he was 'a nigger'".[61]

Egging on such ill-educated and prejudiced people was child's play to Piet Joubert and that perennial troublemaker, Kruger, and Boer rebels moved to attack the scattered British garrisons of the Transvaal and snatch back their independence. Or, more accurately, to replace the relatively equitable and reasonable imperial rule with that of Kruger's corrupt, self-serving clique.

The uprising was little more than the investment of several British-held settlements and a few skirmishes. The first of the latter was the Boer ambush of 240 men of the 94th Infantry at Bronkhurst Spruit which was achieved only by blatant abuse of the white flag, a tactic the Boers would regularly use in the second Boer War. Indeed, the first Boer War gave the British an early indication of the somewhat pragmatic view their foes held toward the accepted rules of war: essentially, 'the enemy must abide by the rules but we don't have to'.

Following hot on the heels of the disgraceful white flag incident at Bronkhorst Spruit (known to the many loyalist residents of the Transvaal as 'the Massacre of Bronkhorst Spruit')[62] came the brutal murder of Captain Elliot who had been captured in that engagement. Elliot and another officer† were given *parole d'honneur* to leave the Transvaal and cross into the Orange Free State. The two unarmed officers were taken to the Vaal River by an escort of eight Boers and forced to try and cross the river in the middle of the night. When they were halfway across, their escort decided it would be good sport to open fire on them, the resultant volley killing the luckless Elliot midstream.[63]

A little later, at the skirmish at Ingogo Heights, the rebels outdid themselves: not only did they shoot under cover of the white flag they had raised, but they

---

* Or 'the first war of independence' if you prefer

† Captain Lambart who had been captured in the separate incident

did so at an unarmed priest who went forward to acknowledge the truce.[64]

Though everyone has heard of the Boer victory at Majuba, the fact is that only one of the small British garrisons—Potchefstroom—fell during the war, and that was due to trickery. The remainder—Standerton, Pretoria, Lydenburg, Marabastadt, Rustenburg and Wakkerstroom—were all still holding out at the end, and giving sanctuary to the many loyalists who wanted nothing to do with Kruger's rebellion.

Normally, this relatively minor insurrection would have been dealt with in the customary imperial fashion, i.e. the British army would have dusted themselves off, sorted themselves out and moved to smash the rebels. A few of the more outspoken and annoying rabble-rousers—like Kruger—would then have been strung up and everything would have returned to normal. This could, and should, easily have been achieved for, while there were only tiny numbers of redcoats in the Transvaal, the British had plenty of troops in the Cape and Natal.[65]

But fortune favoured Kruger, as in London, Gladstone's spineless Liberal administration showed no stomach for the fight. Without a second thought for the thousands of Transvaal loyalists and hundreds of thousands of blacks he was casting aside, Gladstone had been desperate for peace even before Majuba and that defeat was the final straw. His decision was as astonishing as it was pathetically inexplicable, with one reporter writing in disbelief about the British general, Wood, on instructions from London, meeting to parlay with Joubert and his rebels: "The idea of an English General, with 10,000 troops at his back, after the British forces had been thrice beaten in open fight, going to an interview with the leaders of the enemy, for the sake of gaining time to negotiate peace proposals, was thought to be too absurd to be credited."[66]

Many pundits will claim that the British had no interest in fighting for the Transvaal in 1881 because 'no one yet knew there was gold there'. As usual with such simple knee-jerk explanations, and while the Witwatersrand gold rush had not yet started—that happened in 1886—this is utter rubbish. Writing in 1882, a year after the war, Thomas Carter described the continuing development of the gold fields of the Transvaal, such as the 1873 Pilgrim's Rest gold rush in the eastern Transvaal, developments which antedated the 1877 annexation.[67] Similarly, in 1881 Sir Garnet Wolseley counselled Gladstone against his spineless surrender of the Transvaal, pointing out that as gold had already been found there, an influx of English-speaking settlers would soon follow and the voices of the few agitators would be drowned out.[68]

So whatever it was that inspired Gladstone's unpatriotic and gutless decision, it was certainly not a complete lack of knowledge over the Transvaal's gold deposits. Whatever his reasons, in 1881 Gladstone's government threw in the towel, granted a slightly limited form of independence to the ZAR and Kruger became its president shortly thereafter, a position he would hold until he plunged the sub-continent into war at the end of the century. Even as the rebellion was still being fought, Kruger's followers were settling old scores, with numerous cases of murder and pillage being evident. Property belonging to those loyalists who had fled the war was simply seized by Kruger's men; the whole atmosphere should have left no one in any doubt as to the sort of corrupt kleptocracy the newly independent ZAR would become. Two Bechuana chiefs, Montsioa and Mankoroane, who had offered support to the British during the war, were attacked. Loyalists were pressed into service in this conflict "according to the familiar practice of the Boers, who consider excellent policy to make the disaffected fight their battles and save the skins of the good citizens".[69] This policy would also be used during the second Boer War.

But with Kruger's clique in power, no one would suffer more than the Africans who made up the vast majority of the population of the ZAR. A distraught Henry Rider Haggard stated that they deserved "some protection and consideration, some voice in the settlement of their fate. They outnumbered the Boers by twenty-five to one, taking their numbers at a million and those of the Boers at forty-thousand, a fair estimate, I believe … as the lash and the bullet have been the lot of the wretched Transvaal Kaffir in the past, so they will be his lot in the future … after leading those hundreds of thousands of men and women to believe that they were once and for ever the subjects of Her Majesty, safe from all violence, cruelty, and oppression, we have handed them over without a word of warning to the tender mercies of one, where natives are concerned, of the cruellest white races in the world".[70]

It fell to the missionary John Moffat to try to explain to the African chiefs in the Transvaal that they would no longer enjoy British protection or equality before the law. On hearing the news, Moffat described how "for the most part there was the silence of despair. One gentle old man, Mokhatle, a man of great influence, used the language of resignation, 'When I was a child, the

Matabele came, they swept over us like the wind and we bowed before them like the long white grass on the plains. They left us and we stood upright again. The Boers came and we bowed ourselves under them in like manner. The British came and we rose upright, our hearts lived within us and we said: Now we are the children of the Great Lady. And now that is past and we must lie flat again under the wind—who knows what are the ways of God?'"[71]

Emboldened by their victory in the first Boer War, and even before Kruger was formally elected president in 1883,[72] the Transvaal quickly started expanding its western border. An ongoing tribal power struggle in Bechuanaland provided an opportunity for the Transvaalers to get involved, backing one chief against another, with the promise of vast tracts of land as reward.[73] Hundreds of "filibusters and freebooters" from the Transvaal fought a nine-month campaign, which essentially involved the seizing of cattle from the other faction.[74] This raiding and killing continued until the Transvaal government suddenly imposed a peace and, rather conveniently, awarded themselves a large chunk of land as a result. Though patently a colony of the Transvaal, and settled by hundreds of her people, this newly acquired territory was nominally an independent Boer republic, becoming known as Stellaland.

But even grabbing this land was not enough, and the Transvaal quickly involved itself in another power struggle in Bechuanaland. This time the long-running feud was between two rival Barolong chiefs, Moshete and Montsiwa, the struggle having kept southern Bechuanaland in a state of turmoil for many years.[75] Following a now familiar pattern, large numbers of Transvaalers travelled to fight for Moshete, despite protests from the British. So great were their numbers and influence that it was the leader of these Transvaal Boers—the extravagantly named Nicolas Claudius Gey van Pittius—who was directing operations, not Chief Moshete.[76]

An attack by the Transvaalers and Moshete's warriors drove Montsiwa from his main settlement at Sehuba, the victors then burning it to the ground.[77] Montsiwa's followers retreated to Mafeking where, under the supervision of a handful of mainly British advisers, trenches were dug and fortifications constructed. Indeed, Mafeking was so well fortified that Moshete and his Transvaalers had no choice but to lay siege to it, and attempt to starve out Montsiwa's people.* It was an especially savage conflict, with women and

---

* Mafeking would famously be besieged again during the Boer War

children targeted. If caught, the English-speaking advisers to Montsiwa could expect no mercy from the Transvaalers and the brutal murder of one James Scott McGillivray caused a diplomatic outcry. McGillivray appears to have been captured by the Transvaalers, placed in chains and then murdered.

As before, the ZAR forced a peace on the situation and, once again, used this to snatch a large portion of land for itself. Most of Montsiwa's territory was seized, as was a good chunk of Moshete's, and his people placed under the dubious "protection and control of the Transvaal government".[78] To further rub salt into the wound, Montsiwa was also required to pay £16,000 to the Transvaal as a 'war indemnity'.

As with Stellaland, the ZAR went through the charade of pretending that the new territory—Goshenland[79]—was an independent republic, rather than a very obvious colony of the Transvaal. In October 1883 moves were made to unite these two newly acquired mini-republics as the grandly termed, 'The United States of Stellaland'[80], but events moved on before this could come about. Still not satisfied with their expansion, the Transvaal government then petitioned the British to let them take control of the whole of Bechuanaland, claiming this was the only way to 'maintain order' in the area. In reality, Kruger had always intended to annex the Boer republics of Stellaland and Goshen to the Transvaal and continue expanding into Bechuanaland, thereby pushing his border toward the new German colony of South West Africa and the Atlantic Ocean. He was utterly determined to acquire a sea port.[81]

In October 1883 a delegation from the Transvaal, including Kruger and the Reverend Stephanus du Toit,* travelled to London to discuss this and other matters. As well as a reduction in the Transvaal's debt, the delegation managed to renegotiate the Pretoria Convention which had ended the first Boer War. This was followed by the Convention of London which was signed on the 27th February 1884 and which essentially restored the Transvaal to the position of something very close to a fully independent state.[82] The only caveat was contained in the fourth article of the convention, which maintained that: "The South African Republic will conclude no treaty or engagement with any state or nation other than the Orange Free State, nor with any native tribe to the eastward or westward of the republic, until the same has been approved by Her Majesty the Queen".[83]

Writing in 1919, the historian George McCall Theal noted: "In the opinion

---

* Reverend Stephanus Jacobus du Toit (1847–1911) was one of the founders of the Afrikaner Bond

of most people the conclusion of this convention was unquestionably an act of liberality as well as of justice on the part of the British government. It removed from our country the reproach that some foreign people were casting upon us, that we respected treaties with feeble states no longer than suited our own convenience. It was admitted by us that a wrong had been done—though perhaps unintentionally—but that wrong had been redressed, and no apparent reason remained why the most friendly feelings should not in future prevail between the inhabitants of the restored South African Republic and those of the British realm."[84]

Events in Bechuanaland continued to obfuscate and it was decided by London that, rather than let the Transvaal offer their own dubious form of protection over the whole area, southern Bechuanaland should be taken under the wing of the British and annexed to the Cape Colony.[85] As normal, this was to be done with the bare minimum of cost and with no troops being deployed. Indeed, the plan was for the annexation to be done pretty much single-handedly by the Reverend John Mackenzie.[86] Predictably enough, this quickly ran into problems when some of the inhabitants of Stellaland appealed for their territory to be included in the annexation, while others were completely against the idea. To make matters worse, on the 10th May, the Boers of Goshenland again declared war on Montsiwa.[87] When the Reverend Mackenzie arrived in Mafeking a few days later, the crafty Montsiwa instantly agreed to the British annexation and was thus suddenly in the happy position of being under imperial protection. This changed everything at a stroke and, as impressive a man as the Reverend Mackenzie was, it was belatedly realized that he needed a bit of back-up. This was to be supplied by the hundred-strong Bechuanaland Mounted Police (BMP) which was swiftly raised by one Major Stanley Lowe. These troopers were ready for service by late July 1884, their numbers being quickly increased to a hundred and thirty.

Unfortunately, the BMP was not formed in time to prevent the Goshenland Boers launching an attack on Montsiwa's positions. At negligible loss to themselves the Goshenlanders killed over a hundred of Montsiwa's men, though one death was to cause a good deal more consternation than all the others. Mr Christopher Bethell came from a "good family in England", had been an adviser to Montsiwa for some years and "had unfortunately formed a connection with a niece of the chief".[88] He had also recently—and much to the fury of the Goshenlanders—been granted a commission into the BMP.

Though the new unit was still mustering, Bethell was present during the battle and was badly wounded, losing one eye and much of one side of his face. Despite this, he was to receive no pity from the Goshenland Boers, two of whom taunted him after his capture before brutally murdering him in cold blood.[89]

With British prestige counting little, and no imperial troops on hand to enforce a settlement, the crisis spluttered on. The Goshenlanders were warned that, by attacking a chief under British protection, they were making war on Great Britain itself. But this cut little ice. The ZAR stepped in to try and resolve the problem in their customary style. Their shameless proposal was that all the land claimed by Montsiwa and Moshete, including Goshenland, should be simply become a protectorate of the Transvaal.[90] Needless to say, the British didn't concur.

Finally, the imperials acted. It was decided that Montsiwa should have all his territory restored to him, and that the proposed annexation of the whole troublesome area to the Cape Colony should be undertaken. A 5,000-strong expeditionary force was raised, primarily from volunteers in the Cape, but built around a few imperial units. The core of the force was elements of the Inniskilling Dragoons and the Northamptonshire Regiment, both of which were based in South Africa, bolstered by a detachment of the Scots Guards that was shipped in from England. Three regiments of irregular horse were raised from local volunteers and, perhaps with a slight sense of *déjà vu*, the whole was placed under the command of Sir Charles Warren, by then a major-general.*

Warren's force assembled in Cape Town and marched north to Mafeking. Faced with something rather more formidable that Tswana tribesmen, the Goshenlanders thought better of giving battle and dispersed without firing a shot. The event was not entirely bloodless though. Several chiefs who had aligned themselves with the ZAR felt betrayed by this capitulation, and one—Massou—decided to take out his frustration by attacking Boer farmsteads. The Transvaal dealt with this in the usual fashion: an 800-man commando was dispatched under Joubert and Massou's warriors were quite literally blown apart by the State Artillery,[91] with Joubert's men then driving off all Massou's cattle and sheep to cover the costs of the commando.

---

* Warren would later be the Commissioner of the Metropolitan Police during the Jack the Ripper killings, before returning to the army and commanding the imperial forces at Spion Kop. He was promoted general in 1904.

On the 23rd March 1885 a proclamation was issued, declaring a British protectorate over "the whole territory from the western boundary of the South African Republic to the twentieth meridian from Greenwich, and from the Cape Colony to the twenty-second parallel of south latitude".[92] The Transvaal's attempts to snatch Bechuanaland had been foiled.

࿏

Down in Zululand, the expansion of the ZAR proceeded with more success. Exactly as they had done in Bechuanaland, the Transvaal Boers took advantage of inter-tribal chaos and ongoing strife among various competing chiefs, picking a side to support in return for vast tracts of land. Zululand was ripe for the taking as it had been in considerable turmoil since the British victory in the Zulu War of 1879, with various chiefs vying for supremacy.

At a meeting on the 23rd May 1884, a Boer delegation agreed to support Dinizulu in his quest to become supreme chief of the Zulus,[93] the *quid pro quo* being about half of Zululand. It is not clear if Dinizulu simply had no intention of ever honouring the deal or failed to understand that he was cheerfully signing away 7,500 square miles of his land.[94] Either way, just a few months later, hundreds of Boers moved to occupy the new territory, rather unimaginatively named the New Republic.[95] A capital was laid out and named Vryheid (freedom).*

Though their apologists maintained the New Republic was gained and occupied by private individuals, rather than the government of the Transvaal, it was merely the latest in the by-now-familiar method of constant expansion: hundreds of farmers on the border would, one way or another, move in and occupy someone else's land, declaring it yet another mini-republic, though one inextricably linked to the ZAR. Indeed, none other than the commandant-general of the Transvaal, 'Slim' Piet Joubert, was invited to become the president of the New Republic. He declined.

Though events moved too quickly for Stellaland and Goshenland to be formally incorporated into the Transvaal, the same was not the case for the New Republic. On the 11th September 1887 it was suddenly decided that the New Republic was too small to remain independent and was—surprise, surprise—incorporated into the ever-expanding Transvaal.[96]

---

* Vryheid is now in Natal, the border having been redrawn in 1903 in the wake of the Boer War

To the north of Zululand and the New Republic, and between the ZAR and a much-coveted sea port lay the small, sparsely populated kingdom of Swaziland.* For decades the Transvaal Boers had taken advantage of any political power struggle to encroach on Swazi territory, and by these methods had expanded to secure about half of the land once controlled by the Swazi king. Despite the independence and borders of Swaziland having been formalized and acknowledged by the ZAR in both the Pretoria Convention of 1881 and the London Convention of 1884, Kruger remained determined to gain control of the rest of the territory.

In 1886 the paramount chief of the Swazis, Mbandini, informed the governor of Natal that Piet Joubert had visited him, requesting he issue a declaration that "he and all the Swazis agree to go over and recognize the authority of the Boer government, and have nothing more to do with the English".[97] When Mbandini had refused, Joubert asked: "Those fathers of yours, the English, act very slowly; and if you look to them for help, and refuse to sign this paper, we shall have scattered you and your people, and taken possession of your land before they arrive. Why do you refuse to sign the paper? You know we defeated the English at Majuba."[98] Joubert went on to add, rather optimistically, that the British Empire was a "broken reed". By the standards of the Transvaal, Joubert was a moderate, so his remarkable outburst should leave one in no doubt as to the impact of that battle on the mindset of the men who ran the ZAR: after their victory at Majuba, their contempt for the British was such that even relative moderates like Joubert believed that southern Africa was theirs for the taking.

Knowing the intentions of the ZAR, and just like the chiefs of the Basuto and the Tswana, Mbandini repeatedly asked for imperial protection and that a British resident be installed. Unfortunately, and again, just like in the cases of the Basuto and the Tswana, the British were hesitant to get involved. However, the aggressive expansion policy of the ZAR knew no such reluctance and, in the time-honoured fashion, a group of Transvaal Boers moved into Swazi territory and declared yet another mini-republic: this one was called the Klein Vrystaat, the Little Free State, with the tiny settlement of Piet Retief serving as the capital.[99] And just like the New Republic before it, the Klein Vrystaat was incorporated into the ZAR in August 1890. Coming under increasing pressure from the ZAR, Mbandini was coerced

---

* in 1904 the population of Swaziland was reckoned at only 85,000

into granting concessions to the Transvaal to run his "postal, telegraphic, banking, customs", as well as giving mining and grazing rights to increasing numbers of settlers from the ZAR. This sneaky takeover was so successful that, in 1893, the British were essentially presented with a *fait accompli* and their efforts to arrange a system of 'dual control' were too little, too late.

ॐ

The following year, a group of Swazi envoys travelled to Great Britain to beg that HM's government declare a protectorate over their territory, but again this was refused. Later that same year, the British signed a convention with the ZAR granting the latter the administration of Swaziland, against the will of the Swazi people, their king and the queen regent.* Indeed, the queen regent claimed she was prepared to strangle herself to death with a whip rather than be surrendered to the tender mercies of the Transvaal.[100]

Though they had allowed Swaziland to fall into the hands of the Boers, the increasingly hostile attitude of the ZAR finally forced the British to act. In 1895, the British took advantage of a clause in the convention† and moved to annex Amatongaland—a small strip of land which separated Swaziland from the Indian Ocean—to Natal. Indeed, Kruger's drive to the sea was thwarted by none other than the ruler of Amatongaland, the Queen Regent Zambili. She refused to have anything to do with the Transvaal's agents, and instead enthusiastically accepted British suzerainty.[101]

Despite the fantasies of their present-day apologists, the empire of the ZAR was increasing in size year on year, but the British annexation of Amatongaland was a defining moment. Thereafter, the only way Kruger could now acquire an outlet to the sea—and therefore, the outside world— was by seizing land from either the Portuguese or the British. Writing in 1900 Michael Farrelly marked this reality as a turning point on the road to war: "the two Dutch Republics were completely hemmed in by British territory, and the President's dream of his port on the Indian Ocean became no longer realisable by peaceable means."[102] Unfortunately for all concerned, Kruger

---

*   In the Boer War a few years later, Mbandani's widow, Naba Tsibeni, known as the Queen Regent, declared for the British. When the Transvaal was annexed to the British Empire, she requested Swaziland be annexed too.

†   The ZAR had the right to establish a port at Kosi Bay provided they built a railway within three years. Kruger's government had not even started on such a project.

would soon prove he had no qualms about switching to a military solution to achieve his dreams.

Elections were held in the Transvaal in 1893. In a closely, bitterly, and many thought, unfairly, fought contest, Kruger pipped Joubert by 7,911 votes to 7,246.[103] The tiny size of the electorate will leave one in no doubt as to just how restricted the franchise was. It was widely reported, and generally believed, that the scheming Kruger had manipulated the ballot, and many of Joubert's supporters were incensed by what they saw as having been cheated of their rightful victory. Indeed, one who went on to serve in the volksraad offered £1,000 to any man who would shoot Kruger.[104] It is a shame that no one took him up on the offer. Others "implored Joubert to refuse to submit, and to fight it out if necessary; but the General, who was as weak as water, decided that, however great the sacrifice, he could not consent to divide the country on the issue. A stronger man would have hazarded a coup d'état, but Slim Piet was no match for his old rival, whose motto is to get home by any means, fair or foul".[105]

If Joubert—a member of the Afrikaner Bond and a renowned slave owner, yet still a comparative moderate by the appalling standards of the Transvaal—had stood up to Kruger in 1893, another civil war would undoubtedly have been the result. But it is also highly likely there would have been no Boer War.

As well as this political intrigue and the constant expansion of their borders, the 1890s saw the ZAR fight a never-ending series of wars to consolidate their hold on the territory that they already considered theirs. In 1894 the ZAR declared war on Chief Leboho of the Hananwa who lived in the Blouberg Mountains in the northern Transvaal. The objective, as ever, was to extend ZAR influence and dominance over such people. Joubert commanded a force of around 1,800 Boers, complete with artillery, and surrounded the chief's kraal, laying siege to it and cutting off food and water supplies. As usual in such conflicts, and despite their later squeals of protest, Joubert's force was supplemented by 700 black allies. After several months of siege, the chief surrendered on the 31st July and was taken to Pretoria, where his people were essentially enslaved, being divvied up among the members of the victorious commandos and forced to work on Boer farms for five years.[106] Indeed, the treatment of blacks in the Transvaal was brutal in every way. One European visitor approvingly described it thus: "The standing of the Kaffir in the Transvaal is worth notice. While in the English colony they enjoy equal rights with white men, and even have a vote, in the Transvaal their standing is very different. The Kaffir must not walk on the pavement, he must salute every white man, and must not leave his house after 9 PM … every Boer has the tacitly recognized right to punish his blacks. He never does it in passion. When the Kaffir does anything, he is told to appear the next day at a certain hour. He is then tied to the wagon, the braces are dampened, and he gets the necessary number of lashes."[107]

Despite this outrageous racism and the heady enthusiasm for slavery, the Transvaal was essentially a Christian fundamentalist state. Kruger believed absolutely in the divine right of the Afrikaners, somewhat ludicrously considering them to be God's chosen people: "The President really believes, and has always believed, that the Boers are the chosen people of the Old Testament, to whom the people of Ham should be servants, and that they are promised the annexing of the Promised Land."[108] A member of the Orange Free State volksraad wrote that Kruger "made the burghers believe that he was a prophet who, like Moses, was the means of communication between God and his Chosen people. This is literally true. In the earlier days, he often vanished for long periods, and he came back, he made the people believe that he had been communicating with God. It was absolutely believed by the burghers that Kruger, who was in Heidelberg at the time—one hundred miles from the scene—knew the result of the battle of Majuba on the very morning on which it was fought!"[109] Kruger's religious fanaticism was such that it even led the miserable old party-pooper to turn down an invitation to a ball with the excuse that "balls are services of Baal, and God had commanded Moses of old to exterminate all services of Baal".[110] As is to be expected, ignorance went hand-in-hand with this widespread religious fanaticism. Kruger proudly made it be known that the only book he had ever read was the Bible and, despite having travelled to Europe on several occasions, he died firmly believing that the Earth was flat: hardly a suitable man to lead any nation into the twentieth century. When English-speaking residents of Johannesburg fired rockets at clouds in the hope of prompting a badly needed rain storm, the ruling Boer elite reacted with fury. These devil-dodging Calvinists declared the experiment to be "a defiance of God and would most likely bring down a visitation from the Almighty".[111] A Meneer Wolmarans was particularly outraged at such heresy and declared to the volksraad that if any of his children fired a revolver at a cloud, he would thrash the child for mocking the Almighty.[112] Indeed, the Transvaal volksraad was the crucible of such small-minded nonsense. Kruger himself led the (successful) opposition to the introduction of pillar-boxes on the grounds that they were "extravagant and effeminate",[113] while a proposal to formalize a register for births, deaths and marriages was comprehensively rejected by the volksraad for being "an attack on religious principles". Other Luddite volksraad members similarly spoke out against the introduction of railways and trams:[114] "the public was solidly against a steam railway, but not against a horse-drawn one." There were undoubtedly others with keener intellects, but over the years, wide-eyed simpletons of the volksraad earnestly debated such things as the "importance to define the shape and size of neckties", establishing a monopoly to supply jam, outlawing barmaids and whether or not certain words were real if they could not be found in the Bible.[115]

When a plague of locusts caused devastation across the Transvaal, the reaction of the volksraad is instructive. The members generally agreed that this was the work of God and several declared it a sin to try and combat it. One country-bumpkin even announced that rinderpest and the locusts were God's way of punishing the perceived decadence of the growing English-speaking community of Johannesburg: "in former years, before these people and the goldfields were known, there were no plagues."[116] As the debate raged on, another sagely advised that the only way to end the plague was to repent one's sins, while yet another announced: "Everybody knew that locusts were a punishment from the hand of God. They had been away from our country for a long time, and there were reasons for their return. If members read their Bibles, they would know this."[117] Another told a fanciful tale about a man whose farm had always been spared, until the day he killed a locust. Immediately thereafter, his farm was devastated by the plague.[118]

Equally astounding was what happened when a deputation of Johannesburg-based Jews, headed by a Dr Hertz, met Kruger to plead for educational and religious freedoms. Kruger dismissed them out of hand, informing the delegation that, while the Jews were the descendants of Ishmael, the Boers were the direct descendants of Isaac[119] and that therefore it would be against the scriptures for both 'tribes' to live together in harmony.

The Transvaal of the late nineteenth century was in the hands of these religious extremists and it was their brainless fanaticism that was steadily marching southern Africa toward war. One of the more enlightened Afrikaans leaders wrote in frustration that, due to this widespread God-fearing ignorance, "it is easier to mislead [a Boer] than to lead him. A man who plays upon his vanity and prejudice against England quickly obtains influence. A loud talker and blusterer gets a better hearing than a quiet reasoner. I ascribe this to want of education and complete isolation on the veldt, from generation to generation. The depth of their ignorance will hardly be understood by one who does not know them as well as I do ... Unfortunately, the ministers of the Dutch Reformed Church, greedy for the fat lamb, the fowl, and the purse, foster this ignorance. One parson actually had the audacity during the war to tell his congregation that God must help His chosen people, otherwise He would lose His influence".[120]

Throughout the 1890s, the expansionist lust of these puritanical Bible-bashing fanatics continued to be utterly insatiable. In 1891 a trek was organized to seize the newly acquired British territory of Mashonaland, part of what later became Rhodesia.[121] Backed by none other than Piet Joubert, the commandant-general of the ZAR, this trek had originally attracted a couple of thousand Boers, a force which should have swamped the tiny number of British settlers then in Mashonaland. Though their numbers dwindled somewhat before they set off, the trekkers only actually turned back when faced down at the Limpopo River by the doughty troopers of the British South Africa Company Police (BSACP), one Maxim gun and Dr Jameson himself.[122]

Given the incident on the Limpopo River, it is wry to note the self-righteous indignation expressed by Joubert and other ZAR leaders when the roles were reversed just a few years later, and Dr Jameson popped up again to lead a similar—though rather more justifiable—raid against the Transvaal. While it suits pro-Boer writers to claim that the Jameson Raid was a British attempt to steal the Transvaal from Kruger, the reality is rather different. Though the British government undoubtedly had prior knowledge of the coup attempt, they had done nothing to foment the trouble in the ZAR, nor were they in any position to prevent it.[123] The raid was in fact more of a local uprising, and one with some justification. The discovery of the Witwatersrand goldfields had brought huge numbers of English-speaking immigrants to Johannesburg [124]

so many in fact that, by the mid-1890s, these newcomers (dubbed uitlanders, or foreigners) were thought to outnumber the Transvaal Boers.* The skills, investment and hard work of this English-speaking community completely transformed the economy of the ZAR, so much so that by 1895 it was reckoned the uitlanders contributed ninety per cent of the nation's taxes.[125] Despite this, Kruger's clique arrogantly dismissed their perfectly reasonable requests for fair democratic representation, constantly changing the franchise rules to deny them the vote.† This was in stark contrast to the British-run Cape Colony, where Afrikaans-speakers made up a majority of the electorate and the British—quite rightly—made no attempt to challenge this.

With their petitions ignored and finding themselves called up to serve in the Transvaal's never-ending wars of expansion,[126] the uitlanders had had enough and a 'reform committee' was formed to fight this blatant injustice. Despite campaigning for democratic reform against an autocratic, corrupt and highly racist regime, these 'revolutionaries' have never caught the eye of the British Left in the way that all other such groups throughout modern history have. Described by a politically incorrect modern commentator as "the ANC whiteys of the age",[127] Kruger's Boers simply ridiculed their peaceful efforts to prompt change. One member of the volksraad laughed at the presentation of a petition, shouting, "Come on and fight! Come on!" Kruger himself showed similar contempt for the Reform Committee's peaceful demonstrations (and for peaceful government in general), declaring: "Protest! Protest! What is the good of protesting? You have not got the guns—I have."[128]

With peaceful methods getting nowhere, by late 1895, these growing rumblings of discontent in Johannesburg had matured into an uitlander attempt to overthrow the Kruger government. The basic plan was that rifles and machine guns would be smuggled into Johannesburg and the English-speakers would rise up to demand a reformed republic. In support, Cecil Rhodes had organized a force of light horse, under the command of his loyal lieutenant, Dr Leander Starr Jameson, to ride in from neighbouring Bechuanaland.

From the very start, the plan began to unravel,[129] as Johannesburg's cosmopolitan and money-driven uitlander community squabbled over

---

*   In terms of adult males, if not overall. Either way, both white 'tribes' were massively outnumbered by Africans.

†   In 1881, the franchise was available after one year's residency in the Transvaal, subsequently raised to five and then fourteen years.

minutiae.[130] Many reformers simply wanted a fair franchise and to be rid of
Kruger's corrupt regime. Others, like Rhodes and Beit,* wanted the Transvaal
to become British territory. The numerous Irish and American miners made
it clear that had no interest in fighting under the Union Jack[131] and even many
of British uitlanders were individualistic mavericks who were at the diggings
purely to make money, with no pressing desire to risk their lives simply to
replace Kruger's rules and regulations with rather less onerous British rules
and regulations.[132] All in all, this wealthy—in some cases, hugely wealthy—
and diverse population made for unlikely revolutionaries, thus the planned
uprising in Johannesburg fizzled out before it really began. Nevertheless, and
perhaps hoping to galvanize them into action, Jameson crossed the border to
ride to their 'rescue', but his 500-strong force was callously and shamefully
left to its fate by their Johannesburg comrades.†

For reasons known only to themselves, many writers tend to dismiss the
complaints of the Reform Committee,[133] invariably supporting their position
with a single quote deliberately taken out of context, typically Lionel Phillips's
throwaway remark: "as to the franchise, I do not think many people care a fig
for it."[134] What Phillips, who represented the interests of Alfred Beit, actually
said was that they didn't care a fig for the franchise "for fear of irritating old
Kruger", but what they *did* want was reform, a decent administration and
something done to improve the volksraad.[135] Unsurprisingly, even this single
damning quote sounds quite different when you bother to get the full story.

The fact is that the uitlanders had many legitimate complaints and their
plight cannot simply be dismissed as unimportant or frivolous. As even one
of Kruger's most enthusiastic apologists, Thomas Pakenham, concedes: "by
means of a new franchise law, much more restrictive than those of Britain or
America, the Boers kept them starved of political rights."[136] Even those few
moderate members of the volksraad were decent enough to admit that Kruger
was being absolutely unfair. One of them, a Mr Jeppe, said of the uitlanders:
"They own half the soil, they pay at least three-quarters of the taxes. They
are men who in capital, energy and education are at least our equals. What
will become of us or our children on that day when we find ourselves in

---

* Alfred Beit (1853–1906) was a German-born Jew turned passionate supporter of the British Empire in
  southern Africa. Having made his fortune on the Kimberley diamond fields, in 1886 Beit turned his
  attention to the Transvaal gold fields.

† Jameson and his men fought a running battle with Boer commandos before being forced to surrender at
  Doornkop on 2 January 1896. Jameson served time in an English gaol for his part in the fiasco.

a minority of one in twenty without a single friend in the other nineteen, among those who will then tell us that they wished to be brothers, but that we by our own act have made them strangers to the republic?"[137]

Why is it that the uitlanders' very real desire for democracy—the same democracy which, as mentioned, the British Empire afforded to Afrikaners and non-whites in the British colonies of South Africa—is dismissed by modern writers as an irrelevance or an excuse, primarily on the strength of one misquote? Do these same writers also consider the lack of the franchise for blacks in the apartheid period of South Africa as an irrelevance which should be dismissed as a mere excuse for insurrection? Indeed, the situation is remarkably similar, and yet those who championed the right of one man–one vote in the apartheid era appear not to think that those of British stock were equally deserving in the 1890s.

To dismiss the Reform Committee's case for the franchise on the strength of one misconstrued remark does not really explain the tens of thousands of men who petitioned the government of the ZAR, or the establishment of the reform movement. One could certainly argue that the majority of uitlanders made the best of things and did not feel strongly enough about it to take up arms and risk their lives, but then neither did the majority of blacks during the apartheid era.

The only thing the Jameson Raid achieved was to further entrench Kruger's clique in positions of power. The ill-conceived and really rather stupid raid, and the associated Transvaal propaganda[138] surrounding it, prompted even relatively moderate and reasonable voters to turn their support to Kruger. Similarly, in the Cape Colony and the Orange Free State, many of those Afrikaners who previously had no liking for Kruger's corrupt oligarchy suddenly found themselves shifting their support to their kith and kin north of the Vaal.

The Jameson Raid also provided a perfect excuse for Kruger to increase his military capability still further.[139] Despite the claims of those who prefer to explain it away, Kruger's massive programme of building a war machine antedated the raid,* but the moral high ground Jameson's *faux pas* afforded *Oom* Paul justified his ever-increasing spend on weaponry and espionage. With the shame of the raid still raw, the British had little choice but to turn a

---

* The Transvaal's military expenditure in 1895 was over four times that of 1893. Expenditure in 1896 was over four times that of 1895. Many of these contracts would have been signed before the raid.

blind eye. Kruger was happiest playing the part of the victim and the botched raid was a heaven-sent opportunity for him to do just that.

In the wake of the Jameson Raid, the emboldened and increasingly powerful Transvaal took advantage of British embarrassment to engage in yet further intrigue and wars of expansion. As we shall read later, the late 1890s saw the Transvaal's secret service fomenting African rebellions in both Rhodesia and Bechuanaland, their obvious aim being to destabilize these British territories. Transvaal agents were also busy in the Cape Colony and the Orange Free State, spreading anti-British propaganda, smuggling in weapons, bank-rolling pro-Transvaal candidates in elections and funding sedition through the media.[140] One of the most effective ways to disseminate hatred to the poorly educated, God-fearing Boers was from the pulpit, so Kruger's minions turned his venomous loathing of Englishmen into something akin to a crusade. One churchman admitted that "he had to preach anti-English, because otherwise he would lose favour with those in power".[141]

The propaganda fell on fertile ground, as one moderate Orange Free State volksraad member recalled: "This successful anti-British policy of Kruger created a number of imitators—Steyn, Fischer, Esselen, Smuts and numerous other young educated Afrikanders of the Transvaal, Orange Free State, and the Cape Colony, who, misled by his successes, ambitiously hoped by the same means to raise themselves to the same pinnacle ... Krugerism under them developed into a reign of terror. If you were anti-Kruger, you were stigmatized as 'Engelschgezind' [lit. English sympathizing] and a traitor to your people, unworthy of a hearing. I have suffered bitterly from this taunt, especially under Steyn's regime. The more hostile you were to England, the greater patriot you were accounted ... This gang, which I wish to be clearly understood, was spread over the whole of South Africa, the Transvaal, the Orange Free State, and the Cape Colony, used the Bond, the press, and the pulpit to further its schemes."[142]

Enormous sums of money were transferred to the Transvaal's agents in the Europe, forts were built and orders were placed for the latest artillery pieces and new magazine rifles. So many rifles were bought that, by 1894—two years before the raid—the Transvaal already had two modern rifles for every burgher.[143]

In 1898 the ZAR put their newly acquired weaponry to use, invading and seizing the lands of the Venda people.[144] A Boer force of about 4,000 men armed with the new Mauser rifles and modern artillery smashed the Venda of Chief Mphephu,[145] incorporating his territory into the ever-expanding Transvaal. Many Venda fled over the Limpopo to the safety of the British territory of Rhodesia.

Also in 1898, and as we shall discuss in some depth later, Kruger dispatched his men into Swaziland to seize the Swazi chief after he had dared rule in a matter between two of his own subjects.[146] The chief fled over the border to British protection and Milner,* the newly installed high commissioner, issued a stern rebuke to the Transvaal. This enthusiasm to get involved in Swaziland rather makes a mockery of Kruger's stage-managed indignation about British interference in the internal affairs of the Transvaal and the plight of the uitlanders. This then was the Transvaal: an aggressive, warlike and fundamentalist state which Professor Bill Nasson inexplicably declares "asked only to be left alone". And we have met President Kruger, a man Professor Scholtz farcically proclaims "never gazed beyond his own borders".[147] Manfred Nathan, in his sycophantic biography of Kruger, treats us to an equally illogical remark, declaring: "All the Republic wanted was to be left alone."[148]

---

* Alfred Milner, later 1st Viscount Milner KG, GCB, GCMG, PC (23 March 1854–13 May 1925)

CHAPTER TWO

All about gold

"The last thing the capitalists wanted, or needed, in 1899 was a war
—especially one instigated and won by Britain."
—John Stephens, *Fuelling the Empire*

"We seek no gold fields. We seek no territory. What we desire is equal rights for men of
all races, and security for our fellow subjects and for the Empire.
Those are the only objectives that we seek."
—Lord Salisbury, 9th November 1899[1]

"Almost to the very last the capitalists were far more eager to bargain with the Transvaal
Government for reasonable financial and administrative reforms than to clamour for the
franchise … They not unnaturally desired reforms, but they had no craving for war."
—Leo Amery, quoted in *The South African War Reappraised*

"In 1961, in the aftermath of the Sharpville massacre, the writer and caricaturist Osbert
Lancaster depicted this extraordinary transformation in public memory in a sketch of a
London anti-apartheid meeting. Amid placards and posters with the words 'Down with
Verwoerd', an elderly activist turns to the chairman seated next to him and says:
'Oddly enough, the last time I spoke in this hall Lloyd George was in the chair
and the theme was "Hands off the gallant little Boers".'
—*The South African War Reappraised*

"President Kruger is slippery and will have to be watched.
A man who grants reforms against his will must always be watched."
—correspondence of political moderate, Sir James Rose-Innes, 25th July 1899

As discussed, there is a commonly held belief that the British attacked the Transvaal in order to get their grubby little hands on the gold fields. Indeed, this is so widely peddled and repeated that it has become accepted almost as fact. The popularizing of this myth can be traced to a chap called John Atkinson Hobson, a newspaper correspondent for the *Manchester Guardian* who was in South Africa when the war started. As the *Manchester Guardian* morphed into today's God-awful *The Guardian*, it is not surprising that the paper opposed the war and that Hobson himself was a hardline leftie who later joined the Marxist 'Independent Labour Party'. Indeed, Hobson's fervent support for the redistribution of wealth and the nationalizing of industry (those twin pillars of leftist stupidity) led to none other than Lenin himself admiringly describing him as a "social liberal".[2]

Within a few months of fighting breaking out, Hobson had quickly cobbled together a book called *The War in South Africa, Its Causes and Effects*[3] in which he blamed the whole thing on capitalists and, less pleasantly and no more rationally, Jews. Needless to say, this class-war, anti-Semitic drivel was mindlessly lapped up by the usual rabble of assorted liberals, socialists and Marxists and has been ever since.

Rather like the modern obsession of sagely claiming that every single war is 'really about oil',[*] Hobson's book laid all the blame for the conflict on gold, and the desire of guileful Jewish capitalists to snatch it. On the rare occasions he wasn't spitting out his anti-Semitic bile, Hobson asserted that the war was fought in order to "place a small international oligarchy of mine-owners and speculators in power in Pretoria".[4]

Obviously, and despite British victory, this wildly baseless accusation did not come to fruition; in fact, the 'Hobson thesis' has been roundly disproven time and time again in the century since he dreamt it up,[5] but it still holds a magnetic appeal to those who, for whatever reason, choose to believe it.

Hobson and his disciples seem unable to distinguish between the Jameson Raid—most certainly orchestrated and funded by various capitalists, but which fell apart when these same backers got cold feet—and the Boer invasions of the Cape Colony and Natal in 1899. While it appeals to a certain mindset to inextricably link the two, there is little logic in so doing. The

---

[*] This lunatic dinner-party obsession with oil conspiracies even causes some to claim that the British fought the Falklands War of 1982 because of oil. This theory would be fine but for the fact that no one knew there was any oil there, the British had been trying to get rid of the Falklands for years and it was Argentina which started the conflict, not the British.

agitation for reform in Kruger's republic, which ultimately led to the Jameson Raid débâcle, was not about claiming the Transvaal for the British Empire. In fact, the reformers rejected Chamberlain's* and Rhodes's insistence that the rebellion should take place under the Union Flag[6] while Johannesburg's disparate and cosmopolitan digger community couldn't agree on the status any reformed republic should take. All they ultimately could agree on was that they didn't like Kruger but they didn't want to risk their lives to get rid of him.

What the blind acceptance of the 'it was all about gold' theory does best is show just how little its adherents understand of the way the British Empire operated, and how business works. While the investors in southern Africa were a diverse bunch, those of British stock were the largest group and thus many of the Rand gold mines were already owned by British capitalists. Indeed, it is estimated that British investment accounted for between sixty and eighty per cent of that in the territories of southern Africa as a whole. Not only this, but Britain was by far and away the biggest trader with southern Africa, with British exports to the region worth £15 million a year.[7] When the Boers launched their attacks in 1899, seventy-five per cent of the money invested in the Transvaal's gold fields was British.[8] The last thing any right-minded capitalist wanted was to jeopardize his investments and this trade. The gold magnates were especially averse to any sort of conflict, as even a temporary shutdown of the mines would see them suffering enormous losses. Worse still, if they had to abandon their mines for the duration of a war, was the potential for serious damage through either flooding or deliberate sabotage by Boer forces. And in the very worst-case scenario of a Boer victory in any such war the capitalists might have provoked, they obviously stood to lose their investments in their entirety. As respected historian Iain Smith makes abundantly clear in his analysis of the origins of the war, what the British capitalists on the Rand wanted "was not a war but certain clearly and repeatedly stated reforms in the Transvaal's administration".[9] This was also the case at the time of the Jameson Raid: the capitalists wanted change but when push came to shove few of them wanted it enough to fight for it. The last thing any capitalist wants is uncertainty, and armed conflict is about as uncertain as one can get. As with interruption of supply and rising wages,

---

* Joseph Chamberlain (1836–1914). British statesman, one time radical Liberal turned Conservative imperialist. 'Pushful Joe' served as HM government's secretary of state for the colonies from 1895 to 1903.

uncertainty scares investors; for example, the Transvaal's lurch toward war in 1899 led to the Banque Française de L'Afrique pulling back from financing various gold-mining projects.[10] None of this is appealing or sustainable to a businessman caught up in the middle of it.

Obviously there is money to be made during a war if one is supplying one or other of the belligerents and staying well out of it, but the very idea that the gold bugs would profit from even a short conflict—with their investments bang in the middle of it—is nonsensical, Marxist claptrap. In reality, and as everyone had predicted, the war had a terrible impact on the mining operations of the Rand. When 60,000 mine workers[11]—uitlanders and migrant blacks—were either expelled or fled from the Transvaal, mining essentially came to a halt. Any mines which Kruger's clique could link to British investors were refused permission to pump, causing underground flooding.* Even after Johannesburg was captured by imperial forces in 1900, mine owners had to plead with Kitchener to permit workers to return to what was basically still a war zone, thus managing to re-start just three mines and only 150 stamps out of the pre-war total of six thousands.[12]

If the half-baked idea that the capitalists (and Jews) were to blame is baseless, the whole notion that the British Empire wanted to seize the gold mines for their own purpose is further flawed. Other than being able to collect taxes on the profits of the mines—a fairly far-fetched justification for starting a war, given that Britain was the wealthiest country on the planet at the time and that the British quickly granted independence to the defeated republics in any case—the only way for the British government to have benefited from such a scheme would have been if they had nationalized the gold mines of the Transvaal. As the mines were largely owned by British investors, this would see HM's government snatching them off the very people that Hobson would have us believe wanted the war in the first place.

Not only that, the British Empire was the empassioned champion of free trade and *laissez-faire* economics; the notion that they would wish to nationalize the freshly captured mines is fanciful and, more to the point, did not happen. This disinterest in snatching the gold mines from the Boers was comprehensively proven in the peace negotiations of March 1902. Reitz proposed that Johannesburg and the Witwatersrand gold fields should

---

* Those mines owned by French or German investors were allowed to pump and some production continued. The Transvaal attempted to keep a few of the richest mines going for their own profit.

be ceded to the British in return for the Transvaal retaining an 'internal independence' over the rest of their country.[13] This was rejected but the Transvaal was granted self-rule just four years later. Indeed, so wedded was the British Empire to free trade that many ministers—including Winston Churchill* and Charles Ritchie, the president of the Board of Trade at the time of the Boer War and later Chancellor of the Exchequer—were even against the 'Imperial Preference' tariffs that encouraged and supported trade between Great Britain and her colonies. Speaking at an imperial conference a few years after the Boer War, Churchill proudly claimed that he had "banged, barred and bolted the door on Imperial Reciprocity ... they would not give one farthing preference on a single peppercorn".[14] Do these devotees of the free market really sound like the sort of men keen to nationalize a privately owned business? Perhaps Hobson was guilty of judging others by his own sub-standards?

More importantly, if the British plan had been to seize the Transvaal's gold mines, why then did Great Britain grant self-rule to the Transvaal in 1906, just four years after the end of the war, thereby forfeiting any chance of collecting taxes or tariffs off any gold produced? Would this not have been utterly counter-productive and have defeated the whole purpose of the nefarious scheme in a stroke? And the granting of self-rule had nothing to do with the election of Henry Campbell-Bannermans's Liberal government in December 1905: both the newly elected government and the outgoing Conservative one had planned this for South Africa. Indeed, Lord Selborne,† who succeeded Milner as high commissioner to South Africa in May 1905 (when Balfour's Conservatives were still in power), arrived in his new role with letters confirming that self-rule would be forthcoming. Selborne, who had been 'Pushful Joe' Chamberlain's junior in the Colonial Office and who was Lord Salisbury's son-in-law, would remain in his position under the new Liberal government and oversee the granting of self-rule to the former Boer republics and the unification of South Africa,

The man Selborne replaced, Lord Milner, might be seen as a convenient war-mongering bogeyman by some today, but he was by no means ostracized by the newly elected Liberal Party for the part he played in the run-up to the Boer War. Indeed, Milner would later serve the Liberal prime minister, Lloyd

---

*   though Churchill famously crossed the floor twice, he was always an ardent supporter of free trade

†   William Palmer KG, GCMG, PC 2nd Earl of Selborne (1859–1942)

George, as his secretary of state for war, and then secretary of state for the colonies. This would have been unthinkable had the leaders of the Liberal Party considered him part of a Conservative Party conspiracy to force an unfair war of conquest on the Transvaal.

Equally remarkably, another of the Left's favourite 'warmongers', Dr Jameson, held secret talks with King Edward VII before returning to South Africa as a member of the Unification Conference and did more than anyone to unify the various territories of South Africa and set them on the course for independence. Indeed, his arch-enemy, Merriman, described Jameson as the "prime mover" behind the push for a unified South Africa to attain dominion status.[15] The salient fact is that both major parties in Great Britain were only too ready to divest themselves of the newly won territory, which gives a lie to the various conspiracy theories about imperial intentions. Needless to say, none of this is ever addressed by critics in their various brainless rants.

Put simply, no one has ever been able to adequately explain why Great Britain, a functioning democracy with a free press and the undisputed champion of free trade, would provoke an unwarranted war of aggression against what was essentially a sovereign nation, to steal resources which were already largely owned by British investors and then grant it self-rule just four years later, and then independence just four years after that. How on earth does this enthusiasm to divest themselves of the Transvaal with such haste possibly fit the theory that the British had been desperate to snatch it in 1899? Surely even the most wooly-headed critic of the Empire must spot the contradictions in their argument.

Despite the modern myths peddled about the British Empire, a feature of the Victorian period was that London was always keen to rid itself of direct control of colonies, and ever ready to grant responsible rule. Indeed, this desire to grant responsible rule to colonies began with Nova Scotia as far back as 1848. Most of the territories in New Zealand and Australia were granted responsible rule by 1860, though, much to the chagrin of HM's government, Western Australia took a little longer as it was so dependent on funding from the motherland. As far as imperial rule went, the British were always very much hands off. Colonies were expected to stand on their own two feet and pay for themselves: to set and collect their own taxes and tariffs and raise and equip local defence forces, basically causing as little trouble to the motherland as possible. The ultimate manifestation of this was the granting of dominion status to the likes of Australia, New Zealand and Canada. By becoming a dominion, the erstwhile colony was essentially independent of British rule and was, for all intents and purposes, a sovereign nation. Though they might occasionally volunteer money for the Royal Navy or raise volunteer units to support the imperial cause in time of war, neither colonies nor dominions paid any sort of 'rent' to the mother country. As Conan-Doyle rightly asserted in January 1902: "The gold mines are private companies, with shares held by private shareholders, German and French, as well as British. Whether the British or the Boer flag flew over the country would not alienate a single share from any holder, nor would the wealth of Britain be any way greater … how is Britain the richer because her flag flies over the Rand? The Transvaal will be a self-governing colony, like all other British colonies, with its own finance minister, its own budget, its own taxes, even its own power of imposing duties upon British merchandise … We know all this because it is part of our British system, but it is not familiar to those nations who look upon their colonies as sources of direct revenue to the mother country."

Conan-Doyle would be disappointed to know that this inconvenient reality is equally unfamiliar to, or ignored by, many present-day commenters. Iain Smith concedes:

> The evidence so far produced does not support the view that the British government went to war* in 1899 to bring the gold supply or the gold fields under British control or to protect British trade or the profits of cosmopolitan capitalists in the Transvaal. None of these was under serious threat, even if it was acknowledged that the capitalists did suffer from unnecessary impositions at the hands of a corrupt and inefficient government. The Transvaal was not the only part of the world where this occurred; despite their justifiable complaints, the capitalists on the Rand not only made sizable profits, under Kruger's government, but were also successful in attracting the large-scale private investment which was so essential to their operations. While some of their leading members, by 1899, certainly looked to a British takeover in the Transvaal as likely to benefit their interests, there is as yet no evidence that their views formed a significant part of the British government considerations in its mounting conflict with the

---

* except, of course, that the British did not go to war in 1899: they were attacked

Transvaal government of President Kruger. Transvaal gold formed only a small proportion of the low level of British gold reserves, which was a deliberate feature of Bank of England policy before, during and after the South African War.[16]

The British Empire's response when there really was a threat to the world's gold supply is illuminating. In the worst sovereign-debt crisis of the century, the Argentine economy collapsed in 1890–1, sparking turmoil in Britain's financial markets. London's Baring Bank looked set to fold as Argentina defaulted on £48 million of foreign debt, and—unlike in 1899—the British Chancellor of the Exchequer was deeply worried about the gold supply. Despite the fantasies of various Marxists, Britain's response was not to launch a war of conquest or steal someone else's mines, but rather to have the Bank of England organize a rescue package in conjunction with the Bank of France and Russia's central bank. It was a rational and peaceful response which reassured and steadied the markets. Another expert on the subject, John Stephens, agrees that the Great Britain of 1899 had no burning need to increase her gold reserves:

Britain based the defence of her monetary stability, in the event of international gold rushes, on her position as a creditor nation, but did not build up a massive gold reserve beyond what was required for the issue of currency … France too defended the stability of her currency based on a status as a creditor nation, but in addition, she built up a massive gold reserve as a second line of defence. France, not Britain, was the greatest European purchaser of new gold for strategic purposes … there were no compelling reasons at that particular moment for Britain to wish to control the government of the Transvaal in order to have control over its gold mines. Whatever gold was mined in the Transvaal would in any event find its way to the international gold market and the European monetary system, to which Britain had as much access as anybody else. Moreover, whoever bought the gold had to pay the companies that mined it. The mining companies made profits from selling gold, not those who controlled the governments of the producing countries. For Britain, there would thus be enormous disadvantages in taking over the Transvaal, but no conceivable economic advantage to governing a gold-producing colony—it was a much better proposition to hold prime trading rights with a gold-producing colony. There was thus no economic imperative driving Britain to covet the Transvaal for its gold.[17]

Despite admitting that the British had no reason to bring the Transvaal's gold fields under the imperial wing or to support the investors on the Rand, Iain Smith nevertheless goes on to assure us that "historians have been in broad agreement that Britain provoked the war",[18] before admitting that no one can agree on exactly why this would be and dismissing Hobson's theory about it being a capitalist's war as nonsense. Indeed, Smith concedes that "only after the war had begun did the British Government decide to annex the Transvaal, and her ally and sister republic, the Orange Free State. This had not been the original objective".[19]

Yet despite all this splendid and laudable pooh-poohing of various conspiracy theories and wild Marxist fantasies, Smith never seems to pause for a moment to think that the side which actually *did* start the war—the Transvaal—might possibly bear some responsibility for their actions. Given the Transvaal's propensity for violent expansion and the glaring reality that Boer invaders swarmed over their borders to invade the Cape Colony and Natal in 1899, why do historians tie themselves in knots, desperately trying to prove that the British were really responsible for it all? Why is the perfectly plausible notion that Kruger's Transvaal is to blame for the war so readily dismissed by so many historians?

෨

While any right-thinking person must therefore concede that Great Britain did not go to war to grab the Transvaal's gold, gold was still very much a catalyst for the war. For a start, it was the lure of gold which had brought the uitlanders to the Transvaal, which in turn raised tensions when Kruger's medieval oligarchy refused them basic rights. Just as importantly, taxes raised from the gold revenues meant that the Transvaal's economy in 1895 was twenty-five times the size it had been in 1887,[20] which permitted Kruger to invest heavily in his military and secret service. Writing in 1900, Michael

Farrelly described the Transvaal's military build-up prior to the war: "it is quite easy to prepare for war if you have gold, with which to obtain cannon and rifles, and ammunition, and skilled strategists, veterans in stricken fields and expert artillerists. There is no necessity, if things go well, of declaring war until the British Empire is at war with another Great Power."[21]

CHAPTER THREE

Warmongering and the Bond

"They want to sweep the English into the sea, to lick their own nigger and to govern
South Africa with a gun instead of the ballot box. It is only the Little Englanders in London
who say that the Transvaal is merely fighting for its independence,
but here both sides realize it is a question of which race will run the country."
—Rudyard Kipling, 1900[1]

"The Boer ideal was 'Anti-British Federation in South Africa'. Mr Secretary Leyds has
been appointed a kind of a Boer Minister in Europe, where he will no doubt do his utmost
to encourage the idea that the federated Dutch Republics can be relied upon by anyone
who wishes to destroy British supremacy in South Africa."
—writing in 1897, viciously pro-Boer journalist William T. Stead* lets slip that
the republican plan was to challenge British hegemony in southern Africa.

"You might as well expect us to be at war with Switzerland."
—prominent Conservative MP, and later prime minister, Arthur James Balfour, 1899,
when asked about the chances of war with the Orange Free State

"Freedom will rise in Africa like the sun from the morning clouds, inasmuch freedom
rose in the United States … Then it will be from the Zambesi to Simon's Bay:
Africa for the Africander."
—President Paul Kruger gives a lie to modern claims that there was no plan to build an
Afrikaans empire in southern Africa[2]

"The Bond was intended to be Pan-Afrikaner and in spirit bitterly anti-British."
—Professor Eric Walker describes the reality of the Afrikaner Bond

---

* William Thomas Stead (1849–1912), one-time passionate imperialist turned pacifist and Boer-
sympathizing pioneer of investigative journalism. Stead perished in the sinking of the *Titanic*, having
gallantly given his life jacket to another passenger.

"A Century of Wrong—a malicious book with some, but very little truth in it, which was
translated into various languages at great expense to vilify the British."
—Hugh Abercrombie assesses Reitz's widely distributed propaganda work[3]

"You cannot simultaneously prevent and prepare for war."
—Albert Einstein

"It would be a misuse of terms to call the general Boer designs against the British a
conspiracy, for it was openly advocated in the press, preached from the pulpit, and
preached upon the platform, that the Dutch should predominate in South Africa,
and that the portion of it which remained under the British flag
should be absorbed by that which was outside it."
—writing in 1902, Sir Arthur Conan-Doyle tells it how it is

In December 1895, prior to the Jameson Raid, a certain Henning Pretorius,[*]
lieutenant-colonel of the Transvaal Staats Artillerie, entered Rhodesia.
Though ostensibly on a hunting trip, the colonel's busy mind was concerned
with greater matters than shooting game, for he was actually an agent in the
Transvaal's secret service.[4] According to the *Daily Telegraph*'s correspondent,
Pretorius and his agents smuggled 175 rifles and thirty cases of ammunition
into Rhodesia, all "bearing the Transvaal government mark" and "made in
Germany". These were drawn from the Transvaal's magazine at Middleburg
to be distributed to potential rebels and troublemakers in Rhodesia.[5]

Given Kruger's fury at Rhodes stymieing his chance to expand his nation
northward by setting up his personal fiefdom, it is reasonable to assume that
the aim of these agents was to destabilize Rhodesia and to spark insurrection
that would ultimately drive the British out. This would, it was no doubt hoped,
leave a vacuum which the Transvaal would fill. Indeed, when the Matabele
rebelled in 1896, the Transvaal poured yet more weapons into the hands
of the insurgents, with another 200 rifles and sixteen cases of ammunition
delivered. Coming just a few years after Joubert's thwarted attempt to occupy
Mashonaland, Pretorius's mission also ended in failure when British and
Rhodesian forces put down the insurrection. The devious efforts of Henning
Pretorius in this shadow war were duly recognized, however, and a statue of
him was erected in Pretoria.

The agents of the Transvaal's secret service—including Kruger's son,

---

[*] Henning Petrus Nicolaas Pretorius (1844–97). His father, Marthinus Pretorius, was killed in the first
Boer War, while his maternal grandfather was the famous Voortrekker, Piet Retief.

Tjaart[6]—were also busy elsewhere, actively assisting rebels in the Langberg revolt of 1896–7. Situated in the Bechuanaland protectorate, the rugged Langberg Mountains were the scene of a rebellion against imperial steward-ship. Like the Matabele rebellion, one of the catalysts for this uprising was the rinderpest outbreak* and the British response to it. And again, like the Mata-bele rebellion, Transvaal agents were at work behind the scenes, whipping up resentment and supplying weapons to the rebels.

All this was confirmed when the prinipal rebel chief, Galishiwe, was finally arrested and confessed. In a statement Chief Galishiwe admitted that he had been actively encouraged to fight the British by another Transvaal secret agent, a Meneer Piet Bosman. At first, Galishiwe had rejected Bosman's advancces, claiming, "I cannot fight the Englishmen, I am the Englishman's child." Bosman dismissed this, using the veterinary culls implemented by the British to tackle the rinderpest outbreak in order to trick Galishiwe. Bosman then offered to purchase powder and ammunition for Galishiwe, providing him "six bags of powder, five boxes of caps, and five packets of Martini-Henry cartridges",[7] later providing additional Westley-Richards ammunition. Indeed, a feature of the rebellion is how well supplied the insurgents were with ammunition.

Galishiwe asked Bosman to also provide him rifles. However, this was refused, as Bosman feared the British would be able to trace this back to the Transvaal: "The Englishmen will see the guns. I will get my people together and come myself to your assistance when you fight the Englishmen." Despite having a 200-strong commando at his disposal, and perhaps needless to say, Bosman did not honour this promise and left the unfortunate Galishiwe and his people to carry the can.[8]

As we have seen, the Transvaal had always been an expansionist state, but for some reason one of the great sacred cows of the Boer War is that it was in no way the fault of Kruger's Transvaal. Despite Kruger overtly announcing that the "manifest destiny" of his people was to form an Afrikaner empire from the Zambezi to Simon's Town,[9] many modern-day writers squawk indignantly that it has somehow been proven that the Boers were the innocent victims of the piece, the commonly held view of the time that there was a conspiracy to create an Afrikaans South Africa is nonsense, and

---

* This highly infectious virus rampaged throughout much of southern Africa in the 1890s, killing somewhere around 80 to 90% of the cattle in the region.

that no further discussion on the subject will be entertained. By the way of example, Kruger's biographer, Johannes Meintjes (whose sympathy for his subject runs to the point of sycophancy), quotes his hero as saying: "Even should President Steyn try to restrain his burghers from closer union [with Kruger's Transvaal], God will bring it about." And then, immediately after citing Kruger's belief in this divine plan, he bizarrely postulates: "so much for the Great Afrikaner conspiracy to form one vast Republic."[10]

Similarly, the war diary of burgher Jack Lane, a man who was forced against his will to fight in Kruger's army and who repeatedly referred to the Krugerite plan to build an Afrikaans empire, was re-released in 2001 by the Van Riebeeck Society. Rather than let the reader make up his own mind on Mr Lane's views and first-hand experience, the foreword categorically states that everything Mr Lane said on this subject, and this subject alone, was wrong,[11] basing this extraordinary whitewashing on a single quote from a modern book on the war.

It is certainly unlikely that the wilder fears of the uitlanders of the time were realistic, that there was not some vast, all-encompassing octopus-like conspiracy being hatched beneath their feet. But it all depends on one's definition of 'conspiracy'. The Transvaal secret service was very active in British territory, weapons were being smuggled hither and thither and there was a good deal of anti-British propaganda being bandied about. There were large, vocal elements in the Cape who supported Kruger over British rule, but it cannot be confirmed whether these were spontaneous and self-contained, or encouraged and supported by the Transvaal. There is plenty of evidence that clergymen did engage in rabble-rousing, but it is unclear if this was part of a grand master plan or took the form of personal crusades. Many in the Afrikaner Bond did switch their allegiance to the invaders, with much secret contact between the Bond and Kruger's clique. Does this all add up to a master plan to oust the British from South Africa? Who knows, but it is obvious that something was afoot.

Most modern histories of the conflict barely glance at this subject. Instead they concentrate exclusively on the British pro-war elements—of which there were undoubtedly plenty—while completely ignoring what was happening on the other side of the fence. As such, the recent revisionist spin on the war has placed virtually all the blame for the conflict on the British and, especially, Lord Milner. But is this entirely fair? Why is it that, what Andrew Porter calls the "Afrikaner interpretation of the origins of the war", so widely accepted, despite it being "a view produced by historians who, standing too close to the minutiae of events, have placed too great a weight of interpretation on too narrow a base"?[12] Why is it that most of these historians fail to even examine the part that the Boers, and especially Kruger, played in stoking the flames of war? Why do the real aims and objectives of Kruger and Steyn remain unquestioned? Why is the mass of evidence that clearly shows that the ZAR bore at the very least partial culpability for the war so readily brushed under the carpet?

Rather than allow ourselves to be swept along with this, let us instead look at some of the background to the Transvaal's role in the events leading to war. By the mid-1890s, bolstered by a massive military build-up paid for by gold revenues (and the warm glow of victory in the first Boer War), Kruger's ambitions knew no bounds. The Transvaal's ongoing shadowy intrigue, espionage and war-by-proxy of the 1890s is largely ignored, but there is little doubt that the ZAR's long-term wish was to deprive the British of their dominant position in southern Africa.

In fact, it is clear that Kruger had been actively planning for an offensive war against the British as far back as 1887. Two secret conferences were held in Pretoria on the 31st May and the 2nd June 1887, when Kruger met with his counterpart from the Orange Free State, President Jan Brand,* the object being to persuade Brand to agree to an offensive and defensive alliance[13] between the two Boer republics. Brand, a wise and decent man who presided over a comparatively stable and well-run state, was understandably amazed at this proposal. A defensive alliance was one thing, but the only possible target of an offensive alliance could be Great Britain, a nation with which the Orange Free State had never been at war, which was by far their largest trading partner and with which they were on very friendly terms. Indeed, Brand's policy of friendship towards the British Empire had seen him awarded a GCMG in 1882.

Kruger went on to declare his intention of gaining a sea port[14] before clambering up into the pulpit to announce: "The future will provide greater blessings if you work with us. Let them [the British] keep their money. Let them not bind you. The Lord reigns—none other—the deliverance is near at

---

* Sir Johannes Henricus Brand GCMG (1823–88). In 1871 Brand was approached to become president of the ZAR in one of the many attempts to unite the two Boer republics. He declined.

hand." One of his advisers, Meneer F. Wolmarans, went even further: "We are still insufficiently prepared. We wish to get to the sea … you know our secret policy. We cannot treat the Colony as we would treat you. The Colony would destroy us. It is not the Dutch there that we are fighting against. Time shall show what we mean to do with them."[15]

Though Jan Brand rejected the proposal, Kruger did not give up. In October 1887 he travelled to Bloemfontein to stress once again the urgent need for the offensive alliance. Brand replied that he would never be party to attacking British territory, so an offensive alliance was pointless. In respect to the defensive alliance, Brand pointed out that the Orange Free State was on excellent terms with all her neighbours and thus had no need for that either. He went on to tell Kruger that the Transvaal would also have no need for a defensive alliance if their policy remained peaceful and cautious.[16] There was, unfortunately, more chance of Jan Brand stepping in rocking horse shit than of the Transvaal becoming "peaceful and cautious". Indeed, even the pioneering social worker Mary Brown, a Kruger sympathizer, declared him to be a "relic of a past order" and an "intriguer".[17]

When Jan Brand died suddenly in July 1888, the presidency of the Orange Free State passed to Francis Reitz.* Reitz was elected unopposed and would later serve as state secretary of the ZAR and pen the declaration of war against Great Britain—but this was all still in the future. Despite Reitz being born a British subject in the Cape Colony and having studied law in London, he harboured a deep hatred of all things British and a fanatical desire that the Afrikaners—not the British—should dominate the sub-continent. One who met him described him as being "full of disinterested, fiery zeal … certainly the greatest fanatic in the country. His hatred towards England flashed in his eyes … he had all the doctrines of the First Revolution in his blood: he believed in them firmly, and seemed to be ignorant of those lessons which Europe had learned … the pleasures of alcohol and female company he thoroughly despised. Such a real Puritan one but rarely comes across".[18]

As we know, the Orange Free State and Great Britain had been on the friendliest of terms for many years, but Reitz used the occasion of his inauguration to make a truly remarkable speech. He declared that it was his "fervent desire to see the day when the United States of South Africa

---

* Francis William Reitz (1844–1924) served as the president of the Orange Free State from 1889–95 and as secretary of state for the Transvaal from 1898–1902.

should have become an accomplished fact". Reitz's dream did not, of course, envisage this new nation being under the Union Flag; indeed, he expressly declared that his aspiration excluded British power from any part or lot in its accomplishment.[19] Despite using his speech to openly announce his wish to see British power driven out of southern Africa, Reitz did rather sportingly declare that Great Britain could stay on as the "coast protector".

Unsurprisingly, Reitz's first significant act as the new president of the Orange Free State was, in March 1889, to sign the Convention of Potchefstroom, Kruger's much-longed-for defensive alliance with the ZAR.[20] This was as far as Reitz dared go at that time,* as the late Jan Brand's supporters were ably led by the impressive John Fraser† and, other than a few fanatics, no one in the Orange Free State had any interest in war with Great Britain.

Reitz's enthusiasm to sign the alliance with the Transvaal is not unexpected, given that he was one of the founders of the shadowy Afrikaner Bond. Part quasi-secret society, part pressure group, part political party, the Afrikaner Bond was formed shortly after the first Boer War. The first congress of the Bond was held in Graaff-Reinet in March 1882, where the fledgling organization defined its aims as "The formation of a South African nationality by means of union and co-operation as a preparation for the ultimate object, a United South Africa".[21] Obviously, and like any group, there were members in it who were more extreme than others, but its aims, as stated by a contemporary observer, were simple: "The goal, held steadily in view, was the establishing of an independent nation ruling all South Africa, from the Zambesi to the sea."[22]

Another of the founding fathers of the Bond was a Bloemfontein-based newspaperman, Carl Borckenhagen.[23] His paper, *De Express*, openly stated this aim, advocating the formation a Dutch United States of South Africa and the expulsion of British imperial power from the region.[24] The motto of the Afrikaner Bond should leave no one in any doubt of its objective: 'Africa for the Afrikander'.[25]

On the 12th March 1899, Cecil Rhodes made a speech some time after Borckenhagen's death:

---

* As well as signing up to this highly provocative and, in the case of the OFS, utterly unnecessary, alliance, Reitz repeatedly clashed with the British over his harsh 'Bantu policy'. In 1890 he forbade Indian immigrants to settle in the OFS and was locked in a perennial argument with the British high commissioner over such matters, always seeking to push the limits of the British.

† Sir John George Fraser (1840–1927) was a pro-British member of the Orange Free State Volksraad. Remarkably, Fraser's niece was married to Marthinus Steyn, the man who defeated him in the 1896 presidential election.

I remember that we had a great meeting at Bloemfontein, and in the usual course I had to make a speech. I think I was your Prime Minister. And this speech pleased many there, and especially—and I speak of him with the greatest respect—a gentleman who is dead, Mr Borckenhagen. He came to me and asked me to dictate to him the whole of my speech. I said, "I never wrote a speech, and I don't know what I said; but I will tell you what I know about it." He wrote it down, and afterwards came to Capetown with me … He spoke very nicely to me about my speech. "Mr. Rhodes, we want a united South Africa." And I said, "So do I; I am with you entirely. We must have a united South Africa." He said, "There is nothing in the way." And I said, "No; there is nothing in the way. Well," I said, "we are one." "Yes," he said, "and I will tell you: we will take you as our leader," he said. "There is only one small thing, and that is, we must, of course, be independent to the rest of the world." I said, "No; you take me either for a rogue or a fool. I would be a rogue to forget all my history and traditions; and I would be a fool, because I would be hated by my own countrymen and mistrusted by yours." From that day he assumed a most acrid tone in his *Express* towards myself, and I was made full sorry at times by the tone. But that was the overpowering thought in his mind—an independent South Africa.[26]

Byron Farwell makes this excellent, and oft-overlooked, point in his book, *The Great Boer War*: "Both sides wanted a united South Africa, though, of course differed in their ideas of who should dominate it."[27] Eminent Historian Andrew Roberts agrees: "As the year 1899 progressed, British policy-makers became convinced that British paramountcy in southern Africa, so crucial for the future development and protection of the Empire, was under growing threat … This racial antagonism between Boer and Briton was, it was felt in Cape Town, Pretoria and London, leading inexorably towards a clash."[28]

This is the very crux of what caused the Boer War, yet this simple reality is utterly ignored by many of Kruger's apologists today. Of course, everyone is well aware of British imperial possessions in southern Africa, but for some reason, the empire-building schemes and fantasies of the Afrikaner Bond and the Boer republics are disregarded. Though it has become fashionable to paint the British as the sole aggressors in the run-up to the war, the fact is that there were factions on both sides who wanted their 'race' or faction to dominate all southern Africa; the governments of the Transvaal and the Orange Free State (and their European backers) were by no means the innocent parties they have often been so carefully portrayed to be. Well before the Jameson Raid, both the ZAR and Germany were endeavouring to improve their economic and political strength in the region, and to weaken that of Great Britain's.[29]

Germany was putting constant pressure—including naval demonstrations off Delagoa Bay—on Britain's weak Portuguese allies, and was encouraging the Transvaal to assert itself against the existing British paramountcy.[30] In 1894 the favouritism shown by the Transvaal to German interests (at the expense of British ones) was a source of tension, and all the while France, Germany and the Transvaal hovered in readiness to snap up possessions from the perennially cash-strapped Portuguese,[31] this despite the ridiculous claims that the Transvaal never gazed beyond its own borders. Obviously not a man who shared Professor Scholtz's wishful thinking, the British consul in Lourenço Marques summed up the Transvaal's policy of as "one of quiet acquisition aimed at undermining Great Britain's right of pre-emption should Portugal decide to sell".* The policy which had won Kruger virtual control of Swaziland was slowly being applied to Portuguese East Africa.[32] Indeed, such was the "intimidation practiced by Transvaal and German Governments through their respective Consular Agents"[33] that it became necessary to register British companies abroad in order to conduct business in the Portuguese colony.

Writing in March 1896, Lord Selborne declared that the creation of a United States of South Africa† was inevitable but warned that French and German intentions were to ensure that any such union would be outside the British Empire by supporting the ZAR in these efforts.[34] Ever canny, Kruger, via his special envoy, Dr Leyds, was also circumventing the suzerainty restrictions by endeavouring to sign treaties with European Powers through the Orange Free State. In a speech to a secret session of the volksraad in 1897, Kruger crowed that this arrangement seemed destined for success, then referred to

---

* The 1891 Anglo-Portuguese Treaty gave Great Britain pre-emptive rights to take control of what is now Mozambique in the event of Portuguese financial difficulties.

† Far from considering a British-dominated Union of South Africa as unambiguously preferable and beneficial, both Selborne and Salisbury acknowledged that a standing threat from the Transvaal would encourage Natal and the Cape Colony to remain loyal to the Empire.

the planned land grab at the expense of the Portuguese when he boasted, "we shall then settle our affairs, internal and foreign, without British intervention … we shall have what is unquestionably our right, and with the concurrence of the European nations, a voice in securing proper administration in Delagoa Bay, our own port."[35]

Such was the ongoing intrigue and scheming that one alarmed British observer was moved to remark that the Transvaal was being "made a nursery that could be used by continental powers to destroy our interests in Africa",[36] and Kruger certainly gave every appearance that it was his intention for the republic—with German backing—to replace Great Britain as the paramount power in southern Africa. Understandably enough, Britain, under the resolute leadership of Salisbury, was equally determined that this should not occur.

಄

The role of the Afrikaner Bond—members of which occupied high office all over South Africa in the late 1890s—is generally ignored, too. In fact, the mere possibility that a group which openly called for a United South Africa and 'Africa for the Afrikanders' might have had anything to do with starting the war is simply dismissed out of hand by most writers on the subject. Despite the stated aims of the Bond, one modern history of the movement cheerfully absolves its members of all responsibility, declaring, "It is impossible to take the charge of insidious republicanism seriously."[37]

Suffering from delusions of grandeur after the rebels' unlikely victory over the British in the first Boer War, the ultimate aim of the influential—and increasingly highly placed—group of Young Afrikanders who dominated the Bond was the unification of all the territories and states of southern Africa into a single Afrikaans state. Though Kruger was undoubtedly the figurehead of the Boer people and Piet Joubert, the commandant-general of the Transvaal, a Bondsman,[38] it was well-educated and highly intelligent men such as Smuts, Reitz and Steyn* who were the driving force behind the push for a showdown with the British in order to snatch her territories.

Writing in 1902, Iwan-Müller summed this up by stating: "There can be little doubt that Mr Smuts was one of the foremost, if not the foremost, of

---

* Marthinus Theunis Steyn (1857–1916) served as the last president of the independent Orange Free State from 1896–1902

the abettors of Mr Kruger [and] his violently anti-English policy. It is an unquestioned fact that he was also on terms of the closest intimacy with Mr Hofmeyr and the wire-pullers of the Afrikaner Bond."[39]

No doubt many modern readers—and plenty of allegedly esteemed authors—will scoff at this, dismissing it as a conspiracy theory that has been 'proved' to be without foundation. A lot of the evidence is certainly circumstantial, and there is little doubt that some of the rest is the product of anti-Transvaal propaganda, but there is so much other evidence that to mindlessly disregard it, and the stated aims of the Bond itself, is ludicrous. Indeed, the editor of *De Patriot*, the Bond's newspaper, declared: "We have often said it, there is just one hindrance to Confederation, and that is the English flag. Let them take that away, and within a year the Confederation under the free Afrikaner flag would be established. But so long as the English flag remains here, the Afrikaner Bond must be our Confederation. And the British will, after a while, realise that Froude's advice* is the best for them: they must just have Simon's Town as a naval and military station on the road to India and give over all the rest of South Africa to the Afrikanders."[40]

In the years after the first Boer War, *De Patriot* also issued a vile little pamphlet called *De Tranvaalsche Oorlog* which had been produced by the nascent Bond. A copy of the pamphlet was obtained, translated into English and released as, *The Birth of the [Afrikaner] Bond*, with the foreword declaring, "Fortunately the grand conspiracy [British annexation of the Transvaal] has failed, but we earnestly desire that our countrymen should realise the danger from which South Africa has had a narrow escape; and there can be no better means to this end than the universal perusal of the following pages." Those who indulged in such perusal would see that the pamphlet contained sections with such delightfully unambiguous sub-headings as 'Disgrace to Speak English', 'The English Governess a pest', 'No Land to be Sold to the British', 'War Against the English Language', 'The Anti-British Campaign—No Trading with the British' and 'Preparations for War'. This hateful little document openly advocated driving the British out of South Africa, declaring that the British "must be content with Simon's Bay as a naval and military station on the road to India and give over all the rest of South Africa to the Afrikanders". This notion of the Royal Navy retaining their

---

* In 1877, the English writer and historian, James Anthony Froude, had proposed the Empire turn its back on South Africa, build a line of forts between Table Bay and False Bay and retain only the Cape peninsular.

base in the Cape is certainly in line with Reitz's magnanimous suggestion that the British should hang around as the 'coast protector'. The authors of the pamphlet longed for a South Africa with "No English signboard, no English advertisements in English newspapers, no English bookkeepers; no—all Dutch or Afrikander". It brazenly espoused that "the object of the Afrikander Bond is the establishment of a South African nationality ... the Bond must be our preparation for the future confederation of all the States and Colonies of South Africa. The English Government keeps talking of a Confederation under the British flag. This will never happen ... within a year the Confederation under the free Afrikander flag would be established".

The English language was declared to be "miscellaneous gibberish, without proper grammar or dictionary", English books to be "the greatest mass of nonsense that you can find anywhere" and English history a "concatenation of lies and misrepresentations". Illustrating the authors' questionable understanding of geography, England itself was dismissed as "nothing more than an island in the North Sea".[41]

The Afrikaner Bond presented itself as a harmless society which only wished to preserve old Boer traditions and, indeed, many of its members no doubt coveted only this. However, it seemingly did not take President Jan Brand long to suspect the true nature of those driving the movement:

> In 1883 President Brand officially opened the new wagon-road bridge over the Caledon River at Commissie drift, near Smithfield, Orange Free State. Towards the conclusion of the ceremony, one of the other speakers, Mr. Advocate Peeters, member of the volksraad for Smithfield district, in the course of his speech formally suggested that President Brand should accept the leadership of the Orange Free State section of the Afrikaner Bond. The President, addressing the burghers and all present, replied in about the following terms: The proposal just then made by Advocate Peeters had pained and offended him; the festive event would be marred by that incident were it not that it afforded him the opportunity, which he otherwise would have missed, of telling them all what he thought of the Afrikaner Bond— that it was an evil thing; he could not find terms strong enough to warn the people against its subtle seductions. The Afrikaner Bond professed its objects to be peace and harmony, but it really contained

the pernicious seeds of division and strife, to set up enmity between English Afrikaners and Boer Afrikaners. He pointed out the sincerity of friendly relations on the part of England towards both the Orange Free State and the Transvaal Republics. The peace which restored to the Transvaal its independence a few years before was one big proof; his Government had many proofs of England's good will, too. It suited both parties to maintain harmony—it behoved every Afrikaner to be one-minded in friendly reciprocation. Through a gracious Providence both Republics were prosperous and enjoyed independence. All over the world the prosperity of States depended upon good relations with their neighbours—this was especially so as regards the Orange Free State. They knew what kind of bond the Bible enjoined. It was the bond of peace and concord; and he concluded by declaring his well-grounded fears that the Afrikaner Bond was a device of the devil directed against the well-being of the entire Afrikaner nation. Instead of being encouraged, it should, like the 'Boete Bosch' [*Xanthium spinosum*, burr weed], be extirpated from the soil of South Africa.[42]

Brand went on to declare that he was a "patriotic Free Stater, so that Bond membership was no necessary badge of patriotism. On the contrary, its organization seemed to presage the establishment of a state within a state and to threaten the authority of the established government".[43]

This quote was used by the same author who cheerfully declared, "It is impossible to take the charge of insidious republicanism seriously." By the author's own carefree admission, President Jan Brand completely disagreed with that position.

Another who openly warned against the dangers of the Bond was John X. Merriman.* Like any politician, he, like Rhodes, would later prostitute his ideals for the sake of political power, forming an uneasy political partnership with the Afrikaner Bond in the Cape parliament. But in 1885, when he still had the courage of his convictions, Merriman made a very enlightening speech:

---

* John Xavier Merriman (1841–1926) was a one-time political ally of Rhodes but later his bitter political opponent

the situation is a grave one. It is not a question of localism, it is not a question of party politics, but it is a question whether the Cape Colony is to continue to be an integral part of the British Empire. The question is whether we intend to progress along the lines of freedom, of civilization, and respect for law and order, or whether we are ready to take the Transvaal for a model, and have our policy shaped by the Africander Bond.

There is no begging the question. That has been the plain question before the colony, and there is no use hiding it. That is the question said out of doors, and it should be said in public. It is said at the corners, and should be said from the platform. That being the case, strong language might be excused, but I will endeavour to be studiously moderate. It is not a time when any citizen can sit with his hands folded. They would have to keep the public men up to the mark, and each one of you will have to make up his mind whether he is prepared to see this colony remain a part of the British Empire, which carries with it obligations as well as privileges, or whether he is prepared to obey the dictates of the Bond?

From the very first time, some years ago, when the poison began to be distilled into the country, I felt that it must come to this—was England or the Transvaal to be the paramount force in South Africa? In any other country such an organization could not have grown, but here among a scattered population it had insidiously and successfully worked. What could they think of the objects of the Bond when they found Judge Reitz advocating a Republic of South Africa under one flag, and the Rev. Du Toit spluttering out his disloyalty? No man who wishes well for the British Government could have read the leading articles of the *Zuid Afrikaan*, the *Express* and *De Patriot*, expounding the Bond principles without seeing the maintenance of law and order under the British Crown and the object they have in view are absolutely different things.

As to the other doctrines of the Bond in reference to the restriction of commercial progress, and the non-education of women, they were errors of judgment. My quarrel with the Bond is that it stirs up race difference. Its main object is to make the South African Republic the paramount power in South Africa. That is the reason of its hostility to John Brand—John Brand, the Africander of Africanders; a true friend to the English, and one who has governed his State and is jealous of all its privileges. He is as much opposed to the Bond as I am, and the Bond is as much opposed to him. Stanch Burgers is not a Bondman, and the Bond did all they could to keep him out. They turned out Mr. Luttig, a most excellent member, because he would not work with the Bond. As I said before, the only advantage derived from the Rooi Grond negotiation is that it has brought us face to face with the actions of the Bond, and it is better to have an open enemy than an insidious foe.[44]

Advocate J. W. Wessels[*] will feature several times in our tale. This proud Afrikaner and leader of the Pretoria bar campaigned tirelessly against Kruger's clique for years, imploring reason and conciliation. He described the whites of pre-war southern Africa as falling into three distinct groups. The first were those of British stock, whom he described as having strong attachment to the Empire and no interest in cutting these ties. The second group was those of Dutch or Huguenot descent but who shared this affinity to the British Empire and were described by Wessels as "Loyal Dutch Afrikanders". In his opinion, the third group was the most dangerous: Afrikaners "who are anxious to establish a United South Africa entirely free from British rule. Many people identify the Bond party with this class, though I think this too sweeping a statement … They hate with a bitter hatred everybody who is not of their way of thinking, and they would impose their will on their fellows, not by persuasion, but by brute force. To them the Mauser is a holy symbol … their aspirations are to pull down the British flag, to impose the Dutch language on all, and to establish a reign of barbaric terror".[45]

It is remarkable that a gentleman called Michael Farrelly[†] is completely overlooked by most recent histories of the conflict. Neither Pakenham nor Nasson consider him worthy of mention, which is truly astounding given the position he held in the run-up to the war, and the insights he had into the inner thoughts of both Kruger's clique and the Afrikaner Bond. Born in 1859, Farrelly was an Irish barrister who immigrated to South Africa in 1896

---

[*]   Later Sir Johannes Wilhelmus Wessels (1862–1936)

[†]   Michael James Farrelly (1859–1903), brilliant Irish barrister, studied at Trinity College, Dublin and became a recognized authority on international law.

and became an advisory counsel to the government of the ZAR. He served in this capacity in the years prior to the war and would later be admitted as an advocate of the Cape Supreme Court.[46] Far from being a Jingo, Farrelly always supported the Krugerite view that the British claim of 'suzerainty'* over the Transvaal was meaningless and, indeed, wrote to Chamberlain on the subject. Despite this, Farrelly's close contact with Kruger quickly gave him cause for concern. He repeatedly challenged Kruger's unreasonable stance during negotiations with the British,[47] though to no avail. Indeed, such was Kruger's fury at Farrelly's attempts to convince him to take a conciliatory path that the young barrister quickly realized that Kruger simply had no interest in reaching a peaceful settlement.

Like Jan Brand, Farrelly had had an early introduction to the realities of the Afrikaner Bond. In 1891, while working at the Middle Temple in London, Farrelly became acquainted with an Afrikaans fellow-lawyer who was a member of the Bond. During a discussion on international law, Farrelly's new friend boasted that by the millennium "in South Africa, we shall drive the British into the sea". They met again in Bloemfontein in March 1897, by which time Mr Farrelly's friend was holding high office in Steyn's Orange Free State government, which had just signed the offensive alliance with the Transvaal. Again, his friend mentioned the threat, though generously announced that the British "can keep Simonstown and the bay" – the Afrikaner Bondsmen certainly seemed to have made up their minds on this point. Farrelly remembered that this exchange took place during "the Confederation Week of March 1897, which linked the Orange Free State to the fortunes of the Vaal River Republic". The two met again in September 1899 in Johannesburg, in the weeks leading up to hostilities. Faced with the reality of war, Farrelly's highly placed friend's bravado seemed to be waning, and he confided that "we should have preferred this war twenty years later; we may fail, but we shall do our best. You did not believe my prophecies years ago; you believe them now".[48]

Of course, those who so chose can simply dismiss these recollections as one man's word against another's, though one might agree that the evidence of a man like Farrelly should carry a fair amount of weight and there is no reason to simply dismiss it out of hand. And he was not alone. A most remarkable

---

* Suzerainty was the ill-defined concept contained in the conventions following the first Boer War. It basically meant that Britain retained a degree of hazy stewardship over the foreign affairs of the nation, rather than it having full, unqualified independence.

letter was published in the *Cape Times* of the 31st October 1899, a few weeks after the Boers invaded British territory. Penned by Theo Schreiner,* a longtime acquaintance of Reitz's (one of his brothers was married to Reitz's sister), it declared that he felt

> impelled to write the following lines … to throw a little personal historic light on the question as to who is responsible, for the present war, which may serve to show that not England, not England's Queen, nor England's Government are the real originators of the same.
>
> I met Mr. Reitz, then a judge of the Orange Free State, in Bloemfontein between seventeen and eighteen years ago, shortly after the retrocession of the Transvaal and when he [was] busy establishing the Afrikander Bond. It must be patent to everyone that, at that time at all events, England and its Government had no intention of taking away the independence of the Transvaal, for she had just 'magnanimously' granted the same; no intention to seize the Rand gold-fields, for they were not yet discovered.† At that time then I met Mr. Reitz, and he did his best to get me to become a member of his Afrikander Bond, but after studying its constitution and programme, I refused to do so, whereupon the following colloquy in substance took place, which has been indelibly imprinted on my mind ever since:
>
> Reitz: "Why do you refuse? Is the object of getting the people to take an interest in political matters not a good one?"
>
> Myself: "Yes it is, but I seem to see plainly here, between the lines of this constitution, much more ultimately aimed at than that."
>
> Reitz: "What?"
>
> Myself: "I see quite clearly that the ultimate object aimed at is the overthrow of the British power, and the expulsion of the British flag from South Africa."
>
> Reitz (with his pleasant conscious smile, as of one whose secret thought and purpose had been discovered, and who was not altogether

---

* Theophilus Lyndall Schreiner (1844–1920), teacher, temperance worker and elder brother of both Olive Schreiner, anti-war troublemaker and author of *The Story of an African Farm*, and William Schreiner, prime minister of the Cape Colony from 1898–1900 and brother-in-law of Francis Reitz. Their wildly differing views on the war caused a family rift.

† gold had been discovered in other parts of the Transvaal by then

displeased that such was the case): "Well, what if that is so?"

Myself: "You don't suppose, do you, that that flag is going to disappear from South Africa without a tremendous struggle and fight?"

Reitz (with the same pleasant, self-satisfied, and yet semi-apologetic smile): "Well, I suppose not; but even so, what of that?"

Myself: "Only this, that when that struggle takes place, you and I will be on opposite sides, and, what is more, the God who was on the side of the Transvaal in the late war, because it had right on its side, will be on the side of England, because He must view with abhorrence any plotting and scheming to overthrow her power and position in South Africa, which have been ordained by Him."

Reitz: "We'll see."

Thus the conversation ended; but during the seventeen years that have elapsed I have watched the propaganda for the overthrow of British power in South Africa being ceaselessly spread by every possible means—the press, the pulpit, the platform, the schools, the colleges, the legislature—until it has culminated in the present war, of which Mr. Reitz and his co-workers are the origin and the cause. Believe me, Sir, the day which F.W. Reitz sat down to pen his ultimatum to Great Britain was the proudest and happiest moment of his life, and one which had for long years been looked forward to by him with eager longing and expectation …

My object is to show that, not the British Government, but the Republics, led by Kruger, Reitz, Steyn, and their co-workers, have been steadily marching on towards this war, and consciously plotting for it, ever since the 'magnanimous' retrocession of the Transvaal by England, and even before the Witwatersrand gold-fields were discovered.[49]

Theo Schreiner's mention of propaganda being preached from the pulpit is especially noteworthy as many contemporary accounts refer to the influence wielded by churchmen. Tom Vinnicombe was a Natalian who, before the war, moved to the Transvaal to build a Dutch Reformed Church in Bethal. His writings offer a fascinating insight to the mood in the small towns of the Transvaal and he sums up the ceaseless rabble-rousing of the churchmen:

"For weeks before war was declared Dutch parsons preached the sword."[50] The Reverend Horace Orford,* canon and chancellor of the Bloemfontein Anglican cathedral, agreed: "The Boers knew that the crisis would come, and they knew also that it had been precipitated three years too soon for those who had dreamed of extending Boer rule to Table Bay and to the Zambesi. The ministers of the Dutch Reformed Church were more terribly responsible than any other class for the war."[51]

The Reverend John Moffat offered a similar opinion of the Dutch Reformed Church, "from the pulpits of whose church open sedition has been preached at the present juncture—men who in this very manifesto menace us with the disaffection of their people and with a long vendetta of race hatred and woe and sorrow".[52]

Many of the Boers were poorly educated and deeply religious and the impact of this endless preaching of divine approval and encouragement cannot be underestimated. Indeed, while there is no doubting the intelligence and cunning of the urbane Young Afrikanders, many of their followers were simple, easily led men. It is perhaps not surprising that those tempted by the extremist rhetoric of the Bond were described in a speech given to the Cradock farmers' association as "nearly illiterate, ignorant, and governed almost entirely by emotion instead of by reason". The speech was made on the 7th October 1893, over two years before the Jameson Raid, by a Mr Cronwright who went on to say that the Afrikander Bond was "anti-English in its aims; its officers and its language are Dutch; and it is striving to gain such power as absolutely to control the Cape Parliament".[53] Bear in mind that the Cape Colony was British at this time, giving an indication of the reach, ambition and intentions of the Bond, theirs was no simple desire to maintain the independence of the ZAR and the OFS: their long-term dream was quite clearly to dominate and control all of southern Africa.

In the Cape Colony the Afrikaner Bond took the more moderate form of a legitimate political party and felt the need to tone down its public image as a result.[54] The Cape branch therefore adopted the following aims and objectives: "The Bond knows no nationality of any kind save that of the Afrikaners, and considers as belonging it to everybody, of whatever origin, who aims at the welfare of South Africa. The object of the Afrikaner Bond is: the formation of a South African nationality, through the nurturing of true patriotism …

---

* when the war began Orford was only permitted to remain in Bloemfontein by doing ambulance work

The Bond will strive towards this objective, by encouraging the Afrikaners to assert themselves as a nation on both political and on social grounds."[55]

Despite some objection, the following clause of the Transvaal Bond was subtly left out of the Cape branch's constitution: "The immediate objective of the Bond is the formation of a South African nationality; by joining together and co-operating, as preparation for the achievement of the final goal: a United South Africa under its own flag."

As South Africa did not exist at that time—the area was a patchwork of several states and colonies, two of which were British—the formation of a 'South African Nationality' and a 'United South Africa under its own flag' would therefore require dramatic change in the *status quo*, whether by war or peaceful means. British control of her two South African colonies would have to be relinquished one way or another as the retention of these was utterly incompatible with the stated aims of the Afrikaner Bond. Interestingly, and once again, these quotes are used by the same author—Davenport—who sagely assures his readers that he considered it "impossible to take the charge of insidious republicanism seriously". Quite why is rather difficult to understand as it is certainly not based on the reality he himself presents.

Led by Jan Hofmeyr,* the Afrikaner Bond of the Cape often held the balance of power, forming coalitions with other parties and acting as king-maker in the Cape parliament. As we have seen, at various times, the Bond allied itself to both Rhodes and his arch-rival, Merriman.

In 1884, during the Goshen crisis, the Cape Bondsmen showed where their loyalties lay, as they supported the interests of the expansionist Transvaal over their own Cape Colony's.[56] Afrikaner Bondsmen from the Transvaal were heavily involved in the annexation of Goshen where the Bond even set up a local branch. During the crisis, Hofmeyr proved that the loyalty of his party was to his fellow Bondsmen rather than to the territory he had been elected to serve, passionately arguing against proposals to annex the territory to the Cape Colony and instead championing the case of the Transvaal's freebooters.[57] Indeed, at the height of the crisis, a delegation of Transvaal Bondsmen travelled to Cape Town to hold secret talks with their Cape brethren. Remarkably, the visitors refused to meet with the official representatives of the Cape parliament, bizarrely declaring them to be "not authorized by the Colonial Parliament".[58]

---

* Jan Hendrik Hofmeyr (1845–1909)—'*Onze Jan*', 'Our Jan'

❧

President Reitz of the Orange Free State was taken seriously ill in late 1895, prompting his retirement and presidential elections which were held in February 1896. Coming just after the fiasco of the Jameson Raid, and the resultant tide of anti-British feeling, the pan-Dutch party (by then led by another Afrikaner Bondsman, Marthinus Steyn) duly romped to victory over John Fraser's moderates. Fraser was "one of the most experienced, able and reliable men in the State, but was now completely deserted in favour of a young lawyer, whose views appeared so much to coincide with those of President Kruger that, when Mr Steyn was sworn in on March 4, 1896, the former sent a telegram of sincere congratulation, and at the same time expressed a hope that the two Republics would now be more united than heretofore".[59]

Sure enough, in March 1897 the Orange Free State and the Transvaal joined in confederation and Steyn signed the offensive alliance with the Transvaal which Jan Brand had rejected ten years earlier. John Fraser remained bitterly opposed to the treaty, stating that it put the Orange Free State at the mercy of the Transvaal, supported a government which was shamefully corrupt and jeopardized the friendly relations the Orange Free State had previously enjoyed with Great Britain.[60] Though Fraser was later proved to be right on all counts, Kruger's persistence had finally paid off. *Oom* Paul celebrated this pivotal moment by drinking a glass of champagne—the only time in his life he ever consumed alcohol.[61]

Paul Botha was a proud Afrikaner who served in the Orange Free State volksraad for twenty-one years as the member for Kroonstad. He had his own theories on the unknown Steyn's remarkable victory over Fraser, which were

due to the influence of Paul Kruger, who, by his emissaries, agents, and secret service money undermined the Free State. His subsidized organ, the *Bloemfontein Express*, was the first to advocate his candidature. Paul Kruger did not want an honest Free State patriot like Fraser, whose first thought would have been his own country, at the head of the sister Republic. He wanted a servile tool. Steyn's ambition did the rest. He sold his country, body and soul, to the

Transvaal, in the hope that Paul Kruger's mantle would fall on him. The first time that Kruger visited the Orange Free State after Steyn's election, the latter introduced him with these words, "This is my father." The thought occurred to me at the time, "Yes and you are waiting for your father's shoes." He hoped to succeed 'his father' as President of the Transvaal, of the combined republics, aye, even of United South Africa! For this giddy vision he ignored the real interests of our little State—he was false to his oath, and dragged the country, whose integrity and independence he had sworn to uphold, into a wholly and absolutely unnecessary and insane war.[62]

Though few realized the danger that this new offensive alliance presented, it did not go entirely unnoticed. In 1897 the expensive new Royal Navy dockyard facilities which were planned to be built in Cape Town were instead switched to the facility at Simon's Town, on the Cape peninsular, south of Cape Town itself.[63] The thinking at the Admiralty seemed to be that, even if Britain was forced out of the rest of southern Africa, they would be able to negotiate to retain the peninsular—and with it, the new £2.5-million facilities[64]—as some sort of 'Gibraltar of the South'. Though many scoffed at this notion—and the idea that a united Afrikaans South Africa would even allow the British to retain the peninsular—it would appear that the Admiralty, at least, took the threat from the Boer republics seriously.

Those who place all the blame for the war on Milner's shoulders tend to ignore the fact that Kruger and his 'servile tool' signed their offensive alliance two months before Milner* even arrived in South Africa. And, more to the point, Kruger had first started pushing for it a full decade before Milner appeared on the scene.

With Kruger's offensive alliance finally in place, things moved quickly. The Transvaal began to fund a programme of military expansion in the Orange Free State,[65] turning what was a sleepy backwater in 1897 into a force to be reckoned with by 1899. In January 1898 the executive council of the Transvaal passed a resolution stating that they must strengthen their connection with the Afrikaner Bond, who would undoubtedly "render them loyal assistance". They also resolved to "continue to acquire all the latest

---

* After the resignation of Hercules Robinson, Milner was appointed to the twin roles of high commissioner of southern Africa and governor of the Cape Colony in his place. Milner arrived in the Cape in May 1897.

improvements in armament, remembering that they had to provide arms for more than themselves".[66]

The Reverend W. Tees, Presbyterian minister in Durban, was later given first-hand evidence of the 'conspiracy' by one of his congregation. This fellow had formally been the attorney-general of the Free State, was passionately pro-Boer in his leanings and made no secret of his satisfaction as the republicans poured into Natal in October 1899. The churchman fell into conversation with this chap about how well-prepared the Boer commandos were and was told:

"This has been preparing since 1884."

"In both states?"

"Yes, in both, and in the Colony also. The Transvaal has been the arsenal, but those in the know in the Free State and the Colony have worked in unison with Kruger."

"And the object was to oust the British from South Africa?"

"Precisely, but it was not intended to do it all at once. The first step was the consolidation of the two Republics as a sovereign international state, and later on an Afrikaner rising at the right moment."[67]

It is, of course, just about possible that every single one of these highly placed witnesses was lying about the shadowy influence of the Afrikaner Bond, that their various manifestos were all faked, that they didn't really want to form a 'United South Africa under its own flag' and that they never held any secret meetings with the volksraad. Equally, it is not completely impossible, I suppose, that the Transvaal executive council's resolutions about arming others were entirely innocent and that Kruger worked assiduously for ten years to gain an offensive alliance with the Orange Free State just for a bit of a giggle. We shall perhaps never know if the conspiracy to oust the British from South Africa was indeed quite as formal, far-reaching and Machiavellian as some of the uitlanders and loyalists claimed at the time. That there was plenty of anti-British scheming and plotting going on behind the scenes during the late 1890s is as undeniable, however, as was the pervasive desire to create a united, Afrikaans-dominated South Africa. To claim that the Transvaal's leaders and the extreme wing of the Afrikaner Bond were blameless in the run-up to the war is simply to ignore the evidence.

Things soon started hotting up again. In February 1898 Kruger dismissed

John Kotzé,* the chief justice of the Transvaal. A moderate and decent man, Kotzé clashed with Kruger over the independence of the judiciary in the ZAR, infuriating Kruger by ruling against the government in a case on mining rights. The pair also banged heads over Kruger's penchant for simply passing new legislation through the volksraad without bothering to get approval from the high court. Kotzé's questioning of this was enough to get him fired, with Kruger inexplicably comparing him to the devil in the Garden of Eden.[68] Though *Oom* Paul certainly had no interest in the normal trappings of a democracy, Kotzé's real mistake had been standing against Kruger in the 1893 election[†] and for daring to speak out against his victimization of the uitlanders. In a further stab in the eye of the Reform Committee, Kruger replaced Kotzé with Gregorowski, the judge who had recently sentenced several leading Johannesburg reformers to death in the wake of the Jameson Raid.[‡] Another judge, Mr Justice Ameshof, was also fired after speaking in support of Kotzé.[69]

This outrageous intervention in the judiciary did not go unnoticed by Milner, convincing him that Kruger's corrupt oligarchy was beyond negotiation.[70] On the 23rd February 1898 Milner wrote to his boss, 'Pushful Joe' Chamberlain, in London, warning him that "there is no way out of the political troubles of South Africa except reform in the Transvaal or war … [Kruger] has immense resources of money and any amount of ammunition for war, to which he is constantly adding. Politically he had strengthened his hold on the Orange Free State and the Colonial Afrikaners continue to do obeisance to him … Kruger will never take any step which he thinks will provoke us to fight. But if he is assured that our hands are full in other directions, he will certainly seize the opportunity".[71]

This letter was not well received by Chamberlain, who instantly fired back a telegram, reminding Milner that "The principal object of HMG in South Africa at present is peace. Nothing but a most flagrant offence would justify the use of force".[72]

As HM's government disregarded Milner's warnings and sleep-walked blindly toward war, Kruger was re-elected as the Transvaal's president

---

* John Gilbert Kotzé (1849–1940) was chief justice of the Transvaal between 1881 and 1898 and later served as the attorney-general of Rhodesia. He was knighted in 1917.

† Kotzé's election chances were sabotaged by Kruger's supporters spreading rumours of his 'ungodliness'

‡ later commuted to prison sentences

later that year, helped by two rival candidates splitting the vote and, more importantly, by the fact that the overwhelming majority of adult males in his country were denied the franchise. These elections also saw the key Young Afrikanders enter high office in the ZAR. Reitz, former president of the Orange Free State, came out of retirement to become the Transvaal's state secretary; Smuts was appointed as the state attorney and Grobler* the foreign secretary. These three lost no time in testing the resolve to the British and rattling sabres at their neighbours.

As we have learned, the ZAR had recently gained *de facto* control of Swaziland. Though tolerated by the British, this was subject to certain restrictions, primarily connected to the rights of natives, as described by our friend Michael Farrelly: "certain stipulations had been made in favour of the Swazis, including the preservation of their native usages, so far as they were not in conflict with civilised laws and customs … the privileges of the principal chief of the Swazis were specially guarded, and by an express article it was stipulated that the Imperial Government retained the right of diplomatic remonstrance, in case the provisions of the Convention touching the reserved rights of the Swazis were not observed."[73]

When the principal chief of the Swazis ordered the execution of one of his people, the new militant regime in Pretoria decided it was time to test these restrictions. The ZAR's new high court of Swaziland had previously considered such matters as outwith its jurisdiction, being that it was between Swazi and Swazi. With Kotzé's voice of reason now out of the way, the Young Afrikanders advised the government of the Transvaal to arrest this principal Swazi chief—a man called Bunu—with the intention of hanging him. Given the Transvaal's cavalier attitude to native welfare, it is difficult to imagine that their intervention was inspired by concern for human rights, but rather motivated more by a desire to stamp their authority, tweak the nose of the British and see how far they could push the imperial power.

Sure enough, Milner intervened, pointing out the terms of the 1894 convention and that the high court had already decided there was no jurisdiction. This intervention was not well received by the Transvaal government, no remonstrance from the imperial government would be entertained and—as usual—the ZAR turned to its burgeoning military might to enforce its wishes.[74] Commandos were deployed to Swaziland to snatch

---

* Piet Grobler, Kruger's nephew

Bunu, who in turn fled to British territory in August. Milner was in no doubt that, by openly flouting the convention, the Transvaal was challenging British imperial authority in the region and was highly alarmed by this development. The British agent in Pretoria, Edmund Fraser, was instructed to deliver what was essentially an ultimatum to Kruger and the Transvaal. Kruger was caught wrong-footed and backed down, pulling the ZAR commandos out of Swaziland. An arrangement was then reached whereby Chief Bunu was merely fined, rather than strung up.[75] A new protocol was signed in October 1898, extending the jurisdiction of the Transvaal-run high court of Swaziland to cover all cases of violent crime, even when only Swazis were involved.

The Young Afrikanders had tried to twist the lion's tail but, not being ready to risk war at that stage, were forced to back down. The crisis in Swaziland was not the only time Kruger had tested imperial resolution in the years leading up to the Boer War; he had previously been faced down over the Drifts crisis in 1895.* Far from putting Kruger back in his box, however, these stand-offs actually seem to have convinced both sides that the other would never risk actual conflict: the British came away thinking that Kruger was all talk, while Kruger was left with the impression that the Empire was a toothless tiger, happier to negotiate than fight. Despite the ever-growing tensions between the Transvaal and the British, and his telegram to Chamberlain telegram, Milner was one of the few who took the threat from Kruger seriously.

Michael Farrelly, by then advisory counsel to the government of the Transvaal, was another of that small group who clearly saw that Kruger was preparing for war. In early 1899 he tried to warn many of the leaders in British South Africa: "Among those whose views I sought were the Governor of Natal, Sir Walter Hely-Hutchinson, and the Acting High-Commissioner, [General] Sir William Butler; the leading members of the past and the present Governments, and of the legislative bodies, as well as of leading lawyers, of

---

* This spat between the Cape Colony and the Transvaal was caused by Kruger's closure of the drifts (fords) over the Vaal River in an attempt to force traffic onto his (massively overpriced) railway. The Cape government appealed to London for support and tensions ran high for a time, with even the Afrikaner Bond in the Cape supporting military action against the Transvaal. In a similar event a few years earlier, Kruger showed preference to the Cape railways over those of Natal, despite the latter providing a much shorter route to the sea. At a meeting in Pretoria to discuss this, the Natal delegation, headed by a Mr Binns, was told that this would only be revised when Natal became a self-governing colony (which happened in 1893). This is yet another example of Kruger's interference in the affairs of his neighbours and his attempts to undermine the position of the British Empire. As Hugh Abercrombie wrote in 1900: "This is another proof of the President's unswerving policy. Railway interests, commercial interests, race interests, must all be used to secure the ultimate success of his plans, but under no circumstance could deals take place through the Imperial Government."

leading merchants, and landowners in Natal, the Eastern Province and the Cape. With only two exceptions, I was assured that the prospects of war between the two Boer States and the Empire, or between Dutch and British in South Africa, were so remote that no sensible man would think about them."[76]

As late as June 1899, Chamberlain was still absolutely convinced that there would be no shooting war: "there will be no fighting. We know that these fellows won't fight ... we are playing a game."[77] Later still, in the weeks just before the invasion, with Boer commandos mustering on their borders and refugees fleeing Johannesburg, both Rhodes and Dr Jameson dismissed the very notion that war would really happen. Jameson confidently wrote to his brother that Kruger would back down once again,[78] just like he had over the Drifts and Swaziland. The day after the war began Jameson was still unable to believe it, again writing to his brother to tell him, "I cannot believe the Boers will be foolish enough to begin shooting."[79] Indeed, such was the sheer disbelief with which war was greeted that the troopers of the Natal Mounted Police were ordered not to fire on the invaders unless they were themselves fired upon.[80]

Though perhaps surprising to a modern mind, these games of brinksmanship were a common feature of the late Victorian period, where the threat of war (as distinct from war itself) was an oft-used tool in colonial diplomacy. Describing the tensions and sabre-rattling of the uitlander crisis in mid-1899, Frank Welsh states in his history of South Africa: "Up until the last minute there was a strong possibility that the British government would not assume responsibility for giving the order to fire," and the feeling was that "the threat of war would suffice".[81] One senior British diplomat stated that any imperial military force "should be sent chiefly for political reasons" and "none of us believe the Boers would take the offensive".[82] When the Boers did actually attack, London was "surprised and alarmed; it had never been their plan that actual fighting should break out".[83]

In such relations between the Great Powers this brinksmanship worked because both sides understood the game and knew that such threats would never really be carried out. Indeed, the late Victorian era saw nations almost going to war with one another on a regular basis. In 1893 Britain and France almost went to war with one another in Siam and again in 1898 over the Fashoda incident.[84] France and Germany almost went to war in 1875, with

Belgium, Italy and Austria all involved, too. Germany and the USA almost went to war over Samoa in 1897, Russia and Great Britain almost went to war in 1885 over the Panjdeh incident, while the USA and Britain almost went to war over Chile in 1891 and then again over the drawing of the Venezuelan border in 1895. This was just the way governments interacted at the time and these events did not have any lasting impact on relations between the countries involved—everyone seemed to accept that this chest-beating and sabre-rattling was just the way affairs were conducted. Despite almost going to war over the Fashoda incident of 1898, for example, Great Britain and France agreed an alliance* just a few years later with the British supporting France against Germany in the first Morocco crisis of 1905.

Unfortunately, Kruger didn't seem to understand the rules of the game and, though the ZAR had backed down in 1898, the British tendency to threaten but not actually attack only served to strengthen Kruger's contemptuous regard for them. Far from living in constant fear of British invasion as some commentators often claim, after the crisis in Swaziland, Kruger—and as ridiculous as this might sound—convinced himself that the Transvaal was perfectly safe from British attack because of Queen Victoria's hearty dislike of war.[85] Kruger persuaded himself that, such was her determination that her long and glorious reign should end peacefully, she would never permit her armies to go to war. In one respect he was absolutely right, though for absolutely the wrong reasons. While certain writers attempt to portray the Boer invasions as 'pre-emptive attacks', as we shall see later, the pitiful size of the imperial forces in South Africa—even including the reinforcements that were mobilized—are proof enough that there was never really any threat of a British attack on the Transvaal.

Michael Farrelly, who as we know was very closely linked to all the major players, saw that the confrontation over Swaziland could only ultimately lead to war:

> So within two months of succeeding to office in Pretoria, the Young Afrikanders had brought South Africa and the Empire to the verge of war ... it was at that point, in October 1898, after many doubts and long enquiry, that I realized the real trend—notwithstanding the most pacific professions—of the Afrikander movement. It meant

---

* the 1904 *Entente Cordiale*

war. The question was one only of time. That the leaders were
absolutely assured that actual fighting would be necessary is another
matter. If the Empire were at war with another Great Power, possibly
the Imperial Government would peaceably cede South Africa to the
Dutch-speaking dominion, and even accept a subsidy for policing the
sea by its fleet, until the new dominion could spare time to create one
of its own.

My absolute conviction that there would be war was induced by the
fact that I had learned to know the mind of the Young Afrikander, and
well knew the mind of the British people. It was as if one were looking
through a stereoscope, from two points of view at once. In England,
no one could believe in the combined ignorance and audacity of two
petty States, rashly challenging the world-wide Empire; and so, no
one dreamt of war. In the Transvaal and among the mass of half-
educated Afrikanders, not to mention the veldt Boer, although war
was conceived as possible, their invincible ignorance of the extent of
the resources, of the reserve of military power, of the determination
of the Imperial people was as great as British incredulity as to the
magnitude of an audacity, the result of a hundred years of Imperial
mistakes.[86]

CHAPTER FOUR

The road to war

"But the stranger that dwelleth with you shall be unto you as one born among you,
and thou shalt love him as thyself; for ye were strangers in the land of Egypt;
I am the Lord, your God."
—Leviticus. xix.33

"I will make you go to the front if I have to tie you up with my own hands
and throw you onto the wagon."
—Hendrik Schoeman, addressing uitlanders who refused to be commandeered, 1894[1]

"The greatest danger lies in the attitude of President Kruger and his vain hope of building
up a State on a foundation of a narrow unenlightened minority, and his obstinate rejection
of all prospect of using the materials which lie ready to his hand to establish a true
republic on a broad liberal basis. Such a state of affairs cannot last.
It must break down from inherent rottenness."
John X. Merriman to President Steyn, 11th March 1899

"It was recognized by all members of the Cabinet that any actual breach with the
Transvaal would not be cordially supported here, and would divide the
Colonial community at Cape Town into two hostile camps.
For those reasons war would be very much to be deprecated."
—Prime Minister Salisbury to HM Queen Victoria, 13th May 1899[2]

"a Boer Machiavelli, astute and bigoted, obstinate as a mule, remarkably opinionated,
vain and puffed up with the power conferred on him, vindictive, covetous and always
a Boer, which means a narrow-minded and obtuse provincial of the illiterate type."
—Henry Morton Stanley on Paul Kruger[3]

"I cannot abandon my own subjects who have appealed to me for protection.
If President Kruger is reasonable, there will be no war."
—Queen Victoria to Queen Wilhelmina of the Netherlands

"I began to perceive that signs of any inclination seriously to meet the grievances were altogether wanting; and that in this, and many other directions, there unmistakable signs coming into view of a spirit very far removed from conciliation or yielding on the part of the South African Republic. It seemed plain that it was no longer a question of a five years' or a seven years' franchise. It was a question of who was to dictate to South Africa."
—Arthur Hamilton Baynes DD, Bishop of Natal, 1900[4]

"We have committed one of the greatest blunders in war, namely, we have given the enemy the initiative. He is in a position to take the offensive and, by striking the first blow, to ensure the great advantage of winning the first round."
—Lord Wolseley to the secretary of state, 3rd September 1899

The catalyst which finally brought this long-simmering cold war to the boil, and prompted Kruger to launch his invasion, was the plight of the uitlanders— the non-Afrikaans, mainly English-speaking residents of the Transvaal who were almost entirely responsible for the economic boom that the country had enjoyed. Kruger's constant upping of the length of residency-qualification requirements—from one year to five, and finally up to fourteen—meant tens of thousands of these men were essentially denied the franchise.[*] The summation of Kruger's regime by esteemed historian, Andrew Roberts, probably puts it best: "The Transvaal was in no way a democracy. No Catholic or Jew was allowed to vote or hold office. Every Boer was compelled to own a rifle, no non-Boer was allowed to. Johannesburg, with 50,000 mainly Uitlander inhabitants, was not even allowed an unelected municipal council. English was banned in all official proceedings. Judges were appointed by Kruger, who controlled all the government monopolies from jam to dynamite. By far the largest proportion of the tax burden was carried by the Uitlanders, yet no open-air public meetings were permitted. Newspapers could be closed down arbitrarily without any reason given. Above all, full citizenship was almost impossible to gain for non-Boers. Pretoria ran a tight, tough, quasi-police state."[5]

An Austrian visitor to the Transvaal described the situation of the uitlanders who, despite "owning property, paying taxes etc, are barred from the right of voting, and enjoy no more political rights than the Kaffir ... that radical

---

[*] Unlike in the British territories of South Africa, non-whites were also completely denied the vote in the Transvaal. For some reason, this reality is generally ignored by Boer apologists as they fall over themselves to defend Kruger's regime.

reform was absolutely needed in the Transvaal everyone who has been there will admit".[6]

It had not always been this way. When gold was first discovered in the Transvaal, prior to the 1877 annexation, a community of English-speaking miners (mainly Scotsmen) established themselves in the area around Pilgrim's Rest. When they approached President Burgers to request representation in the volksraad, he agreed, and two representatives were elected from the digging community.[7] The later Witwatersrand gold rush occurred under the rather less benign regime of President Kruger, however, and there was no such enthusiasm to accommodate the newcomers. Indeed, Kruger's repeated changing of the franchise law made it obvious he had no intention of ever letting significant numbers of uitlanders get the vote.

In 1894, when the Transvaal went to war with yet another African chief, large numbers of British uitlanders were called up to fight for the republic. Uitlanders of all other nationalities were exempt,[8] so this was seen by many as a calculated insult to Great Britain and a deliberate attempt to test her resolve. Understandably enough, many of those conscripted in this fashion refused to fight, declaring that they had no intention of bearing arms for a country which denied them the vote. Meetings were held and an uitlander association was formed to challenge the conscription. This had the support of various churchmen and of Advocate J. W. Wessels, (whom we met earlier) who stated: "It is not at all clear to me that the Government can commandeer any but burghers to suppress the kaffir rebels."[9]

Tensions were high and the uitlanders were in what was described as a "state of unarmed uprising". In scenes which would be repeated in the 1970s and '80s, July saw the Transvaal police—the much hated ZARPs—cracking down on demonstrations with considerable brutality. On the 8th October that year, an Englishwoman called Mrs Simpson attempted to come to the aid of her servant girl who was being attacked by a ZARP officer. The brute kicked Mrs Simpson so hard in the stomach that she would die from her injuries.[10] Danie Theron, a Krugersdorp lawyer who would later gain notoriety during the guerrilla war, physically assaulted the anti-Kruger editor of the Johannesburg Star, only to have his fine paid by his cheering supporters who packed the courthouse.[11] It is small wonder that the uitlanders had had enough.

When the state attorney took action against a group of uitlanders who refused to fight, the uitlander association raised funds to defend them. Nevertheless, they were found guilty and taken to the front under military escort. Others were thrashed for the same offence.[12] When this situation was reported to London by the British resident, Sir Jacobus de Wet, the imperial response was somewhat pathetic. Far from seizing on this as a *casus belli*, and to the fury of the uitlanders, all the British government did was courteously request that British subjects be exempted from service. Needless to say, this was simply ignored by the Transvaal until secret talks were held between Kruger and Sir Henry Loch,* British high commissioner for southern Africa.[13] It was a typical Kruger bargaining tactic: by conceding on one point—and only to what was reasonable in the first place—he made it look as though he was the one prepared to be conciliatory. By 'graciously' exempting the uitlanders from conscription, he hoped to pull the rug from under their feet. Kruger's supporters and apologists elsewhere, both then and now, seemed to think the uitlanders should have been grateful and given up their aspirations to gain a fair franchise requirement.

Though no longer liable for conscription, the vast majority of uitlanders was still denied the vote, and still responsible for virtually all the tax paid in the Transvaal—so, by any standard, their continued demands for reform were entirely reasonable. Kruger had even introduced additional taxes aimed at the uitlanders after the end of commandeering.[14] The farce of the Jameson Raid of 1895/6 had not helped their cause, for it allowed Kruger to play his favourite role—that of the victim, valiantly standing up to the British bully. But as 1899 began, the underlying problem had not gone away: the uitlanders were still being unfairly treated, and Kruger still had no intention of addressing this issue.

Not surprisingly, and despite various pro-Boer writers claiming that their cause was just an excuse for war, the uitlanders enjoyed widespread support across the spectrum of the popular press: "In London *The Times*, the newly-founded *Daily Mail*, the Liberal *Daily News* and the judicious *Westminster Gazette* were alike beginning to agitate their cause as the 19th Century came to a close. In South Africa, Garrett's *Cape Times* took the same line (as did the Rhodes' controlled Argus group)."[15] Similarly, their plight struck a chord with their kith and kin across the Empire and "petitions poured in from the Cape Colony, Natal and Rhodesia praying for redress of uitlander grievances,

---

* Henry Brougham Loch, 1st Baron Loch GCB, GCMG (23 May 1827–20 June 1900), high commissioner for southern Africa, 1889–95

and the distant Canadian Parliament expressed sympathy with uitlander aspirations".[16] As previously mentioned, do those modern writers who think that Kruger was right to deny the franchise to the uitlanders, or think that they were motived by 'greed', also think the later apartheid regime was right to deny the franchise to non-whites, and that Mandela's ANC was 'greedy' to demand the vote? The principle is exactly the same; this rank hypocrisy tells us a lot about those who dismiss the situation of the uitlanders with such cavalier disregard. The usual excuse given by such apologists is that the uitlanders were 'newly arrived' and only after a quick buck. John Stephens comprehensively refutes this argument:

> It is easy to forget that when dealing with the ZAR of the 1880s, one is not dealing with a long-established country, suddenly overrun by fortune-seekers who try to take over the reins of state. In the 1880s, the ZAR was never more than a collection of admittedly growing, but still far-flung, isolated communities. Due to their greater access to modern weapons, they could dominate to subjugation their surrounding black communities, extracting labour from them as tribute, but not much more. The ZAR was only regarded as a state because Britain, for its own purposes, had seen fit to recognize it was such, and that recognition only pre-dated the arrival of the first Uitlanders by five years. Even then, all are agreed that the ZAR's independence was conditional and that it lacked sovereignty. There was no good reason why people, coming to what can at best be described as a nascent state, perennially indigent, with no industry, no commerce or economy, and no expertise to change said situation, should be denied full participation in that state by those whose only claim was that they had arrived a few years earlier. Even more so, when those earlier arrivals had in the space of those years not achieved anything constructive, except for the fact that they had survived.[17]

With their efforts to secure some sort of reform mocked and rejected by Kruger's oligarchy, in February 1899 the uitlanders felt they had no choice but to turn to the Motherland to support their case. It was the first direct appeal to London by British residents of the Transvaal since the war of 1880/1—a momentous event from which there would be no turning back.[18]

Thousands of uitlanders signed a petition which was sent to Queen Victoria, urging her government to intervene. Though many like to portray Rhodes and the other Randlords as the driving force behind this agitation, "the mine magnates held aloof so rigidly that the Consolidated Goldfields, Rhodes's own Company, dismissed an employee who had taken the chair at the Amphitheatre meeting".[19] In March, another petition, this one consisting of 21,684 signatures, was drawn up before a group of leading uitlanders made their way to deliver it to the British vice-consul in Johannesburg. This trip was enough for two of the men involved, Messrs Webb and Dodd, to be prosecuted on the orders of Jan Smuts (the Transvaal's state attorney) on a trumped-up charge of conducting an illegal public meeting.[20] With tedious predictability, Kruger's apologists seek to dismiss these huge petitions by claiming that some of the names were faked[21]—as if a few falsified names invalidate the reasonable demands of tens of thousands of tax-paying adults.

The reason for Kruger's continued oppression of the uitlanders was simple: he knew that if they got a fair franchise then his party would lose power, and with this loss of power would vanish all the long-planned schemes and dreams of dominating southern Africa. As Michael Farrelly—who was uniquely well placed to comment—wrote in 1900, "The Afrikaner party kept steady in view the Pan-Afrikaner anti-British goal. To preserve the nucleus round which was to group the Dutch domination from the Zambesi to the Cape, from the Atlantic to the Indian Ocean, a most jealous grasp was to be kept on political power, on the gold in the reef, on the command of rifles, forts and armaments, on the exclusive use of the Dutch tongue."[22]

With his country in turmoil and in a bid to buy time, Kruger offered to replace the fourteen-year residency requirement for the franchise with a nine-year one. Everyone involved must have known that this would be completely unacceptable to the uitlanders. The fact that the new law would be non-retrospective and, worse still, that those enfranchised in this fashion would be denied a vote in presidential elections[23] made it even less appealing. Not surprisingly, these 'reforms' were roundly rejected by the uitlanders, all the more so because Kruger also sought to link this 'concession' to a renewal of the much-hated dynamite monopoly.*

---

* Recognizing that the gold mines had an insatiable demand for dynamite, Kruger established a monopoly on supply, handing the concession to French and German investors. This led to the Transvaal having one of the largest explosives factories in the world. The monopoly kept dynamite prices outrageously high, generating an annual profit of £2 million, and greatly annoying the Randlords.

But Kruger's agents were simultaneously working behind the scenes, trying to drive a wedge between the Randlords and the uitlander rank and file. When this proved futile, they then tried to sow dissent within the powerful Jewish community. Again, this failed.

Mass meetings of uitlanders across Johannesburg[24] resolved to settle for nothing less than a five-year residency qualification for the franchise (i.e. the same as in the Cape Colony and the Orange Free State). This, they stated, would be their "irreducible minimum" and it was by no means unreasonable. Milner noted that the agitation of the uitlander groups had grown to "formidable proportions".[25] In Natal a meeting was held in Pietermaritzburg "to express its strong sympathy with British subjects in the South African Republic in the grave difficulties and dangers under which they are suffering". Similar meetings were held in Cape Town and other parts of the Cape Colony.[26] A rival, pro-Kruger rally in the centre of Johannesburg organized by trouble-making Irish nationalists quickly descended into violence as patriotic British uitlanders clashed with the Fenian rabble-rousers. The leader of the Irish dissidents tried to open fire on the uitlanders but was disarmed before he could, while mounted ZARPs charged to break up the riot.[27] Kruger's intransigence and determination to deny the uitlanders even the most basic rights was stoking the flames of war.

∂

Our friend Michael Farrelly, in his role as advisory counsel to the government of the Transvaal, attended the opening of the Orange Free State volksraad in April 1899.[28] Just as he had done a few weeks earlier in British South Africa, he took the chance to broach his fear of impending conflict with the leading men in the Orange Free State, advising them of the "extreme gravity of the situation".

As a simple and elegant way of solving the franchise issue at a stroke, Farrelly quite logically pushed the leaders of the Orange Free State to convince Kruger to introduce the Orange Free State franchise laws to the Transvaal, something which would have solved the problem in an instant. As we shall soon see, however, Kruger simply never had any genuine interest in addressing the grievances of the uitlanders. Farrelly also

endeavoured to convey to them my own conviction of the imminent risk of war; and that the calculation obviously being made by the militant Afrikanders that, once again, the Imperial Government would waver and retreat, was due to an absolute want of knowledge of the courage and resolution of the British people or Government, when once roused ... I pointed out, too, the boundless wealth and the reserve military force of the Empire in the case of the war, towards which militant Afrikander policy in Pretoria was impelling the two Republics. I found that, with the exception of certain progressive members of the Volksraad, including Mr. J. G. Fraser, there was not the least confidence in the resolution of the Imperial Government. And as to the chances of [winning the] war, that they inclined in favour of the Boer States; more especially in view of the likelihood of foreign complication. For much of this I was prepared, but I confess I was surprised to find the President [Steyn] holding—as he told me—that the presence of the [Afrikaner] Bond Ministry in office in the Cape would interfere with Imperial troops making use of its railways. [29]

In May 1899 Schreiner's Bond-backed Cape government felt compelled to intervene in the crisis. The chief justice of the Cape Colony, Sir Henry de Villiers, travelled to the Transvaal for talks with Kruger, but was unable to meet with the president. He did, however, manage to talk with Reitz and Smuts, and returned to Cape Town satisfied that they would press Kruger to offer a reasonable five-year franchise.[30] These men had backed down over Swaziland the year before and seemed ready to do so again. Were the Young Afrikaners worried things were moving too quickly, that the demands of the increasingly bellicose uitlander lobby would provoke a war before the British Empire was embroiled in conflict with another Great Power?

Milner sent a long telegram to his London masters in that same month. Parts of it are instructive in terms of his desires and intentions:

The true remedy is to strike at the root of all these injuries—the political impotence of the injured. What diplomatic protests will never accomplish, a fair measure of *Uitlander* representation would gradually, but surely, bring about. It seems a paradox, but it is true

The Vanquis Bank App

For day-to-day banking on the go, whenever and wherever you want, download the Vanquis Bank App today.

3 simple steps to register

Step 1 — **Validate** - Enter your mobile number

Step 2 — **Secure** - Create passcode

Step 3 — **Activate** - Enter your card number and CVV number (3 digit number on the back of your card)

Download the app for free from the App Store or Google play

You can also register at www.evanquis.co.uk for free email and SMS alerts, quick access to your last 6 months' statements and to switch off paper statements.

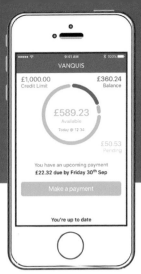

VANQUIS BANK

The Vanquis Bank App
for better banking
on the move

With the app you will be able to:

 Activate your card using the
Vanquis Bank App

 View your balance and see how much
you have available to spend

 Make debit card payments

 View your recent transactions
including pending transactions

 Schedule a future debit card payment

 Set up a Direct Debit

 Login securely with your fingerprint
or passcode*

*Fingerprint login - A quick, easy and convenient way to log in to the new Vanquis Bank
 App, if available on your mobile device.

Download for free from the App Store or Google play

that the only effective way of protecting our subjects is to help them to cease to be our subjects. The admission of the Uitlanders to a fair share of political power would, no doubt, give stability to the Republic. But it would, at the same time, remove most of our causes of difference with it, and modify, and the long-term entirely remove, that intense suspicion and bitter hostility to Great Britain which at present dominates it internal and external policy ... A certain section of the press, not in the Transvaal only, preaches openly and constantly the doctrine of a republic embracing all South Africa, and supports it by menacing references to the armaments of the Transvaal, its alliance with the Orange Free State, and the active sympathy which in case of war it would receive from a section of Her Majesty's subjects. I regret to say that this doctrine, supported as it is by a ceaseless stream of malignant lies about the intention of the British Government, is producing a great effect upon a large number of our Dutch fellow-colonists. Language is frequently used which seems to imply that that the Dutch have some superior right even in this Colony to their fellow citizens of British birth. Thousands of men peaceably disposed, and, if left alone, perfectly satisfied with their position as British subjects, are being drawn into disaffection, and there is corresponding exasperation on the side of the British.

I can see nothing which will put a stop to this mischievous propaganda but some striking proof of the intention of Her Majesty's Government not to be ousted from its position in South Africa. And the best proof alike of its power and its justice would be to obtain for the Uitlanders in the Transvaal a fair share in the government of the country which owes everything to their exertions. It could be made perfectly clear that our action was not directed against the existence of the Republic. We should only be demanding the re-establishment of rights which now exist in the Orange Free State, and which existed in the Transvaal itself at the time of, and long after, the withdrawal of British sovereignty. It would be no selfish demand, as other Uitlanders beside those of British birth would benefit from it. It is asking for nothing from others which we do not give ourselves. And it would certainly go to the root of the political unrest in South Africa, and though temporarily it might aggravate, it would ultimately extinguish the race feud which is the great bane of this country.[31]

These words certainly do not leave one with the impression that Milner had a burning desire to invade the Transvaal and add it to the British Empire, or that his intentions were anything other than simply to gain a fair franchise for the uitlanders.

On the 16th May sensational news broke in the European press of a British plot to seize power in Johannesburg. With echoes of the Jameson Raid, the dastardly scheme involved a group of imperial officers smuggling arms into the town, snatching the fort and holding out until the arrival of troops from Natal. The arrest of these plotters was trumpeted by the Transvaal government and reported across the world, with every effort made to foster the suspicion that the British were behind a treacherous attack on the South African Republic.[32]

Strangely, this wicked plot is overlooked in most modern accounts, for the simple reason that it was a false-flag, put-up job, dreamed up by Kruger's spooks. The main players in what became known as the 'Bogus Conspiracy' were Chief Detective de Villiers, Kruger's youngest son, Tjaart, and Commissioner of Police Schutte. The so-called conspirators were all members of the Transvaal Secret Service,[33] though a Mr Nicholls, a respectable miner who had talked about raising a corps for the defence of the town, was slung into gaol. This was nothing less than a blatant attempt to turn international opinion against the British, whip up the people of the Transvaal in readiness for war, and to justify an attack on Natal. That it is not even mentioned by either Nasson or Pakenham or any other modern accounts of the war is mind-boggling and one is left wondering if this critical event is deliberately overlooked so as to maintain the fiction that Kruger's regime was the innocent party.

It was in the wake of this clumsy attempt at warmongering that Milner and Kruger met to discuss the uitlander situation in Bloemfontein in June 1899. A clash with the undiplomatic and outspoken Reitz in the run-up to the conference poisoned the mood still further and led to Milner talking of a "one in ten chance of war". In what can only have been a calculated attempt to taunt Milner, on the very eve of the conference the Transvaal brazenly tampered with the franchise enjoyed by a few lucky uitlanders.[34] In this atmosphere Milner's line during the conference was one of making his demands clear, and resolutely sticking to this position. He was certain that the previous vacillation of the British was responsible for many of the problems in South Africa, and that this dithering had only served to fuel Kruger's territorial ambition and contempt for the Empire. Even Steyn—who hosted the conference—admitted that Milner's strong, decisive line was the only way to deal with Kruger;[35] he had previously pleaded with Kruger to make concessions, pointing out that "Franchise after a residence of fourteen years is in conflict with first principles of a republican and democratic government".[36] Kruger assured Steyn that he was prepared to concede on some matters, but would not give up his independence. Milner himself reckoned that "the odds were 20 to 1 in favour" of Kruger climbing down, as long as the British showed "absolute downright determination".[37]

Faced with a determined British representative for the first time, the Young Afrikaners realized that the rules had changed. Steyn and Smuts both pleaded with Kruger to agree to the straightforward demands made by Milner: a retrospective five-year franchise, which would only have brought the Transvaal into line with the rest of southern Africa, and reasonable representation for the mining areas.[38] This would have meant that any white man who had settled in the Transvaal before 1894, and had enough property to qualify, would have a vote. A distraught Kruger reckoned these numbers at over 60,000,[39] inadvertently admitting just how many uitlanders his regime discriminated against. Milner even proposed that any uitlanders desirous of the vote should take "an oath to obey the laws, undertake all obligations of citizenship, and defend the independence of the country".[40] Hardly the words of a man determined to annex the place. Despite enjoying the support of Steyn and Smuts, it is this eminently reasonable demand which has caused pro-Boer writers to paint Milner as a warmongering psychopath. Though some of the leading Young Afrikaners pleaded with Kruger to accept the proposal, other Boers, perhaps blunter and less Machiavellian, were having none of it. Schalk Burger and Andries Wolmarans led such a backlash: a large petition landed on Kruger's desk, demanding he make no concessions whatsoever. Indeed, resistance to any and all meaningful reform was not merely confined to a few extremist nutters: the Transvaal volksraad quickly passed a resolution which would have created new seats the following year and which was "clearly intended to swamp those that might by then have been granted to the gold-fields".[41] In his memoirs Kruger would later whine that "in spite of all the concessions, all the patience and indulgence of the Republic, the war broke out",[42] yet the reality was completely at odds with his ludicrous claim. The truth is that the president of the Transvaal quite simply had no intention of loosening his vice-like grip on the reins of power. Sure enough, Kruger rejected Milner's reasonable proposal, instead offering a highly conditional seven-year franchise qualification and seeking to make even this contingent on British agreement of a whole raft of other thorny issues, including Swaziland. Most importantly, thanks to the peculiar semi-retrospective element of Kruger's offer, no uitlander could expect the right to vote for another two years, and the vast majority would have to wait another five years.[43]

Predictability, Kruger's arch-cheerleader, Pakenham, once again chooses to ignore the facts and fallaciously claims the only difference was "five years for the franchise against seven", thereby heaping all the blame for the disagreement onto Milner.[44] While accepting that even this was an improvement on the current fourteen-year franchise rule, Milner stuck resolutely to his line— exactly as Kruger knew he would—and thus the conference ended in deadlock. Quite why Pakenham thinks Milner should have given in to Kruger's unreasonable offer is not explained. Chamberlain had wanted Milner to continue until Kruger talked himself out[45] but the discussions had broken up before his message arrived. Milner later told James Rose-Innes that he would have come to an agreement had he been able to trust Kruger.[46] Even senior men within Kruger's own regime saw the president's proposals for what they were. Wessels, the leader of the Pretoria bar, "denounced them as ridiculous, and it was calculated that if similar provisions were in force in Cape Colony, not one man in fifty now on the register would ever get there".[47]

Always one for melodramatics, Kruger—his eyes glistening with crocodile tears and acting for all the world like a spoiled brat who hadn't got his way— ended the conference by blurting out, "It is our country you want!"[48] 'Our country', the reader will remember, was the one from which, only a couple of generations earlier, the voortrekkers had driven the ruling Ndebele, and which their descendants had continued to expand by violence ever since. 'Our country' was one in which Kruger's clique not only denied the vote to all non-whites (who formed the vast majority of the population) but also to the overwhelming majority of non-Afrikaans white residents, despite this latter group being almost entirely responsible for turning what had recently been little more than a few scattered, fratricidal Boer communities into something approaching a modern state.

Even as Kruger pretended to negotiate in Bloemfontein, the Transvaal was in reality preparing for war. Though he would have preferred to delay another two or three years until his massive military expansion was finished and the preparations for an uprising in the Cape were ready,[49] Kruger knew that Milner had forced his hand. Bill Nasson talks about Kruger's fear that control of the Transvaal would pass into British hands and claims that the president was taking "a desperate gamble by a cornered opponent, and one which simply had to be taken".[50] Though it made a convenient rallying cry to whip up the hoi polloi, the independence of the Transvaal was never in doubt; however, Kruger's gang would quickly lose power if he conceded to the franchise conditions demanded by the uitlanders.

For many months before the fighting started, the Transvaal volksraad had been meeting in secret sessions, debating and passing new enactments, provisions and laws, all of which would suddenly come into force upon the declaration of war.[51] As one resident of the Transvaal town of Belfast wrote in 1900, these months of endless secret sessions and careful preparation for martial law clearly prove "at least a studious purpose months beforehand to be in complete readiness, for it obviously took no little time to prepare all those laws, and have them ready in type for despatch and publication as has been done. It accords with the assumption that war had been predetermined, and this is further confirmed by numerous statements, publicly made by Volksraad members".

Long before the first shots were fired, the ZAR's large, well-financed secret service was hard at work down in the Cape,[52] agitating malcontents in the belief that they would rise up against British rule in the event of war. It is instructive to note that some sources claim the Transvaal Secret Service had an annual budget of as much as £300,000.[53] In stark contrast, and to put this into perspective, Britain—with her vast global empire and the long-simmering 'Great Game' against Russia—spent just £20,000 a year on such things.[54] The Transvaal Secret Service also sponsored various dissident Irish republicans in southern Africa. Months before the war, British army intelligence reported that these troublemaking traitors had been sent over the borders to test the loyalty of the Irish regiments of the imperial garrison, and to foment mutiny. These endeavours were entirely unsuccessful.[55] A Cape hotelier wrote to his friend Sir Bartle Frere,* urgently warning him that Mausers had been smuggled into the Cape Colony and distributed as far south as Paarl.[56] Pro-Kruger newspapers all over the subcontinent talked of "Boer opinion" as though it were a national movement, while the *Dagblad*, a free Dutch-language newspaper with loyalist sympathies, was boycotted and even condemned by the Afrikaans clergy in the Cape.[57]

Agents of the Orange Free State were also busy in Basutoland, and reports were spread through native workers that "the Boers would soon be the undisputed masters of southern Africa".[58] So much for the bizarre, though currently trendy, idea that the federal attacks which started the war were in some way defensive. These Free State agents also approached one dissident Basuto chief, Joel Molapo, and agreed a deal whereby a 500-strong commando would be sent to aid him against his half-brother, the pre-eminent pro-British chief, Jonathan.[59] These two had been in conflict for almost twenty years, and so the Boer agents implemented their time-honoured tactic of supporting one faction against the other. It was well known to Jonathan that Joel was in close contact with several farmers over the border in the Orange Free State; he became very alarmed when it emerged that federal agents had supplied Joel's rebels with Mausers. It was this latest bout of Boer intrigue and gun-running which drove Jonathan to declare his unconditional support for the British government.[60]

In the wake of the failed Bloemfontein conference, leading Cape Bondsmen were summoned to Pretoria for secret talks. The subject was their enthusiasm for an uprising against the British. Like the Johannesburg reformers before them, however, any would-be revolutionaries in the Cape were getting cold feet as war looked more and more like a reality. The Cape Dutch enjoyed prosperity, democracy, freedom and the rule of law under the Union Jack and so the thought of taking up arms to help Kruger conquer an empire stretching from the Zambezi to the Cape was beginning to lose any glamour it might once have held. No doubt much to Kruger's fury, these senior Cape Bondsmen warned him to expect no armed help from them.[61]

While these secret talks were being held and armaments continued to flood into the Boer republics—"Steyn returned from his leavetaking with the

---

* Major Sir Bartle Compton Arthur Frere, 2nd Baronet (1854–1933), son of the more famous Sir Henry Bartle Edward Frere, 1st Baronet (1815–84) of Zulu War fame.

High Commissioner to order Mausers and cartridges from Germany"[62]—the British government and Her Majesty's forces remained blissfully unprepared for, and oblivious to, the impending conflict. When a million rounds of Mauser ammunition destined for the Orange Free State arrived at Port Elizabeth on the 8th July[63]—having obviously been ordered several months before—the Cape Colony authorities made no effort to stop the consignment. William Schreiner, the Cape premier, later defended this by claiming he simply had no reason to anticipate war with the Free State.

The officer commanding Her Majesty's troops in South Africa, Lieutenant-General Sir William Butler, had also "been informed that there was no special reason to fear immediate war and was ordered to curtail long-authorized military expenditure".[64] Though the Rhodesian authorities asked the imperial government for arms, the War Office continued to cut down establishments.[65]

Underfunded and scattered across the world in penny packets, the British army was in no state to fight a major war in late 1899. The Royal Artillery's three howitzer batteries had just one spare gun, one carriage and two ammunition wagons between them. Ammunition supplies for artillery were just 200 rounds per gun, meaning the army would be forced to beg and borrow ammunition from the Indian army and Royal Navy barely a fortnight into the conflict. As there were not enough machine guns to equip a field force, these would have to be taken from fortresses in the Motherland.[66] There were similarly alarming shortages in saddlery and harnesses, wagons, tents, hospital marquees and infantry accoutrements. There was no reserve stock of khaki uniforms, and British industry, even working night shifts and Sundays, would later prove unable to keep up with the supply of small-arms ammunition.[67]

There was also a chronic shortage of engineering equipment—the army held just eighty yards' worth of pontoon bridges, and yet the Orange River, for example, was 300 yards wide.[68] And far from being evidence of blasé arrogance, these shortcomings horrified the high command. Lord Roberts summed up this shocking lack of readiness: "I was astonished beyond measure to hear of our utter unpreparedness, and it makes me tremble to think of what might happen if France or Russia had any idea of the wretched state we are in regards stores, munitions of war etc. How could this have been permitted? And who is responsible for it?"[69]

Not all on the British side were so blind to the threat of the ZAR. By July loyalist farmers in northern Natal had become increasingly concerned with developments over the frontier.[70] The veldt had been burned unusually early to encourage a speedy grass crop after the first rains, and those farmers of the Orange Free State, who normally grazed their livestock in Natal during the winter, had driven them to safety behind the Drakensberg Mountains.[71] By September the colonial authorities in Natal were reporting Transvaal Secret Service agents to be spreading sedition among the "loyal natives" and endeavouring to "set tribe against tribe in order to create confusion and detail the defensive forces of the colony".[72] Elsewhere, a group of leading Johannesburg uitlanders raised funds sufficient to mount and equip a regiment of a thousand light horsemen, the plan being to fill the ranks of this new unit with those uitlanders who had been forced to leave Johannesburg. The backers of this potential regiment headed to Cape Town and met with Milner* and General Butler, offering them the services of a thousand men. Butler wouldn't hear of it though, dismissing the delegation with the remarkable and noteworthy statement: "England is not preparing for war, even if the Transvaal is preparing."[73]

Fortunately, these uitlanders were not men to take no for an answer, and instead left Cape Town for Natal, keen to present their offer to the governor of that colony, Sir Walter Hely-Hutchinson. With the requisite backing of Hely-Hutchinson, the military authorities in Natal agreed to accept the unit, but with a reduced complement of only 500 men.[74] They further stipulated that the commanding officer should be a regular soldier.

The new regiment was named the Imperial Light Horse,† a name personally approved by Queen Victoria and on the 21st September, recruiting finally commenced at the Pietermaritzburg showground, with over 5,000 men applying to join.

Even then, with war less than three weeks away, the new regiment faced practical difficulties: "there were no modern rifles, bayonets, or other equipments in the whole of South Africa to arm the newly formed Imperial Light Horse. When this regiment took the field in October 1899, it was armed

---

* Pakenham's claim that the unit was formed at Milner's suggestion is simply untrue

† The Imperial Light Horse served with distinction throughout the Boer War, with a second battalion being formed in 1900. Known to their enemies as 'the Uitlander Regiment', there was no love lost between the Boers and Imperial Light Horsemen. The ILH served in both World Wars and, though the 'Imperial' was dropped in the apartheid era, the unit still exists today as the Light Horse Regiment of the South African army.

with out-of-date Martini-Metford* rifles without bayonets, and saddlery was purchased as and where obtainable."[75]

After the war, a royal commission was set up to examine the lessons that could be learned from the conflict. One of their most remarkable findings—and one which gives a lie to the oft-peddled nonsense that that British had been desperate to force war on the Boers—was that while there were various intelligence briefings and the like, "no plan of campaign ever existed for operations in South Africa".[76]

In the wake of the Bloemfontein conference, meetings were held all over the Transvaal to discuss Kruger's offer of the seven-year franchise. A witness at one reported that the *landrost* (chief official) of the ward took the chair, and four members of the volksraad attended. These members took turns to convince the audience to approve the seven-year franchise, gradually swaying them in that direction. One burgher spoke against the proposal, however. In an impassioned speech, he declared that "it is the Boer nation which is entitled to supremacy, not only in the Transvaal but right to the sea. The Cape Colonies are ours by divine right, and so is Natal, and no Afrikaner may rest until we are reinstated". This outburst met with "general approbation and stamping of feet" and not one of the volksraad said a word against it. On the contrary, when the volksraad members rose to speak again, it was to reassure the audience that they could "safely approve of it [the seven-year franchise], it can result in no harm, it will only strengthen our course ... this law will contribute to thwart her [Britain], though will not avert war";[77] the rabble-rousing continued: "we have become strong and united since, it will be soon seen that our people have to be reckoned with among the other nations of the earth; we have right on our side and, with God's help, we are certain to prevail. Burghers, you may trust us as your representatives; we are all of one mind with you."[78]

If the Boer hoi polloi were worried that Kruger's condition-laden, seven-year franchise offer was a concession too far, the Johannesburg uitlanders dismissed it as laughably insufficient. Mass meetings were held in the wake of the failed conference, with the *Sydney Morning Herald* reporting on one such event: "A meeting of 7,000 Uitlanders was held at Johannesburg last night (July 27th) at which resolutions were passed condemning the franchise

---

* The Martini-Metford was a half-arsed attempt to add the .303 rifled Metford barrel to the old Martini-Henry rifle. Retaining the Martini falling-block action, it was a single-shot weapon and thus utterly outclassed by the modern magazine rifles of the Boers.

concessions as inadequate, and demanding workable reforms imperially guaranteed."[79]

These illegal mass rallies give the lie to the oft-repeated idea that "no one cared a fig for the franchise" and also the notion that Milner alone was the driving force behind rejecting Kruger's concessions. All the uitlanders wanted was a five-year franchise rule similar to those in place in the rest of South Africa, and for this to be retrospective and not tied to so many conditions as to be worthless. Would an observer in the 1980s have congratulated the apartheid government for offering some grudging, conditional semi-reform? The same sort of people who were rightly insistent on full (and instant) democracy in that case seem to think the uitlanders and Milner should have been delighted with the very limited and highly conditional reforms Kruger offered.* If the apartheid-era South Africa had then lashed out militarily at its neighbours due to sanctions or political pressure,† would this also have been excused by the British Left?

In early July Hofmeyr of the Cape Bondsmen and representatives from the Orange Free State were invited to yet more secret talks with Kruger.[80] In an attempt to pull the rug from under Milner's feet and split his opponents, Kruger emerged to announce that, despite no agreement having been reached at Bloemfontein, he would introduce the new seven-year franchise law anyway. When Hofmeyr declared that this would be free of all the conditions which had caused Milner to reject it at the conference, Schreiner felt "at liberty to say that the Cape Government regards the Reform proposals of the Transvaal Government as adequate and satisfactory, and as such should secure a peaceful settlement".[81] Salisbury recorded that he felt war had been averted and "a satisfactory solution" had been found. Chamberlain agreed, "I am really sanguine that the crisis is over" and declared Kruger's latest climb-down "a triumph of moral pressure—accompanied by special service officers and three batteries of artillery". Queen Victoria had perhaps not been told how 'sanguine' the colonial secretary felt, as, on the 18th July, she wrote in her diary: "The country, as well as the cabinet, excepting perhaps Mr Chamberlain, were against a war."[82]

---

* Interestingly, the same reason given for denying the uitlanders the vote was one of the excuses the apartheid-era government used to deny the majority the vote, i.e. that their Afrikaans culture would be swamped. British liberals approved of this stance in 1899, but—with their trademark hypocrisy—vehemently opposed it post-1948.

† which it arguably did

All seemed good. Surely no one would think of going to war if the only difference between the proposals genuinely was just two years? But there remained the troubling and ominous fact that the Transvaal refused to make clear the precise nature of the revised offer. Was it *really* the same as Milner's proposal but with seven years substituted for five? Chamberlain's request for details was brushed aside by Reitz who airily declared that "the whole matter is out of the hands of the Government, and it is therefore no longer possible for this Government to further satisfy the request of the Secretary of State".[83] A further request was similarly rebuffed. What was Kruger's clique trying to hide?

The mysterious new law was passed on the 23rd July, but an explanatory memorandum only reached the British Colonial Office on the 11th August. Kruger seemed in no hurry to resolve the crisis and his constant delaying tactics should have rung alarm bells in London. That the new law required an explanatory memorandum in the first place amazed Sir Henry de Villiers, chief justice of the Cape Colony. Sir Henry wrote to a highly placed friend in the Orange Free State: "Surely a law should be clear enough to speak for itself, and no Government or court of law will be bound by the State Attorney's explanations. I do not know what these explanations are, but the very fact that they are required condemns the Bill … If you can see your way to bring about a settlement to all concerned, you will be a benefactor to South Africa. I don't think that President Kruger and his friends realize the gravity of the situation. Even now the State Secretary is doing things which would be almost farcical if the times were not so serious … the time really has come when the friends of the Transvaal must induce President Kruger to become perfectly frank and take the newcomers into his confidence. It may be a bitter pill to swallow, in yielding to further demands, but it is quite clear to the world that he would not have done as much as he has done if pressure had not been applied."[84]

The fact that the British government seemed to be ready to listen to the new seven-year franchise proposal at all deeply worried the uitlanders. They saw this as contrary to the line Milner had drawn in the sand at Bloemfontein and, readying themselves for yet more vacillation and back-tracking by the Colonial Office, a despairing telegram was sent to Chamberlain.[85] On the other hand, pro-Boers were delighted at what seemed like a victory, while moderates hoped against hope that Kruger's latest proposal was sincere.

To try and unravel the enigma which was the new law, the Colonial Office proposed to Kruger that an impartial international commission investigate it. Even the German government encouraged Kruger to agree to this eminently reasonable suggestion, as did the outrageously pro-Boer and utterly loathsome Henry Labouchère:*[86] "Don't, for goodness sake," Labouchère counselled a leading republican, "let Mr Kruger make his first mistake by refusing this; a little skilful management, and he will give Master Joe another fall ... you are such past-masters in the art of gaining time, here is an opportunity ... you ought to spin out the negotiations for quite two or three months."[87]

Reitz was approached to persuade Kruger to agree to the commission, but, according to Sir Henry de Villiers, "seemed to view the whole thing as a joke. He is a danger in the present situation".[88] But in any case Kruger was not interested in anyone unpicking the details and hidden ramifications of his latest proposal. He explained this untenable position to the Dutch consul-general: "By accepting it a very direct encroachment of the English in internal affairs would result." More tellingly, he went on to make clear he had no fear about any war his intransigence would provoke: "Defeats such as the English had suffered in the war for freedom, and later under Jameson, had never been suffered by the Boers."[89] Kruger's reluctance to make the full text of the new law public—and his objection to an impartial inquiry into it—can only have been because it was a sham. As the details of the new law slowly began to dribble out, it became obvious to all that it was yet another smoke-screen. Far from being a simple seven-year version of Milner's proposal, according to the leader in *The Times*, the new law was "of such a character as to make the period of qualification utterly unimportant. It might almost as well be seventy years as seven".[90] It was by no means a general enfranchisement of those uitlanders who had resided in the Transvaal for seven years, but instead applied only to those who had enjoyed "the personal acquaintance of the Field Cornets and Landdrosts of the wards and districts in which they lived". Furthermore, these officials were called upon to certify entirely from personal knowledge the domicile, continuous registration and obedience to the laws of the uitlander in question. Another demand made of the prospective voter was the vague and unqualified criteria that insisted he should never have been "guilty of any crime against the independence of the country". An alternative was that the uitlander of seven

---

*   Henry Du Pré Labouchère (1831–1912) was a self-loathing, pro-Boer, British Radical politician, magazine editor, theatre-owner and hater of the British Empire in general and Rhodes in particular. His legacy to British life was to pass a law outlawing male homosexuality.

years' residence could be recommended for the franchise by two "notable" burghers, officially defined as needing to be "more than respectable" in their ward and who had personally known him for the entirety of his residence.[91] The reality—as everyone knew—was that the vast majority of uitlanders were separated from the Transvaal burghers by both geography and language. Precious few Johannesburg mine-workers or merchants could possibly meet these demands, however long they had lived in the Transvaal—as well Kruger knew. But this was not all. If any uitlander achieved the impossible and actually managed to meet these criteria, he still had to produce "proof of good behaviour such as will satisfy the State Attorney". In essence, what the proposal did was permit Kruger's clique to grant the franchise to the small number of uitlanders who were known to be hostile to Britain, and effectively deny the rest—the large majority—the franchise for as long as they wanted. It is thus quite obvious why Kruger was so determined that his new law would not be scrutinized by an independent commission.

Meanwhile, the fall-out of Kruger's farcical 'Bogus Conspiracy' plot continued. The unfortunate Mr Nicholls, already in gaol for two months, now faced some serious irregularities during his trial. Luckily for Nicholls, the British agent had appointed a very capable lawyer and, despite the best efforts of the Transvaal Secret Service, the case was eventually thrown out on the 25th July. One witness later signed an affidavit stating that he had been offered £200 by Tjaart Kruger to lie in court and claim the plot had been a conspiracy hatched by the British government and the uitlanders.[92] This amateurish plot, widely reported,[93] would have brought down most governments, but Kruger's was not a normal regime. The secret service agents and various other Transvaal officials were not reprimanded in any way and no apology was made to the British government or to Mr Nicholls. Some in South Africa were left in no doubt that the plot was evidence of Kruger's determination to force a war on the British.[94] If, on the other hand, the British were desperate to provoke war with the ZAR, nothing would have been easier than to have sent an ultimatum demanding a public apology, an indemnity for Mr Nicholls and the immediate dismissal of all those involved in the Transvaal Secret Service and the police.[95]

Despite this, and much to the continued chagrin of the uitlanders, the British government still appeared prepared to accept a genuine seven-year franchise deal. However, they had plenty of reason to doubt the validity of Kruger's offer, especially when he refused to accept the independent commission. But Kruger had one more trick up his sleeve: in early August he suddenly suggested that he would agree to a five-year franchise if the British agreed to drop any inquiry into the law.[96] The *Cape Times* summed this up in quaint terms: "A countryman who had some claim against a neighbour was once offered a florin for full discharge. He suspected the florin. 'Let us drop any enquiry into that,' said the donor, 'and I will make it half a crown instead.'"[97]

Pakenham and others try to convince us that, as the new offer involved the phrase 'five-year franchise', it was surely exactly "the same franchise … that Milner had demanded at Bloemfontein".[98] Pakenham must have known that his statement was simply untrue: it was in fact the same mysterious seven-year franchise discussed earlier, but with the qualification period dropped to five years; and so complex and convoluted were the other criteria that the qualification term "might almost as well be seventy years as seven".

Nevertheless, news of this latest proposal was initially gratefully received in London, especially because the British government had begun to realize just how hopelessly unprepared they were for any sort of conflict. Wishy-washy General Butler had been replaced, but few of the reinforcements Milner had been asking for had materialized. The newly appointed officer commanding in Natal, Major-General Penn Symons,* had requested an extra 5,000 men, but so far had been fobbed off with a re-deployment of just 500 men from the garrison in the Cape Colony. To be fair, the imperial government was in a difficult position. Sending even relatively small numbers of reinforcements to South Africa risked bringing matters to a head with Kruger; on the other hand, if they waited until the ZAR declared war the delay might well prove fatal. It was reckoned that the Transvaal outnumbered the British regulars of the normal garrison by four to one; if the Orange Free State threw its lot in with the Transvaal, the ratio became seven to one.[99] If these numbers looked bad enough, there were also the Cape Afrikaners to consider. Thanks to the tireless work of the Transvaal Secret Service and the enigmatic influence of the Afrikaner Bond, many feared that the Cape Afrikaners would at the very least declare their neutrality. Others thought it more likely that a large number

---

* Major-General Sir William Penn Symons KCB (1843–99). Named after William Penn, Quaker big-wig and founder of Pennsylvania, Symons was—somewhat unusually for a soldier—himself from a Quaker family too. Though strictly speaking not his surname, he preferred to be known as 'Penn Symons'. He was mortally wounded at the battle of Talana Hill very early in the war.

would actually join the fight in support of their kinsmen and so the already over-stretched imperial garrison would have to be ready for this threat too.

Worse still, in London, the War Office had finally admitted that mobilizing an army corps (roughly 35,000 men) for South Africa would take four months—or three months, provided a million pounds' worth of mules, carts, clothing and so on were ordered immediately. Needless to say, the prime minister was not about to approve this additional expenditure[100] and—with a solution to the crisis seemingly in sight—was more interested in spending the glorious summer at his country residence. At the risk of sounding like a broken record, these are hardly the actions of a regime thirsty for a war of conquest.

The problem was that this latest offer was just yet another delaying tactic from Kruger, and Milner was one of the few to see this. Pakenham paints Milner's realization of this reality as 'evidence' that he had always wanted to start a war, but none of the quotes Pakenham uses actually support this. Instead, what comes across is Milner's frustration at the Colonial Office's readiness to accept any old concession from Kruger, rather than being willing to see the crisis through to the end and actually achieve meaningful reform for the uitlanders.

Had Milner not shown resolution and determination not to "assume, even to pretend, that we had secured all we wanted"[101] then perhaps the crisis might have subsided for a time, but the underlying problem would have remained, only to bubble up once again, perhaps when British forces were embroiled elsewhere. And the underlying problem—the lack of the franchise for the tens of thousands of tax-paying uitlanders—was not Milner's fault: it was entirely Kruger's.

In an attempt to get to the bottom of the new five-year offer, Conyngham Greene,* the British agent in Pretoria, held exhaustive meetings with the Kruger cabal, finally emerging with what seemed like a new and more reasonable, proposal which he telegrammed to Milner on the 15th August.[102] Indeed, so reasonable did he understand the revised proposal to be, that Conyngham Greene considered it "a bona fide attempt to settle the political rights of our people once and for all, the Government of the South African Republic need not fear that we shall in future either wish or have cause to

---

* Sir William Conyngham Greene KCB, GCMG, PC (1854–1934) was a long-serving diplomat and later British ambassador to Japan.

interfere in their internal affairs. I have said, as regards suzerainty, that I feel sure Her Majesty's Government will not and cannot abandon the right which the preamble to the Convention of 1881 gives them, but that they will have no desire to hurt Boer sensibilities by publicly reasserting it, so long as no reason to do so is given to them by the Government of the South African Republic".[103]

Far from indulging in warmongering, Milner instructed Conyngham Greene: "If the South African Republic Government should reply to the invitation to a joint inquiry put forward by Her Majesty's Government by formally making the proposals described in your telegram, such a course would not be regarded by Her Majesty's Government as a refusal of their offer, but they would be prepared to consider the reply of the South African Government on its merits."[104]

But just as it seemed the Transvaal had finally made a genuine concession to the uitlanders, things began to unravel. On the 19th August, Reitz sent through the formal proposal, but this was substantially different from what had been agreed in the meeting with Conyngham Greene. Reitz had added various conditions and additions, the thrust of which was that Great Britain had to give up any suzerainty over the Transvaal and agree to never again interfere in its internal affairs. Reitz also dropped the clause which agreed "as regards language, the new members of the Volksraad to use their own" and, most importantly of all, ditched the statement that the new franchise law would be "simplified immensely" compared to the previous enigmatic seven-year one.[105]

If this was not bad enough, only two days after these eleventh-hour changes had been sent to the British, another telegram arrived from Reitz. This contained so many more changes, demands and pre-conditions that the whole tone of the agreement was altered: the changes were certainly not calculated to increase the chances of an immediate or friendly settlement. An exasperated Conyngham Greene declared his efforts at diplomacy to have been "reduced to a regular kaffir bargain".[106] Michael Farrelly, who knew the methods and slippery tricks of the Young Afrikaners better than anyone, had warned the British negotiators they would be better served to conduct the discussions in writing, rather than in face-to-face talks: "Sir Conyngham Greene's diplomatic experience in civilized lands, such as Holland and Greece—and Persia—had misled him as to what he was reasonably justified in expecting. A veneer of European civilization is at times disconcerting."[107] Sure enough, Conyngham Greene quickly spotted numerous discrepancies between what he had agreed to and what appeared on the formal proposal, and pointed this out. Jan Smuts himself replied to tell him there was not "the slightest chance of an alteration or amplification of those terms".[108] It was not only the career diplomat, Conyngham Greene, who greeted all this with disbelief and annoyance. Sir Henry de Villiers, chief justice in the Cape, declared that "something happened between the 19th and 21st which led the Transvaal Government to think they had yielded too much. I have heard it said that between these dates a cablegram from Dr Leyds gave hopes of European intervention, and the return of Wolmarans from the Orange Free State gave hopes of assistance from that quarter".[109]

William Schreiner, premier of the Cape Colony and by no means a friend of Milner's, also believed that information from Europe had suddenly convinced the Transvaal to change their proposal and instead to play for time. "He firmly believed that the unfortunate Republics had been led to suppose that the Great Powers in Europe were about to interfere on their behalf, and they must have been misled by the assumptions and assurances conveyed to them by their emissaries."[110] Indeed, Schreiner considered the Transvaal's confidence in receiving help from a European Great Power to be "the chief influence in causing the war".*

Interestingly, Pakenham fails to mention any of this in his 'magisterial' book on the war. Instead, he pays scant heed to all these changes and problems, stating only that the scheming Milner convinced Chamberlain that the proposal was "full of traps and pitfalls"[111] without seeming to think for a moment that Milner said this precisely *because it was*. He thus peddles

---

* Though the German foreign office had officially ruled out intervention in a message sent on the 15th August, Germany's history of trouble-making and egging on the Transvaal still made it the most likely to have been the mystery European Great Power. Germany had recently established a colony in what is now Namibia, and newspapers and periodicals of the time talked of flooding South Africa with German immigrants. During the Jameson Raid, the Kaiser had told his ministers that "The moment has come when Germany can obtain the Protectorate over the Transvaal, and later on, over the Orange Free State," and had advocated seizing Delagoa Bay. The German army also supplied battle plans to the Boer high command via Dr Leyds. However, and though she was rapidly building a fleet to challenge the Royal Navy, Germany was not quite ready for war with the British Empire—this was admitted by Prince von Buelow in 1897. So exactly from which Great Power the Transvaal expected help remains a mystery. Other than Germany, Russia is perhaps the most likely candidate, given the long-running tensions on the border of British India. On the very eve of hostilities, General Joubert informed his men that there would be no war, as the European Powers were bringing pressure to bear, and that the United States government had promised to intervene. So who knows. For more on this fascinating subject, read *The Secret History of the Transvaal*.

his inexplicable falsehood that this five-year franchise offer was 'the same' as Milner had demanded at Bloemfontein.

It was becoming clear to even the most sympathetic observer that this diplomatic ping-pong was just a waste of everyone's time and that Kruger had no intention of ever offering any meaningful concessions. Sir Henry de Villiers, who was no enemy of the Transvaal and was, indeed, disliked by the Jingoes for being overly enamoured of Kruger's regime,[112] perhaps put it best: "Throughout the negotiations, they [the Transvaal government] have always been wriggling to prevent a clear and precise decision,"[113] and, "The very best friends of the Transvaal feel that the Bill providing for the seven years franchise is not a fair or workable measure. It is this manoeuvring to escape an unpleasant decision which has more than anything else driven the British Government into its present attitude."[114] That attitude was demonstrated by a speech Chamberlain made in Birmingham on the 28th August: "We have been, as you know, for the last three months negotiating with President Kruger. We have made perhaps some progress; but I cannot truly say that the crisis is passed. Mr Kruger procrastinates in his replies. He dribbles out reforms like water from a squeezed sponge, and he either accompanies his offers with conditions which he knows to be impossible, or he refuses to allow us to make a satisfactory investigation of the nature and character of these reforms."[115]

The British dispatch sent on the same day summed up the situation, and proposed a way forward which involved an inquiry into the new (and oft-changed) five-year franchise and an independent court of arbitration to rule on the differing interpretations of the suzerainty question. Again, it was hardly a warlike or sabre-rattling communique—especially given the un-ending stream of nonsense coming out of Pretoria.

The Transvaal's response was a long-winded message dispatched on the 2nd September, in which the British proposals were reject-ed, and their own offer of the five-year franchise was withdrawn.[116] The British response to this, sent on the 8th September, was about as con-ciliatory as was possible. There was no mention of suzerainty; that trouble-some word was tactfully dropped. The British repeated their readiness for an independent arbitrator and expressed their willingness to accept at least part of the latest proposal from the Transvaal, "provided that the inquiry which Her Majesty's Government have proposed, whether joint—as Her Majesty's

Government originally suggested—or unilateral, shows that the new scheme of representation will not be encumbered by conditions which will nullify the intention to substantial and immediate representation to the Uitlanders".[117]

The British proposal of the 8th September was widely seen as a fair and moderate response, even by the most fanatical of pro-Boers. Speaking in Manchester, one the oldest and most stalwart supporters of the Transvaal's cause in Britain hailed it with satisfaction, declaring it to be "a rebuke to the fire-eaters, and a rebuke, most of all, to … Sir Alfred Milner. [He was] glad of the last despatch of Mr Chamberlain, and wished Paul Kruger could control his Boers sufficiently to induce them to accept the proposals of that document".[118] His audience of ghastly Little-Englanders stopped wringing their hands long enough to applaud loudly. If even these self-loathing lefties thought the British offer was fair, it is hard to see what the problem was. As one canny observer remarked, "It is difficult also to see why the Transvaal Government should not be satisfied, except on the hypothesis that something more was wanted than appeared on the surface."[119]

Indeed, it was becoming obvious to many that there was something brewing behind the scenes and few of those in the know had any confidence that the latest British proposal would be accepted. Sir Henry de Villiers, who worked tirelessly for a peaceful solution throughout the crisis, gloomily wrote: "The manner in which the latest proposals were rejected does not give me much ground for hope. Take such a reasonable proposal as that members should be allowed to address the Volksraad in the English language. Surely it ought not to have been rejected in such a summary, I might almost say, contemptuous, manner."[120]

Sir Henry was right to be worried, for when the response from Kruger (via Reitz) finally came, it was to reject the British proposal—the "rebuke to the fire-eaters" so heartily approved by British pro-Boers—absolutely. Once more, it was a verbose, waffle-ridden communiqué, but the long and the short of it was that the all the key proposals were dismissed out of hand. The Transvaal would not agree to a retrospective five-year franchise, a reasonable number of seats for the goldfields or, indeed, any new volksraad members being permitted to speak in their own language. Instead, the Transvaal's latest horse-trading move was to renege on their offer of a five-year franchise and return to their earlier offer of a seven-year term.

Kruger's supporters among the British Left had been sure that the five-

year offer would not be withdrawn, assuming—naturally enough—that
what had been offered one day could not be withdrawn the next. But these
naïve Little-Englanders had wrongly presumed both the peaceful intentions
of the Transvaal government and its sincerity during the negotiations.
An increasingly distraught and exasperated Sir Henry de Villiers saw this
latest delaying tactic for exactly what it was, writing to a friend that "I confess
I look with horror on a war to be fought by Afrikanders to bolster up President
Kruger's regime. I could understand a war in defence of the South African
Republic after it has made reasonable concessions to the demands of the newcomers, and after it has displayed the same desire to secure good government
as is seen in the Orange Free State; but of such a desire I have not seen the
faintest trace".[121]

An equally infuriated Michael Farrelly agreed with Sir Henry, describing
the Transvaal's tactics throughout the negotiations: "Understanding, so well
as I do, the series of evasions and devices the kaleidoscope succession of
supposed offers of franchise really were, I could not find patience to attempt
to summarize them, but that it is alleged even by some people in England that
the faulty diplomacy of the Imperial Government caused the war. There was
no faulty diplomacy on the British side after the Conference at Bloemfontein
… if anything, it was too patient. As I have shown, war was forced on the
Afrikander leaders by the veldt Boer. But it was they who sent the veldt Boer
to the border; and there would have been no war if they had agreed to treat
the Uitlander as a political equal."[122]

Other moderate observers outside the Transvaal also struggled to
understand what Kruger's problem was and racked their brains to work out
what was "the rock on which the British proposals of September 8 had broken
up". The leader in the *Daily News* asked rhetorically what Kruger's difficulty
in accepting the proposals was: "Is it future interference? Is it suzerainty?
Is it arbitration? These, it will be remembered, were the three points which
formed the subject of the conditions attached to President Kruger's own offer
of August 19. On each and all of these points the British Government has
gone a long way to meet the President's demands. Wherein is it that the British
propositions and assurances are so unsatisfactory to him as to make him prefer
a rupture? … In the absence of any intelligible and coherent reply to these
questions, it will be difficult to resist the conclusion that the real issues lie far
behind; that either President Kruger has not yet sincerely convinced himself

of the necessity of doing prompt and substantial justice to the Uitlanders, or that he is only prepared to do it at the price of extorting from Great Britain concessions inconsistent with her present position in South Africa."[123]

Around the 10th September the Young Afrikanders decided to up the ante. As Michael Farrelly mentions, Boer commandos were ordered to the Natal frontier, the thought being to "frighten the Imperial Government out of its supposed policy of pretence and bluster".[124] But the British—and Lord Milner in particular—were not pretending or blustering. In the eyes of Michael Farrelly, it was the Transvaal's aggressive deployment of these forces that finally made war unavoidable.

A secret memorandum sent by Jan Smuts to the Transvaal Executive on the 4th September suggests that all these negotiations were only ever a time-wasting exercise in any case, and leaves one in no doubt as to the imperial ambitions of the Boers: "South Africa stands on the eve of a frightful blood-bath out of which our Volk shall come … either as … hewers of wood and drawers of water for a hated race, or as victors, founders of a United South Africa, of one of the great empires [*rijken*] of the world … an Afrikaans republic of South Africa stretching from Table Bay to the Zambezi."[125]

Blind to the empire-building ambitions of the Boers, the British cabinet met on the 22nd September and, unsure exactly how to proceed, it was decided an interim dispatch should be sent to Pretoria. This was merely to acknowledge the Transvaal's rejection of the latest proposals and to inform Kruger's gang that London was now deliberating on the way forward. The interim dispatch clearly stated that Great Britain had "not asserted any rights of interference in the internal affairs of the Republic, other than those which are derived from the Conventions between the two countries, or which belong to every neighbouring Government".

The message reasserted the position the British had adopted throughout the "four months of protracted negotiations", *viz.* "to obtain such a substantial and immediate representation for the Uitlanders in the South African Republic as Her Majesty's Government hoped would relieve them from any necessity for further interference on their behalf, and would enable the Uitlanders to secure for themselves that fair and just treatment which was formally promised them in 1881".[126]

Again, this communiqué was regarded as reasonable and fair by most observers except, perhaps, some of the more enthusiastic Jingoes who by then had had more than enough of Kruger's antics and were openly calling for war. But, judging from the tone of Britain's newspapers at the time, these voices were a small minority. Indeed, this latest dispatch was approvingly described as a "golden bridge" in the British press,[127] as it was seen to offer Kruger a chance to return to his five-year franchise offer with dignity and honour.

While supportive of London's latest attempt to continue negotiations, the *Daily News* also reminded its readers that

> It takes two to make an honourable peace. We are afraid that some of those who are loudest in their professions as friends of peace do not always remember this simple fact. Of course, if Great Britain is to pursue peace at any price, then she alone—without any corresponding goodwill on the part of the Transvaal—can secure peace. She has only to withdraw from her position, or to go on negotiating for ever, and the peace thus need never be broken. But if the task to which she has set herself is just and right, what then? Mr Morley [a leading British pro-Boer and outspoken champion of the Transvaal] says that Great Britain must "insist" on the five year franchise. But if President Kruger "insists" on withdrawing his offer, what is then to be the issue? … The weakness of Mr Morley's case is that he is afraid to say what he knows to be true—that we cannot go on forever with diplomacy. We have asked nothing but what is reasonable, and we mean to have it. They are the best friends of the Boers at the present crisis who urge them to yield gracefully and to trust our country. The British Cabinet by its decision of yesterday has left a way open for peace. The next move is with President Kruger. It is to him that peacemakers should now address their articles, their resolutions, their memorials.[128]

Our old friend, Sir Henry de Villiers was endeavouring to do just that. Sir Henry was about as far from being a Jingo as is possible to be. He was a decent and tireless worker for peace, and his natural affinity to his Afrikaner kinsmen lends a certain weight to his views, and the statements he made, throughout the crisis. On the 28th September, Sir Henry wrote to his friend

Abraham Fischer,* a member of the Orange Free State's executive council, imploring him to talk some sense into Kruger: "I do not, of course, know what the contents of the next British despatch will be, but if they be such as can be accepted without actual dishonour, I hope they will be accepted. The South African Republic cannot go to war if your Government should consider the despatch one which ought not to be rejected … Judging from the forecasts given of the intended despatch, it will, at all events, formulate all the British demands. If that be so, there will not be the danger of further demands being sprung on the South African Republic. It will surely be for the interests of South Africa that a full and final settlement should now be arrived at … My fear is that the fresh proposals will be summarily rejected, but that the day will come when everybody who has had a hand in such rejection will bitterly regret his action."[129]

Unfortunately, Sir Henry's wise counsel was destined to fall on deaf ears. While de Villiers was vainly trying to encourage Pretoria to show a modicum of conciliation, the Cape government instead sent their appeals to London. The Cape premier, William Schreiner, urged "consideration and compromise" from the British government (but didn't seem to feel the Transvaal should be asked to display either), prompting the following reply: "Her Majesty's Government have shown, and will continue to show, every consideration to the Government of the South African Republic consistent with the maintenance of British interests; that they profoundly deplore the fact that up to the present, all their efforts to secure a peaceful and satisfactory settlement have been unsuccessful, but this is still open to the Government of the South African Republic to do so without any sacrifice of its independence."[130]

While all this was going on, the Transvaal was readying its war machine, for the timing of war was absolutely critical. As tensions continued to rise, British reinforcements, totalling about 10,000 men, were finally en route to South Africa while, behind the scenes, the general staffs of several European powers were urging the Boers to invade Natal before these units arrived.[131] But the Boers dared not launch their attack before with the start of the spring rains,

---

* Abraham Fischer (1850–1913), long-serving politician in the Orange Free State and later the first (and only) prime minister of the Orange River Colony, from 1907–10

else their ponies would struggle to find enough to eat during the advance. A reluctant and apprehensive Joubert, in command of the Transvaal forces massing on the border with Natal, kept a close eye on the grass as it slowly turned green.[132]

An ultimatum was drafted on the 26th September, but disagreement with the Orange Free State and a lack of transport meant this was not issued immediately. The 'cowardice' and 'stupidity' of the reluctant Orange Free State volksraad was infuriating to the firebrands of the Transvaal, and threatened to derail the "dreams of a Dutch Dominion throughout South Africa".[133] After much persuasion and 'lubrication' from the Transvaal, the Orange Free State volksraad finally voted to go to war—but only by the narrowest of margins.

Nevertheless, the ZAR mobilized on the 27th September,[134] and their military took control of the nation's railways on the 29th. Tens of thousands of uitlanders had fled Johannesburg in the weeks before the war, and thousands more were now expelled—though Kruger made no provision for their transport: "Consequently the scenes which were enacted at the railway stations on the departure of the ordinary passenger trains were of the most harrowing description. Men, women and children were knocked about, and hustled by railway officials, by 'ZARPs', and by members of the gathering commandoes … many of the last batch to leave, which included many women and children, were obliged to travel in open coal trucks, where thirty or forty would be huddled together, and have to remain in this state for perhaps thirty hours without food or water."[135]

One such refugee recalled, "The Boers were commandeering all the Outlanders' property as a war tax; they claimed all the horses on the mines, and behaved most insultingly to any Englishman they could come across. The way the Boers were treating us was simply outrageous. They are worse than Kaffirs."[136] This fellow and thousands of other such unfortunates descended on Natal and the Cape Colony, many forced to exist purely on the kindness of strangers. Though this is never mentioned by Kruger's present-day supporters, thousands of others who were "friendless and homeless, penniless and helpless"[137] were forced to live in tented refugee encampments—long before any Boer civilians ended up in such things. Writing from Port Elizabeth, one newly arrived uitlander wrote to his parents: "There are about 5,000 refugees from the Transvaal down here, and I hear that at Cape Town and Durban people are sleeping in churches, warehouses, and, in fact, anywhere they can get a covering for their heads. People who came down here two or three months ago are at their wits' end, their money being finished, and they are having to rely on charity for a bite to eat. Whole families are starving."[138]

As this exodus began, a member of the Transvaal judiciary expressed his regret to Michael Farrelly that Kruger's "war party" had been too powerful and that Farrelly's pacific counsel had been dismissed out of hand. This fellow went on to claim that "we cannot help it now; we shall win in the beginning and for a long time, and then the British will get so tired of the loss of lives and expense, that we shall get better terms and a new Convention".[139]

By the end of September, perhaps 30,000 white uitlanders had left. Many of these were directly involved in mining, and Johannesburg had essentially shut down, with the mine workings grinding to a virtual halt and most of the shops boarded up.[140] Of course, the many non-white workers suffered badly too and it is reckoned that in September and October some 78,000 fled Johannesburg,[141] including 7,000 blacks led to safety by a young Natal colonist, a J. Sydney Marwick.[142] The treatment these refugees received at the hands of the Transvaal authorities was shocking: it had been decreed that no money was to leave the republic and so every effort was made to seize the wages carried by blacks departing for the frontier. Railway officials and commandos enforced this with rigorous brutality, and in many cases the refugees were sent on their way barely clothed, their garments having been confiscated lest there was money secreted therein. These poor souls arrived home destitute, exhausted and emaciated.[143]

On the 2nd October Kruger informed the Transvaal volksraad that war was now inevitable. The next day, the 3rd October, the Orange Free State mobilized and Kruger's agents brazenly seized a gold shipment worth around £500,000. The burghers of both republics were now massed on their borders, the belligerent Transvaalers jeering at their more hesitant southern allies.[144] Indeed, so widespread was the enthusiasm and lust for war in the ZAR that few risked speaking out against it. One who lived through it all remembered: "If you dared to lift up a voice against the powers that be, you would simply be torn to pieces, and vengeance wreaked upon your innocent wife and children … not one, but many, since declaration of war, have told me openly: 'If you don't come, we will take good care you don't go anywhere else' … Many of the Boers, I know, are hard against this war, but what can they do?"[145] Perhaps unsurprisingly, those who did the most talking in favour of war had cunningly ensured that they would be nowhere near the front: "These same class (and I am sorry to say some of them born Englishmen) have been agitating the ignorant Boer, and telling them they must drive the *verdomd Engelsh na de zee* [drive the damned English into the sea], keeping them up to boiling point, and I am pretty certain, should the British happen to march into Klerksdorp (which I think is pretty certain, sooner or later) will be the first to cry out: 'I never was against you, and was always against the war.'"[146]

It was not until the 7th that the British began to mobilize their reserves,[147] without which her regiments were woefully understrength. This was in itself a lengthy process and even after that, these men would take several weeks to be transported to the theatre. Despite this, some of the more insane pro-Boer writers claim it was this mobilization which caused the war—which goes to show that such people never let the facts get in the way of their opinion. Indeed, fanatical Irish republican, Michael Davitt, offered a typically blinkered summary of the run-up to the war, lumping the blame on the British mobilization and the "English army headquarters in Natal" being moved up to the Transvaal border,* while completely disregarding the fact that both Boer republics mobilized first.[148] The rest of his book, *The Boer Fight for Freedom* is similarly one-eyed, violently anti-British propaganda.

Portugal, England's oldest ally, had been holding up munitions in Delagoa Bay, but was forced to release them to the Transvaal under intense German pressure. Fortunately, an order placed in July for another twelve 'Long Toms'† and an incredible eighty-two 75mm Creusots never made it to the Transvaal in time for the war.[149] Members of the volksraad were puffing out their chests and indulging in ever-more bellicose speeches. Those like Joubert and de la Rey who had counselled restraint and caution were ignored as Kruger sent his laconic message to President Steyn: "We must begin."[150] Kruger's use of the phrase 'we must begin' is noteworthy, especially as it comes from the correspondence of Leyds. Kruger did not say "we have no other choice" or "now we're buggered"—but rather, "we must begin".

As late as the 5th October, Milner—whom Pakenham would like us to

---

* Presumably this is Davitt's crackpot interpretation of Yule's 8th Brigade being deployed to defend the coal mines around Dundee.

† This French 155mm artillery piece was to become an iconic weapon of the war. Flinging a 94lb shell out to about 10,000 yards, it utterly outclassed any field piece the British army deployed throughout the war. But it was a heavy, relatively immobile weapon, more suited to siege and trench warfare than the Transvaal's usual actions against their African neighbours. The only possible motivation for this enormous order was for war against the British.

believe was a deranged, swivel-eyed warmonger—was writing to President Steyn, urging peace: "The present position is that burgher forces are assembled in very large numbers in immediate proximity to the frontiers of Natal, while the British troops occupy certain defensive positions well within those borders. The question is whether the burgher forces will invade British territory, thus closing the door to any possibility of a pacific solution. I cannot believe the South African Republic will make such aggressive action, or that Your Honour would countenance such a course, which there is nothing to justify. Prolonged negotiations have hitherto failed to bring about a satisfactory understanding, and no doubt such understanding is more difficult than ever today, after expulsion of British subjects with great loss and suffering; but until the threatened act of aggression is committed I shall not despair of peace, and I feel sure that any reasonable proposal, from whatever quarter proceeding, would be favourably considered by Her Majesty's Government."[151]

The much-delayed Boer ultimatum was finally sent to the British Colonial Office early on the 10th October. Written by Reitz, it was as verbose as ever, but was nevertheless a remarkable communication. Giving a hint that the war had nothing to do with independence, and everything to do with building an Afrikaner empire in southern Africa, the ultimatum declared that the Transvaal was acting "in the interest not only of this Republic, but also of all South Africa".[152] The demands of the ultimatum were so outlandish that its authors knew the British could never agree to them. One commentator declared it would have been "rejected with scorn by Montenegro"[153]—thus it was more a declaration of war than a true ultimatum. Among various other demands, the Transvaal called for the British to withdraw any troops who had arrived in southern Africa after the 1st June and to turn round those troop ships currently en route.

Milner immediately contacted President Steyn, who confirmed that the Orange Free State would also be declaring war on Great Britain. On the face of it, Steyn was committing his nation—a nation which had always enjoyed friendly relations with Britain—to war so as to defend the Transvaal's right to implement far harsher franchise rules than the Orange Free State itself. In fact, if the object was truly to defend the Transvaal from British invasion, then the greatest service the Orange Free State could have done their kinsmen was to have declared its neutrality. The easiest and most logical route to the Transvaal was through the Orange Free State and, had the British been denied this, they could only have attacked through the mountains that formed the Natalian border.[154] This area was perfect for defence, described by one reporter as "rocky bewildering chains of hills and mountains … deep-dented interlacing of spruits are so many natural fortified positions waiting to be occupied".[155] And while the Transvaal Boers occupied such impregnable sites, Orange Free State volunteers could always have made their way into the Transvaal to assist in repelling any British invasion.[156] All the while, of course, the British would still have had to guard against a sudden intervention by the Orange Free State government.

This would have been the logical course of action had the object of the war really been to protect the ZAR from invasion, but of course it wasn't. In reality, and as Steyn announced to his own burghers on 11th October 1899, the Orange Free State was going to war to challenge Britain's position as the "Paramount Power" in South Africa.[157]

Never a man to use one word when fifty would do, Reitz went even further in one of his trademark rants, calling on his "Brother Afrikaners! The Great Day is at hand! The God of our fathers will be with us in our struggles … Has the British Government been a blessing or a curse to his sub-continent? Brother Afrikaners! I repeat, the day is at hand on which great deeds are expected of us! WAR has broken out! What is it to be? A wasted and enslaved South Africa, or—a Free, United South Africa?"[158]

In an utterly bizarre interview published in the French newspaper, the *Echo de Paris*, Reitz tried to whip up support to turn the conflict into a something approaching a world war: "Great Britain is most gloriously isolated, and the British Empire itself runs considerable risk of being vanquished. France and Russia have never had a finer chance to get rid of a troublesome enemy. Does France mean to allow this opportunity—the last she will ever have, perhaps—to pass without taking her revenge on the British? No! I am sure you will not, for such conduct would be nothing less than criminal. It would mean your destruction. Make a bold attempt for Egypt then, and extend your possessions in Tripoli. Fight, I say, even at the very improbable risk of being beaten. Follow our example. As for Russia, anyone can see that it is in her interest to incite India to rebellion."[159]

৯

Count Adalbert Graf Sternberg, the Austrian war correspondent, travelled to both Pretoria and Bloemfontein in December of 1899, in a quest to "discover the ultimate objects of the Boers"—something historians have argued about ever since. The count came away with no definitive answer: no two seemed to share the same idea but many wanted a United States of South Africa in some form—and this was certainly what the popular press was calling for. Others in the Transvaal wanted to nationalize the goldfields, feeling that they had in some way been cheated out of them. Sternberg spent a good deal of time with Kruger, a man he appears to have admired. Tellingly, he reported that "Kruger himself only wanted Natal, with the port of Durban"[160]—suggesting some of his circle wanted more.

Sternberg also spent time with President Steyn, describing him as "a fine man, a European with a clever, striking face … a model of sincerity and candour, and a Boer President par excellence".[161] Steyn admitted to the count that the Orange Free State had always enjoyed good relations with Great Britain and that "the present state of affairs is quite artificial". During their meeting, Steyn told the count that his nation was poor and that "their first object was the annexation of the diamond fields. This war made possible the attainment of their wishes, and before their eyes hovered the possibility of re-establishing the old frontiers, so that Kimberley would belong to the Free State". So that would be a war of territorial expansion, then.

Steyn went on to explain to the count that the Afrikaner movement embraced everyone in South Africa, that the centre of the movement was in Cape Town, and that the colony was far more hostile to the English than the Orange Free State itself. Steyn believed that the war would "strengthen the loose organization of the Afrikander Bond, and he had no doubt of the final result". Sternberg also came away from his meeting with Steyn with his own ideas as to why Kruger dragged the Orange Free State into the war, when strategically—and as already mentioned—a neutral Orange Free State would have been far more useful. The count was convinced that Kruger calculated that the war—even if lost—would serve to unite the Afrikaners of South Africa: "a conquered Free State, over which the horrors of war had passed, would remain true to the Boer cause until the last drop of blood had been spilt."[162]

It is instructive that Count Sternberg is mentioned by General Ben Viljoen in his *Reminiscences of the Anglo-Boer War*. Viljoen criticizes the count's mem-

oirs for all manner of things, such as "extraordinary tales" about '"the galloping and trotting feats of the Basuto ponies" and claims that the closest Sternberg came to action was when his cigars were stolen by a German ambulance
man.[163] What General Viljoen does not do, however, is contradict or challenge
any of the comments the count made about the Boer war aims and objectives.

Writing in 1905, Leo Amery* sums up the confused war aims of the Boers
rather well: "The more sanguine 'young Afrikanders' and enthusiastic
fanatics like Mr Reitz thought that the time had already come for the final
expulsion of the British Power from South Africa and the creation of the
great Afrikander Republic, and their sentiments were freely expressed in
the Republican Press."[164] Only slightly less ambitious, states Amery, were
the dreams of Kruger, who was determined to win an outlet to the sea
and, if possible, secure the annexation of Natal, as well as Mafeking and
Bechuanaland. Similarly, the leaders of the Orange Free State considered
Kimberley and Griqualand West as "definitely Free State territory, while the
more forward spirits among them insisted that the invaded districts south of
the Orange River should, on the conclusion of peace, be allowed to decide for
themselves whether they would remain British territory or not".[165] Given that
all loyalists were quickly driven out and non-whites would have been denied
any say in the matter, this was only ever going to be a formality.

Sir William Dunn, who served as the consul-general of the Orange
Free State in London offered his own view: "While the [Jameson] Raid
undoubtedly hastened the outbreak in hostilities, the Dutch had, long before
that date, been doing all they could to undermine British supremacy in South
Africa, and were simply biding their time until they saw their way clear to
striking an effective blow."[166]

Though he never seemed able to make up his mind if he had plunged
his country into war for the sake of independence or for conquest,[167] Steyn
twice—first in November 1899 at the height of republican success and again
in February 1900—openly called for the Cape Colony to become another
Boer republic.[168] Furthermore, it is known that this idea was again discussed
and formally agreed to at a council of war held at Waterval later in the war.[169]
The aim of creating an Afrikaans-dominated South Africa was also the
subject of letters between senior republicans: de Wet, for example, wrote to

---

* Leopold Amery (22 November 1873–16 September 1955), correspondent for *The Times* during the war
  and later a long-serving MP, including stints as First Lord of the Admiralty, Colonial Secretary and
  Secretary of State for India.

Commandant Badenhorst to assure him that "It is certain that the ways of the Lord are mysterious, but from it all it appears to me that the day of a united South Africa is not far off".[170] At the other end of the spectrum was Dr Leyds, Kruger's man in Europe. He claimed that the republics would be satisfied with a payment of their war expenses and recognition of full sovereign status.[171]

And yet, despite Leyds being something of a lone voice, it is his slightly more palatable objectives that have been seized upon by most modern writers. The common modern view is that the Boer War was caused by the gold-bugs, the British, or was somehow 'Milner's War'—it speaks volumes of the power of propaganda and wishful thinking that relatively intelligent and well-educated people still trot out this rubbish even today. When you read the outbursts and dreams of Kruger, Reitz and Steyn, and consider that the reasonable, clear demands of the British were rejected out of hand, and that the counter proposals from the Kruger gang were opaque, mysterious and ever-changing, it is hard to ignore their culpability. At no point during four months of negotiations did Kruger, Reitz or Smuts make a genuine, clear and sincere offer which would have secured peace in the Transvaal; instead, their intention throughout the months of talks appears to have been to obfuscate and procrastinate.

It is also worth remembering that the Transvaal of 1899 had an even more restricted franchise than the South Africa of the apartheid era. Pretty much the whole world agreed that the latter was wrong, so why—we may ask—is it that so many commentators fall over themselves to defend Kruger's right to preside over an even more exclusive and odious regime? Why do they dismiss the genuine grievances of the uitlanders so readily? Overall, it is difficult to disagree with the assessment of George Gibson, regimental historian of the Imperial Light Horse: "The Transvaal Republic went to war rather than concede a measure of reform in favour of the Uitlanders, and had no sooner declared war that it openly avowed that the object of the war was not so much the maintenance of the Transvaal franchise in its existing form, as the destruction of British power in South Africa."[172]

No less a man than Commandant-General Joubert admitted that the war was caused by Kruger's "blind obstinacy"[173] and said that all it would have taken to avoid it was for the Transvaal to adopt a five-year franchise law.[174] When Joubert received the order to invade Natal, he initially refused, pointing out to Kruger's cronies that, by so doing, all chance of foreign intervention or mediation would be gone. He received a strongly worded telegram from Kruger, and—unfortunately for all concerned—backed down.[175] One Free State burgher remembered that "The Transvaalers were also spoiling for a fight, and, from what I saw in Pretoria during the few weeks that preceded the ultimatum, I feel sure that the Boers would in any case have insisted on a rupture".[176] Former chief justice of the Transvaal, John Kotzé, declared that it was Kruger's "autocratic bearing and obstinate character that ultimately led to his downfall, and that of the second Republic".[177]

There were some in the Transvaal brave enough to raise dissenting voices, arguing that Kruger was entirely to blame for the lack of a peaceful solution as he knew that any change in the franchise law would mean "the weakening of the Kruger party". These dissenters were demonized by the Kruger clique, however, and Progressives were dismissed as "traitors". One such internal critic of the Kruger regime, the prominent attorney, Ludwig Krause,* was convinced that the cabal had "engineered the war as an ill-judged trial of armed strength in order that the Kruger party might remain in power".[178]

Joining in the prevailing mood in the Transvaal, the Pretoria *Volksstem* published a delightfully bloodthirsty poem on the 26th August 1899, several weeks before Kruger launched his invasion. The cheery doggerel translates:

> *Then shall our ears with pleasure listen,*
> *To widow's wail and orphan's cry;*
> *And shall we gird, as joyful witness,*
> *The death-watch of your villainy*
>
> *Then shall we massacre and butcher,*
> *You, and swallow glad your blood;*
> *And count it 'capital with interest'—*
> *Villain's interest—sweet and good,*
>
> *And when the sun shall set in Heaven,*
> *Dark with the clouds of steaming blood,*
> *A ghastly, woeful, dying murmur,*
> *Will be the Briton's last salute*[179]

---

* In his book, *The War for South Africa*, Nasson stops short of calling Krause a 'traitor'; however, he does declare him to have been a "bilious anti-Kruger Progressive".

Despite all this, there have recently been many writers determined to twist themselves in knots to paint the Transvaal as the victim of the piece. Ignoring that the independence of the Orange Free State was not in any way an issue, Professor Scholtz claims: "The Boer leaders did not wish to wage a war of conquest. Their aim was to defend their own independence. According to the Dutch journalist Frederik Rompel, who in all likelihood obtained his information from Abraham Fischer (a member of the Free State Executive Council), the Boer leaders regarded a war of conquest as directly opposed to the Afrikaner's conception of Christianity and civilization."[180] Building up a head of steam, Scholtz goes on to assure us that President Steyn posed "moral objections" to the invasion.[181] This is of course to completely disregard what he told Count Sternberg about snatching the Kimberley diamond fields and, if Steyn genuinely had moral objections to a war of conquest, why did he sign up to the offensive alliance in 1897? Were these moral objections not more accurately 'cold feet' or perhaps a desire to stick to the plan and wait for the British to get embroiled in another conflict? What is the purpose of an offensive alliance other than to embark on wars of conquest? Though Piet Joubert was certainly opposed to the war, even he admitted that the masterplan was to "advance rapidly on Cape Town, Port Elizabeth, East London and Durban. Smuts also stated that it was planned to advance to the coastal ports of Natal and the Cape".[182] And despite his reservations about the whole scheme, on the 10th November 1899, Joubert would himself issue a proclamation declaring that the northern portion of Natal had been annexed to the South African Republic.[183] What was that if not an act of invasion and conquest?

Indeed, so peculiar are his claims that again one cannot be entirely sure if Scholtz is joking or not; but if he meant this statement sincerely, and put any store in these holier-than-thou quotes, then it is truly odd. For a professor of history not to know that the Boers had only obtained and expanded their republics by wars of conquest in the first place is beyond rational belief. As we have seen, the Transvaal, in particular, had spent the previous generation fighting endless wars of expansion, snatching pieces of Zululand, Bechuanaland and Swaziland, launching abortive invasions of the Orange Free State and Mashonaland, gun-running and rabble-rousing in British territory and indulging in the enthusiastic capture of, and trade in, slaves. That Scholtz genuinely considers such people "too Christian" to embark on a war of conquest stretches the imagination. Or perhaps the professor simply doesn't count those wars fought against 'natives'? Either way, Scholtz contradicts himself just a couple of pages later: "The Free State juts deep into the Cape Colony, and therefore the Cape heartland, with the ports, was within reach of the Boer commandos ... the Transvaal Department of Justice under Attorney-General Smuts was well-prepared. Some considerable time before the war Smuts ordered his secret service to investigate the political sympathies of the Cape Afrikaners."[184] Smuts believed that "by such action the interior districts of the Cape Colony would be encouraged to rise and to form themselves into a third great republic". And yet the professor still thinks the war was fought merely to preserve the independence of the ZAR?

Even the estimable Iain Smith cheerfully dismisses the notion that the Transvaal wanted to establish her dominance over all southern Africa. Despite grudgingly admitting that "Smuts and others" attempted to rally "all Afrikaners from the Zambesi to Simon's Bay" under the slogan "Africa for the Africander", Smith rather curiously goes on to assure us it was all a "convenient myth developed by the British".[185] Given that this dream was a stated aim of the Afrikaner Bond, and was openly admitted by numerous senior figures in the Transvaal, it is curious that Smith is so ready to dismiss this as a "convenient myth". It is certainly true that when push came to shove, many in the Cape Colony chapters of the Afrikaner Bond wanted nothing to do with the war, but that does not absolve the organization of its mischief-making prior to the conflict. As Smuts's invasion plan called for the capture of Natal and the Cape Colony, and the foundation of a "United South Africa",[186] Steyn confessed he wanted to grab the diamond fields and Kruger admitted he wanted to annex Natal, it seems fanciful that this was all a myth developed by the British.

It is also worth noting that if the Transvaal Boers were as pious as Scholtz ludicrously claims, they would be aware that their determination to deny the uitlanders (as well as anyone without a white skin) the vote was firmly against of the teachings of the Bible. For a man who proudly claimed it was the only book he'd ever read, it is remarkable that Kruger glibly ignored the various references that pepper Numbers, Leviticus and Exodus, warning against denying rights to newcomers; for example: "Ye shall have one manner of law as well for the stranger as one for one of your own country; for I am the Lord your God" (Leviticus xxiv. 22); and "One law and one manner shall be for you and for the stranger that sojourneth with you." (Numbers. xv. 16) Quite simply, if Kruger had embraced the teachings of the Good Book, rather than hypocritically adopting the moral high ground, there would have been no Boer War.

As it was, such was the enthusiasm in the Transvaal for war that her forces did not even wait for their thirty-six-hour ultimatum to lapse before commencing hostilities. A Natalian civilian train was seized by Boer forces at Harrismith several hours before the deadline had expired,[187] leaving no doubt that the republicans had no interest whatsoever in peace. The captured train would later be used to ferry troops, guns and supplies during the siege of Ladysmith.

The stark contrast in the relative states of preparedness of the two sides was illustrated in the first couple of days of the war. After the capture of the civilian train at Harrismith, Boer forces pushed over the border into Natal at various points. At De Jager's Drift, and demonstrating their usual cavalier disregard of the accepted rules of war, the invaders used two civilians to distract the five officers of the Natal Mounted Police who were stationed at the crossing. While they were chatting, a group of thirty armed Boers rode up and demanded that the mounted policemen surrender. What was remarkable about the event was that no one had informed the NMP post that war had been declared—such was the lack of readiness for war on the British side. The idea that vast numbers of imperial troops were poised on the borders of the Transvaal, ready to pounce and steal the gold mines is completely fallacious.

Kruger's apologists have always sought to excuse the Boer ultimatum, the declaration of war and the invasion by claiming that the British were preparing their own ultimatum. It is indeed true that Chamberlain was drafting another proposal when Kruger's ultimatum arrived, but the new convention being drawn up in London should not be considered an ultimatum as such. Instead, it was a list of seven provisions, relating to such things as the franchise laws, the end of religious discrimination against non-Protestants and the independence of the Transvaal's courts of justice.[188] Also, as John Stephens wrote in *Fuelling the Empire*, "in return the British Government would fully guarantee the Transvaal against any attack on its independence, whether from any British dominion or from the territory of any foreign country … nothing in the draft seemed in any way to suggest a desire by Britain to annex the Transvaal. Also, from the draft form of the document it does not appear to be an ultimatum, since no sanction is included should the reaction from the Transvaal not be favourable."[189]

For reasons known only to themselves many writers are blind to the aggressive nature of the Transvaal. Pakenham's history of the conflict, for example, would leave one believing the Boer War was actually 'Milner's War'. This is gross exaggeration. None other than the leading Cape Bondsman, Jan Hofmeyr, admitted that the "High Commissioner would much prefer to gain concessions and settlement without war, but will not shrink from war if object cannot otherwise be obtained".[190] Milner was undoubtedly a hard-nosed diplomat, and resolute in his aim to gain fair rights for the uitlanders. His steely determination to drag Kruger's corrupt oligarchy into the modern, democratic, age—and not shrink from the Transvaal's challenge to British supremacy—certainly hastened the start of hostilities* but this was by no means the root cause of the problems in South Africa. These stemmed directly from the desire of a group of influential Transvaal Afrikaners (and their supporters in the Orange Free State and the Cape Colony) to establish their ever-expanding republic as the pre-eminent power in the subcontinent. This was incompatible with the fact that the British Empire held this position, and could hardly be expected to simply relinquish it. Tensions had been rising throughout the 1890s and, as we have seen, the Transvaal had been building her forces and indulging in intrigue, propaganda, espionage and war by proxy for years prior to the Jameson Raid or Milner's arrival on the scene. As long as the Transvaal was run by men whose dream was to build an Afrikaans empire stretching from "the Zambesi to the Cape, from the Atlantic to the Indian Ocean",[191] then war was coming to South Africa sooner or later—it was only a matter of when. As one contemporary observer stated, "Of course the war could have been avoided. Of course, it would have been quite possible [for Britain] to voluntarily retire from the Cape and allow South Africa to become entirely Dutch. In the same way we could give up governing India and hand it over to Russia and confine our expenses and our energies to Great Britain, the water supply, the development of national cookery, and the propagation of cabbages."[192]

One of the inner circle of the Orange Free State leadership wrote a very telling letter on the 25th September, betraying fears that the Boers might be

---

* "I precipitated the crisis, which was inevitable, before it was too late … It was not very agreeable, and in many eyes, not very creditable piece of business." Milner to Lord Roberts, June 1900.

denied their war by an eleventh-hour British climb-down: "The only thing that we are now afraid of is that Chamberlain, with his admitted fitfulness of temper, will cheat us out of the war, and consequently the opportunity of annexing the Cape Colony and Natal and forming the Republican United States of South Africa."[193]

As we know, the Austrian traveller and war correspondent, Count Sternberg spent time in South Africa during the war—his account of the war was originally published in German with the catchy title of *Meine Erlebnisse und Erfahrungen im Boerenkriege*—enjoying close contact with many of the leading Boers for much of the conflict. He offered his opinion on where the culpability lay: "There can be no doubt that England was long-suffering; and that, as far as this war is concerned, she was justified in the eyes of God and man. The Boers base their arguments on the right of the landlord to do what he likes in his own house. The foreigner is a lawless stranger. Their laws are the unalterable precepts of Calvin, founded on the Psalms of Holy Writ, and all other views are heretical."[194]

Despite all this, it is fashionable to simply absolve Kruger's gang of all responsibility and instead heap all the blame for the war on the British and on Lord Milner in particular. Though appealing to those of a rabidly anti-British persuasion, this is to ignore the simple reality that both sides wanted to dominate southern Africa, to disregard the Bogus Conspiracy and all of Kruger's scheming, dreaming and intransigence. While Milner certainly played a significant part in bringing matters to a head, overall policy was made in London, not Cape Town, and Salisbury personally approved every communication before it was sent to Pretoria.[195] Salisbury and Milner can only really be accused of starting a war in that they refused to bow to Kruger and were unwilling to surrender British power and prestige in southern Africa.

In the cast of culpable characters there were empire-builders, idealists and patriots like Smuts, Reitz, Steyn, Leyds, Jameson and Rhodes, ambitious born-again Jingoes like Chamberlain, rabble-rousing London newspaper editors, trouble-making Afrikaner Bond members, exasperated Johannesburg uitlanders, meddling emissaries from Germany, Russia and France, ill-educated, uncompromising and extremist backveldt Boers, and naïve, head-in-the-sand generals like Sir William Butler. But if one was to identify the main culprit, it would undoubtedly be the president of the Transvaal. As Andrew Roberts asserts, "the two obstinate bearded old patriarchs, Salisbury and Kruger, both knew that this struggle was actually about ultimate regional paramountcy, about showing who was 'Boss' in South Africa".[196] From start to finish, Kruger had been resolutely determined that he would become the Boss and that his nation would replace Great Britain as the pre-eminent power in southern Africa. The Boer War was not Milner's War—it was Kruger's War.

"We admit that the British soldiers are the best in the world"—imperial infantry find what cover they can.

"... and your regimental officers the bravest"—some rather dapper-looking imperial officers ready to have a go.

Left: "Jolly pig-sticking"—many Boers proved to be utterly terrified of the sabres and lances of imperial cavalry.

Below left: "... dashing, fiery, brilliant"—the Jocks of the Highland regiments were some of the finest troops in the British army.

Below: Tommies skirmish up a rocky hillside with fixed bayonets—almost all such photographs were staged for the benefit of the press corps.

'Hairy Mary', a Heath-Robinson attempt at an early armoured train, using heavy ship's rope to render the locomotive bullet-proof.

The sort of image of a clean-cut, gallant bitter-einder favoured by post-war propagandists—in reality, many were little more than murdering bandits.

A rather more impressive-looking armoured train. Though badly handled at first, imperial forces learned the optimum use of these assets, which later proved their worth in protecting supply lines.

One of the famous Boer 94-pounder Creusot guns, or 'Long Toms'. The Transvaal had another twelve such guns and a further eighty-two 75mm pieces on order when Kruger launched his invasions.

The victor of Stormberg, General Olivier, was later sent to what appears a very comfortable exile in Ceylon (Sir Lanka) after his somewhat shameless offer to switch sides and join the British was rejected.

Another formidable-looking armoured train and her crew.

Armoured trains could not be everywhere and railway bridges were a favourite target of the Boers. Such attacks impacted on getting supplies to imperial troops, but also to the residents of the concentration camps.

Despite the modern-day perceptions, the British army was quick to embrace the latest innovations. Here, an observation balloon—'the scaly, brown-coloured monster'—is readied for use.

Despite the post-war spin, many bitter-einder attacks against trains were arbitrary acts of terrorism and banditry. Note the female civilian on the right.

CHAPTER FIVE

Arrogance, over-confidence and the Kruger raid

"the most costly, unsatisfactory, and difficult of all the little wars
which we could possibly undertake."
—Joe Chamberlain, describing any potential war against the Transvaal[1]

"he commenced the war with a firm trust in God, and the most gross negligence."
—an anonymous Hollander's assessment of President Steyn of the Orange Free State[2]

"We are now practically masters of South Africa from the Zambesi to the Cape. All the
Afrikaners in the Cape Colony have been working for years past for this end ... For thirty
years the Cape Dutch have been waiting their chance, and now their day has come;
they will throw off their mask and their yoke at the same instant,
and 200,000 Dutch heroes will trample you under foot.
We can afford to tell you the truth now, and in this letter you have got it."
—comment in the *Pretoria Volksstem*, 20th November 1899

"our leaders underestimated the magnitude of the task on which they were embarked."
—Boer commando, Deneys Reitz

"The Transvaaler, accustomed to fight against natives, welcomed the war;
for them it was more sport than anything."
—Count Sternberg, 1901

Depending on what point they are trying to make at the time, it suits today's
Kruger apologists to paint the British army in a variety of ways. HM forces
are generally dismissed as having been no match for the republicans, unable
to shoot straight, too scared to fight fair and led by a horde of idiotic, chinless
wonders. When such sages are trying to explain the uncomfortable fact that the
Boers lost, however, the imperial troops suddenly find themselves described

as being all-powerful, professional soldiers, far better equipped than the poor
old Boers. And when discussing the start of the war, it invariably pleases such
observers to espouse that the imperial troops were so arrogantly cocksure as
to be absolutely certain of victory. The image they like to draw is of preening,
red-faced, port-swilling buffoons strutting about in mess-dress, guffawing
loudly and more concerned with a regular ice supply for their G&Ts than
worrying about anything Kruger's working-class heroes might do. Of course,
it amuses such Krugerphiles to then declare that the upper-class twits who led
the imperial army were swiftly put in their place by the plucky Boers—with
the tacit implication that the British Victorian army was only ever any good at
mowing down spear-wielding tribesmen. But merely stating something often
enough does not necessarily make it true. What is this assertion based on?
And was all the arrogance on the side of the British?

Jonathan Hyslop, in his biography of extremist socialist traitor, James Bain,
claims that "the British position was based on a misplaced contempt for Boer
military capacities"[3] but does not trouble himself to back up this statement
with any evidence. Scholtz also grandly declares that the British "completely
underestimated their opponents' tenacity",[4] supporting this somewhat
sweeping statement up with a single quote from Lord Milner—who was
not, it will be recalled, a soldier. In *The War for South Africa*, Bill Nasson says
that the Salisbury government figured on 75,000 men being required, the
war lasting "between three and four months" and costing "perhaps £10m or
£11m". He then asserts that the British assumed "victory would be secured
for no more than £600,000 a month".[5]

All very damning at first glance, but as we shall see, the figure of 75,000
men is contradicted by those numbers put forward by military planners;
one doesn't need to be a rocket scientist to realize that Nasson's financials
don't quite add up—£600,000 into £11m is eighteen months, not "between
three and four". Talk over after-dinner cigars is one thing, but as the Zulu
War of 1879 had lasted six months, Kitchener's reconquest of the Sudan had
taken over two years* and the second Matabele War / Mashona Rebellion had

---

* Kitchener won his first significant battle at Ferkeh in June 1896. The final battle at Omdurman was in
  September 1898.

dragged on for eighteen months, it is highly unlikely that anyone seriously considered a war against the Boer republics lasting for such a short period.

Pakenham, on the other hand, gives a lot of weight to his selective reading of a secret report called 'Military notes on the Dutch Republics of South Africa'.[6] Originally produced in April 1898 by Britain's underfunded War Office intelligence division (which had no professional agents in either of the said republics),[7] it was revised and re-issued in June 1899.* Pakenham roundly ridicules this document, making all manner of claims to perpetuate the myth of British army arrogance and crass stupidity. He remarks that the report only predicted a Boer attack on Ladysmith in a footnote and that it stated that the main threat would be from smaller raiding groups of between two and three thousand men. Pakenham mocks the report for pointing out the lack of Boer experience of handling large bodies of men, inexperience in logistics and a lack of military discipline. He also derides the document for claiming the federals would not be strong enough to successfully invade British territory and, in contrast, that when the British could gather "adequate" forces, they would be able to invade the two Boer states. He, with matchless impudence, alters what he declares to be the report's "majestic conclusion" in his book—only slightly but tellingly. Eager to make his point, and seemingly conceited enough to think he alone knew what the author *really* meant, Pakenham scoffs that the report said the Boers would collapse "after [one] serious defeat",[8] rather than "after serious defeat". Predictably enough, Pakenham's gleeful interpretation of this report is woefully twisted and self-serving. When one looks at it rather more dispassionately, little of what is contained in the report is unreasonable or arrogant and most was ultimately proved correct. The Boers did fight better in small units, and never managed to use their forces in divisional-sized units in the way the British could. For example, though the republican forces besieging Ladysmith eventually totalled around 22,000 men, they were only ever able to coordinate attacks by small fractions of this number, with many Boers simply refusing to take part in assaults[9] or disappearing without permission.

As the report predicted, the Boer invasions did indeed prove to be unsuccessful and, as soon as they had enough men in theatre, the British managed to destroy the federals in the open terrain as predicted, smashing

---

* Perhaps hoping his readers will be dissuaded from trying to buy a copy and checking for themselves, Pakenham airily suggests that this report is very difficult to obtain. Maybe it was in 1979, but not now.

them in a month of relentless victories in early 1900. The damning "majestic conclusion", which caused Pakenham such amusement, and which he felt the need to correct, actually occurs on page 52 of 119[10] and was not far from reality. Boer morale did indeed collapse terribly during their 'Black Month' and their men surrendered in far larger numbers than the British ever did during their darkest hour.* During this period, and seeing the war couldn't now be won, many burghers simply went home: essentially they deserted in their hundreds and thousands in a fashion unthinkable to the British Tommies. While imperial forces showed grit, resolve and determination, enduring months of sieges and fighting tooth and nail to defend several inconsequential little towns, the demoralized federals failed to make a serious attempt to defend the gold fields of Johannesburg or even their capitals of Bloemfontein and Pretoria.

The report states that it is "not improbable" that the Boers will "boldly take the offensive against Natal or Kimberley"[11] which proved to be perfectly true. The 'footnote' at which Pakenham scoffed relates to this prediction, suggesting the most likely axis of attack to be against Ladysmith. There is also an enormous amount of detail on the Boer forces, including equipment, orders of battle, ammunition stocks and sketches of forts. In addition, the report contains information on the numerous German and French advisers operating in the republics, in some cases even naming such officers and their parent regiments in Europe. The chapter on logistics contains an interesting discussion on the number of mules available and that the Transvaal found imported donkeys to be unsuitable and prone to foot rot.[12]

So determined is Pakenham that this report contains all the evidence he needs to prove British imperial arrogance, that he bandies about its statements on the need for "adequate" forces without feeling the need to quantify them. If he had, he would have had to tell his readers that General Sir John Ardagh, head of the British army's intelligence branch, informed the War Ministry that it would require 200,000 men to defeat the two republics.[13] Though not convenient for Pakenham's tiresome Brit-bashing thesis, these were the numbers that imperial military planners considered "adequate". Not much evidence of arrogance there, given that this number proved almost spot on.

Similarly, the report warns that the tactics of the republicans presented

* Over 4,000 Boers surrendered at Paardeberg on the 27th February 1900 and another 4,150 with Prinsloo on the 29th July in the same year. In contrast, the largest British surrender of the war was at Nicholson's Nek, where around 900 men were taken prisoner.

great danger to infantry operating without mounted troops protecting their flanks and of the Boer 'genius' for fighting from cover.[14] Though the report claims the federals might not be as individually formidable as they were in 1880/1, "on the other hand they will have a better rifle in their hands, an unlimited supply of ammunition, and the advantage of modern field artillery and machine guns".[15] The author has an especially high regard for the men of the Orange Free State, praising their horsemanship, their marksmanship and their "natural eye for ground".[16]

'Military notes on the Dutch Republics of South Africa' is a fascinating report. Far from ending with Pakenham's "majestic conclusion", the document actually goes on to describe the details of rivers, tunnels, railway track inclines, lengths of sidings and carrying capacity. One chapter investigates a hypothetical Boer raid to snatch Delagoa Bay and the issues faced by a British force tasked with driving them out of that area. There is great detail on the towns and villages of both the Transvaal and the Orange Free State, recording such things as churches, hotels and shops. Bridges are discussed in minutiae, with the number and width of their spans recorded, and the materials of their construction documented. The report continues to detail the livestock in various districts and even the population breakdown of individual villages. Reddersburg, for example, is described as containing "1 doctor, 1 butcher and baker, 2 farriers, 2 millers, 1 saddler and 3 general stores".[17] There is whole chapter on communications, detailing railway junctions, those stretches of track which required additional locomotives to ascend inclines and even the various types of girders used on railway bridges in the Orange Free State.[18] Another table reports the "pumping stations between Volksrust and Heidelberg". By way of example, one such station, Paarde Kop, is described thus: "Well, 30 feet deep; hand pump. Four tanks holding 6,300 gallons. Yield sometimes fails partially, when it is supplemented by a hand pump 1½ miles beyond the station."[19] There are also notes on the locations of telegraph offices and a chapter on the "Climate and Seasons" of the region. This recommends that extra blankets for the troops "would be an absolute essential" in winter. It is difficult to agree with Pakenham's assertion that the report proves the British army thought the whole thing would be a picnic.

Pakenham also ignores various other British intelligence reports, none of which give the reader any impression of imperial arrogance. Major E. A. Altham, DAAG Military Intelligence, produced a memorandum entitled

'Remarks on the Present Strategical Situation in South Africa' as early as the 11th June 1896. This report warned of the increase in Boer military strength and of the possibility of the two republics making a dash for Natal and the port of Durban. Altham also pointed out the necessity for specialized troops, including the Aldershot-based mounted infantry units, which would be tasked with guarding the railways. Later that same month, Captain H. R. Gale, RE reported to Major-General G. Cox, then officer commanding Her Majesty's troops in Natal and Zululand, on the state of the Natal railways, including cuttings, culverts, watering places and the measures necessary for their defence. Of crucial importance was the safeguarding of the supply of coal from the Dundee coalfields.

Major-General Ardagh had produced another memorandum, 'The Transvaal Boers from a Military Point of View', dated the 13th November 1896, which pointed out that the South African Republic had spent £1.5 million on military preparations and set aside a further £850,000 for the provision of artillery, rifles, ammunition and fortifications. With remarkable foresight, Ardagh highlighted that, "as the Transvaal is almost entirely surrounded by British territory, this large expenditure can have no other explanation than an anticipation of war, or an intention of aggression against this country, and its supremacy in South Africa".[20]

As regards the men on the ground, one British general who is often accused of outrageous over-confidence is Penn Symons. It was reported that the newly arrived British commander in Natal farcically claimed that he could defend to the colony with just 5,000 men[21] and that a British infantry brigade could defeat a Boer force five times its size.* On the other hand, the Bishop of Natal noted in his diary that Penn Symons was fastidious in making his regiments practise skirmishing drills: "I want you to practise your men in trying to get to the top of that hill [pointing to the slopes of Impati] without exposing themselves, taking advantage of every bit of cover, so that if possible they shall get to the top without being seen from it."[22] But even had the self-confidence of Penn Symons bordered on arrogance, this attitude does not

---

* To be fair, this might have been taken out of context, and Penn Symons may have meant it could fight off a Boer force five times its size—a very different prospect from attacking such a force.

seem to have been widespread among the British high command in South Africa. Sir George White, who arrived just before the war and assumed command over Penn Symons and of imperial forces in Natal, fretted that the British had 20,000 too few troops in South Africa and feared they might have to "reconquer it from the sea".[23] These are not the words of a man who was confident of a quick and easy victory, or who considered the Boers to be no match for British troops. One of White's staff officers, Colonel Rawlinson, went a little further, dismissing the low opinion Penn Symons held of the republicans as "silly rot".[24]

Buller—who knew Natal and knew the Boers[*]—considered it impossible to defend northern Natal against the superior numbers of highly mobile Boers, and passionately advocated withdrawing to a defensive line along the Tugela River instead. He also pleaded for additional troops to be sent to the theatre—over and above those already en route—declaring, "We are in a very uncomfortable military position—if the Boers are bold ... they have now a chance of inflicting a serious reverse upon us in Natal."[25] That Buller's sound advice was not heeded had less to do with arrogance and more to do with political considerations, as we shall soon see.

There were, of course, officers and soldiers who talked of giving the Boers a hiding or of enjoying their Christmas dinner in Pretoria, but no army holds a monopoly on such semi-drunken, bravado-fuelled outbursts. Those who like to paint the British as being wildly over-confident of a quick victory in 1899 tend to focus on such things and of talk of it being a "tea-time war".[†]

More relevant than a few anecdotes of Jingoistic remarks made over a whisky and soda, however, was the size of the force that the British Empire was scrambling to send out to South Africa. The title of one of the chapters in Pakenham's history of the conflict is 'Preparing for a Short War', but the truth is that Britain's reserves were being mobilized for the first time in a generation and, when the Cavalry Division and the nation's one and only standing army corps[‡] started shipping out from Great Britain on the 20th

---

[*] Buller had served with Boer irregular forces in the Zulu War of 1879 in which he won a VC. He had the utmost respect for, and knowledge of, their war-fighting methods.

[†] This phrase was coined because the Boer ultimatum expired at 'tea time' in England. It did not mean that the war could be fought and won quickly, or would be an effortless victory.

[‡] The Army Corps comprised 1st, 2nd and 3rd Infantry divisions, plus additional support elements. Those troops already in Natal formed the 4th Division, a division being roughly 10,000 men strong. Eight additional independent infantry battalions (800–1,000 men each) were mobilized to protect lines of communication.

October, the Empire was sending its biggest expeditionary force since the Napoleonic Wars, bigger even than that sent to the Crimea for war against Russia.[26] On the 11th November the 5th Infantry Division was mobilized, along with an additional brigade of artillery. Orders to mobilize the 6th Division were issued on the 2nd December[27]—well before the 'humiliations' of Black Week. This huge commitment of troops should be evidence enough of the respect the British army held for the Boers—even before the reverses suffered in mid-December. Two additional divisions were mobilized shortly thereafter, virtually emptying Great Britain of regular troops.

❖

In stark contrast, Kruger did not hesitate to ditch the long-held plan that the Boer republics would only spark the war once the British Empire was otherwise engaged against another Great Power.[28] As we have seen, abandoning this logical plan caused consternation in some circles, for it was an act of supreme arrogance if not outright stupidity. Some leading uitlanders believed that the Kruger clique had decided on their invasion of Natal during the Fashoda Crisis of 1898,[29] so convinced were they that Great Britain and France would soon be at war. To carry on with the plans despite the Fashoda incident being peacefully resolved defies logic.

As we know, a few years previously, someone else had tried something remarkably similar to what Kruger now planned. In the early hours of the 30th December 1895, Dr Leander Starr Jameson led some 500 Rhodesian police troopers over the border into the Transvaal. His fellow, Transvaal-based conspirators had long plotted a revolution in that state, and the Doctor was confident that the uitlanders, who most believed outnumbered the ruling Afrikaners, would rise up to support his small force. In fact, they didn't and Jameson was abandoned. Outnumbered, exhausted and outgunned, the raiders were forced to surrender.

The Transvaal's master plan in October 1899 was by no means dissimilar. After years of plotting, gun-running and propaganda, Boer forces were to be unleashed into the Cape Colony and Natal, fully expectant of sparking a general rebellion against British rule. The rearmament splurge of the 1890s had left the Transvaal with tens of thousands of excess rifles, which many assumed—understandably enough—were retained for distribution to the

Cape rebels. One famous and highly knowledgeable veteran of the war, Sir Winston Churchill, took this line: "Cannon, ammunition, rifles streamed in from Holland and Germany in quantities sufficient not only to equip the population of the two Boer Republics, but to arm a still larger number of the Dutch race throughout the Cape Colony."[30] Some have tried to explain away this massive over-stocking of rifles by claiming that it was the natural result of the Transvaal switching from the Martini-Henry to the Mauser, and that the excess rifles were merely these old Martini-Henrys. This would make sense but for the fact that in early 1898 the Transvaal volksraad attempted to buy "60,000 obsolete Werdl rifles from the Austrian government ... the surplus is intended to arm the disloyalists from Cape Colony and Natal".[31]

There was, however, one crucial difference between Jameson's raid and what we might call 'the Kruger raid'. For while the Afrikaans-speakers Kruger banked on to support his scheme made up a majority of whites in the Cape Colony*, unlike the uitlanders of Johannesburg, they were by no means subjugated or denied simple rights. If the down-trodden English-speaking majority† of the Transvaal had failed to rise up in support of Jameson's raid, what made Kruger so sure that the free and franchised Afrikaners of the Cape would be keen to swap relatively benevolent and democratic British rule for that of his corrupt oligarchy? It was an act of astonishing conceit on Kruger's part, made more remarkable by the fact that he had specifically been told not to expect any military help from that quarter; a few weeks before the war, and in a meeting that echoed those held by panic-stricken Johannesburg reformers attempting to stop Jameson from launching his raid, "Hofmeyr and Albertus Herholdt, an Afrikaner member of the Cape Ministry, were in Pretoria to tell the Raad in secret session to look for no armed help from the Colony and to induce Kruger to modify the franchise bill and appoint a commission to deal with [the] dynamite [monopoly]".[32] That is not to say there wasn't a section of Afrikaans opinion in Cape Colony that sided with Kruger, of course. As early as 1897 Milner—who was still on his way to start his new role in South Africa—had worried about the "Kruger Raid", writing to Lord Selborne on the 20th April of his fears about "a Boer incursion into Cape Colony and a rising to meet it".[33]

But the Kruger masterplan was entirely dependent on the success of

---

* though certainly not Natal, where the vast majority of settlers were staunchly pro-British

† in terms of adult males

his invasion. Though thousands of rebels did indeed join his armies, the overwhelming majority of Cape Boers remained loyal or at least neutral[34] and, indeed, many even fought for the British.* Rather than waiting to pop up behind the British lines, many of those Cape Dutch who supported Kruger's schemes headed up to the Transvaal in the days prior to the war, meaning that those who stayed behind were generally those less inclined toward the invasion. The prime minister of the Cape, William Schreiner, was "convinced that the Dutch farmers of the Cape would understand their own interests too well to join in a mad attempt to expel British authority from South Africa"[35] and stated that "to get to the sea was the life and hope of Paul Kruger".[36] So it would seem Schreiner, like everyone else at the time, also knew what the real aims of Kruger's invasion were too, and that he did not subscribe to the present-day delusion that the invasion was in some way defensive.

In areas which the republican invaders managed to occupy, however, there were indeed some who welcomed them with open arms. When Boer forces occupied Colesberg, for example, a gushing Mr van der Walt declared, "The star of liberty has arisen at last—it had been the nation's desire and prayers during the past fifteen years. I could thank God with tears of joy for having granted those prayers."[37] As an elected member of the Cape's legislative assembly, van der Walt's oath of allegiance to the Queen doesn't seem to have troubled him much—which leaves one in no doubt as to the calibre of the man.

While plenty of these traitors (or patriots, if you prefer) were motivated by genuine enthusiasm for an Afrikaans South African empire, numerous others were press-ganged, intimidated or joined for fear of seeing their property torched and their belongings seized. This fear was not irrational: loyalist civilians, be they English- or Afrikaans-speaking, were driven from their homes by the invaders, forced to abandon everything they owned and make their own way to the British lines. When a Free State commando captured the small town of Lady Grey, loyalist inhabitants were given just a few days to evacuate.[38] Similarly, at Burghersdorp, Colesberg and Aliwal North, any residents who refused to side with the invaders were forced from their homes, arriving at British-held Queenstown as destitute refugees.[39] Forced mass recruiting led to a situation in which "Septuagenarians and striplings were drafted into the commandos, while at Burghersdorp the Town Guard

---

* many locally raised imperial units had large numbers of Afrikaans speakers

was composed of lads of about thirteen years of age".[40] When there were insufficient volunteers, Boer commandants simply forced "Dutchmen all and sundry to serve with the Transvaal colours. 'There is no such thing as a loyal Dutchman,' declared Olivier, and promptly commandeered young and old on pain of fine or imprisonment".[41]

What went wrong is that, as we shall soon see, the invading columns wasted their energies on pointless sieges and the recently reinforced imperial forces proved able to block the invading Boer commandos, thus preventing them from spreading their seditious poison and press-ganging to most of the colony. And just like the Transvaal uitlanders before them, the Cape Boers showed little inclination to rise up, meaning that areas which were free of invading forces remained essentially loyal. With no burning desire to shake off British rule, the vast majority of Cape Afrikaners adopted a wait-and-see attitude, resigned to making the best of whatever the end result was. Had Kruger's men managed to penetrate deeper into the Cape, there can be little doubt that greater numbers of supporters would have emerged from the woodwork; but this didn't happen spontaneously and nor was it ever likely to.

Indeed, the 'Kruger Raid' was fatally flawed from the start. The invasion plans had been finalized by Jan Smuts in early September 1899,[42] before any meaningful British reinforcements had arrived. This offensive planning was by no means the last-minute act of desperation some writers would like to pretend: none other than Joubert admitted that detailed invasion plans had been drawn up by a German staff officer as early as March 1898.[43]

Smuts's plan was based on there being only three small bodies of imperial forces anywhere near the republics: 500 regular troops at Kimberley, 2,000 in northern Natal and 500 irregulars at Mafeking. In a thunderous blitzkrieg it was envisaged that Boer invasion forces would shatter these scattered units and press on to the ports of Natal and the Cape. It was further assumed that the capture of these ports would prevent any additional British reinforcements landing and, as mentioned, it was hoped that the invasion of Cape Colony would prompt a general rebellion, with tens of thousands (some spoke of hundreds of thousands) of rebels joining the fight. Rather amusingly, it will be recalled that Professor Scholtz nevertheless declares that this blitzkrieg was defensive in nature.[44]

By the time the attack was launched, however, the strategic picture of South Africa had changed considerably. Recently arrived reinforcements meant that, rather than the 3,000 or so envisaged in Smuts's plan, there were instead perhaps 13,000 imperial troops holding blocking positions near the borders of the Cape Colony and Natal (as well as others in more distant locations). The republicans still held a large numerical advantage, of course, but nothing like the invasion plan had assumed. Such things seemed to be of little concern to Kruger's clique though. They were still dining out on tales of their victory over 400 redcoats at Majuba almost twenty years earlier (while conveniently ignoring their inability to win any of the siege actions of that war) and no one appears to have felt the need to change Smuts's basic plan. Whether it was 3,000 or 13,000 British troops, what did it matter? Even the alleged arrogance of Penn Symons pales next to this.*

Of those burghers mobilized by the time the attack was launched, some 21,000† were assigned to the invasion of Natal[45]—with more to follow. These units were under the indolent command of General Joubert, a man bitterly opposed to Kruger's insane war of conquest in the first place. The enormous commitment to invade Natal left only about 15,000 Boers to mount the invasion of Cape Colony, despite this being the source of all the potential rebels. The plan, the allocations of troops and the choice of military leadership were completely flawed from the outset.

None of this seemed to bother the average Boer, however. Modern accounts prefer sharing tales of British arrogance, but largely ignore the fact that the republicans were also supremely confident of victory, despite the arrival of imperial reinforcements. One observer recalled that in the Transvaal "the people were not only perfectly willing to go to war, but that they absolutely wished for it". As one Boer put it to the same observer: "'We look on fighting the English as a picnic. In some of the Kaffir wars we had a little trouble, but in the Vryheids Oorlog [the first Boer War] we simply potted the Rooineks as they streamed across the veldt in their red jackets, without the slightest danger to ourselves.' They had the utmost contempt for Tommy Atkins and his leaders, many of them bragging that the only thing that deterred them from advocating war instanter was the thought that they would have to kill so many of the soldiers, with whom individually they said there was no quarrel."[46] A resident of Bethal remembered the pre-war boasting of his fellow

---

* This outrageous over-confidence was nothing new: during the Zulu War, Kruger had boasted to Sir Bartle Frere that 500 Boers could do the work of the British army.

† 15,000 Transvalers backed by another 6,000 from the Orange Free State

townsmen: "One of us shall drive three score, and five a thousand drive ..."[47] This supreme confidence was again in evidence when the Bethal Commando mustered and rode out to the front. After offering prayers, the commando "rode out in the early morning, in all kinds of clothes, with saddlebags slung over the front of their saddle, all full of hope and big talk of driving the Rooineks into the sea".[48] Though a proud Afrikaner himself, Advocate J. W. Wessels made a speech in 1900 in which he described this rather unpleasant trait found in many of his countrymen:

> There is, however, one bad quality which has become prevalent amongst us Afrikanders, and that is the quality of conceit. It is especially noticeable in the rising generation of Afrikanders ... the Young Afrikander reminds me of the fable of the frog that felt so confident that it could rival a bull in size, that it blew itself out until it burst ... the young Afrikanders in the Transvaal and Free State gradually came to believe that they knew everything better, and could do everything better than any Englishman. They thought that because they, or rather their fathers, could hit a bottle at 200 yards there was no limit to their capacities ... to suggest to the young Afrikander that he was not omnipotent was to be a traitor to one's race. To tell the Kruger oligarchy at Pretoria that it was quite impossible to prevent the active and intelligent majority of the community from obtaining a voice in the future government of the State was enough to be jeered at called a fool ... to point out their folly and to caution them that if they persisted in their foolish course, ruin would stare them in the face, was a sin that merited the contempt of every Afrikander. This conceit has brought ruin to many a Transvaal, Free State and Colonial home.[49]

A remarkable letter was sent to the *Cape Times* just after the invasions. Though of course this by no means represents the views of every Boer, it does perhaps serve to illustrate the attitude that their lunatic fringe held toward the British Empire, an empire they considered to be in terminal decline, ravaged by decadence, torn apart by class warfare and teetering on the edge of collapse. In a deranged, rambling, though still rather entertaining, rant, the author claimed that Britain's "lazy, dirty, drunken working classes will never again permit themselves to be taxed to support your Empire, or even to preserve your existence as a nation" and that Great Britain exists "as an independent Power merely on sufferance, and that at any moment the great Emperor William can arrange with France or Russia to wipe you off the face of the earth. They can at any time starve you into surrender". According to this letter-writing twit, the supposed decline in British manhood was because "you have had no civil war like the Americans and French to tone up your nerves and strengthen your manliness, and consequently your able-bodied men will not enlist in your so-called voluntary army. Therefore you have to hire the dregs of your population to do your fighting, and they are deficient in physique, in moral and mental ability, and in all the qualities that make good fighting men". He went on to claim that "Your military officers we know to be merely pedantic scholars or frivolous society men, without any capacity for practical warfare with white men. The Afridis were more than a match for you, and your victory over the Soudanese was achieved because those poor people had not a rifle amongst them". While entertaining, these claims are obviously completely untrue. After this ahistorical swipe at the officer class, the deluded diatribe turns its attentions to British troops, which being "the dregs of your people, are naturally feeble, and that they are also saturated with the most horrible sexual diseases ... and that they cannot endure the hardships of war". Not even British children were safe from his bizarre attentions, dismissed as being "born weak, diseased and deformed and the major part of your population consists of females, cripples, epileptics, consumptives, cancerous people, invalids and lunatics of all kinds". In a truly surreal allegation, the fool then declared, "We know that nine-tenths of your statesmen and higher officials, military and naval, are suffering from kidney diseases" and, only slightly more reasonably, "We know that your Navy is big, but we know it is not powerful and that it is honeycombed with disloyalty". Sticking to the party line that the war would be a walkover, he snatches up an atlas and begins to work himself up into a fury, trumpeting, "We know that British soldiers and sailors are immensely inferior as marksmen, not only to Germans, French and Americans, but also to Japanese, Afridis, Chileans, Peruvians, Belgians and Russians," before the grand crescendo of fevered lunacy: "We Boers know that we will not be governed by a set of British curs, but that we will drive you out of Africa altogether ... for thirty years the Cape Dutch have been waiting their chance, and now their day has come; they will throw off their mask and your yoke in the same instant, and 300,000 Dutch heroes will trample you underfoot."[50]

&

Keen for a scoop from the thick of the action, war correspondent Bennet Burleigh travelled up to Pretoria from Cape Town in the days before the war. He shared the long journey with a train full of Cape Afrikaners, all heading north to join Kruger's crusade. He described his companions as "noisy and boastful … but to that they were urged, openly and secretly, by Colonial Dutchmen, and later on by their own people. It is not pleasant to reflect that, for years past, a stream of mawkish sentiment has been allowed to flow unchecked (nay, has often been encouraged) that a Dutch South Afrikander nation were the heirs of the whole country, from the Cape to the Zambesi, from the Atlantic to the Indian Ocean".[51] He recalled the supreme confidence of these men, each brainwashed so as to be totally convinced he was "invincible because of his powers of marksmanship, and the special aid on his behalf of Providence. Said one of this fanatical type the other day to a Britisher, 'I suppose the English can send an army of 20,000 soldiers against us?' 'Oh yes—500,000 troops, if necessary,' answered the patriot. 'Verdompt!' rejoined the Boer, in unconscious humour, 'it would take us three months to kill them all.'"[52] This utter contempt for imperial troops led the burghers to dismiss the dashing blue jackets of the naval brigades as "fish" and the stalwart, kilted men of the Highland regiments as "women".[53]

After a few days in Pretoria, Burleigh travelled to the Natal front on a Boer troop train carrying men of the Middelburg Commando. With a very human mix of admiration and regret, he described the naïve young men of this contingent as being "an excellent yeoman type of burghers, the best among the Boers, simple good-hearted fellows, with a foolish belief that England was a wretched and cowardly country they could put down any day. They were going to invade Natal, eat fish in Durban, and then, if the English did not submit to be thrashed, sail over to London and finish the job! It is sorrowful to think that so few of them realized what they were under-taking".[54] Such was the wholly misplaced optimism of those boasting that they would "eat fish in Durban" within a month that "many of them carried tin cases containing dress suits and new clothes in preparation for that convivial event".[55]

Our Austrian friend, Count Sternberg, had initially travelled to the Transvaal to fight for the Boers. When he was denied a field command, he instead attached himself to the federal armies for much of the war, acting as a war correspondent. This remarkable man enjoyed access to many of the most senior Boer leaders and even prior to his departure from Europe, he met Dr Leyds in Brussels, remembering him appearing "quite confident, relying mainly on the inevitable European intervention"[56]—this despite his repeated warnings to Pretoria that no such help would be forthcoming. If the calm and urbane Dr Leyds was only "quite confident", others were more so. On his arrival in the Transvaal in December, the count met F. W. Reitz and recalled that he had "no doubt as to the final victory of the Boers, of which he was so convinced that he would not even allow the possibility of the fortunes of war changing".[57] Other, more lowly, Transvaal Boers shared this conviction, with the count remarking that the outbreak of the war had been greeted with great enthusiasm by many, and that there was no doubt as to their ultimate success.[58] Others were so confident of an easy victory that they bragged they were not going to wash until they reached the Indian Ocean, or even Cape Town. There was a "feeling rampant in young Transvaal that they would sweep the British into the sea and compel the officials at Cape Town to speak Cape Dutch".[59]

In his magnificent personal account of the conflict, *Commando*, Deneys Reitz* is not too proud to admit that he embarked on the war "with the eyes of youth, seeing only the glamour, but knowing nothing of the horror and the misery".[60] Reitz would later serve in the British army in the First World War, rising to the rank of colonel, but was just a precocious seventeen-year-old when he joined the commandos. Reitz proudly told none other than President Kruger that, not only would he account for three British soldiers, but he would do so with one shot.[61]

A long-term resident of the Transvaal, Ulsterman Jack Lane, was commandeered against his will, and sent to fight against the nation of his birth. He recorded his bitter skepticism and contempt for Kruger's invasion and the triumphant mood prematurely sweeping the Transvaal in his diary: "I do not doubt that, the Boers may have a bit of a success for the first three months. But then, the time will come for reverses, when there will be another story to tell, when there will be a 'howling and gnashing of teeth'. And, in my humble

---

*   son of F. W. Reitz

opinion, the non-existence of their beloved South African Republic, and no one to blame but themselves and the Afrikaner Bond of the Cape Colony, combined with the Hollanders, and miserable Germans, who are making leaders believe that European nations will take up the quarrel against Britain. The Afrikaner Bond has poisoned the mind of the uneducated Transvaal Boer, with its papers and pamphlets, and lies they circulate. The ordinary Transvaal Boer believes it is impossible for any nation to beat them."[62] In another entry, he wrote: "The crowd are talking very big and from their talk Cape Town and Durban will be their first stopping place!!"[63] And nor was it only the rank and file who thought the invasion would be a turkey-shooting cakewalk. As Boer forces pushed into Natal, their commanders telegraphed Kruger to say that the Vierkleur (the four-coloured flag of the Transvaal) would soon be flying over Durban.[64] The chief justice of the Transvaal, Mr Gregorowski, was equally confident, boasting that the war would "be over in a fortnight. We shall take Kimberley and Mafeking, and give the English such a beating in Natal that they will sue for peace".[65]

Leaving aside his penchant for slave-trading, General Joubert was regarded by most as a rational and intelligent man, yet even he proved hopelessly out of touch. With astounding naïveté, he believed that the easily obtainable little red army lists contained details of the full might of imperial forces.[66] In reality, the army lists only showed an officers' graduation list (i.e. a list of serving officers in order of seniority, with dates of birth and promotions) and brief details of their service record.

Not all the Boers treated the affair in such a cavalier fashion, however. Koos de la Rey,* who would later become a famous guerrilla commander, spoke in the volksraad against Kruger's war, only to be shouted down and accused of cowardice by Kruger himself. De la Rey calmly replied that, as a loyal Boer, he would fight in the war and, what is more, he would still be fighting long after Kruger had fled to safety; this later proved to be absolutely true as Kruger scarpered with undue haste as soon as the tide turned against the republicans. Another who bitterly opposed Kruger's war, but would later be made famous by it, was General Louis Botha. His outspoken opposition had excluded him from high command at the start of the war, but he loyally served in the ranks[67] during the invasion of Natal. Such was the chaotic nature of the Transvaal's command structure that he would find himself serving as a

---

* General Jacobus Herculaas de la Rey (1847–1914)

general just days later.*

Other than the occasional exceptions like de la Rey and Botha, the senior men of the Transvaal demonstrated a quite astounding misunderstanding of the world at large. It was widely believed in Pretoria that, with Britain's attention focused on the Transvaal, Canada, India and Australia would seize their chance to escape the jackboot of the British Empire. This fallacy was encouraged by their Continental allies, few of whom seemed to grasp that, unlike their own empires, the British Empire was not held together by military force but rather by bonds of loyalty. One Frenchman, rather more enlightened than most of his countrymen, summed up this mindset: "he cannot be made to see that all these countries scattered over the surface of the globe can form a whole; he is always expecting a break up, and is firmly persuaded that the smallest event might bring it about … his prophetic vision sees Ireland, India, Burmah, Jamaica, Australia, New Zealand, the Cape, Egypt, Canada, proclaiming their *independence*, as if that magic word expressed the highest hopes of all these countries. You cannot get it into his head that they are all loyal to England, because they are happy under her rule and because there is something quite wonderful in her power of organization and administration."[68] In reality, far from seizing their chance to 'escape' the British Empire, the colonies sent thousands of volunteers to fight in South Africa.

On the 2nd October, the most deluded of them all, President Paul Kruger, addressed the two volksraads of the Transvaal in special session, assuring his God-fearing audience that their invasion was fully supported by the Almighty. In an address which was genuinely harebrained even by Kruger's standards, he reminded the members that the Lord had "transplanted the people to this country, and led it here amid miracles … He is waiting for our prayers and He will be with us".[69] Kruger went on to remind everyone that the Lord had been on hand to help them win the first Boer War and to defeat Jameson's raiders: "They aimed thousands of shells and balls at us, while we only shot with rifles; and how wonderfully was the course of the bullets ordered! Three of us fell, while the enemy had hundreds killed and wounded. And who ordered the flight of the bullets? The Lord! He spared us then, to prove that He rules all things. The Lord will also protect you now, even if thousands of bullets fly around you … I will say once more that the Lord will guide us."[70]

---

* to be fair, in the case of Botha it worked out well; he proved to be one of the better republican generals

But even leaving aside letter-writing cretins, drunken bravado, Bible-bashing rants and mind-blowing naïveté, the decision of the Transvaal and the Orange Free State to start a war against the British Empire, rather than grant meaningful democratic reform, remains one of the most ill-considered decisions in military history, even more loony, perhaps, than Hitler's 1941 invasion of the Soviet Union. Kruger and his ilk made their choice because they had utter contempt for the British army, wildly misplaced confidence in their own troops, an unshakeable belief that the Cape Dutch would rise up in revolution and, viewing the whole enterprise as something akin to a crusade, a quasi-lunatic belief that God was on their side. As is to be expected from a man who firmly believed that the earth is flat, Kruger seemed totally unable to grasp the vast, near-limitless power that the British Empire could ultimately bring to bear. Perhaps he had been fooled by Gladstone's spineless capitulation in 1881, or maybe he found himself sucked in by events and simply did not understand the rules of the brinkmanship game, but either way, his contempt for British arms seemed to know no bounds. Even Joubert was unable to comprehend the sheer resources that could be brought to bear against Boers raised to believe in their God-given invincibility, based on their defeat of large numbers of poorly armed blacks and a remarkable victory over a tiny force of redcoats at Majuba.

CHAPTER SIX

Opening shots

"the militant Afrikander led his misguided people into striking the first blow, by seizing,
annexing, and renaming British towns and territory in Natal and Cape Colony;
and by looting and destroying houses and property of British citizens."
—Michael Farrelly, 1900

"In consequence of the armed forces of the South African Republic having committed an
act of war, by invading British territory, I give notice that a state of war exists,
and that the civil law is for the time being suspended."
—Colonel Baden-Powell, October 1899[1]

"I thought it quite sporting of the Boers to take on the whole British Empire,
and I felt quite glad they were not defenceless and had put themselves
in the wrong by making preparations."
—Winston Churchill, October 1899[2]

"I would remind you that the present war is of one government against another—not of
people against people. Now you propose to inflict damage upon private property in a
peaceful town, and possibly to injure women and children under the excuse of war.
If you do this it will justify us (although such method of retaliation is repugnant to me)
in ordering similar methods to be taken in a wholesale manner
when the time comes for our forces to enter the Transvaal."
—Baden-Powell protests to General Piet Cronjé about
Boer shelling of Mafeking, October 1899[3]

"They were fighting man to man; they had human beings to deal with,
and they dealt with them as the British soldier does."
—Major-General Sir H. E. Colville, describing the Guards Brigade
at the battle of Belmont[4]

"The Franchise and Independence is our cry, then on the other hand, by sending
England an ultimatum, and invading her territory, it does not look like it.
In my opinion, it is nothing more or less than the whole of South Africa
to be cleared of the British rule, and the Pretoria clique to be the rulers."
—conversation between two Boers, recorded in the diary of Burgher Jack Lane

"The moment has arrived for deciding whether the future of South Africa
is to be a growing and increasing Dutch supremacy or a safe,
perfectly established supremacy of the English Queen."
—Salisbury addresses the House of Lords, 17th October 1899[5]

Since the 1960s, the British Left has delighted in telling anyone who will
listen that the British army of the First World War was useless, led by
Bertie Wooster-style twits, hide-bound by tradition and generally utterly
incompetent. The main problem with this commonly peddled myth is that
the British won, which leaves those who swear by it as gospel in a rather
awkward position. Flapping wildly and clutching at straws, they generally
wriggle out of this by giving credit to someone else or, more ridiculously,
by claiming that the war just sort of ended, and then go back to watching
Oh! What a Lovely War to learn a bit more military history. A similar myth
exists about the Boer War. Again, the British are dismissed as being wholly
outclassed by the Boers, routed and scattered with gay abandon by Kruger's
men, the troublesome reality of British victory cheerfully explained away by
the 'fact' that the British brought in so many men that they outnumbered
the Boers by a hundred to one. Now if there was any truth in all this, then
the opening weeks of the war—where Kruger's forces enjoyed a numerical
advantage of somewhere between two and three to one—should have seen
the republican armies smashing British units left, right and centre. Indeed,
many histories of the war declare that the first few months of the war were
a never-ending string of losses for the British. Perhaps, therefore, it will be
interesting to examine the opening engagements—those fought by Kruger's
invaders against an outnumbered and unprepared imperial garrison, many of
whom had just stepped off a ship.

But before we look at what happened, let us consider what the point of the
invasion was. To this day, as we read in the previous chapter, it is implausible
that the war aims of the Boers are still the subject of debate. Ignoring their
blatant land-grabbing, Bill Nasson feels confident enough to assure his

readers that "Boer War aims were simple and straightforward—the retention of the internal political independence of the Transvaal, respect for its post-1881 independent status, and a repudiation of imperial suzerainty".[6] Despite admitting that both Reitz and Smuts both declared the aim was to bring about "a Free, United South Africa, an ambitious national Afrikaner republic stretching from the Zambesi to Table Bay",[7] Nasson simply dismisses this as presumably having been said for a bit of a laugh. Even though he devotes much attention to Smuts's plan to invade Natal and capture Durban,[8] Nasson still assures his readers that "On the Boer side, the war which came was entirely defensive" and then ties himself in knots by saying, "even if the chosen method of defence would be the invasion of British colonial territory, it was widely understood to be a defensive enterprise."[9] Presumably this was not widely understood by anyone in Natal at the time.

Pakenham takes a similar line, assuring us that the Boer war aims were "more limited than Milner ... could ever have grasped",[10] before going on to state that half of the Boer invaders was ready to go home and the other half was ready to ride to Durban, neither of which in any way supports his claims regarding the aims and objectives of the invading republicans. Nevertheless, Pakenham airily declares that Milner, Amery, Reitz and subsequent British historians are all wrong, and—like Nasson—contends that the aims of the invasions were strictly defensive. He only quotes one source to back up this startling bit of historical revision, so it would seem the origin of this 'defensive invasion' idea is a set of books called *Geskiedenis van die Tweede Vryheidsoorlog, 1899–1902*. Written a couple of generations after the war by the apartheid regime's state-approved historian, J. H. Breytenbach, and published by the then government printers, to say it therefore lacks a degree of objectivity would not be unfair. Nevertheless, the 'defensive invasion' theory Breytenbach adduced has been unthinkingly lapped up by many writers ever since. Despite avowing that there was "no evidence" that the republicans wanted to capture Natal all the way to Durban, Breytenbach even admits: *"As die Boere besef het dat Natal op die tydstip letterlik aan hul genade oorgelewer was, sou hulle ongetwyfeld vinnig suidwaarts opgeruk endie gebied tot by Durban van die vyand gesuiwerhet"* (If the Boers realized that Natal at the time was delivered literally at their mercy, they would without a doubt have quickly marched south and cleared the enemy from the area up to Durban),[11] a claim which fully contradicts his own remarkable 'defensive invasion' theory and one presumably ignored by Pakenham in his selective reading of the tome. Those with rather more open minds might think it reasonable to say that—whether the plan was take Durban or 'just' northern Natal—any invasion and conquest of someone else's territory is not generally understood to be a defensive enterprise. It is mind-boggling that some seek to excuse Kruger's invasions by saying he only planned to take 'some' of Natal and the Cape Colony, as if grabbing just part of a neighbouring territory is okay. This argument is especially absurd when—as we shall soon see—there was no suggestion that any such grabbing was to be a temporary affair.

Though they cannot quite agree on the details, other Kruger apologists, both then and now, are amusingly determined to paint the invasion as having been in no way aggressive and that the republicans were forced to act while they still significantly outnumbered the imperial forces in southern Africa, i.e. it's all the fault of the British. Most therefore perversely adopt the view that this made the invasion plan somehow entirely 'defensive' but some go even further into the realms of fantasy, claiming the aim was only ever to advance a few miles, then take up easily defendable positions, all of which— surprise, surprise—just happened to be in British territory.

However, no one ever really specifies where these supposed defensive positions were: they certainly cannot have included the Tugela River line, for example, as the republican invaders pushed well past that, before coming up against imperial reinforcements and then *retreating back* to the Tugela and digging in there. Similarly, the formidable Magersfontein position was only occupied after the invading commandos had been thrown back in three actions, so this cannot possibly have been part of any initial master plan to seize valuable defensive terrain. Nevertheless, the argument, such as it is, postulates that the plan was for these sites to be occupied and for imperial troops to then throw themselves at these allegedly pre-determined defensive positions, lose heavily in several battles and then sue for peace.[12]

Though a convenient, if lame, excuse to absolve Kruger's invaders of any blame whatsoever, it is a peculiar argument for many reasons. Firstly, as we have seen, the best defensive terrain between Natal and both the Orange Free State and the Transvaal were the Drakensberg Mountains that in any case formed much of the frontier. Republican riflemen in such territory would have been able to fight off a British invasion force many times their number and any invading columns would have been funnelled into the few passes through the mountains. Only two railways wound their way through the range, one of which terminated just twenty miles over the border of the Orange Free State at Harrismith and was therefore of little use to an invader. The other line crossed into the Transvaal under Laing's Nek and Majuba through a tunnel over 700 yards long*—an outrageously vulnerable spot which could have easily been dynamited by a raiding force, meaning that, even if the British did manage to break through, there was no way the invading columns could have been adequately supplied for weeks, perhaps even months.[†]

Boer forces had indeed pushed a few miles into Natal to successfully defend these passes in the first Boer War, but the scope, scale and extent of their invasion of Natal (and elsewhere) in 1899 was completely different—thereby torpedoing the 'defensive invasion' theory at a stroke. Far from adopting defensive positions 'not too far from their borders' as some claim,[13] the 1899 invaders of Natal advanced deep into the colony, annexing territory, renaming towns and looting as they went. Others even rampaged and pillaged their way almost as far as Mooi River, just forty miles from Pietermaritzburg, only retreating in the face of imperial reinforcements. It was Smuts's stated aim to capture Durban,[14] while General Louis Botha[‡] had assured Kruger that the flag of the Transvaal would soon "wave over a free harbour"[15] and later claimed that only General Joubert's timidity had prevented him from "coming to Durban in 1899 to eat bananas".[16]

None of this should be surprising, however. As we have seen, the invasion plans—which were based on those drawn up by German advisers the year before—called for the capture of the Natal ports, as well as those of the Cape. One German 'Boer' who took part in the march on Durban even described the enterprise as a "*Lumpen Kreuzug*", a 'Tramps' Crusade'.[17]

And Botha's was not the only command to penetrate deep into Natal. The eastern prong of the Natal invasion force rampaged their way to Pomeroy, which they burned and looted[18] before being halted by the Umvoti Mounted

---

* at 2,231 feet long, the Laing's Nek tunnel was opened in 1891

† During their retreat from Natal, the Boers did indeed make an attempt at destroying the Lang's Nek railway tunnel by placing a truckload of dynamite in the middle and sending in a train from either side. This action caused a week's delay in restoring rail traffic and, ultimately, the British supply route. A less hasty attempt might have been more devastating.

‡ Breytenbach said there was "no evidence" that the republicans wanted to capture Natal all the way to Durban—presumably the words of the man who finalized the invasion plans, and of the man who led the drive south, do not count as evidence.

Rifles at the Tugela. Other raids were made into neighbouring Zululand, targeting the trading post at Mhlatuze and burning down the magistrate's office at Ingwavuma. These were followed up by the seizing of the whole Ingwavuma district by a 400-strong commando.[19] Further raids were launched against the trading posts at Rorke's Drift* and Vaant's Drift, both of which were looted. When a small force of Colonial Scouts was moved into the area to deter further such raids, republican forces responded by invading and occupying the districts of Nquthu and Nkandla in western Zululand. True to form, these captured districts were formally annexed to the South African Republic and placed under the control of two veldkornets who supervised the collection of a hut tax. One of this duo, Veldkornet van der Berg, even boasted to the Zulus of Nkandla: "the Boers intend to crown Dinuzulu king over the whole native population, and there would be only two kings in the whole of the land—Paul [Kruger] over the whites, and Dinuzulu over the blacks."[20] Even the most hare-brained Kruger apologist would struggle to claim that any of these raids, invasions and annexations were in anyway designed to occupy defensive terrain to block an imperial advance: they were looting sprees and territorial land-grabs, pure and simple.

Over on the western front General Cronjé was equally unambiguous in terms of his aims. After a few weeks of war, he treated his burghers to an hour-long rah-rah session in which he declared the plan was that "the 'Rooinek' must be driven into the sea" and that he, and he alone apparently, would do it and be in Cape Town within a month. Getting rather carried away with himself, Cronjé also went on to assure his men that France, Germany and even Russia were all coming to help and, indeed, had already started landing troops at Delagoa Bay.[21] Many of the republican rank and file certainly thought that they were fighting to drive the British out of southern Africa altogether. One such burgher assured our friend Jack Lane that they were fighting a just cause and would drive the Rooineks out and be in Cape Town by the end of January. His personal motivation was that he would then be able to get his father's old Cape Colony farm back, a farm which the family had sold to enable them to move to the Transvaal. He felt that Boer victory would fully entitle him to seize it from the English settler who had bought it from them fair and square.[22]

---

* Rorke's Drift is more famous as the site of the 1879 battle depicted in the Michael Caine film, *Zulu*

⊷

In the case of the Orange Free State, the Orange River provided a natural defensive obstacle along much of the border of the Cape Colony. Again, the logical way to conduct a defensive war would have been to blow the railway bridges over the river at Norval's Pont and Bethulie, and mount a raid on the railway which ran through British territory along the western frontier of the Orange Free State connecting Cape Town to Kimberley, Mafeking and, ultimately, Rhodesia. This extremely vulnerable railway crossed the Orange, Vaal and Limpopo and the bridges over these could have been blown by raiding parties. With the railway bridges thus sabotaged, the Orange Free State commandos could have dug in along the natural defensive barrier of the Orange River.

Instead, the Boers of the Orange Free State hung around for three weeks before breaking the promise Steyn had given the Cape parliament and invading the Cape Colony proper* on the 1st November, suddenly keen, presumably, to occupy undefined defensive positions therein. Some even claim that the aim of the 'defensive invasion' of the Cape Midlands was to seize the railway junctions at Stormberg, Naauwpoort and De Aar, but this fails to withstand scrutiny. Firstly, if these were genuinely considered important objectives, why did the Orange Free State not grab these in the first few days of the war? Also, it is not explained why the loss of these railway junctions would have been in any way devastating for the imperial cause, thus forcing the British to the negotiating table. Their loss would—and did—certainly inconvenience the British, but was far from being a tactic which justified starting the war, rather than holding a defensive line along the Orange and waiting for any British invasion. Even with the junctions in Boer hands, the British were able to move units up and down the coast at will, redeploying forces to and from Cape Town, Port Elizabeth, East London and Durban. These forces would then advance up the railway lines from these ports and clear the Boers from these junctions in any case.

The 'defensive invasion' argument also fails to address the salient fact that Boer forces invaded territory in every direction—not only Natal and the Cape Colony whence imperial 'invasion forces' might theoretically appear, but also Rhodesia, Zululand, Bechuanaland and Griqualand West. More

---

* as opposed to Griqualand West

importantly, it completely ignores the war aims which Steyn and Kruger confessed to Count Sternberg: to annex the Kimberley diamond fields, all of Natal and the long-held ambition of Kruger to snatch a sea port.[23] It similarly disregards wartime speeches given by leading Boer generals and brushes under the carpet the post-war memoirs of Jan Smuts and a volksraad member called P. C. Joubert,* both of whom confessed that the real war aims had been discussed in various secret sessions of the two volksraads: to capture the ports of Natal and the Cape Colony, including Port Elizabeth, East London and Cape Town itself.[24]

Colonel Villebois-Mareuil† was a French mercenary who fought for the Boers and took a similar line. Villebois-Mareuil would be promoted to the rank of general,[25] enjoyed personal contact with President Kruger and worked closely with Joubert, Cronjé and Botha, so his opinion can hardly be dismissed. Known as 'the French Colonel', he wrote that their war aims were "simply a matter of grabbing back the whole of South Africa from the British … a case of the hatchet in the big oak".[26]

Even those who did not advocate snatching British South Africa in its entirety were only marginally less ambitious. Speaking in Berlin at the end of January 1900, Dr Leyds confidently, though prematurely, predicted that if victorious the Transvaal would demand "the strip of coast between Durban and Delagoa Bay, with the harbours of Lucia and Kosi … together with parts of Natal and the northern districts of Cape Colony". How does this support the notion that the republicans were only interested in adopting defensive positions not too far from their borders? Writing in the same year, the eminent American historian, Captain A. T. Mahan, USN, broadly agreed with Dr Leyds, stating that the Boer war aims had been "to force the British out of Natal, thus closing access by Durban from the sea, and at the same time to seize the pass of Cape Town known as Hex River".[27] A quick glance at the map will show that this would have left the British with only a small fraction

---

* not to be confused with General Piet Joubert

† George Henri Anne-Marie Victor de Villebois-Mareuil (1847–1900) fought in the Franco-Prussian War before service in Tunisia and Madagascar. In 1892 he became the youngest colonel in the French army before leaving and volunteering for service in the Transvaal. He was killed in action at the battle of Boshof on the 5th April 1900 and was buried with full military honours by the British with his gravestone paid for by Lord Methuen. The colonel's ADC, Lieutenant Comte Pierre de Bréda (who had been captured in the action), thanked Methuen for his chivalry and declared: "We thank you for your courtesy. We recognize that we are prisoners of an army which is the bravest of the brave." The chivalry shown by Lord Methuen is all the more remarkable given that one of his officers, Lieutenant Williams of the Yeomanry, had been shot by a Boer after the white flag had been raised.

of their South African colonies. There is nothing especially defensive in any of this; Breytenbach's bizarre contention of there being no evidence of a plan to capture large swathes of British territory is rubbish. And if the intention of the various invasions was indeed defensive, this is inexplicable from a military point of view: by launching their attack on British territory, the republicans cast themselves as the aggressors of the piece, meaning they forfeited much of the sympathy they would have enjoyed had they waited for any potential imperial attack. This cost Kruger any chance of third-party intervention. It is also doubtful whether the various colonies of the British Empire would have rallied to the cause with such enthusiasm had the British started the war.

So in the Blue Corner we have the historical reality of a series of invasions which pushed deep into British territory on several fronts, together with unambiguous statements and memoirs of countless Boer generals and politicians, all of which say the capture of all or a large chunk of British South Africa was the aim of the invasion. And in the Red Corner we have a version written over sixty years later by a government-approved historian who— using just a couple of telegrams as his evidence—conjures up the far-fetched claim that the Boers only ever wanted to defend their borders, a claim completely at odds with what actually happened and which he contradicts in his own work. One can understand why an apartheid-state-approved historian would want to come up with something to excuse Kruger's aggression, but quite why such hogwash is entertained by so many modern historians is baffling. With no organized military staff, a rather strained alliance and cursed with more chiefs than Indians, the Boer invasion plans were haphazard, chaotic*, poorly coordinated and lacked a clear overall objective, but one thing they were demonstrably not was in any way defensive.

It often appears that the various Boer generals were making things up as they went along, and the overall strategy fell to pieces pretty quickly as some commanders settled into the relative comfort of siege warfare while others embarked on looting sprees. Nevertheless, the best description of the initial Boer plan of campaign is perhaps that given by Leo Amery in 1902: "A large

---

* Michael Farrelly even claims that Kruger was forced into agreeing to the invasion by the belligerence
   and enthusiasm of the Boers he sent to the Natal frontier, suggesting that Kruger had completely lost
   control of his men.

force was to invade Northern Natal from west, north and east, crush the little garrisons at Dundee and Ladysmith, and then rapidly overrun Natal down to Durban. Other forces, drawn from the burghers of the western frontier of both States, should capture the British towns strung along the Bechuanaland railway, Mafeking, Vryburg and Kimberley, and should then advance southwards to help the general armed uprising of the Cape Dutch which would follow upon the successes in Natal and the West. With Natal and almost the whole of the Cape Colony in their hands, with 70,000 or 80,000 mounted men in the field, the Boers had every reason to hope that they could hold their own till the European Powers interfered or till England abandoned the contest."[28]

Kruger's ultimatum expired on the 11th October and the massed Boer armies crossed into the British territories of Natal and the Cape Colony* the next morning. Smaller Boer forces also pushed into Bechuanaland, Zululand and Matabeleland in the opening period of the war. As we have seen, the largest Boer commitment was to the invasion of Natal, and so we shall cover that first.

~

Imperial reinforcements had been rushed to Natal, meaning that Sir George White, the newly arrived overall commander in that colony, had about 12,000 men under him by the time of the Boer attack. As we know, Buller had rightly counselled that White should adopt a defensive line along the Tugela River, but the government of Natal, led by Hely-Hutchinson, had insisted that the valuable coal fields in the Dundee area must be defended[29] and thus Penn Symons was to hold the exposed town with the 8th Brigade. It is interesting to take a moment to ponder what might have happened had Buller's advice been taken, and the coal fields of Dundee—as well as the garrison town of Ladysmith—been abandoned. With White's command—including Penn Symons's force—pulled back to the southern bank of the Tugela and dug in to protect the railway crossing at Colenso, it is highly doubtful that the invading Boers could have crossed the river. There is little reason to doubt that White could have held this position while Buller landed at Cape Town and pushed

---

* Though President Steyn hesitated to attack the Cape Colony proper, Boer forces immediately attacked Griqualand West which was part of the colony. Boer units would cross the Orange River to invade the midlands of the Cape Colony in early November.

up the railway line to Bloemfontein with the Army Corps. With no siege of Ladysmith and White's division content to hold the Tugela line, there would have been no imperial defeats at Nicholson's Nek, Colenso or Spion Kop. Similarly, without the need to relieve a beleaguered Ladysmith, the whole Army Corps could have been landed in the Cape and committed to the advance on Bloemfontein rather than being scattered about in penny packets. Concentrated thus, it would have been highly unlikely that the republicans could have checked the imperial advance as they did at Magersfontein.

Though he must take a share of the blame for this strategic blooper, it would be unfair to overly criticize Hely-Hutchinson. He had long warned of the threat of a Boer attack and, indeed, it was only thanks to his insistent protests that the garrison had been reinforced. As we have seen, few others had taken the threat of war seriously and, even as the Boers poured into Natal, the most basic steps were not taken: imperial units had not in any way attempted to defend, or even block, Natal's mountainous borders with the Transvaal and Orange Free State, "no passes were mined, tunnels blocked or bridges blown up. The railway line was left intact".[30] The regimental historian of the Imperial Light Horse recorded this insanity: "The blunders were all part of the tragic lack of preparations for the campaign and the direct results of crying 'Peace! Peace!' when there was no peace."[31] Indeed, so complete was the lack of preparation for war on the British side that it was reckoned there was less than two weeks' worth of coal in the colony,[32] so one can understand the reluctance to abandon the mines. However, with his trademark breezy confidence, Penn Symons* reported that he was confident of holding Dundee with his force of 4,000 and the newly arrived White courteously decided not to overrule him. With Penn Symons's brigade out on a limb at Dundee, the only other significant imperial force in Natal were the 8,000 men under Sir George White, forty miles to the south in Ladysmith. If the federals could shatter or mask these two contingents, all that lay between them and the Indian Ocean were a few small, scattered local units.

The Boers invaded Natal from three points, with Joubert's main force pushing through Laing's Nek in the shadow of Majuba and other, smaller units crossing the border through Botha's pass and Van Reenan's pass. Accurate records were not kept, but their numbers were somewhere between

---

* Penn Symons splendidly declared that he only ever thought of two things: "his duty, and doing it in the spirit of a high-minded, chivalrous gentleman"—so it is difficult to think too ill of him.

21,000 and 30,000 men. With each man being mounted, they also had the huge advantage of mobility. Given that time was of the essence, the Boers advanced at a surprisingly leisurely pace. Much has quite rightly been made of the ponderous way that British units would later operate, but the dawdling advance of Joubert's army was every bit as risible. Every day they wasted was a gift to the hard-pressed British as imperial reinforcements disembarked in Durban, yet it was only on the 17th that the Boers occupied Newcastle[33] - just some fifteen miles from the border. The town had been abandoned but, despite Joubert's pleas, the Boers went on a looting spree, plundering whatever they chose. Despite the fantasies of those who claim that the Boer invasion of Natal was purely defensive, efforts were made to establish a new administrative structure in the occupied areas, with rebels appointed to serve as veldkornets, landdrosts and the like, belying the notion that this would be a short-lived situation. Newcastle would remain under Boer control until May 1900, with the republican invaders even going to the trouble of renaming it Viljoensdorp.[34]

It was not until the 18th October that the Boer invaders of Natal first clashed with imperial units and in so doing gave an early indication of how they intended to fight the war. The main body of the invading Boer army bumped into a small force of colonial light horse units and a small, fast-moving skirmish action ensued. The four-hour-long running battle became known as the 'Carbineer Engagement' and ended when the outnumbered colonials conducted a well-executed and plucky fighting retreat, using their Maxim gun to great effect. Though one remarkable feature of the action was the poor marksmanship of the republicans, it was quickly realized that Lieutenant W. J. Gallwey of the Natal Carbineers was missing. Surgeon-Major Buntine and two others went back under a white flag to try and find the missing officer, but immediately came under fire from the Boers and were forced to abandon their search.[35]

The poor shooting reported by the Natal Carbineers is perhaps explained when one examines Joubert's army in more detail. Many of his men did indeed adhere to the stereotypical image of the Boers: "the sunburnt, tangle-haired, full-bearded farmers, the men of the Bible and the rifle, imbued with the traditions of their own guerrilla warfare. These were perhaps the finest natural warriors upon earth, marksmen, hunters, accustomed to hard fare and a harder couch."[36] But even the Transvaal was changing and, unlike the Boers in the 1880/1 war, many others in Joubert's army were townsmen, unused to a life in the saddle and by no means as formidable an opponent as his backveldt cousin. The army also contained a good number of the Eurotrash troublemakers, described by Milner, not unreasonably, as "disagreeable foreign riff-raff"[37] who had flocked to Kruger's standard. There was a German corps a few hundred strong, as well as a Hollander corps of about 250 and an Irish corps of a similar number. There is no reason to assume that these men were any more at home in the South African veldt than was the rawest British Tommy. Nevertheless, "by all accounts, they were of an astonishingly high heart, convinced that nothing could bar their way to the sea. If the British commanders underrated their opponents, there is ample evidence that the mistake was reciprocal".[38]

One explanation for the sloth-like pace of the Boer advance into Natal was that many Boers were more interested in garnering loot than risking their necks in battle. As well as the plundering of Newcastle, the commandos pillaged their way through the rest of northern Natal, helping themselves to whatever they fancied from each village they captured, looting any farmsteads they came across[39] and driving terrified refugees before them. On the 19th October a republican patrol entered Elandslaagte, chancing upon a packed civilian train as it entered the station. Nevertheless, the Boers disgracefully poured rifle fire into it as the driver made full steam toward Dundee, escaping in the nick of time.[40] Elandslaagte lay about fifteen miles north of Ladysmith, on the railway line to Dundee, and its capture meant that rail and telegraph communication between White's main force and Penn Symons's isolated brigade had been severed.[41]

The following day saw the first major engagement of the war. In the early hours of the 20th October, elements scouting ahead of Lukas Meyer's Vryheid Commando bumped into a standing patrol of the Royal Dublin Fusiliers outside the town of Dundee. The full significance of this encounter was not realized until at first light the men of Penn Symons's brigade saw that the crest line which dominated Dundee was crammed with Boers. Worse still, Meyer's men had dragged two 75mm Creusot field guns up during the night and quickly commenced a bombardment of the British positions. Penn Symons's force was based on the 8th Brigade, commanded by Brigadier J. H. Yule, comprising the 1st Leicesters, 2nd Dublin Fusiliers, 1st Royal Irish Fusiliers and 1st King's Royal Rifle Corps,* three of which included one mounted infantry company. In addition, there was cavalry support in the form of the 18th Hussars, commanded by Lieutenant-Colonel Möller, and three batteries of the Royal Artillery (13th, 67th and 69th) all manning 15-pounders.[42] Facing them, mainly on the ridge formed by Talana and Lennox hills, were about 3,000 Boers under Lukas Meyer, together with the two field guns and a 1-pounder 'pom-pom'.[†] Another commando, about 2,000 strong and commanded by General D. J. E. Erasmus, occupied Impati Hill, a few miles to the north-east of the main body.

Whatever his other alleged faults, Penn Symons reacted to this unexpected attack with dynamism and resolution. While the Hussars were ordered off into cover, the Royal Artillery quickly came into action against the Boer guns and absolutely flayed the ridge line with shrapnel. Indeed so effective was this thunderous bombardment that the republican guns were silenced almost immediately and, what is more, hundreds—perhaps as many as a thousand—of Meyer's men fled in panic.[43] One such chicken-hearted wretch rode as fast as he could for fifty miles and reported Meyer's whole force was destroyed.

Others were made of sterner stuff, however, enduring the shrapnel shells that exploded above them and remaining in place on the rocky ridge line awaiting the inevitable infantry assault. Penn Symons's plan of attack was a simple one: a frontal infantry assault under cover of the fearsome artillery bombardment. The 2nd Dublins, 1st Royal Irish and the 1st King's Royal Rifle Corps formed up to advance, with the Leicesters told off to defend the camp.[44] The assaulting khaki waves[‡] came under effective fire throughout their advance, being forced to ground time after time. The Royal Artillery batteries also limbered up and moved forward to support the attack, their shrapnel raking the hillside like deadly hailstones. Penn Symons was in the very thick of the action, his personal gallantry inspiring his men. Not only did he refuse to dismount amid the fusillade, he insisted on being accompanied

---

* The King's Royal Rifle Corps was often referred to by the abbreviation 'KRRC' but also simply as 'the Rifles' or by their old designation, 'the 60th'. The regiment was unusual in having four battalions at a time when most others had only one or two. All four battalions of the KRRC would ultimately serve in South Africa, though the 4th would only arrive in theatre in December 1901.

† essentially a large-calibre (37mm) machine gun which spat out 1lb shells at an impressive rate of fire

‡ As mentioned earlier, one South African battlefield guide assured me that the British fought in scarlet at Talana. This is quite simply untrue, as was his other, equally ludicrous, claim that Penn Symons' brigade was a "peacekeeping force in the ZAR—just like the UN". Unfortunately, there is little to stop such self-appointed experts peddling this sort of tripe to tourists.

by an orderly carrying a red pennon. "Forward the Rifles, the gallant 60th, and take that hill!"[45] he cried, driving the stalled attack forward once more. The outrageous gallantry of Penn Symons was always going to end in tears and sure enough he took a bullet in the stomach. Even as he was carried away to the rear, he continued to shout encouragement, demanding, "Have they got the Hill? Have they got the Hill?"[46] From then on, it was an infantryman's battle. The ordered lines that had commenced the attack became bunched and confused, but the bravery of the junior officers and NCOs and the dogged determination of the men, kept them moving forward. As the Tommies pushed on through a plantation, the rifle fire from the Boers was so intense that the "green of the trees cut by the bullets fell like autumn leaves in England".[47]

The battle of Talana not only proved the grit and fighting spirit of the much-maligned British Tommy, but also showed the glaring failings in the Boer armies. As if the panic-stricken rout of a large chunk of his force was not enough, Meyer was to find no support from General Erasmus's commando over on Impati Hill.[48] Though their view of the action was blocked by fog, Erasmus had heard the fearful artillery bombardment and knew full well that battle had been joined. Several of his men tried to persuade Erasmus to ride to Meyer's assistance, but the general was having none of it. Deneys Reitz, who served under Erasmus, recalled, "President Kruger's son Caspar, who was serving with us as a private, and who for once in his life showed a little spirit, went up and implored them to march us to the enemy, [Erasmus] curtly ordered him off."[49]

The Boers' individualism and lack of normal military discipline was also a factor. As units of the KRRC forced their way out of the plantation, they dashed across some open ground and reached a stone wall. Amazed to find this obstacle undefended, the riflemen dived into shelter behind it and took the opportunity to sort themselves out and reorganize for the final push. The Dublins had taken quite a mauling and were essentially out of the battle by that point, but the men of the Royal Irish Fusiliers saw the success of the Rifles and followed their lead.

The wall would have offered defending troops a perfect killing zone over the open ground between it and the plantation and Meyer had indeed ordered that it be manned. His burghers, however, had realized that there was no easy avenue of retreat from such a position and had thus flatly refused to line it.[50]

Had they done so, it is likely that the British would have lost the battle of Talana.

As it was, the hiatus at the wall lasted two whole hours. Reinforcements were brought up and units hastily reorganized. The gunners moved their 15-pounders up to yet another position, more suitable to covering the final assault. As the Royal Artillery brought their guns into action once more, the infantrymen surged forward with a roar, the cold steel of their bayonets glinting in the hazy sunshine. This was too much for the republicans and they melted away long before the Tommies could have at them with the bayonet. That part of Meyer's force which occupied neighbouring Lennox Hill had no interest in making a fight of it and also took to their ponies.[51]

Penn Symons would die of his wounds three days later, but his men had won a hard-fought victory, though this is not the way some modern writers describe it. In *Buller's Campaign*, we are told that "the attack was not a success" even though we are then informed, just two lines later, that "The British reached the crest of Talana and the Boers fled", which would seem rather successful. Though the khakis had proved to be more than a match for the Boers, the victory was certainly not as complete as it might have been. The moment Talana Hill was taken the Royal Artillery batteries moved up and unlimbered on Smith's Nek, between Talana and Lennox.[52] This position gave them a perfect view of the retreating Boers as they streamed away in a confused rabble, presenting an ideal chance for the gunners to utterly pulverize them with shrapnel. The fleeing republicans, however, shamelessly put up Red Cross flags[53] to cover their retreat and, assuming an armistice had been declared, the chivalrous British artillery commander ordered his guns to hold their fire.[54] Just as in the 'Carbineer Engagement' a couple of days previously, the Boers were giving an early indication that they felt the accepted rules of war quite simply did not apply to them.

Though General Erasmus's men had been happy to leave Meyer's commando to their fate, they did play a part later in the day. A mounted force—made up of elements of the 18th Hussars and the MI (mounted infantry) companies of the Rifles and the luckless Dublins—had been given vague orders to follow up the retreating Boers. Losing their bearings in the fog, a group of these horsemen ran into Erasmus's men as they came down from Impati Hill,[55] retreated to a farmhouse and were cut off and surrounded. After a firefight of several hours, the Boers brought up a field gun to bombard them,[56] and surrender was the only practical option. Sending the small mounted force off with imprecise orders and no local guides was an unforgivable error.

The battle of Talana Hill was a tactical victory for the British, and perhaps for the republicans a rude awakening that their contempt for the British army was hopelessly misplaced, but it achieved little of strategic value. Such was the advantage the invading Boers enjoyed in terms of numbers and mobility that Brigadier Yule, who had assumed command from the mortally wounded Penn Symons, had little choice but to retreat toward Ladysmith or risk having his brigade cut off.[57]

⌘

The Boer patrols that had seized Elandslaagte on the 19th called for the main body of their force to join them. General Koch* marched his men through the night, arriving on the 20th, the day the battle of Talana Hill was being fought. Koch's force was a powerful one, comprising the Johannesburg Commando, the ZARPs, some 170 Germans under Colonel Schiel, seventy Hollanders and some Free-Staters from Vrede, in all, about 1,250–1,500 men,[58] and three 75mm guns. Koch's troops made themselves comfortable at Elandslaagte, even holding a smoking concert at the village hotel and sportingly inviting some British prisoners to attend.[59]

Down the line in Ladysmith, another Boer patrol was captured by imperial troops and revealed that Elandslaagte had been seized, but the captives were unaware that Koch's main force was now in position.[60] Based on this incomplete intelligence, General White determined to drive off what he thought were only patrol-sized republican forces from Elandslaagte and thus clear the way for Yule to bring the 8th Brigade down from Dundee to Ladysmith. The man White sent to retake the station was General Sir John French,† who had arrived in Ladysmith that day to take command of White's cavalry. French would later command the British Expeditionary Force in the First World War, while his chief of staff, a Major Douglas Haig, was destined to become even more noteworthy.‡ Haig would take over command of the BEF from French in 1915 and lead the British armies to victory in 1918.

---

*   some reports refer to him as General Kock

†   General John Denton Pinkstone French (1852–1925)

‡   or infamous if you prefer

On the morning of the 21st, French advanced north from Ladysmith, travelling along the Newcastle road. Expecting only to have to clear out a small Boer patrol, French's force was not huge: just a squadron each of the 5th Dragoon Guards and the 5th Lancers, five squadrons of the Imperial Light Horse,[61] a battery of the Natal Volunteer Field Artillery and, chuffing along in a train behind them, half a battalion of the Manchester Regiment.[62] It will be recalled that the newly raised Imperial Light Horse had recently been formed from uitlander refugees. After just a couple of weeks of rudimentary training, the unit had been flung into the line,* such was the desperation to stop the Boer invasion. Whatever the troopers of the Imperial Light Horse may have lacked in training, they more than made up for in heart: these men had a score to settle.

The little 7-pounder guns of the Natal Volunteers were brought into action to bombard Elandslaagte. Though the Boers quickly scuttled from the town, their artillery on some nearby hills soon replied to these obsolete field pieces, and a most unequal artillery duel ensued: "Bang came another, and another, and another, right into the heart of the [Natal] battery. The six little guns lay back at their extremist angle, and all barked together in impotent fury. Another shell pitched over them and the officer in command lowered his field-glass in despair as he saw his own shells bursting far short upon the hillside."[63]

But for all the obsolescence of the Natal artillery's guns, the battle of Elandslaagte was a thoroughly modern engagement. Indeed, it flies in the face of the oft-peddled myth that the British commanders were stuck in another era, still fighting the Crimean War. On seeing that the Boers actually occupied the nearby hills in force, and realizing he had not the strength to drive them out, French had his signallers tap into the telegraph line to Ladysmith and request reinforcements.[64] Far from playing the part of a dithering donkey, White reacted with alacrity: the 7th Brigade was loaded onto trains and was soon steaming up the line. Commanded by the dashing Colonel Ian Hamilton†—who would go on to command Allied forces at Gallipoli in

---

* 'A' Squadron ILH had ridden out of the regimental depot at Pietermaritzburg on 13 October and was patrolling south of the Tugela, guarding against an incursion from the Orange Free State. The five squadrons of ILH which fought at Elandslaagte were 'B', 'C', 'D', 'E' and 'F', all of which had arrived in Ladysmith on the 16th October.

† later General Sir Ian Standish Monteith Hamilton GCB GCMG DSO TD (1853–1947)

1915—this comprised the rest of the Manchesters,[*] the 1st Devons and the 2nd Gordon Highlanders. Two batteries of Royal Artillery 15-pounders (the 42nd and 21st) were also sent, along with a small contingent of the Natal Mounted Rifles.[65] By 1530 hours, the reinforcements were in place and ready to attack. Not a few years earlier it would have been impossible to signal for and receive reinforcements in such a timely fashion. The telegraph and the railway were revolutionizing warfare and General French took full advantage.

The Devons and Gordons were the most valuable addition to French's command. These regiments had only just arrived in Natal, shipped in from India,[66] before being rushed up from Durban to Ladysmith. Fresh from fighting Pathans on the North West Frontier, the men of both regiments were bronzed and tough, but in very different ways, the Devons "quiet, business-like, reliable", the Gordon Highlanders "dashing, fiery, brilliant".[67] They were formidable troops, among the best in the British army.

A Gordon Highlander himself—who had been at the débâcle of Majuba—Colonel Hamilton addressed his brigade before the attack, telling them that the Devons would attack the Boers' hilltop position frontally while the Manchesters and Gordons would work their way round to the south and roll up the Boers on their flank. The batteries of the Royal Artillery would support the attack while the regular cavalry of the dragoons and lancers would operate out on the left flank, with the gifted amateurs of the Imperial Light Horse operating on the right. The plan was simple and straightforward—as all such plans should be—and the men cheered their colonel, waving their helmets aloft: "We'll do it, sir! We'll do it!"[68]

As at Talana Hill, the 15-pounders of the Royal Artillery quickly silenced the Boer guns and the infantry pushed forward with grim determination. The Devons, attacking frontally, trudged forward in very open order, completely contrary to both Continental practice at the time, and modern-day myth. Even still, they began to take losses and came to a halt about 800 yards from the Boer positions, diving behind anthills to return fire.[69] Meanwhile the flanking move of the Gordons and Manchesters was hampered by a series of fence lines and broken ground.

Boer sharpshooters fired on the advancing troops from a farmhouse and casualties began to mount. A storm suddenly broke over the battlefield and the Germans under Colonel Schiel gallantly attempted a counter-attack. This

---

[*] the 1st Manchester Regiment had been rushed to Natal from Gibraltar, arriving just before the invasion

was broken up by the Imperial Light Horse, the Germans being shot down almost to a man.

Colonel Hamilton was on hand to keep the attack moving, shouting and encouraging his men forward. The effect was electric. The Gordons and Manchesters fixed bayonets and surged forwards in great style, cheering and roaring as they came. Eager for his men to play their part, the commander of the Imperial Light Horse requested permission to join the attack. French acceded and the ILH troopers dismounted and charged up the hillside alongside the regular troops. As at Talana Hill, it was all too much for the Boers. Many who had been content to shoot at the attacking troops until they were fifteen yards away suddenly threw up their hands and demanded quarter. Colonel Hamilton and his officers ensured that these men were spared, a tribute to the discipline and professionalism of the imperial troops.[70]

Yet again, the republicans used their favourite white-flag trick. A flag of surrender was raised and the British troops cheered their victory, waving their rifles and helmets in the air. Men were gathered around the captured Boer guns, enjoying the thrill of their achievement when suddenly a group of about fifty Boers, including General Koch himself,[71] opened fire on the celebrating troops, emptying their magazines into them. Such was the confusion caused by this filthy trick that the British were driven off the summit. Once more the ubiquitous Colonel Hamilton was on hand to rally the waverers, and General French, who had moved up with the advancing Devons, was there to drive the men back into the fight. A confused mass of Manchesters, Gordons, Devons and Imperial Light Horse men surged back up the hill, shouting, "Majuba! Majuba!" Many Boers had taken advantage of the lull to flee, while those who had stayed quickly surrendered once again. It was a dirty, deceitful trick and it is to the credit of the imperial troops that they did not bayonet every prisoner they took. Again, the imperial troops celebrated a hard-fought win, with the pipers of the Gordon Highlanders striking up with 'Cock of the North'.[72]

By now it was almost dark, yet there was still time for a final act. The 5th Dragoons and 5th Lancers had been waiting for their moment all afternoon and were finally pitched into the fight to attack the routing Boers. Charging through the fleeing rabble, the cavalrymen cut, thrust and skewered for a frenzied few minutes. It was a devastating attack and one which the Boers would never forgive nor forget, vowing to kill any lancer they took prisoner after that day.[73]

The outrage felt by the Boers[74] and their supporters in Europe at this cavalry charge is flabbergasting. Every major army deployed cavalry and the sabre and lance had been accepted weapons of war all over the world for centuries. The republicans, however, seemed to think they had the right to shoot at advancing troops for hours on end then demand individual quarter as soon their life was endangered. Furthermore, their outrage came after their own white-flag trick. At the height of the cavalry charge itself, one burgher furiously waved the Lancers away from a group of tents he claimed to be a hospital. When the troopers obeyed and rode past, he opened fire on them with a revolver. Luckily, an officer saw this and shot the man dead.[75] The terror-stricken Boers fled in all directions, one fellow running all the way to Dundee, while two others made it all the way to Pretoria. Their tales of the thrashing caused such panic in the capital that they were locked up until they calmed down a little.[76]

Elandslaagte was a crushing British victory, more conclusive than the one at Talana Hill the day before. The newly formed Imperial Light Horse had performed with extreme valour and was delighted in their part in cutting up their arch enemies of the Johannesburg Commando. The lighthorsemen may have lost their colonel but they won two Victoria Crosses, their fighting spirit impressing even the doughty men of the Gordon Highlanders: "On the day after the battle the ILH reached camp weary and worn and dismounted alongside the Gordons' lines as that Regiment was on the point of drawing a beer ration. Spontaneously as each Gordon received his measure he carried it across and gave it to a comrade in the ILH—a generous self-denying tribute."

Bill Nasson in *The War for South Africa* does not trouble himself to relate General Koch's despicable misuse of the white flag and does his best to downplay the British victory, rather oddly claiming that the result was "mixed" and the British were "hardly unscathed".[77] It would be difficult to imagine an infantry assault where the attackers emerged unscathed, and the result was anything but mixed. Once more the pluck, determination and fighting spirit of the imperial troops had been too much for the federals and their hyperbolic nonsense about driving the British into the sea had been exposed for the hot air it was. Even if present-day historians refuse to accept this, Ben Viljoen—who, unlike Nasson, fought at Elandslaagte with the Johannesburg Commando—described the action as a "splendid success" for the British.[78] Viljoen also described how the defeat had a "disastrous moral effect" on the shattered Johannesburg Commando, and that thirty of the survivors simply refused to fight any more and were sent back home.[79] Boer General Joubert also saw these opening battles for what they were: in an official communiqué to Kruger, Joubert described Elandslaagte as "a total defeat as great as has ever yet befallen the Afrikaner volk".[80]

࿇

Though much equipment and regimental paraphernalia was left behind, Yule extracted his isolated command from Dundee with a fair degree of aplomb. Leaving the tent encampment intact to fool the Boers, the 8th Brigade set off in the evening of the 22nd, embarking on a sixty-four-mile roundabout route to Ladysmith through incessant rain and heavy, clinging mud. Yule was lucky to have the services of Colonel Dartnell of the Natal Police who knew the territory like the back of his hand and guided the battered 8th Brigade along half-forgotten back roads. Chastened by the lesson they had been given at Talana Hill, the federals were none too keen to approach Dundee too closely.[81] By the time a Boer patrol realized that the bird had flown and Erasmus's commando moved in to occupy the town, Yule's command was ten miles away, but still strung out and an easy target. Fortunately, the indiscipline of the Boers played a role once more: they proved far more interested in rampaging through the streets of Dundee on a looting binge than following up the retreating British troops.[82] "There was no attempt at exercising any control over the Burghers, who ran riot in the town and camp, drinking, plundering and wrecking. Even the hospital failed to escape the attention of the looters. The orgy went on all night and next morning. In order to put an end to it, Erasmus ordered all spirituous liquors in the town to be destroyed."[83]

Deneys Reitz took part in this lawless free-for-all, gleefully recalling: "1,500 men were whooping through the streets and behaving in a very undisciplined manner. Officers tried to stem the rush but we were not to be denied, and we plundered shops and dwelling houses … the joy of ransacking other people's property is hard to resist."[84]

To cover Yule's approach, troops from Ladysmith sallied out to fight a small but successful action at Rietfontein on the 24th October. The brunt of the fighting was borne by the Gloucesters and Imperial Light Horse, and a Free

State commando was held off long enough to allow Yule's men to slip past. Though they were hungry and exhausted, Yule's force made it safely into Ladysmith at lunchtime that day. It was a brilliantly conducted extraction of a force which should never have been left out on a limb in the first place, but none the less the 8th Brigade was saved.[85]

Some latter-day writers make the remarkable claim that Yule left the invasions plans for the Transvaal and Orange Free State behind in Dundee.[86] While he certainly left behind code books, no such invasion plans ever existed,[87] so this cannot be the case.* Pakenham mentions that Yule left behind his copy of *Military Notes on the Dutch Republics of South Africa*[88] but this, as we know, was purely an intelligence briefing and not a set of invasion plans. It would no doubt have been seized upon by the busy propaganda machine of the Boers, however, and it is probable that this is the origin of this wild claim.

🍙

Contrary to the myth, it would seem that the British had started the war reasonably well: despite being substantially outnumbered and woefully unprepared, their troops had yet to lose a battle. The pluck and grit of the Tommies had proved too much for the invaders when it came to set-piece actions and even the most delusional of Boers must have begun to realize that the war might not be a picnic after all. Nevertheless, and displaying a remarkable disregard for reality, one modern writer claims that the republicans were "jubilant" after Talana Hill and Elandslaagte, dismissing the Boer defeats by muttering that retreating was "their usual tactic".[89] Despite this nonsensical claim, the opening weeks were far from being a string of Boer victories as is generally portrayed. A somewhat less-than-jubilant General Joubert wrote to the state secretary in Pretoria on the 27th October to say: "Our case is serious. We are now even as Napoleon in the time in Moscow."[90]

Though they had been unable to win any tactical victories and for all the despondency of their commander, Joubert's invasion force still enjoyed a considerable strategic advantage due to its sheer weight of numbers and superior mobility. Though White had managed to consolidate his forces in Ladysmith, Joubert's commandos were able to roam across northern Natal

---

* The 1904 Royal Commission into the war highlighted this failing as one of its primary findings: quite simply, there was no plan in place to invade the two Boer republics.

at will and the encirclement of Ladysmith was a racing certainty. If he could bottle up White's force in that town, there was very little standing between the Boers and sea: aside from White's division, there were just 2,300 other imperial troops in all of the rest of Natal, of which only 300 were mounted.[91]

By the 29th October, Boer laagers surrounded Ladysmith. They had cut the town's water supply and were emplacing their guns on Pepworth Hill, about 7,000 yards from the town centre.[92] The Boers quizzically named one of these siege guns 'Franchise', ridiculing the uitlanders for their aspirations.[93] Sir George White faced an impossible decision: whether to stay on the defensive in Ladysmith and allow his division to be cut off entirely, or to sally out and force a general action, an action that might shatter Joubert's resolve after the two recent republican defeats. Though outnumbered, White chose the latter, perhaps reasoning that one more decisive victory on the scale of Elandslaagte might well have seen the brittle Boer morale shatter completely.

Fought on Monday, the 30th October, the action is known variously as the battle of Ladysmith, the battle of Nicholson's Nek or—more accurately— 'Mournful Monday'. In contrast to Talana Hill and Elandslaagte, the plan of attack was overly complicated, the general idea being that the 8th Brigade, recently arrived from Dundee and now commanded by Colonel Geoffrey Grimwood,[94] would storm Boer positions on Long Hill, while the 7th Brigade under Hamilton would create a diversion. Another force would make a night march on Nicholson's Nek and from there engage the Boers as they, or so it was hoped, retreated from Long Hill in panic and disorder.

The plan started to go wrong almost from the start. The republicans had already retreated from Long Hill so Grimwood's men took it without a fight, but in the confusion got separated from their artillery.[95] They came under heavy enfilading fire from other Boer positions, however, and French had to move his cavalry up in support. Colonel Hamilton's brigade was also sucked into this now-pointless engagement. Boer artillery on Pepworth Hill began to bombard both British positions and the town of Ladysmith. The 42nd and 67th batteries of the Royal Artillery quickly came into action against the Boer guns, rapidly silencing them and causing losses among the gun crews. Deneys Reitz left his commando to look for his brother who was serving in the Boer artillery and described the scene: "six or seven dead artillery men, some horribly mutilated, were laid out on a square of canvas to which they had been carried from above, and Ferdinand Holz, the German military doctor, was attending to a number of wounded also brought down from the emplacements … I found my brother, and the surviving artillerymen, crouching behind the wall, unable to serve their guns under the storm that was lashing the position … more dead lay about and wounded men were sheltering with the rest in the lee of the parapet."[96]

When it was realized that there was nothing to be gained from the infantry staying in place on Long Hill, it was decided to pull them back to Ladysmith. Though Hamilton's brigade was extracted without incident, some reports claim that the retreat of Grimwood's brigade threatened to become a rout as the Boers tore into them with rifle and artillery fire. One eyewitness disagreed, claiming that the retreating men were "fighting grimly, not hastening a step … the cool steadiness of the men was magnificent, and though the Boers fired rapidly, and their machine cannon made a tremendous row, the British soldiers took matters very leisurely".[97]

Either way, the infantry could be thankful for the gallantry of the Royal Artillery: the 13th and 21st batteries covered the retreat, drawing the Boer fire and withdrawing in stages through the smoke and dust. In the middle of the action a Royal Navy contingent* arrived by train at Ladysmith and immediately brought their long-range guns into action, once more silencing the Boer artillery on Pepworth Hill.[98] Joubert is said to have watched the retreat but refused to have ordered a pursuit, thereby missing a chance to inflict a telling blow on the British.[99] When asked why, the old man pontificated, "When God holds out a finger, don't take the whole hand." Joubert had about 15,000 men at his disposal and though perhaps humane, his decision not to pursue was arguably the biggest mistake of the campaign.†

Though the main British forces had thus successfully withdrawn to Ladysmith, the whole thing had been a confused mess, a "scrambling, inconsequential, unsatisfactory action".[100] The official history of the Imperial Light Horse stated that "the British had been outmanoeuvred by the tactics and the mobility of their opponents—*but not defeated*", though this would be putting the best possible gloss on the action. Nevertheless, and thanks entirely

---

* The Naval Brigade consisted of two 4.7-inch guns, four 12-pounders and about 280 men of the HMS *Powerful*, the force being under the command of Captain the Honourable Lambton.

† Joubert was not the only Boer commander to come out of the battle badly: Lukas (also Lucas) Meyer, who had previously failed so miserably at Talana Hill, suffered a breakdown and retired to Pretoria to recover. Louis Botha took over his duties until he returned.

to Joubert's inexplicable decision, no irreparable harm had been done.

Unfortunately, the smaller, secondary force which had been tasked to take Nicholson's Nek fared far worse. The column sent to seize Nicholson's Nek was about a thousand strong,[101] commanded by Colonel Carleton and made up of elements of both the Gloucester Regiment and the Royal Irish Fusiliers. They were supported by No. 10 Mountain Battery of the Royal Artillery,[102] which operated dismantleable 2.5-inch screw guns carried by mules. The mountain battery had only arrived in Ladysmith the previous day after a long sea and rail journey and the irascible mules were in no mood to play the game. During the night march to the position the witless beasts panicked, stampeding off into the night carrying the precious mountain guns, a large chunk of the spare rifle ammunition and, worst of all, all the signalling apparatus.

Daybreak revealed that the night march had stopped well short of the desired location with Carleton's men now overlooked by the Boers. Undeterred, the infantrymen quickly began to build sangars out of rock before the inevitable Boer attack commenced.[103] One by one the sangars were taken and the troops driven back. For nine and a half hours, Carleton's men clung on, their ammunition pouches empty and reduced to scavenging cartridges from their dead comrades.[104] The Boers showed impressive field craft and marksmanship as they stalked and sniped their way forward. But the real turning point of the battle was not Boer brilliance but British misfortune and their sense of honour. One unit of the Gloucesters, divorced from the main body, became convinced they were cut off and that the rest of the force had retreated to Ladysmith. Considering they had fought a good fight and were wholly surrounded, this small unit raised a white flag. The Boers stood up to accept the surrender, waving their hats in acknowledgement.[105] The rest of the British force—that is, the vast majority of it—was stunned into inaction by this strange turn of events. Unlike the republicans at Elandslaagte, the British troops could not bring themselves to open fire on such easy targets presented to them. Confusion reigned, with many of his officers imploring Carleton not to recognize the surrender. Some even broke their swords in indignation and disgust. But Carleton was a decent, honourable man and the white flag had forced his hand. He ordered his bugler to sound the surrender and around 900 British troops[106] were marched off into captivity. It was the biggest British capitulation since the Napoleonic Wars.

❧

Though much is made of the defeats of Black Week, the loss at Nicholson's Nek was undoubtedly a more serious reverse for the British: indeed, it was arguably their worst defeat of the war. Few could believe that troops who had fought so brilliantly at Elandslaagte and Talana could suddenly be on the wrong end of such a caning, and much was made of the tactical superiority of the Boers during their attack on Carleton's column. This would be to overstate matters though: there was no evidence of this tactical superiority ten days earlier and the republicans were fortunate that Carleton lost his artillery under such bizarre circumstances. When White's over-complex plan unravelled, Carleton's men were left out on a limb, fighting a very different action from what they had expected. Christiaan de Wet claims that the position was stormed by only 200 Boers,[107] but this is patently untrue and typical of the exaggeration peddled in such memoirs. A British doctor who was captured was told by his captors that the Boers had heard Carleton's men in the night and by the time day broke, there were 2,000 Boers closely investing the British positions.[108] Other sources confirm that, though only 1,000 Boers took part in the close fighting, 4,000 in all were involved, meaning they actually outnumbered Carleton's isolated force fourfold.[109] Furthermore, the Boers by no means defeated his whole force, but were granted their victory due to British respect for the white flag.*

Launching the twin battles of the 30th October was a serious error by White. Perhaps he was emboldened by the recent victories and confident of delivering a knockout blow. There can be little doubt that he felt the need to do something before the Boer net closed around Ladysmith: to have sat back and done nothing would have been equally unforgiveable. But throwing outnumbered and in many cases newly arrived troops (and mules) into a complicated series of coordinated night marches and attacks was a major blunder. Ever a gentleman, however, General White sent a dispatch in which he took all the blame for the fiasco, thus disarming the usual tirade of criticism in the British press.[110]

Lieutenant-Colonel Sir Henry Rawlinson, who served on White's staff and had counselled against such a convoluted operation, wrote in his diary: "This has not been a successful day. As a matter of fact we were so greatly

---

* though it is of course debateable how much longer the remainder of Carleton's force could have held on

outnumbered that it would have been impossible for us to hope for success in the open field against a mounted and tactically very mobile force"[111] The official history of the Imperial Light Horse takes a similar line: "It was primarily an encounter between 15,000 riflemen [Joubert's Boers] opposed to some 8,000 infantry, supported by some 2,500 cavalry and two brigades of Field Artillery. The issue should never have been in doubt. In an action of this nature, one mounted man is calculated to equal three infantrymen."[112] Deneys Reitz, on the other hand, saw it as an opportunity lost, rather than a stunning victory: "With that lack of vision that marred most of our doings in the early stages, we hailed the Ladysmith battle as a great victory, and we acted as if we had a broken and defeated enemy before us. It certainly was a notable success, but in the end it would have been better for us had the British smashed our line that day, for our leaders would then have followed a better plan of campaign than sitting down to a prolonged and ruinous siege … Had the Boers made for the coast, instead of tying up their horsemen around towns that were of no value to them, the outcome of the war might have been different, but they sacrificed their one great advantage of superior mobility … at a time when our only salvation lay in pushing for the sea."[113]

With the victory at Nicholson's Nek, the Boers had finally bested a British force. In truth, they were gifted the victory as, with his whole force back in Ladysmith and British reinforcements arriving in Durban every week, there was no pressing reason for General White to have taken the offensive. As Deneys Reitz mentioned, rather than screening Ladysmith and pushing on, Joubert's army now settled into a pointless siege, though not before General French had left the town on the last train out on the 2nd November.*

On the 9th November the Boer bombardment was much heavier than usual and their long-range guns absolutely hammered Ladysmith throughout the morning.[114] This barrage was followed up by the first Boer attempt to assault British positions on the southern portion of perimeter. The sector was manned by the regulars of the Manchester Regiment and the 1st Battalion

---

* General French's and Major Haig's train came under heavy fire from the Boers as they tried to complete their encirclement. An unexploded 75mm shell was later found lodged in Haig's kitbag. French had been ordered to leave the town so as to command the Cavalry Division then forming in the Cape.

of the King's Royal Rifle Corps* who opened up on the attackers at around 800 yards. As one commentator noted, "The Boer, however, save when the odds are all in his favour, is not, in spite of his considerable personal bravery, at his best in attack." Sure enough, the assaults were broken up and driven off without difficulty.[115]

Whatever his alleged faults, the British Tommy has always been stubborn, steady, bloody-minded and formidable in defence. The attacking republicans learned the hard way that occupying trenches and sniping from hilltops is a whole lot easier than advancing over open ground and storming prepared positions, and they suffered heavily. Though this cannot be verified and is probably an exaggeration, several hundred were reported killed against British losses for the day of just thirty killed and wounded. It is certainly infeasible that their losses were not "very much more severe" than those of the defending Tommies. To make matters worse many burghers simply decided not to bother joining the attack in the first place,[116] leading to the usual recriminations and accusations. One again, the federals had proved that they were a highly individualistic bunch with little or no semblance of military discipline. It is possible to get away with this when fighting from defensive positions, but this failing is cruelly exposed when troops are called upon to advance to contact. The battle of the 9th November was a serious defeat for the republicans, but despite suffering perhaps hundreds of casualties, this action is virtually unknown and is not even accorded a name.

After the bloody nose his men had been given on the 9th, Joubert was more content than ever to starve Ladysmith into submission. Not everyone agreed with this policy of inactivity and after much pleading, Louis Botha was given permission to lead a force of around 3,500 men toward Durban. These men appear to have been more interested in plunder than fighting, side-stepping the small imperial garrison of Estcourt and pushing south toward Nottingham Road, a small town just forty miles from Pietermaritzburg. The wanton destruction visited on Natal by this force will be covered elsewhere, so we shall concern ourselves here only with their military actions. The raiders made a half-hearted attempt at taking British-held Mooi River before themselves being attacked at Willow Grange. Fought in the early hours of the 23rd November 1899, the battle of Willow Grange was little more than a confused, inconclusive skirmish, but none the less marked the

---

* most accounts of the action still refer to the KRRC by their old name of the 60th Rifles

high-water mark of the Boer invasion of Natal.* Planned as a night attack by the West Yorks and East Surreys[117] against about 2,000 Boers[118] holding positions near Estcourt, General Hildyard's men were led to their start lines by a Mr Chapmen, a local farmer who thus had more reason than most to want to be rid of the invaders.[119] Despite this local knowledge, the night-time action was ill-coordinated and, besides driving a Boer picket from a hilltop, achieved little. When dawn broke, the imperial forces found themselves in the unpleasant position of being under Boer artillery fire they were unable to answer. General Hildyard thus had little choice but to pull his men back.

Willow Grange was a most rare occurrence, for though the imperial forces sustained a tactical defeat, they won a rather surprising strategic victory, the exact opposite of what had happened in some of the earlier engagements in Natal. The numbers involved on either side were small and casualties insignificant but the attack seemed to have made the leaden General Joubert even more nervous than usual. The ultra-cautious commandant greatly feared that Botha's raiding force would soon be cut off and therefore ordered his men back north of the Tugela to dig themselves in to await the inevitable British counter-stroke. During this period Joubert had also suffered a serious fall from his horse and effective command of the Tugela line passed to Louis Botha.[120] The Natal front thus stagnated for a couple of weeks, so we shall turn our attention elsewhere.

Rhodesia and Bechuanaland were threatened by a Boer force of about 1,300 strong under Commandant van Rensburg and another of about 600 strong under Assistant-Commandant General Grobelaar. One of Kruger's grandsons, Veldkornet Sarel Eloff, served under van Rensburg, as did a German artillery expert named von Dalwig.[121] For most of October, van Rensburg remained static, fooled into thinking the British force on the other side of the Limpopo was too strong for him to risk taking the offensive. In reality, imperial forces in the region were woefully weak. As war loomed, the now-famous Colonel Baden-Powell had been sent to the region to raise two irregular regiments: the Protectorate regiment in Bechuanaland and the Rhodesia regiment in

---

* Willow Grange was also noteworthy as the brother of Percy Fitzpatrick, uitlander leader and later the author of *Jock of the Bushveld*, was killed there while serving in the Imperial Light Horse.

Bulawayo. It had been a difficult task as good men did not want to lose their jobs on the off-chance of war, so the regiments initially attracted 'loafers and wasters'.[122] When the Protectorate regiment's 447 soldiers were listed by their previous profession, they included "26 farmworkers, 16 carpenters, 16 decorators, 18 diggers, 12 engine drivers, 11 storemen, 12 masons, 10 electrical engineers; and among the others 2 jockeys, 2 vets, 1 tripe dresser, 1 male nurse, 1 florist, 1 hair dresser, 1 riding master and several musicians".[123]

In the weeks before the Boer invasion, Baden-Powell moved the Protectorate regiment under Lieutenant-Colonel Hore into Mafeking, while the Rhodesia regiment under Lieutenant-Colonel Plumer* was tasked with patrolling the frontier in such a manner as to mislead the Boers into believing his force was far greater than it actually was. When the war began the only troops standing between the federals and an invasion of Rhodesia were the 450 men of the recently Rhodesia regiment. It is testimony to Plumer's constant, aggressive patrolling that the Boers were fooled into thinking he actually had 1,400 men under his command. So successful was this deception that it was not until the 2nd November that Grobelaar finally managed to spur van Rensburg into action. Van Rensberg's and Grobelaar's combined forces of just under 2,000 men struck over the border into Rhodesia, capturing a small convoy of wagons at Bryce's Store. A simultaneous attack on the squadron of the Rhodesian regiment holding Rhodes's Drift was less successful.[124] Under the command of Colonel Jack Spreckley†, the Rhodesians held off the invaders until nightfall before withdrawing in good order to Tuli. Perhaps the bloody nose at Rhodes's Drift had been too much for them but, either way, the bickering, indecisive republican commanders entrenched their forces at Bryce's Store[125] with van Rensberg showing little resolution to do much else. Grobelaar was by far the more martial of the two and submitted a plan to Pretoria which involved the destruction of Plumer's Rhodesia regiment and raids against Bulawayo and the railway. With the invasions of Natal and Cape Colony stalling in the face of British reinforcements, this aggressive, daring plan was rejected.

---

*   Later Field Marshal Herbert Charles Onslow Plumer, 1st Viscount Plumer GCB, GCMG, GCVO, GBE (1857–1932). Plumer had served with distinction in the Matabele War of 1896 and would go on to command the British Second Army in the First World War.

†   Colonel Jack Spreckley was one of the original Rhodesian Pioneers

Boer forces of between 6,000 and 8,000* under Piet Cronjé marched against Mafeking, just eight miles over the border. Cronjé's force was supported by ten field pieces[126] with the dashing General de la Rey marching with him.[127] Indeed, in what is generally regarded to be the first action of the war, de la Rey captured an armoured train at Kraipan, thirty-five miles south of Mafeking. Named the *Mosquito*, this train had been bringing two more precious guns to Mafeking but was halted by a torn-up track, ambushed and surrounded.[128] Though outnumbered and with no hope of relief, the fifteen-man crew of the train only surrendered after an hour when nine of them, including their commander, had been seriously wounded.[129] General de la Rey also captured the town of Vryburg to the south of Mafeking. Such was the enthusiasm with which the Afrikaans residents of the town greeted de la Rey's men that the British commander, Assistant-Commissioner Scott, shot himself in shame.[130] De la Rey then read a proclamation declaring that "the Republican flag was flying over all the land north of the Orange River and would continue to fly there for ever".[131] This would indicate that the annexations of Bechuanaland and Rhodesia were part of the plan. Indeed, Conan-Doyle, who served in the conflict, remarked, "The policy of the instant annexation of all territories invaded was habitually carried out by the enemy, with the idea that British subjects who joined them would in this way be shielded from the consequences of treason."[132]

The garrison of Mafeking was—as every school boy knows—commanded by Colonel Baden-Powell himself. He had at his disposal fewer than 1,000 auxiliaries and two dozen regular soldiers.[133] As well as the aforementioned Protectorate regiment, the garrison included a mixed force of colonial police units and a hastily raised militia.† The artillery consisted of just four obsolete muzzle-loading 7-pounders and a few machine guns. It was still as though no one in the Cape was ready to accept the reality of war and hence a battery of 12-pounders remained in storage in Cape Town despite Baden-Powell's pleas for guns.[134] Trains full of refugees were departing the town but the Cape authorities refused to pay their fares.[135]

The investment of Mafeking began on the 14th October with Baden-Powell

---

* The Boers failed to keep accurate records throughout the war, so this figure is at best an educated guess. Baden-Powell's report to Lord Roberts gave the figure as 8,000 while the *Times Official History of the War* gives 6,750.

† To these troops, Baden-Powell would later controversially add the 'Black Watch': some 700 Africans were armed during the siege.

noting a "smartly fought little engagement" on the same day. Supported by an armoured train, elements of the Protectorate regiment clashed with Boer units in a fairly confused skirmish that halted a republican attack on the town. Once again, the Boers ignored the Red Cross flag and opened fire on British stretcher bearers who were trying to attend to the wounded.[136] The belligerence and bravery of the Protectorate regiment seemed to come as a shock to the federals[137] who had perhaps been expecting to stroll into Mafeking and who showed little of their famed martial prowess during the battle. The *London Gazette* laconically reported "the moral effect of this blow had a very important bearing on subsequent encounters with the Boers".[138] Indeed, the timidity of the republican attackers baffled many, with one witness recalling that "had the Boers pushed home their attack in the first instance, nothing could have stopped them from riding straight into the town". Baden-Powell was more sanguine and, knowing his enemy's preferred way of fighting, informed his garrison, "The Boers will never come on and storm a position. They cannot possibly get in or even near the place if everyone sticks to his post and shoots straight."[139] As it was, both Cronjé and Baden-Powell seemed happy to settle down for a long siege.

Many latter-day critics of Baden-Powell have claimed it was pointless to defend Mafeking and that he exaggerated the numbers of Boers he tied down during the long siege. This is unreasonable criticism. Not only was Mafeking chock-a-block with supplies but it was the administrative centre for the Bechuanaland Protectorate and the north-eastern region of the Cape Colony; it also contained valuable railway stock.[140] As importantly, the administrator of Rhodesia, Sir Arthur Lawley, warned that if Mafeking was lost, the tribes of northern Bechuanaland and the Matabele would rise in rebellion. As if not justification enough, every day that several thousand Boers wasted their time at Mafeking was a day they were not following the plan of striking for the Cape. Though the Boer numbers involved in the siege dropped in later months, to assign over 6,000 men to capturing Mafeking—and at the most important time of their campaign—showed the value the Boers placed on the town.

Since the publication of Pakenham's *The Boer War* in 1979, it has also become fashionable to blame Baden-Powell for all the suffering endured by the blacks during the siege. Pakenham made a few of his trademark wild, sensational and poorly researched claims that essentially accused Baden-Powell of starving the town's blacks to enable the whites to live it up. In fact, the blacks who suffered were non-local refugees* recently arrived from the Transvaal and who were shunned by those local Africans able to supplement their diets with their crops and cattle.[141] Muddling up local Africans and refugees, Pakenham claims that Baden-Powell allowed these 2,000 black refugees to go without free food rations altogether, which is quite simply untrue† and was comprehensively refuted by Tim Jeal in his magisterial 1989 biography of Baden-Powell. It is certainly true that Baden-Powell was forced to make some tough decisions and prioritized "useful mouths" over "useless mouths" but even those on a full ration suffered terribly and this distinction had little to do with racism; a young Sol Plaatje,‡ for example, lived through the siege before going on to become a founding father of the ANC. Though African, his employment as a court interpreter meant that he received a full ration.[142] Indeed, so brilliantly does Jeal torpedo Pakenham's farrago of misquotes, misunderstandings, half-truths, untruths and fallacious allegations that this nasty little myth should be put to bed once and for all. We shall allow the impressive Mr Jeal to have the final word on the subject: "Baden-Powell's treatment of the blacks in Mafeking does not seem particularly reprehensible, and the more extreme charges against him are unfounded."[143]

Cronjé began shelling the town on the morning of the 16th October, initially with two 12-pounders that were well out of range of the garrison's little 7-pounders. Despite claims that the Boers did not consider Mafeking of any importance, when Cronjé requested additional heavy artillery to subdue the garrison, he was assigned one of the Transvaal's four Creusot 'Long Tom' guns. This piece arrived on the 23rd and joined the bombardment. The shelling of Mafeking was a terror tactic, pure and simple: Cronjé reckoned that it would only take a few civilian deaths to persuade the townspeople to urge Baden-Powell to surrender.[144] When a traitorous pro-Boer Briton called Everitt entered the town under a white flag and invited Baden-Powel to surrender to "avoid further bloodshed", the indomitable colonel asked him

---

* These poor devils had fled from the Boers and were now besieged by the Boers in a war started by the Boers, so it is surely reasonable to suggest that the republicans should bear more than a little responsibility for their suffering.

† soup kitchens were established to dispense free rations to them, and 1,300 out of the 2,000 given employment

‡ Solomon Tshekisho Plaatje (1876–19 June 1932). Highly talented linguist and intellectual, Plaatje was a founder member and first general-secretary of the South African Native National Congress (SANNC), the forerunner to the ANC.

what he was talking about as the only blood shed to date had been a dead chicken and a wounded donkey.[145] With admirable panache, he then invited Everitt for lunch.

Another republican attack on the town was made on the 25th October, but was driven off with ease.[146] The advancing Boers came under fire at the extreme range of 2,000 yards, decided it wasn't to their liking and retreated.[147] The next day another Boer attack was cancelled when it started to rain, thus making the ground "too slippery for military operations".[148] In stark contrast, on the 27th October, a night raid by 'D' Squadron of the Protectorate regiment on Boer trenches was a marked success.[149] The troopers—who only weeks before had been florists, tripe-dressers and riding masters—stalked though the darkness toward the republican positions unseen then leapt in to butcher them with their bayonets. Suddenly set upon by cold steel in the middle of the night, no mercy was shown to the terrified Boers: in a few horrifying minutes sixty republicans were either killed or wounded.[150] The raid commander* was the first into the trenches and killed four Boers with his sword, one of whom he decapitated with a single swing.[151] His valour earned him a VC.[152]

Cannon Kop was the southernmost point of the British defensive perimeter around Mafeking. It was a small, rocky hillock which, though insignificant in itself, overlooked the town, meaning its loss would have been devastating for the defenders. The stony ground had made it impossible to dig proper trenches, so ramparts had been built instead. A photograph taken in 1899 shows stone parapets topped with sandbags and a steel windmill, perhaps forty feet tall and devoid of its fan, which served as a lookout post.[153] The position was held by forty-five men of the British South Africa Police† and half a dozen of the Protectorate regiment. The only protection from artillery fire was a slit trench some forty yards back from the summit and a small scrape dug between two rocks where the BSAP colonel sheltered. When under fire all the men—except their commander and the man up in the lookout tower—were held back in the slit trench for safety. For several days Boer artillery had steadily flayed the hill but, at 0430 hours on the 31st October, five Boer guns opened up on it with a vengeance. The BSAP lookout bravely stayed at his post throughout, his tunic torn with shell splinters and

---

* Captain (later Brigadier) Charles Fitzclarence (1865–1914) whose courage and penchant for aggressive raiding during the siege earned him the sobriquet 'The Demon of Mafeking'

† originally raised to escort the Pioneer Column in 1890, the BSAP was the mounted police force of Rhodesia

his telescope shattered. The observing Boers who witnessed it remarked that this courageous fellow looked like a monkey in a tree, and thus christened the Cannon Kop defences 'Babiaan's Fort' or Baboon's Fort. The half-hour bombardment covered the advance of up to 1,000 Boers[154] who approached "in a great half moon".[155] When the attackers were about 300 yards away—and with the artillery barrage still under way—the stalwart BSAP troopers were called out of their slit trench to man the ramparts. Shrapnel splintered over the hilltop but the defenders unleashed a furious fusillade into the Boers. Incredibly, this tiny group managed to halt the republican assault, sending them to ground. Baden-Powell quickly moved up two of his 7-pounders to support the BSAP detachment and these guns began to lob shells into the stalled, huddled mass. After only a couple of minutes, "the Boers rose en masse out of the long grass, appeared for a moment to hesitate … and then turned and fled towards their horses".[156] Completely disregarded by both Pakenham and Nasson,* an attack by 1,000 burghers supported by five field guns had been driven off by just fifty imperial troopers.[157] It is curious why British defeats like Colenso or Magersfontein are invariably described as humiliations, but the inability of the Boers to storm Cannon Kop is simply brushed under the carpet; presumably a Boer defeat, despite outnumbering their opponent twentyfold, does not warrant a mention or qualify as a humiliation. (One recurring theme throughout modern histories of the conflict is that only the imperial forces were capable of being humiliated.) But more than just the pluck of the BSAP, the defeat had been due to the utter disinclination of the assaulting Boers to display any determination or fighting spirit. As *The Times History of the War in South Africa* recorded: "The achievement of the Police was as notable for its good fortune as its valour; for nothing could have saved them from an enemy but half as resolute as themselves." A contemporary Dutch report entitled '*Die Beleg van Mafeking*' agreed, laying the blame for the defeat on a "lack of stimulation from Veld-Kornet Martins and other Potchefstroom officers to fulfil the task".[158] Unfortunately for the Boers, and despite the usual fables, they rarely showed either valour or resolution in the opening battles of their invasions.

With the attack on Cannon Kopje driven off with fairly heavy loss, Cronjé was more determined than ever to wait out Baden-Powell. One burgher

---

* Nasson does, however, find time to claim that Baden-Powell was a "dab hand at releasing outnumbered, poorly briefed and ill-prepared forces to attack well-fortified Boer positions to negligible gain".

reported in his diary: "When in laager, watching Mafeking, it was nothing but a large picnic … [the besiegers] took good care never to come within range of the British guns. Lots to eat and drink, and giving out of clothing galore, all looted stuff."[159] The duty of the besiegers was not unpleasant or especially hazardous as the Boers enjoyed firing into the town at long range. On the 17th November our friend Sol Plaatje recorded in his diary: "Mausers were also very brisk today. Goodness knows what these Boers are shooting: they kill on average only one goat, sheep or fowl after spending five thousand rounds of Mauser ammunition—but very rarely a man."[160] As the thousands of Boers surrounding Mafeking settled in to the fairly jolly task of besieging the town, we shall turn our attention farther south.

Though not quite as exposed as Mafeking, the diamond town of Kimberley also presented a juicy target for the invading Boers and, as we have seen, Steyn admitted that its capture was one of his primary war aims.* Seeking as always to justify the republican invasions, and displaying his traditional cavalier disregard for historical reality, Pakenham claims that Kimberley was only British because it had been "grabbed from the Free State when it was found to contain the largest diamond pipe in the world".[161] The truth is no less dramatic but the only 'grabbing' involved was an early attempt at empire-building by the Transvaal.

In the 1860s diamond deposits had been discovered in the lands belonging to the chief of the Griquas, Nicholas Waterboer, whose territory lay in the midst of the poorly defined borders between the newly independent Orange Free State, the Cape Colony and the Transvaal. True to form, and as we have already touched on briefly, 1870 saw the Transvaal simply announce that the area belonged to them, with President Marthinus Pretorius personally leading an armed force to snatch the diamond fields.[162] This attempt was foiled by the diggers themselves, the majority of whom were of British extraction. The Transvaal flag was seized by an angry mob before it could be hoisted, a few shots rang out and the Transvaalers beat a hasty retreat. Needless to say, none

---

* When the invading republicans captured the town of Barkly West—about twenty miles northwest of Kimberley and Cecil Rhodes's seat in the Cape parliament—they even took the trouble to rename it Nieuw Boshof. The whole 'defensive invasion' theory begins to look very stupid when you start to scratch the surface.

of this is mentioned by Pakenham. Though the Orange Free State certainly claimed the area as well, they by no means controlled it. Indeed, in the wake of the attempted invasion by the Transvaal, the diggers actually set up their own diggers' republic and elected an ex-seaman, Stafford Parker,* as their 'president'. An increasingly nervous Waterboer, who was counselled by an extremely able and intelligent Cape Coloured lawyer called David Arnot,[163] requested that his territory be taken under British protection. Even the diggers were relieved to see the end of their short-lived, bizarre and rather lawless republic, with 'President' Parker greeting the first British resident magistrate under a banner that read, "Unity is Strength".[164] It was initially administered as a separate entity, but a bill annexing Griqualand West to the Cape Colony had been passed by the Cape Assembly in 1877, though nothing had really been done to effect this.† It was not until the 15th October 1880 that Griqualand West was officially incorporated into the Cape Colony. Despite the fact that Waterboer had asked to be taken under British protection and the fact that the diggers wanted this, the British still voluntarily forked out £90,000 in 'compensation' to the Orange Free State.[165]

As at Mafeking, the Cape authorities failed to take the threat to Kimberley seriously, belittling the concerns of the townspeople and refusing to prepare for the coming attack. It was only when a Colonel Kekewich of the 1st Loyal North Lancashire Regiment arrived in the town in mid-September 1899 that things started to happen. He reported that the town, and the diamond fields in general, were "dangerously vulnerable" and demanded troops be sent immediately. Just half of his own battalion was sent to him, along with some artillery, service and medical units.[166] Though sorely lacking in regular troops, Kekewich raised a town guard of about 2,500 men. The considerable resources of Rhodes's De Beers Company also swung into action, with the technical knowledge of their mining engineers being used to good effect in the construction of defensive positions and shelters. Rhodes himself arrived in the town the day before the invasion. On the 14th October Boer forces cut the telegraph line, isolating Kimberley—the most "English—that is, British, town in Cape Colony"[167]—from the world.

---

* Parker, who would later serve as mayor of Barberton during the 1884 gold rush, is perhaps better known for his Saturday night duties in auctioning off Cockney Liz, a barmaid who had previously worked in Kimberley.

† As strange as this will no doubt sound, there was actually a good deal of reluctance on the part of the Cape government to assume control of Griqualand West as it was heavily in debt.

Though Kekewich declared a state of siege on the 15th, once more the Boers showed little dash or drive and so the investment of the town was a slow process. The republicans seemed more interested in issuing proclamations declaring the annexation of British territory than actually fighting for it, with Kekewich moved to issue his own counter-proclamations to repudiate these.[168]

The first clash of the siege occurred on the 24th October, when 300 mounted infantry under Major Scott Turner located the Boshof Commando some miles to the north of Kimberley. Turner signalled back to Kekewich who had established a 'conning tower' on the headgear of one of the mines, giving him an impressive vantage point. Kekewich then dispatched reinforcements in the form of the half-battalion of the North Lancashires, two guns and an additional hundred mounted infantry. These troops attacked in great style, driving the Boshofs from their ridgeline positions with considerable loss.[169] Once more, the Boers—even the raffish de la Rey—were more inclined to settle down for a long siege than to force the issue.

Not content with wasting their effort at Ladysmith, Kimberley and Mafeking, the Boers also invested the tiny settlement of Kuruman. Originally a mission station, by 1899 Kuruman was an administrative centre for a large farming area. When a 700-strong Boer force under Commandant Visser attacked on the 13th November, they were held at bay by a miniscule force of police and loyalist settlers, both white and coloured,* perhaps eighty armed men in all.[170] Commanded by Major A. Bates of the Cape Police, this scratch force was kept under fire for the next four days, though the republicans, despite their overwhelming numbers, never dared to mount a close assault.[171] On the 18th Visser's force retired a few miles and awaited reinforcement in the form of some local rebels. His numbers thus swelled to 1,000 men, Visser continued to besiege this irrelevant outpost. (Except for Kimberley, Kuruman and Mafeking, the whole of British Bechuanaland and Griqualand West were annexed to the two republics.)[172] From the 5th to the 17th December Visser's men kept the defenders under fire, launching four assaults during this period, all of which were repulsed with losses.[173] In desperation, Visser then demanded heavy artillery and sat back to await its arrival.

One of the ladies of Kuruman wrote to a friend: "Our men fought bravely

---

* These Kuruman coloureds were often referred to as 'Bastards', a name which, remarkably enough, seems to have held no malice.

for six days, after which the Boers departed, and we don't know if they intend returning or not. Charlie is at the Police Camp and looks well and happy. He is very proud of our men. Our men are still on the alert, and are strengthening their forts, as the Boers will not return without a cannon. They quite expected this place to be handed over to them at once."[174]

The defence of Kuruman is an epic of the period: a handful of plucky loyalists holding out for weeks against all odds. Strangely, and exactly like the gallant defence of Cannon Kop, this sublime defensive action is not even mentioned by Pakenham.

⁊

Elsewhere in the Cape Colony, the border regions were in a state of "suppressed ferment". A prominent Afrikaans resident of Colesberg was on trial for seditious language, giving the disloyal inhabitants of that town plenty of opportunity to show their true colours. Republican agents had long operated in the border region, whipping up unrest where they could and encouraging it where they found it. As early as July 1899, agents had begun to distribute rifles to rebel groups and, as ridiculous as this sounds, the rebels engaged in target practice under the noses of colonial forces.[175]

Elements of the Cape Police dug in to protect the bridges over the Orange River, but were largely unable to prevent rebel leaders communicating daily with their Afrikaans brothers over in the Free State and urging them to attack. President Steyn came under increasing pressure from his commanders to cross the Orange and commence the invasion of the Cape to free their "oppressed Afrikander brethren".[176] Steyn gave the word and, supported by a commando from the Transvaal and a battery of artillery from Pretoria, his men swarmed into the Cape Colony on the 1st November, seizing the railways bridge at Norwal's Pont before pressing south.[177] Others crossed the Bethulie bridges and pushed on toward Naauwpoort and Stormberg. With only tiny numbers of troops in the region,* the diminutive garrisons of Naauwpoort and Stormberg were ordered to retreat to De Aar and Queenstown respectively.

The republicans pressed on and, somewhat perversely, blew up some other bridges just outside Colesberg. The retreating British blew up the railway

---

* the only major unit, the 1st Border Regiment, had recently been pulled back to East London and shipped to Natal

line to protect Naauwpoort and a bridge a few miles south of Burghersdorp. Nevertheless, the invaders advanced, entering Aliwal North on the 13th November. They had been egged on by disloyalists, including the mayor, a Mr Smuts, who had been constantly sending invitations and promises of help. A day later, another commando entered Colesberg amid similar scenes of enthusiasm from disloyalists. Indeed, these traitors formed a committee to assist the Boers in administering the town, foremost among who was Meneer Ignatius van der Walt, one of the most respected senior members of the Cape Legislature.[178] On the 15th Boer forces occupied Burghersdorp, much to the delight and relief of the Dutch Reformed Church clergymen who had for weeks been preaching rebellion from their pulpits. (However, we have been told *ad nauseam* we are not allowed to take seriously any suggestion whatsoever of Afrikaans sedition in the Cape.)

In the town of Lady Grey, occupied on the 18th November, the invaders were met by a defiantly courageous postmistress, Mrs Sarah Glueck. She refused to hand over the post office, and re-hoisted the Union Flag which the republicans had hauled down.[179] Others showed less loyalty and a large number of Lady Grey rebels joined the invasion, marching on Barkly East where rebels there were already prepared for their arrival, having seized 350 rifles from the magistrate. Upon arrival at Barkly East, the republican commander announced that he had "annexed this splendid tract of country".

It is clear that, as in northern Natal, the triumphant federal invaders had much grander ideas for their new territory than a fleeting occupation. Local rebels were appointed as veldkornets and landdrosts and an administrative structure was quickly put in place. Worse, the invaders brought their oppressive, racist laws with them, enforcing them on the non-whites of the Cape. Or, as Bill Nasson puts it: "the imported doctrine of white supremacy and the repeated desire to assert what commandants habitually termed Republic Native Law."[180] Unknown under imperial rule, this involved the federals introducing and rigorously enforcing a system of passes on the black population, as well as conscripting non-whites to work as unpaid labour wherever they saw fit. Essentially slave labour, these workers were provided with food and permitted to retain loot,[181] invariably taken from other blacks or loyalists. Though residents of the Cape Colony had enjoyed a colour-blind franchise system under British rule, in those districts which had been annexed to the federals, the disenfranchisement of non-whites was authorized and steps taken to systematically enforce this.[182] The invaders were clearly not planning on leaving any time soon.

One Cape Coloured, Cornelius Olifant, remembered the arrival of the Free State invaders in November 1899. With them were two local rebels, one of whom, Abraham Cronjé, told Olifant that all his land was now Orange Free State property and that he was now subject to the laws of that state. He was told to write his name on a piece of paper bearing the names of other "better class Natives" which was to signify his acknowledgement that he had been stripped of the vote: "When I did not want to do this thing Maree [the other local rebel] and the Free State Boers said they would shoot me. I was very afraid to lose my vote as I would then have no rights and just be a common Native and have to work as a slave for these white men. These Boer soldiers who came here to steal our goods and our rights as civilised Natives were not even white men really, but many had some Native blood in them, they were not really white men, just Boer Natives."[183]

Though senseless in many ways, the one thing the sieges did achieve was to alter British strategy. On the 31st October General Sir Redvers Buller VC had arrived to an uproarious reception in Cape Town to take command of imperial forces in southern Africa. He was cheered through the streets by people who viewed him as their saviour.[184] Buller's initial plan was for the Army Corps, following in his wake on the Atlantic, to land in the Cape and march on Bloemfontein and Pretoria along the line of the rail, roughly the line the N1 highway takes today. With White's command bottled up in Ladysmith, however, Buller was forced to divide his forces and attempt to achieve several things at once. It was never likely to be an easy task.

While Buller concentrated on events in Natal, the western front and, specifically, the relief of Kimberley became Lord Methuen's responsibility. The newly arrived Lieutenant-General Gatacre* was given command of what one might term the central front, that is the area between Methuen's advance and the Natal front sometimes referred to as the Cape Midlands.[185]

On the western front Methuen commenced his march north on the 21st November, his objective Kimberley. A Colonel Gough had tried a

---

* known as 'Back-acher' to his men, due to his tireless love of long route marches

reconnaissance in force as far north as the Orange River Station on the 9th November but this was driven off with several officers killed. Indeed, the Boers seemed to be well aware of Methuen's movements: on the 19th November, having made no further serious attempt to assault the town, General Cronjé withdrew 4,000 men from the siege of Mafeking and redeployed them to face Methuen's advancing columns.[186] At first glance Methuen's command was impressive, about 8,000 strong.[187] A Guards officer himself, Methuen must have been delighted to have several Guards battalions in his force, as well as several other British infantry regiments. Where the force was weak, however, was in the all-important mounted troops: he had just one regular cavalry regiment, the 9th Lancers, supported by a single squadron of the New South Wales Lancers and a small, locally raised corps of guides called Rimington's Tigers*—just 900 horsemen in total.[188] This otherwise formidable command marched north along the railway line, supported by an armoured train and followed by supply wagons and livestock.

The Boers' first attempt to block Methuen's advance was at Belmont, seventeen miles north of the Orange River. A force of Free-Staters under Commandant J. Prinsloo occupied a strong position on a trio of hilltops. They had dug themselves in and had orders to hold Methuen up until Cronjé's men could arrive from Mafeking.[189] The Free-Staters held a naturally formidable position: the steep-sided hills were a jumble of broken ground, completely dominating the railway below and the crests had been further strengthened by trench lines and breastworks. The British plan was a frontal attack, with the 9th Infantry Brigade[†] on the left and the Guards Brigade[‡] on the right. The 15-pounders of the 18th and 75th Batteries, RA, and some Royal Navy long-range 12-pounders provided support.[190] The infantry pushed forward, played into battle by the regimental band of the Guards. Despite this archaic though magnificent flourish, the officers and men of even the most traditional regiments had already begun to cover their shiny buttons, dull their belts and

---

*   The 'Tigers' were raised by a regular army officer, Major Rimington (often misspelled—then and now—as Remington), their slouch-hats sporting a leopard-skin puggaree. Despite this rather dubious knowledge of zoology, these were locally raised colonials who knew the ground and were fluent in Afrikaans and/or native languages.

†   The 9th Brigade was commanded by Major-General Pole-Carew and comprised the 2nd King's Yorkshire Light Infantry, 2nd Northamptons, 1st Northumberland Fusiliers and half a battalion of the Loyal North Lancs (the other half being bottled up in Kimberley under Colonel Kekewich).

‡   The Guards Brigade was commanded by Brigadier Colville and comprised the 3rd Grenadier Guards, 1st and 2nd Coldstream Guards and the 1st Scots Guards.

stain their white kit; officers had largely swapped their conspicuous swords for rifles.[191] Lieutenant Barton of the Northamptons recorded the orders given to his regiment: "Officers are to discard their useless swords and carry rifles or carbines so as to confuse the Boer marksmen. All the Aldershot Drill Book Tactics are to be abolished and we shall adopt very extended order, men getting quickly from rock to rock, irregularity of line being sought and 'regular dressing' avoided."[192] Essentially, 'fire and movement' in today's military parlance. Unperturbed by the musketry of the Boers, the men doubled forward in open order. Pausing at the bottom of the first hill to fix bayonets, they then surged up the slope in great style. A loyalist South African member of the 'Tigers' described the action in his diary: "The British infantry, without bothering to wait till the hills had been shelled, walked up and kicked the Boers out."[193] The sight of a several thousand bayonets was indeed too much for Prinsloo's men and they began to fall back. The third hill was not contested as the retreat turned into a something approaching a rout with the Boers scrambling for their ponies and fleeing. Methuen's paucity of cavalry meant no meaningful pursuit was possible.

Yet again, the republicans used their favourite white-flag trick to shoot dead two Tommies and Methuen formally protested to Prinsloo over the use of dum-dum ammunition. The Boers even managed to combine these two war crimes in the same incident: the war correspondent, Mr E. Knight of the *Morning Post* was fired on by Boers from under the white flag, losing his right arm to a dum-dum round.[194] In an equally unsavoury incident, an officer of the Guards was shot by a wounded burgher while offering him a drink from his water bottle.

Keen as ever to paint even this clear-cut British victory in as dim a light as possible, Pakenham dismisses this two-brigade attack on a 2,000-strong force as a "minor victory". Showing an astounding lack of understanding of matters military, he then goes on to compare Methuen's casualties (297) with those of the Boers (under 150), before rhetorically asking, "What went wrong?"[195] Far from anything going wrong, Belmont was yet another example of British infantry storming well-placed Boer entrenchments. Prinsloo's men, who had been ordered to delay Methuen, fled rather than face the British bayonets. Indeed, many republicans had taken the defeat as their signal to urgently check on their crops and families, and large numbers kept on fleeing and simply evaporated.[196] Furthermore, it is only to be expected that in an infantry assault, an attacking force will take higher casualties than the defenders and total casualties of 297 (the majority of whom were only wounded) out of a force of 8,000 is an insignificant loss for the storming of such a position. Brigadier Colville, commanding the Guards Brigade, said that the men had "done for themselves what no general would have dared asked of them" and later wrote that "unlike most 'soldiers' battles', it had not the drawback of being someone's mistake".[197] Methuen addressed his victorious men: "With troops like you no general can fear the result of his plans."[198]

Some claim that the Boers never really wished to hold the position at Belmont in the first place and that their withdrawal was therefore not the rout that the evidence suggests, but instead was a cunning plan. Though no doubt an appealing hypothesis in some circles, the facts simply do not support this. Methuen's cavalry strength was insufficient for a proper pursuit, but none the less imperial mounted troops captured a laager that had been abandoned in the panic: "It seemed evident, from the number of wagons and the amount of clothing and stores left behind and littered in every direction, that the Boers had not expected to be shifted nearly so suddenly as they were. There were heaps of provisions, quantities of coffee tied up in small bags, sugar, rice, biltong … there were waggons loaded, or half-loaded, with old chests and boxes, and many heaped about the ground … we also found a lot of abandoned ammunition, shell and Mauser."[199]

Two days later, on the 25th November, Methuen's men repeated the trick at Graspan,* this time against a rather larger Boer force. De la Rey's commando held the position initially, but he finally managed to persuade some of the demoralized survivors of Belmont to join him, taking the defending force up to 2,300 and supported by three Krupp 75mm guns and a couple of pom-poms.[200] This time it was the 9th Infantry Brigade which did the lion's share of the fighting. The 300 hardy sea-dogs of the newly arrived Naval Brigade had been attached to 9th Brigade and distinguished themselves in leading the attack. Despite taking a hammering from de la Rey's marksmen, the infantry, marines and bluejackets stormed the Boer position with astounding gallantry. Once more the Boers broke and ran,[201] having managed to hold their positions for just thirty minutes.[202] For the second time in forty-eight hours Methuen's men had brushed aside a strong, well-placed Boer blocking force with relative ease.

---

* this action is sometimes referred to as 'Enslin' as the fighting took place between Graspan and Enslin

None of this prevented the republicans from convincing themselves that they had won a great victory. One reluctant burgher told of an old Boer of over sixty who arrived at his position with dispatches after the battle: "Stands up in his cart, hat off, and makes a speech to this crowd, telling them in thousands, of how many British were slain at Graspan and Belmont and he said: 'We are the victors.' Query, 'How is it we are retreating, if victors?' Winding up with, 'God gave us the Bible and now he has added the Mauser. The British have no chance against us.' Alas, a large majority of these misled Boers believe all this as gospel truth."[203]

As Methuen's command again pushed forward, the Boers once more attempted to block his advance, this time defending positions along the Modder River. Given the Boers penchant for defending hilltop locations, digging in on the river was a fairly surprising departure and one which was only decided upon after a great deal of argument. The idea was de la Rey's with the thinking being to take advantage of the flat trajectory of the Mausers by placing the defensive positions low down. The commonly held notion of the war is that it was the British high command which was inflexible and resistant to change, but the Boers had their own such stodgy generals. Cronjé dismissed de la Rey's plan out of hand, despite the fact that the republicans had been driven from two hilltop positions in the space of two days. It took the personal intervention of President Steyn to persuade the more conservative elements to try something new.[204]

Numbering about 3,500 men with six guns and several pom-poms,[205] the federals dug in on both banks of the Modder, either side of the railway bridge and on the far bank of the Riet River.[206] The Boer trenches stretched for about four miles, with the Riet River one of the keys to the position, as it effectively prevented a British move on their right flank. Numerous false trenches and positions were also dug and the real positions well camouflaged. So effective was this deception that it was later discovered that the Northumberland Fusiliers had directed return fire at unoccupied positions for several hours.[207] It has been said that Modder River demonstrates the inflexibility and limitations of Lord Methuen and there is a great deal of truth in this accusation. It is true that Methuen attacked the Boer positions exactly as de la Rey had presumed he would. Again, however, it should be remembered that the British were sorely lacking in mounted troops and reliant on the railway for their supplies, meaning sweeping flanking moves were somewhat impractical. Pre-empting uninformed criticism of the strategy adopted throughout the advance as a whole, L. March Phillips, one of Rimington's Tigers, summed up the lack of options available to Methuen: "First, we are bound to keep our line of communication, that is, the railway, open, and hold it as we advance … second, we are not strong enough, and above all not mobile enough, while holding the railway to attempt a wide flanking movement which might threaten the Boer retreat, or enable us to shell and attack from two sides at once … so you must figure to yourself a small army, an army almost with no cavalry, and an army tied to the railway on this march; and if we bring off no brilliant strategy, but simply plod on and take hard knocks, well, what else, I ask, under the circumstances can we do?"[208]

Methuen also believed the crossing to be held by just 500 men and his maps were inaccurate in their placement of the Riet River.[209] Though the Riet prevented much opportunity for work on the right, Methuen could—and should—have screened the Boer positions with his Guards and pushed his 9th Infantry Brigade out farther to the left, not in a wide flanking manoeuvre, but far enough to turn the position. This is easy to say in hindsight, however. Perhaps after the victories of Belmont and Graspan—both won with simple frontal assaults—Methuen might have thought he had found a winning formula, but his predictable and unimaginative approach was to cost his men dear.

As it was, the Tommies trudged toward the railway bridge early in the morning of the 28th November, with the Colville's Guards Brigade on the right and Pole-Carew's 9th Infantry Brigade on the left. One witnessed described "the country is like what one imagines a North American prairie to be, a sea of whitish, course grass, with here and there a low clump of bushes (behind one of which we are halted as I write this). One can see a vast distance over the surface. Along the north horizon there is a ripple of small hills and kopjes, looking blue, with the white grass-land running up to them. It is a comparatively cool morning with a few light clouds in the sky and a pleasant breeze. On our left is the railway, and all along our right, extending far in front and far behind, advances the army".[210]

The 'army' was still far too small for the job it had been tasked with. There was still a terrible paucity of mounted troops, though the infantry losses of Belmont and Graspan had been made good by the arrival of the dashing men of the Argyll and Sutherland Highlanders. The artillery support consisted of two batteries of 15-pounders and four naval guns.[211] As the long, widely spaced lines of infantry plodded forward, all was quiet for a while. Indeed, it was so quiet that Methuen turned to Colville and murmured, "They are not here." The unflappable Colville replied, "They are sitting uncommonly tight if they are, sir."[212] And then all hell broke loose. The hidden Boers opened a thunderous fusillade on the advancing Tommies, with the Guards being forced to ground immediately. The Scots Guards bore the brunt as their machine-gun section was "swept away" by a burst from the Boer pom-pom gun. With the Guards Brigade stalled all along their front, their reserve battalion, the 1st Coldstream Guards, was ordered to try and work their way round the flank but their path was blocked by the unfordable river Riet. Pinned in place, the Guards were reduced to sitting it out and exchanging ineffectual fire with their unseen tormentors. Once again, however, the indiscipline of the republicans was decisive: had they held their fire until the guardsmen were close to the Modder River as they had been ordered, the ambush would have been truly devastating. Instead the Boers nervously sprang their trap too early, opening fire when the Guards were still 1,000 yards away.[213] Interestingly, Colville also mentions that the Boers were "weak in 'fire discipline' and wasteful of ammunition",[214] though this seems a mite churlish. On the left the 9th Brigade was also being flayed by artillery and rifle fire, though was partly shielded by a fold in the ground. As the day wore on, some units of the 9th slowly managed to work their way round to their left. Facing them were the increasingly unreliable Free-Staters under the command of Prinsloo; and Cronjé, now in overall command, had placed much of his artillery in such a way that they could not support Prinsloo's men.[215] In contrast, the 15-pounders of the Royal Artillery hammered Prinsloo's position, silencing the few guns they had in support,[216] and the dramatic arrival of the 62nd Battery halfway through the action gave the British another six guns.* The 62nd had travelled thirty-two miles in eight hours and in marked contrast to the attitude of the Boers at Talana, trotted toward the action as soon as they heard the sounds of battle.[217]

After many hours, Pole-Carew's men drove Prinsloo's Free-Staters back across the Modder before managing to get some of his own units over the river. Scattered elements of the Yorkshires, Argylls and North Lancs acted with great pluck and resolution, forded the river and drove the Boers[218] from

---

* unfortunately, their first contribution was to mistakenly shell some of their own men

the fortified village of Rosmead.* Though both Methuen and Pole-Carew led from the front, the battle was won by the drive and grit of the regimental officers and NCOs pushing their men on and not accepting defeat. Major Coleridge of the North Lancs cheerfully encouraged his men to follow him into the river, asking, "Now, boys—who's for otter hunting?"[219] before plunging in. Faced with this gathering threat to their flank, Prinsloo's Free-Staters had had enough[220] and some began to slip away, leaving their more stout-hearted brethren in the lurch. This spontaneous retreat in turn threatened the loss of their precious artillery and so the Boer guns were also withdrawn. A furious de la Rey pulled his men back as the rest of 9th Brigade crossed the Modder. The federal trench lines were completely abandoned during the night. For all the claims of the brilliance of the Boer commanders, they seem to have had no way in preventing their men from running away when the fancy took them.

Indeed, the main reason that more burghers did not desert was fear of the retribution that would be wrought upon their families. In the wake of this latest defeat, reluctant burgher Jack Lane tried to persuade his friend to join him in making a break for the imperial lines but his mate would not be convinced: "'Don't you see, these fellows would give us a bullet. As it is, by their looks they take us for Free Staters. They say that the Free Staters left them yesterday in the lurch. They are swearing at them for running away. Besides, you must remember your family at home. If our people found out you had gone over or surrendered, your family at home would simply suffer. I am a Boer,' he said, 'myself, and I am sorry to say, the devil is loose amongst us, If this war continues, God alone knows what they will turn into.'"[221] This would prove prophetic.

Some later claimed, once again, that slipping away in the night was all part of the Boer master plan and was yet another stroke of genius by de la Rey. But this was certainly not the case: after the battle, locals told the imperial troops that the Boers had thought their position impregnable.[222] Even more tellingly, de la Rey was utterly opposed to abandoning the Modder River positions:[223] "At a *krygsraad* [council of war] held at 2000 hours, Cronjé decided, in view of the defection of the Free Staters, that is was necessary to evacuate the position and retire on Jacobsdal to meet the strong reinforcements which were still coming up. This decision, approved by the rest of the commandants, met with

---

* today the village of Rosmead is called Ritchie and is in the Northern Cape province

the bitterest opposition from de la Rey. That stern old warrior had seen his eldest son mortally wounded during the day, but, as he declared afterwards to a friend, that loss did not affect him as keenly as the abandonment of the position. In his view the British would not only fail to dislodge the Boers from the position, but would be compelled in consequence, for want of water, to fall back all the way on the Orange River."[224]

Far from the retreat being part of a cunning plan, the flight of the Free-Staters and the fact that many of their number had simply sat out the battle in their laagers, caused something of a diplomatic rift between the two Boer republics. Kruger fired off a thundering telegram to his ally, complaining, "I am convinced it is the want of unity that compelled us to abandon our positions."[225] President Steyn in turn sent a truly insane telegram to be read out to the wavering Free-Staters, declaring that the battle had not in fact been a reverse, that Irish regiments were mutinying and that most of the English soldiers had also refused to fight further.[226] The claim that the republican retreat was in any way intended is yet another fable dreamed up to explain away uncomfortable facts. Equally strange are the claims by Bill Nasson. Firstly he announces that the Boers were not "panicked into flight" when quite clearly large numbers of Free-Staters were, and secondly, he asserts that "the Boers can hardly be said to have been beaten in battle" when quite clearly they had[227]—being driven from an 'impregnable' position after a large chunk of your army has run away is generally considered a loss.

Despite these wilder claims, Modder River was another British victory but the cost had been far heavier than either Belmont or Graspan. Total British casualties were around 460, compared to reported losses of about eighty on the Boer side.[228] As fifty Boer dead were left on the field, it is likely that their actual loses were closer to two hundred. Either way, this disproportionate ratio is only to be expected: the Boers were fighting from dug-in positions and most fled long before the British could have at them with the bayonet. The resolution and determination of the Tommies was remarkable: they endured hour after hour of rifle and artillery fire under a blazing sun but emerged victorious. The 9th Brigade won the battle by turning the Boer flank, but the Guards also played their part by pinning the Boers in place; this was more by good luck than good management but, still, was only possible due to the bravery and steadiness of the troops, and the inspired leadership of their officers. Colville's ADC, Captain George Nugent, displayed magnificent courage when the Guards were pinned down under heavy fire. A rather foul-mouthed guardsman described Nugent's supreme nonchalance under fire: "He rides about on his ******* old white horse, and don't care a ****, and just says: "Let the ******* shoot."[229]

In contrast, though the Boers had fought long and hard, their lack of discipline, brittle morale and elementary mistakes cost them any chance of victory. Under de la Rey's keen eye their defences had been masterfully constructed, but leaving Prinsloo's force without sufficient artillery support was an oversight on Cronjé's part, and no effort was made to reposition the republican guns to cover them. This is especially strange as the Boer left (the British right) was effectively screened by the unfordable Riet River. So why put a preponderance of guns on that flank instead of their more vulnerable right? Worse still was the way the federals sprang their trap too early for it to be truly effective. Their sheer dread of the British bayonets undoubtedly played a role, and there was little their commanders could do to instil any semblance of military discipline in the individualistic burghers.

Modder River is often cited as an example of British ineptitude and Boer martial brilliance. It is undoubtedly the case that the victory was gained despite Methuen's tactics rather than because of them, for he made a series of inexcusable errors. But again, we cannot ignore the salient fact that Methuen won and de la Rey lost. Not only did Methuen's forces triumph, they did so against the odds: the standard ratio considered necessary for a successful infantry assault is 3:1; against well dug-in positions—such as those the Boers held at Modder River—this can be raised to at least 5:1 and sometimes higher. Methuen, however, only had an advantage of around 2:1, though some accounts put the numbers of troops actually involved as essentially even.

Paying scant attention to reconnaissance, Methuen cheerfully blundered into the Boer trap as de la Rey and Cronjé had predicted he would. But that was really the only part of the federal plan that went right. With the nervous republicans springing the trap prematurely, there was no danger of the British infantry being destroyed once they had gone to ground. Had the 9th Brigade been pinned at, say, 300 yards from the Boer positions instead of 1,000 yards then there is no way they could have executed the flank movement that ultimately won the day for the British. Likewise, on the right, though the Guards endured a miserable day under constant rifle fire, there was never any pressing need to extract them. They could lie still and exchange long-range fire with the Boers all day, taking some casualties but nothing compared to those they would have suffered at 300 yards. Similarly, when the 9th Brigade began pressing to their left in small groups, there was very little reaction from the federals: essentially, there was no Plan B. A localized counter-attack was indeed launched by units under the command of de la Rey, but it is remarkable that there were no significant reserves which might have been committed to drive the Tommies back nor was there any attempt to redeploy the artillery to counter this new threat. Once elements of the 9th Brigade were over the Modder and had driven the Boers from Rosmead, there seemed to be an acceptance of defeat, rather than any resolute response to push the Tommies back again. The initial deployment and siting of republican trenches was very good, but if Methuen's plan of attack was predictable and unimaginative, once battle was joined Cronjé and de la Rey's fighting of a defensive action was just as much so, with no semblance of an active defence. Basically, if the British would not play ball and retreat under the hail of gunfire then there was little else that de la Rey and Cronjé had up their sleeves. Their decision not to keep any men in reserve gives a lie to any claims of tactical brilliance.

Methuen has been roundly criticized for lacking grip and not having control of the action. This is certainly a fair comment as he spent the day in the very thick of the action—being wounded as a result—rather than stepping back, viewing the big picture and directing the battle.[230] Needless to say, had Methuen not been in the thick of the fighting, he would have been criticized in some quarters for that, but that is exactly where he should not have been. What is not often appreciated is that the British infantry retained their resolve and determination, and Methuen's presence in the front lines must have had an impact on this. In contrast, the much-vaunted Boer commanders proved unable to inspire and motivate their wavering troops despite all the advantages they held.

And so ended the opening phase of the war. The Boer invasions had been stopped and on the western front even pushed back. The offensive had not captured anything like enough territory to force the British to the bargaining table: there had been no 'Majuba Hill' for Dr Leyds and others to exploit and force a settlement on the imperial government.[231] Far from the common myth of it being one British thrashing after another, the khakis had proved more than a match for the Boers more often than not. Talana Hill, Elandslaagte, Belmont, Graspan and Modder River, as well as the numerous unnamed battles in defence of Kuruman, Mafeking, Kimberley and Ladysmith, were all hard-fought British victories and all won long before the British had any sort of numerical advantage in the theatre. There were a few inconclusive actions, but the only significant Boer victory in the opening weeks was Nicholson's Nek, achieved by the most fortuitous of means.*

Apart from the odd exception, time after time the federal invasion forces had proved timid in attack and brittle in defence: they were happy enough to blaze away at long range but quick to withdraw at the first glint of a bayonet or if their flanks were threatened. Their generals were shown to be ponderous or lacking in tactical acumen. Even the much-admired de la Rey had been driven from two defensible positions. There was a distinct lack of strategic planning: driven by his desire to seize Kimberley, Steyn dithered elsewhere until early November, forfeiting any chance to push into the Cape Colony and spark a rebellion. Rebels in the Cape pleaded for help but by the time this came British reinforcements were in place. Many thousands of Boers idled away their time in the carefree investments of Kuruman and Mafeking. Though Kruger, Smuts and Botha all wanted to snatch Durban and annex Natal, Joubert was content to tie up the lion's share of his army in besieging Ladysmith. Those units he did permit to advance into Natal were more focused on plunder than any obvious military objective and were pulled back after encountering negligible resistance, instead digging in passively along the Tugela. On a tactical level Boer attacks were rarely pressed with any conviction or courage. Though their excellent marksmanship and field craft made them a deadly foe in defensive actions, when the going got tough, units simply withdrew with no regard for their comrades, or refused to march in support of their friends. The white and Red Cross flags were abused on numerous occasions. Many burghers were far more interested in looting than in fighting.

And all this occurred, it must be remembered, when the Boers enjoyed considerable numerical advantage. Writing in 1901, Lieutenant-Colonel Henderson remarked that "it is doubtless true that, had Natal been garrisoned

---

* it would be fair to say that the republicans won at Willow Grange too, but this was a small, fairly indecisive action and prompted the Boer retreat

by 20,000 men, and Ladysmith adequately fortified"[232] then the British would have won the war very quickly. As it was, the outnumbered and ill-prepared imperial troops had somehow managed to fight the Boers to a standstill, but would now have to drive the invaders back whence they came.

CHAPTER SEVEN

Black Week and Black Month

"There are few pleasanter sights for an Englishman than that of our artillery moving under fire. Nearly everybody gets cool when 'the guns begun to shoot', but I know of nothing that conveys by its manner such an utter disregard for the enemy's efforts as a British battery quietly trotting along under a heavy shower of shells."
—Major-General Colville, describing the Royal Artillery
withdrawing under fire at Magersfontein[1]

"The cavalry must relieve Kimberley at all costs …
If it fails, neither I nor the Field Marshal can tell what the result on the Empire may be."
—Major-General Lord Kitchener of Khartoum

"I am going to give you some very hard work to do, but at the same time you are going to get the greatest chance cavalry ever had … You will remember what you are going to do all your lives, and when you have grown to be old men, you will tell the story of the relief of Kimberley … The enemy are afraid of the British Cavalry, and I hope when you get them out into the open you will make an example of them."
—Lord Roberts, addressing the officers of the Cavalry Division, 10th February 1900

"the English possess better scouts and a better intelligence department than we do."
—Boer secret telegram, 7th December 1899

"I am glad to see you. You made a gallant defence …"
—Lord Roberts to General Cronjé, 27th February 1900

"The English have taken our Majuba Day away from us."
—President Kruger after the surrender at Paardeberg

"Every man for himself, we will meet the other side of Kimberley."
—according to a Boer deserter, this was the last order issued
by General Cronjé before abandoning Magersfontein

"I cannot catch a hare with unwilling dogs; and whatever I had said or done,
the burghers would have gone home."
—General de Wet explaining his decision to let
his commandos go home after Paardeberg

For most modern writers on the Boer War, the three British defeats of 'Black Week' are the highlight of the conflict, and all the evidence needed to prove the theory of British military incompetence and Boer brilliance. While the innumerable republican defeats can be explained away or simply ignored, the British losses during Black Week—like any other British defeat—are invariably, and with undisguised glee, described as 'humiliations'. There is certainly no doubt that after the victories enjoyed by the imperial forces in October and November (victories which are either down-played or completely overlooked by most such writers), the events of Black Week came as a rude awakening for imperial cause. It is equally true to say that they were greeted with disbelief and horror at the time.

But how bad were the Black Week defeats really and what else was happening in early December? Why has attention tended to focus on this period of the war and why has there been comparatively little interest in the 'Black Month' suffered by the Boers shortly thereafter?

First, let's have a quick recap of events in early December. Operations in Rhodesia and around Mafeking had largely settled into something approaching a stalemate. The Boer offensive on the western front had been checked and, in the latter half of November, driven back in a series of engagements as Lord Methuen advanced to raise the siege of Kimberley. The situation on the central front had seen the Boers push south into the Midlands of the Cape Colony, but there had been no significant actions in the area up to this point and British reinforcements had been deployed to block any major drive in this region. On the Natal front, Ladysmith was besieged, but imperial forces had won two tactical victories and the Boer drive to Durban had fizzled out like a damp squib. Botha, who had by then effectively replaced Joubert, continued the investment and bombardment of Ladysmith and had dug in along the line of the Tugela River in anticipation of the British counter-offensive. It is worth mentioning that the British by no means enjoyed any significant numerical advantage by this stage. Troops were arriving in Cape Town and Durban every day but in the three main areas of operations the front-line imperial forces were still inconsiderable. In the west Lord Methuen commanded about 15,000, while strung out along the vast central front, generals Gatacre and French had only a few thousand between them.[2] The largest British force was in Natal: in addition to the 12,000 men bottled up in Ladysmith under General White, General Buller had assembled a field force of just over twenty thousand.

The first 'disaster' of Black Week was an attempted night attack on Boer positions near Stormberg Junction on the 9th/10th December. General Gatacre led about 2,000 British troops* against around 2,300 Boers and in a confused action the attack was repulsed. British casualties were very low, with twenty-six killed; it would have been an insignificant action but for the fact that in the confusion about 560 Northumberland Fusiliers were cut off and left behind to be captured.[3] Despite this haul and though they outnumbered the retreating British, the Boers under Commandant Olivier had been given quite a scare and showed no inclination to follow up. Indeed, Gatacre's subsequent actions held the line until the great advance on Bloemfontein began. It was a severe defeat and the loss of the Fusiliers was a serious blow given the paltry numbers of British forces in the region, but as disasters go, it was a fairly minor one.

On the 11th December, over on the western front, Lord Methuen recommenced his advance toward Kimberley after a fortnight's delay. Recent reinforcements meant that his force was now around 15,000 strong, though still lacking in mounted troops. Facing them were about 8,500 Boers under Cronjé and de la Rey who had dug themselves in on the Magersfontein hills, just a few miles north of the Modder River. Again, de la Rey's influence had led to the Boer trenches being cleverly sited and numerous rather more obvious dummy positions prepared to draw British artillery fire.[4] As mentioned earlier, and as any student of tactics will tell you, it is generally accepted that a threefold advantage in numbers is required for a successful attack, and against positions such as those held by Cronjé's men at Magersfontein, military planners might even up this ratio to 5:1—an incredible 45,000 men. As it

---

* Gatacre's force was built around the Northumberland Fusiliers, Royal Irish Rifles and two batteries of 15-pounders

was, the only British force fully committed to the action was the Highland Brigade of around 3,500 men.* The Guards Brigade acted in reserve and saw little action, while the 9th Infantry was largely held back to secure the newly repaired bridges over the Modder. Since the great victory at Tel el Kabir in 1882, when faced with entrenched positions many British generals adopted the practice of a night march to a jumping-off point close to the enemy positions, followed by a dawn attack. This is what Gatacre had attempted at Stormberg; it was also the plan at Magersfontein.

Far from the oft-trotted-out myth of the British being supremely confident of victory, General Wauchope, commanding the Highland Brigade which was to do the lion's share of the fighting, was very realistic about the task ahead. He told the commander of the Guards Brigade: "Things do not always do as they are expected; you may not be in reserve for long."[5] Wauchope could not have been more right as the attack was a complete failure. The Highlanders had marched up in column to preserve their order in the darkness, which was entirely sensible. The problem was that, as dawn broke, Wauchope was unforgivably slow in dispersing his men into looser order.[6] They were thus still closely packed when the federals opened fire on them at about 400 yards, driving them to ground and breaking up the attack. Despite the inexplicable failings of their commander, the Highlanders tried to keep the momentum by charging in short rushes, but even these attempts were beaten off about 250 yards short of the Boer trenches.[7] After many hours pinned down, a Boer attempt to outflank the Highlanders was the straw that broke the camel's back, and an attempt to realign to face this threat turned into a rout, the Highlanders being knocked down in their dozens as they fled. General Wauchope was one of those killed, shot just 200 yards from the republican positions.

The British, mainly the Highlanders, lost 220 killed with total casualties of 902, compared to Boer losses of 236, with the Scandinavian Corps being essentially destroyed. Though the Highlanders had had a dreadful time of it, the Guards had been under-utilized, their commander recalling that the day had been "only a trying one for us. We were ordered not to advance, and had nothing much to look forward to, so we simply lay in the sun till our clothes were dry, and when it got hot wished they were wet again. We were under

---

* The Highland Brigade comprised the 2nd Black Watch, 1st Argyll and Sutherlands, 2nd Seaforth Highlanders and the 1st Highland Light Infantry.

fire all day, but it was never as heavy as at Modder River, and there was more cover".[8]

The battle had gone wrong from the very beginning. If Wauchope had timed his approach march with greater precision and shaken his men out into open order before they came under fire, it is entirely possible that the Highlanders might have stormed the Boer trenches and taken them at bayonet point. When they were instead scythed down and left under heavy fire at 400 yards the result was never in doubt. It is interesting to note the difference between Modder River and Magersfontein in this respect: perhaps a daylight approach would actually have been less damaging as the Boers would most probably have opened fire as soon as they could. Lord Methuen showed no inclination to use the majority of his forces, incxcusablc as they had been resting for two weeks since Modder River. Despite the legendary gallantry and dash of the Highlanders, sending 3,500 of them against 8,500 dug-in burghers was never likely to end well. It is also fair to criticize Methuen for delaying for so long after the battle of Modder River. Admittedly his force had taken quite a mauling in that action, but dithering for a fortnight was a gift to the Boers and allowed them to reinforce and prepare their positions at Magersfontein. Had Methuen driven his troops forward after Modder River he may well have smashed his way through to Kimberley before Cronjé and de la Rey could reorganize.

There was another side to the defeat though. Even though Magersfontein had been a case of 'fourth time lucky' for the Boers, beating off the attack of the Highlanders convinced Cronjé that he had finally found the key to success. Much is rightly made of the unimaginative tactics by some of the British commanders in the war, but the federals were to show similar traits in the wake of their victory. Cronjé was outrageously complacent for a man whose troops had won just one battle out of four, dismissing concerns voiced by his junior officers as to the limitations of the Magersfontein defences.[9] Supremely confident that the British would obligingly attack his position head-on once again, Cronjé naïvely declared, "The English do not make turning movements; they never leave the railway, because they cannot march."[10]

More effort was put into rounding up local loyalist farmers than preparing for an imperial turning movement. One burgher remembered some of these fellows being brought into their laager, musing: "they will send them to

Pretoria to swell the list of prisoners of war. This is the worst of this war. If you don't join the Republicans, you are made prisoner, your wife and children turned out homeless, your farm destroyed."[11] Others who refused to switch their allegiance to the federals were driven out of their homes and forced to make their own way to the imperial lines: "Men, women and children, all hunted together in a flock without any shelter. Because they stick to their government, this is the way they are treated. Cronjé says the 'duivels' must suffer. I wonder what he would say if the British were to do the same … Judgement is sure to fall on the Boer shoulders for this, and worse things."[12]

As well as such ethnic cleansing and the complacent arrogance of their commander, the poor discipline of the republican troops quickly manifested itself after the victory. With so many Boers in a small area, the veldt was quickly grazed away to nothing, meaning that many horses were soon cheerfully dispatched to other pastures. Supremely confident in their ability to hold their positions, many burghers summoned their wives and children to join the party, and enormous amounts of baggage soon arrived. The result of turning the Magersfontein position into a vast jamboree was a steady deterioration in the mobility, dynamism and the aggressive spirit of Cronjé's forces.[13]

As Cronjé's men relaxed, over on the Natal front the third and final 'disaster' of Black Week was taking place. On the 15th December General Buller made a half-hearted attempt to break General Botha's defence line on the Tugela near the village of Colenso. Buller had earlier declared that a frontal attack on Boer positions on the other side of the Tugela would be too costly and had been planning a move off to one flank to skirt them. Perhaps prodded into action after the defeats at Stormberg and Magersfontein, however, Buller decided to have a go. It would appear that he retained plenty of doubts, cabling the War Office the day before to inform them: "From my point of view, it would be better to lose Ladysmith altogether than to throw Natal open to the enemy."[14] On the day of the battle he signalled: "I fully expect to be successful but probably at heavy cost."[15] He had about 20,000 men under his command but, rather like Methuen at Magersfontein, he only committed two of his four infantry brigades to the assault, with many of his men spending the day waiting and watching. The 5th (Irish) Brigade* was to ford the Tugela at a crossing called Brindle's Drift, while the 2nd Infantry Brigade† was tasked to make the main assault at Wagon Drift. The small Cavalry Brigade was to demonstrate on the British right, but had very little impact on the battle.

Facing the imperial troops were 4,500 Boers with five artillery pieces under the command of Louis Botha. A couple of days earlier, when the British attack began to appear likely, men of the Soutpansberg and Boksburg commandos withdrew from their exposed hilltop positions on the southern bank of the Tugela and no one else could be persuaded to reoccupy these posts. The crisis was only solved when Kruger intervened by telegram and the Boer commandants agreed to draw lots to decide who should occupy these positions.[16] The hill in question, Hlangwane, was actually the key to Botha's position for it overlooked the main Boer trench lines on the northern bank;[17] had the British captured it and dragged artillery up it then Botha would have had to abandon these positions. Unfortunately for Buller, his maps incorrectly showed Hlangwane to be on the northern side of the river, and thus no serious attempt was made to storm it.

In the event, Buller's attack went wrong from the start. Advancing in close order, General Hart's 5th (Irish) Brigade blundered into a loop in the Tugela and, unable to find a crossing point, came under fire from three sides. As General Hildyard's 2nd Brigade advanced on Colenso village, Botha's plan had been for them to be allowed to cross the iron bridge before they were fired on. Cut off on the wrong side of the river and under close-range fire from several sides, it would have been utter carnage. Once more the Boers struggled to hold their fire as ordered[18] and instead opened up on the advancing Tommies at long range. This poor discipline again prevented the ambush from being anywhere near as effective as it could have been; nevertheless, Hildyard's brigade was unable to make any significant progress.

To add to Buller's woes, two batteries of 15-pounders had been moved too far forward and came under heavy Boer rifle fire, and it was at this point— just a couple of hours into the battle—that he decided to call the whole thing off. Hart's 5th Brigade was ordered to retreat and attempts were made to rescue the guns. Again the timidity of the Boers prevented Hart's brigade

---

* The Irish Brigade consisted of the 2nd Dublin Fusiliers, 1st Inniskillings, 1st Connaught Rangers and the 1st Border Regiment.

† The 2nd Infantry Brigade consisted of the 2nd Devonshires, 2nd Queen's, 2nd West Yorkshires and the 2nd East Surreys.

being cut off and captured; Botha ordered Commandant Fourie to move and cut the Irish off in the loop but Fourie's men had no intention of leaving the safety of their trenches and remained serenely immobile. An outraged Botha later furiously declared that Fourie's men had "continued to watch the battle, sitting manfully on the mountain".[19]

In the event, once Buller had called off his attack both British brigades extracted without too much difficulty. To the intense embarrassment of the Royal Artillery and despite several gallant efforts to recover them, only two of the 15-pounders were recovered with ten left on the field to later be captured by the Boers. Mistakenly deployed too far forward,* the gunners came under a storm of republican rifle, pom-pom and artillery fire.[20] Nevertheless, and despite taking crippling losses, the 15-pounders had been handled with incredible bravery, returning the Boer fire, silencing their guns and subduing the marksmen[21] until their ammunition was all but exhausted.[22] Buller's decision to abandon the 15-pounders was astonishing: there was no reason why they could not have been kept under fire until night fall and then recovered.

But it was not just the loss of the guns which demonstrated Buller's half-heartedness. The attack had never been pressed with much enthusiasm, and Buller never deployed his reserves. Losses were comparatively light given the size of the imperial forces involved: 143 men killed with several hundred more wounded and missing. As usual, Boer losses are uncertain, but thought to be in the region of fifty, though one contemporary Boer account claimed they were much higher: "115 killed, mostly by shellfire".[23] It is as though Buller realized very early in the piece that Botha's positions were too formidable for a frontal attack and called the whole thing off; and there was no doubt that Botha's men held a very strong position. On seeing the Colenso line, the German military attaché, von Luturz, remarked, "It is a natural fortress. I could not have believed it so perfectly defensible and almost impregnable if I had not seen it."[24]

Though it had happened inadvertently, Modder River had shown how Colenso should have been fought: an infantry brigade should have advanced to contact in the centre, springing the Boer ambush, going to ground and pinning the bulk of the Boers in place. Buller would then have had the chance of getting one or two of his other brigades over the Tugela on a flank. Even

---

* though at Modder River the Royal Artillery had deployed guns much farther forward and to great effect

allowing for the benefit of hindsight, it is difficult to understand why Buller did not adopt this plan of attack. Equally lamentable was Buller's lack of reconnaissance: had he known that Hlangwane was on the southern bank of the river, surely he would have seen that its capture was critical and would have assaulted it in force. Given the number of Natal loyalists in Buller's force, it is perplexing that no locals were able to point out this fact.

Despite the British losses being relatively light—about five per cent of his force, with only one per cent killed[25]—the Boers made enormous propaganda capital from the victory. In Pretoria it was announced: "Twelve guns and 750 prisoners captured" which, as only about 200 were captured, was the predictable exaggeration.[26] Deneys Reitz remembered that many thought that this victory meant the war was over: "These tidings caused universal rejoicing, and there were few of us who did not believe that peace would soon follow, as it had after the battle of Amajuba in 1881 … we confidently awaited the opening of peace negotiations and the surrender of Ladysmith, both of which events we expected to take place at any moment."[27]

Other rumours quickly spread through the ranks of the superstitious, naïve Boer commandos, telling of mass British mutinies and that Great Britain was bankrupt and would need to sue for peace. More bizarrely, there were widely believed rumours of two ghostly horsemen who helped the republicans in every battle, apparitions which appeared whenever the fighting started and were utterly impervious to British rifle fire.[28] Strangely no record of this gruesome twosome is found in any regimental histories of the conflict.

But what did the three Boer victories of 'Black Week' actually achieve? Firstly it is often forgotten that all three were defensive victories: by winning these battles the Boers captured no towns, ports or even an inch of ground. Though Magersfontein and Colenso had delayed the British advance,* they had little impact on the eventual result. As one observer pointed out, the Boers made no effort to follow up on these successes, dealing a fatal blow to their chances of victory: "to remain purely on the defensive was 'to suffer war, not make it'."[29] Winning only defensive battles is not a normal way to win a war, and as long as British political will stayed strong then the three republican victories

---

* bizarrely, Stormberg delayed the Boer advance if anything

of Black Week were largely a military irrelevance, despite what the Boer
propaganda machine claimed. Indeed, far from causing British resolution to
crack, if anything the defeats stiffened British determination for victory.[30]

There was certainly something approaching a frenzy in the British press at
the time, or as close as the Victorians ever got to such emotional, sensationalist
nonsense. It must be remembered that the British army had only lost over a
hundred men killed in a single action twice since the Indian Mutiny, so it
is perhaps understandable that the press should over-react. But for all the
fuss, the losses sustained at Magersfontein, Stormberg and Colenso were
insignificant by contemporary standards; during the Franco-Prussian War of
1870/1, for example, the French suffered around 13,000 casualties at the battle
of Mars-la-Tour and a staggering 37,000 at the battle of Sedan two weeks
later. In the wake of Sedan, the remainder of a 120,000-strong French army
surrendered and the French went on to sustain total casualties of 750,000 in a
war that lasted well under a year. Britain had not seen anything approaching
such carnage in generations, nor would she during the Boer War. As Colonel
F. N. Maude declared, decades of relative peace or fairly painless colonial
wars meant that the British public "did not know that bloodshed was a usual
consequence of the armed collision of combatants. Hence, the outbreak of
hysteria with which they received the news of our casualties".*

Another aspect of the tale of Black Week is that the period is generally
portrayed as a never-ending string of British thrashings. It is perfectly true to
say that Stormberg, Magersfontein and Colenso were heavy British defeats.
It is perhaps even fair to say that Magersfontein was a disaster, maybe even
a humiliation, but that is to ignore other events that occurred during Black
Week. It would be a bit like telling the tale of the British in the Second World
War but only mentioning the defeat at Narvik, the sinking of the HMS *Hood*,
the loss of Crete and the surrender at Singapore, before leaving the reader
to conclude that His Majesty's forces were defeated at every turn. It is not
lying as such, but it certainly presents the facts in such a way as to suit a given
argument. So while it doesn't fit with the usual tale of Black Week, let us take
a moment to look at what else was happening in southern Africa during early
December 1899.

---

* There is a similar reaction in the press today, with every single fatality suffered in Afghanistan reported
by the British press; to a nation which has not experienced a major war for almost three generations,
such extremely light losses are shocking and enough to prompt calls to pull out.

∂

Though by far the more famous action, Magersfontein was not the only battle fought on the western front during Black Week. On the 7th December General Prinsloo, with around 1,000 Boers and three guns, attacked Enslin Station. The position was held by just two companies of the Northamptons—perhaps 200 men—under the command of Captain H. C. Godley. Nevertheless, the steady fire of the Northamptons broke up Prinsloo's attacks, holding them off for six hours.[31] When the 12th Lancers and a battery of the Royal Artillery arrived on the scene Prinsloo quickly scurried back to Jacobsdal.[32] Despite their fivefold advantage, the Boers found it no easier to storm British trenches than the British found it to storm Boer ones. This latest fiasco was the last straw for the republican high command and the hapless Prinsloo was dismissed as head commandant of the Free-Staters for "incapacity and cowardice".[33] He was replaced by Commandant Ferreira of Ladybrand.

Over in Natal the defenders of Ladysmith were striking back at their besiegers. On the night of the 7th/8th December 500 troops of the Imperial Light Horse* and the Natal colonial regiments raided the heavy gun positions on Gun Hill. The plucky troopers picked their way through the night, advancing stealthily toward the Boer lines. While 300 men were told off as flank guards, the ILH and a hundred Natal troops advanced on the guns. A sentry was surprised, some shots were fired and the officers shouted, "Fix bayonets!" and "Give them the cold steel!"[34] The colonials had not one bayonet between them but the very thought was too much for the Boers and they fled in panic. The raiders blew up a Long Tom and a howitzer then triumphantly retired to Ladysmith, dragging a captured 7-pounder[35] (some accounts claim this was a Colt machine gun) and carrying the Long Tom's 180lb breech block with them as a souvenir.† When safely back in Ladysmith, three lusty cheers were given for the Queen.[36] The raid had been as close to perfect as could ever have been hoped, with imperial casualties of just seven men wounded.[37] In a simultaneous attack two companies of the 1st Liverpool Regiment, supported by a squadron of the 19th Hussars,[38] attacked and captured Limit Hill. The cavalry raided four miles beyond the hill, destroying the telegraph

---

* The Imperial Light Horse was called on to supply a hundred men for an "immediate risky adventure"; every man in the regiment volunteered.

† For years this breech block would grace the table top at ILH mess dinners and was later presented to Jan Smuts.

lines and shelters that were being used by the enemy.[39] On the night of the 10th/11th December, the regulars of the Rifle Brigade repeated the trick, striking a howitzer on Surprise Hill.[40] Though the howitzer was knocked out, the Boers reacted more quickly than in the previous attack and tried to cut the raiders off. The riflemen fought their way through the darkness, killing or wounding perhaps thirty Boers in close-quarter bayonet fighting. One Tommy described the action: "Colonel shouted out: 'Fix swords and charge!' and in we went … the enemy had got right up all around us, never was in such a hot place in my life … I am so glad that the RB [Rifle Brigade] have had a chance at last."[41] Deneys Reitz was one of those Boers who tried to trap the raiders, later claiming that he and just ten others "accounted for more than eighty opponents".[42] In this case the usual tiresome hyperbole is perhaps forgivable given the confusion of the action, but only sixteen riflemen were killed in the raid,[43] a considerable number of Boers had been bayoneted and, most importantly of all, the British got the gun.

Likewise, Gatacre's attack on Stormberg was not the only action on the central front during Black Week. On the 7th December mounted units of General French's command recaptured Arundel, a small town some twenty miles south of Boer-held Colesberg. The following day French himself arrived on the scene from Naauwpoort and ordered a reconnaissance in force against Boer positions on the hills at Rensberg,[44] three miles north of Arundel. In a well-coordinated action, imperial cavalry and mounted infantry* drove the Boers from their positions and took possession of them.[45] No further advance was possible as the British came under republican artillery fire but they retained possession of the hills they had captured. A prisoner disclosed that French's diminutive command was faced by about 3,000 Boers under Commandant Schoeman plus some locally raised rebels. He also revealed that Schoeman's artillery train consisted of four field pieces and three smaller guns. Furthermore, the 1,700 Boers under Commandant Grobelaar holding Burghersdorp, some eighty miles to the east of Arundel, were expecting to be reinforced by another 600 men from the Orange Free State in short order, after which this combined force would start operating in conjunction with Schoeman's command. Despite being outnumbered French remained

---

* Commanded by Colonel T. C. Porter, this *ad-hoc* mounted force was about 1,200 strong and comprised the New Zealand Mounted Rifles (about 400 men), the 6th Dragoon Guards (Carabiniers) (about 550 strong), a squadron of mounted infantry, a troop of the New South Wales Lancers, a handful of Royal Engineers and a field telegraph unit.

determined to take the fight to Schoeman, noting in his diary that "to establish a moral superiority" over the enemy is an object of the "first importance".[46]

Over the next few days French's mounted units were reinforced by 'R' Battery, RHA, three companies of the Royal Berkshires, and two squadrons each of the 10th Hussars and the Inniskilling Dragoons.[47] Early on the 11th December Colonel Porter's mounted units drove the Boers from three outposts, one of which was the hill of Vaal Kop, which was then occupied. On the 13th Schoeman made a push for Naauwpoort with 1,800 of his men. While the rest of the imperial troops held their hilltop positions, Colonel Porter met this advance with six squadrons of cavalry of perhaps 800 men and four guns of the Royal Horse Artillery. In a most satisfactory action Schoeman's two guns were quickly silenced by the British artillery and his commandos were mauled[48] and driven off by the imperial cavalry. On the west of the British position a Boer force which had captured Kuilfontein farm was blasted out of it by the two British guns on Vaal Kop, sustaining "considerable loss" as a result.[49] Imperial losses for the day amounted to just eight wounded. None of the series of actions fought by French's cavalry around Arundel during Black Week was a major engagement, but his outnumbered force had successfully out-fought and out-manoeuvred his adversary, foiling Schoeman's attempts to push deeper into the Cape Colony.

None of this is to suggest that the three British defeats of Black Week were not canings of the first order. What is however worth noting was that while most histories focus their attention on the events at Stormberg, Magersfontein and Colenso, other imperial troops were fighting and defeating their enemies on all three fronts. Black Week was certainly the nadir of imperial fortunes in the Boer War, but it was by no means the one-way street of Boer martial brilliance it is so often portrayed.

Just as the British had endured a black week in early December 1899, the Boers were to suffer their own black month in early 1900. This unremitting string of Boer defeats is largely glossed over in many histories, certainly not given anything like the attention festooned on the three British defeats during Black Week. In his account of Buller's Natal campaign, for example, Julian Symons devotes about 120 pages to describing the British defeats of Colenso,

Spion Kop and Vaal Krantz in intimate detail. In contrast, the series of battles fought constantly for sixteen days during February that saw Buller's men finally smash through the Boer's Tugela defence lines, are skipped through in just fifteen pages—less than a page a day.

Buller launched this series of actions on the 12th February. Over on the western front Lord Roberts commenced his advance the day before, and the month that followed would prove to be infinitely worse for the Boers than Black Week had been for the British. The Boer armies began February occupying large chunks of captured territory and holding formidable defensive positions in the Cape Colony and Natal. Morale was high as the burghers were flushed with the warm afterglow of their Black Week victories and confident of soon forcing the surrender of the besieged towns. A month later their commandos had been shattered and were in full retreat, with one of the Boer capitals in imperial hands.* At the end of 'Black Month', while it was still a long way off, the result of the war was no longer in any doubt.

The front lines remained largely static during the two months between Black Week and Black Month. The tiny garrison of Kuruman finally surrendered on the 1st January 1900 after holding off ten times its number for over six weeks and only after the Boers had brought up artillery to bombard the village into submission. Roberts and Kitchener arrived in Cape Town on the 10th January and took a firm grip of the western front, reorganizing their troops after the débâcle of Magersfontein. In the centre Schoeman had pulled back on Colesberg and French continued to vex the Boers, fighting a series of actions in the first days of January 1900, carrying the fight to the enemy. A sharp fight on New Year's Day was a marked success and a hill—named 'McCracken's Hill' after the assaulting commander—was taken. On the 4th a Boer counter-attack was driven off, costing the republicans some hundred killed and wounded and no less than forty prisoners.[50]

Though these actions were largely successful, on the 6th January a night attack by four companies of Suffolks went awry and a hundred men were left behind to be taken prisoner.[51] Despite this, Schoeman was kept on the back foot and his outposts were slowly herded back toward Colesberg. French continued to innovate and surprise his enemy, and on the 12th January a 15-pounder was dragged up onto the top of Cole's Kop—a feat few believed possible—and began shelling the Boers below.[52] French's operations in the

---

* Bloemfontein was captured by imperial forces on 13th March 1900

Colesberg area have largely been forgotten but they were remarkable in many ways. Though mounted troops only accounted for half his strength and his forces were always outnumbered by about three to one, French had checked the Boer invasion of the Cape Colony, bridged the yawning gap between Methuen and Gatacre, drawn Boer reinforcements into the area and achieved an "almost unbroken series of successes".[53]

On the Natal front, on the 6th January, the republicans made a determined assault against Ladysmith. A bombardment was unleashed on all parts of the perimeter and in an action now known as either 'Caesar's Camp' or 'Wagon Hill', 4,000 Boers (2,000 from each republic) were tasked to storm imperial positions on the southern defences of the town. It was a poorly coordinated assault with many Boers simply refusing to take part, or doing so very half-heartedly. A diversionary attack on Observation Hill was broken up, with the Boers, including young Deneys Reitz, fleeing in confusion[54] and leaving a score of dead in front of the imperial trenches. On the main objective of Bester's Ridge,* however, the fighting raged all day. With only about 1,000 men initially at their disposal, the British were lucky that the local commander was the gallant Colonel Ian Hamilton, though General White reacted with commendable alacrity in rushing reinforcements to the scene. White was able to communicate, coordinate his defence and direct the battle by telephone from his headquarters, something which would have been unthinkable just a few years earlier.[55]

Wagon Hill was one of the few occasions in the war where the Boers went toe-to-toe against the Tommies in close-quarter fighting, initially driving the defenders from several strongpoints. There were examples of valour and cowardice on both sides, many positions were taken and retaken throughout the battle and the result hung in the balance for much of the day. The fighting along Bester's Ridge lasted sixteen hours, finally ending when a counter-attack by three companies of the Devons cleared the last of the federals in a bayonet charge.[56]

The Boers were routed, suffering terribly as the whole British line opened up on them.[57] Five VCs were awarded in the action, including a posthumous one for Trooper Albrecht of the Imperial Light Horse,[58] the uitlander regiment's third VC of the war. A letter from one of Albrecht's comrades vividly illustrates the ILH's part in the action:

---

* Bester's Ridge was formed by the peaks of Wagon Hill and Caesar's Camp

Our squadron and another were picketing Wagon Hill … when the naval guns were being changed from their old place to this hill—when the Boers made a most determined attack about 2 am—The Hill is almost vertical and consists of big rocks and it is about 150ft high. They got right up to the top—our 2 sqdrns being only 65 strong (reduced by sickness etc.) and were shooting at 6–7ft interval[s], we being severely handicapped by not being armed with magazine rifles—Our chaps stuck to their place like men despite losing half their men … the Boers holding the crest of the hill all day. Gradually reinforcements came to us and we had an easier time—but the Boers (all Free-Staters) were splendid brave fellows;—again and again charging up only to be shot down—it was a beastly time … They kept up the attack till dark and finished with another charge in the midst of a tremendous thunderstorm—they were met by the Devons with bayonet, who shoved them back over the Hill … The Boers were splendid brave fellows and several of them were old grey-bearded chaps—they told us afterwards that their orders were to take the hill and stay there—There was a general attack all round by the Transvaal Boers—but only half-hearted—the Free Staters expressed great disgust at their behaviour.[59]

The republicans suffered dreadfully at Wagon Hill, with the cream of the besiegers being wiped out. After the battle, the British assisted the Boers to recover their dead who had been left behind, "as each succeeding hero was brought down—they *were* heroes—the Boers wrung their hands and owned that we had killed their best."[60]

To the south of Ladysmith, and after the fiasco at Colenso on the 15th December, Buller made two more attempts to break through the Boer positions on the Tugela line: General Warren's attack on Spion Kop on the 24th January and a decidedly half-hearted attempt at Vaal Krantz between the 5th and 7th February.

Though now considered a great Boer victory, Spion Kop really should have been a British triumph, and seen the lifting of the siege of Ladysmith: all the hard work had been done but no one realized it. The plan was to break the Tugela line to the west of Colenso by seizing commanding high ground.

The 11th Lancashire Brigade* under Major-General E. R. P. Woodgate, along with around 200 Natal colonials of the newly raised Thorneycroft's Mounted Infantry and a half-company of Royal Engineers, drove a Boer picket from Spion Kop on the night of the 23rd/24th January[61] and got ready to defend the peak. Oversight or incompetence meant the Lancastrians were "without machine guns, sandbags or a field telegraph unit, and with only twenty picks and shovels to entrench 2,000 men"[62]—an inexplicable mistake which was to cost them dear. Throughout the 24th, Boer artillery on neighbouring hills relentlessly bombarded this poorly entrenched force, with numerous attacks launched to drive the Lancastrians from the hill. Despite their fearful losses, however, the Tommies would not be budged. The 10th Brigade[†] under Major-General J. Talbot Coke was sent to reinforce the 11th as the 60th Rifles drove the republicans from their positions on the nearby Twin Peaks, causing panic among their ranks. A republican council of war described the situation as hopeless.[63]

By 2200 hours on the 24th, the Boers had given Spion Kop up as lost. 'Red' Daniel Opperman of the Carolina Commando ordered a withdrawal as the burghers began abandoning neighbouring positions. The shattered Boers had loaded their wagons and were fleeing as General Louis Botha arrived on the scene, begging the disheartened commandos to stay at their posts, spending the whole night going from commando to commando, imploring them not to retreat.[64] What Botha did not know, however, is that—with Major-General Woodgate mortally wounded—a comedy of errors leading to a complete mix-up was taking place among the defending force on the summit. No one seemed entirely sure who was now in command, and in the confusion the British also began to withdraw their battered but undefeated force. Incredibly, even as this was happening, a battery of mountain guns arrived and four were being carted up to reinforce the infantry. A Royal Navy 12-pounder was also being dragged up the hill under the guidance of Natal farmer who knew a route.[65] In the midst of this chaos, however, Spion Kop was abandoned. It was with disbelief that at first light Botha's men saw the hill was free to be reoccupied. Only Botha's perseverance turned defeat into victory.

A few days later Buller tried again, this time attempting to capture the ridge

---

* The 11th (Lancashire) Brigade was made up of the 2nd Royal Lancaster Regiment, 2nd Lancashire Fusiliers, 1st South Lancashire Regiment and the 1st York and Lancaster Regiment.

† The 10th Infantry Brigade was formed from the 2nd Middlesex Regiment, 2nd Dorsetshire Regiment, 2nd Somerset Light Infantry and the Imperial Light Infantry.

known as Vaal Krantz. As at Colenso, Buller seemed to lose heart early in
the piece and the attempt was limp at best. Lyttelton's 4th (Light) Brigade*
crossed the Tugela on pontoon bridges and seized their objectives but Buller
did not grasp the opportunity that Lyttelton's men had won for him.[66] Buller
convinced himself that to take the next objective, Green Hill, would cost the
lives of 2,000–3,000 of his men[67] and instead called the Light Brigade back
across the Tugela once more.

ȣ

The battles of the opening months of the Boer War illustrate that the advent
of the magazine rifle,[†] smokeless powder and field communications had
shifted the balance of power decisively in favour of defending troops. Imperial
defensive victories at Wagon Hill, Cannon Kop, Kuruman and Enslin Station
clearly demonstrate that it made little difference if the defending troops were
Boers or British: storming any fortified position was an immensely difficult
undertaking. Like the Germans fifteen years later, overall it was the Boers
who benefited most from these technological advances, however. They had
invaded and taken someone else's territory, meaning that they had the luxury
of having to be driven out of their positions. Like the British troops in the
First World War, sitting back in trenches was simply not an option for the
Tommies in the Boer War: the only way the war could be won was by forcing
the republican invaders out of Natal and the Cape Colony. The war is often
portrayed as illustrating Boer brilliance in defence and British ineptitude in
attack, but this ignores the reality that both sides struggled to assault defensive
positions. Indeed, and despite their numerous setbacks, the British infantry
consistently proved to be much better at it than the Boers, especially during
the Black Month.

The republicans had held the initiative for the first few months of the
war. Their superiority in numbers and mobility had left the imperial forces
dancing to their tune and, largely, fighting battles where it suited the Boers
to fight them. With the arrival of Lord Roberts, this changed. The day after
his arrival in Cape Town, Roberts sent the following telegram to Methuen:

---

* Commanded by Major-General the Hon. N. G. Lyttelton, the 4th (Light) Brigade was formed from the
2nd Scottish Rifles, 3rd King's Royal Rifle Corps, 1st Durham Light Infantry and the 1st Rifle Brigade.

† although the Imperial Light Horse did not have them, virtually all other units did

"I have come to the conclusion that I must ask you to act strictly on the defensive, and as it may be even necessary for me to withdraw a portion of your force, you should consider how your line of entrenchments could be sufficiently reduced to enable you to hold the position with two, instead of three, brigades, and possibly with one or two batteries and one regiment of cavalry less than you have at present. Your request for four of the siege 4.7-in. guns will be complied with, and when these reach you, you will doubtless be able to make your position practically impregnable."[68]

There would be no more piecemeal attacks or half-baked attempts to break through the Boer defences: Roberts would spend the next month planning and preparing for his attack, and doing so in complete secrecy. Undetected by the enemy, an enormous stockpile of supplies was gathered in the area of Graspan, ready to support the long-awaited thrust toward Kimberley. By use of clever troop movements and the issuing of false orders, which he knew would be intercepted by the enemy, Roberts convinced the Boers that this thrust, when it came, would be in the centre in the Colesberg area and not in the west. The republican high command was duly fooled, with President Steyn ordering General de Wet to redeploy the Free State commandos from the Magersfontein defences to Colesberg. Though de Wet refused, railway records later proved that 1,500 burghers were redeployed to the Colesberg defences between the 25th January and the 8th February 1900.[69] From the 28th January to the 12th February, however, Roberts was assembling his forces at the Graspan camp, not in front of Colesberg.

As Roberts laid his plans, the imperial forces finally had a reasonable number of troops in theatre. A colonial division had been raised from South African loyalists and more regular infantry units were converted to mounted infantry. More artillery was arriving at the front, and the ammunition for such was ameliorated. After the surprise of facing them in Boer hands, forty-nine Vickers-Maxim pom-poms had been bought and rushed to South Africa. Roberts also overhauled the transport system and set about reorganizing the running of the railways.[70]

Roberts assembled his forces, ready for the big push in the west. General French had been summoned to command a cavalry division comprising three cavalry and two mounted infantry brigades. There were also two infantry divisions available: the 6th under Kelly-Kenny, the 7th (Tucker) and another, the 9th (Colville), being formed.[71] Including Methuen's 1st Infantry

Division[72] (comprising the Guards and the 9th Infantry brigades) which was
left to screen the Magersfontein defences and thus would not play an active
part in the offensive, the total force was about 40,000 strong, and all this
remained undetected by Cronjé as he sat blissfully unaware at Magersfontein,
cheerfully convinced that his men could repulse any frontal assault. Despite
the modern take on the conflict, however, the force Roberts commanded was
by no means an overwhelming; indeed, on the 4th February, Roberts sent
a telegram to the War Office, to point out the paucity of forces available in
South Africa.[73]

As well as reorganizing his command, establishing a supply depot and
deceiving the enemy into where his killer blow would be delivered, Roberts
took the time to reinforce the lessons of the conflict thus far. Various 'Notes
for Guidance in South African Warfare' were issued for each of the fighting
arms:

INFANTRY

As it is desirable that full advantage should be taken of the experience
gained during the past three months by our troops in South Africa,
the following notes are issued for the guidance of all who may find
themselves in command of a force (large or small) on service in the
field. We have to deal with an enemy possessing remarkable mobility,
intimately acquainted with the country, thoroughly understanding
how to take advantage of ground, adept in improvising cover, and
most skilful in the use of their weapons.

Against such an enemy any attempt to take a position by direct
attack will assuredly fail. The only hope of success lies in being able to
turn one or both flanks, or what would, in many instances, be equally
effective, to threaten to cut the enemy's line of communication.
Before any plan of attack can be decided upon, the position must
be carefully examined by reconnoitring parties, and every endeavour
must be made to obtain all possible information about it from the
people of the country. It must, however, be remembered that the
position ostensibly occupied is not always the one the Boers intend to
defend; it is often merely a decoy, a stronger position in the vicinity
having previously been prepared upon which they move rapidly, and
from which they can frequently bring a destructive fire to bear upon

the attacking line. Their marvellous mobility enables them to do this without much risk to themselves, and also to be in strength at any point of the position that may be seriously threatened.

It follows, therefore, that our object should be to cripple the mobility of the Boers, and to effect this, next to inflicting heavy losses on the men themselves, the surest means would be the capture or destruction of their horses. When the extreme rifle range from the position is reached (1,500 to 1,800 yards) by the advance troops, or before, if they find themselves under artillery fire, all column formations must be given up, and, when advancing to the attack of the position infantry must be freely extended, even on occasions, if necessary, to six or eight paces, the front and both flanks being well covered with scouts. This extended formation will throw increased responsibility on battalion and company commanders. The objective aimed at, therefore, should be carefully explained to them. They should be allowed to make use of any opportunity that may offer to further the scheme, on the distinct understanding that no isolated acts are attempted, such as might endanger the general plan. During the attack commanding officers must be careful not to lose touch with the troops on their right and left, and they should, as far as possible, ensure their co-operation. Every advantage should be taken of cover, and battalion and company commanders should look out for and occupy positions from which they would be able to bring an enfilading fire to bear upon the enemy. The capacity of these officers will be judged by the initiative displayed in seizing rapidly every opportunity to further the general scheme of attack.

An essential point, and one which must never be lost sight of, is the power of endurance of the infantry soldier. If infantry soldiers (carrying as they do a considerable weight on their backs) are called upon to march a longer distance than can reasonably be expected from men in a normal state of health, or if they are injudiciously pressed as regards the pace, they will necessarily commence to feel the strain before they reach a point where their best energies are required to surmount the difficulties which lie before them. If at such a period a man feels exhausted, moral deterioration and the consequences to our arms which such deterioration entails, must readily supervene.[74]

It is difficult to disagree that this was anything other than sensible advice. The gunners and mounted troops got similarly good advice:

ARTILLERY

As a general rule the artillery appear to have adapted themselves to the situation, and to the special conditions which present themselves in a campaign in South Africa. The following points, however, require to be noticed:

1. At the commencement of an action artillery should not be ordered to take up a position until it has been ascertained by scouts to be clear of the enemy and out of range of infantry fire.

2. When it is intended to take a position with infantry the preparation by artillery should be thorough and not spasmodic. Unless a strong force of infantry is pushed within 900 yards of the position, the enemy will not occupy his trenches and the guns will have no target. It is a mere waste of ammunition also to bombard an entrenchment when the infantry attack is likely to be delayed, even for a short time. To be of real value the fire of the guns should be continuous until the assault is about to be delivered.

3. The expenditure of ammunition is a matter which can only be regulated by the circumstances of the moment; officers commanding should, however, always bear in mind that the supply of artillery ammunition in the field is necessarily limited.

4. It is of great importance that artillery horses should be kept fit for any special effort. They are not easily replaced, and it is the duty of artillery officers to represent to the commander of the column whenever they consider that their horses are being unduly worked, as regards either pace or distance.

CAVALRY AND MOUNTED TROOPS

Similarly with cavalry horses. Every endeavour should be made to save them as much as possible, for unless this is done they cannot be expected to last through a lengthened campaign. The men should dismount on every available opportunity, if for a few minutes only at a time, and, on the line of march, it will be advantageous for them to occasionally lead instead of riding their horses. Horses should be fed at short intervals, and not allowed to be kept too long without water. A sufficiency of grain is necessary to enable horses to withstand hard work, but they will never keep in condition unless they have an ample supply of hay or some bulky equivalent.

On the line of march scouting must be carried out by the mounted troops in the most searching manner, in front and on both flanks. All high ground should be visited and, whenever practicable, horsemen should ride along ridges and hills. As soon as parties of the enemy are observed the mounted troops (after sending back word to the commander) should make a considerable detour round the position occupied by the Boers, endeavour to estimate their numbers, and to ascertain where their horses have been left. They should also see whether, by threatening the Boers' line of communication, they would not be forced to fight on ground unprepared for defence.[75]

Many other communications followed, detailing such things as how infantry should take the opportunity to dig in whenever they could, suggesting methods to improve ammunition supply to the forward troops and combating the problem of retaining 'grip' of troops in the new, extended orders. Roberts was not a man to leave anything to chance. Some claim that the British won because they massively outnumbered the Boers, but this is simply not the case. The outnumbered garrisons of Natal and the Cape Colony had checked the Boer invasions and indeed even driven them back. It was only in early February that Roberts had collected and organized a large enough force to mount a determined offensive. Most importantly, Roberts finally had enough mounted troops and transport to allow him to leave the critical railway lines. Even then the numbers of imperial troops were in no way overwhelming: total imperial forces in southern Africa (including those bottled up in Kimberley and Ladysmith) at the beginning of Black Month were only around 90,000,[76] with some of these units still forming. Talk of 'divisions' and 'brigades' is also misleading. On paper, for example, French's Cavalry Division should have boasted 8,500 horsemen: in the event, he only had 4,000 and seven batteries of horse artillery.[77]

The shortage of water was another huge problem for Roberts. The Orange

Free State in mid-summer is a hot and dusty place, and the lack of water would force the British to keep their units well spaced as they advanced.

On the 11th February Roberts's great flanking move began as, led by the slouch-hatted troopers of Rimington's Tigers, French's Cavalry Division set off in an easterly direction toward the farm of Ramdam. From there and over the following days French would continue east, striking toward Waterval Drift on the Riet River before turning northward past Jacobsdal to seize Klip Drift on the Modder River.[78] The plan called for the 6th and 7th Infantry divisions—the 9th Division was still forming—to follow the cavalry at intervals and hold these drifts while the cavalry pushed on to relieve Kimberley, simultaneously cutting off Cronjé's force at Magersfontein which was to be destroyed in detail. Rather like the paratroopers at Market Garden in 1944, the cavalry was tasked with bursting through enemy-held territory to capture and hold the river crossings, and doing so on an extremely tight schedule due to the limited supplies that they could carry. It was as audacious as it was brilliant.

There had been some limited skirmishing, but on the 13th French's cavalry were closing in on the drifts over the Modder River. By means of a feint toward Klip Kraal Drift, a few miles farther east, French threw the Boers off balance before striking toward his real objective of Klip Drift. The burghers holding Klip Drift were taken completely by surprise and fled, abandoning their laager. French took the crossing at the cost of just three men wounded. The cost in horses had been higher, however: 500 of the wretched beasts were unable to continue, with forty dying of exhaustion on the march.[79]

As the Cavalry Division paused to await the arrival of the infantry which would secure the crossing at Klip Drift, Cronjé dithered at Magersfontein, some ten miles to the west. He had initially sent de Wet with just 450 men to drive back the British cavalry,[80] which unsurprisingly de Wet had proved completely unable to do. He did, however, send a panic-stricken message to Cronjé, informing his commander that French's force was 40,000–50,000 strong. De Wet, who had the benefit of writing his own history of his part in the war, later claimed he knew exactly what French's aim was, though this is by no means borne out in his actions at the time or by the orders that he gave.[81] Seemingly unable—or unwilling—to believe what he was told by those who had fled Klip Drift, and not grasping the severity of the position he was now in, Cronjé still dismissed French's thrust as a mere feint. Cronjé's inactivity may well have been inspired by a bizarre arrogance: he cheerfully informed Count Sternberg that the British forces threatening his flank were "only cavalry—who we shoot and capture".[82] Despite the much-vaunted mobility of the Boer commandos, Cronjé showed no inclination to leave his fortifications on the Magersfontein ridge and in so doing surrendered the initiative to Roberts and French.

A series of hills to the north and east of Klip Drift was held by republican forces, as was a ridge which stretched away to the west toward Cronjé's main position at Magersfontein. Between these, however, was a long valley about a mile wide which pointed almost directly toward Kimberley. This was not considered to be strongly held by the enemy and so, during the morning of the 15th, French ordered his division to advance through it at a "fast gallop". This charge was covered by both his horse artillery batteries and the artillery of Kelly-Kenny's newly arrived 6th Infantry Division.[83] The Boers on the high ground opened fire as best they could, but were fairly ineffective against the charging horsemen. The dust, open order and considerable British artillery support all worked against the republicans and, led by the 9th and 16th Lancers, the horsemen swept up the valley like a latter-day charge of the Light Brigade. Those Boers unfortunate enough to be in the valley were ridden down, speared or taken captive. British losses in the action were just two killed and seventeen wounded, and the way to Kimberley lay open.[84] That evening French rode into town to be met by the mayor.[85] More important even than the relief of Kimberley, however, was that Cronjé's force at Magersfontein was now all but cut off.

French's cavalry action at Klip Drift was greatly admired, with *The Times History* saying: "The charge at Klip Drift marks an epoch in the history of cavalry … the quick insight that prompted it, the instantaneous decision that launched it against the enemy, the reckless dare-devil confidence that carried it through … the thin line of unseen riflemen, with its wide gaps covered by converging fire, which had proved so unapproachable to the slow, short-winded foot soldier, availed nothing against the rushing speed and sustained impetus of the wave of horsemen."[86] Captain Foster of the Royal Horse Artillery recorded the charge in his diary: "General French decided to risk a bit & make a dash up a plain about 2 miles broad with all his cavalry … the move was entirely successful and it was a grand sight to see line after line of cavalry galloping as hard as they could for 5 miles up the plain. Kopjes lined both sides of the plain & the Boers blazed away from either side but we soon cleared them out ... the Lancers had managed to spear some twenty odd Boers."[87]

Technically it was not really a cavalry charge as such: it was not aimed at shattering an enemy force but was rather directed at the weakest point in the enemy line so as to break through. Indeed, had the Boers strung just a few strands of wire across the valley floor, it might have all ended differently. But it was still a brilliant example of dash, determination and courage. Indeed, French's march as a whole had been the most dynamic and resolute move of the war to date. Modern writers tend to pour cold water on his achievements, pointing out that by thrusting forward so quickly, he exhausted his horses. But this is to completely misunderstand the point: if French hadn't driven his division on he would not have achieved his objectives, Cronjé would have been able to pull back from the Magersfontein fortifications and set up blocking positions at Klip Drift. It doesn't make sense to criticize other imperial commanders for plodding forward at a snail's pace, and to criticize one when he acts with flair, drive and dash; and the sacrifice of the horses would not be in vain.

Cronjé's reaction to this *coup de main* was a mixture of disbelief and panic. One witness recorded: "It appears to me that the General has lost his head and seems as helpless as a little child. Now is the time he should show his generalship, at all events keep a little order and discipline, and make his people face the music. They are spanning in like blazes already, seem not to know where to go, instead of the General giving some definite orders, he is going about like a beaten dog with his tail between his legs. He got us into this hole and should, at all events, have some plan formed to get us out."

When the French military adviser Colonel Villebois advocated a counter-attack to let the majority of his force escape, Cronjé rejected this.[88] The republicans finally began to react but it was too little too late. Not eager to take on the fighting Tommies who were bursting forward,[89] de Wet instead contented himself with attacking a supply column at Waterval Drift.[90] While the 500-strong escort held their own against de Wet's 1,000-strong force, the Boers managed to drive off or kill 800 out of 1,600 oxen needed to move the British supplies forward. Rather than slow the advance, however, Roberts ordered that the supplies be left where they were and pressed on.[91] The republican garrison was driven out of Jacobsdal[92] on the 16th and, unnoticed by Lord Methuen, Cronjé had finally abandoned the Magersfontein defences the following day, also managing to slip past Kelly-Kenny's slow-moving 6th Infantry Division.

Cronjé's rearguard was harried by imperial mounted infantry all the way, however; later that day the head of the fleeing column was intercepted by French's cavalry as they attempted to cross the Modder River drifts to safety. Such was the suffering endured by French's horses on his flank march that, when he was ordered to move back from Kimberley to block Cronjé, he could only muster 1,500 men and twelve guns. Nevertheless, French rushed this scratch force south-east in time to catch Cronjé's men crossing Vendutie Drift. The 12-pounders of the Royal Horse Artillery opened up on the leading Boer wagons as they picked their way across the river, causing panic and disorder. Many of the Boer oxen and horses, outspanned and waiting on the far bank, bolted.[93] Again, when he should have attacked to repulse French, Cronjé dithered. With another 2,000 Boers in the area, he outnumbered French by three to one, but instead chose to dig in on the riverbanks near the drift at Paardeberg. Cronjé's decision to entrench rather than break out was undoubtedly the wrong one, but it was probably the only one available to him. Though fearsome in defence, the Boers were a fairly one-dimensional army; as one British officer observed: "The Boer is a very practical sort of man, and, although he can be as brave as anyone else if he thinks it worthwhile, does not seem to get any pleasure out of being shot at, and generally thinks out for himself the best way of avoiding that condition at the moment. Finding himself in a tight corner, therefore, his first idea was to put his body in a safe place, and his second was to make that place as poor a target for our guns as possible."[94]

By the following morning, as Cronjé's men dug in, both the 6th and 9th Infantry divisions had arrived on the scene to seal the deal. Rather than bombard the Boers into submission with artillery, Kitchener, temporarily standing in for Roberts, made the remarkable decision to storm Cronjé's position that afternoon, an attack which ended in predictable and costly failure. While Kitchener's determination to assault the Cronjé's position at Paardeberg seems peculiar, it must be compared to the dithering and indecision that marked other battles. Kitchener was resolved not to let victory slip through his fingers and allow Cronjé to escape or the numerous other Boer forces in the area to break through to rescue him. Calmer heads quickly prevailed, however, and Roberts returned to command to order that the Boers entrenchments should be bombarded by artillery, directed by an observer up in a balloon.[95]

An attempt by de Wet to break through to Cronjé on the 21st was driven off by French's cavalry. Another led by Commandant Steyn was broken up by the 81st Battery, RA; so heavy was the bombardment that Steyn was forced to abandon his guns, only recovering them after nightfall.[96] Over the next few days the imperial infantry tightened their stranglehold on Cronjé's position, nudging their trenches forward.

On the night of the 26th/27th some of Roberts's Canadian troops had pushed their saps to within just ninety yards of the Boer lines. When day broke on the 27th—Majuba Day—Cronjé surrendered with around 4,000 men and four guns. The surrender at Paardeberg was a devastating blow to the republican cause.*

The effects of Roberts's march were soon felt on the central front. The Boers had been forced to redeploy their men from the Colesberg area and that town was recaptured by General Clements (who had replaced General French) on the 26th February. Stormberg was also abandoned as the republicans fell back on positions inside the Orange Free State.[97]

General Brabant's newly formed Colonial Division had also been on the move, attacking and defeating a Boer force at Dordrecht on the 16th and liberating Jamestown a week later. The Boers retreated before the colonials, heading for the Orange River. The Cape rebels in Barkly East had the temerity to ask for terms and were informed there would be none other than unconditional surrender.[98]

As Roberts was commencing his great advance in the west, Buller was also active in Natal. After the still-born attack on Vaal Krantz, Buller had again moved his field force back across the Tugela, essentially back to where he had been before the battle of Colenso. There is a commonly held view that the wily Boers were always one step ahead of the pedantic British, though this was certainly not the case here. General Meyer was perplexed by Buller's

---

* Amazingly, one modern writer even tries to put a positive spin on this crushing defeat, declaring that the British failed to capture those enemy armaments and equipment which had been "shrewdly" thrown in the Modder River.

redeployment, as revealed in a telegram he sent on the 10th: "It is not impossible they will now entrench themselves on some place or another, and that the greater part of them are going to Cape Colony."[99]

On the 12th February, the day after Roberts unleashed French's cavalry on the western front, Buller sent Dundonald's Mounted Brigade* to make a reconnaissance in force against Boer-held Hussar Hill. On the 14th Dundonald's men occupied the hill and were soon reinforced by some naval guns and two infantry brigades.[100] Though no one perhaps realized it, these were the opening moves in what would later be named the battle of the Tugela Heights. Though virtually unknown today, this hard-fought battle would last for two weeks, and see the republicans turned out of one defensive position after another in some of the hardest-fought infantry actions of the war.

The Boer command structure during the battle of the Tugela Heights was a confused one. After Joubert's illness, command had passed to General Lukas Meyer, though General Louis Botha was Joubert's first choice and was effectively in charge. Meyer and Botha had around 7,000 burghers[101] to hold the Tugela defences, while Buller faced them with around 25,000 men. Though these numbers look overwhelming at first glance, it should be remembered that the Boers were holding well-fortified positions and, unlike the British, all their troops were fighting men. They were also highly mobile and thus easily able to reposition to counter any potential British thrust, whereas Buller had to keep half an eye on his lines of supply at all times. Also, a sizeable chunk of Buller's force were engineers, balloon detachments, telegraph companies, ammunition companies, medical staff and the like and the lion's share of the actual fighting would be done by his five infantry brigades of perhaps 19,000 men.[102] It should also be remembered that many thousands more Boers were camped around Ladysmith just a few miles to the north, and it is reckoned that between 1,500 and 2,000 of these were redeployed to the Tugela line during the battle, giving a total federal strength of nearer 9,000 men-at-arms.[103] This number also excludes the thousands of blacks who accompanied the Boers, and whose exertions permitted the rapid digging of extensive entrenchments. The positions held by the Boers were indeed formidable. When later examined by Royal Engineers, they were described as being "about four feet deep, with a parapet three feet in height,

---

*   later Lieutenant-General Douglas Mackinnon Baillie Hamilton Cochrane, 12th Earl of Dundonald
    KCB, KCVO (1852–1935)

and several feet in thickness. Their occupants stood up to fire through small loopholes. In selecting sites for these entrenchments, the Boers had shown their usual skill, and to conceal them and blur their outline, bushes, rocks and boughs of trees had been scattered in front of them. Good use was made of dummy trenches, ostentatiously built in open ground to draw artillery fire".[104]

The guns of the Royal Artillery hammered republican positions on Cingolo Hill throughout the 15th and 16th February before Hildyard's 2nd Brigade* assaulted it early on the 17th. Colonel Norcott's 4th (Rifle) Brigade† pushed forward toward the defile between Cingolo and Monte Cristo while Barton's 6th Brigade‡ remained in support. The Boers were driven from Cingolo that afternoon, with the Tommies shouting "Majuba! Majuba!" as they advanced. The next part of Buller's puzzle had fallen into place and Louis Botha began to realize things were serious, requesting reinforcements from the besiegers of Ladysmith.

Buller's next objective was Monte Cristo, a peak a mile or so to the north-west of Cingolo. Supported by machine-gun fire from Cingolo, the British 2nd Infantry Brigade surged up its southern slopes in the early hours of the 18th. Monte Cristo was secured by midday, the bag of prisoners including one Constantine von Braun, a colonel in the German army who was clad in an "an oilskin coat with steel netting".[105] With Monte Cristo taken, the 4th and 6th brigades then stormed the ridge known as Green Hill. These Boer positions were also masterfully constructed, as a witness described: "the surface soil was extremely shallow, not 6" in places, and as the trenches were sunk to the depth of about 5 feet, they had for the most part to be hewn out of the solid rock. This seemed to have been done entirely by manual labour, as mark of picks were apparent on the stone … although there were some two miles of trenches, none of them were straight, but cut in zigzag fashion to avoid enfilading fire … the width of the trenches at the top was never more than 2 feet, and they widened out at the bottom to nearly 4 feet, being, in fact, so hollowed out as to afford excellent protection against shell-fire. The clay and rocks removed to make the excavation were thrown up in front in the

---

* The 2nd Infantry Brigade consisted of the 2nd Royal West Surrey Regiment (the Queen's), 2nd Devons, 2nd East Surreys and the 2nd West Yorkshires.

† The 4th (Rifle) Brigade was made up from the 1st Durham Light Infantry, 1st Scottish Rifles, 3rd King's Royal Rifle Corps and 1st Rifle Brigade (The Prince Consort's Own).

‡ The 6th Brigade comprised the 2nd Royal Fusiliers, 2nd Royal Scots Fusiliers, 1st Royal Welsh Fusiliers and the 2nd Royal Irish Fusiliers.

form of a solid embankment, which was in many cases surmounted by sacks full of clay, with sods, cut grass, and bushes in front to conceal the ridge."[106]

By nightfall, however, both Monte Cristo and Green Hill were firmly in British hands and a pair of naval guns was being dragged up to the summit of the former. Buller sent a congratulatory message to the assaulting troops: "Shall you be able to make yourself comfortable there for the night? Dundonald knows where water is. We see many mounted Boers running away from your front."[107]

The Boer hilltop defenders had indeed fled across the Tugela, leaving Hlangwane as the only Boer-held peak south of the river. Hlangwane was occupied by the Bethal Commando; realizing how critical it was that this position be held, Botha ordered the Heidelberg Commando to cross the Tugela and reinforce them, but for one reason or another, the Heidelbergers never arrived.[108] The following day Hlangwane was assaulted by the Tommies and, after a sharp fight, the Bethal Commando abandoned their sangars and fled across the Tugela. In their haste they left behind an enormous quantity of entrenching gear, some sixty horses and a large amount of ammunition, including considerable quantities of expanding rounds which were forbidden by international law.[109]

The newly emplaced 12-pounder naval guns on Monte Cristo began shelling Boer gun positions on the northern bank of the Tugela that morning. Later in the day they were joined by a pair of RN 4.7-inch guns and two batteries of Royal Artillery 15-pounders.

By the 20th, the village of Colenso was recaptured and, in so doing, the last remaining Boers had been driven from their positions on the southern bank of the Tugela. When imperial troops entered Colenso they found an apocalyptic scene: "The village had been shamefully looted and polluted. What had once been a peaceful and picturesque little hamlet was now a mass of foetid ruins ... the enemy had dragged their dead horses into the interior of the houses and they lay in the rooms among broken furniture and debris. The corrugated-zinc roofs had been torn off the buildings, all the available woodwork had been removed for fuel, window and doors were wantonly smashed ... some Boer prisoners were afterwards employed, while waiting for their train to Durban, by the officer in charge to drag these putrid horses away and bury them."[110]

Buller's advance had not been dramatic or dashing like French's sweeping right hook, but was rather a steady, methodical and ultimately irresistible, unlocking of the Boer positions, taking each in turn. His staff urged him to follow the retreating Boers over the Tugela, but the general remained cautious and had no intention of throwing away his advantage on a whim. Though they had been driven from their positions, leaving behind enormous stocks of ammunition and stores,[111] the Boer retreat across the Tugela was by no means a rout, and there was no reason to assume Botha's force was shattered. Buller was also well aware that there were many thousands of Boers encamped around Ladysmith and understandably assumed that they would be marching south to support their comrades manning the Tugela defences. In reality, the series of defeats south of the river had taken a serious toll on the Boer force, and it is reckoned that only about 3,000 remained to defend what was left of the Tugela line; over half of Botha's men had either become causalities or—more likely—had deserted during the first week of the battle. Kruger sent a typically unrealistic 'stand and fight' order to his beleaguered burghers, treating them to a bit of an Old Testament rant in so doing. Joubert got off his deathbed to review the defensive positions but Botha was too busy to even meet his former commander. In contrast, clearing the southern bank of the Tugela had cost Buller 305 casualties, with only twenty-five killed.[112]

On the 21st Buller's engineers constructed a pontoon bridge across the Tugela just behind Hlangwane. Coke's 10th Brigade was given the dubious honour of crossing the bridge and driving on to the Colenso Kopjes beyond. Once more, the poor fire discipline of the Boers worked against them as Coke's men came under heavy fire far sooner than Botha had planned. Nevertheless, the 10th Brigade could make no progress against the unseen marksmen and pulled back at nightfall. Overnight, more imperial troops crossed the pontoon and on the 22nd Major-General Wynne's 11th Infantry Brigade* was tasked with storming Boer positions on Horseshoe and Hedge hills, positions identified as Wynne's Hill (West), Wynne's Hill and Wynne's Hill (East). The Lancashire men went forward in good style but soon came under heavy rifle fire. Wynne himself was badly wounded in the thigh and handed command to Colonel Crofton of the Royal Lancaster Regiment. The defending Boers fell back to a second line of defence, leaving the Tommies in a very exposed position and one not helped when their own supporting

---

* The 11th (Lancashire) Brigade was made up of the 2nd Royal Lancasters, 1st South Lancashires, 1st York and Lancasters and the 2nd Lancashire Fusiliers whom we last met at Spion Kop.

artillery opened up on them by mistake. A republican counter-attack drove the British back, but they quickly rallied and, with bayonets fixed and cheering as they came, surged back up the slopes, driving the Boers back to their second line of defence once more.[113]

Night fell on the stalemate with the federals still holding sangars on all three hills, and the 11th Brigade clinging on to dearly won positions by their fingertips. The battle continued through the night as Boer raiding parties were driven off by bayonet charges; it was savage fighting with the Boers making widespread use of expanding bullets throughout the defence.[114] There was no let-up in the fighting throughout the 23rd as fresh battalions were brought up to relieve the exhausted men of the 11th Brigade.

Accepting that the attack on Wynne's Hill had got as far as it was going to, Buller turned to General Hart's 5th (Irish) Brigade.* Hart's Irishmen had been seriously mauled at Colenso and, it might be reasonably assumed, had a point to prove. Their objective was christened 'Hart's Hill' and lay a couple of miles north-east of the positions on Wynne's Hill.

Defended by the Rustenburg and Krugersdorp commandos, with some elements of the Boksburg and Wakkerstroom commandos,[115] all under the command of Veldkornet Sarel Oosthuizen, who was promptly made a general by Meyer. Hart's men set off at lunchtime on the 23rd, moving in single file while using the banks of the Tugela to shelter themselves from long-range Boer fire, though still suffering the attentions of a pom-pom gun. Hart urged his men forward, ordering his bugler to call the 'double!' and 'charge!' repeatedly. With only a couple of hours of daylight left, there was little time to lose. At first all went well. The Irishmen surged up the hill with great dash, as the Boers quickly withdrew from their forward positions to their main defences whence they poured a murderous fusillade into the Irishmen. The attack stalled.

The battered 5th Brigade clung on to the ground they had won through the night and, by dawn on the 24th, had thrown up sangars to protect their positions, as reinforcements were pushed up to Hart. Daylight revealed that in places the opposing lines were just 300 yards apart, with the no-man's-land strewn with the wounded, the dead and the dying of the previous day's

---

* The 5th (Irish) Brigade consisted of the 1st Royal Inniskilling Fusiliers, 1st Connaught Rangers, 2nd Royal Dublin Fusiliers and half a battalion of the Imperial Light Infantry. For the attack on the 23rd, the brigade was reinforced by the 1st Durham Light Infantry and the 1st Rifle Brigade, both attached from the 4th Brigade.

carnage. Shortly after first light, the firing stopped when a party of Boers emerged under a Red Cross flag and approached some of these unfortunate souls. After first dragging away their own wounded, the party then sidled over to where the British casualties lay and started "despoiling the dead and wounded, taking off their boots and emptying out their pockets".[116] Needless to say, this so incensed their khaki comrades that a fearsome fusillade was unleashed on the ghoulish looters. This in turn incensed the republicans in the trenches, who oddly considered it a breach of the flag of truce, and they brutally shot down several wounded Tommies who were trying to crawl toward the Irish sangars.

There was little evidence of a 'Gentleman's War' being fought on Hart's Hill. One British prisoner who endured two days of captivity in a Boer trench stated that he was denied food or water throughout his ordeal, and that "there were a number of our wounded lying close to the trenches, and asking for water all the time, which was always refused. If any of the wounded moved, they were shot at. Most of them died for want of assistance, as they had to lay there for two days and two nights. The Boers said, 'Let them die, and give them no water.'"[117]

The bad blood continued into Sunday, the 25th. Buller requested an armistice to enable the wounded lying out on Wynne's and Hart's hills to be attended to. This was formally refused, but Meyer and Botha did consent to the wounded being removed as long as no attempt was made to attack.[118] The refusal of a full armistice helped both sides: the Boers used the chance to improve their fortifications and the British redeployed their artillery to cover the next phase of the battle. Buller had banged his head on the federal defences and not broken through, but he retained the initiative and calmly reorganized and redeployed for another crack.

On the 27th he unleashed ten battalions (perhaps 8,000 men) against Pieter's and Railway hills on the extreme right of the Boer defences—the extreme left as viewed by Generals Botha and Meyer. The massed artillery batteries opened up on the Boer positions at 0800 hours, with a line of twenty-two machine guns adding their own deadly contribution[119] as the dauntless Tommies formed up for the assault. Lead by Barton's 6th Brigade,* the infantry surged up the steep slopes, brushing aside a small outpost and

---

* The 6th Brigade had been reorganized and was now just three battalions strong: the Royal Irish Fusiliers, 2nd Royal Scots Fusiliers and the 2nd Royal Dublin Fusiliers which had transferred from Hart's 5th Brigade.

heading for Pieter's Hill. The 11th Brigade,* now under Colonel Kitchener†
due to Wynne's injury, followed the 6th and assaulted Railway Hill. The
Tommies pushed forwards despite the hail of gunfire which swept over them.
Railway Hill was taken at bayonet point by the South Lancashires and the
West Yorks. The defenders fled, sparking a similar reaction from the Boers on
the eastern defences of Hart's Hill.[120] Norcott's 4th Brigade‡ was then flung
into action to take Hart's Hill. The objective was secured by 1800 hours.

Over on the far right, the republicans clung to their posts on Pieter's Hill,
but were forced to abandon them by midnight. Deneys Reitz witnessed the
attacks, and described "British infantry swarming over the skyline, their
bayonets flashing in the sun ... a rout of burghers broke back from the hill,
streaming towards us in disorderly flight. The soldiers fired into them,
bringing many down as they made blindly past us, not looking to right or left
... Of our Pretoria men who had been on the ridge not one came back".[121]

The loss of Railway, Pieter's and Hart's hills rendered the whole Tugela
line indefensible; the Boers were in full retreat by daybreak on the 28th as
imperial mounted units pressed forward to relieve Ladysmith that afternoon.

Buller's victory came at a high price but it was still a remarkable feat. In two
weeks of almost non-stop fighting, he had smashed the near-impregnable
Tugela line and raised the siege. The Boers had been soundly beaten, as
recorded by one of their officers: "All our best efforts did not avail, we had
lost the battle—hopelessly lost—we had to retire. The Standertonians retired
first, then the Johannesburgers, the Krugersdorpers followed (nearly all killed
or captured) and Pretorians ... the enemy was the master of the battlefield
and we had to flee."[122]

It was a battle which belonged more to the First World War than a colonial
campaign, fought over a number of days along a broad front, demanding close
cooperation between the infantry and the artillery. There had been setbacks
but Buller had plugged on methodically and resolutely, shifting the axis of
advance this way and that, probing for a weak point until he broke through.

Two weeks into Black Month and the republican forces were reeling on all
fronts. Kimberley and Ladysmith had been relieved, Cronjé had surrendered

---

* The 11th Brigade consisted of the 1st South Lancashires, 1st York and Lancasters, Royal Lancaster and
  six companies of the 2nd West Yorks.

† Lord Kitchener's brother

‡ The 4th Brigade had been reorganized as follows: the 1st Durham Light Infantry, 1st Rifle Brigade,
  four companies of the Scottish Rifles and six of the 2nd East Surreys.

with 4,000 men, Colesberg had been liberated, the Tugela line had been shattered and Boers were deserting in their thousands. The difference between the two armies, and the spirit that kept the British going throughout the defeats of Black Week and into the victories of Black Month, is perhaps best summed up by an exchange which took place at the impromptu armistice on the 25th February. Some Boers suggested to Major-General Lyttelton that they were giving the British a rough time of it. The general replied: "A rough time? Yes, I suppose so. But for us, of course, it is nothing. We are used to it, and we are well paid for it. This is the life we lead—always, you understand." To which the burgher replied "Great God." Lyttelton continued, "Why not? This is our life, whether we are at Aldershot or India, or wherever we are. We are just settling down to this campaign."[123]

The imperial forces had certainly settled into the campaign, and there was more to come. Lord Roberts had spent the week following the Boer surrender at Paardeberg reorganizing. His horses had been in a shocking state and the rapid advance had outrun his supply chain.

By the 7th March, however, he was on the move again. General de Wet commanded a Boer force reckoned to be in the region of 14,000 men with twenty guns holding blocking positions in the area of Poplar Grove, perhaps forty miles from Kimberley and fifty miles west of Bloemfontein. The positions were in a run of kopjes on either side of the Modder River, extending perhaps twenty-five miles in all.[124] The plan was simple but, given the state of French's Cavalry Division, overly ambitious. Seeking to repeat the trick which had isolated Cronjé at Paardeberg, French's horsemen would push round to the republican left in a wide arc, cutting off their retreat as the infantry divisions assaulted them frontally.[125] Though French had received remounts which brought his number of horses up to 5,655, many were of poor quality, others were sick and there was a general shortage of fodder. French declared that his division was "quite inadequate for the purpose"[126] but did his best in any case. However good the British cavalry horses had been, it is doubtful that the trap could have worked. French set off at 0300 hours on the 7th, reaching Kalkfontein farm by 0700. At the first sign of imperial troops, however, de Wet's Boers began to abandon the Poplar Grove position and, by

0730 hours, his disordered men were streaming away toward Bloemfontein. President Kruger, on a morale-boosting visit to the front, joined the panic-stricken retreat in his Cape cart.[127]

The appearance of French's cavalry on their flank had certainly greatly alarmed the Boers, and in their flight abandoned large quantities of ammunition, cooking utensils, cooked food and tents.[128] The cavalry was in no shape to effectively pursue the fleeing republicans, however, and the day saw only saw small skirmishes here and there, with losses on both sides of only about fifty.

Wars are not won by retreating though; de Wet desperately tried to rally his demoralized forces for a last stand before Bloemfontein. At Abram's Kraal, some thirty-five miles from the capital, de Wet, de la Rey and Kruger himself tried to stop the rout. Witnesses recalled that Kruger was almost frantic as he moved among the fleeing Boers: "he lifted his heavy stick against the fugitives whom no one seemed able to check; at last he ordered the ZARPs to shoot anyone who attempted to flee." It was to no avail though; the ZARPs would not shoot and the retreat continued in a cloud of dust.[129] Some were made of sterner stuff, however, and de Wet managed to establish a defensive line based on three kopjes, the central one being on a farm called Driefontein, while one flank rested on the Modder River.[130] His forces had been reinforced by a commando under his brother, Piet de Wet, and some 1,000 ZARPs under de la Rey.

On Steyn's orders, de Wet rode back to Bloemfontein to assist in preparing the capital for defence, while the 9th was spent siting entrenchments and organizing the forces there.[131] Some have attempted to explain away the fact that the republicans didn't force the British to fight for their capitals because towns were meaningless to the Boers as they had already cleverly decided on a course of guerrilla warfare. Steyn's and de Wet's frantic attempts to fortify Bloemfontein give a lie to this claim.

De Wet returned to the Driefontein position on the morning of the 10th to find his troops in a state of disorder. Of the 380-strong Ladybrand Commando, 265 had simply gone home, while another unit of 163 had only seventeen men left at the front. The Boer army was disintegrating before de Wet's eyes. Nevertheless, the timely arrival of Piet de Wet's men and the ZARPs still allowed the position to be held in some strength and de la Rey had been busy in de Wet's absence. Federal artillery consisted of two Krupp

75mm guns and a pair of 15-pounders, two of the guns captured at Colenso three months earlier.[132]

Elements of the Cavalry Division encountered the Driefontein defences early on the 10th and alerted the 6th Infantry Division. As the British had not fallen into the trap of frontally assaulting the position, and finding the cavalry working round his flank, de Wet was forced to hurriedly redeploy his force to counter this threat. At about midday the 18th Brigade launched their attack, taking their objectives with ease as the Boers had fallen back. At 1400 hours the infantry assaulted the main republican positions, driving the burghers before them at bayonet point. De Wet wrote bitterly of his men that "once more panic seized them; leaving their positions, they retreated towards Bloemfontein, now again only a disorderly crowd of terrified men blindly flying before the enemy".

Total British casualties at Driefontein were 438, including eighty-seven killed. As usual, the official Boer casualty figures were typically implausible: just seven killed. Despite the usual poppycock of the republican propaganda machine, the British buried 102 dead Boers and took thirty prisoners. A neighbouring farmer would later claim that a "great number" of Boers had also been left unburied.[133]

With de Wet defeated at Driefontein, the way to Bloemfontein was open and Roberts made his formal entry into the capital of the Orange Free State on the 13th March. Despite the plans of de Wet and Steyn, nothing could stop the fleeing burghers and no attempt was made to defend the city. Unlike the British Tommies, who endured months of siege to defend villages like Mafeking and Kuruman, thousands of Boers kept on trekking, passing through Bloemfontein in their desperation to escape. Steyn himself had fled on the 12th, setting up a new capital in Kroonstad. Rather than facing weeks of siege therefore, the imperial forces marched through streets decorated with bunting and were greeted by cheering crowds.[134]

There can be little doubt that there was an element of realpolitik about this sudden change of loyalty, but some of it was genuine. The Orange Free State had decided only by the narrowest of margins to join Kruger's war, and Bloemfontein was home to large numbers of moderates and English-speakers who were opposed to the invasion of British territory and viewed the imperial troops more as liberators than conquerors. One mounted infantry officer remembered his arrival in the town:

instead of sullen, downcast faces awaiting us as [we] passed under the fort and entered the capital, we met with a most enthusiastic welcome. An excited crowd lining the route cheered again and again. Women and children, decked with red-white-and-blue rosettes and ribbons, crowded round us waving handkerchiefs amid all possible manifestations of delight. Could this be the surrendered capital of the Free State, or was it all a dream from which we should be awakened by the screeching of a shell, to find ourselves on a lonely sangar-crested kopje, the sport of the Boer guns? No. That warm shake of the hand was real. We were indeed treading the streets of Bloemfontein.

The long-stifled feelings of these people (the town seemed peopled with English) broke out in a warm-hearted welcome the like of which we never met with in any other part of South Africa. Women and children pressed forward and enthusiastically shook us by the hand. "Our mouths have been shut for months," one said to me. "We cannot restrain our feelings any longer. We have been living in a reign of terror, and had but to bestow a friendly smile on the English prisoners of war passing through on their way to Pretoria, to feel a tap on the shoulder and be told that our names had been noted. The next warning would be in the form of an order to leave the town within twenty-four hours, and be put across the border."

I hadn't been standing on the market square five minutes before one Dutchman after another came up and asked me to go to the nearest hotel and have a drink ... one man followed me about protesting that he had not been fighting, pulling out a red-cross badge.[135]

Lieutenant Ronald Charles, Royal Engineers, similarly remembered the welcome: "the town council came out in all their glory of white top hats etc. about 10.30 am on the 13th & solemnly handed over the keys of the capital to Lord Roberts, who promised to respect life and property & all the rest of it & the Advanced Guard of the British Army marched into Bloemfontein in rather scattered detachments to the accompaniment of the ringing cheers of the inhabitants, black & white. I never heard such cheering, though doubtless many of them were cheering the Boers a week before we arrived—everyone was wearing tricolour favours, brand new Union Jacks were being flown, people were singing 'God Save the Queen', 'Rule Britannia' & other patriotic & marshal airs. I don't suppose we could be given a more hearty reception even on returning home: & mind you we were entering the [enemy's] capital as victors, not as a relieving force."[136]

Sir John Fraser, who had lost the previous election to Steyn—an event which plunged the Orange Free State on the course to war—actively assisted the occupying forces and Bloemfontein was quickly returned to a semblance of normality. Markets, banks and schools quickly reopened and those Boers combatants who had had enough were encouraged to surrender their rifles.[137]

In the month since Roberts had started his march and Buller had seized Hussar Hill, the whole complexion of the war had changed. The republicans had been defeated in all parts of South Africa and were in headlong retreat, their armies shattered and disordered. There was no way back for the Boers after Black Month but, unfortunately for all concerned, some of their leaders refused to accept reality. Instead they mindlessly opted to drag South Africa through another two years of a war they simply could no longer win.

CHAPTER EIGHT

Guerrilla war or terrorism?

"When will it all be over?" said a Boer to someone.
"As soon as you get tired of it and give in," was the reply.
—overheard during a brief armistice[1]

"By God, these English, I have known them for fifteen years …
You cannot beat the English without deceit."[2]
—Ansar General Osman Digna, before the battle of Omdurman, 1898

"I am entitled by law to force every man to join, and if they do not do so,
to confiscate their property and leave their families on the veldt."[3]
—Louis Botha explaining his persecution of *hendsoppers* ('hands-uppers')
to Lord Kitchener

"We went as far as Sand Spruit Railway Station and stopped there last night close to
some farms. The inhabitants consisted only of women and children who fully expected
the Boers to blow up their houses. However, they consented to sell us a goose for 3s."[4]
—diary entry of Captain George Clarke, Royal Artillery

"What the bulk of the people [in the Orange River Colony] require is protection not
punishment. I do not mean to say that they do not all hate us. They do.
But they love their property more than they hate the British and
would be glad to see the back of the Guerrillas."[5]
—Milner gives a pragmatic assessment to Lord Kitchener

"The logic of facts was inexorable, and the cold still voice of common-sense had more
power than all the ravings of enthusiasts. The vote showed that the great majority of the
delegates were in favour of surrender upon the terms offered by the British Government."
—Conan-Doyle sums up the final surrender at Vereeniging

"the sustained use of violence against symbolic or civilian targets by small groups for
political purposes, such as inspiring fear, drawing widespread attention to a political
grievance, and/or provoking a draconian or unsustainable response."
— James D. Kiras's definition of terrorism in *Understanding Modern Warfare*

"being shot by an Indian from behind a rock,
and having your name spelled wrong in the newspaper."
—a US Cavalry veteran of the Plains Wars describes the grim reality of
another guerrilla campaign of the age[6]

After the fall of Bloemfontein, there was a lull while Roberts sorted out his forces. Hoping, not unreasonably, that the Boers would accept the reality of the situation, Roberts issued the following proclamation on the 15th March: "All Burghers who have not taken a prominent part in the policy which has led to the war between Her Majesty and the Orange Free State, or commanded any forces of the Republics or commandeered or used violence to any British subjects, and who are willing to lay down their arms at once and to bind themselves by an oath to abstain from further participation in the war, will be given passes to allow them to return to their homes and will not be made prisoners of war nor will their property be taken from them."

The difficult bit was to spread this message to the scattered commandos and it was harder still to protect those who had had enough from their more extreme comrades. To this end, imperial columns were sent out to various parts of the newly captured territory, with one having an early taste of what to expect during the rest of the war: on the 26th March Lieutenant-Colonel Pilcher led around a hundred men to Ladybrand to arrest the landdrost. The village was bedecked in white flags and Pilcher and fifty men—the other fifty plus a Maxim gun covered the advance—were received "with open arms" and "enthusiasm". As Pilcher was leaving the village with his captive, news came of the approach of a 1,000-strong Boer commando. As soon as this force hove into view, the good people of Ladybrand instantly switched their white flags for Mausers, and opened fire on Pilcher's rapidly retiring party.[7] An officer of the 10th Hussars had an especially lucky escape, having been "told off to search the landdrost's house, in so became suspicious, owing to the palpable and persistent manner in which the landdrost's daughter, while pretending to be friendly, delayed him in his search by pointing out one thing and another of interest in the house and endeavouring to hold him in conversation.

On leaving the house, he found his suspicions only too well founded. No sooner had he put his foot outside the door than someone shouted, "Hands Up!" Paying no heed, he jumped onto his pony—to find Colonel Pilcher's small escort leaving the town in desperate haste. The Boers were sweeping down on the town in hundreds. The friendly shopkeeper of a minute before, dashing behind his counter, picked up his Mauser lying in readiness there, and emptied his magazine at the men as they clattered past down the street. The local chemist, who was better suited to the concoction of pills than to the use of a rifle, in his hurry shot a passing Boer lady; this regrettable incident, I believe, was the only serious casualty".[8]

Though it was admirably gallant of the witness, a Captain St Leger, to regard this fratricide as "regrettable", the incident serves to illustrate the problems faced by the imperial troops as the war took an unpleasant and distinctly dirty turn. A man could be a friendly chemist one moment and an enemy combatant a second later. If the chemist had been shot or detained before he grabbed his rifle, the British would no doubt be accused of barbarity by today's armchair critics. Though dignified to an extent by the term 'guerrilla warfare', much of what happened after the fall of Bloemfontein would be described as terrorism today. One can, of course, argue that the Boers were 'forced' to fight this way, but equally one must accept that the British were forced to react accordingly. If a man living in a village bedecked with the white flags of surrender can be a pharmacist one moment, a rebel the next and then change back to an 'innocent' civilian the instant it suits him, it was obvious that the imperial troops could not counter this by conventional means. Had Ladybrand's chemist been shot down in the exchange, some latter-day apologist would almost certainly have written a book about the 'outrage' and would be squawking about the murder of an innocent man, blissfully ignoring the fact that many other armies of the period would have razed the village to the ground for such an act.

The Boer high command was busy reorganizing to fight this next phase of the conflict. A council of war was held in Kroonstad on the 19th March, attended by both presidents and various generals. Steyn surreally assured the gathering that if they could just hold on for another six to eight weeks, a Russian move on India would force the British to accept terms.[9] Incredibly Joubert, de Wet,

Botha and de la Rey all went along with this chimera and vowed to keep fighting. De la Rey then declared that their defeats were attributable to the large size of their commandos with their cumbersome ox-wagon trains and their accompanying families. These, he insisted, should be broken up into nimbler units. Essentially, they would be become raiding forces which would strike at the vulnerable supply lines of the British and, more importantly but generally overlooked today, intimidate their countrymen against accepting Roberts's amnesty or from cooperating with the imperials.[10]

It was the first step to abandoning the normal rules of war and is today called the guerrilla war.* When this phase of the conflict is written about today much attention focuses on plucky raids against lumbering supply columns, or well-executed attacks on imperial outposts by gallant figures like de la Rey and de Wet. But, and as much as this is unpalatable for modern-day Boer sympathizers to admit, a primary motivation behind adopting the new tactics was to bully, cajole and terrorize their own people into continuing what was by then already a futile, unwinnable conflict.

Throughout March imperial troops on the central front pushed the Boers back, recapturing Aliwal North on the 11th. Until the railway lines were cleared and in imperial hands, Roberts's army relied on wheeled transport for supply, a highly unsatisfactory situation.[11] On the 10th March, British scouts arrived at Bethulie just in time to see the railway bridge being blown up. The Boers then turned their attention to the nearby road bridge and would have blown that up too had the dozen or so scouts not gallantly attacked the demolition team. With no idea just how tiny a force they were being assailed by, the burghers crowding the bridge fled in panic, and in an action worthy of the SAS of the Second World War, the crossing was taken intact.[12] Gatacre took his main force across the Orange on the 15th.

Several spans of the Norval's Pont bridge had also been blown, but by means of a hastily built pontoon bridge, General Clements's force also crossed the Orange on the 15th. These troops pushed forward, quickly linking up with the main body at Bloemfontein. Back on the Orange River engineers worked to repair the sabotaged bridges; a temporary railway bridge was in operation at Norval's Pont by the 27th while the line at Bethulie was diverted to cross

---

* Though the term 'guerrilla' (literally 'little war') originates from actions by Spanish irregulars against Napoleon's occupying army, guerrilla warfare is as old as war itself and was by no means 'invented' by the Boers as some claim. The first documented reference to this sort of warfare dates from the fifteenth century BC.

the road bridge. Though ingenious, this Heath-Robinson solution was not considered sturdy enough to take the weight of a train, and so wagons were pushed across by hand then hooked up to another engine on the other side.[13]

On the 31st March the British suffered a serious reverse at Sannah's Post outside Bloemfontein when de Wet ambushed a British column under Colonel Broadwood which was escorting surrendered Free-Staters into the capital.[14] Though Broadwood fought an admirable rearguard action, 400 prisoners, seven guns, and eighty-three wagon-loads of stores were taken by de Wet; his men also destroyed the Bloemfontein waterworks.[15] More than this though, de Wet's success allowed him to put "strong pressure upon the considerable numbers of his fellow countrymen who, declaring themselves tired of the war, had given in their rifles to the British troops, and had been allowed to return to their farms as peaceful non-combatants".[16]

Three days later de Wet attacked the 600-strong garrison at Reddersberg, thirty miles to the south. After holding out for twenty-four hours, 546 of the Royal Irish Regiment were taken prisoner.[17] Though these successes, and others, led some to claim de Wet to be a military genius of the first order, de Wet was achieving little of strategic importance. He failed to cut the vulnerable railway line or attack the Bethulie bridge over the Orange and Kruger himself felt obliged to intervene. In a telegram sent to Steyn, Kruger questioned the wisdom of de Wet using his powerful commando to attack isolated British garrisons in the southern Orange Free State when the main British thrust was to the north. It was undesirable, read the telegram, that de Wet's force "should be so far south while the great movement of the enemy is northward. The danger in this is that a difficulty may arise similar to that after the retreat from Magersfontein. I think that as soon as he has broken up the railway beyond Bloemfontein, or if this takes too much time without doing so, he must join the forces north of Bloemfontein".[18]

Nevertheless, and for no discernible reason, de Wet instead opted to attack the small imperial force at Wepener, arriving there late on the 4th April with about 6,000 men, a number which soon swelled to between 8,000 and 10,000[19] with ten to twelve guns. Rather than striking immediately, however, de Wet dithered until the 9th before starting his bombardment and it wasn't until the 10th that he got around to launching an assault on the village. This inexplicable delay was absolutely critical for the outnumbered imperial garrison of around 1,800 men who took the chance to dig themselves some formidable defences. After two days of failed attacks, de Wet continued to closely invest Wepener but proved utterly unable to break through. After sixteen days, the siege was raised by General Brabant with around 1,200 men of the Colonial Division and General Hart with another 2,800. At a time when he was needed in the north de Wet wasted weeks on a target he proved singularly unable to take, and which—even had he captured it—would have achieved nothing.

Despite it being a completely botched attempt from start to finish, Pakenham nevertheless paints de Wet's failure at Wepener in the most glowing of terms. To him, de Wet did not fail to take the town or—heaven forbid—suffer a 'humiliation'; instead, Pakenham says, "After sixteen days, de Wet *let go* [author's italics] of Wepener, and swooped back to his eyrie in the north."[20] One wonders what on earth would have had to have happened for Pakenham to ever declare that the republicans had cocked up. We shall examine this remarkable action, and others, in more detail later.

Exacerbated by the loss of the waterworks—only retaken on the 23rd April—typhoid spread through the imperial troops in Bloemfontein, meaning that it was not until the 3rd May that the march on Pretoria finally commenced.[21] In addition to this outbreak of sickness, which Nasson predictably attributes to "Roberts' bungling"[22], it was not until late April that sufficient supplies had been gathered in Bloemfontein to support an advance. Ammunition was in especially short supply and the horses were in a shocking state. There were not even adequate stocks of new boots or uniforms to re-clothe the tattered Tommies.[23] The British army had simply been in no state to fight an offensive war at the time of the Boer invasions, and was still not really ready six months into the conflict. Manpower was also still short. Roberts had originally estimated he would need a force of 50,000 (of which 15,000 were to be mounted) before he could march on Pretoria.[24] As it was, he set off with perhaps 43,000 men,* and even this army shrank with every mile as units were told off to defend the lengthy lines of communication and form garrisons. He commanded the main body, which consisted of French's

---

*   The 6th and 3rd divisions were left in the area of Bloemfontein to garrison the town, while the newly arrived 10th and 8th divisions operated in the south of the Orange Free State.

cavalry and two infantry divisions, the 7th and 9th—about 25,000 men in all. General Ian Hamilton commanded an independent mounted infantry division which, with supports, was about a further 18,000 strong. Despite the name, only around 6,000 of Hamilton's men were mounted.[25]

It is difficult to know how many republicans were still in the field, as their numbers fluctuated wildly day by day. Many had gone home, though would later return to the fight—whether by their own volition or 'encouraged' so to do by their erstwhile comrades. At the time, however, British intelligence reports reckoned on Botha holding a position on the Zand River with about 6,000 men and (a somewhat improbable) eighteen guns, and a like number of Boers with between eight and ten guns in the Kroonstad area. Smaller units covered the gap between these forces. De Wet was known to be active somewhere on the border with Basutoland near Ladybrand with about 6,000 men and about ten guns. General du Toit was thought to have another 4,000 men and nine guns near Warrenton, on the railway some thirty miles north of Kimberley. As well as these main groups, there were also a number of smaller commandos, some 500 to 1,000 strong, still at large and roaming behind the imperial lines.[26] Roberts's 300-mile advance on Pretoria was not therefore an inconsiderable task, and nor was it done with the overwhelming numbers so often mentioned to dilute his victory.

The first objective of the march was Brandfort, held by about 450 of the republican Irish Brigade and a slightly larger force under de la Rey. Roberts's force ejected this garrison from Brandfort on the first day of the advance in a lengthy but fairly bloodless engagement, with more skirmishing ensuing the following day. On the 5th, about 5,000 republicans, under de la Rey and Lukas Meyer, were skilfully turned out of formidable positions along the Vet River by a flanking move, leaving a small bag of prisoners as they fled.[27] Roberts had no intention of launching costly frontal assaults when he could manoeuvre the enemy out of his defences, and the Boers had little answer to this.

The capture of Brandfort and the advance toward Wynburg caused the federal forces in the southern Orange Free State to head north and join the defence line on the Zand River. Many foreign observers saw this somewhat helter-skelter flight north as the beginning of the end, with scenes of disordered chaos as large numbers flooded back with scant semblance of discipline. Many less ardent burghers chose this point to slip back to their farms.[28] When imperial troops marched into Wynburg, they were cheered by the townspeople, with one Gordon Highlander remembering: "Reached Wynberg [sic] about 2pm, a good looking place with a lot of British women in it. As we marched through the streets a young woman shouted three cheers for the British. Some of them were handing packets of cigarettes to us. We camped about half a mile on the other side of the Town. We were told the Boers were only two hours out of it."[29]

On the 9th Roberts advanced to the Zand River which was strongly held and considered by the British as where the Boers would offer their main effort to halt the advance. Where Methuen had suffered from a lack of horsemen, Roberts was luckier, and the cavalry under French and the mounted infantry under Hamilton pushed out on either flank. Drifts were quickly secured and the attack was launched the following morning. In a well-coordinated series of assaults the defenders were driven from their positions, a reasonable enough bag of prisoners was taken and imperial losses were slight. Though they had turned the Boers from their positions, Roberts had been unable to trap a truly significant number of them. His lack of confidence in the replacement cavalry horses prevented him launching French on a really daring flanking move: the Boers had in any case been more than ready to retreat as soon as it looked like their flanks were in any danger.[30]

Nevertheless, Kroonstad, the impromptu capital of the Orange Free State was taken without a fight on the 12th May. As one witness recalled when President Steyn fled: "Kroonstad that night found itself face to face with pandemonium let loose. The great railway bridge over the Valsch was blown up with a terrific crash. The new goods station belonging to the railway, recently built at a cost of £5,000, and filled with valuable food stuffs … was drenched with paraffin by the Boer Irish Brigade, and given to the flames; while five hundred sacks of Indian corn piled outside shared the same fate. No wonder that, as at Bloemfontein, the arrival of the Guards' Brigade was welcomed with ringing cheers, and the frantic waving by many a hand of little Union Jacks. Our coming was to them the end of anarchy … It is, however, worthy of note that the Boers who thus gave up food stuffs to the flames, and strove continually to tear up the rails along which food supplies arrived, yet left their wives and children for us to feed. About that they had no compunctions and no fear, in spite of the fabled horrors ascribed to British troops. They knew full well that even if those troops were half-starved, these non-combatants would not be suffered to lack any good thing. Even President Kruger, though careful to carry all his wealth away, commended his wife to our tender keeping."[31]

The advance to, and capture of, Kroonstad had cost just 242 imperial casualties, of which only thirty-two were killed. Again, however, Roberts had to call a halt and wait for his supply lines to be repaired. Though much is made of the later 'scorched earth' tactics of the British, and as just mentioned, the retreating Boers had done a pretty good job of destroying their own country in their wake: "Between Bloemfontein and Kroonstad no fewer than twenty-seven spans of four great bridges, some of them seventy feet above the water and totaling 670 feet in width, with twelve piers of massive masonry, lay in ruins in the river beds. Culverts to the number of sixteen had been blown up, most of the water tanks and pumps shattered, rails torn up and twisted, the permanent way and points damaged, signalling instruments broken, in short, all things destroyed with almost as much care and science as had gone to the construction of them."[32]

Of course, one can argue that this was a sensible military necessity, but the same argument can also be made for the destruction imperial troops would later wreak on the Orange Free State. Either way, the railway repair department got to work with alacrity. There was also, once again, the problem of horses. French's Cavalry Division had lost about half its mounts in the march from Bloemfontein to Kroonstad, and again these would have to be made good. Though the main body was thus halted, Roberts sent Hamilton's mounted infantry off to the east to seize the village of Lindley which had been grandly declared the latest capital of the Orange Free State. This was done and a haul of Boer leaders and prisoners taken.[33] A sharp fight with a commando under Piet de Wet on the 20th ended when the Boers got turned, and broke and fled from the field.

With Heilbron now revealed as the new capital-of-the-day of the Orange Free State, Hamilton rushed his force there, desperate to trap President Steyn and the rest of the government. Though he took Heilbron on the 22nd, Steyn had once more made good his escape. Worse still was that, due to the pell-mell nature of the chase, Hamilton left the Lindley area after just two days, and had not taken the time nor had the troops available to garrison and pacify the area. This sudden occupation and abandonment left a lot of loyalists in the lurch, and did nothing to encourage others to show their true colours in the weeks and months ahead.[34] Winston Churchill, who was there, described with his trademark elegance how suddenly allegiances could switch: "All kinds of worthy old gentlemen, moreover, who had received us civilly enough the day before, produced rifles from various hiding-places and shot at us from off their verandas."[35]

❧

At about the same time, Roberts sent a 1,150-strong flying column under Colonel Mahon to join with Plumer's Rhodesians and finally relieve Mafeking. Mahon's command was built around three squadrons of the Imperial Light Horse and the Kimberley Mounted Corps,* making this almost exclusively a colonial affair.[36] As Mahon's column pushed north, they were well received by most of the locals, both black and white. Sergeant David Maxwell[†] of the Imperial Light Horse wrote to his sister to tell her of the march: "nice open country full of small game, very loyal natives who sold and gave fowls and eggs readily. Next day marched at 3 am & got 10 prisoners, as many horses and rifles. On the 9th left at 6.30 & arrived Vryburg at 3.30 being received with open arms and much show of Red, White and Blue rosettes and ribbons … On the 12th we started again at 5 am, took any amount of prisoners (rebels) arms—carts & horses … The most loyal old Brit owned the hotel & refused to fight for the Boers, telling them they might cut his throat first—this from the Kaffirs—the old gent and his wife not mentioning this little affair. They refused payment for everything—giving us eggs, fowls, butter & an excellent dinner to the Officers … Marched at 6 am on 13th to Brodie's farm where another loyal man entertained us royally."[37]

Not everyone was as welcoming, of course. Another letter from an Imperial lighthorseman declared: "Every day we captured a few Boers, principally rebels found on their farms with arms in the possession and in nearly all cases their farms were burnt."[38]

As Mahon made rapid progress, Mafeking's besiegers opted for a last-ditch effort to storm the town before relief arrived, something they might have been better served attempting some 200 days earlier. The plan called for a

---

* Colonel Mahon's command comprised 780 from the Imperial Light Horse, 120 from the Kimberley Mounted Corps, four Royal Artillery 12-pounders, one company of infantry and two machine guns: a total of 1,149 officers and men. They were supplied by fifty-two mule wagons.

† later Colonel Maxwell

feint that would cover the main attack by Commandant Eloff at the head of 700 republicans who would push through some native villages. On the 12th May this was attempted, though—true to form—few of the burghers had any interest in such a dangerous scheme, and Eloff could only persuade 240 to join him.[39] Nevertheless, the assault was still launched but was quickly contained and then pinned by a vigorous counter-attack. The Boers surrendered, having sustained sixty causalities and 108 taken prisoner. Baden-Powell's losses were twelve dead and eight wounded.

The ubiquitous de la Rey had been rushed to the scene and, with 2,000 men and seven guns, was confident of being able to defeat Mahon's force. Despite assuring the burghers that "all would go well", de la Rey's men were driven back during the fighting of the morning of the 17th. It was yet another of those nameless republican defeats which are simply never mentioned in modern histories of the conflict, and forgotten in the myth created around de la Rey. With the Boers broken up and retiring, a detachment of the Imperial Light Horse entered Mafeking that evening, lifting the siege which had lasted 217 days.[40]

As the army of the Orange Free State disintegrated, Roberts and Hamilton were again on the move, pushing on toward Pretoria. Hamilton's mounted infantry crossed the Vaal on the 26th May and fought a sharp action at Doornkop on the 30th. The Gordons fixed bayonets and charged to the skirl of the pipes. It was a relatively costly manoeuvre, but the Boers fled before the oncoming Highlanders.[41] Hamilton's victory was well received, as it was at Doornkop that Jameson's raiders had surrendered a few years earlier.[42]

By now the morale of the republicans was almost completely shattered. Hilder of the Royal Canadian Dragoons noted that though his unit was less than a hundred strong at that point, they fell upon a retreating Boer convoy as it struggled across a river crossing. These burghers had no fight left in them and the Canadians captured three guns, a number of wagons and a hundred prisoners.[43]

Johannesburg was taken the follow day, and Pretoria on the 5th June. Pretoria contained all the Transvaal's currency reserves, ammunition stocks and surplus food stocks.[44] Far from not considering their capital worth defending, the Transvaal volksraad had met to urgently discuss the matter, appointing Lukas Meyer as the man to lead the defence. In the years prior to the war, four forts had been built for the express purpose of defending the capital: Klapperkop,* Shanskop, Wonderboompoort and Daspoortrand. All were built atop hills and were of the latest design, being sturdily built and equipped with bombproof casemates and ammunition stores. No expense had been spared in their construction: they were connected to one another by telephone and had electric power. Most of their heavy guns had been sent to support the invasions, but efforts were made to get at least one Long Tom in place again, though Roberts had reacted too quickly for this.[45]

Events were swiftly overtaking the republicans. In scenes of chaos the defeated, demoralized commandos who limped into the capital showed more interest in drinking and looting sprees than defending the city.[46] With the Tommies pressing inexorably and thousands of other Boers deserting or surrendering, there was no way any organized resistance of Pretoria could be mounted. Louis Botha accepted that the war was lost and had sensibly counselled suing for peace.[47] Smuts and Botha telegraphed Kruger—the president had already fled east to Machadodorp (with Bible and the Transvaal's gold reserves but *sans vrou*)—from Pretoria on the 1st June, recommending surrender. Had this wise advice been taken, it would have been far better for all concerned. Instead Kruger consulted with Steyn who told Kruger in no uncertain terms that he would not hear of such a thing. Staunchly backed by de Wet, Steyn pointed out that the Transvaal had dragged his country into the war but was now ready to give up.[48] Steyn's misplaced pride prolonged the war for another two years, achieving absolutely nothing.

When imperial troops entered Pretoria, Lord Roberts was presented with a petition by two black clergymen, who requested on behalf of the townspeople that the British alleviate the distress they had suffered under the Boers' conscription of labour: "A very large majority of us were commandeered for Government and private work, such as rendering of menial services at the front, at the Artillery Camp, in town, and even at private farms, without any remuneration whatsoever; and in consequence whereof, many of us find ourselves quite destitute and on the brink of starvation."[49]

The fall of Pretoria is often considered to mark the end of the conventional war and the start of the guerrilla war. This is broadly true, though, as we

---

* Fort Klapperkop has been preserved and is now an excellent museum

have seen, de Wet and others had been fighting guerrilla-style actions in the Orange Free State for weeks and there was still the occasional larger-scale battle to come.*

æ

The latter phase of the war is often portrayed as being a gallant David-versus-Goliath-type affair, with Robin-Hood-like bands of Boers skipping merrily about the veldt, dealing out defeats to the blundering British as and when it suited them, adored by the people and welcomed wherever they went. We shall soon see that there is little truth behind such claptrap.

There is no doubt that the imperial forces did not immediately switch from conventional to counter-insurgency mode, nor could they have been expected to. The whole situation was massively confused: peace overtures were being made by the republicans with the fall of Pretoria, and though guerrilla attacks had started in the Orange Free State, there were still large units of 'formed' Boers in the Transvaal. In the follow-up after the battle of Diamond Hill, General French talked of de la Rey being Botha's "right flank", whereas in fact de la Rey's command was, by then a semi-independent group living off the land.[50] There were certainly some noteworthy Boer successes but these have largely been blown out of all proportion to their impact. Piet de Wet's capture, for example, of several hundred Imperial Yeoman near Lindley was spectacular[51] but essentially militarily irrelevant. Where the bitter-einders[†] were able to assemble a large enough force they could strike at more substantial targets, and Boer victories like Nooitgedacht[‡] were impressive. Though they made headlines around the world and were embarrassing to the imperial generals, such major triumphs were far from commonplace. Conversely, as well as Boer spectaculars like Nooitgedacht, there were significant imperial victories like Bothaville[§] where de Wet came a cropper.[52] In the main, the bitter-einders were elusive, but from a military point of view rarely able to

---

* Roberts drove Botha from positions at Diamond Hill on the 11th/12th June 1900 and Buller defeated Botha at Bergendal two months later.

† 'bitter-enders', those who fought to the last

‡ On the 13th December 1900 de la Rey led 2,100 Boers in a highly successful attack on General Clements's force of 1,500 encamped at Nooitgedacht.

§ On the 6th November 1900 de Wet's commando was surprised by a smaller force of mounted infantry and fled, leaving behind over a hundred prisoners and several artillery pieces.

inflict little more than pinpricks, and even these were generally delivered against isolated rear-echelon garrisons or poorly protected supply columns.

But for all the confusion and bickering in the imperial high command,[53] and less trumpeted than the occasional Boer triumph, the Tommies were grinding down the bitter-einders. Modern histories of this period of the war are anxious to relate the intimate details of any Boer successes, tauntingly highlighting the blundering British columns which fruitlessly pursued them. But this is to completely miss the point of how the guerrilla war was fought and won and is to blatantly ignore the hauls of prisoners the imperial forces were garnering, week in, week out, month after month. Though by no means as dashing and appealing as the sporadic exploits of de la Rey, Smuts or de Wet, the British army slowly, surely and inexorably destroyed the Boers as a fighting force throughout the guerrilla war in hundreds of skirmishes no one has ever bothered to name.

Oft overlooked is that bickering and confusion also occurred within the Boer high command. The defeated Boers did not suddenly and effortlessly metamorphose into a guerrilla army at the drop of a hat. During the initial phase in the Orange Free State, brothers Piet and Christiaan de Wet quarrelled bitterly about the best way to combat the British advance, Piet advocating concentrating all available forces to halt the imperial push head-on, while Christiaan was keener to strike at their rear. When overruled Piet found himself marginalized, began to communicate with the British and ultimately switched sides to fight for them against his brother.[54] Piet wrote to Christiaan in early 1901, desperately trying to persuade his brother that continuing the war was pointless and, worse still, was destroying the country. His letter makes interesting reading, and it is a shame for all concerned that Christiaan ignored it:

"Which is better for the Republics—to continue the struggle and run the risk of total ruin as a nation or to submit? ... Put passionate feeling aside for a moment and use common sense, and you will then agree with me that the best thing for the people and the country is to give in, be loyal to the new government, and try to get responsible government ... [the British] consider the matter ended, and they only try to treat magnanimously those who are continuing the struggle in order to try to prevent unnecessary bloodshed ... If you consider the Free State you are not sensible, and do not act sensibly. Are you blind? Can you not see that you are being deceived by the Transvaal generals and burghers? What are they doing? They do not fight a tenth as much as we do."[55]

Though the guerrilla war was generally one of small actions, there was one major coup early in the piece. In July 1900 imperial troops took Frankfort and then drove a large body of Boers out of Bethlehem into an area known as the Brandwater Basin. As well as President Steyn and Christiaan de Wet, 9,000 burghers were hemmed in, with around 16,000 British soldiers trying to cut off their escape. Though Steyn and de Wet got away with a few thousand, Commandant Prinsloo was left to surrender with about 4,500 of his men,[56] an even larger number than Cronjé turned over at Paardeberg:

> On July 30th the motley army which had held the British off so long emerged from among the mountains. But it soon became evident that in speaking for all Prinsloo had gone beyond his powers. Discipline was low and individualism high in the Boer army. Every man might repudiate the decision of his commandant, as every man might repudiate the white flag of his comrade. On the first day no more than eleven hundred men of the Ficksburg and Ladybrand commandos, with fifteen hundred horses and two guns, were surrendered. Next day seven hundred and fifty more men came in with eight hundred horses, and by August 6th the total of the prisoners had mounted to four thousand one hundred and fifty with three guns, two of which were our own. But Olivier,* with fifteen hundred men and several guns, broke away from the captured force and escaped through the hills. Of this incident General Hunter, an honourable soldier, remarks in his official report: "I regard it as a dishonorable breach of faith upon the part of General Olivier, for which I hold him personally responsible. He admitted that he knew that General Prinsloo had included him in the unconditional surrender." It is strange that, on Olivier's capture shortly afterwards, he was not court-martialled for this breach of the rules of war, but that good-natured giant, the Empire, is quick—too quick, perhaps—to let byegones be byegones.[57]

Though General Olivier briefly got away by means fair or foul, he shamelessly offerered to join the imperial cause when he was captured just a

---

* General Jan Hendrik Olivier, who had defeated Gatacre at Stormberg during Black Week

few weeks later. Perhaps due to his 'dishonourable breach of faith', however, Olivier's proposal that he would switch sides and use his commando to maintain peace in their home district was rejected by the British[58] and he was shipped off to a PoW camp in Ceylon instead. Other groups, disheartened by this massive capitulation, also quietly slipped away to surrender to Hunter's troops, or simply headed home. Although a defeat many times greater than those suffered by the British at Colenso or Spion Kop, this mass surrender is virtually unknown. Indeed, the action doesn't really even have a name.*

But the coup at the Brandwater Basin was the exception; this new type of war soon put the imperial troops in an almost impossible position. Suddenly the enemy was nowhere, but everywhere at once. The British were essentially now stuck in the middle of a civil war, unsure who could be trusted and never knowing whether the innocent-looking school teacher who had wished them good morning would shoot them that afternoon. Having a large army in theatre meant having a large supply network, and a large supply network needed protecting, which meant it needed to be even bigger still to supply those guarding it. With many reserve and volunteer units having reached the end of their terms of service, units were leaving South Africa at a time when they were most needed. Throughout most of the guerrilla war, there were about 195,000 imperial troops in southern Africa, but with so many towns and villages to garrison, and supply lines to protect, this left only 22,000 available for offensive operations, and only 13,000 of these were combat troops.[59] With men needed to form flying columns to take the fight to the Boers there was no way that every culvert, railway bridge, loyalist farm or surrendered town could be protected from an enemy that had abandoned the normal rules of war. This was quite simply asking the impossible, especially when the penny-pinching London government reduced the commitment to 189,000 men, and was pressing a further reduction to 140,000.[60]

---

* In 2013 I helped organize an off-roading competition in the area and, as part of it, drew up a short quiz on local points of interest. One question asked: 'Forces from which army surrendered at Surrender Hill near Fouriesburg?' Only one team got the correct answer, another guessed it was the Basuto, while all the rest picked "the British". The power of the myth of the Boer War is so deeply ingrained in South African society that this massive republican defeat seems to have been airbrushed from history and it is noteworthy that virtually all those who were not sure automatically assumed the British *must* have been the ones to have surrendered.

Back during the Boer invasions and occupations of British territory, a proclamation was made by President Steyn on the 14th October 1899, the most important paragraph of which read:

> All persons who do not constitute a portion of the British Army, or who (a) serve the enemy as spies; (b) cause the burghers and men of the South African Republic and Orange Free State to lose their way when acting as guides; (c) kill, murder, or rob persons belonging to one of the Republics, or forming part of their following and train; (d) destroy bridges or damage telegraph lines, heliographic apparatus, or railways, or in any way cause damage to parts or portions of the same, whereby the Republics may be hindered or their people or property damaged, or even in any endeavour to repair or make good the damage done by the Republican forces to property or apparatus, or who set fire to the ammunition, war supplies, quarters or camps of the Republican forces, or in any way damage them; (e) take up arms against the forces of one of the said Republics shall, at the discretion of a Council or War, be punished by death or imprisonment not exceeding fifteen years.[61]

This is how the republicans had threatened to deal with anyone who dared indulge in guerrilla warfare against them, so it is curious that they objected so vehemently when far less draconian methods were employed against them. Unsurprisingly, the guerrilla war soon became a very nasty, dirty conflict, but, even still, the British largely fought the bitter-einders as though they were a uniformed, regular enemy, despite the Boers' clear breaches of the Hague and Geneva conventions—and others—in this regard.[62] Indeed, if anything, many considered that this perceived leniency only served to prolong the war. On the 18th June one Royal Horse Artillery officer wrote to his wife in frustration at being ordered to fight the war with one hand tied behind his back: "some things are inexplicable to us of the rank & file—we do not seem to inflict any punishment on the inhabitants of the district & to such an extent spare their feelings that no officer or man is allowed to go into Wakkerstroom and I don't think the Union Jack had been hoisted. The inhabitants of course say they can't control the commando which is somewhere in the hills & that when we go the commando will return & loot cattle & do damage to them for having surrendered."[63] This was an ongoing problem. Far from being gangs of rob-from-the-rich-to-give-to-the-poor-types, the bitter-einders exacted terrible revenge on any of their countrymen who did not share their enthusiasm for extending the war. One American war correspondent, Frederic Unger who reported from both camps, remembered: "On entering the Free State and taking Bloemfontein, Lord Roberts had issued a proclamation to the effect that if the burghers would come in, surrender their arms, and take the oath of neutrality, they would receive passes from the Provost Marshall, and be allowed to go back to their farms. Many of the burghers did this. Afterwards, owing to Lord Roberts' failure to give them the promised protection, Boer raiders swept down, accused them of disloyalty, looted their farms and escaped before troops could arrive."[64]

Where there were no imperial troops available to protect them, other hendsoppers were forced to return to the fight against their will: Many of the passive hendsoppers who had surrendered fairly early on in the war often found themselves back on commando. For those who did so unwillingly, it was often due to British inability or unwillingness to guarantee their safety against active burghers.[65]

Much is made of the large army that the British employed during the guerrilla war, but it quite simply could not be everywhere at once. Unger reported on farms belonging to surrendered Boers around Bloemfontein being given their own mini-garrisons of imperial troops.[66] Of course, all this did was offer up penny packets of Tommies to be pounced upon by larger gangs of marauders and still there was simply no way every loyalist or surrendered farm could be protected from the unpleasant attentions of the bitter-einders; and many of the bitter-einder gangs had no hesitation in sucking others into their terrorist campaign. Frederic Unger wrote about a disgraceful episode where some rebels used a surrendered farm to ambush a British patrol:

> General French's Chief of Staff was talking to the burgher, who was one of those who had surrendered his arms and taken the oath of allegiance. Several white flags were flying overhead as a sign of neutrality. [The next time I saw it] This place was entirely in ashes, still smoking. The farmer's wife and children were camped in an outbuilding, with a few articles of bedding saved from the house … I

learned that just after I left the place a party of Boers had occupied the farm, and one of their pickets had fired on the scouts of the passing army. Information of this was conveyed to the British General. He ordered out a squadron of horse to clear the farm of the Boers, which they did. Then the place was burned; the old burgher and his son were made prisoners. I afterward met the officer who had charge of this work, and he said, "It was the most miserable piece of business I ever had to do." … the burgher who had owned the farm, and his son also, were actually acquitted, as it was shown that they had taken no part in the firing on the troops, and had protested against it.[67]

Unger tells of another incident where the farmer had a lucky escape after an imperial patrol came under fire from his farmhouse: "the house was searched after the women were told to surrender any arms or ammunition they had. A few cartridges were brought out, for they had been told 'if we find a single cartridge, we will burn the house over your heads'. The horses in the stable and two handsome wagons were commandeered; then the officers and scouts rode on."[68]

As well as flagrantly abusing the white flag, firing from the farm of a loyalist or a hendsopper was a sure fire way to get the British to punish them, thereby devastating a decent family who simply wanted to get on with life, and turning them against imperial rule for ever. And when they were not tricking the British into doing it for them, the bitter-einders simply targeted the farms of hendsoppers themselves. General Louis Botha issued an instruction on the 6th October, ordering his commanders to "Do everything in your power to prevent the burghers laying down their arms. I will be compelled, if they do not listen to this, to confiscate everything movable and also to burn their farms".[69] There was nothing admirable or gallant about this type of warfare: it was quite simply terrorism—ugly, dirty and underhand.

Though some of the bitter-einder leaders might have been patriots, many of their followers were a less pleasant, less idealistic bunch. Even before the war, a British military intelligence report had warned of the dangers of the large number of poorly educated young Boers who essentially had nothing to lose by engaging in a protracted guerrilla war.[70] While those with families, businesses or professions had reason to surrender and return to normality, international troublemakers, those with criminal backgrounds and the 'under class' had no such motivation. Rural violence in the western Cape became endemic as bands of guerrillas and rebels roamed the countryside, seizing produce and livestock from natives, either for their own use or for redistribution to local Afrikaner farmers.[71] "These were roaming, thieving bands of rebels, grouped roughly under Conroy, Van Zyl and Jan Louw, parties with no aim but looting."[72] There was no discernible military objective behind this: it was pure banditry. Mission stations were a particularly favoured target for the bitter-einders and many were brutally attacked. When the Reverend C. Schröder returned to his Gordonia congregation after the war he was horrified to find most of his flock had been killed by Boer raiders. A bitter-einder attack on the Methodist mission station at Leliefontein in Namaqualand was especially savage. This outpost produced corn and vegetables and was mercilessly razed and plundered by guerrillas and local rebels, with the indiscriminate violence shocking even young Deneys Reitz: "We found the place sacked and gutted, and, among the rocks beyond the burning houses, lay twenty or thirty dead Hottentots … Maritz had wiped out the settlement, which seemed to many of us a ruthless and unjustifiable act … we lived in an atmosphere of rotting corpses for some days."[73] The wretched refugees of this massacre were pitilessly hunted down by parties of Boers. Those unfortunate enough to be captured were brought back to work as slave labourers, feeding and cooking for the bitter-einders. Indeed, they were even shackled in irons forged at the mission station's smithy.[74]

These barbaric attacks on black and coloured farmers are instructive. Contrary to their carefully cultivated latter-day image, the bitter-einders were largely the poorest and least educated whites, those with nothing to lose by dragging on the guerrilla war: essentially White Trash. Paul Botha, ex-volksraad member for Kroonstadt, described his frustration at the situation: "It is impossible to reason with the men who are now at the front. With the exception of a few officials, these men consist almost exclusively of the poorest and most ignorant class of bywoners [sharecroppers], augmented by the desperate class of men from the Cape Colony, who have nothing to lose, and who lead a jolly, rollicking life on commando—stealing and looting from the farmers who have surrendered, and whom they opprobriously call Hendsoppers but doing very little damage to the English. The officials gull them with promises of farms belonging to the landowners—most of whom have surrendered to the British—which the Orange Free State Government intend on confiscating after the war! These bywoners believe any preposterous story their leaders tell them in order to keep them together. One of my sons, who was taken prisoner by Theron because he had laid down his arms, told me, after his escape, that it was common laager talk that 60,000 Russians, Americans and Frenchmen were on the water and expected daily, that China had invaded and occupied England, and that only a small corner of the country still resisted, that God was killing the British all over the world with the bubonic plague."[75]

To these desperate, ill-educated men, the war was more about pillaging from those even less well off than themselves than about airy-fairy notions of independence and franchise. Weeks after the end of the war, poor white farmers in the area were found to be using over a hundred ploughs pillaged from Leliefontein, others were found to have had even stolen clothing and cooking utensils from the mission station. One leading historian of the war goes as far as to state that the war by this stage had actually become "a desperate, undeclared civil war between rural whites and rural blacks"[76] and that these poor whites were "often eager and predatory followers of Republican forces, seizing chances to enlarge their meagre resources from the ruin of black competitors".[77]

When an exasperated Kitchener was asked if he thought the Boer leaders encouraged such actions or disapproved of them, he responded, "Even if they disapproved, they had no control over their men."[78] This was the crux of the matter, though Botha claimed to be able to coordinate simultaneous attacks all over the country.[79] By the time of the guerrilla war, many of the so-called bitter-einders were not fighting for any ideals but were simply lawless bandits, roaming about attacking mission posts, blowing up trains, looting and burning—a profitable and far from unpleasant existence for some of these fellows. As Bill Nasson concedes, many were tempted to rejoin the fight as there were "Crown loyalist stores to plunder, and foodstuffs to be carried off from luckless African peasants".[80]

Other, less well-educated, burghers were fooled by the firebrand oratory of fanatical zealots like Smuts and de Wet. Either way it was a far more glamorous and exciting a life than many had ever known; what's more, they were even able to claim that they were doing it for a noble purpose even if they had long since forgotten what that was.

One of the most notorious guerrillas was a renegade Scotsman called Jack

Hindon, a deserter from the British army who had switched his allegiance to the Boers by the time of the Jameson Raid. In contrast to those bitter-einders who suffered terribly, this turncoat and his gang enjoyed a rollicking time, blowing up trains and living the high life on the plunder they looted: "they never wanted for supplies. Apart from what they looted from trains, they had a few men farming for them. At the German mission station at Botshabelo, near Middelburg, one Mr Weiner ground mielies for them at night and corps members were treated by a Mr Beaurten's family as if they were relatives."[81]

Though Kitchener is alleged to have stated that Hindon had caused him more problems than any other Boer,[82] the renegade's campaign of attacks on the railways were really only "petty but exasperating"[83] and ultimately achieved absolutely nothing other than perhaps providing amusement and enrichment for Hindon and his men. There were a few attacks on armoured trains but Hindon's men generally shied away from tougher targets; indeed, throughout the whole campaign they only made four half-arsed attempts at attacking fortified posts, all of which were repulsed with ease.[84] A more typical Hindon attack was that on a train on the 31st August 1901. It was a mixed goods–passenger train, escorted by forty-five men of the West Riding Regiment under Lieutenant-Colonel Vandeleur.* The train left Pretoria at 0400 on the 31st, bound for Pietersburg and consisted of three wagons full of heavy logs, then the locomotive and water tank, then an armoured wagon carrying the escort, some goods trucks, two carriages of civilian passengers and finally another armoured wagon.[85] The three wagons at the front were a rudimentary anti-mine measure, the idea being that they would take the brunt of any explosion on the line, and thus save the engine. Hindon's men, however, detonated their mine by command wire, exploding it directly underneath the first armoured wagon. The devastation was almost total with much of the train derailed and upset and most of the soldiers in the first armoured wagon killed or stunned. Hindon and seventy of his gang members, mostly clad in British khaki, descended onto the scene along with thirty blacks. Hindon's men opened fire on the stricken train, killing wounded soldiers and civilians alike. Realizing that there was no way of fighting back, Vandeleur instead tried to limit the carnage, emerging from cover to shout that one carriage contained only women and children. His reward for this gallantry was to be shot dead along with a male civilian. The train-wreckers

---

* Lieutenant-Colonel Cecil F. S. Vandeleur DSO (1869–1901)

then entered the women's carriage. Recognizing one of the occupants as a nurse named Jacoba Page, one of the Hindon gang shot her, presumably as some sort of act of revenge. Realizing his first shot had not killed the poor girl, he fired again before the pleading of the other female passengers in the compartment persuaded him to stop.[86] The bitter-einders then stripped rings, money, trinkets and private papers from the dead and wounded, even taking all the luggage belonging to the female passengers. Incredibly, Hindon and his bandits then sang a hymn and offered a prayer of thanks for their "great victory" before fleeing the scene.[87] Other attacks saw Hindon's gang murder in cold blood civilian train drivers, firemen and guards.[88] Despite these, and numerous like acts of terrorism and murder, Hindon's antics were later honoured by the apartheid-era government and a Jack Hindon medal was struck.*

ঌ

Of course, attacking trains and railway lines is a legitimate tactic in war, and was widely employed by the bitter-einders across the theatre.† These attacks were the IEDs of their time: striking at supply lines and causing terror and disruption was the whole intention.

As one rarely knew if a given train was carrying troops, wounded soldiers or civilians, it was an indiscriminate way of waging war,[89] and, as we have seen, civilian trains were just as vulnerable as military ones. An attack on a mail train was described in a letter written on the 22nd February 1901: "On Wednesday morning, the mail train steamed in here about eleven o'clock. There were a good many people in it, including two women, a girl and a small boy. The train started off for Heidelburg. It went merrily past Snickerbosch Spruit and when it nearly got to Kraal—Bang!—one of the three trucks was blown up by dynamite and at the same time a volley of bullets was poured into the train."[90]

Stevens, in his *Complete History of the South African War, in 1899–1902*, gives other examples of when train-wrecking was nothing more than simply banditry: "Here is an instance of brutal brigandage on Feb. 7th. A

---

*   Today, a group called the Jack Hindon Scouts calls for "Boere-Afrikaner self-determination".

†   Indeed the British would later use similar tactics in, among others, Lawrence of Arabia's campaigns of the First World War, though these were invariably directed at Turkish military trains.

Durban train, proceeding to Pretoria, was attacked between Greylingstad and Heidelberg, by a party of ambushing Boers who riddled the carriages with shots, and wounded six civilian passengers. The object was robbery, for as soon as the train was held up every passenger was searched, £25 being taken from a nurse, and all the luggage in the train was stolen ... Two other trains were wrecked on the same line that week, and one with supplies was only saved by an armoured train coming to the rescue. Similar outrages were often repeated on the Delagoa and other railways. At Taaibosch, C. C [Cape Colony], railway passengers were robbed, train wrecked, and natives shot in a pit. Three of the Boer miscreants were punished by Court Martial, being sentenced to death, and two were imprisoned for five years. Mr. Kruger justified the plunder as a necessary act of war."[91]

Kitchener took a slightly different view "although it may be admitted that the mining of railways and the derailment of trains is in no way opposed to the customs of war wherever any definite object is in view, it is impossible to regard senseless and meaningless acts of this nature, which have no effect whatever on the general course of operations, as anything better than wanton murder".[92]

Train-wrecking became so widespread that the British were forced to start carrying Boer hostages on some routes, the idea being that these would dissuade the terrorist attacks. Needless to say, this somewhat hardline tactic caused much wringing of hands, agonized wailing and gnashing of teeth from the usual suspects in the British pro-Boer lobby, but did prove highly effective. Suffice to say, there was no such bleating about the regular murder of civilians by gangs such as Hindon's.

Indeed, as the guerrilla war dragged on, lingering thoughts of the conflict being a 'Gentleman's War' faded fast. Though always ready to squeal about the supposed mistreatment of their womenfolk, gangs of bitter-einders specifically targeted the wives and children of any burgher suspected of loyalist sympathies. Many such unfortunates were seized and carried away, to be used as bargaining chips to persuade husbands and fathers to join or rejoin the commandos.[93]

The British entry into Wolmaranstad led to the capture of the landdrost, a notorious man called Pearson who already been connected with the murder of five loyalist citizens of that town:

The particulars of this dastardly murder of these men must be recorded, as they serve to show the innate brutality of the Boers, which in the earlier part of the war had been suppressed in the hope to seduce the sympathy of the Powers. The news of the execution of five British subjects—so-called rebels—by De La Rey's commando was brought to Klerksdorp by Mrs McLachlan, whose husband, father and brother had been among the victims. Most of them were burghers who had surrendered or left the country prior to the war, while the others were alleged to have taken up arms. The man Boyd, a British subject, had been detained in jail since July 1900 by the Landdrost, who induced him, with two others, to write a message to the English, praying them to come to their rescue. This was afterwards made the plea for sentencing the three to death. Among others sentenced were two burghers named Theunissen, well-known farmers of Klerksdorp, who had surrendered with General Andreas Cronjé's commando in June, and had taken the oath of neutrality and refused to break it. Mrs McLachlan, the daughter of the elder Theunissen, gave an account of her loss, narrating how she had taken coffins to the place of execution to bury the bodies of her father, brother and husband, to whom she had been married only two years, while another lady made the following statement: "The Boers have forty of our men prisoners there. Eight or ten have been condemned to be shot. They were tried by the late Landdrost of Klerksorp, a man name Heethling, in conjunction with other members of the Court. The sentences were confirmed by Generals Smuts and De La Rey, who sent men to carry them out. The four who were shot were Mr Theunissen, his son, his son-in-law, Mr McLachlan and Mr Boyd. From the first to the last, they were brutally treated. The execution was a sad spectacle. The prisoners, on being taken out of jail, grasped one another's hands. They were placed in a row and shot down one by one. Mr Boyd received three bullets, but was still alive when put into the grave. The Boers fired again and it was all over."[94]

By all accounts, Pearson was a prime actor in the barbarous drama.[95]

A surrendered burgher, Mr Prosser, and his wife were attacked twice by bitter-einders. Prosser had been granted permission to return to his farm by the British, on condition that he acted as a guide or interpreter as required but was quickly visited by a party of Boers who demanded all his horses then tried to shoot his wife. Others returned the following month and murdered Prosser himself.[96]

In another ugly episode, a gang of bitter-einders attacked the house of a loyalist who was away serving in the South African Constabulary, snatching his wife and two-year-old child as hostages. The loyalist and his police comrades tracked the bandits to their laager and attacked it, freeing the woman and child. One Boer even tried to make off with the infant in the middle of the action but was luckily foiled.[97]

Not only loyalists and hendsoppers were targeted. Even those Boers who tried to negotiate a peace were viewed by the increasingly irrational bitter-einders as deserters or traitors. Their pacific overtures to the commandos led to some being taken captive and, in that favourite terror tactic, their farms destroyed. Others were flogged and some murdered.[98]

Blacks and coloureds could expect to be especially savagely treated by the bitter-einders: "a small party of twenty-one Imperial Yeomanry was captured, after a gallant resistance, by a large force of Boers at the Doorn River on the other side of the Colony. The Kaffir scouts of the British were shot dead in cold blood by their captors after the action. There seems to be no possible excuse for the repeated murders of coloured men by the Boers, as they had themselves from the beginning of the war used their Kaffirs for every purpose short of actually fighting."[99]

In August 1901 a detachment of British auxiliaries was defeated near the village of the Shangane chief, Mpisana. The fifty blacks who were taken prisoner were all subsequently murdered by General Viljoen's men.[100] In other incidents, forty native auxiliaries captured near Queenstown were lined up and shot in November 1900, thirty-seven unarmed scouts were murdered near de Aar in August 1901 and the following month, sixteen black dispatch riders attached to the 17th Lancers were killed in a variety of horrific ways, including disembowelment and mutilation.[101]

And it wasn't just those blacks who actively served the Empire in some way who could expect to be butchered. One of the leading missionaries in the Transvaal, Canon Farmer, wrote of the murderous terror the bitter-einders inflicted on the natives of that area. The blacks welcomed the security of the British columns but when the Tommies were not around to protect them they faced a stark choice of abandoning their livestock and fleeing to the British-held towns, or being killed.[102] The missionary concluded that the Boers "look upon the Kaffirs as dogs & the killing of them as hardly a crime". One example of this cheerful butchery occurred in July 1901 when Veldkornet Dirk Brits murdered twenty-nine blacks—men, women and children—at Dordecht. Brits declared these poor devils were "in league with the British" and, when he cruelly turned their bodies over to their families, the rest of the settlement bolted for the hills.[103] This penchant for off-the-cuff brutality against blacks had long been reported: war reporter Bennet Burleigh described the Boers has having a "notorious and almost innate habit of terrorizing, beating, and even killing without mercy, any native who may have happened to have aroused his suspicions or incurred his ire".[104] In addition to this casual murder, rural non-whites could expect the bitter-einders to descend on their settlements and commandeer anything they fancied. Among many others, raiders paid unwelcome visits to the towns of Maraisburg, Steynsburg, Colesberg, Molteno, Albert, Dordrecht, Aliwal North and Barkly East, stealing wagons from the locals and often forcing them into slave labour as drivers. One victim of such raids was Jonas Mungawara, who testified in November 1901: "the Boers came here some time ago and took from me one mare, nineteen horses, thirty-five bags of grain, my Cape carts and mule spans, and two of my servants. For four weeks they made me drive for them, saying they would shoot me if I did not do so."[105] Whenever these forced labourers managed to escape they were cruelly hunted down by pursuit parties. Those who did manage to escape often staggered into imperial territory in such a shocking condition that even British military doctors were distressed.

Many of these native escapees proved to be very useful to the imperial intelligence services and later served as scouts, spies, interpreters and even interrogators—despite the horrific retribution they could expect if recaptured.[106] Some escaped former servants to the Boers went even further, forming their own irregular mounted unit and waging a private war against the guerrillas around Beaufort West during 1901.[107]

Coloured Bastards, who were used as scouts and in defensive positions in what is now the Northern Cape, could expect no quarter from Boer raiders either: as far as they were concerned, it was a "war to the knife".[108] Coloured civilians also suffered, the most famous such incident being the torture and murder of a blacksmith called Abraham Esau who lived in the small town of Calvinia in Namaqualand. As the guerrilla war spluttered on, there were ongoing Boer raids in the area, with tribute demanded and whippings, looting and even exemplary executions common.[109] Staunchly pro-British, Esau was blessed with formidable leadership skills and became a prominent figure in his small town, rallying and organizing a militia force to resist these incursions. This patriotism and bravery brought him to the attention of both the raiding Free Stater bitter-enders and local rebel Boers and he quickly became a marked man. When a commando fell on Calvinia on the 7th January 1901[110] Esau was one of those sought out amidst the wholesale plunder of the town. The Boer raiding party—which grew to 600 strong—occupied Calvinia for some weeks, terrorizing the local population. Local rebels took the chance to settle old scores—real and imagined—with the coloured community. During this period Esau was beaten, bludgeoned and lashed. Incredibly, this astonishing man endured this torture until the 5th February when he was shackled in irons and dragged for five miles behind a pair of horses. After a final beating, he was shot dead.[111] The following day the raiders fled Calvinia as an imperial relief column approached. Pakenham ignores this incident altogether, while other modern accounts suggest that the British latched onto this as a propaganda coup, almost as though this in some way excuses the weeks of torture Esau endured. Bill Nasson, for example, says that Lord Milner "made a great show of revulsion and immediately seized upon the atrocity story as a suitably decent stick with which to beat the Boer Republics as bloody and barbarous" before going on to quote the high commissioner's denouncement of the act.[112] It doesn't seem to occur to anyone that Milner, like any other civilized and decent man, might genuinely have been revolted by this savagery or that the "atrocity story" made a "suitably decent stick" with which to beat the bitter-enders precisely because they did indeed prove, time and time again, to be "bloody and barbarous".

And these examples of savage brutality were not just the occasional excess, but rather official—or, at least, semi-official—policy. A particularly brutal commandant testified on his capture that "General Smuts personally gave me orders to shoot all unarmed natives who might be working for the British who should fall into my path".[113] Likewise, bitter-einder General Kritzinger issued a proclamation in July 1901, ordering that all blacks captured in the service of the British, whether armed or not, should be summarily executed. During November a further proclamation was issued, ordering that any black or coloured persons betraying the whereabouts of Boer commandos to the British should be executed when caught.[114] One later pro-Boer history of the conflict states with the indignation: "The British reacted to this proclamation by executing all Boers found guilty of 'murdering' [note the quotation marks] coloured people or blacks."[115] Quite why this writer thinks that executing an unarmed person because of his skin colour is 'murder' rather than plain murder, or why those who did the murdering are in any way deserving of our pity, is a mystery. This was the level the bitter-einders sank to, and the level their current apologists will go to to defend their actions.

One such Boer leader who was to face British justice was Commandant Gideon Scheepers. This young man was an especially loathsome fellow who raided all over the Cape, train-wrecking, looting and burning down public buildings and houses belonging to loyalists. Native policemen were murdered because of their colour. Scheepers also attempted to rob the Murraysburg branch of Standard Bank, sjambokking the manager when he refused to comply.[116] He avoided battle where possible and instead "confined his attention to the more genial work of robbing, burning and devastating. In his operations there was no military object; he meant, he said, to make Cape Colony a desert".[117] Even as imperial columns began cutting up his raiding parties and running his gang to ground, Scheepers found time to commit one last atrocity. When two coloured scouts were captured, Scheepers decided it was his right to murder them, despite their being in uniform. The two were forced to draw lots, and the loser was immediately shot. The other was beaten and released to stagger to the nearest British outpost.[118] Scheepers was finally captured and tried at Graaff-Reinet "for repeated breaches of the laws of war, including the murder of several natives. He was condemned to death and executed in December. Much sympathy was excited by his gallantry and his youth—he was only twenty-three. On the other hand, our word was pledged to protect the natives, and if he whose hand had been so heavy upon them escaped, all confidence would have been lost in our promises and our justice".[119]

Despite his horrific catalogue of murder and mayhem, the pro-Boer press in Britain shrieked that he should be spared. More recently he is defended in the book *Innocent Blood*, despite the writer acknowledging his admittance to executing several coloured 'spies'[120] and that standing orders among the bitter-einders were to execute any black or coloured person betraying their positions to the British. According to the author's curious logic, "The fact that Scheepers admitted to the execution of some spies did not make him guilty of murder." Quite how a scout wearing military uniform can be classed as a spy is anyone's guess: if the justification is that they were not wearing uniform then, by that token, virtually every Boer taken prisoner could equally have been executed by imperial forces.

While it is difficult for a rational person to feel much sympathy for Commandant Scheepers, other, more senior, Boers literally got away with murder. When Jan Smuts's commando fell on the native village at Modderfontein, for example, they butchered the 200 or so black inhabitants,[121] leaving their bodies strewn around, unburied. Smuts would never be punished for this; indeed, he would later become a field marshal in imperial service. Even General Kritzinger himself, one of the leaders of the Boers within the Cape Colony and the man who had issued the odious order mentioned above, somehow managed to escape the hangman's noose. His fate turned upon how far he was responsible for the misdeeds of some of his subordinates. His defence team somehow managed to prove that he could not be held accountable for the excesses of his scattered command, and was acquitted by the military court.[122]

Like many guerrilla wars since, the British were caught trying to fight a war and a police action at the same time. Though their opponents fought by whatever rules suited them, the British were expected to conduct fair trials through the judicial system. By rights, any Cape colonial who took up arms against the Crown could be treated as a traitor and hanged. In the black-and-white view of many imperial officers this is exactly what should have happened and was considered the only way to discourage others. Politicians, especially those who were trying to build a future for the region, saw this more in shades of grey: Kitchener was instructed that hanging should only be used in cases of conduct which was "markedly mutinous". Echoing this, Milner wrote to French: "Whatever we may think of our Dutch friends, it won't pay to treat every Dutch-speaking man as a rebel unless his proves the contrary."[123] Like any army fighting a guerrilla war, the British were performing a balancing act between decisive action to destroy terrorist units on one hand, and leniency to win the hearts and minds of their would-be supporters on the other. Few would claim they always got the balance right, but none has ever suggested an alternative way the war could have been won.

~

By the end of 1900, the British held 15,755 Boers as prisoners of war and reckoned a further 21,239 had been lost as casualties.* Post-war analyses, based on how many Boers were in the field at the final surrender and how many prisoners had been taken up to that point, suggest that on the 1st January 1901 there were still 50,371 active guerrillas.[124] This is a far cry from the normal claim that the British were fighting a handful of Boers during the latter stages of the war. That is not to suggest, however, that all 50,000 were galloping about the veldt on the 1st January; that is not how guerrilla wars are fought. The huge advantage the Boers held was that their men could be everywhere and nowhere at once, disappearing for a while, popping up to cause mayhem and then blending back into the general population again. Others had surrendered only to later break their oath or be forced to break it at gunpoint. Others might simply have gone home to tend to their farms and then opted to rejoin for a raid as and when it suited them so to do. Indeed, if all 50,000 bitter-einders had remained in the field at all times, the imperial forces would have had a much easier time of it.

What these figures do not cover are those Boers who, between the 1st January 1901 and the surrender in May 1902, were not captured and were not in the field at the end. We shall never know how many men slipped quietly away and returned to their life when it was obvious they were fighting in a lost cause. We also cannot be sure about other men, like perhaps the Ladybrand chemist we met earlier and who might never have left home but was happy to loose off a few rounds whenever it suited him. In this way, at least, the British were still firmly stuck in the past, naïvely believing that chivalrous, honourable behaviour was the norm. As such, they unthinkingly trusted that the word of a surrendered Boer was his bond, whereas, in reality, they were facing a foe with a very different set of morals. "It was a very common trick on the part of surrendered burghers who took the oath of neutrality and gave up their arms, to hand in weapons that were thus worthless, and to hide for future use what were of any value. We did not even attempt to take possession of any such burgher's house. We found him a soldier, and when he surrendered we left him a soldier, well horsed, well armed, and often deadlier as a pretended friend than as a professed foe. Because of that exquisite folly,

---

* this figure will include a large percentage of wounded and missing, rather than killed

which we misnamed 'clemency', we have had to traverse the whole ground twice over, and found a guerrilla war treading close on the heels of the great war."[125]

With all right-thinking men now realizing that the republicans could not possibly win the war, Lord Kitchener* held peace talks with General Louis Botha at the Middelburg conference in late February 1901. Unfortunately for all concerned, this olive branch was rejected, despite the conditions offered by Kitchener being virtually the same as those eventually accepted by the bitter-einders over a year later. The commander-in-chief was undeterred, however, and as 1901 wore on, Kitchener's new tactics began to have an effect and the numbers of Boer prisoners taken continued to mount. The combination of more imperial mounted troops, the 'drives' of the flying columns, the network of blockhouses and the infamous scorched-earth policy had tipped the scales in favour of the British. We shall cover the details of Kitchener's somewhat controversial tactics later, but there is no denying their impact.

In the first quarter of 1901, Boer losses were 4,103, including 2,223 who were either taken prisoner or voluntarily surrendered. In the second quarter total losses were 7,299, of which 6,138 ended up in British captivity. Though enormous fuss is made over de la Rey capturing a couple of hundred soldiers here, or a few wagons there, much less attention is paid to the literally thousands of Boer prisoners who were being taken month in, month out. Though there were occasionally larger bags, these were prisoners generally captured in small numbers in countless and unnamed patrol actions and skirmishes—but it was happening day in, day out all over the theatre. Raids on farmhouses often netted prisoners, fighting patrols would return with two or three captives and sometimes dozens simply arrived at an imperial post and gave themselves up. None of these actions was ever honoured with a name, or given any real attention, but this was how the imperial forces slowly but surely won the guerrilla war. By the end of 1901, the British had inflicted total casualties of 22,417 for the year, of whom 17,715 were either taken prisoner

---

* Kitchener replaced Roberts as commander-in-chief in South Africa in late 1900. Roberts returned to Britain assuming the war was essentially over and only a limited police action remained. Though he is often portrayed today as being a cold-hearted fellow, it was Kitchener who pushed for the peace talks with Louis Botha in early 1901, and it is a great shame that these came to nothing.

or surrendered of their own accord: almost 1,500 a month, or fifty a day.[126]

W. S. Carr, who served with the South African Light Horse during the guerrilla war, recalled one such small, unknown and virtually forgotten action: "At eight-thirty that night all available men except outlying pickets left camp, going through farm after farm without any luck until well after midnight. Our normal procedure, dashing across the clear, flattening against walls, bursting open a door, finally met with luck and we collared fifteen armed men and their mounts at one place without firing a shot. It turned out they were part of Hertzog's rearguard, left behind to watch our movements, but we caught them napping. There was a large number of women and children at this farm and there was some wailing when we took their menfolk away with us."[127]

As well as prisoners taken on such raids, quantities of war-making materials were regularly seized: "One farmhouse we searched during our bolt across the flats proved to be quite a young arsenal. Bullets for all types of rifles had been manufactured wholesale—Martini, Westley-Richards, Lee-Metford or Enfield, Mauser and other moulds. None of the bullets was nickel coated and they made frightful wounds if they hit a bone. Sheet lead, melting pots and ladles were all on the premises ... This was the only farmhouse I was ever to see deliberately burned by our troops."[128]

Another night patrol of SALH saw the troopers visiting various Boer farms: "The sky was lighting up on the hilltops when we came to the farms Schietfontein and Kafferfontein, whose homesteads lay but 300 yards apart. Dogs again heralded our approach. We found a horse, saddled, with strips of biltong or dried meat hanging from the 'Ds'. The rider we never saw. He was probably a watcher, fallen asleep and awakened by the baying just as we were upon him, but managed to find a hiding place. Food was on the table, coffee quite hot, but our quarry had fled."[129]

The troopers were just too late on that occasion, but the SALH's tactic of aggressively targeting Boer homesteads at night to catch their quarry sleeping in them was a successful one, with Carr reporting that they had "captured one hundred and fourteen prisoners in night marches alone during the past two months".[130]

Though fighting imperial troops by any means possible can be understood and justified to a greater or lesser extent, the treatment the bitter-einders meted out to hendsoppers and loyalists can only really be defined as terrorism in the truest sense of the word. As the net tightened throughout 1901, the bitter-einders became increasingly ruthless in their attacks against their own people. Paul Botha described them as "men who are ruining the country, stealing from and terrifying their own people, at the instigation of Steyn, Hertzog, and others. They are encouraged to roam about the country in small parties for this purpose. If I had space, I could instance hundreds of cases to show their atrocious conduct. Notorious thieves and cowards, such as Commandant Nel, of this district who has never been in a single fight, are allowed to clear the isolated farm houses of every valuable. Even widows whose husbands have been killed on commando are not safe from their depredations, and there have been cases, such as Prinsloo's, of this district, where they have even set fire to the dwelling houses while the inmates were asleep inside. As I have said, these marauders possess no property, and have the natural delight of the bywoner class to injure anyone better off than themselves".[131]

Kitchener reported to Lord Salisbury that "Numerous complaints were made to me in the early part of this year by surrendered burghers, who stated that after they had laid down their arms, their families were ill-treated and their stock and property confiscated by order of the Commandants-General of the Transvaal and Orange Free State".[132] When a band of bitter-einders arrived in town, even Afrikaners could expect to be relieved of their belongings: "On Tuesday a band of robbers (15 of Oom Paul's soldiers) came into the town and went into people's stables and took everyone's best horses. People went to the Landdrost and complained, but the only thing he said was: 'What can I do against so many?'"[133]

On the 2nd June, after a long and rapid march, a Boer commando threw itself upon Jamestown, overwhelmed the sixty part-timers who formed the guard, and looted the town. Carrying as much as they could and stealing a hundred horses, the rebels left the town gutted and vanished into the hills once more;[134] these were men who had "flagrantly and treacherously broken their oath of neutrality or those who are simply making the war into an excuse to rob, loot and steal".[135]

In what he describes as a reign of terror, one historian describes how the predatory bands of bitter-einders made rural life impossibly dangerous. One such gang fell upon Jagersfontein and, though unable to flush the imperial troops out of the two forts they held in the town, took the opportunity to shoot ten unarmed natives with expanding bullets.[136] Other gangs roamed about the north-east of the Orange River Colony, and the burning and looting of houses and stores was commonplace. When his commando was driven off by the defenders of Frederikstad, de Wet flew into a rage and demanded the place be smashed by artillery. The town of Lindley was also "wantonly wrecked" by these "noble" marauders and Harrismith was in a state of siege.[137]

When British columns managed to catch up with the commandos, the fighting was more savage than ever. 'B' Squadron, Imperial Light Horse was badly cut up in a Boer attack at Naauwpoort in January 1901. While the lighthorsemen reorganized to retake their positions—which they duly did four hours later—the wounded who had been left behind told how the bitter-einders walked among them: "Practically all of them were dressed in khaki and had the water bottles and haversacks of our soldiers. One of them snatched up a bayonet from a dead man, and was about to despatch one of our wounded when he was stopped in the nick of time by a man in a black suit, who, I afterwards learned, was De la Rey himself."

Nevertheless, when a British counter-attack retook the ridge, they were horrified to find "some seventy killed and wounded, many of them terribly mutilated".[138] It should be remembered that there was no love lost between the Boers and the uitlanders of the Imperial Light Horse, but this was not a unique incident.

On the 28th May 1901 an action was fought near Vlakfontein, immediately south of Oliphant's Nek. The Boers, under Commandant Kemp, initially captured two British guns, turning them back onto their previous owners. The guns were quickly recaptured by imperial forces under General Dixon and forty-one dead Boers—other reports say fewer—were left lying on the field as their comrades fled, though not before they had brutally murdered a number of the wounded Tommies. One officer was shot through the head with his own revolver after he had surrendered and many others were finished off as they lay on the veldt. Sergeant Chambers of the Yeomanry saw "a Boer, a short man with a dark beard, going around carrying his rifle under his arm, as one would carry a sporting rifle, and shoot three of our wounded".[139]

Controversy has raged over this incident ever since, with Kitchener first seeking to suppress reports of the outrage as he worked on a peace treaty with the Boers.[140] There were many eyewitnesses who described in detail what happened, however, with several describing a Boer whose hat rather incongruously sported a "pink puggaree" as one of the main culprits.[141] A sickened Conan-Doyle stated: "there is one subject which cannot be ignored in discussing this battle, however repugnant it may be. That is the shooting of some the British wounded who lay round the guns. There is no question at all about the fact, which is attested by many independent witnesses … it is pleasant to add that there is at least one witness to the fact that Boer officers interfered with threats to prevent some of these outrages. It is unfair to tarnish the whole Boer nation and cause on account of a few irresponsible villains."[142]

It is certainly unfair to suggest that all the bitter-einders behaved so abominably, but there were a lot more than 'a few' villains. When de Wet surprised a slumbering unit of imperial Yeomanry near Tweefontein, the result was more of a massacre than a battle, as described by our friend Sergeant Maxwell: "The whole of the sentries must have been asleep, as it was full moon & on a clear bright night. The Boers climbed up one of the precipices—formed line about 200 of them & then walked through the camp—shooting down everyone that got up—most were shot in their tents. 60 were killed, 68 wounded & 15 natives killed … I am afraid that there is no doubt that they killed numbers of wounded—as many of the dead had bayonet wounds as well as bullets—& the Boer doesn't carry bayonets—also many heads smashed in with butts of rifles—One of the surviving gunners states that many of them got drunk on the officers' whiskey & rum for issue on Xmas day & then rushed about, killing the wounded."[143]

A detachment of Victorians who were overrun also reported atrocious acts of murder. One private soldier had surrendered and stood with his hands up; in full view of his comrades a bitter-einder casually placed the muzzle of his rifle against the Australian's chest and shot him dead.[144] Despite this brutality, amazingly there were still occasional vestiges of the 'Gentleman's War' to be found. Deneys Reitz recalled that the "English soldiers, both officers and men, were unfailingly humane. This was so well known that there was never any hesitation in abandoning a wounded man to the mercy of the troops, in the sure knowledge that he would be taken away and carefully nursed, a certainty which went so far to soften the asperities of the war".[145] Similarly, when the bitter-einders withdrew from Carolina in May 1901 they had no qualms about leaving their women and children behind: "the burghers always showed by their acts that they had perfect confidence that their non-combatants would not be ill-treated."[146]

അ

As 1901 wore on, imperial successes slowly began to take their toll. General Kritzinger was driven out of the Cape Colony in mid-August; on the 5th September Lotter's commando was surprised, shattered and captured by the 9th Lancers under the hard-riding Colonel Scobell.[147] By deceitful use of captured uniforms,[148] Smuts managed to cut up a squadron of the 17th Lancers at Elands River just two days later,* but the murderous Gideon Scheepers was captured on the 11th October and the equally odious Kritzinger a month thereafter.[149] At least in battles in the field the imperial troops knew who their enemy was. Other bitter-einders were shiftier as described in this incident which took place in Pietersburg in May 1901: "two officers were going out to a magazine on the outskirts of the town, and were sniped at and shot dead by a Dutch schoolmaster who lay hidden in the long grass. When the troops ran up to see what was the matter, this gentleman jumped up and shouted, "I surrender! I surrender! I surrender!" The men walked up to him and without hesitation ran a bayonet through his body, and in the heat and stress of the battlefield, this action of the soldiers is to be applauded."[150]

Another Tommy wrote home to tell of coming under fire from a 'surrendered' farm. When stormed, the farm, bedecked in white flags, contained no less than seventeen Boer snipers, all of whom "begged for mercy". At least one was denied this, killed by a wrathful Hussar.[151]

And it was not only male 'civilians' of whom the Tommies had to beware: Boer women were sometimes even more hardline than their menfolk. Their habit of smuggling Mausers under their dresses led one letter-writer to demand that no lady in a captured town should be permitted to wear a dress longer than six inches below the knee—something outrageously risqué to the Victorians—before going on to bemoan the fact that "all the regulations out here are far harder for Loyal Englishmen than the Boers".[152]

Though they certainly had plenty of support in some areas, the perception that the bitter-einders skipped about South Africa to be greeted with joy wherever they went is utter rubbish. The overwhelming majority of South Africans wanted nothing to do with their pointless and increasingly brutal campaign and lived in terror of their visitations. The padre of the Guards Brigade recorded a visit made by another chaplain on a Boer farmstead: "At

---

* we will examine this action in more depth later

Hoekfontein he called at a farmhouse close to our camp, and in it he found an old woman of seventy, and her husband, of whom she spoke as nearly ninety. 'Do you believe in God?' she asked the Chaplain, and added, 'so do I, but I believe in hell as well, and would fling De Wet into it if I could.' Then she proceeded to explain that her first husband was killed in the last war: that of her three sons commandeered in this war one was already slain and that when the other two returned from the fighting line De Wet at once sent to fetch them back."[153]

Most Afrikaners were heartily sick of the fighting, which only continued thanks to the intransigence of the bitter-einders, who dragged on their campaign with no regard to the suffering of their own people.[154] Captain George Clarke of the Royal Artillery also recorded meeting some prisoners who had had more than enough of the war: "Early yesterday a train came from the north pushed by men. The oxen, who were acting as engine, broke down a mile or two back. The train had some 150 released prisoners and about 30 Boers who had either given themselves up or who were taken prisoners. Several of them spoke English very well, including an officer of the Staat's Artillery, who was chiefly concerned about the loss of his house, furniture and garden at the Barracks at Pretoria. They were all very sick of the War and had lost all faith in Kruger."[155]

For non-whites, the arrival of bitter-einders was even worse news. One plucky native police constable in Barkly East was ordered to pay tribute by raiders. He replied: "Kruger is not baas here and I am not going to pay him a penny, he can do what he wish I am a Government man and not yours, and I am under the English Government, not him. I am sick of these Boers with their nuisance towards me."[156]

Even many of the womenfolk in the concentration camps had had enough of the futile war, and wished the bitter-einders would call an end to it. Relations between women with spouses still out on commando and those whose men had capitulated were reportedly "very poor", with the latter snooping and informing on pro-fighting sentiment to camp authorities. One Transvaal bitter-einder noted that they were "berated for forcing them to keep on living in the midst of misery and the dying".[157]

The reception the bitter-einders received elsewhere was often considerably worse. When General Botha invaded Natal in September 1901, he was misled by the locals into attacking two British positions on the border of Zululand, having been falsely told they were lightly held.[158] In a pair of battles which is completely overlooked by most accounts of the war, Botha's attacks were driven off with very heavy loss, as we shall later examine in more depth.

And it was not just in staunchly pro-British Natal that the bitter-einders could expect little support. During Commandant Lotter's raid into the Cape Colony, imperial troops were led to his hiding place by a local Afrikaner loyalist.[159] A few months later, when Jan Smuts embarked on his invasion of the Cape Colony, he hoped to spark a general uprising and that hordes would rally to his banner. Several thousands in fact did; Milner reckoned that it was "plain fact that the rebels are still in undisturbed possession of about one-third of the Colony"[160]—but roaming about in semi-populated wilderness areas was not the same as sparking a revolution. And though a few thousand rebels joined Smuts, the response from the Cape loyalists is less known: when the Cape had first been threatened earlier in 1901, 10,000 loyalist volunteers came forward in just three weeks. These men were enrolled, and dispatched in detachments to hold the towns and villages which stood in the path of the invading commandos.[161] Civilian telegraph operators bravely raised the alarm when Smuts's raiders burst onto the scene. One especially courageous young lady, Miss Devenish, continued to send reports even as the bitter-einders entered her house, tapping away as her father delayed them.[162] Her telegraph machine was smashed by the raiders shortly thereafter. In a similar incident another young female operator managed to send off her message, causing Smuts's men to reach for their sjamboks.

As British flying columns—especially those of Lord Lovat and Lieutenant-Colonel Baillie—and the local town guards slowly took their toll on this latest incursion, Smuts headed for the mining town of Okiep. Though his men quickly subdued the nearby towns of Springbok and Concordia,* Okiep would prove a much tougher nut to crack. Okiep was surrounded on the last day of March but the prompt landing of a party of blue jackets from HMS *Barracouta*† at Port Nolloth managed to deny the raiders entry to the town. The locally raised men of the Namaqualand Border Scouts also reacted quickly, securing the railway bridges to facilitate the advance of any relief column.[163] In Okiep itself the small imperial garrison was bolstered by 275

---

* the Springbok town guard resisted for sixteen hours and Concordia fell without a shot being fired

† HMS *Barracouta* was a 1,580-ton 3rd class twin-screw cruiser, commanded by the superbly named Commander S. H. B. Ash, RN.

volunteers, predominantly miners. Okiep held out for thirty days before the besiegers retreated in the face of a relief force.

ঌ

By early 1902, Kitchener's men had built 8,600 blockhouses covering 3,700 miles of fence. This system was manned by around 50,000 white troops, supported by another 16,000 armed Africans.[164] Many bitter-enders later claimed the blockhouse system was a white elephant, but this is nothing more than sour grapes: Kitchener's drives were bringing in more and more prisoners each week. On the 27th February 1902—Majuba Day—one of Kitchener's columns surrounded Meyer's laager at Lang Riet, capturing 650 bitter-enders at a stroke. And even though bands of bitter-enders often did manage to break through the lines, they frequently took casualties in the process.[165] For all their misplaced bravado the statistics tell the story: the first three months of 1902 saw 3,533 prisoners taken, with a further 861 Boers voluntarily turning themselves in.[166]

More telling still, many former commandos had actually switched sides and joined the imperial cause, the most famous of which was General Piet de Wet as mentioned earlier. Indeed, by early 1902, so many 'joiners' had changed their allegiance that two new mounted units were added to the imperial order of battle: the (Transvaal) National Scouts and the Orange River Colony Volunteers. Dressed in British uniform and subject to military discipline, these regiments of *joiners* were of more political significance than military, though they did score a noteworthy victory on the 2nd February 1902 when a strong detachment of National Scouts helped capture a commando of 164 burghers.[167] Unsurprisingly, they were hated with even more vehemence than the hendsoppers and any unlucky enough to fall into the hands of the bitter-enders was generally murdered as a traitor.[168] In one particularly grisly incident, twelve captured National Scouts were castrated by their erstwhile comrades.[169] Though the bitter-enders reserved a special hatred for their former friends who joined such units, hendsoppers also served the British as scouts, guides and intelligence officers throughout the guerrilla war.[170]

Despite the unglamorous, though relentless, steamroller of grinding imperial success, there were still moments of triumph for the Boers. General de la Rey pounced on a supply column in February 1902, losing fifty of his force killed but capturing over 300 men. More spectacularly, on the 7th of March, he then ambushed the relief column, falling on Lord Methuen's 1,250-strong force at what became known as the battle of Tweebosch. De la Rey swooped on Methuen's outnumbered command and the British were badly mauled, losing over 200 prisoners and six guns. Methuen himself was severely wounded in the battle, and was taken prisoner. Many of the Boers wanted to murder him on the spot, but de la Rey gallantly sent him back to the British lines under a flag of truce so that he could receive medical attention. While this act of humanity is admirable, a cynic might wonder if de la Rey knew the end was nigh and whether there was an element of self-preservation in his action.

Less trumpeted is what happened a few weeks later. General Hamilton commanded several columns sent to avenge Tweebosch, one of which hammered a Boer commando at Rooiwal on the 11th April 1902, recapturing the guns taken at Tweebosch. It was the last significant action of the war.

It is fair to say that the bitter-einders fought a very dirty and unpleasant campaign. Many had reduced themselves to the level of common criminals, more concerned with larceny than combat; others had indulged in the mass murder of blacks or the savage execution of wounded prisoners, with civilians across South Africa living in fear of their visitation. One contemporary observer, summing up the widespread murder of imperial wounded, and the equally widespread use of expanding bullets and khaki uniforms, declared: "the pro-Boers on every occasion strove to justify these practices, as they strove to justify whatever the enemy did, and to attack the British army, however forbearing it showed itself."[171]

But were the bitter-einders fighting a guerrilla war or a terrorist campaign? This is something of a moot point, as one man's terrorist will always be another man's freedom fighter. The rallying cries may have been 'independence' and 'freedom' but in reality the republican hardliners were fighting for nothing of the sort. Those bitter-einders who still fought for a political purpose, rather than simply for loot, were desperate to ensure that the Boer republics would continue to be ruled by a small minority of their people. If we look at James Kiras's definition of terrorism, "the sustained use of violence against symbolic or civilian targets by small groups for political purposes, such as inspiring fear, drawing widespread attention to a political grievance, and/or provoking a draconian or unsustainable response", then the methods and tactics of the bitter-einders undoubtedly fit the bill. Civilians, loyalists, surrendered Boers and, most savagely of all, non-whites, were targeted in a sustained campaign of intimidation and murder, and such tactics certainly prompted a draconian response from the imperial high command. That said, the tactics of many later 'liberation movements', such as the African National Congress, would also fit Kiras's definition, so in the end it all comes down to personal persuasion.

However one choses to term it, it was a confused, regrettable and highly unsavoury phase of a war which should have ended two years earlier but for the pride, obstinacy and commitment to racial supremacy of a handful of charismatic hardliners. Though the post-war regimes did a magnificent job in rebranding these disparate bands as romantic idealists, the truth is less palatable. It is often forgotten that the bitter-einders were not fighting, as is so often claimed, for their independence: that had long since been accepted as lost by all but the most unhinged. The terms offered the bitter-einders at the Middelburg peace talks in February 1901 had included, in a rather roundabout way, the proposal that a colour-blind franchise—similar to that in the other British territories of South Africa—would be implemented after representative government was granted to the two Boer states.[172] At the insistence of London, Kitchener had also been forced to include a statement confirming that "the legal position of Kaffirs will be similar to that which they hold in the Cape Colony",[173] something which would never be accepted by the bitter-einders. Sure enough, the peace offer was rejected and another thirteen months of brutal fighting, massacre and murder ensued. In what was one of the few significant changes* between the Middelburg offer and the peace proposal which was finally signed at Vereeniging in May 1902, the troublesome clause was subtly changed to "no franchise be granted for natives until after self-government" and any mention of the legal position of natives was quietly omitted.[174] As no Boer-dominated government was going to give the vote to Africans in a hurry, the bitter-einders could safely agree to the revised proposal. One of the leading historians examining the impact that the war had on the black population of South Africa declared this to be the most significant clause of the surrender.[175] More than anything else—aside perhaps

---

* the only other significant change concerned the amnesty of Cape rebels

from the joy of looting—what motivated many bitter-einders to continue fighting tooth and nail was their determination that non-whites should not be given the vote in the post-war Transvaal and Orange River Colony.

For this reason, and many others, it is a period from which neither side can take any great pride. Undoubtedly, unspeakable brutalities were committed, but there were also glimmers of decency and honour. Frederic Unger attended an oyster supper at the Bloemfontein town hall at the height of the guerrilla war, arranged as a fundraiser for Boer prisoners on St Helena. Not only did the British permit this to occur, but imperial officers even attended the party.[176]

Though few would agree with him today, perhaps Conan-Doyle put it best: "when one remembers the condonation upon the part of the British on the use of their own uniforms by the Boers, of the wholesale breaking of paroles, of the continual use of explosive bullets, of the abuse of the pass system and of the red cross, it is impossible to blame them for showing some severity in the stamping out of armed rebellion within their own Colony. If stern measures were eventually adopted it was only after extreme leniency had been tried and failed. The loss of five years' franchise as a penalty for firing upon their own flag is surely the most gentle correction which an Empire ever laid upon a rebellious people."[177] Of course, Conan-Doyle's assessment of imperial leniency is utterly at odds with today's commonly held notions of the British conduct in the war. To examine this further we must now turn our attention to the main cause of this controversy: farm-burning.

CHAPTER NINE

Methods of barbarism

"As soon as we sent Pres. Kruger out of the country, and his money-grabbing,
traitorous hangers-on were out of the way, the whole tone and
aspect of things altered for the better."[1]
—Jan Smuts's assessment of the Kruger clique

"Every farm is an intelligence agency and a supply depot."[2]
—Lord Kitchener, December 1900

"At Estcourt, we passed four trucks of Boer prisoners recently captured.
Most of them wished the war was over, but others were indifferent."
—Diary entry of Corporal Albert Hilder, Royal Canadian Dragoons, 26th February 1902[3]

"In spite of all the real and imaginary horrors recorded in 'War Against War',
this has been the most humanely conducted struggle the world has ever seen."
—Padre Lowry of the Guards Brigade, 1901[4]

"Every day we see how much the Pro-Boers are answerable for the prolongation of the
War. The Boers read the accounts of their speeches and naturally
expect that we will give them back their independence."
—diary of Captain George Clarke, Royal Artillery, 19th September 1901

"How else could the British cope with burghers who were in the field one day
and the next on the stoeps of their homes, each of which was a potential fort
and a permanent source of information and supply?"
—Eric Walker in *A History of Southern Africa*

"a striking feature of the Boer rebel conduct towards black civilians is that it did not
consist only of a mass of randomly directly vendettas; actions and demands
carried the flavour of a generalized repressive determination."
—Bill Nasson in *Abraham Esau's War*

"One can hardly trust the Boers to act on the methods of civilized warfare.
Their leaders might, but some of them are half civilized."
—Bishop of Natal, Arthur Hamilton Baynes, 1900

"The British have been too merciful, and I believe, had a more rigorous course been
adopted when the Army first entered this capital and the enemy been
thoroughly stampeded, the war would have been materially shortened."
—Captain Slocum, American military attaché, writing from Bloemfontein

... safes had been blown to pieces with dynamite; the lamps and
furniture had been smashed to atoms; the papers, tickets and books
had been torn to pieces and lay strewn over the floors. The farmhouses
had also suffered in a like manner, valued trinkets and ornaments
lying smashed among the debris of furniture etc. The doors and
windows had been burst open and broken into pieces with crowbars.
But it is impossible to adequately describe the heartrending scenes
which were enacted. To understand fully the wanton devastation
which had been made in many a happy country home, it would be
necessary to witness the scene of desolation ... the enemy had not
restricted these wicked acts of destruction to the interiors of the
farmhouses only, for in some cases orchards of young fruit trees
had been chopped down and utterly destroyed, and iron rain-water
tanks had been pierced through the sides, rendering them useless.
Many a heart was bowed down with grief on beholding the home,
which had meant years of work, thus destroyed in a few moments by
a ruthless foe. Much of the livestock, that had not been driven away,
had also been destroyed. Dead poultry were lying about in heaps at
one farmstead, among them being fifty young turkeys. Cattle and
sheep lay rotting in the paddocks. On another farm three hundred
head of cattle and sheep had been destroyed with arsenical poison.[5]

This is more like it, many readers will be thinking: at last, we're going to
hear how ghastly the Tommies really were. This is the sort of the thing one
will read in many recent histories of the Boer War and, at this point, most
readers will be indignantly imagining the raiders as ruthlessly rapacious Brits,
sweeping down onto Boer farmsteads to jubilantly visit destruction on the
poor, downtrodden inhabitants. Photos of the burning farm and the plucky,

innocent—always innocent, of course—Boers watching their life's work go up in smoke are iconic images of the war, rivalled only in their power to enrage by those of the concentration camps. There is, however, rather more to this than meets the eye, as the above extract was written in 1900, describing the devastation inflicted on Natal by—wait for it— the invading republicans.

Though strangely ignored by most modern historians, and long before imperial troops burned any farms, Boer invasion forces cheerfully looted and plundered those areas of Natal they had seized and declared to be part of the South African Republic. The commandos that streamed into British territory pillaged as they went, helping themselves to whatever they fancied from each village they captured, ransacking any farmsteads they came across,[6] and driving terrified refugees before them. "Boer women followed the Commandos, with their waggons, joyfully loading up with food and furniture, a splendid shopping-spree with nothing to pay! The piled-up carts and waggons passed through Bethal, arousing feelings of pleasure" from the townspeople.[7]

When the town of Dundee was captured, the looting which followed was so bad that the Boer commander, Commandant Joubert, furiously attempted to demote the leaders of one of the commandos responsible.[8] Joubert had to back down, however, when the loot-laden men of the commando threatened to desert *en masse* if any action was taken against their leaders. Similarly, when Joubert tried to remonstrate with some Boers who had raided and pillaged a farm, they took the dressing-down light-heartedly, one admitting that "no one treated our Commandant in Chief very seriously".[9]

While he was generally regarded as a gentleman, Joubert had little control over his forces, but the pillaging might have been even worse had a more dashing and aggressive leader been in command. As we know, with the vast majority of Natal's imperial forces bottled up in Ladysmith, the exasperatingly cautious Joubert inexplicably settled down to besiege them, ignoring the fact that the rest of Natal was open for the taking. Even when he was finally pricked into action by his more aggressive subordinates, Joubert still left some 18,000 of his men to continue the siege, leading a force of around only 3,500 to drive deeper into Natal and press on to seize Durban. As they advanced once more, Boer raiding parties roamed the country, "capturing the whole of the livestock that they came across, and ruthlessly destroying the homesteads … the road going south from Mooi River to Nottingham Road presented a most remarkable appearance, for it was crowded with thousands of horses, cattle and sheep being driven by the flying farmers to positions of safety from the Boer raiders".[10]

Elements of the Piet Retief and Bethal commandos[11] sacked the village of Pomeroy, leaving the settlement almost entirely destroyed as the Boer raiders "looted every building, and burnt down the gaol, post-office, hotel, and sundry other buildings".[12] The Boer capture of Weenen also saw the burghers indulge in a looting spree, helping themselves to anything that took their fancy and loading their booty onto requisitioned wagons. They then smashed their way into the public houses[13] and went on the sort of riotous drunken bender possible only when someone else is paying for the booze. The wife of one Natalian farmer remembered a visit from a republican raiding party who interrupted the family at breakfast time. She ran outside to find them "cutting fences and riding in all directions, anywhere through the homestead, no discipline whatsoever, just like a pack of hounds when the fox is lost ... three men came to commandeer our carriage horses, one riding-horse, and my youngest boy's pony ... when they entered the stable, I stood by my favourite and slated them. The men were not Boers, but some of the scum who have joined". These raiders then helped themselves to "anything the wretches could lay hands on". This plucky lady described how they had occupied a neighbouring farm and had "broken and destroyed everything about this place, killed off his sheep etc ... the descriptions they themselves gave of wrecked homes was heart-rending. Some of them sported all sorts of loot, and were dressed in clothes that were never bought by them".[14] Barely able to believe what the average burgher was capable of, reporter Bennet Burleigh recorded this "wild, criminal destruction of property ... the Boer was addicted to lifting cattle, confiscating forage, food and other articles belonging to private persons ... he often wasted what he could not carry away, or pressed natives to "help themselves". In this last raid of Joubert's commando another stage has been reached. From Mooi River to Frere, not only has there been wholesale looting of cattle and all kinds of private property, but there have been repeated instances of wanton destructiveness. Judged by the canons of European or civilized warfare, the acts were those of brigandage, and the culprits, had they been caught red handed, deserved trial by drum-head court martial, and to be led out for execution".[15]

The diary of the Bishop of Natal, Arthur Baynes DD, is peppered with accounts of the looting and wanton vandalism suffered by his flock. He writes of one stud farm where the invaders helped themselves to £15,000-worth of high-quality horses[16]—an enormous sum of money at the time. A few days later, the frustrated bishop angrily declared, "The Boers have been making free with my diocese and with all the farmers' stock quite long enough."[17] Later still, when the imperial troops reoccupied Chieveley, the bishop described the state of the stationmaster's house in which he spent the night: "The house was in a sad state of dirt and disorder. The Boers had been in possession of it a little while back, and had ruthlessly destroyed everything they could lay hands on in the most wanton and brutal manner. They had hacked down the marble mantelpiece and left the pieces in the grate, had broken his cupboards and windows, torn the locks off his drawers and (most childish and wanton of all) had destroyed his cases of stuffed birds by pulling the heads off them all."[18]

But this free-for-all binge of looting and vandalism—and Joubert's dithering—had cost the Boers their chance to capture Natal. At the start of November, when the encirclement of Ladysmith was complete, there were just 2,300 imperial troops to defend the rest of Natal, and only 300 of these were mounted.[19] Reinforcements were steadily landing in Durban, however, and, a mere two weeks later, imperial forces south of the Tugela totalled around 14,000 men. Joubert's invasion only got as far as Willow Grange before faltering in the face of the imperial reinforcements. No sooner had the new regiments disembarked than they were pushing northward to hold the line, before advancing, ready to drive the invaders back whence they came. Joubert had, quite frankly, made the most dunderheaded mistake of the war. Needless to say, this retreat came as an enormous relief to the people of Durban and Pietermaritzburg and all the other Natalians who had thus far been spared their brutal attentions.

Though this Boer strike force had, just a couple of weeks earlier, departed from their positions around Ladysmith with little encumbrance, they were to return absolutely laden with all manner of pillage. The vast column of the stolen goods was testament to the enthusiastic theft in which the Boers blatantly engaged throughout their invasion of Natal. As the commandos trudged their way back north with their ill-gotten gains, imperial forces missed a golden opportunity to pounce on them, a mix-up which almost caused a mutiny among the furious Natalian troops: "The Commando had come out lightly equipped; it returned heavy with hundreds of wagons loaded with looted goods and chattels and droves upon droves of raided cattle, a great straggling procession. Here was opportunity for a swift stroke—the Composite Regiment* took up position on the heights commanding a narrow defile about 10 miles to the west of Estcourt, through which the only available road passed, and as they were on the point of surprising the enemy and probably engaging them successfully, just such an opportunity as soldiers dream, the OC Mounted Troops arrived on the scene and refused to allow them to fire. The OC explained to the dismayed McKenzie [Major McKenzie of the Natal Carbineers, senior officer of the Composite Regiment on the spot], in hearing of some of the equally astonished troopers, that his instructions were not to engage, but merely to shepherd them back to Colenso. Remembering the ravaged farms, the troops bitterly, almost mutinously, watched the enemy straggle away with their loot unmolested."[20]

When the Boers were finally driven from their positions on the Tugela in early 1900 the imperial forces discovered yet more shocking examples of republican looting and destruction. As we read earlier, when Colenso was recaptured British troops found every attempt to render the village uninhabitable. Another witness recorded that "every house was more or less ruined. Everything of any value within the houses had been smashed or torn to atoms. In the station-master's office, his papers were torn and strewn about the floor, and in the centre of the room was the partially decomposed carcass of a horse which and been tied by the halter to the letter-press and left to die, presumably of starvation. The railway bridge over the Tugela River was also completely destroyed; the whole village and surroundings thus presenting a scene of wanton destruction".[21]

While the wartime destruction of a railway bridge is certainly a permissible—indeed, perfectly sensible—act, the rest of the Boer pillaging is harder to forgive. As Buller's forces steadily drove the republican invaders out of Natal,

---

* The Composite Regiment was formed from 'A' Squadron of the Imperial Light Horse (the rest of the regiment being stuck in Ladysmith), one squadron of the Natal Carbineers, a company of the Dublin Fusiliers Mounted Infantry and the 2nd 60th Mounted Infantry. The regiment numbered 450 all ranks, and was commanded by Brevet Major Hubert Gough—later Lieutenant-General Sir Hubert Gough who commanded the British Fifth Army in the First World War.

each mile the British advanced brought more horrifying revelations: "Signs of devastation on the farms around Ladysmith was evident on all sides. As they had done in the Estcourt districts, so they have done here—ruthlessly looting and destroying everything they could lay their hands on. At Elandslaagte, beyond which they had now retreated five or six miles, two stores and the railway station had been burnt to the ground. At the coal mine the winding machinery and electric light plant had been blown up with dynamite. Along the railway line from Ladysmith to Elandslaagte and on to Sunday's River, every bridge and culvert had also been blown up, and all the damage that their hasty retreat admitted of had been done."[22]

Again, the destruction of bridges and the like is perfectly acceptable within the rules of warfare, but there is also no doubt that the Boers indulged in a fairly coordinated effort to lay waste to farmsteads and other civilian property. For many burghers, the invasion was seen as nothing other than opportunity to enrich themselves at the expense of the colonists of Natal. An hotelier in Waterval Boven who lived through the war described the invaders in terms one is unlikely to read in many recent histories: "this whole war has been nothing but a war of loot from the very start. Why, when the invasion of Natal began, the burghers looted every place they came to. Every man in the Federal army had his Cape-cart, drawn by two horses, and one or two nigger servants behind with two or three extra riding horses. Some of the men had two or three carts, and every one of them was piled and loaded down with loot."[23]

A few Natalians of Dutch extraction treacherously threw their lot in with the invaders, grasping what they could in the free-for-all. One such traitor, "evidently thinking that the Boers were going to be victorious, and would establish Dutch supremacy throughout the whole of South Africa, wrote to his neighbour—an English farmer—and offered him ten pounds for his large farm, at the same time pointing out that he would get nothing for it after the war was over, as it would be taken off him".[24] Another turncoat was found to have acquired no less than five pianos, all looted from the houses of neighbouring farms.[25] Apart from a music-hire business, quite what he planned to do with them all is anyone's guess.

Conan-Doyle noted that he later met numerous Orange Free State farmers who acknowledged the suffering endured in their country was "just retribution" for what the Boers had inflicted on the people of Natal.[26] This is far from the popular view of course: though we have suffered endless self-righteous clamouring about the Kitchener's 'methods of barbarism', reaction to the burning and looting of northern Natal has always been one of deafening silence. Emily Hobhouse, in *The Brunt of the War and Where it Fell* even goes so far as to dismiss any criticism of the Boer invaders, declaring that no Natal farms were destroyed by them.[27] This clear falsehood forces one to question the veracity of the rest of her tome. In stark contrast to Hobhouse's reality-airbrush, a contemporary letter perhaps best sums up the fury and frustration of the Natal loyalists:

DEVASTATED NATAL

It is almost impossible to know how to begin a letter when placed in the position that we Loyalists occupy in Natal, and, I may as well say, the whole of South Africa. To say that we have been ruined is practically nothing. The circumstances of each individual case are far more heartrending than the total result. Not only does there seem to be very little sympathy in the hearts of those who hold the high offices in this country and at home, but, further, the military authorities both here and at the Cape have peculiar methods of their own in dealing with the several matters entrusted to them. We who are loyal are expected to sit down and be content, although we have no homes, very little food, less clothing, and no money. Some details may be of interest. Imagine yourself in a newly-built house, with every room neatly and comfortably furnished, your business bringing in sufficient to enable you to live without anxiety. Then try, if it be possible, to imagine yourself and family flying for your life with less than an hour's notice, leaving everything and escaping with only the clothes you stand upright in, to tramp sixty miles through a country such as this without the slightest shelter, and with only what food could be placed in your pockets before starting. Hurrying through the terrible heat of the day, walking through rivers, and lying on the grass for a bed, with a heavy rain descending to add to its discomfort, we finally arrive at a town where we are allowed a shilling each adult per day to provide for all our wants.

On returning to our homes, we find that after the semi-savage Boer has occupied them for a time the best of our furniture has been taken into the Transvaal, even by some of the members of the First Raad—that is to say, the Boers' House of Lords. Other furniture has been taken by the disloyal Natal Boer, and what could not be taken has been destroyed for fire purposes. To add to our distress and disgust, sick horses or cattle have been taken into our houses and starved to death, so that they should die inside, and the terrible remains of these poor animals have floated about our floors, so that the rooms cannot again be used without new woodwork. Not only so, but the wretches have violated all decency in every room, so much so that it will be sickening ever to remember it. The walls have been plastered with the same filth as lies upon the floors. The window-sashes are smashed, doors broken down and burnt, ceilings destroyed, and sometimes floors broken up to provide fuel for the fire. The kitchen range is smashed, the garden devastated, choice fruit-trees, grape vines, etc., chopped down, and fences destroyed. The wreckage is beyond description, and all this by the saintly Boer, so much worshipped by the ignorant in our own country.

THE QUESTION OF COMPENSATION

Now, turning to the high officials, we hear something of compensation. Someone in the House of Commons says full compensation must be exacted; another says the Loyalists must be compensated; and another says there are great difficulties in this question of compensation; but I have not heard anyone say, "What are these loyal people doing to obtain food? Can't we give them immediate help?" People at home cannot realize what misery we have to endure. This is our position to-day: The Mansion House Fund allows each woman one shilling per day, each child sixpence per day, with one or two rooms, according to the size of family. The men get nothing, save one or two free meals per day. There being so many men from upcountry, the Transvaal and Free State, etc., it is impossible to get work at any price, so we live in a state of semi-starvation, and get what old clothes we can to cover our nakedness. While we are enduring this the Home Government says, "You shall be compensated"; but we say, "How shall we exist until that time comes?" I know men whose income was nearly one hundred a month now living on borrowed money; but it is not all of us who can raise money on our property, considering that it is in the hands of the Boers, and may be completely destroyed. How the up-country towns are going to start again I do not know, unless the Home Government comes to our rescue at once. So far we have suffered and paid dearly for our loyalty, while the rebel has grown rich and fat before our eyes.

CLEMENCY FOR REBELS

Now comes the third point concerning the military. Their doings with the rebels and others simply confound us. The rebels are treated with the utmost consideration; it curdles our blood to see this, for we who live here know what it means. The treatment meted out to these vile creatures is unrighteous and unjust, and will be the cause of bloodshed after the war is over. The military authorities, as you have doubtless seen, accept the surrender of men anywhere without their arms or ammunition, which they have buried in some secret place, and these men are allowed to return home even without a cross word to take up their arms at a time that will suit them. On other occasions they are allowed to surrender with the oldest rubbish in the shape of arms that can be scraped together, while their Mausers are at home. Can you wonder, then, that we who are to live here when the military are gone are disgusted at their ignorance or weakness. Further, as regards the Boers who have surrendered, they will every one of them take up arms again when Roberts and Buller have got further up-country. It is good policy for a lot of them to stay behind; but our Generals don't know the Boer, and will not be told.

THE PENALTY OF LOYALTY

It makes our blood boil to see some men in our House of Commons continually asking of the welfare of the Boer prisoners, but very seldom do we see much said concerning our prisoners at Pretoria. You who live at home do not know and feel as we do. You have only newspaper reports to read, and different statements made in the House, many of which are radically misleading, because written and spoken by men whose experience in South Africa may run into one or two months, and perhaps not even that. For instance, take Mr

Churchill, the correspondent of the Morning Post. He has hardly been here sufficient time to know where he is, knows nothing of the country, the people, or customs, has no interest in or care for the country, and will soon be gone; yet he desires to counsel us, who have been years in the colony, and know everything concerning it, and have our all invested here; and yet thousands at home will think him correct.

It is a grand thing to talk of loyalty at home, where it costs nothing; but be here at the present time, and you will see that loyalty means a different thing altogether. It does not pay to be loyal. The disloyal always comes off the best. If you were here you would not ask an explanation. It was so before I came into the colony, and during the ten years that I have been here it has been the same. Do you wonder, then, that our feelings are strong against the disloyal, and that we are hurt at our own country compelling us to suffer, while it seems afraid to punish the rebellious.[28]

As we have seen, even after they had been driven out of Natal and the Cape Colony, federal forces continued to indulge in the burning and looting of farms and other property, using such methods to terrorize waverers among their own people. Indeed, it was these continual attacks on the farms of surrendered Boers that first prompted the British to set up the refugee camps to protect these unfortunate souls. As well as terrifying those who had had enough of the war, this constant threat tied down large numbers of imperial troops who had to be posted in penny packets to protect the farms of surrendered Boers.[29] Nor was this the work of a few villains, but was rather a considered policy of the Boer leadership to ensure that the war dragged fruitlessly on. As we saw in chapter eight, General Louis Botha himself issued an instruction to his subordinates, demanding that they take drastic measures to prevent any burghers from giving up the fight, and ordering them "to confiscate everything movable and also to burn their farms"[30] if needed.

The Boer invasion of the Cape Colony was slightly different from that of Natal, in that significant numbers of Cape Dutch threw their lot in with the invaders. While many of these traitors were motivated by genuine enthusiasm for an Afrikaans South African empire, others were intimidated, or joined for fear of seeing their property torched and their belongings seized. This fear was not irrational: as we saw in chapter five, loyalist civilians were driven from their homes by the invaders, forced to abandon everything they owned and make their own way to the British lines, often arriving as destitute refugees.[31]

As we know, the British repulse at Magersfontein in December 1899 had led to something of a stalemate on the western front, with Lord Methuen digging in on the Modder River and awaiting reinforcements. Several small cavalry actions punctuated this hiatus. On the 9th January a British flying column raided into the Orange Free State.[32] Comprising elements of the 9th and 12th Lancers, the colonials of the Victorian Mounted Rifles and 'G' Battery, Royal Horse Artillery, Colonel Babington's force burned down a farmhouse owned by Boer Commandant Lubbe.[33] Despite the fact that Lubbe's farm had been used as a base by Boer forces and that the federals were indulging in unfettered looting and burning in Natal, Babington's actions raised eyebrows in London and Pretoria; even the *The Times History* disapproved, stating that the burning of Lubbe's farm "cannot be regarded as warranted by military exigencies". Though the raid was a mere pinprick compared to the wholesale pillage by Kruger's men in Natal, the grumpy old bugger shamelessly reacted with his trademark sanctimonious outrage, condemning Babington's actions.

For the Boer propaganda machine to seize upon the burning of this single farm, obliviously disregarding their own actions in Natal, is only to be expected. Likewise, the unpatriotic windbags of the British Left are always mind-numbingly predictable in their efforts to outdo each other in their passionate belief in 'my country—always wrong', and their feigned outrage and hysterical ranting can never be taken too seriously.*

That even as rational an organ as *The Times* should sniffily disapprove of the burning of Lubbe's farm, however, showed the impossible task which imperial troops would find themselves facing throughout the war. Essentially, Her Majesty's forces were expected to fight in an absolutely and unrealistically irreproachable fashion, while the actions of their enemy would always be explained away as the justifiable actions of desperate men. While it was not (and, indeed, is still not) unreasonable to expect the very highest standards of honour from Her Majesty's forces, those keen to criticize seem to have no concept that war is a very ugly thing and unpleasant things tend to happen.

---

* Regretfully, this passionately held attitude of 'my country—always wrong' continues through to the present day. The Falklands War of 1982 provides a splendid example of this, with various loathsome Labour MPs in uproar over the sinking of the *Belgrano*, while wordless about the sinking of the British ships, *Atlantic Conveyor*, *Sir Galahad*, HMS *Sheffield*, HMS *Coventry* and others.

It is undeniable that the Boers were the first to indulge in farm-burning and looting in the war. Equally undeniable is that as the war went on, the republicans used farm-burning and looting as a terror tactic, openly sanctioned and approved of by their high command, as well as being a convenient method of personal enrichment. It was designed to strike fear into the hearts of loyalists, punish hendsoppers and terrorize waverers among their own people, the object being to maintain the struggle long after anyone with half a brain had realized it was futile.

In stark contrast, when imperial troops were later forced to also adopt the practice, it was a matter of simple military necessity, not the joyful pillage in which the invading republicans had eagerly indulged during the opening months. On the 16th June 1900 Lord Roberts proclaimed that he would raze those farms which were closest to the places where railways lines had been sabotaged. By today's standards this was unquestionably a heavy-handed and arbitrary response to acts of terrorism, but Roberts was not the first to find himself forced to employ it—his proclamation was inspired by the Prussian military in the Franco-Prussian War.[34] Other farms were destroyed where there was evidence that they were supporting or harbouring the guerrillas, reasonably so. Separating the guerrilla from the population is standard practice in counter-insurgency warfare,[35] and striking the supply source of the enemy is military stratagem as old as war itself—indeed, throughout the guerrilla war, the bitter-einders themselves preferred striking at ponderous British supply columns and depots safely out of range of imperial combat troops. By the time of the guerrilla war, many Boer farmsteads were nothing less than mini-fortresses, serving as supply points for those bitter-einders still in the field. Is it in any way reasonable to suggest that the imperial forces should have ignored these bastions and permitted the commandos to pop round whenever they fancied stocking up on food and ammunition, or wished to spend the night in relative comfort and security? Surely even the most wide-eyed critic of the tactic will agree it would have been completely and utterly illogical for the imperial forces *not* to have targeted such farms?

It was certainly a harsh aspect of the war and was considered so by most of the Tommies who had to do it. Undoubtedly mistakes were made: imperial troops were human beings after all. They got tired and hungry, they got fed up of chasing an enemy who tended to avoid taking them on in a straight fight, their nerves were frayed by living in perpetual fear of the farmer who smilingly offered them coffee one day and shot them in the back the next. As we have seen, at times bitter-einders callously sniped from surrendered farms so as to provoke retribution from the British. Needless to say, there were instances of Tommies over-stepping their orders, whether through frustration, devilry or a combination of both.

But few things in war are pleasant, and one will never win a war by tip-toeing around social niceties. Just as the RAF and USAF spent years pulverizing entire German cities and killing tens of thousands of civilians to destroy Hitler's vile regime, so the imperial forces in South Africa had to take harsh measures to bring the war to a close. And that is the crux of the matter: it was a war, and the bitter-einders were quite happy to fight it in as dirty a fashion as possible. It is difficult to think of an alternative to the action the British were forced to take.

When faced with a similar situation, for example, the US army was unable to find a solution more palatable to modern commentators. Indeed, the American-Philippine War of 1899–1903 (fought almost simultaneously with the Boer War) saw US troops adopting tactics far harsher than those employed by imperial forces in South Africa: "the behaviour of American soldiers in the Philippines was officially governed by General Orders 100. GO 100 had been written during the Civil War to help Union forces deal with the task of controlling occupied Southern territories. The author, a distinguished lawyer named Frances Lieber, had had sons fighting both sides, and he aimed the orders to be stern but fair … GO 100 demanded the fair treatment of enemy soldiers and of civilians in occupied terrain. But it also required that those enemy soldiers and occupied civilians meet certain rules of behaviour. Enemy soldiers had to wear uniforms. Occupied civilians could not act to hide or assist enemy soldiers without fear of repercussion … if the civilian population acted to hide or assist such guerrilla forces, the occupying army was justified in punitive destruction of civilian property, as long as that destruction was not 'wanton' … captured insurgents could be executed summarily. Towns giving support to Aguinaldo's forces could be destroyed"[36] and "the population [of one area which was an insurgent stronghold] was forced into zones of concentration around the major towns and anything left outside was considered fair game. American units burned villages, killed animals, and destroyed crops … one officer who took part in the campaign, recalled, 'We did not take any prisoners. We shot everybody on sight.'"[37]

And this was by no means the occasional excess: Major Littleton Waller of the US Marines received the following orders from his general: "I want no prisoners. I wish you to kill and burn, the more you kill and burn, the better it will please me." When Waller questioned what the lower age limit there was on the killing, he was told "ten years of age".[38] After an insurgent attack on American forces at Balangiga in the Philippines left forty-eight US troops dead, "the town of Balangiga was razed to the ground, such that nothing there remains to this day but the bare walls of the church used to conceal the ambushers".[39] One American officer had cages constructed from railway tracks, measuring fifteen by thirty feet and six feet high with up to fifty prisoners crammed in for months at a time. The architect proudly posed in front of his cages for a press photographer, and cheerfully answered questions about the death rates they caused.[40] An American soldier wrote home to tell his family that "The town of Titatia [sic] was surrendered to us a few days ago, and two companies occupy the same. Last night one of our boys was found shot and his stomach cut open. Immediately orders were received from General Wheaton to burn the town and kill every native in sight; which was done to a finish. About 1,000 men, women and children were reported killed. I am probably growing hard-hearted, for I am in my glory when I can sight my gun on some dark skin and pull the trigger".[41]

American "soldiers derisively labelled this kind of fighting 'amigo' warfare because, after inflicting casualties, the insurgent force would fade away into the jungle, and when the Americans pushed on into the nearest town, all they would find were Filipinos in civilian clothing crying out 'Amigo, amigo!' as a sign of friendship".[42]

The point is not to suggest that the Americans did it so it is okay that the British did it too; rather it is to demonstrate that this was depth of barbarism to which the American army plunged when placed in a similar situation. Even if the British army was at times less than blameless, no one else had found a credible alternative. As an aside, the infinitely more heavy-handed tactics of the Americans rarely attract the same level of criticism as is directed at the British in South Africa. Despite criticism in the press at the time, few Americans feel any guilt over the tactics their soldiers employed in the Philippines; no one ever claims that the Americans invented the concentration camp, even though they were also forced to employ them at exactly the same time as the British. It is interesting to ponder the differences in the way the two conflicts are now commonly perceived. No storm of indignation surrounds the American-Philippine conflict, despite the Filipinos having to wait a generation longer for independence than the Afrikaners. Is this perhaps down to simple racism: the suffering of the white Boers is somehow viewed as less acceptable than the— much worse—suffering of the brown Filipinos? Or is it perhaps testament to the success of the apartheid regime's determination to portray the *Boerevolk* as the victims of British imperial brutality?

⋙

Either way, it was not just the Americans and British who discovered the hard way that fighting a guerrilla campaign meant rewriting the normal rules of war. Indeed, when the Boers forces had previously found themselves in a similar position they too adopted similar tactics. Let us turn back the clock to 1865. There had existed an uneasy peace between the Orange Free State and Basutoland since their war in 1858. Various border clashes had brought matters to a head and, in June 1865, the Orange Free State invaded their neighbour once again. The men of the Orange Free State were assisted by a large contingent from the ZAR under Kruger and—somewhat more remarkably— several hundred Barolongs, Fingos, Batlokua and Bamonaheng warriors.[43] It is noteworthy that the Boers never seemed to have a problem with blacks joining a fight as long as they were on their side. Despite these allies, the invaders were still heavily outnumbered but managed to trounce the Basuto in a series of open battles. Realizing the superiority of the Boers' marksmanship, the Basuto changed tactics and retreated to several mountaintop redoubts, positions which the Free-Staters proved unable to breach.[44] With their easy victories behind them, the morale of the besieging Boers started to flag, with rifts and desertions becoming commonplace. At the end of October Kruger's commando withdrew and returned to the Transvaal,[45] leaving the Orange Free State without enough men to continue the war. This situation led to an attempt by the Orange Free State to recruit a corps of mercenaries, the vast majority of which would necessarily have been British subjects from the Cape Colony and Natal. This did not sit well with the British high commissioner[46] who moved quickly to seek an armistice between the Orange Free State and the Basuto, requesting permission from the secretary of state for the colonies to take the latter under British protection. Unluckily for the Basuto and before the British could implement this, the Orange Free State attacked with renewed vigour in February 1866 and what was already a very savage conflict worsened. Denied outright military victory, the Free-Staters cast about for an easy target and the supposedly God-fearing Boers turned on the missionaries: "There was a general impression among the burghers that the missionaries acted as special pleaders for the Basuto, regardless altogether of the merits or demerits of their case, that they gave advice on military matters, that some of them took part in the fighting, and that in consequence they were more hurtful than the Basuto themselves."[47]

Needless to say, the expulsion of these churchmen and the destruction of their mission stations, caused outrage overseas. The mood of the British was not helped when they learned the details of a peace treaty that the Orange Free State had forced on the Basuto, a treaty which signed over a large chunk of Basuto territory to the Orange Free State.[48] The armistice was only temporary, however, and fighting soon broke out again. Boer commandos moved against the Basuto again in March 1867, this time targeting their crops, using what could rightfully be termed 'scorched earth' tactics.[49] Again, with the Basuto eager to avoid a 'fair fight', the invading Boers were reduced to chasing shadows, destroying crops and seizing cattle; those prisoners that they did manage to take stood a good chance of being shot in cold blood.[50] The Basuto, like the later Boer guerrillas, had no choice but to adopt hit-and-run tactics, striking at lonely homesteads or careless travellers. Again, as a foretaste of the Boer War, as the Free State columns cast about for an unseen enemy, "sentinels on every hill gave notice of the approach of the burghers, who soon found that their only chance of meeting the enemy was by quick and stealthy night marches".[51]

The Basuto women and children suffered terribly in this bitter conflict, their plight reaching the editor of the *Natal Witness* who was scathing in his condemnation of Boer atrocities. In truth, and exactly like the British in the Boer War, it would have been impossible for the Free-Staters to prevent all such suffering of non-combatants. If women and children happened to be in a mountaintop fortress when it was shelled or stormed, they were obviously as likely to get blown to pieces as their menfolk. When the Boers were trying to starve an impregnable fastness into submission, it stands to reason that any Basuto women or children sheltering therein suffered as much as, if not more, than the combatants. Writing in 1899, the British historian George

Theal commented on this harsh reality and the outrage it provoked, with admirable pragmatism: "In this condition of warfare, it sometimes happened that women and children lost their lives, and for this the Free State forces have been severely blamed. But no one has as yet devised a plan by which hostilities with a people like the Basuto can be carried on without such casualties."*

જ

As the British tried to find a solution, the Basuto war dragged on. Boer commandos moved about Basutoland at will, unable to engage their foe in battle but attempting to starve the Basuto into submission by destroying grain, capturing cattle and burning kraals.[52] This nasty little war was finally brought to an end in March 1868 when, after years of appeals from Basuto chiefs, the British declared a protectorate over Basutoland. And such 'methods of barbarism' were not limited to the Free State. That same year Kruger was again leading ZAR commandos against a neighbouring tribe. Upon seizing the kraal of Chief Mapela, his men torched it and made off with the women and children they had captured. Kruger would later use these wretched hostages as bargaining chips to force Mapela to accept peace terms.[53]

Much sneering is directed at the British army of the Boer War for struggling to fight an enemy who wouldn't run onto their machine guns, but as the war with the Basuto shows, the Boers struggled just as much to win a guerrilla campaign. Only the most slow-witted will have failed to notice that when the Basuto enemy was no longer keen to engage in conventional battle the Boers found themselves forced to adopt exactly the same tactics that they would later, with shameless hypocrisy, pillory the British for using. With the Basuto refusing to have anything to do with set-piece battles (which they always lost), the Free-Staters were forced to target the supplies, kraals and cattle of the Basuto—a course of action which obviously caused untold misery, suffering and death to the women and children of Basutoland. This is not to criticize the Free State as such, for really what choice did they have? But what made it alright for the Boers to use such tactics but unacceptable for the British to? Skin colour?

---

* Theal was right, but such pragmatism is rarely encountered today when discussing the impact of the Boer War on civilians, despite even Ben Viljoen acknowledging in his memoirs that the British had no choice but to strike at those who supplied and supported the guerrillas: "the enemy could not be expected to do otherwise than devastate the country."

For all that, no one would say that such tactics were pleasant or especially honourable, only that both the British and the Boers* found them necessary and that both were sooner or later forced to adopt them. The word 'forced' is used deliberately: Kitchener appealed directly to Louis Botha to have all farms declared off-limits during the guerrilla war. During the Middelburg peace talks in February 1901, Kitchener said that he would stop his troops burning farms as long as the Boers stopped using them as bases and—more importantly—stopped using the farm-burning tactic themselves: "I told him that if he continued such acts I should be forced to bring in all women and children, and as much property as possible to protect them from the acts of the burghers. I further enquired if he would agree to spare the farms and families of neutral or surrendered burghers, in which case I expressed my willingness to leave undisturbed the farms and families of burghers who were on commando, provided they did not actively assist their relatives."

Botha was not going to give up his favoured method of subjugating his own people, however, and rejected Kitchener's proposal out of hand: "I am entitled by law to force every man to join, and if they do not do so, to confiscate their property and leave their families on the veldt." When Kitchener asked him how best he could protect the surrendered burghers and their families, Botha callously declared: "The only thing you can do is to send them out of the country, as if I catch them, they must suffer."[54] It is therefore fair to lay a good chunk of the blame for the devastation of large areas of South Africa squarely at Botha's feet of and his equally hardline and hard-headed confederates.

While in 1899 many of the invading Boers had been a lawless mob that had looted the farms and towns of Natal with gusto, farm-burning was not work that the Tommies enjoyed.[55] Diaries are full of their grumbling at having to do what they considered dirty work, but they—unlike their enemy—had to follow orders, and those orders were strict. Roberts issued this instruction in August 1900: "Buildings harbouring the enemy would be liable to be razed to the ground. Burghers not notifying the presence of the enemy on their farms would be treated as aiding and abetting."[56] And this one in November of that year: "No farm is to be burnt except for an act of treachery, or when troops have

---

* and the Americans, Prussians, French, Spanish etc.

been fired on from the premises, or as punishment for breaking of telegraph or railway line, or when they have been used as bases of operations for raids, and then only with the consent of the General Officer Commanding, which is to be given in writing; the mere fact of a burgher absent on commando is on no account to be used as reason for burning the house."[57]

Though military discipline generally remained strict, various accounts suggest that the locally raised South African units were keener to engage in farm-burning than British regiments, mainly due to ill-feeling about what the Boers had done to their people earlier in the war. Filson Young of the perennially disapproving and staunchly anti-war *Manchester Guardian* reported: "We have been marching through a part of the country where some mischievous person has been collecting and encouraging insurgents. And in the course of about ten miles we have burned no fewer than six farmhouses. Care seems to have been taken that there was proper evidence against the owners, who were absent, and in no case were people actually burned out of their homes … The effect on those of the colonial troops who, in carrying out these orders to destroy, are gratifying their feeling of hatred and revenge, is very bad. Their discipline is far below that of Imperial troops and they soon get out of hand … yesterday some of them were complaining bitterly that a suspected house, against the owner of which there was not sufficient evidence, was not delivered into their hands."[58]

When General de Wet formally complained to Lord Roberts about the burning of certain farmhouses, Roberts replied, explaining the details of each case, including fodder stocks which were "burnt at Perzikfontein to prevent them falling into the hands of the enemy". Others at Paardekraal, Leeuw Kop and Kroonstad were burned "because British troops had been fired on whilst the white flag was flying from the homestead".[59] De Wet wrote to Roberts again shortly thereafter, complaining about farms being burned near Middelburg and Standerton. This was passed to Buller, as the 'outrages' had occurred in his area of responsibility. Buller quickly responded, confirming he had indeed given orders to burn six farms: "Shortly after our arrival at Standerton our telegraph line was cut on several nights following, and attempts were made to damage the military line by placing dynamite cartridges with detonators attached upon it. The attempts were all made on or in close vicinity to the estates above named. A watch was kept and it was found that the attempts were made not by any formed force of the enemy, but by a few scattered banditti who were given shelter during the night in the houses I afterwards had destroyed, and who thence, when they could, tried to murder our patrols, and sallied out at night to damage the line." There can be no doubt that Buller was, with respect to both military logic and to Article XXIII of The Hague Convention, perfectly entitled to destroy these farms.

In another example, two members of the Imperial Yeomanry who had become detached from their unit, stopped at a farm to ask for water. The occupants instead directed the two stragglers into an ambush which left one Yeoman dead and the other wounded. The farm was subsequently burned as punishment for this act.[60] Though many thousands of farms were torched, the fact that both Roberts and Buller replied in detail to de Wet's complaints also suggests that such burnings were far from some random, uncontrolled act. Indeed, so many imperial patrols came under fire from so-called surrendered farms that Roberts was forced to write to de Wet to point this out. In a letter dated the 3rd August 1900, Roberts stated: "Latterly, many of my soldiers have been shot from farmhouses over which the white flag has been flying, the railway and telegraph lines have been cut, and trains wrecked. I have therefore found it necessary, after warning your Honour, to take such steps as are sanctioned by the customs of war to put an end to these and similar acts, and have burned down the farmhouses at or near which such deeds have been perpetrated. This I shall continue to do whenever I consider the occasion demands it. The remedy lies in your Honour's own hands. The destruction of property is most distasteful to me, and I shall be greatly pleased when your Honour's co-operation in the matter renders it no longer necessary."

Farms were also widely used by the bitter-einders as rendezvous points, victualling stations, stores, armament factories and headquarters. Diaries recording the hundreds of nameless skirmishes of the guerrilla war invariably talk of groups of bitter-einders being holed up at this farm or that: many—though by no means all—were therefore perfectly legitimate military targets.

One of the first significant battles of the guerrilla war, Bothaville, was fought at a farm on the 6th November 1900. Christiaan de Wet's men were surprised there by a mounted infantry column under Lieutenant-Colonel Le Gallais and hundreds fled in panic. Those who remained held positions in the main house and cattle kraal, while a pig-pen had been loop-holed and served as a troublesome strongpoint throughout the action. Though Le Gallais was shot at close range personally leading an attack on the farmhouse, the Boers surrendered after four hours of bitter fighting. The haul was impressive: "ninety-nine Boers and four Kaffirs, together with five guns and one Maxim. Two of the guns were twelve-pounders which once belonged to 'Q' Battery and one to 'U' Battery Royal Horse Artillery. 'U' Battery Royal Horse Artillery was the Battery now with us. These three guns were some of those captured by the Boers during the recent disaster to our forces at Sannah's Post. The number of dead Boers, which we collected at this point, was sixteen."[61] In addition, all de Wet's wagons and supplies were captured.

But larger-scale actions like Bothaville were very much the exception. In the main, the guerrilla war was one of small, half-forgotten, nameless actions, of fighting patrols and searching farms thought to be supporting the bitter-einders. For the imperial troops this shadow war was a dangerous business. Albert Hilder, who served with the Royal Canadian Dragoons, remembered that in a fifteen-week period "there was hardly a day without some shooting going on".[62] He also recorded how one of their patrols near a surrendered farm between Dewetsdorp and ThabuNchu suddenly came under fire from the farmstead. This was, despite the white flag flying above it, by no means an unusual event.[63]

We met W. S. Carr of the South African Light Horse in the previous chapter. Some of his other diary entries are enlightening on just what it was like to search farmsteads. Here he describes a typical approach to a farm suspected of harbouring bitter-einders:

> the order was sent back from the leading officer: "No talking or smoking." We then travelled in silence, except for the pad of the horses' hooves. Successive orders were given in whispers.
>
> "B3, dismount. Number threes to remain mounted and lead the troop's horses to stone-post fence at back."
>
> Then there followed an investigation by officer and sergeant through the aloe tangle. We dashed across the clearing at top speed, flattening ourselves against the walls of the buildings on either side of the doors and windows. The nearest trooper to the officer would bang on the door with the butt of his rifle and the OC would call out: "Open in the Queen's name." Sometimes a volley from doors and windows and one or two would bite the dust. Not even a dog's bark They had somehow got wind of our coming and decamped.

The same patrol pushed on and, at about 0500 hours, approached another farm. This time things were very different: "Riding down the narrowing field between the converging hills, six to eight paces apart, our rifles held across right thighs at the 'ready', we were suddenly in the midst of pinging bullets from a heavy fusillade from the hills above the house ... The sergeant and his horse went down. Four men on either side of him spurred forwards to the shelter of a loose-stone cattle kraal, from which we poured forth rapid magazine fire at moving specks on the hill and at figures running between the main building and outhouses."[64]

During one night patrol to check Boer farmsteads, three members of a four-man section of South African Light Horse had dismounted to check the buildings, leaving their horses under the control of the fourth. As his comrades tried to gain entry into the farm house, the mounted horse-holder was suddenly blasted down by a fusillade from within. The farmer "disclosed later that he was sheltering seventeen burgers who, when they heard hooves and men's voices, clustered about window and door, fired into the group of horses and then bolted into the darkness".[65] "'D' Squadron followed up with the hunt during the night and at a mêlée at a farmhouse took fourteen prisoners after losing a Lieutenant killed and a Sergeant shot through the leg. The leader of the men captured was a Veldcornet 'wanted' by the British on two charges of murder ... we were taking a few prisoners daily and had twenty-eight when we marched through the little town of Luckhoff, eight days after leaving Priors."[66]

And even when the menfolk were nowhere to be found, searching farms was still a deadly business: "I thought of the Mounted Infantryman who a week or two back had made a similar inspection by himself and who had carried a ladder in that he might have access to a trap door in the cloth ceiling. He leaned his loaded rifle against the ladder while he climbed and the *huisvrou* picked it up and shot him from below. His comrade, left on watch outside, entered and took the rifle from the woman, turned over the body for a brief examination and then rode off to rejoin his squadron, leading the spare horse. The woman had decamped when an ambulance corporal came to the farm to bury the corpse."[67]

Another who served during the guerrilla war was Captain St Leger of the MI. He recorded similar thoughts:

To those of us who had the painful duty of searching Boer farms, numbers of which were found to be nothing but arsenals and granaries, many pathetic scenes presented themselves. The farms were invariably left in charge of the women and children, and one can imagine how they must have hated the sight of us … it fell to [a brother officer and his men] to search a large farm which belonged to the field cornet of the district. I don't remember the reason why, but, at any rate, in accordance with one of the various Proclamations issued on the subject of the liability of farms to this penalty, this particular farm was ordered to be burnt. All the furniture that could be taken was removed from the condemned building by the troops, and then, when the dense black columns of smoke arose, and the hungry flames crackled and leapt from basement to roof of her home, what do you think this field cornet's wife did? She did not give way to hysteria—she was far too brave a woman for that—but sat down and made coffee for this officer and his man at the same time saying: "I know you are only doing your duty as my husband is doing his"[68] … the women living on these farms were always treated with the utmost consideration. As much of their furniture and personal belongings as possible was invariably taken out of the condemned portion of the farm and stored in the building left for them to live in.[69]

Captain St Leger's claims of treating the Boer womenfolk as well as possible will no doubt be scoffed at but it would appear that this was often indeed the case. In February 1902 a meeting was held in Bloemfontein, presided over by Dr Kellner, one of those who had formally surrendered the capital to Lord Roberts in 1900. A member of the late government of the Orange Free State proposed the following resolution, which was passed unanimously: "We, the citizens of Bloemfontein, having had our attention drawn to certain statements made in England and on the Continent of Europe, accusing the British army of barbarous and wanton cruelty to defenceless women and children, take this opportunity of publically denouncing such statements as wholly untrue, so far as our experience and knowledge of the conduct of the British troops in this part of the country are concerned. We would further like to record our appreciation of the humanity and good conduct of all the troops passing through or stationed here, and our conviction that if there had been any truth in the slanders referred to, we should have been fully acquainted with the facts."[70]

Another eyewitness, our friend Frederic Unger, the American war correspondent, had similar recollections: "During this futile pursuit of De Wet, the raider, I had spent sufficient time on the extreme advance line to be an eyewitness to the great consideration shown to the families of the warring burghers whenever the troops came up to a farmhouse. Everything the advance line took for their use, from eggs to chickens and forage, was paid for on the spot."[71] Not all imperial troops were as as well behaved, of course, and though his memoires are full of tales of eating geese and pigs taken from abandoned farms, Corporal Hilder makes it clear that those who indulged in it could expect to face serious consequences: "This, [the colonel] said, was against the army orders and he wanted to make it clear that, if any of his men were caught looting, he would have to make an example of them."[72] The Guards Brigade padre agreed with this: "at the head of the Brigade there marched a strong body of Military Police whose one business it was to see that these famished men [the British Tommies] looted nothing. When a deserted house was reached no pretence at protecting it was made. Such a house of course never contained food, and our men sought in it only what would serve as firewood … but if a man, woman or child were in the house, a cordon of police was instantly put round the building. The longing eyes and tingling fingers passed on, and absolutely nothing was touched except on payment."[73]

Despite these efforts, there was obviously still a fair degree of looting by imperial troops. When an elderly Boer woman complained to another British army padre that imperial scouts had broken a panel in her door and stolen some fowls, she was directed to take her complaint directly to General Ian Hamilton. She was given the enormously inappropriate sum of £20 compensation which would be levied from the scouts responsible.[74] Occasionally, a degree of looting was permitted as a punishment for a violation of surrender terms, which though unpleasant, is perhaps not unreasonable. Even this did not come naturally to British troops though, with one diary entry stating: "Some of Plumer's men were fired on from the farms. In consequence the farms are being burnt down and we have been told to do as much looting and damage as we like. I am afraid my men up to now have been held with too tight a hand to be much good at looting."[75]

We shall give the last word on the subject to our friend the padre: "Later in the day, to my sincere grief, a beautiful Boer house was set on fire by our men, after careful enquiry into the facts by the provost-marshal, because the farmer occupying it had run up the white flag over his house, and then from under that flag our scouts had been shot at. Such acts of treachery became lamentably common, and had at all cost to be restricted by the only arguments a Voortrekker seemed able to understand; but the Boers in Natal had long before this proved adept at kindling similar bonfires, though without any such provocation, and cannot therefore pose as martyrs over the burning of their own farms, however deplorable that burning be."[76]

The padre would be interested to learn that the Boers and their supporters have indeed posed as martyrs on this account for the past 110 years. What else were the British expected to do? If their men came under fire from the white flag of a surrendered farmer, what sympathy did he really deserve?

Though they get all the limelight, the British scorched-earth tactics were not the only methods of barbarism employed in the guerrilla war. Though never deemed worthy of attention, bitter-einder gangs were indulging in their own version of the tactic, regularly targeting farms belonging to loyalists, surrendered Boers and non-whites. After the butchery of the Leliefontein massacre (more later), for example, the bitter-einders gutted all the dwellings, smashed up furniture and burned any books they could find: "The fields were razed, grain pits sacked, stock butchered or run off and agricultural tools expropriated ... Bywoners and other nomadic poor whites trudged across the reserve to capture horses, mules and wagons and supplies of wheat, grain and barley."[77]

Bands of bitter-einders raided all over the Cape, targeting loyalists and burning down their property. One such victim was a Mr Herrholdt who, along with his wife, was turned out of his house at gunpoint. The bandits then stole whatever they fancied and burned the house to the ground.[78] As they pillaged their merry way across the colony, one local observer wrote: "the bandit forces of Boers and Colonial rebels are scouring the country in every direction, robbing, looting and house burning—brutally assaulting defenceless Colonists, and plying the sjambok wherever their demands are not immediately complied with ... in the face of such cruel outrages it is little wonder that the inhabitants of the numerous dorps and villages scattered over the present area of operations are bitterly complaining of the incapacity of the military to safeguard their interests."[79]

Another incident saw Commandant Fouché and the Rouxville Commando attacking the African settlements at Molteno. The unfortunate residents were flogged, huts were burned down and crops destroyed.[80] In other districts "where guerrillas were unable to consolidate control or scare the populace into docility, commandants tended simply to rampage onwards, spreading havoc. In some areas, the fabric of peasant communities was shredded as Boers razed crops, plundered stock and sacked homesteads. Not only were poultry and agricultural produce snatched as food and pigs and goats slaughtered on the spot to provide meat, but entire flocks and herds were liable to be scattered, driven off or wantonly butchered".[81]

Elsewhere, entire settlements were robbed of their able-bodied men and boys as bitter-einders swooped and drove them off as slave labour. When Boer gangs approached Wupperthal, Genadendal, Elim, Tulbagh and Riversdale the village menfolk fled into the hills until the coast was clear. In other villages, resisting the conscription gangs led to headmen being whipped by the bitter-einders. Others were shot, dwellings burned down and women and children taken hostage to force communities to offer up slave labour.[82]

Republican bitter-einders not only indulged in farm-burning, murder, massacre and slavery on a horrific scale, but also broke many other accepted rules of war. As we have seen, the misuse of the white flag by the federals was so widespread that it essentially lost its meaning. So many Tommies had been shot from under cover of the white flag that Buller was repeatedly forced to warn his men that they were facing "a clever unscrupulous enemy; let no man allow himself to be deceived by them. If a white flag is displayed it means nothing, unless the force who display it halt, throw down their arms, and throw up their hands ... we are fighting in defence of the flag against an enemy who has forced war on us from the worst and lowest motives, by treachery, conspiracy and deceit. Let us bear ourselves as the cause deserves".[83]

And this was not born of desperation: Buller first started warning of the Boers' flagrant contempt for the white flag very early in the war, stating that "from personal experience it was already stained with the blood of two gallant British officers, besides many men, in this campaign".[84] The Red Cross flag was also frequently ignored by federal troops, long before their cause was lost. During the siege of Ladysmith, the Boer gunners "began to turn their attention to those buildings which were flying the Red Cross flag, and which were being used as hospitals for the wounded. The Town Hall and Sanatorium were both struck three or four times. One shell entered the Town Hall and killed a wounded man who was lying in bed, and wounded eight others. The churches also, which were used as hospitals, were struck, so that Sir George White ordered that all the Red Cross flags were to be taken down, as they were disregarded by the Boers and only tended to attract their shell fire. In reply to Sir George White's remonstrance, General Joubert stated that he would respect no Red Cross flag in the town".[85]

At Mafeking civilians also suffered terribly from Boer shelling in defiance of the Red Cross flag: "for two days in succession, has he made the hospital and the women's laager the sole object of his attentions ... Your correspondent very much regrets to have to state that though the shelling of the women's laager many children's lives have been sacrificed, many women mutilated ... The children of some of the most respected and most loyal townspeople have been killed in this manner ... For two hours this morning, the quick-firing guns of the enemy fired into the laager, creating scenes of panic and consternation which it is not fitting to describe ... impossible for us to regard our foe as other than one which is inspired with the emotions of a degraded people and the crude cruelty and vindictive animosity of savages."[86]

This casual disregard dated back to the previous Boer War. Across the theatre and throughout the conflict extra precautions had to be taken by imperial troops with regard to the white flag: "It began to be believed at last that the Boer would take an unfair advantage of the Briton whenever he should get a chance. Strangely enough, our officers seemed to have forgotten or disregarded the object-lesson of the tragic affair of Bronker's Spruit [sic]. Yet Boer 'slimness' was then well enough established. The unfortunate Colonel Anstruther caused to be printed in the Transvaal Government Gazette a bi-lingual proclamation, informing the Boers that, in consequence of the many treacherous uses to which the white flag had been put, he would in future recognise the emblem only under the following conditions: two Boers accompanied by an officer, and all unarmed, must approach the lines bearing the white flag aloft. The British soldiers were also advised to keep well under cover whenever the flag was displayed. This showed that reliance on Boer honour would in no case be attempted. At the present date Boer morality had not improved, and it was even declared that the Free-Staters had made their women boil down their national flag, so that in its pallid state it might at a little distance be mistaken for the white flag, and come in handy in case of need."[87]

The widespread wearing of captured uniforms was also completely contrary to the accepted rules of war and, though they rarely exercised their right, the British would have been completely justified in executing anyone caught so doing. There is a very fine line between a clever *ruse de guerre* and a war crime: if such a deception works it will be remembered as a great success, but by engaging in such trickery, you are essentially forfeiting your rights as a soldier.

And it was not just the use of captured British khaki that was highly dubious. The fact that vast majority of Boers commenced the war without any sort of uniform at all led Leo Amery to note:

> It is to be regretted that the British Government did not at the outset declare that it would refuse to treat the ununiformed commandos of the Boers as belligerents on British soil. The right of a population to take up arms to repel invasion of its own territory is one that the British representatives strongly urged at The Hague Convention. But the invasion and occupation of another country by bands of armed men in ordinary clothes, indistinguishable from the civilian population of the country, for whom they would frequently pass themselves off for purposes of espionage, was a very different matter. A declaration that all armed men made prisoners on British territory, and not wearing some permanent and easily recognisable uniform or badge marking them as belonging to the Republican forces, would be treated as bandits and be liable to be shot without ceremony, would have had an excellent effect and might have delayed or possibly even have prevented an invasion, while it would have been in perfect harmony with The Hague Convention on the Laws and Customs of War (articles 1 and 2).* That no steps at all were taken, and that in consequence British generals had to fight at a most serious disadvantage, is simply another instance of the casual and haphazard fashion in which the war was taken in hand by those in supreme

---

* The Hague Convention clearly stated that the rules of law only protected those who, among other things, "displayed a fixed distinctive emblem recognizable at a distance". The vast majority of federal invaders wore no such uniform or armband.

authority. The British government was not, strictly speaking, bound to observe the rules of the Hague Convention toward the Boers. But if it had announced its intention of both observing and enforcing those rules strictly, it would not only have gained European sympathy but would have derived substantial advantages, and might even have averted or kept within limits the long guerrilla campaign, with all its regrettable concomitants, which followed the break-up of the Boer armies. In war severity, if based on clearly defined rules, is often far more humane in the end than mere easy-going contempt of one's enemy masquerading as clemency.[88]

Amery's suggestion that all federal prisoners captured while not wearing uniform should have been shot will strike most as outrageously extreme, but the imperial high command would certainly have been well within their rights to have done this. Indeed, compared to the reaction of other nations when faced with an un-uniformed enemy, the British were amazingly lenient. In the Franco-Prussian War of 1870/1, for example, Prussian troops simply executed French guerrillas, or *franc-tireurs*, out of hand.[89]

The German army did likewise in the First World War, torching entire French or Belgian villages in retribution for the actions of a handful of *franc-tireurs*.[90]

The American-Philippine War saw 117 documented atrocities against insurgents,[91] while in the latter stages of the American Civil War, irregular Confederate forces, or 'bushwhackers', could expect no mercy and were routinely shot or hanged.[92]

During Napoleon's occupation of Spain any man reported to be absent from his home was assumed to be a guerrilla and was summarily executed if later captured. In October 1810 one French general decreed that four guerrillas would be hanged for every French soldier killed; if insufficient guerrilla prisoners were available, civilians were simply hanged in their place.[93]

During the French Revolution a law was passed by the new republican government which stipulated the death penalty for all rebels: "the war was carried to the population as a whole through the operations of General Turreau's twelve so-called *colonnes infernales* [infernal columns] killing, deporting, burning and confiscating as they marched. Those who took advantage of a proffered government amnesty in early 1794 were simply executed, and the troops ordered to kill anyone found in areas already cleared. Atrocities against women were all too common, mothers and their 'wolf cubs' alike slaughtered, and priests drowned. Indeed, such was the lack of control that republican supporters were frequently killed as well. All livestock and other supplies were removed by the *commission civile et administrative* [civil and administrative commission], ironically often depriving their own troops of sustenance. The campaign of suppression has been characterised as 'ideological genocide', costing perhaps 250,000 lives."[94]

In contrast, the British were actually very indulgent indeed. Despite this relative leniency in respect of repeated, widespread and flagrant republican breaches of the established rules of war, many still insist on excusing the war crimes committed by the bitter-einders. Possibly the worst of such books is a self-pitying publication called *Innocent Blood* by Graham Jooste.

Blasphemously claiming to be a "commemoration of innocent blood split for God, family and fatherland", the book is in reality 230 pages of poorly researched, anti-British propaganda, of which even Dr Goebbels would be proud. Peppering his work with such references as another page in his own book and a comment he once heard a DJ make on the radio, Mr Jooste essentially claims that the "at least sixty" Boers* executed in the war were all completely innocent and that therefore the British were evil murderers. Jooste endeavours to substantiate this somewhat illogical position by sagely informing us that some of those executed liked reading the Bible—pretty much like everyone else at the time—and can thus only have been wonderful, pious people; this despite their being executed for such things as "shooting a wounded prisoner" and "firing under a white flag" and leaving aside the fact that sixty-odd executions during the course of a bitter three-year war in which thousands of men broke oaths of allegiance and committed mass murder and acts of terrorism, is a remarkably small number. Indeed, it would be even smaller but Mr Jooste, desperate to inflate his paltry numbers, shamelessly includes the execution of a British army deserter. As a postscript, Jooste grudgingly admits that a further 335 Boers condemned to death were reprieved.

Let us randomly select one of Mr Jooste's miscarriages of justice. His feathers puffed up with self-righteous indignation, he tells us of the case of

---

* i.e. far less than the number of black civilians murdered by bitter-einders in one afternoon at Modderfontein

Mr Piet Schuil, a man who was seemingly so unbelievably stupid as to tie a white rag to the end of his rifle in an alleged attempt to surrender during the middle of a skirmish. One would have thought that if Mr Schuil had indeed really been intent on surrender it might have been more prudent to throw down his rifle; if he was, for some bizarre reason, resolutely determined to use a flagpole, perhaps even Mr Jooste will agree that a stick might have been a more sensible choice than a Mauser. The two British soldiers who moved forward to accept his surrender swore under oath that Schuil then, either foolishly or treacherously, changed his mind and took a pot shot at them. Schuil was thus, not unreasonably, tried for abusing the white flag, found guilty and shot.[95]

Jooste does not point out any inconsistencies between the testimonies of the two British witnesses. Indeed, the sole basis of his argument is that they can only possibly have been lying, because Mr Schuil had been a teacher who enjoyed poetry and "was more interested in literature than warfare". Mr Jooste does not trouble himself to explain why British soldiers would lie in the case of Mr Schuil, but not in the case of the other republicans captured that day, or indeed the tens of thousands of other Boers who were taken prisoner during the conflict. He also fails to explain why, if these two Tommies had been so determined to murder Schuil, they did not simply shoot him on the spot—after all, the incident took place in the middle of a skirmish—rather than taking him prisoner.

Instead, they reported his behaviour and an, albeit fairly brief, trial found him guilty, which on the basis of what Mr Jooste tells us seems a fair verdict. A man being executed is never a trivial event, but it is not entirely clear why Mr Jooste gets his knickers in such a twist over Schuil.

Another classic from Mr Jooste are those few Boers who were executed for wearing captured British uniforms, executions which were completely acceptable by the standards of the day. Jooste, however, tells us that those few poor, innocent souls who were shot for this crime "had not had time" to cut off the insignia, buttons and regimental flashes, leading the British, quite reasonably one would think, to conclude the uniforms were being used for deception rather than warmth. Quite how long Mr Jooste considers it takes to cut off a button is anyone's guess.[96] Apologists for the Boer penchant of wearing captured uniforms tend to claim that the Boers had no choice as they were short of supplies and were very cold. There is certainly a degree of truth in this later on in the war, which is precisely why executions for wearing khaki were so few and far between. But such claims also ignore the inconvenient fact that these dubious activities started long before the guerrilla war began. As early as the battle of Wagon Hill, for example, a Boer was caught trying to sneak through the British lines wearing a captured khaki uniform. In another instance from that period: "In the distance from the British outposts a Highlander was observed in the act of driving cattle. As the proceeding was contrary to orders, the manoeuvres of this man were carefully observed and he was discovered to be a Boer masquerading in Highland uniform. He was at once fired upon and he fell."[97] This was long before even the most rabid of Boer apologists could claim he was wearing the uniform because his own clothes were rags; apart from which, a kilt and sporran is far from being the most practical outfit.

In a rather far-fetched effort to juxtapose the very occasional execution of Cape rebels and war criminals to an example of the Boers' magnanimous treatment of a prisoner, Mr Jooste goes on to tell us the tale of Koos de la Rey's chivalrous treatment of Lord Methuen after the latter was badly wounded and captured at the battle of Tweebosch. Jooste neglects to mention that only de la Rey's intervention prevented Methuen being shot in cold blood by other Boers, but nevertheless de la Rey's actions were undoubtedly magnificently noble and were acknowledged as such by the British army and the press. Indeed, such was the widespread acclaim that de la Rey's actions can hardly be portrayed as typical.* Incidentally, it should also be remembered that Methuen had earlier spared de la Rey's farm from destruction.[98]

Tellingly, Jooste prefers to use the fairly remarkable example of how Methuen was treated rather than perhaps citing what happened to any blacks or coloureds who fell into the hands of the bitter-einders. Another example Mr Jooste might have picked was that of Private Roberts of the Worcestershire Regiment who was left on the field of battle after receiving no less than seven bullet wounds, one each in the head, shoulder and a leg, and four in the stomach. When a party of Boers found it too much trouble to take him prisoner, they broke four of his ribs in their enthusiastic looting of his personal belongings. Unable to fight back, Roberts was partially stripped and, while stealing his ring, his attackers broke his finger before leaving him on the veldt.[99]

---

* after the war the two would become friends

Jooste could equally have used the treatment of the wounded Captain Hunt of the Bushveldt Carbineers as an example of how the bitter-einders sometimes treated their prisoners. His men having been ambushed and forced to retire, Hunt was left wounded and moaning on the field, his men confirming he had taken a bullet in the chest. His body, stripped completely naked, was later found lying in a gutter by a local missionary, a Mr Reuter. Hunt's men were shocked to see that body was battered, his face repeatedly stamped on by hobnailed boots,* his legs slashed and mutilated with knives and his neck broken.[100]

There is a postscript to the discovery of Captain Hunt's mutilated corpse. In a unChristian act which rather flies in the face of Jooste's fantasies, the Bible-bashing bitter-einders threatened to burn down Mr Reuter's mission station—with him inside—as punishment for recovering Captain Hunt's body and for fraternizing with the Tommies. British guards thus had to be posted to protect the poor preacher from the attentions of these republican diehards.[101]

Another recurring war crime was the widespread Boer use of 'dum-dum' rounds. Often called exploding rounds by the Tommies, these were, more correctly, expanding bullets, but whatever their name, they caused horrific injury and were outlawed by the Hague Convention. Signed by twenty-five nations, including most of the major powers, on the 29th July 1899, one of the declarations of the convention was specifically "On the Use of Bullets Which Expand or Flatten Easily in the Human Body". The British had previously used such bullets—the Mark IV round to be precise—at the battle of Omdurman in 1898, but had quickly reverted to the standard Mark II full metal jacket round in the face of German protests. Though the British army had ceased using expanding rounds by the time of the Boer War, there are endless reports of such ammunition being used by federal forces, and—once again—it was a practice that commenced long before anyone could claim they had been forced so to do. After Ladysmith was relieved, for example, imperial troops searched the abandoned Boer positions surrounding the town: "Ammunition of all kinds was lying about in large quantities, much of it being of the sorts condemned for usage in civilised warfare. Whole cases of Mauser cartridges were found with verdigrissed bullets, others with soft-

---

* some prefer to claim that Hunt was actually mutilated by Africans, presumably ones wearing hobnailed boots

nosed or expanding bullets. Many of the verdigrissed bullets appeared to have been used; for, lying about the tents were bandoliers full of them; and this accounted for the frequent cases of blood-poisoning which occurred among the wounded British soldiers."[102]

Despite such reports being largely dismissed as British propaganda, there were so many that it is nonsensical to simply ignore them; the outrage felt by British Tommies discovering such arms caches was genuine enough.[103] This is not to say that the imperial troops were blameless, or that only the Boers were the ones breaking all the rules, but merely to try to balance the current perception which is completely tilted in favour of the bitter-einders.

❧

Though today it is pleasing for some to paint the Tommies as a universally hated enemy, this was not the case at the time. Shortly after the war a message was sent to Mr Chamberlain by the loyal burghers of the Orange River Colony—not latter-day left-wing academics but rather people who had lived in the midst of the very worst of the scorched-earth campaign. Signed by P. de Wet (ex-General), F. Schimpers, S. Jacobs, C. Cloete (ex-member of the volksraad), S. Benkes (ex-member of the volksraad), W. Richter, Van Wyk (ex-member of the volksraad), J. Els, J. Heilbron (ex-Commandant), J. Cloete, F. Cloete, Dr Leech and the Reverend du Plessis, the message read:

> We loyal Dutch residents and ex-burghers of the Orange River Colony who surrendered under Lord Roberts' proclamation when we realized that the Constitutional Government of the Orange Free State had ceased to exist and that further warfare could not affect the result, but would certainly add further to the bloodshed and the ruin of the country, and who have kept our oaths, beg to thank you for according us an interview to enable is to place before you points in which those whom we represent are specially interested.
>
> We are aware that you are kindly receiving many deputations from the old residents of the country, but we feel that the special interests of our friends may perhaps not be fully represented by the delegates who have not been specially elected by our section of the people. We therefore respectfully claim the right to speak for ourselves and for

those whom we represent, as we are satisfied with the Government, its actions, and its policy and do not wish to ask for changes.

We recognise that to-day all the residents of the Orange River Colony are passively loyal to the Crown, but our past record does, we trust, entitle us to claim that we represent a section whose loyalty has been voluntarily assumed, and we cannot too strongly condemn any action which may keep alive or may again stir up the embers of dissention between Boer and Britisher … We are grateful for what has been done by the Government in its recognition of the loyal Dutch people whom we represent, and we beg that the Government will always recognise our desire to co-operate with it policy to further the prosperity of this colony, and to lay the foundations of a United South Africa under a British Flag.[104]

And it was not just the loyal Dutch of the Orange River Colony pledging their allegiance to the British cause and eager to move on: throughout the long and bitter guerrilla war, sick and wounded imperial troops benefited from subscriptions of money and gifts made by various native chiefs, committees and other groups in South Africa.[105] The details of these donations make fascinating reading: Chief Ndgungazwe, for example, handed over £8.9s.10½d. "for the sick and wounded". More tellingly, the "Loyal Dutch round Tugela district" raised £41.7s.6d. for the British wounded, and the Berlin Mission in New Germany donated another £8.[106] Other donations ran well into the hundreds of pounds—big money at the time.

By indulging in massacres, terrorism, constant abuse of the white flag, the widespread use of dum-dum ammunition and a near-systematic onslaught against black and coloured farmers, it is difficult to share the commonly held view of the bitter-einders being the goodies in the guerrilla war. The Boer attitude might be summed up as 'all's fair in love and war, as long as we're the ones doing it'. In stark contrast, modern writers are quick to lambast imperial troops and tactics, expecting the Tommies to have behaved in a completely unrealistic fashion, allowing surrendered burghers to fire at them from farmhouses displaying white flags, with no consequence.

Few would argue that Kitchener's scorched-earth campaign was something to be proud of, but it was a necessary evil of war and one forced upon the imperial forces by republican tactics. A viable alternative is yet to be suggested;

indeed, if anything, a common theme in diaries and letters is the feeling that the British were too lenient in their dealings with the diehards. One undeniable consequence of the farm-burnings was to produce thousands of refugees, many of whom would be housed in what infamously became known as the 'concentration camps'.

And it is to these that we must now turn our attention.

CHAPTER TEN

The concentration camps

"'The number'—that is, the Vrouemonuent and its number—has continued over the time since then to accrue public meaning around repetitions and reinterpretations, the most powerful of which involved the strategy under apartheid to legitimize Afrikaner nationalism and racism by reference both to the past history of the concentration camp deaths, and also increasingly by reference to viewing 'the number' as inscribed on the Vrouemonument as 'a story of the facts' in and of itself. This has been supported by the huge comparison that has been made through repetitions of the words 'concentration camps', which by their post-Nazi meaning and power seem to have explanatory power in association with 'the number' of an 'it was genocide' kind by claiming tacit kindred between these deaths and the six million in the Nazi camps."
—Liz Stanley and Helen Dampier in
The Number of the South African War (1899–1902) Concentration Camp Dead: Standard Stories, Superior Stories and a Forgotten Proto-Nationalist Research Investigation

"The first of them had been opened at Krugersdorp as a shelter for refugees, whose numbers grew after Kitchener had failed to persuade Botha to leave surrendered burghers unmolested on their farms."[1]
—Eric Walker in *A History of Southern Africa*

"Their sufferings are among what we may call the necessary circumstances of the war."[2]
—Christiaan de Wet, dismissing any concern for the Boer women and children and arguing in favour of continuing the guerrilla war

"one is only too thankful nowadays to know that our wives are under English protection."[3]
—Louis Botha, describing his gratitude for the British camps

"Concentration camps in the Boer War must not be confused with the German camps of the Second World War. The British camps were set up for an entirely different reason and were meant to house the refugees in comfort and safety."
—Emanoel Lee in *To the Bitter End*

"[The Boers] should have thought of its horrible significance
when they invaded the Queen's dominions."[4]
—British prime minister, the Marquess of Salisbury, responding to criticism of the camps

"I have served President Kruger a long time and got nothing,
and now the new King, as soon as he is our King,
thinks of the old people and gives us a dinner, he is the King for me."[5]
—an elderly resident expresses his feelings after a party held
at Irene camp to celebrate the coronation of King Edward VII

Ask most people about the Boer War and you can be pretty sure that the concentration camps will come up early in the conversation. You will often then judiciously be informed that it was "not the Nazis who invented the concentration camp—oh no—it was the British". Like most leftist mantras, however, this is both factually incorrect and a disingenuous misuse of terms. Firstly, there is absolutely no resemblance between Hitler's death camps and the concentration camps the British set up in the Boer War. The inmates of the British camps were not murdered, and though people certainly died of natural causes therein, to this day people die of natural causes in hospitals, prisons and old-age homes too. Secondly, and though widely trotted out,[6] the idea that the British were the first to employ concentration camps—as distinct from the very different death camps—is historically incorrect in any case.

As we have seen, such camps were widely employed by the American military in the American-Philippine War which ran concurrently with the Boer War. Many of the American camps were massively overcrowded, with one report declaring 8,000 Filipinos were held in a camp just two miles long by a mile wide. One church in the camp housed 127 females, while 270 men shared a house.[7] Civilian death tolls in that conflict dwarf those of the Boer War and are estimated at anywhere between 200,000 and over a million: it was reckoned that 100,000 civilians perished in Batangas province alone.[8] Indeed, the very term 'concentration camp' derives from the Spanish *reconcentration camps*[9] as such establishments were named during the Spanish-Cuban War fought a couple of years earlier. Introduced by the governor of Cuba, General Valeriano Weyler[10] in 1897, the Spanish camps were also infinitely deadlier than those established by the British in South Africa, and it is estimated that hundreds of thousands of Cubans perished in them. Though their introduction earned him the nickname 'Butcher', even General Weyler was by no means the inventor of such camps. It is said that Weyler was given the idea by General Sherman while assigned to the post of military attaché in the Spanish embassy in Washington. Sherman, the American Civil War general, had widely employed such camps during that conflict.[11] Indeed, America has a long history of such things, with concentration camps—known as 'emigration depots'—established during the Plains Wars, where large numbers of Native Americans were interned and died. The French established concentration camps in Algeria in the 1830s and would do so again in the 1950s. It has been estimated that from 1830 to 1900, between fifteen and twenty-five per cent of the Algerian population died in such camps. But even these were not the first: an attempt at establishing concentration camps had been tried by the Paraguayan military as early as 1813.

None of this of course makes the British use of concentration camps any pleasanter, but it is important to put their introduction into context, and to torpedo the myth that they were a dastardly British invention. Despite all the attention given to the camps in South Africa, there is one which never gets a mention, no one talks about and few have ever heard of: the internment camp at Nooitgedacht. That it is utterly overlooked by modern historians is undoubtedly because it was set up by the Boers to house imperial prisoners of war; the mistreatment they endured does not fit with the fashionable view of the conflict. While always eager to hammer endlessly on about the turpitude of the British concentration camp system, no hand-wringing liberal or apologist for Kruger's regime ever seems interested in exposing the way the republicans treated their PoWs. Pakenham does not mention their plight at all, their suffering is not considered worthy of mention in Nasson's *The War for South Africa* or in Barthorp's *Slogging Over Africa*. Quite why these fellows choose not to touch upon the subject is open to conjecture. Sir Arthur Conan-Doyle did, however, feel the way his kith and kin were treated worthy of mention: "nothing can excuse the harshness which the Boers showed to the Colonials who fell into their power, or the callous neglect of the sick prisoners."[12] The reason for Conan-Doyle's disgust is obvious: Nooitgedacht was essentially nothing more than a large barbed-wire pen, out on the open veldt north-east of Pretoria.[13] There was absolutely no protection from the elements and the imperial PoWs suffered terribly in the cold.[14] Each man could expect just a pound of meat a week (compared to between three and four pounds of meat per week issued to adults living in the British concentration camps),[15] but in reality lived mainly on mealies.[16] Shocked at the conditions in which the PoWs were being kept, patriotic subjects of the Empire rallied to provide supplies through the Absent Minded Beggars' Fund. However, it would seem that these supplies were simply seized in their entirety by the grateful Boers.[17] When the condition of the PoWs became known to Lord Roberts he contacted Kruger, requesting they be released on condition that they be sent to England and pledge to take no further part in the war.[18] Despite this meaning that the Boers would be relieved of the burden of feeding and guarding them, as well as instantly removing the possibility of their rejoining their regiments upon liberation, Kruger did not take up the offer.

On the 30th August 1900, with Buller's troops occupying the hills above Nooitgedacht and poised to break through and liberate the prison camp, General Viljoen decided to release the PoWs. Conveniently deciding that this was a good time to claim he was ashamed of the treatment they had received at the hands of his government[19] and with more than a hint of self-preservation now that the winds of war were blowing against the Boers, Viljoen remarked to the PoWs: "You know why you have been released. I hope the British and the Boers will be friends."[20] Quite how this statement was received by the ravaged, emaciated survivors is not recorded. Viljoen's shame did not prevent him from jubilantly seizing the ambulance mules which had been sent forward to convey medical supplies to the PoWs and using the beasts to move his heavy guns.[21] Buller's men were stunned by the appearance of the fifty-five officers and 2,788 men who staggered their way to the imperial positions. The prisoners were in a shocking condition, half-starved[22] and dressed in tatters. Almost three-quarters of the PoWs were in such poor condition that they were declared unfit for duty[23] and had to be invalided home. It is worth remembering that these were soldiers of a volunteer army and, by definition, fit, hardy, young men. Had Buller's advance been delayed by another week or two, there is little doubt that hundreds more would have perished at Nooitgedacht.* Of course, the appalling treatment of imperial prisoners in no way justifies any mistreatment of Boer civilians, but is—yet again—included to give a sense of perspective and context: it's a bit rum of the republicans to play the victim when their own record shabbily speaks for itself. Not only

---

* Given that HRH the Duke of Edinburgh was badgered into issuing an apology for the concentration camps, perhaps the British people might expect a similar apology from Jacob Zuma over the treatment of British PoWs?

did the federals treat the imperial prisoners of Nooitgedacht terribly, but they also bear a huge and oft-overlooked part in the establishment of the British concentration camps.

Despite the determination of many to paint Kitchener as an evil bogey-man, he cannot reasonably be held responsible for the establishment of the camps. Though the first camps were set up while his predecessor, Lord Roberts, was still in command, they were not the brainchild of Roberts either. Indeed, more than anyone, it was the diehard Boer high command which was responsible for their coming into being. Poverty among the white population was an enormous pre-war problem in the Transvaal[24] and, as Roberts advanced into the Boer republics in 1900, he inherited a massive refugee problem at the outset. Thousands of destitute republican non-combatants were fleeing the fighting; 1,200 such refugees arrived at Klerksdorp alone, for example, but the republican leadership showed neither the inclination nor the means to care for these unfortunates. Botha urged would-be refugees to remain where they were, announcing, "the time has come that they had to sacrifice families, cattle and everything, in order to retain their independence." President Steyn coldly agreed: "We must not think of our wives and children anymore ... it is but a short time that our women and children will suffer."[25]

As the British pushed into the Transvaal, far from capturing and imprisoning these wretched refugees, Roberts arranged transport for over 2,000 such women and children to be sent to their menfolk in republican-held Barberton. When this town was captured a few months later, however, the Boers simply again abandoned these refugees, and the British were once more left with around 2,500 poverty-stricken women and children to care for.[26] As Elizabeth van Heyningen states in her groundbreaking study of the camps: "Boer leaders had in fact already taken their first difficult decision in the policies that would lead to the camps: to leave their families to fend for themselves." As the conflict descended into guerrilla war, surrendered Boers and loyal Afrikaners, or those who simply wanted to be left in peace, increasingly came to the British for protection. Even Emily Hobhouse conceded that "men, with several women and children, had come into the camp, bringing with them their cattle, waggons and carts ... in various localities a few men appeared and sought protection for themselves and their goods. It became an instant duty to provide for them, and on 22nd September General Maxwell issued the order which established the system of Refugee Camps".[27]

General Maxwell's order read: "Camps for Burghers who voluntarily surrender are being formed in Pretoria and Bloemfontein." Once again, even the disapproving Hobhouse conceded that "they really were Refugee Camps"[28] and grudgingly attributes a good chunk of the blame to the intransigent Boer bitter-einders: "From the date of the Middelburg Conference the Boers washed their hands, as it were, more completely of the families of surrendered burghers, and, regarding them as English subjects, sent them into the English lines."[29] This is the point so often overlooked. As the guerrilla war spluttered on, and as we have already seen, the imperials were by no means the only ones burning farms. Loyalists and surrendered burghers lived in perennial fear of a commando turning up and razing their property to the ground. While the British targeting of farms used to support the Boers still in the field at least had some military justification and rationale, the bitter-einder attacks on loyalist farms were nothing less than calculated acts of terror.

Shortly after the capture of Bloemfontein, Roberts issued a proclamation which allowed those burghers who laid down their arms and took the oath of neutrality to return to their farms and carry on their ordinary peaceful occupations. It was not surprising that many thousands, believing the war already lost, availed themselves of the terms. But when the bitter-einders continued with war, these burghers now found themselves in an extremely awkward position: to break their oaths to the British or face the murderous wrath of their erstwhile brothers-in-arms.[30] Botha quickly issued a counter-proclamation, ordering his commandos to terrorize any waverers into rejoining the struggle or face being burned out of their homes.[31] In contrast, and as we have witnessed, during the tentative peace talks with Botha at the Middelburg conference after a few months of guerrilla war, the much-maligned Kitchener endeavoured to have all farms declared off-limits. As we saw in chapter nine, and due entirely to the bitter-einders' savage reprisals against loyalists, and their habit of forcibly press-ganging surrendered Boers back into service, Kitchener warned Botha that he would soon have to take drastic action to protect these unfortunates. As we know, Botha refused to agree to spare the farms and families of neutral or surrendered burghers, despite Kitchener offering to declare the farms of burghers who were on commando off limits.[32]

Kitchener confirmed what had been discussed at Middelburg in a letter to Botha dated the 16th April 1901: "As I informed your Honour at Middelburg, owing to the irregular manner in which you have conducted, and are conducting, hostilities by forcing unwilling and peaceful inhabitants to join your commandos ... I have now no other course open to me except to take the unpleasant and repugnant step of bringing in the women and children."[33]

Botha's role in creating the concentration camps is completely overlooked: had he agreed to Kitchener's proposal to declare all farms off-limits during the guerrilla war, there would have been no scorched-earth policy and consequently the camps would have needed to cope with far fewer refugees. Indeed, had Botha agreed to leave surrendered Boers in peace on their farms, the major cause of the refugee crisis would have disappeared at a stroke, as the camps were initially established to protect and care for those who voluntarily entered them to escape the raiding and killing of the bitter-einders. As the war dragged on, these camps were rapidly expanded to cope with increasing numbers: in addition to the families of those burghers who had surrendered of their own volition, two other groups were forcibly brought in: families who had habitually engaged in passing intelligence to the enemy, and families from farms which had been constantly used by the enemy either as shelter from which to fire upon British troops, or as commissariat depots. The refugees could therefore be split into three groups: 1) self-supporting refugees who had voluntarily sought protection for themselves and their stock, 2) refugees who were unable to support themselves, but who had sought the protection of the camps, and 3) families of persons who had been brought into camp against their will—either for protection or for the two reasons given above. This latter group was the minority in most camps and, unsurprisingly, principally malcontents.[34]

The bitter-einders actually took advantage of the shelter and relative safety the camps offered. An imperial intelligence agent, Napier Devitt, captured an order written by Louis Botha; the original was in Dutch but the translation read as follows: "In consequence of the moving about of commandos many of the wives and families of the burghers are disposed to attach themselves to our forces and thereby cause hindrance to our operations. As the enemy has destroyed our farms, thereby causing the families of the burghers to be homeless, all officers are requested to see that such persons do not follow the commandos as the responsibility for their food and shelter rests upon the enemy."[35]

Though completely disregarded today, the simple reality is that many thousands of those who lived in the camps really did approach the British, seeking the protection they offered—a situation caused largely by the marauding antics of the Boer hardliners. Indeed, the turnaround from viewing the British as the enemy to a protector was startling. In October 1900, in the Barberton district, for example, a strong force of bitter-einders was making trouble: "These commandos have been raiding cattle and horses every day, keeping well out of the reach of our guns; many rumours of their intent to attack us at Grass Kop have been brought in but we are quite ready for them. This raiding has had the effect of bringing all the Dutch farmers and their sons flying back to their farms to look after their stock; they are highly indignant with the looters, have all surrendered and taken the oath at Volksrust, and ride up here to the foot of the hill every day with many reports and much advice about their former comrades' movements, and how to attack and kill them! Many old Dutch women have come also to the hill in tears over their losses from Boer marauders and say they are starving. All this gives Major Dawson and Lieutenant Poynder, Adjutant of the Queen's, a great deal of work and many walks down the hill to interview these people."[36]

It is also ignored that, ever fearful of raids from bitter-einders, most camps actually employed numbers of surrendered Boers as camp guards and police, and who were paid for their service. The sixty inmates who served as camp police in the Krugersdorp camp, for example, cost around £180 a month.[37] These hendsoppers usually served in camps away from their home districts and, having taken the oath of allegiance, were entrusted to protect their fellow refugees. The resident magistrate of the Middelburg camp recorded an incident when one such camp guard—a man named Gouws—stuck to the letter of his orders and refused entry to the Lord Kitchener himself as the commander-in-chief did not have written approval from the camp medical officer. When this was sorted out Kitchener sportingly congratulated Gouws for his professionalism.[38] But it was not just attacks from their former brothers-in-arms that the surrendered Boers had to fear. Toward the end of 1900 native attacks in the western Transvaal saw increasing numbers of hendsoppers in a desperate plight. A report declared that the blacks "in many places are active in hostility against, and a standing danger to, the Boers. Last week four Boers were wounded and one killed by Natives at different places about the Pilansberg; most of the Boers from that neighbourhood have come to live under our protection". And far from encouraging such attacks as some prefer to claim, both Baden-Powell—who commanded the newly formed South African Constabulary—and Roberts did all they could to disarm these natives.[39]

Even as Boer refugees sought protection in the camps from native attacks, there were also huge numbers of natives who sought imperial protection from the brutal attacks of the bitter-einders: "Following the British annexation of the Transvaal and Orange River Colony and the beginning of the guerrilla war, the military administration was faced with two immediate problems concerning black refugees: first, to alleviate hardship and destitution among those Africans whose livelihood had been destroyed by military operations; and secondly, to give protection to black communities in danger of suffering at the hands of the Boer commandos for the assistance they had given to imperial forces. Already by the end of July 1900 groups of blacks had begun entering the British lines and garrison towns to seek protection from military operations and punitive raids on their settlements."[40] Large numbers of such refugees flooded into Vryburg, with similar scenes in the western Transvaal, where many blacks with their herds of livestock sought military protection with the British columns. Many refugees staggered into British-held towns, starving and destitute. "The inhabitants of Zwaartboys, their stad having been destroyed by General Grobler, were permitted to settle close to Wolmaransstad and some assistance given them."[41] In garrison towns attempts at relief were made by district commissioners but, by the end of 1900, it was apparent that a coherent policy was needed to deal with the tide of black refugees fleeing from the guerrilla onslaught: this was a humanitarian crisis caused almost entirely by the murder and mayhem of the bitter-einders.

And not only did the terrorism of the bitter-einders directly prompt the establishment of the refugee camps for blacks, but the Boers then went on to cheerfully target the blacks therein as a handy source of supply, stealing food from those already in a desperate condition. Pickets were raised from the refugees to defend the camps against night raids but still there were many successful attacks. In early 1901 three raids by bitter-einders on the black refugee camp at Potchefstroom netted 258 cattle and 400 sheep, as well as leaving one refugee dead.* Attacks on other black refugee camps saw the bitter-einders make off with

---

* In a similar incident the Belfast concentration camp was raided by *bitter-einders* on 15 September 1901; one woman was killed and two children injured.

hauls of money, food and clothing, while one such raid resulted in the death
of thirteen residents,[42] their deaths undoubtedly included in the statistics
of those 'murdered' by the British. Even black refugees outside the formal
British camp system were considered fair game by the Boers. In February
1902 a raiding party fell on an unofficial refugee settlement in the Thabu
Nchu area in the Orange River Colony, stealing 590 cattle, thirty-two horses
and 6,625 sheep and goats from these poor wretches.[43]

None of this is to suggest that imperial forces did not also create refugees
by way of their scorched-earth tactics: of course they did and many tens of
thousands of them. It should always be remembered though that many of
these were as a direct result of the bitter-einders sniping from 'surrendered'
farms, using others farms as depots and such like. Also, and as we saw in
the previous chapter, the refugee crisis has to be understood in context:
Kitchener's memorandum of the 21st December 1900, for example, called
for: "the removal of men, women and children and natives from the Districts
which the enemy's bands persistently occupy. This course has been pointed
out by surrendered Burghers, who are anxious to finish the war, as the most
effective method of limiting the endurance of the Guerrillas, as the men and
women left on the farms, if disloyal, willingly supply Burghers; if loyal, dare
not refuse to do so. Moreover, seeing the unprotected state of women now
living out in the Districts, this course is desirable to ensure their not being
insulted or molested by natives."[44]

This frustration is obvious in a message an increasingly exasperated Milner
wrote to Chamberlain: "Every farm had become a supply depot for the
enemy, enabling him to concentrate at will and refit his commandos with
food and munitions of war ... to have denuded the farms and left the women
and children to subsist as best they could would have been entirely within
the military rights of the British ... the women had actively assisted the
combatants by furnishing them with exact information regarding all British
movements. The military situation demanded that the enemy should be
deprived of such a system of intelligence, and humanity induced the British
Commander to remove the inhabitants from the farms and assemble them
in concentration camps, where they have at all times received food similar to
that provided for the British soldier, as well as shelter and other comforts."[45]

Though the scorched-earth tactics are often criticized, even the generally
rather critical *The Times History of the War* concedes: "To strike at an enemy's

sources of supply is and must be one of the principal aims of a belligerent. The regular sources of supply once possessed by the Boers—towns, railways, magazines—all, or nearly all, had been lost. Their new base was the farmstead and all pertaining thereto; private property had become indistinguishable from the magazines, stores and depots of an army in the field."[46]

Given that the bitter-einders were returning to farms to stock up on supplies and rest and refit, what alternative did the imperial commanders have but to destroy these depots? The burning of farms which provided succour and support to the guerrillas was undoubtedly unpleasant, perhaps even harsh, but what did the bitter-einders really expect?

So this is how the camps came about, but what of the other myth that they were a deliberate genocidal plot to exterminate the *Boerevolk*? To apartheid-era nutters the concentration camps were a propaganda godsend and blatant use was made of them to excuse and justify everything they did: "nationalists made it clear that Britain ought not even to dare to criticize 'race' politics in South Africa when it had earlier attempted genocide against the Afrikaners."[47] But was there really any attempt at ethnic-cleansing?

For a start no one was imprisoned in the camps. In 2008 an Afrikaans singer called Bok van Blerk released a fairly controversial song called *De la Rey*, which called on someone to rise up and lead the *Boere* again (presumably it wouldn't be Bok). Designed to tug at the heart-strings of any young Afrikaner after he's nailed a few Klippies* and Cokes, the music video shows some women and children stuck behind the wire fence of a camp, while outside a group of Boers wave about the flag of the old Orange Free State. In reality, camp inmates were not imprisoned behind barbed wire. Even in camps close to areas where bitter-einders remained active, residents were free to leave the camp twice a week, despite the obvious opportunity this presented to pass information and supplies to the guerrillas.[48] In camps in safer areas, and aside from the night-time curfews, the inmates were free to come and go exactly as they pleased: "The camp people also come into Krugersdorp and spend money in the shops there. In one very good tool shop which we visited the man spoke bitterly of the camp women coming

---

* Klipdrift, a popular South African brandy

in and spending 'money by the sovereign'.[49] Inmates were encouraged to find work locally or within the camp itself. Of the 262 men housed at the Pietermaritzburg camp, "a large proportion was employed, some on railway, some on steam trollies, some in breweries". Though often to the annoyance of local community, the official policy was "whenever work was required for the general permanent improvement of the camp, such as building huts, or preparing land for growing winter vegetables, or for any useful work to be done for the Government in the vicinity of the camp, preference was to be given in employment to occupants of the camps".[50] Indeed, so many of the inmates were working that imperial authorities in the Transvaal calculated the wage bill for residents and black employees was higher than that of the staff. In November 1901, for example, camp staff were paid a total of £5,633 while inmates and black employees received £7,232.[51]

Where possible, the imperial authorities actually preferred to house people with relations in towns, rather than in the camps and a good many people were rehoused in this way.[52] Indeed, as the war progressed, it became a matter of policy to permit refugees to reside with relatives or friends as long as they were not considered to present a security risk.[53] Locals were also encouraged to take the refugees in as lodgers, with the wife and children of Burgher Jack Lane, whom we met earlier, being placed with a Mrs Bell of Colesberg, for example. It is noteworthy that the reason Mrs Bell was able to accommodate the family was that her own children had recently died in the various epidemics that rampaged through South Africa at the time. Despite never staying in a concentration camp, the Lane children also suffered: all fell sick and the youngest one, little Maxwell, died.[54] Of the twelve children the Lanes and the Bells had between them, three died in infancy before the war, and another three died of measles during the war—a mortality rate of fifty per cent—and this despite none of them ever having been in a concentration camp.

Despite the twaddle one can read on extremist Afrikaans websites today, and hear in the fifth-hand family anecdotes which have been passed down like Chinese-whispers through the generations, people were not murdered in the camps and, other than a few, isolated cases, people did not starve in them. Some died of old age, but overwhelmingly those who died did so as a result of the various diseases that swept through the sub-continent at the time.[55] A measles epidemic was ravaging South Africa before the war began and, unsurprisingly, this was the single biggest killer in the camps, accounting for forty-three per cent of the deaths.[56] Pneumonia, dysentery, diarrhoea, typhoid and whooping cough were also major causes of death.

The understanding of nutrition was in its infancy in the 1890s. Even in Great Britain scurvy and rickets remained commonplace[57] and famines had really only ended in the 1870s when grain from Canada and Australia became more readily available when British harvests failed.[58] No one seemed to think that adding chalk to watered-down milk to improve its whiteness was a bad thing, nor was it unusal to add ground-up bones to dough for the same reason.[59] Such was the lack of understanding of diet at the time that the Victorian housewife's bible, Mrs Beaton's *Book of Household Management*, warned of the dangers of serving ice-cream to children or the elderly after a hot meal for fear that the rapid change in food temperatures would be too great a shock to their systems.[60] Diseases like measles, which are today considered almost comical in nature, were still massive killers at the end of the nineteenth century and it is small wonder that thousands of deaths occurred in the concentration camps—just as they did elsewhere across southern Africa: "Medical science had yet to find antidotes to typhoid, dysentery, pneumonia, bronchitis, whooping cough, diphtheria and malaria. Antiseptics were little understood and the importance of aseptic surgery was not yet generally realized. Ignorance of the laws of hygiene was common, and dieticians had not yet heard of vitamins. Typhoid killed about one in five that it attacked; diphtheria and pneumonia generally killed one in three."[61]

It is thus impossible to consider the mortality rates of the camps without being cognizant of the impact that outbreaks of disease had in South Africa before the advent of modern medicine. Back in the days of the Great Trek, measles swept through a laager of some 1,000 wagons—perhaps 5,000 people—leaving hundreds dead.[62] In another example, early in 1870 fever made its appearance at the tiny settlement of Potgieter's Rust. By April, eighty-one of the ninety-three European inhabitants were either dead or ill, and in May the hamlet was abandoned.[63] A few years later, 700 were confirmed dead in a smallpox outbreak in the Kimberley area.[64] In 1893 an outbreak of measles in northern Natal killed 163 girls between the ages of twelve and fourteen, with other age groups suffering similarly. One family lost all eight of their children, the eldest of whom was sixteen, in the space of ten days.[65]

During the war, a party of twenty-one would-be bitter-enders was afflicted by malaria on a trek to meet up with a commando near Pietersburg. Eight died on the way and by the time the group surrendered to the British, another was lying dead in a wagon. They were taken to a hospital where another six died shortly thereafter.[66]

Today's annual mortality rates are a fraction of what they were a century ago, with some poorer areas of Victorian Britain registering overall peacetime mortality rates of around forty per 1,000, compared to under six per thousand today.[67] A study into pre-war life expectancy in the Soutpansberg district of the Transvaal revealed men could only expect to live to thirty-nine, while women only averaged thirty-six[68]—roughly half what one would expect in a Western country today. Remarkably, female life expectancy in Britain at the time was around fifty-three—an incredible seventeen years higher.

It should perhaps not be surprising therefore that, even in peacetime, southern African infant and maternal mortality rates of the period were truly shocking, yet this is generally overlooked in the mindless clamour to blame the camps for all such deaths. Modern maternal mortality rates* in the West are around ten per 100,000 births. In the early 1900s, and even in the best of times, it was more like one in a hundred—a hundred times as common—which goes some way in explaining the three-year difference in life expectancy between the genders mentioned above. Due mainly to improved asepsis, fluid management and blood transfusion, and better pre-natal care, it is only relatively recently that such rates have plummeted and then only in the developed world.[†]

Infant mortality was even worse. Neither Boer republic troubled itself to monitor infant mortality before the war, but the 1890 Transvaal census reveals an astoundingly low number of infants[69]—an indication of chronic infant mortality described as a 'real anomaly'. The figures from the more settled, developed and generally healthier climate of the Cape Colony are also instructive. Infant mortality is defined as the number of deaths of children under one year against every 1,000 births; the figure for Britain today is around four and a half, with South Africa ten times worse at around forty-two per thousand. In contrast, the rates in Victorian Britain were shocking

---

* Defined by the World Health Organisation as the death of a woman while pregnant or within forty-two days of termination of pregnancy, irrespective of the duration and site of the pregnancy, from any cause related to or aggravated by the pregnancy or its management but not from accidental or incidental causes.

† South Africa still has maternal mortality rates of around 300 per 100,000 births

with the national average at 150 per 1,000, and in some slum areas around 250 per 1,000—fifty-five times as bad as the current British average.[70] Incredibly in the Victorian-era Cape Colony, the figures were even worse: between 1896 and 1898 the average infant mortality rate among white children in the Cape was 180 per thousand.[71] Between 1896 and 1900 in the town of Cradock, it was 395 per 1,000; that is to say that almost forty per cent of European children born in Cradock did not make it to their first birthday during that period.[72] The figures for coloured babies were even more shocking, with an average infant mortality rate across the Cape of 332 per 1,000 between 1896 and 1898, so even in peacetime one in three coloured babies did not live past one. War or peace, South African infants of all colours died like flies at the *fin du siècle*.

It is also often forgotten or overlooked that British troops suffered equally as severely from disease during the Boer War. After the capture of Bloemfontein, enteric fever swept through the ranks, with fifty men a day dying at the height of the outbreak, with one 500-bed hospital trying to cope with 1,700 patients.[73] Overall, 13,720 imperial soldiers died of disease—almost twice as many as were killed in action—over the course of the conflict. A further 66,500 were invalided home.[74] It is also worth noting the high death toll of doctors and nurses working the camps: in one month alone it was recorded that one doctor, one camp superintendent and four nurses died of either measles or enteric fever.[75]

The Boer War was by no means unique in this regard. Elsewhere in the period, disease—especially in time of war—had an equally devastating impact. In the Philippines, for example, "with the warming of the spring of 1902, all the above factors came into play. The result was a catastrophic outbreak of disease. The culprit was cholera, a disease spread through contaminated food and water ... the most plausible estimates for cholera deaths seem to be in the range of 150,000 to 200,000".[76] In 1862, Henry Morton Stanley—later the famous explorer—ended up in Camp Douglas prisoner-of-war camp during the American Civil War. In his first week there, 220 of his fellow inmates died of dysentery and typhoid.[77] Sixty thousand Austrians were taken prisoner by the Serbs in the opening battles of the Great War; one in five would die of typhus by the end of 1914, with many more to follow.[78]

Obviously, war made the impact of killer diseases even worse: it is claimed that the camps caused disease to spread more readily by bringing people into closer proximity. There is no doubt plenty of truth in this. However, the deaths in the Boer War concentration camps pale into insignificance compared with those of the 1918 influenza epidemic in South Africa. In just a few short weeks, and without a concentration camp in sight, 142,000 South Africans died[79] (a staggering fifteen millions perished in Europe).

Of course the camps would not have attracted media attention and outrage had there not been significant suffering, but one must also endeavour to disregard the rampant pro-Boer European propaganda. Conversely, if the imperial authorities had something to hide, why would ardent critics like Emily Hobhouse have been permitted to publicize what was happening: why would she—and the equally formidable women of the Ladies' Commission*—have been permitted to travel to South Africa to study and report on the camps? Why would the anti-war press in London have been able to freely report on the situation? Would the now-infamous handful of photographs of emaciated children[†] have been permitted to be taken had there been some sort of desire to hide such things? This was long before the age of the camera phone: setting up a bulky old plate-camera-type affair—not to mention setting off an exploding magnesium flash—would have been virtually impossible to do without the knowledge and approval of camp authorities.[80]

Indeed, Sir Arthur Conan-Doyle, who served as a doctor during the war, provides a more plausible explanation for one of the most famous such photographs in his 1902 *The War in South Africa: Its Causes and Conduct* in that it was taken "by the British authorities on the occasion of the criminal trial of the mother for the ill-usage of the child". That this photograph was subsequently used as a stick with which to beat the British, Conan-Doyle describes as "characteristic of the unscrupulous tactics which have been used from the beginning to poison the mind of the world against Great Britain". Conan-Doyle might not be surprised to know that such unscrupulous tactics continue over a century later. Less attention is paid to the many hundreds of photographs of camp residents that do not fit the myth: pictures of healthy-looking children, of camp sports teams and societies, or of family groups dressed in their Sunday best, are airily dismissed as British propaganda.[81]

---

* Under the presidency of Mrs Fawcett, the Ladies' Commission was established by the War Office in July 1901 and sent to South Africa to report on the conditions in the camps.

† There are three such photos which one can expect to find in every single book, article or webpage on the subject, the most famous of which is that of little Lizzie van Zyl who—like 8,020 imperial soldiers—tragically died of typhoid.

৯৯

It is often deemed unfair, arrogant or uncaring to point out that a major reason behind the spread of disease in Boer concentration camps was the widespread lack of basic hygiene and understanding of such things by many of the residents. It would certainly be unfair to make note of this but for the fact that there is so much evidence to support it; indeed, the commandos had also exhibited this trait throughout the war: "Close to the Gatsrand Commando trenches, dead horses are still lying thick. Burghers are too lazy to make an effort to remove them, the consequence will be an outbreak of fever, and, as for the sanitary arrangements, it is simply disgusting. Any ordinary white man would have been dead long ago."[82] And: "Orders issued this morning, laager was to be removed two miles further down river. I hear several burghers asking each other, what the devil the General means, taking the laager nearer the British, are they not near enough? The Doctors advised that the laager to be removed on sanitary grounds, and I don't wonder at it, it is simply awful, the lazy brutes, Kaffirs are more particular."[83]

When the British drove the Boers off Monte Cristo, prior to the relief of Ladysmith, they were appalled by the condition of the republican camps: "the filthy condition in which the camps were found surprised the British soldiers; every place was in a most insanitary state, the stench arising therefrom being noticeable at a great distance."[84] After Ladysmith itself was relieved, the situation was discovered to be same in federal positions around the town: "The Boer camps were in a most insanitary condition, and it is a matter of surprise that there was not more sickness among the enemy."[85]

These bad habits were brought to the concentration camps, as reported by the Ladies' Commission: "it is necessary to put on record the insanitary habits of the people. However numerous, suitable and well-kept may be the latrines provided, the fouling of the ground, including river banks, and slopes and trenches leading to the water supply, goes on to such an extent which would probably not be credited except by those who have seen it … the extensive fouling of the floors of tents and the ground of camps by it has been the direct cause of a devastating attack of enteric in more than one camp."[86] One recent examination on the history of the camps concedes: "Boer farms often lacked any form of sanitation. Accounts of Boer sanitary practices, though much resented by middle-class Afrikaners then and later, are so graphic and so frequent that there can be no doubt that most Boers in the camps, who were bywoners (landless farmers) rather than middle class, lived in comfortable association with human and animal excrement."[87]

As well as simply living in "comfortable association" with it, animal excrement was viewed by many inmates as something of a cure-all. One medical historian recorded: "The intestinal contents of different animals or their excreta were believed to possess almost magical healing qualities." The rather less-than-yummy-sounding goat-dung tea was a popular remedy for measles, while pieces of raw meat were bandaged over eyes to cure conjunctivitis, and all manner of things were inserted into babies' ears.[88] Though Hobhouse and other pro-Boer sources remain resolutely silent on the subject for fear of torpedoing their own case, these peculiar Boer remedies greatly exacerbated the death tolls of the concentration camps: "It was to this hospital in July last that unfortunate children were brought, whose mother had painted them with common green oil paint as a remedy for measles. There were three of these children, one died in the tent; the other two were brought into hospital, but their lives could not be saved. They died from the effect of arsenic poisoning. Not content with painting their bodies, the mother had, in the case of one child, added a plaster of American cloth thickly daubed with the same paint. The nurses told us that it was very common among the Boers to tar a patient's feet as a remedy for fever. Dogs' blood was recommended for fits and so on. The nurses spoke of one case where a child in a tent was in a high fever (temperature 104) from measles. The mother utilized the heat thus generated by putting the bread, which she had just made, inside the child's bed to cause it to rise."[89]

Though happy to inflict green oil paint, goat-dung tea, tar and dog's blood on their children, many residents were deeply suspicious of more logical remedies: British attempts to introduce a lime-juice ration and the insistence of boiling drinking water both met resistance.[90] Worse still, camp doctors struggled to stop the practice of large numbers of inmates gathering round a seriously ill patient, cramming into the tent and thus vastly increasing the chances of the disease spreading.[91] Predictably, most writers ignore all this and dutifully spout the party line. One such luminary heaps all the blame on the British: "The conditions in these camps was [sic] uniformly appalling. The camps lacked even the most basic of sanitary and medical amenities."[92] But on the same page the imbecilic commentator unthinkingly presents a quote which completely contradicts his own outlandish statement: "I spent some time during the last two days in the Bloemfontein camp, and can honestly say that everything possible in the circumstances is done for the unfortunate people. The hospitals [basic medical amenities?], for which the Boers are slowly overcoming their dislike, are in perfect order. The doctors have a free hand to prescribe everything necessary for both in-patients and out-patients … The advisability of closing the schools during the epidemic of measles has been under discussion. It is hoped that the measure will not be found necessary. The children seem to take readily to the schooling and it gives an excellent opportunity to a large number to learn English." So here is an historian mindlessly assuring his readers that the camps lacked "even the basic of medical amenities" and in the same breath idiotically presenting evidence which states that there were hospitals and doctors. Such is the power of propaganda on the gullible. The same writer later cheerily dismisses the eyewitness account of a lady who does not share his jaundiced view on the camps as a "backwoods imperialist".[93]

It is quite possible that this writer, and his equally sheeplike ilk, were influenced by a school textbook approved by the Transvaal Education Department during the apartheid era. Though works by respected South African historians such as professors Walker, Macmillan, Keppel-Jones and Fouché were all excluded from the approved list, *Die Konsentrasiekampe* was eagerly snapped up.[94] Written by one Dr J. C. Otto, it was a work of myth-building propaganda so appalling that a fellow Afrikaans historian described the error-strewn drivel as an "emotional outburst from beginning to end".[95] Nevertheless, Otto's ahistorical rubbish fitted the apartheid regime's determination to squeeze every drop of political capital they could from the Boer War, and this was considered exactly the sort of thing all South African school children should be studying. Undeterred by the facts, Otto supports his case—such as it is—by using an unending string of mistruths and blatant misquotes. For example, the general superintendent of the Transvaal camps, and later mayor of Johannesburg, Mr W. K. Tucker, is quoted as saying: "The formation of the Concentration Camps should be regarded as an evil." In fact what he *actually* said was: "The method of warfare adopted by the Boers inevitably brought ruin and death upon their women and children. The formation of the Concentration Camps should be regarded as an evil of far less magnitude, however, than those from which the inmates were saved by this means, and itself the creation of military necessity."[96] Otto also disregards his own quoted sources, for example claiming that there were no doctors in the Bloemfontein camp; indeed, he claims there was only one "over worked and underfed" nurse there during the first half of 1901. However, Dr Otto's own quoted sources do not support his claims, stating that in June 1901 there were three doctors, five trained nurses and twelve untrained nurses. These numbers increased throughout the rest of the year and, by the time of the Ladies' Commission visit in September, were confirmed as "five doctors, two dispensers, one matron, five head nurses, twenty-five local assistants".[97] In reality, the British authorities moved quickly to address any initial shortages, recruiting large numbers of doctors and nurses in the UK to serve in South Africa. Nurses, many of them very experienced professionals in their late thirties, were attracted by the high salaries on offer: £10 a month[98] in the Orange River Colony and £12 a month in the Transvaal—far more than they would earn in Great Britain and about four times what the British army paid a private soldier. It is also worth noting that these nurses lived in bell tents just like the inmates, and received the same rations.[99] Doctors were even better remunerated, earning over £40 a month—more than many of the camp superintendents. There was also a big drive to recruit hundreds of local Afrikaans girls to be trained as nurses[100]—a profession virtually unknown in the pre-war Boer republics. The camp administrators provided training in sanitary practice and nutrition, the recruits were given lectures, tests were written and the girls issued with certificates. Initially taken on as 'probationers', many of these young ladies swiftly proved efficient enough to be promoted to nursing assistants, earning £6 a month. It is also worth noting that camp residents were recruited and paid to work as medical assistants.

The employment of large numbers of these Afrikaans girls is contrary to the enduring lie that the camps were run by cruel, uncaring Britons. The reality is that many camp doctors and superintendents were not British at all, but rather Afrikaans or European. Brandfort camp, for example, and which was the scene of a short-lived rebellion, was run by a Cape Afrikaner called Jacobs.[101] The senior doctor at the Mafeking camp was Dr Kaufmann, an Austrian, and his deputy was a German.[102] Other examples are Dr van der Wall, an Afrikaner who worked at the Kroonstad camp, Dr Martinius at Brandfort and Minister Lückhoff at Bethulie.[103]

Nevertheless, Dr Otto's surreal offensive against continues with his declaration that the hospital accommodation at one concentration camp "consisted of three little zinc huts, each with 16 beds, and a few marquee tents and they were, as may easily be appreciated, all regularly full". A report from March 1901 and acknowledged by Otto as one of his sources, confirmed that the hospital was "clean and well kept". Another report, from June, which Otto also cites as a source (though presumably never bothered to read), gives lots of detail on the hospital buildings: "The measles hut is 112' 5" long, 24' 1" broad, 7' 9" to the eaves, 11' 9" to the roof ridge and provided a cubic space of 454.8 cubic feet per patient. There were six open fire places to control the temperature. There were 63 beds of which 43 were occupied. There were one trained and three untrained nurses. An extremely clean, bright, and cheery appearance was presented. The bedding arrangements are identical with those of any permanent hospital, the patients being very comfortable and extremely contented." The typhoid wards are described as being "considerably smaller than the huts described above, but are built on the same principle. The internal dimensions are length 36', breadth 18'. Height to the eaves 9', height to roof ridge 12' 6" … cubic space per head in the adult wards is 497.5 cubic feet, in the children's ward 409.7 cubic feet … The wards are extremely neat, bright, cheerful and comfortable".[104] Other than the obvious explanation that he simply pulled it out of his arse, one is left wondering where Dr Otto got his own alternative description from. He does similar injustice to several other camps, cleverly expounding that there were no doctors present, but forgetting to inform his readers that the period to which he is referring was when the camp was still being established. For example, he damningly pontificates that, in late June 1901, Bethulie camp had no doctor. In fact, at that time the newly established camp had one doctor, two trained nurses and two untrained nurses and by August this had increased to four doctors.[105] Though for various reasons some camps were undeniably worse than others, it is often brushed aside that many camps were well run.

Many families even retained their black servants during their sojourn. Generally the blacks were kept segregated but could attend to their employers during the day. In other instances, the servants shared accommodation with their masters. At the Baberton camp, for example, it was recorded: "there are over a hundred native servants, principally with their families, who have accompanied their employers … there appears to be undue familiarity; some natives sleeping, eating and drinking the same tents as whites".[106] The British concentration camps must have been the only ones in history where inmates retained domestic staff.

In another, one lady seemed to be living very comfortably indeed: "in one very smartly furnished tent with carved oak and red velvet chairs the woman had chickens and guinea pigs inside, the latter of which she was feeding on raw carrots. She was very cheerful and conversational, and said she had plenty of chickens when she first came to camp, but 'though they only had two legs to start with, in camp they quickly got four'."[107]

Though still widely repeated even today, reports of British attempts to poison the food of the residents lack any hard evidence whatsoever. Indeed, it would be utterly illogical to poison people you are paying enormous sums of money to provide medical care for. Poppycock about 'blue poison' in the sugar only started appearing in print in the 1930s[108] and seems to have stemmed simply from unschooled gossiping by people who had never before seen the blue aniline dye crystals added to improve the whiteness of sugar.[109] Incredibly, these sort of "blatant lies about the British putting fish-hooks into bully beef* and ground glass into food, and of pigs devouring the corpses of children, were officially taught in South African schools as late as the 1940s … a myth of deliberate British cruelty was devised and even persists to this day, despite a wealth of well-documented evidence on the subject".[110] As one Afrikaans historian writes in the story of his people, this sort of gibberish was and still is widely believed: "It matters not at all that hardly anyone was deliberately killed in the camps, that most of the deaths were caused by typhoid, malnutrition, and lack of hygiene: we 'knew' perfectly well as children that the British put ground glass into the camp food to cause internal bleeding, diarrhoea, and death … We 'knew' all this was true despite the best efforts of Afrikaner liberals."[111]

The complete lack of evidence or logic remains no bar to perpetuation of such mythology. If the camps were designed to starve (or, even more ludicrously, poison and kill with ground-up glass) the residents to death, then they proved highly unsuccessful. The reality is that the longer people stayed in them generally the healthier they became: the inmates soon began to realize that their children were better off when receiving professional medical care.[112] The highest mortality rates were found in those newly arrived in a camp, as

---

* The corned beef was shipped in from America, so the cans would have had to have been pre-ordered with hooks in them from the suppliers—a truly ludicrous suggestion

they often staggered in half-starved and in a woeful state. Dr van der Wall, an Afrikaans doctor working at the Kroonstad camp, remarked on a group of 800 refugees who were brought in after their laager: "The health of this section is extremely bad. These people came into camp laden with disease and worn out in constitution … I find that all diseases rampant among them now were in evidence amongst them when they came in … in conclusion I wish to point out that the cause of mortality was introduced from outside, and is not due to existing circumstances in the camp."[113] In another of many examples, the superintendent of Brandfort camp reported that those refugees brought in after the capture of a Boer laager near Hoopstad were in a terrible state: "The privations and hardships this had induced had told with great effect on the women and children, many of whom were scantily clad. In some instances, women had clothed their children with sheep skins and roughly dressed hides, and the people, almost without exception, expressed their pleasure at having been taken away from the commando."[114]

Much has been made of the rations issued to the residents but, without fail, it is always left out that even contemporary critics acknowledged that the very lowest of the ration scales were better than those that imperial soldiers enjoyed in peacetime.[115] Indeed, even on operations, British troops existed on very meagre rations: Allenby recorded that his men got "2lbs of meat a day, besides that, they only get 1¼ biscuits" each.[116] When the Ladies' Commission looked at ration scales, they recommended only small changes to the issues: "Considering the ample provision of all necessities for the healthy and of necessities and luxuries for the sick which has been made, it is rather difficult to find a suitable channel into which to direct the flow of private charity … with some trifling exceptions, in which, from the fund placed at our disposal by the Victoria League, we supplemented in a few camps the supply of medical comforts, or established a soup kitchen, we have recommended that the main body of the fund should be used for the promotion and development of education."[117] As critics are forced to admit, "The Boers in the camps were certainly given enough to eat" before explaining that the problems were more concerned with the inexact knowledge of vitamins and nutrition of the time.[118] If vitamin deficiency was indeed a widespread problem, it would stand to reason that there would have been an ever-increasing rise in the mortality rates as long as ration scales remained unchanged and inmates grew weaker and more vulnerable with time. As ration scales remained unaltered in the Transvaal camps from February 1901—and those in the Orange Free State from March 1901—to January 1902 when they were increased, then one would logically expect the highest mortality rates to have occurred in December 1901. Instead, mortality rates peaked in October 1901 and dropped thereafter.[119] Individual camps saw death rates drop as the measles epidemic subsided in their area: for example, thirteen camps saw death rates peak in or before August 1901, so there can be no possible link between the improving health in the camps, and the very slight change in ration scale implemented five months later.[120] There were certainly interruptions to supply, but the British can hardly be blamed for bands of bitter-einders blowing up and looting supply trains. This ongoing terrorist campaign impacted upon some outlying camps, with the standard daily ration occasionally reduced as a result.[121]

As well as the rations they were given courtesy of the British taxpayer, the camp residents were encouraged to supplement their diets by planting vegetable patches which soon became commonplace.[122] Local traders also visited the camps to sell fresh fruit and vegetables.[123] In addition, for the large numbers who found work, or who arrived with money, all the camps had shops with prices approved by the superintendent, or kept low by competition.[124] By all accounts many of these did a roaring trade: "the camp store in Klerksdorp took £30 to £40 per day, Potchefstroom camp store took £50 to £60 per day, whilst Vereeniging store might take as much as £150 a day. Howick and Pietermaritzburg supported three camp shops, Bloemfontein ten or eleven, whilst Aliwal North had as many as thirteen … whilst milk, tinned fish, dates, sweets, Worcester sauce, chow-chow were amongst the most popular items, many luxury articles were also in demand, such as gramophones, watches, concertinas at 25s, silk fronts, photographs. In one camp women's corsets were becoming fashionable."[125] One camp where the shop was rather less successful was Volksrust: as its prices were the same as those in town, many residents preferred to take a pleasant stroll into Volksrust to pick up their groceries.[126]

Adequate water supply was initially a major problem for many camps: when a stream which had been sufficient for a village of 1,000 inhabitants was suddenly called upon to provide water for a camp of 10,000, there were bound to be water shortages, especially when many of the rivers were contaminated with typhoid. Extensive testing of river water was done by the authorities and recommendations regarding filtration acted upon. Engineering works to provide enough water took up a large chunk of the cost of running the camps and, indeed, left a positive legacy in many towns: "By April 1902, the Klerksdorp camp had 10 tanks for boiling water, ensuring that no river water was used at all. Aliwal North, on the confluence of the Kraai and Orange Rivers, could have been expected to have ample water, but, by 1902, an extensive water scheme had been installed, including five miles of pipes, an engine which supplied 20,000 gallons (90,921 litres) a day and £3,150 worth of storage tanks. Since this elaborate scheme, which also included a sand filter, was well beyond the needs of the camp, the authorities began negotiations to supply the town as well."[127]

As well as improving the water supply and providing shops and medical, educational and recreational facilities, the British engaged—and paid for—*predikants* of the Dutch Reformed Church (and ministers of other denominations) to cater for the social and spiritual well-being of the residents. One such gentleman, the Reverend J. C. Hefer, Dutch Reformed minister of Parys, had resolutely refused to take the oath of allegiance and had lost two of his children to disease while working in the Vredefort road camp. Nevertheless, he wrote to the administrator of the Orange River Colony on the 3rd October 1901 to say: "It will always be my happy privilege here, as well as elsewhere, to testify to the good treatment of refugees in the Vredefort Road Camp and the goodwill shown us all by Your Honour."[128]

Schools were established in all the camps, with 42,500 children receiving tuition therein. Before the war there had never been more than 24,000 children attending school in the pair of republics combined.[129] Other facilities provided to the residents included musical centres and reading rooms, with materials provided to inmates to indulge in dress-making, carpentry and so forth. By May 1901, the camp at Aliwal North boasted several tennis courts, while other camp superintendents organized football fields, cricket equipment, croquet sets and quoits for the inmates.[130]

Vryburg camp had a swimming pool where every day over 200 children enjoyed a dip.[131] Indoor activities were also provided for, and the residents were encouraged to enjoy table-tennis, chess, reading and marbles. Other camps had active debating and choral societies, while many held dances on weekends. With the measles epidemic past, and the camps by then well organized and established, Christmas 1901 was celebrated in style by the residents. Christmas trees were decorated, and at one camp 200 plum puddings were dished out.[132]

Interestingly, the Pietersburg camp was actually captured by bitter-einders toward the end of 1901, a time when mortality rates were at their highest. Between 700 and 800 burghers seized the camp, took the superintendent and his staff prisoner and enjoyed a raucous night with their wives and sweethearts—and probably a few other men's wives and sweethearts too. In the morning the superintendent and his staff were released, as the Boer commandant "expressed his appreciation of the manner in which their women and children were being cared for, and stated that he was happy to leave them where they were".[133] When bitter-einder General Viljoen lodged complaints about the conditions in the camps during the epidemic, Kitchener arranged that a Boer nominee, Captain Malan, be permitted to inspect them and investigate for himself. Malan afterward expressed "his entire satisfaction with the arrangements which had been made on behalf of the Boer women and children".[134] Furthermore, when Kitchener wrote to de Wet in December 1901 to say he was more than willing to send "all women and children at present in our camps" to wherever the Boer general specified, no reply was ever received.[135] Of course, it was far easier for de Wet—and all those of his ilk ever since—to spit venom at Kitchener than to actually trouble himself to do anything practical to assist his kinfolk.

It should also be remembered that many thousands of loyalist refugees complained bitterly about the relatively good conditions enjoyed by the Boers in the camps, while they themselves went unfed and unhoused in real destitution. Almost completely overlooked are those refugees of British stock who, driven from their homes in Johannesburg and northern Natal by the Boer invasions, found themselves in "the English refugee camps at Durban, where the people are living like Kaffirs in huts made of tins and boxes. The contrast with the trim rows of tents in the Boer refugee camps with free rations, hospitals etc, is rather too painful. One cannot help feeling there has been a grave oversight on the part of the British Government to support the Boers and do nothing for our own people."[136] Some protested to Lord Milner that by ignoring his own people he was spoiling the Boers in the concentration camps while "leaving the British refugees in idleness and poverty at the coast, in order to keep the people in the concentration camps supplied with every luxury and comfort".[137]

ॐ

Few would suggest that anyone really lived in luxury in the camps, and despite the efforts of the staff it is undeniable that many thousands died in them. No one can really be sure exactly how many, though various figures get thrown about. Figures for non-white deaths in the camps are thought to be around 12,000,[138] controversy has always surrounded the number of Boer deaths, and the many thousands of imperial troops who also died of disease during the war are simply ignored altogether. Between 1906 and 1914, a Mr P. L. A. Goldman was appointed by the Botha–Smuts proto-nationalist Transvaal Het Volk (the People's Union) party to research the numbers of burghers who had served in the war. The political elite of the Orange Free State had a rather different agenda, however, instead kvetching for the numbers of deaths among women and children in the camps to be computed. There were plenty of mistakes in Goldman's figures: "in some cases 'non-relevant' deaths remain included (see for instance RS8, Kestell District enumeration forms, where a death in India is retained … Bloemfontein District enumeration forms, where deaths are included even though all that is recorded is the name with the date and place unknown (*onbekend*)."[139] It is also clear that Goldman "prioritized lists and information received from 'het volk', from Boer sources rather than 'official' British ones".[140]

Before the war, the Orange Free State had legislated that someone stopped being considered a child on their twelfth birthday, while the Transvaal stipulated the sixteenth. Goldman ignored both these existing standards and recorded all deaths under the age of seventeen as children—a more emotive term which no doubt pleased his political masters.[141] Equally importantly, building the myth of a united *volk* required pretending that there were no males of fighting age in the camps; this technique permitted a sixteen-year-old male to be counted as a non-gender-specific 'child' rather than an adult—who would have to be defined as being either male or female. Men actually accounted for about a third of the adult population of the burgher camps.[142] More striking still is that the vast majority of these male inmates were between sixteen and forty-nine, rather than the fragile old men as commonly reported.[143] There is also no sign that Goldman cross-referenced information received from different sources: "If, for instance, deaths of a Coetzee, Coetsee, Coetzer, Coetser, Coetsen, Kotze, Kotzee, are not cross-checked against each other" then the result is to introduce "a major but unpredictable source of over-counting deaths."[144] Goldman's superbly dubious calculations eventually ended up with a figure of 27,927 deaths in the camps—whites only: non-whites didn't count and weren't counted.[145] To further add to the confusion, Bloemfontein's National Women's Monument, unveiled in 1913, asserts the number to be 26,370. It is also worth noting that the construction of this monument was bitterly opposed by loyalist elements on the post-war Bloemfontein town council *and* General Louis Botha as it was considered a form of anti-British propaganda. More tellingly is that the heart-wrenching scene on the monument that depicts Emily Hobhouse's recollection of a girl who died at Springfontein Station, is, to put it nicely, a fabrication: the girl had never entered a concentration camp.[146]

Professor Walker in *A History of Southern Africa* gives a figure of 20,000 deaths in the camps,[147] while in his biography of Salisbury, eminent historian Andrew Roberts dismisses the higher numbers as Afrikaner propaganda and suggests the same figure.[148] No one is saying that a lower figure makes the number of Boers who died in the camps okay, but even if we ignore all the failings in Goldman's techniques and accept that 27,927 Boers did die *in* the camps, then this is completely different from saying they died *because* of the camps. We will probably never know how many died *because* of the camps—it might well only be a few hundred or perhaps even less. Such a statement will no doubt prompt the usual tedious squeals of manufactured indignation but, as we have seen, disease killed those outside the camps (including imperial soldiers) just as readily as those inside the camps (including medical staff). Had the British simply left the refugees on the veldt rather than providing protection, shelter, food and medical care (however flawed this might have been in some cases), then the death toll can only possibly have been higher still.

The actions of the bitter-einders created a refugee crisis—among both black and white—and thus they bear much responsibility for the situation. It is also completely overlooked that, and as the Marquess of Salisbury rightly pointed out, the ultimate responsibility for the camps—and, indeed, for all deaths attributable to the conflict—can be squarely laid at the door of Oom Paul whose intransigence and empire-building ambitions started the war in the first place.

Long-term Transvaaler, Hugh Abercrombie, lived through the Boer War and the dawn of apartheid and knew many of the major players personally. Toward the end of his long life he wrote: "Nobody can doubt for one moment that if Dr Reitz, and Field-Marshal Smuts, at that time State Attorney, had backed up General Piet Joubert [who was always bitterly opposed to Kruger's invasion] there would have been no war. They, with Dr Leyds, must therefore take the responsibility for the conflict, the concentration camps, as they are falsely called, and the racialism which undoubtedly exists in extremist quarters today."[149]

So while the saga of the camps is certainly unpleasant and regrettable, the lingering fables about them need to be busted. Elizabeth van Heyningen's excellent history of the subject describes this myth as resulting from a "haze of informal history", mainly based on poetry and semi-fictional accounts of camp life, many of which were written a generation after the event.[150] Such legends were carefully cultivated by Afrikaner nationalists in the 1920s and '30s and then whipped into a frenzy of extreme exaggeration by the apartheid regime to become what we know today. Given the position that the British found themselves in, it is difficult to come up with an alternative strategy they could have pursued, short of leaving homeless women and children to starve and die on the veldt which would have been utterly reprehensible. As the Boer high command—which, let us not forget, started the war in the first place—had openly and callously simply washed their hands of the problem, it is simplistic and naïve to consider the British as the only bad guys in all of this.

Mistakes were certainly made and there is little doubt that some camps could have been better managed from the outset, but it is also unreasonable to blame the imperial authorities for the deaths of all those who died from measles and typhoid, just because they happened to be living in a camp at the time they succumbed. As mentioned earlier, even now, thousands of people die in refugee camps and hospitals every day all over the world, and rarely is this considered the fault of the institution. It is also unreasonable to put all the blame for the existence of the camps on the British, when they were initially set up to house refugees who were being terrorized, not by imperial troops but by marauding bands of bitter-einders, whose significant portion of the blame is rarely if ever mentioned. Conversely, it is conveniently forgotten that in plans drawn up by President Steyn and General de Wet for the invasion of the Cape Colony, the captured women and children were to be housed in similar camps.[151]

The British concentration camps were never part of any military strategy; they were a "terrible, unexpected by-product of the guerrilla war", a humanitarian response to the refugee crisis started by the Boers and exacerbated by the imperial scorched-earth policy, and as such were essential—in spite of presenting an open goal to the Boer propaganda machine and the anti-war lobby in Europe. If they were a calculated scheme to bring the Boers to the negotiating table then the camps failed spectacularly in this regard. With the British housing, protecting and feeding their women and children, the bitter-einders were able to carry on their aimless guerrilla war with carefree abandon, cheerfully absolving themselves of all responsibility for their civilian population, their own kith and kin. As it was, the imperial authorities proved keener to help Boer refugees than their own, and were understandably criticized for doing so. Arch bitter-einder de Wet took it a step further, openly advocating handing those women and children still with the Boers over to the British—even his own wife was a long-term inmate of one of the camps.[152] Indeed, it was only due to the camps that "Botha was then able to express his thankfulness that so many of the Boers' families were in British hands, and Steyn could urge the fighting-men to go on with the war while the British looked after their families ... less note has been taken of the heavy loss of life in the similar Loyalist and Native camps or among the overworked staffs in all of them".[153] Posterity will, ultimately, judge the likes of Steyn and de Wet with little kindness.

CHAPTER ELEVEN

We rely on your generals

"among the small but restive urban 'educated Afrikander' soldiery, lawyers, teachers,
ordinary state officials, beneficiaries of European travel and the like, there was a
bemoaning of the failings of a band of 'country' or 'bush' Boer generals who were too
pre-modern to ensure success. Inflexible, obstinate and ignorant of anything other than
hugging the ground and holding defensive positions, they were incapable
of addressing fundamental campaign problems."
—Bill Nasson, *The War for South Africa*

"The result was a series of hasty retreats on the part of De la Rey's rearguard,
soon degenerating into a rout which infected the whole force and hurried it in disorder
from the field. This was a heavy blow to De la Rey, whose star was now considerably
obscured by such repeated terminations to forays, the first speed and
spirit of which had died at the moment of action."[1]
—General Maurice describing de la Rey's string of beatings in March 1901

"There have been unfortunate British officers in this war, and there have been occasions
when a disaster to the British has been immediately attributed to the acts or the tactics
of the commanding officer. In this connection, I will cite the regrettable instance
of General Gatacre at Stormberg. I do not think this reverse is to be
attributable to stupidity, or indiscretion, or cowardice."
—General Ben Viljoen

During one armistice at the siege of Ladysmith, one Boer commandant told a
war correspondent of Britain's *Daily News*: "We admit that the British soldiers
are the best in the world, and your regimental officers the bravest—but we
rely on your generals."[2] Pakenham picks up on this theme, trumpeting, "The
great generals of this war were to prove exclusively Boer: Botha, Christiaan
De Wet, De la Rey, perhaps Smuts,"[3] though gives no reasons for his claim,

or any supporting evidence. The 1991 book, *The Guinness Book of Military Blunders*, goes even further, making the extraordinary claim that Buller lost the battle of Colenso because he forbade his men from digging trenches and foxholes. As the British were assaulting dug-in Boer positions, it is unclear how and why the Tommies would need to dig such trenches or how such digging could possibly have aided Buller's cause. What it does illustrate is that the writer of this tripe has absolutely no understanding of military matters in general, and no understanding of the battle of Colenso in particular, yet still feels qualified to write a book about the blunders of others. This is the sort of absolute rubbish which gets written, published and unthinkingly re-hashed about the British generals of the period, even by those who really should know better. On a tour of the battlefield at Spion Kop, for example, the guide quite sincerely informed us that the reason the British officers were so poor was that they had all purchased their commissions, despite this practice having been abolished a generation before the outbreak of the Boer War.*

Of course, this sort of class-war bashing of British officers is always appealing to anti-establishment types, but is there really any basis to it? Again, and just like such claims made about Britain's First World War generals, the argument rather founders on the rock of British victory. Surely if the senior officers on one side were all stupid and all the 'great' ones were on the other, the result of the conflict should never have been in doubt? As normal, this is pooh-poohed away with remarks about the overwhelming numbers of imperial troops, ignoring the fact that several British victories were achieved when the federal forces still had a marked superiority in numbers. Furthermore, the republicans managed to make little use of their intial numerical advantage and achieved none of the aims of their offensive, with their invasions quickly bogging down and stagnating. Worse still, during the Boer rout, their Black Month, the total number of imperial troops in theatre was only perhaps fifty per cent greater than those the Boers could draw upon; so numbers, while certainly a factor, were by no means the be all and end all they are claimed to be.

Let's consider the conventional war first and investigate if there were any 'great' generals on the republican side. For a start, the whole federal strategy

---

* The Sale of Commissions was abolished in 1871 as part of the Cardwell Reforms and had only ever applied to infantry and cavalry units, not the Royal Engineers or Royal Artillery. As the officer commanding at Spion Kop, General Warren, had been commissioned into the Royal Engineers, the guide's comments are therefore even more misplaced.

was hopelessly flawed and muddled from the outset, with little evidence of military genius. Smuts's plan called for republican units to push forward as fast as possible, securing the ports before imperial reinforcements could make landfall.[4] As we saw in chapter five, in the time between conception and implementation of the plan the balance of power had shifted significantly, and yet the invasion was still launched. Furthermore, the offensive only made sense if Boer forces advanced quickly: in reality, the invasion forces in Natal and over on the western front dawdled, while there was no advance on the central front at all until early November.

As well as these delays, the deployment of the Boer forces was also hopelessly ill conceived, with the bulk of the republicans troops committed to an invasion of Natal when it would have made more sense to direct their main effort against the Cape Colony to provoke a popular uprising. Bill Nasson says the Boers were "beguiled by the reclamation of the spiritual lower plain of Natal, by the harvesting of Durban, and by the lure of an artery to the sea. Had more weight been added to the western front, the unleashing of between 30,000 and 40,000 well-prepared riflemen into the Cape Colony might conceivably have radically altered the course of the war".[5] Nasson is undoubtedly correct as there was little point in the republicans seizing Durban without capturing all the Cape ports as well. Even had Durban fallen, as long as the political will to fight remained, the British would simply have poured their reinforcements into the Cape instead and then have fought their way north.

And in any case, the Boer invasion of Natal demonstrated little in the way of direction or dynamism. After their early defeats at Talana Hill and Elandslaagte, there seemed no great enthusiasm to aggressively push on to Durban, without which the whole venture was completely pointless. Instead, the invasion fizzled out into little more than a siege and a looting binge. Besieging Ladysmith (and Mafeking and Kimberley) proved that Boer generals either completely misunderstood or simply ignored the aims of their invasions. Despite the pleading of some of their more aggressive subordinates, the republican high command showed absolutely no drive or determination to aggressively seize their objectives. In the event, and despite the federal preponderance in numbers, not a single port came close to being captured and thus the invasions can only be considered an abject failure. The republican fascination with sieges was remarkable in many ways. By besieging (rather than screening and bypassing) Ladysmith, the Boer high command forfeited any chance of capturing Durban at a stroke. As we have seen, with somewhere around 18,000 of his men irrelevantly investing the town, Joubert only belatedly released a small number to drive on to the coast. Unsurprisingly, this force had little option but to retreat after the battle of Willow Grange, as increasing numbers of imperial reinforcements began to arrive in Natal.

It is often claimed that the Boer way of making war was more astute than that of the British, but this is not borne out by the results in the conventional war. Firstly, and despite their generals displaying a peculiar attraction to it, the lightly equipped republican armies were completely unsuited to siege warfare: they lacked the heavy artillery and matériel required. As Nasson remarked, "As with the other misguided and drifting investments of garrison towns, what the Kimberley attackers lacked as much as anything were the banks of heavy artillery and reserve shell supply necessary to resolve stubborn sieges successfully."[6] It stands to reason that a nimble, fleet-footed force cannot have a vast siege train so it was nonsensical that their commanders engage in such static warfare so readily or indeed become so "hypnotised by sieges".[7]

Worse still, enforcing an effective siege tended to become a meat-grinder and the federal commanders were loath to take casualties: "any attempt to overwhelm the enemy by running at them in preponderant force involved an acceptance of casualties far in excess of those to which the Boers were accustomed. Therefore, if the offensive tactics of Joubert, Cronjé and Wessels were exceptionally cautious, this was due, at least in part, to a sense that they had to go carefully with their men."[8] While this desire to limit casualties is in many ways admirable, it is very difficult to closely invest a besieged enemy, dig saps and assault outlying positions if you are not prepared to accept losses—meaning the capture of a stoutly defended town becomes an almost impossible task.

The Boerphiles spout that the republicans might have been unencumbered by siege equipment and ammunition stocks, but they more than made up for it by being a fast-moving force not tied to railway lines like the British, and that their generals could deploy their commandos on a whim, flitting them around the veldt to pop up where they were least expected. Of course, this all appears sound at first glance, but despite this legendary fleetness of foot, the invading Boers were actually surprisingly ponderous during the conventional war. The invasion of the Cape Colony was inexplicably delayed by several weeks, and we have already seen how slowly Joubert's men probed into Natal. To have any chance of success the invasions called for a thunderous blitzkrieg, with self-supporting columns bypassing imperial strongpoints, slicing deep into Natal with no regard for their flanks. Instead, the Boer generals opted for a slow and steady plod forward, paying no heed to the enemy reinforcements by then pouring in from across the Empire.

For all the much-vaunted genius of the Boer commanders, the one truly brilliant manoeuvre of the conventional war was performed not by the commandos, but by General French's British Cavalry Division. As we saw in chapter seven, and in a move which totally wrong-footed the republicans, Roberts had French's division swing round the Magersfontein defences in a wide right hook, completely cutting off Cronjé's force. The drive and aggression of this move was astounding, with horses literally dropping from exhaustion as French harried his men to achieve their objectives. Leaving Cronjé bewildered, it was a bold and daring masterstroke, unmatched by anything else in the war and showed that there were senior imperial commanders who were every bit as inventive and dynamic as the very best of their republican counterparts. It is also worth noting that though the rapid advance of French's cavalry outflanked the Boer defences, this would have meant nothing if his horsemen had not been followed up by the slower-moving British infantry divisions. Without these heavy units, with their well-provisioned artillery batteries, the freshly captured positions could not have been held, a pitched battle could not have been fought and Cronjé would have escaped.

In contrast to the more multi-faceted imperial forces, the Boers generals commanded a very one-dimensional army. Though generally employed far more timidly, their commandos were akin to imperial mounted units, like French's Cavalry Division, but the republicans had no equivalent to the British infantry, men who were backed by a formidable artillery train and who would storm defences, more often than not carrying them at bayonet point. No less a man than General Ben Viljoen wrote admiringly of their tactics in assault, of their use of cover and their coordination with artillery, admitting that British infantry attacks were "very difficult indeed to repulse".[9] The federals, in contrast, were extremely formidable in defence as long as their flanks were secure, but time and again they proved quite simply unable—or unwilling—to assault.

Though brilliant, French's flanking move was certainly an aberration and it is true to say that the British army was by and large tied to the railway lines throughout the conventional war. It must be remembered that this was a period where machine guns and quick-firing artillery were new arrivals on the battlefield, and aside from a handful of traction engines, everything which could not be put on a train had to be moved by horses or oxen, all of which needed fodder, and the men who fed them needed to be fed, and so on. To switch an axis of attack was a vast undertaking, unless, like the republicans, you employed much lighter forces. The downside of this option, however, was that you needed a large, artillery-heavy, well-provisioned force to break through and actually achieve anything, leading to a classic Catch-22 situation: the longer you took to switch your axis of advance, the more time the enemy had to prepare and thus the more men you needed to be successful, *ad nauseam*.

So does this mean that the Boer method of conventional warfare was therefore better? Patently not. Theoretically, their light, more manoeuvrable forces should have been able to pull off masterstrokes like that of French's Cavalry Division, but in reality they never did. The invaders of Natal, for example, did not cut White off in Ladysmith in a brilliant *coup de main*, but rather by a very methodical advance which permitted imperial naval guns and reinforcements to arrive (and refugees to escape) before the net was finally closed. And even then, with the lion's share of Natal's imperial forces bottled up in Ladysmith, there was no thought of screening the town and thrusting forward with their famed light horsemen to overrun the rest of the colony. With this opportunity missed, the republican commanders—for all their fast-moving mounted units—were also surprisingly passive in their defence of the Tugela line. Despite Botha (one of the 'greats', according to Pakenham) effectively being in command by the end, no attempts were made to mount raids to disrupt Buller's supply lines or flanks, or even just to give him something else to think about. Instead, Botha's plan was essentially to sit and wait, making no use of his mounted units and completely forfeiting the initiative to Buller. The imperial forces were thus permitted to steadily build up their supplies and ready themselves for their counter-strokes which could be delivered wherever and whenever Buller chose.

Indeed, taking the conventional war as a whole, the Boer commanders' way of making war proved fatally flawed. Their units' lack of heavy support, together with a combination of timid leadership, a determination never to be cut off and an aversion to taking losses, meant the republican invasions essentially achieved nothing except starting a war that they ultimately lost. The Boers were not able take a single major town, failed in all three major sieges and were halted, thrown back and comprehensively defeated by the ponderous imperial forces so hastily maligned by modern writers. The one thing they did prove is that there is little point skipping about the veldt if you cannot achieve much when you get there.

Even their most devoted apologists could not reasonably claim that the republicans were well served by their generals during the conventional war. Cronjé and Prinsloo on the western front, and Joubert, Meyer and Erasmus in Natal were all inadequate. Boer general Ben Viljoen put it bluntly: "if we younger commanders had had more authority in the earlier stages of the war, and had less to deal with arrogant and stupid old men, we would have reached Durban and Cape Town."[10]

The idea of tying up 6,000 men and a dozen guns in a siege of Mafeking seems to have been Cronjé's: de la Rey begged him to leave a screening force of "no more than 1,000 Boers" and press on. Instead, and at the most critical point in the war, Cronjé wasted a large chunk of the republican armies by sitting outside Mafeking for weeks with paltry effort to storm the town. Apologists seek to excuse Cronjé's inactivity by claiming that Kruger ordered him not to attack Mafeking if an assault would lose more than fifty lives; this seems to be a completely unfounded excuse for his idleness, with no record of Kruger issuing such a peculiar order.[11] Despite his propensity for dithering, the one thing Cronjé did not lack, however, was self-confidence. Later, while basking the warmth of his victory at Magersfontein (which came after three straight defeats for the Boers on the western front), he declared that Joubert had offered him more men and guns before the battle. Cronjé's answer, or so he grandly claimed, was, "Men I don't require, and guns I will take from the British,"[12]—a plan that did not work too well at Paardeberg.

When Cronjé did finally bow to pressure from Kruger and advanced with several thousand men, he left the besieging force in the hands of General J. P. Snyman.[13] Amazingly, Snyman would prove to be even worse at prosecuting the siege than had Cronjé. Happily settling in for the long haul, his utter lack of energy and determination was such that, while Baden-Powell would become the toast of the Empire, Snyman and his men would "become the scorn of the rest of the Boer army".[14] After months of inactivity and with an imperial relief column finally approaching, Kruger's grandson, Commandant Sarel Eloff, arrived on the scene and proposed storming the town before the siege could be raised. Eloff's plan called for him to lead a force of 700 in a night attack,* but such was his mistrust of his general that he demanded Snyman put in writing that he would move to reinforce him on a pre-arranged signal.[15] In the event, Snyman was happy to leave young Eloff to his fate and made no attempt to actively support the last-ditch attack. When his officers urged him to move up in support as promised, Snyman simply muttered, "tomorrow is another day." A furious Kruger was later informed of Snyman's spineless and incompetent performance: his first reaction was to ask if the general had been drunk.[16]

Snyman might well have been the worst Boer general of the war, but Joubert proved little better. As we have seen, Joubert refused to order a pursuit of the retreating imperial forces on Mournful Monday, completely missing his chance to inflict a knockout blow on the British.[17] When asked why, the old man replied, "When God holds out a finger, don't take the whole hand,"— hardly the soundest basis for a military decision. Joubert later justified calling off the invasion of Natal on the strength of two Boers being killed by lightning at the battle of Willow Grange—'*Slim*' Piet told his astonished men that this "was an infallible sign from the Almighty that the commandos were to proceed no further".[18]

Another Boer general who was more cut out to be a Sunday school teacher than a military commander was General D. J. E. 'Maroela' Erasmus. We met Erasmus earlier when, during the first battle of the war, he had sat passively atop Impati Hill while imperial troops stormed to victory at nearby Talana. Later in the war a Prussian major attached to the Boer forces, and captured during Buller's push to clear northern Natal, told an equally damning tale of General Erasmus. As imperial troops assembled in the area of Laing's Nek and Botha's Pass, the Prussian urged Erasmus to reposition his artillery to counter the deployments: "he thought for a minute and said: 'No, I will not send guns, it is a Sunday and God will stop them.'"[19]

---

* though only 240 bothered turning up on the night

So then, why is it that imperial commanders get so lambasted as incompetent fools, blundering from one disaster to another? Was their record really so much worse than that of their opponents? Buller—the man most often held up as the epitome of the stupidity of the British officer class—certainly did not cover himself with glory in Natal. He has been rightly criticized for permitting the Boers to escape after the relief of Ladysmith and, rather less fairly, for taking several attempts to break through to the town in the first instance. It is often forgotten, however, that Buller ultimately broke through by defeating Botha at Tugela Heights.* The magnitude of this undertaking is generally underestimated: most simply dismiss the achievement because of Buller's weight of numbers, but this is to completely misunderstand warfare of the period. After several hundred pages of delighting in tales of imperial 'humiliation', even Pakenham belatedly admits, "the reason for those humiliating reverses was not the marksmanship of the Boers, not their better guns or rifles, not the crass stupidity of the British generals … It was that the smokeless, long-range, high-velocity, small-bore magazine bullet from rifle or machine gun—plus the trench—had decisively tilted the balance against the attack and in favour of defence."[20] In this he is absolutely right: new technology had shifted the odds enormously in favour of defending troops and the fact that Buller was able to overcome this was no small achievement. One German observer remarked that it was "a wonder" that Buller had broken through the Colenso defences with just 30,000 men.[21] And even Pakenham confesses that after his relief of Ladysmith, Buller enjoyed "eight months of unbroken success in independent command" and, pitted against Botha in the eastern Transvaal, "manoeuvred the commandos out of a series of Spion Kops with less than a hundred casualties".[22] This is hardly the record of the idiot he is so often portrayed as.

Whatever his other failings, Buller was never unduly reckless with the lives of his men, and the morale of his army remained high throughout, despite their initial defeats. One cannot say the same of the Boer armies. Others pointed to Buller's development of the new tactics which—rather than just a pure preponderance of numbers—proved too much for the Boers. Describing Buller's capture of Botha's Pass, Ken Gillings notes: "For Buller, the most important aspect of the successful outcome of the battle was that he had

---

* and then again, some months later, at Bergendal (sometimes known as the battle of Belfast or the battle of Dalmanutha)

managed to gain a foothold in the Free State and finally break out of Natal. His strategy at Helpmekaar, where he used revolutionary tactics in deception, was repeated on a far wider scale in his operations below the Drakensberg. These tactics were very similar to those used later in the First World War. Could it be claimed that they were inspired by these operations?"[23] In 1909 the French general, Langlois, made a similar observation: "it was Buller who was the innovator in countering Boer tactics. The proper use of cover, of infantry advancing in rushes, co-ordinated in turn with creeping barrages of artillery; these were the tactics of truly modern war, first evolved by Buller in Natal."[24] This is not to say that Buller can be classed as a great general, but it is unfair to deride him as a fool based on his defeat at Colenso, a battle which he called off as soon as he realised things had gone awry and at which, as a result, his force suffered less than one per cent killed in action.

Of the other senior imperial commanders in the conventional war, the courageous and dashing Penn Symons was undoubtedly over-confident and arguably arrogant. White was not the most dynamic of leaders and his over-complex plan led to the defeat of Mournful Monday, but he also played his part by holding Ladysmith for many months. French scored a crushing victory at Elandslaagte, outfought the republicans on the central front and led the Cavalry Division on their quite brilliant flank march. Methuen's victories at Belmont, Graspan and Modder River are generally overlooked in the clamour to discuss his defeat at Magersfontein. Though few would claim Methuen to be a military genius, his record was certainly not as dismal as it tends to be painted. Similarly, and though he was later side-lined, Gatacre's defeat at Stormberg overshadows the good work he did in the weeks thereafter.[25] Roberts's remarkable achievements are generally dismissed as being inevitable because of his numerical advantage in troops (the fact that this same advantage was enjoyed by the republicans in the opening weeks and led to nought is never mentioned).

Roberts was more than ready to adopt the latest tactics while he planned and prepared his counter-stroke. By means of an elaborate deception plan, he pinned the complacent Cronjé in place then unleashed French on his wide flanking march, arguably the most striking and dynamic move of the war but one rarely given the praise it deserves.

A few months later Roberts had shattered the federal armies in a string of actions, and taken both Boer capitals. It is hard to find serious fault with either Roberts or French and surely this pair must be considered the best two senior commanders on either side in the conventional period of the war.

ॐ

If several of the imperial commanders were slow in adapting to the realities of modern warfare, the older Boer generals proved to be as bad if not worse. Indeed, as these old warhorses proved completely out of their depth in the opening months, the notion of Boer strategic brilliance tends to focus on a handful of younger men who emerged toward the end of the conventional war. Men like de Wet and de la Rey led their bands of freebooters in a long and bitter guerrilla campaign but does this mean they were great generals and in what way were they so much better than their imperial counterparts? This legend of these brilliant young Boer generals, and utterly incompetent imperial ones, is certainly perpetuated in most accounts. The method employed—whether consciously or not—is simply to devote much attention to British defeats and gloss over the republican ones.

Christiaan de Wet, for example, is one of Pakenham's great generals of the war, which perhaps explains why he pays scant attention to de Wet's complete and abject failure at Wepener—a battle which we touched on earlier and which occurred as the conventional war gave way to the guerrilla campaign. While Pakenham devotes two entire chapters (thirty-five pages) to Buller's defeat at Colenso,[26] the sixteen-day battle at Wepener gets just nine lines and Pakenham somehow even manages to paint de Wet's defeat as some sort of victory.[27] Nasson takes a similar line, paying little regard to the salient fact that de Wet's efforts to take the town were broken up, driven off and completely thwarted: that he was able to flee before being encircled by the relieving troops[28] presumably counted as a victory.

The siege of Wepener was actually an epic of the war. Situated against the border with Basutoland, Wepener was an inconsequential settlement. Units of the Colonial Division had first moved into the area in late March 1900, and had busied themselves with disarming surrendering Boers and rounding up local troublemakers.[29] Though Wepener was a place of absolutely no strategic value, de Wet's irrational desire to strike a blow against loyalist colonials[30] appears to have blinded him against more sensible and practical targets like the railway or the bridges over the Orange River. Had he not wasted his time and resources in attacking Wepener, there would have been nothing stopping his commandos sweeping into the Cape Colony and causing merry hell with Roberts's supply lines, thereby putting a halt to his advance and perhaps even threatening the British position at Bloemfontein.[31] Instead, and with the Boer lines collapsing to the north, de Wet mustered between 8,000 and 10,000 men* with ten or twelve guns and struck against the worthless target of Wepener.[32] Even a furious Kruger signalled that this would achieve nothing,[33] recognizing de Wet's action for what it was: a significant strategic blunder.

With the approach of de Wet's formidable force, the decision was taken not to hold Wepener itself, but to fortify positions in the hills just outside of town, the siting of these defences being supervised by Major Maxwell of the Royal Engineers. As well as Maxwell's small party of sappers, the imperial forces defending the position at Wepener consisted of elements from the 1st and 2nd Brabant's Horse, others from the Cape Mounted Rifles, Driscoll's Scouts, the Kaffrarian Rifles and a company of the Royal Scots Mounted Infantry. The total force was somewhere between 1,700 and 1,850 men, with seven guns (including a pair of redundant 7-pounders) and six Maxims. The garrison was thus overwhelmingly made up of loyalist South Africans, with the officer commanding being Colonel Dalgety of the Cape Mounted Rifles.

On the 4th April a party of Boers—under a German officer—entered Wepener under a flag of truce to demand the imperial surrender. They were sent on their way, though not before Colonel Dalgety, with an admirable flourish of showmanship, had offered to accept *their* surrender instead.[34] Incredibly, the dashing de Wet then wasted another five days dithering before attempting an attack on the imperial positions, five days which Dalgety used to further improve his position, and which relieving forces spent marching to the rescue. It was an inexplicable blunder.

The Boers finally commenced their bombardment on the 9th and it was not until the 10th that de Wet attempted to assault the British positions and fierce fighting raged throughout that day. All de Wet's assaults were repulsed with heavy loss and no ground was gained, despite the fighting raging until 0200 hours on the 11th. Though the onslaught had been intense, all the Boer attacks were broken up and driven off by the imperial defenders, some with the bayonet. Thirty-six hours of attacks against a heavily outnumbered foe had not gained de Wet a single inch of ground. A defender recalled one of the

---

*   Pakenham curiously claims de Wet had just 1,500 men which is at odds with every other account

initial assaults: "Our men allowed them to get right in and then opened fire at fifty yards. Every man had his bayonet fixed and ready, and at the word they went for them. In less than an hour it was all over, and the Boers were beaten back, leaving 300 dead. It was pitiful to hear them crying. They have not the heart of a school-girl, and they cannot stand a beating."[35] Though the figure of three hundred dead should be taken with a pinch of salt, there can be little doubt that the republicans suffered severely; and this carnage was the result of just one assault in one sector on one day of the battle. It is also worth pointing out, by way of comparison, that the British lost just 143 men killed at Colenso, a defeat considered so costly and humiliating as to be worth multiple chapters in the so-called definitive histories.

As well as the constant sniping and bombardment, and the nauseating stench of putrefying horse carcasses, four days of incessant rain added to the defenders' misery, filling their trenches with water and transforming the battlefield into a quagmire. So small was the area defended that troops in some of the more exposed imperial positions were unable to leave their trenches at any time during the siege. These men survived on the cold food and fresh water brought to them by work parties crawling forward under cover of darkness.

An officer of Brabant's Horse remembered the siege: "We fought all day and all night. The big gun and rifle fire were almost deafening, and as we were entirely surrounded, it was pouring in on all sides, a continuous hail of shot and shell. Towards afternoon they directed all their gun fire to one spot, and blew to bits the schances of the CMR [Cape Mounted Rifles], thus leaving them unprotected, and in the night they attempted to take the position by assault. Although the CMR were very considerably outnumbered, the Boers were unable to attain their object. They had not reckoned of the opposition of, undoubtedly, one of the finest regiments in the whole world, as the CMR are."[36] Another officer remembers the depths to which de Wet's men sank to in their desperation: "Coming across from the CMR lines towards the Kaffrarian lines was a stretcher carried by four men with a wounded man on it. As soon as it came from under the shelter of the kopje on which we and the CMR live, about 1,200 yards from the ridge held by the enemy, opposite the open end of the horseshoe, it was received by a hail of bullets. On went the gallant bearers for about a hundred yards, when they came to a sudden stand, put the stretcher on the ground, and seemed to consult. First one ran about twenty yards, to fall, apparently shot dead; then another did the same, and the third; and the three corpses were lying on the ground. The fourth man fell to his knees between the stretcher and the enemy. The Boers, then satisfied that they had disposed of this lot, ceased firing at them for the space of some minutes, when suddenly the four dead men came to life, rushed to the stretcher, and went on with it at the double, though little columns of dust rose thicker than ever round the devoted bearers."[37]

De Wet appears to have had no coherent plan other than to drive his reluctant men directly onto the imperial trenches. The bitter fighting "continued through the ensuing days and even at night, the Boers once storming right up to the British trenches at 2 a.m. to be beaten off at bayonet point. Nor did a four-day downpour of rain stop their persistent attacks under the lash of De Wet who did not hesitate to use his leather thong [sjambok] to enforce obedience to his will."[38]

It is difficult to to find any tactical brilliance to admire in de Wet's bull-headed approach, and despite his efforts, the republicans were unable to capture and hold any ground whatsoever. The gallantry shown by the garrison was remarkable, as was their resilience to the never-ending pressure; the defenders did not just grimly man their trenches, but maintained an impressive aggressive spirit and even sallied forth to capture one of the Boer guns. In the words of one imperial officer who kept a diary during the siege: "In the Crimea, twenty-four hours on and twenty-four hours off was considered hard work. My men have been ten days in their trenches without leaving them, wet to the skin oftener than not, and day and night exposed to shrapnel, not able to raise their hand above without getting a bullet through them, and yet not a grumble is heard."[39]

While not as famous or lengthy as the sieges at Ladysmith or Mafeking, in many ways the defenders at Wepener had an even rougher time of it. The Boer attacks on the first two days were every bit as intense as anything in the more renowned sieges, with many of the imperial troops in place and under fire for the entirety of the action.

உ

Let us briefly turn our attention to the relieving forces which Pakenham claims were plodding toward Wepener. With more units arriving from all over the Empire,* Roberts was ready for a general advance to clear the remaining Boer forces out of the south-eastern Free State. One column was specifically tasked to relieve Wepener, and would fight its way toward the beleaguered garrison from the south. This column was made up of the balance of the Colonial Division—about 1,200 men and two guns under Brabant—together with half of Hart's brigade: two and a half battalions and a Royal Artillery battery. The combined relief force was perhaps 4,000 men in total, with Hart in overall command.

De Wet had told off about 1,300 men and two guns under Froneman to oppose this advance, and the federals made their first attempt to stop Hart's southern column at Rouxville. Froneman's commandos were driven out of that town on the 15th April. His forces then made another stand at Boesman's Kop, some twenty miles south of Wepener.[40] An over-enthusiastic sally by the Boers saw a group of about sixty leave their positions to attack Hart's scouts, thus exposing themselves to the rifle fire of the main body and being shot down in detail. Though never able to get to close quarters and destroy these blocking forces, Hart's men persisted in driving the Boers before them, with Froneman's units disappearing into the night on the 24th. The siege was lifted by Hart's command the following day, with de Wet fleeing north.

So here was a battle which lasted sixteen days, involved around 15,000 troops in all and which was fought at a time when de Wet's large force was urgently needed elsewhere. Despite a fivefold advantage—better odds than Buller faced at Colenso, and without a river to cross—de Wet completely failed to dislodge Colonel Dalgety's small force, and then retreated in the face of a relatively small relief column.

When faced with the facts of Wepener, there is little to support the notion that de Wet displayed any signs of greatness: it was an action which should never have been fought and which he really should have been able to win easily. So why is Wepener not remembered in the same light as Colenso or Magersfontein, and why is de Wet not regarded as a Methuen or Buller? Why is de Wet's victory at Sannah's Post given such attention while his defeat—for that is most certainly what it was—at Wepener is brushed under the carpet?

It is not as though his supporters can even claim that Wepener was a one-off: a few months later, in late October 1900, de Wet united with other Boer

---

* as well as the 8th Division, newly arrived from Great Britain, Roberts received some mounted infantry from Malta and a unit of 'Roughriders' from New Zealand

leaders, including General Liebenberg, to throw some 1,500 men against the small railway town of Frederikstad,* fifteen miles north of Potchefstroom. Again, and as at Wepener, de Wet bit off more than he could chew. Major-General Barton's column† was present in the town and fought off several days of poorly coordinated attacks by de Wet,[41] with Barton's lone 4.7-inch naval gun proving invaluable. After five days, and with the approach of an imperial relief column, de Wet's battered forces fled, leaving behind a considerable number of dead and captured. De Wet also parted company with General Liebenberg whom he tried to blame for the débâcle.

Later in the war, on the 6th June 1901, a patrol of mounted infantry‡ under Major Sladen rode down and captured a Boer convoy near the village of Reitz. Sladen's haul was a hundred wagons and forty-five prisoners; he then sent a party back to report it to his commanding officer, Colonel de Lisle, who was some way off with the rest of the column.[42] Meanwhile, Sladen moved his prisoners and the wagons into a kraal on a farm called Graspan and awaited reinforcement.[43] A Boer galloper quickly brought this news to where de Wet, de La Rey and Steyn were encamped, prompting de Wet and de La Rey to lead some 500 Boers against Sladen's command, which was by then reduced to about a hundred men. "With forty-five Boers [the prisoners] to hold down, and 500 under Fourie, de Wet and de La Rey around them, the little band made rapid preparation for a desperate resistance; the prisoners were laid upon their faces, the men knocked loopholes in the mud walls of the kraal, and a blunt soldierly answer was returned to the demand for surrender. But it was a desperate business. The attackers were five to one, and the five were soldiers of de Wet, the hard-bitten veterans of a hundred encounters … But the men who faced them were veterans too, and the defence made up for the disparity of numbers … Once more, as at Bothaville, the British Mounted Infantry proved that when it came to a dogged pelting match, they could stand punishment longer than their enemy."[44] The battle raged for four hours. With his attacks repulsed, de Wet resorted to trying to recover the wagons. Even this ended in failure when de Lisle and the rest of the column galloped into view and the Boers lost them for a second time that day.[45] Major Sladen's

---

* Frederikstad is today in the North West Province

† 2nd Royal Scots Fusiliers, 1st Royal Welsh Fusiliers, 19th Company Imperial Yeomanry, 200 men of Marshall's Horse, forty Australian Bushmen and eighty mounted infantry. Barton's artillery comprised six 15-pounders, a pom-pom and a 4.7-inch naval gun.

‡ Sladen's force was made up of men from the 6th Mounted Infantry and the South Australian Bushmen

remarkable defence—or, if you prefer, de Wet's remarkable failure—is not even graced with a name.

But even these defeats pale into insignificance when compared to de Wet's greatest folly. Boer agents had long been fomenting unrest in various areas of the Cape, most notably Graaff-Reinet and Worcester[46] and, in late 1900, it was decided to invade to spark an uprising by these elements. De Wet's initial attempts were thwarted by the flood waters of the Orange and Caledon rivers, but two of his lieutenants, Kritzinger and Hertzog, managed to slip into the colony with about 2,000 men, nearly all of them oath-breakers.[47] These bands roamed about, outrunning their pursuers but otherwise not achieving a great deal. What they did manage was to sufficiently alert the British so that when de Wet finally did sneak over the Orange River on the 10th February 1901 they were ready for him.[48] So clearly had de Wet telegraphed his intentions that one of his commandants, Piet Fourie, said that de Wet was out of his mind.[49] Fourie was right: de Wet's invasion proved an unmitigated disaster. Imperial patrols picked up the invaders almost immediately and began shadowing and harrying them. On the 12th a squadron of Imperial Light Horse took up a blocking position and, after a short skirmish, de Wet was forced to change direction and head toward Philipstown. An attack on the town was driven off by the small garrison after an eleven-hour battle. With imperial columns closing in all around him, the invasion had failed utterly within forty-eight hours.

From then on it was merely a battle of survival. Colonel Plumer's men fell on de Wet's rearguard on the 14th, as twenty wagons were abandoned by the fleeing republicans. On the 16th Lieutenant-Colonel Crabbe's column caught up with them near Houtkraal, where his pair of 15-pounders accounted for sixty-five Boer casualties. "The Boer leaders fled helter-skelter, and we captured 100 ox-waggons and carts, also a spring waggon and an ambulance waggon containing 100,000 rounds of rifle ammunition, 6,000 pom-pom shells, several boxes of 15-pounder ammunition, and 30 prisoners in a tattered state, some of them shoeless. Our casualties were two officers of the 3rd Dragoons, one officer of the Australian Bushmen and one private wounded. It was discovered that De Wet, finding himself headed in the chase, had bolted, leaving the fighting to his lieutenant Froneman, with a thousand men, a pom-pom and a 15-pounder, who had been sent against Hopetown on the Orange River colony border. Abandoned by his chief, this poor fellow lost all but a few carts, hundreds of his distressed horses being abandoned in the flight."[50] Imperial intelligence agents kept the columns on de Wet's trail for 300 miles as the raiders desperately sought a way to scurry back over the Orange River. On the 22nd Plumer—who had outrun his supplies and driven his men on to the point of exhaustion—caught de Wet at Disselfontein. A handful of troopers on the best horses charged the straggling rabble, causing sheer panic. As usual, de Wet escaped but left behind his all his guns and ammunition, and 102 prisoners.[51] Desperate to salvage something from the raid, or save his own skin, de Wet then simply abandoned his unmounted men to their fate and pressed on. These unfortunate foot-sloggers were later caught by the horsemen of the Scottish Yeomanry as they tried to cross the Orange in a small boat, with ten shot down and thirty-seven captured.[52] De Wet and the shattered remains of his invasion force finally found a drift over the flooded Orange and reached safety on the 28th but not before thirty of his men drowned during the crossing.[53]

Less than three weeks earlier, he had led 1,500 bitter-einders into the Cape. After a headlong flight, the few hundred that made it out did so by the skin of their teeth. In the rout, hundreds of their comrades had been left behind, either dead or captive. Their guns, transport and many of their horses were lost. De Wet had been "crushed by superior numbers, worn down by men as inexhaustible as himself, warred against by the rivers, until his mere escape from such odds seemed a military miracle. His error lay rather in the initial strategy of his campaign; in the advertisement of his intentions by the despatch of Kritzinger and Hertzog in advance; by the delay in supporting his forerunners until his opponents had ample time alike to comprehend the warning, to reduce his detachments to impotence, and to prepare for himself. His own undisguised and dilatory march from the Doornberg had but intensified the rashness of his passage of the Orange. Not for one moment had Cape Colony been in danger; and if the exertions of the British columns in pursuit of him had been almost superhuman, it was rather in the fervent hope of capturing his person, the highest prize in South Africa, than of foiling his campaign, the futility of which had been apparent from the first."[54] De Wet's only achievement during this crackpot invasion was in evading capture; hundreds of his men were not so fortunate. Other than proving himself an adept escapologist with a burning desire to save his own skin, de Wet's generalship was, at best, slipshod.

❧

Some of the legends surrounding the other Boer 'greats' also seem to be the products of selective reading. Botha, for example, was driven out of Natal by Buller but is lauded for his guerrilla war victories at Blood River Poort and Bakenlaagte, respectively on the 17th September and the 30th October 1901. Though solid victories for the republicans, neither shows any evidence of tactical brilliance. At Blood River Poort, Captain (local Lieutenant-Colonel) Gough's* small command were pursuing a group of fleeing Boers, and in so doing galloped straight into the midst of Botha's main force.[55] It was a confused, swirling engagement rather than a clever Boer trap, with the British defeat caused by Gough's youthful rashness, and overzealous desire to impress, rather than Botha's military genius. Nevertheless, Pakenham describes Gough's defeat at the hands of a much larger force as "the most humiliating reverse since Clements' smash-up at Nooitgedacht nine months before".[56]

A few weeks later, at Bakenlaagte, Botha, with about 2,000 men,[57] fell upon the small rearguard of Lieutenant-Colonel Benson's† column as they tried to extricate a wagon which was stuck in a drift. Benson, one of the most aggressive and feared column commanders,[58] had himself ridden back to oversee this and was killed in the battle. The 280 officers and men of Benson's rearguard fought with unmatched bravery, the remnants only surrendering when sixty-six of their number lay dead and 165 wounded,[59] and having inflicting heavy loss on their attackers.

Botha can certainly be admired for assembling and manoeuvring his men into a position to pounce and overwhelm this small force, but with odds of around seven to one in his favour, there is no reason to trumpet the victory as brilliant. Botha's large superiority in numbers is not even mentioned by Pakenham[60] and thus remains somewhat at odds with the common perception of the guerrilla war, where it is generally assumed that any actions won by the bitter-einders were against enormous imperial forces. One could of course argue that a great general is one who gets himself into a position to overwhelm the enemy with superior numbers and, while there is a great deal of validity

---

* Later General Sir Hubert de la Poer Gough, GCB, GCMG, KCVO (1870-1963). We briefly met Gough earlier, when he was in command of the Composite Regiment in Natal.

† Lieutenant-Colonel G. E. Benson, RA (1861–1901).

to this statement, it is unmentioned in reference to similar imperial victories.

Botha also does not appear to have been able to control his men in the wake of their victory, with some very unpleasant scenes witnessed as the British wounded were robbed and shot. One witness recalled, "There seems no doubt that though the Boer Commandants have the will, they no longer have the power to repress outrage and murder on the part of their subordinates."[61] It is difficult to admire the leadership of a man who has absolutely no control over his troops and who will permit murder.

However, strangely overlooked by his groupies are some of Botha's other actions in the guerrilla war. In the battle fought at Bothwell Farm in the early hours of the 6th February 1901, General Botha "threw himself with great impetuosity" against the encampment of Smith-Dorrien's* column. It was a formidable target, comprising elements from the Suffolks, West Yorks, Camerons, 5th Lancers, 2nd Imperial Light Horse, 3rd Mounted Infantry and attached guns. Botha rather optimistically gambled on panicking and overwhelming Smith-Dorrien's command with a night attack, confidently unleashing his several-thousand-strong force at 0300 hours. The Boers came on in good style, but the steady British infantry quite simply blew them apart, breaking up the attack and leaving dozens of Boers dead on the field. Botha's men then contented themselves with a pointless long-range fusillade on the British positions, but this was "answered and crushed" by return fire from the imperial troops; the republicans had no choice but to slip away into the night.[62] As well as demonstrating misplaced arrogance and underestimating the musketry of the British infantry, Botha's plan was also hopelessly uncoordinated: the main assault was conducted by the Heidelbergers while a supporting attack from the Carolina Commando simply never materialized, leading to serious recriminations among his subordinate commanders. It is unclear quite why Botha is not accused of arrogance or supreme confidence in the way Penn Symons usually is.

Botha's defeat of Gough at Blood River Poort had occurred during the second attempt to invade Natal. Though it was a telling Boer victory, less attention is given to the actions which occurred immediately thereafter when Botha's jubilant men pushed on to attack the tiny imperial garrisons at Itala and Fort Prospect. Botha's invasion force was about 2,000 strong, made up of picked

---

* Later General Sir Horace Lockwood Smith-Dorrien GCB, GCMG, DSO, ADC (26 May 1858–12 August 1930), he was known as 'Smithereens' and went on to command the British Second Army in the First World War.

men from the Bethal, South Middelburg, Ermelo, Carolina, Standerton, Wakkerstroom, Piet Retief, Utrecht and Vryheid commandos.[63] Opposing them at the twin positions of Fort Prospect and Itala was a small detachment of the 5th Mounted Infantry Division under the command of Major A. J. Chapman, Dublin Fusiliers. Chapman was a clean-cut, professional soldier. At thirty-eight he was Botha's junior by three months, campaign-hardened like his men, and with nearly two years of arduous toughening in the mould of veldt warfare behind him. Unlike the commonly held perception of his fellow officers of the period, Chapman was astute, wide awake and extremely capable, as he had already proved in his successful defence of Utrecht.[64] Despite what loyalist locals misled Botha to believe, the positions held by Chapman's small command were well fortified.[65] Around 300 men with a pair of 15-pounders* were in position at Itala under Chapman himself, while Captain Rowley held Fort Prospect with around eighty-five men.† As scouts and locals brought word of the impending attack, the Itala defenders worked feverishly with spades and picks, improving their positions and digging well-sited and mutually supporting trenches to four or five feet deep. Botha only held back 200 men and confidently split his command to attack both targets at once, rather than dealing with them piecemeal. In the early hours of the 26th September, 400 burghers under Emmett and Grobelaar were flung at Fort Prospect, while Botha himself led the balance of some 1,400 against Chapman at Itala.[66]

The assault on Itala was launched at about 0200 hours and raged until daylight, with the Boers throwing themselves forward through the fusillade and being driven back at bayonet point. In his brief mention of it, Pakenham seeks to excuse Botha's defeat by saying he drove his men forward with "British-style recklessness".[67]

Seemingly even when the Boers lose, such things can be blamed on the British. Casualties on both sides were indeed high, but Botha's men were unable to breach the imperial defences. There was a brief lull in the slaughter at around 0600 hours, as Dr Fielding, the British medical officer, set out to attend the wounded.

Almost immediately, however, the attack was resumed and, if anything, more violently than before:

---

* the guns were from 69th Battery RFA

† thirty-five men of the 5th Division MI and fifty of the 2nd Dorsetshire Regiment

The gunners, who had gallantly manned the two 15-pounders during the night, were too exposed now and were soon shot down. The guns ceased firing. The machine gun on the spur became hopelessly jammed and the battle now resolved into Lee-Metford against Lee-Metford, for the Boers were by now nearly all equipped with captured rifles. The Burghers, with the edge on marksmanship, were technically at an advantage.

A tornado of lead enveloped the post. Bullets screamed and howled, the ground rapidly became covered with a shower of broken branches and chopped leaves, the screams and groans of stricken men and of the pathetic unprotected horses filled the air; dust and earth flew in all directions and the constant ear-shattering crash of hundreds of rifles made a sound to match all the thunderbolts of hell, as the Boers tried to batter the defences to pieces with rifle fire. No cover could withstand this inferno, and men fell thick and fast, yet each attack melted away under the galling return cross-fire of the defenders.

The position was reaching a stalemate and a battle of attrition developed. By now, Louis Botha, realising the importance of the sangared spur ordered that it be taken at all costs. This was an almost impossible task, for 600 yards of absolutely coverless ground had to be crossed. The troops behind the sangars were no mean shots themselves and blew each new attack to pieces before it got far.[68]

Desperate attempts were made to get ammunition to the defenders up on the spur, with Chapman calling for volunteers. Driver F. G. Bradley of the Royal Artillery stepped forward and, ignoring the fusillade, repeatedly carried ammunition boxes up and dragged wounded comrades down. He was awarded the Victoria Cross.[69] By late afternoon, Botha had no choice but to call off the attack. Seventeen hours of heavy, unrelenting fighting had shattered his commando. Chapman—himself shot through the leg—was down to half his strength and his ammunition was almost exhausted. But it was Botha who blinked first and the Boers began to melt away. During the battle, the two British 15-pounders had fired sixty-three shells and the small garrison had blasted off 70,040 rounds of rifle ammunition, about 230 rounds per man.* British losses were twenty-two killed and fifty-nine wounded. In addition six native servants died and four were wounded. One hundred and forty-nine Boer bodies were found, though it is likely others were removed or died later of their wounds. Conservative estimates of republican wounded were two hundred and seventy.[70]

The simultaneous attack against Fort Prospect was a less bloody affair but equally unsuccessful. Two assaults were made against the fort and both were driven off. Despite their preponderance in numbers, the Boers were soon reduced to long-range sniping before withdrawing altogether late in the afternoon. The defenders lost one man killed and nine wounded. Boer losses were estimated at around forty.[71] Botha ludicrously declared that he had only suffered two men wounded at Fort Prospect, which rather begs the question how both assaults were driven off and why his men were completely unable to get into the British position. In a letter to the state secretary on the 28th September 1901, Botha excused these defeats to his government, blaming false information and the unfavourable weather. In the wake of these battles, he had little choice but to call off his invasion of Natal and ordered a general retirement, falling back with a small following.[72]

Assuming just ten Boers were killed during their two failed assaults against Fort Prospect, this would bring the total killed in action for the two battles to 159, or almost nine per cent of Botha's force. It should also be borne in mind that Botha had better odds (around 5:1) at the twin battles of Itala and Fort Prospect than Buller had at Colenso (around 4:1). Also, Botha was not attacking across a river as was the case at Colenso. So why are these actions not given more attention? Why is Buller's defeat at Colenso invariably declared to be a humiliation, but Botha's far heavier defeats at Itala and Fort Prospect not considered worthy of a mention? Nasson ignores them altogether, while Pakenham, who devotes just half a dozen lines to them, contriving an inane dig about "British-style recklessness", considers Botha a great general, but French not.

---

* The true fury of this defence can be gauged by comparison with the battle of Kambula, a bloodbath in the Zulu war, where the 2,000 British troops fired just 66,400 rounds, around thirty-three apiece.

So what of the two other famous guerrilla leaders, Smuts and de la Rey? Smuts served for much of the guerrilla war as de la Rey's second-in-command[73] and, arguably, their most famous victory was Nooitgedacht. Fought on the 13th December 1900, the action was an attack on General Clements's camp in the Magaliesberg Mountains of the western Transvaal. The Boer attackers only outnumbered the defending British by a little more than two to one[74] and though they dealt him a severe blow, Clements was able to withdraw most of his force, displaying what Smuts described as "insight and soldierly qualities"[75]. While Clements certainly extracted his battered command with aplomb, his escape was primarily due to the inability of de la Rey and Smuts to control their men: there was nothing they could do to prevent them looting the abandoned camp rather than pursuing the retreating Clements.[76] Nevertheless, Nooitgedacht is still described as a humiliation for the British.

A few days earlier, on the 2nd, de la Rey had pounced on a supply convoy, making off with 126 wagons and either driving off or killing 1,862 oxen. Yet again, the victory was incomplete. The remnants of the escort, consisting of a small twenty-one-man detachment of the King's Own Yorkshire Light Infantry and two guns of the 75th Battery Royal Field Artillery,[77] occupied a kopje and showed no intention of giving up. De la Rey was determined to seize the guns but all such attempts were driven off: "Encircled by the enemy, the rapidly diminishing infantry shot back as fast as their magazines could be emptied and re-charged. The guns—finely commanded by Captain H. J. Farrell, RA, an intrepid officer, who when many of his men were down, armed the rest with rifles taken from the slain and laid the field-pieces himself— were run trail to trail, and with depressed muzzles shattered the front of the charge at only forty yards' distance with case shot and shrapnel fused to zero. The infantry around the guns showed equal valour. Of the twenty-one men of the King's Own Yorkshire Light Infantry, who formed the escort, eleven fell; but of the soldiers of this regiment it was to be known that so long as any remained alive guns were safe in their keeping."[78] As night fell, de la Rey had no choice but to abandon his attempts to storm the kopje. His men, though they outnumbered the tiny band by six to one, were exhausted and shattered.

De la Rey's success as a guerrilla leader was as attributable to his brutality as his brilliance. Colonel Woolls-Sampson, the British intelligence officer *extraordinaire*, had built a vast network of African contacts in the eastern Transvaal, allowing the imperial columns to hunt down and destroy the bitter-einders in that region. When he later endeavoured to build a similar network in the western Transvaal to track down de la Rey, he found it much harder: de la Rey had ruthlessly cleared the whole region of native families in order to protect his band.[79] But even his willingness to adopt such extreme measures did not mean de la Rey was anything like the invincible leader he is portrayed as today. Earlier that year, he had tried to take the imperial positions at Elands River. Held by just 300 Australians and Rhodesians, with one Maxim and a 7-pounder, the camp was on a slight rise which dominated the nearby water source, but was overlooked by hills on three sides. On the 4th August 1900, a 500-strong commando with four guns, three pom-poms and a machine gun began bombarding the garrison. De la Rey's arrival brought the besieging force to 2,000, with seven guns.[80]

An imperial relief column was driven off and de la Rey ordered night attacks to capture the garrison's water supply, but these were all broken up and beaten off. Nevertheless, on the 9th, after five days of non-stop bombardment, de la Rey demanded the imperial surrender. This was politely declined, the garrison commander allegedly saying, "I cannot surrender. I am in command of Australians who would cut my throat if I did."[81] De la Rey continued to bang his head against the colonials until the 15th when he retreated in the face of another relief column. His apologists claim that, by forcing the British to divert these troops to relieve Elands River, de la Rey scored a great success. There is no doubt that his attempt to capture Elands River interfered with imperial plans to trap de Wet's commando, but this is another case of twisting the facts to fit the myth. Given de la Rey's advantage of over six to one* and his overwhelming superiority in artillery, one would think it should have been a doddle, but the engagement is generally ignored; one website even concludes that the battle represents "a monument to British bungling and ineptitude,"[82] which sums up prevailing attitudes to the war rather well: even when the bitter-einders lost, they are said to have won, and even when the imperials won, they are accused of bungling and ineptitude.

1901 begun badly for the guerrillas in the Transvaal. In early January various troupes of bitter-einders launched attacks against Belfast, Zeerust, Kaalfontein and Zuurfontein, all of which were repulsed with heavy loss.[83] It would be fair to say that these actions are unheard of by all but the most

---

* Some sources claim the defenders were 500 strong and de la Rey was 3,000 strong, but either way the ratios all remain essentially the same.

avid Boer War enthusiast. Though de la Rey is today lauded as some sort of unbeatable genius, even 'The Lion of the West' suffered a string of serious hidings in the first few months of 1901. At the end of January his second-in-command, Smuts, led a 1,000-man commando in a successful attack on the 200-strong imperial garrison[84] at Modderfontein but any military glory was overshadowed by the subsequent horrific massacre of around 200 black villagers. After this, things started going badly wrong.

In mid-February the much-maligned Lord Methuen received intelligence that de la Rey's force was lying in wait for him at Haartebeestefontein, having left his laager only weakly guarded. Lord Methuen struck at the laager first, quickly overwhelming the guards in a night attack during the early hours of the 18th February, capturing the camp and thirty-six prisoners, sixty-seven wagons and cart-loads of stores. Next, Methuen struck at de la Rey's blocking force which numbered around 1,400 men. Though Methuen only had around 900 troops, he launched his attack by sending the 5th Imperial Yeomanry against the western Boer positions. When the 5th were unable to make any headway because of the hotness of the fire, Methuen then sent the 10th Imperial Yeomanry and the Victorian Bushmen against the other flank, their attack supported by four field guns. The attack was brilliantly delivered and the crest was taken. After a counter-attack led by de la Rey failed, the republicans abandoned their positions and retreated. The road to Klerksdorp thus lay open. Lord Methuen marched into town the following day "with all his forces and an immense mass of captured stock, forage and Boer families".[85]

A Boer attack on Lichtenburg on the 3rd March 1901 also ended in dismal failure.[86] De la Rey and Smuts led some 1,500 men against the 600-strong garrison, the defenders consisting of a detachment of Paget's Horse and three companies of the 1st Battalion Northumberland Fusiliers. The garrison as a whole was under the command of Lieutenant-Colonel C. E. Money of the Northumberlands.[87] Initially all went well as the bitter-einders pushed forward and attempted to rush the British pickets—outposts which were widely separated because of the extensive perimeter of the town's defences. The Boers planned to surround each in turn and cut them off from all communications with headquarters. The pickets, however, were strongly entrenched and the Tommies fought valiantly. Despite twenty-four hours of effort, de la Rey got nowhere. The steady, unflappable northerners proved more than a match for de la Rey's guerrillas and the commandos retreated, having suffered around sixty casualties and leaving seven prisoners behind. The impact on their morale remains unquantified.

Chastened perhaps by their inglorious defeat at Lichtenburg, de la Rey and Smuts turned their attention to easier targets. On the 22nd March 1901 de la Rey, with 500 men and three guns, pounced on a patrol of the Imperial Light Horse under Major C. J. Briggs (King's Dragoon Guards). Despite their being at a disadvantage of at least two to one,[88] the Imperial Light Horsemen "by virtue of their steadiness and gallantry ... succeeded in withdrawing themselves and their pom-pom without a disaster. With Boers in their front and Boers on either flank they fought an admirable rearguard action. So hot was the fire that A squadron alone had twenty-two casualties. They faced it out, however, until their gun had reached a place of safety, when they made an orderly retirement towards Babington's* camp, having inflicted as heavy a loss as they had sustained".[89] One eye-witness stated that the ILH had "knocked the stuffing out of De la Rey near Klerksdorp ... Our fellows had a warm time of it, but being well handled by Major Briggs beat off the attack ... [the Boers] charged right through the Imperial Light Horse, whose ammunition was exhausted, but were driven back by the fire of about twenty-five men who were holding the horses."[90]

If his inability to defeat this small patrol in the open was not enough to shake de la Rey's confidence, the Imperial Light Horse quickly exacted their revenge. Early on in the morning of the 24th, these ILH squadrons formed part of Colonel Gray's vanguard of Babington's column which caught part of De la Rey's commando strung out on the move in the open near Wildfontein.[91] There was a slight moment of disbelief on both sides, but Colonel Gray reacted by far the better and ordered the charge. With a yell, his horsemen dug in their spurs and galloped toward the bewildered bitter-einders. The Boers attempted to get one of their guns into action but it was quickly overwhelmed by the charging horsemen. The rest of the commando broke and fled in a panic-stricken rout, their guns and wagons abandoned in their flight:[92] "Hardly a shot was fired at the pursuers, and the riflemen seem to have been only too happy to save their own skins. Two field guns, one pom-pom, six maxims, fifty-six wagons and 140 prisoners were the fruits of

---

*   Later Lieutenant-General Sir James Melville Babington (31 July 1854–15 June 1936) KCB, KCMG. After the war, Babington commanded the New Zealand Defence Force and during the First World War he commanded the 23rd Division before being promoted to commander of imperial forces in Italy.

that one magnificent charge, while fifty-four stricken Boers were picked up after the action. The pursuit was reluctantly abandoned when the spent horses could go no farther. While the vanguard had thus scattered the main body of the enemy a detachment of riflemen had ridden round to attack the British rear and convoy. A few volleys from the escort drove them off, however, with some loss. Altogether, what with the loss of nine guns and of at least 200 men, the rout of Haartebeestefontein was a severe blow to the Boer cause."[93] Though de la Rey lost all his guns and a couple of hundred of his men, and just like de Wet, he did manage to successfully do what he always proved best at: avoiding capture himself. And if this string of defeats was not bad enough, less than a fortnight later imperial troops rushed Smuts's laager in daylight, capturing another two guns and thirty prisoners.[94]

The pair of 15-pounders taken from de la Rey that day were two of those captured at Colenso,[95] but, for whatever reason, the action at Wildfontein* is not deemed to deserve anything approaching the sort of attention lavished on Colenso, or any other imperial reverse, for that matter. Indeed, de la Rey's string of defeats in March 1901 simply goes unmentioned in most current histories of the war.

So if most recent histories of the conflict give a distinctly unbalanced account of the guerrilla war, what *was* actually happening? Though he became especially feared, Babington's hard-riding column was not the only imperial force inflicting defeats on the republican bands: "All over the country small British columns had been operating during these months—operations which were destined to increase in scope and energy as the cold weather drew in. The weekly tale of prisoners and captures, though small for any one column, gave the aggregate result of a considerable victory. In these scattered and obscure actions there was much good work which can have no reward save the knowledge of duty done. Among many successful raids and skirmishes may be mentioned two by Colonel Park from Lydenburg, which resulted between them in the capture of nearly 100 of the enemy, including Abel Erasmus of sinister reputation."[96]

---

* The action is known variously as Wildfontein and Haartebeestefontein, which creates considerable confusion, as both the two earlier actions are also sometimes referred to as Haartebeestefontein.

During the few days that a correspondent of the London *Times* rode with them, Colonel Woolls-Sampson's men captured a Boer commandant and forty-nine men of the Pretoria Commando one day then, the same night, another twenty. By the end of the sweep, the 'bag' was 105 bitter-einders and some thousand cattle,[97] and all in actions without a name that no one has ever heard of. It was a grinding war of attrition and the commanders of the British flying columns generally proved rather good at it.

One who proved especially effective in the guerrilla phase was General French. If we consider the conventional and guerrilla wars together, one could certainly say that Methuen and Buller had a somewhat mixed records— though Buller departed South African before the guerrilla war really got into full swing. The same cannot be said of General French, however. As we have seen, though outnumbered, he fought and beat the Boers at their own game on the central front before leading his Cavalry Division in the most striking move of the war. French remained in South Africa and continued this good work into the guerrilla war. Despite truly atrocious weather, a sweep through the eastern Transvaal in the first months of 1901 saw a never-ending series of successes. By the end of February, French reported his monthly results as being 292 Boers killed or wounded, 500 captured, three guns and one Maxim taken, together with 600 rifles, 4,000 horses, 4,500 trek oxen, 1,300 wagons and carts, 24,000 cattle and 165,000 sheep. The vast expanse of the eastern veldt was dotted with the broken and charred wagons of the enemy.[98] Though spread out over a month, French's achievements in February 1901 were as decisive as any of the much-heralded republican triumphs of Black Week, yet remain virtually unknown.

Elsewhere, in the first couple of days of March, Dartnell's column bagged a Maxim and fifty prisoners, and Smith-Dorrien's another eighty. French reported fifty more prisoners on the 3rd March. Just three days later, French captured two more guns and, shortly thereafter, he reported having inflicted another forty-six casualties and taken 146 prisoners, 500 more wagons and a large number of sheep and oxen. The indefatigable French pushed on to Vryheid by the end of March, his supplies suffering as the incessant rain made wagon transport nigh on impossible. Nevertheless, by the end of the month, he reported inflicting another seventeen casualties and capturing 140 prisoners, one gun and two pom-poms. On the 4th April, French captured the last Boer artillery piece in the region and 200 more bitter-einders surrendered.[99] In total, French's drive through the eastern Transvaal netted a bag of 1,100 Boers killed or captured, and the seizing of seven guns, two Maxims, two pom-poms and thousands of horses.[100] In an unrelenting series of nameless, unknown actions French's men captured a haul of guns and prisoners unmatched by any victory of the bitter-einders—ever—and it was a blow from which the guerrillas never recovered. French's sweep puts the achievements of de Wet and de la Rey, or guerrilla war 'humiliations' like Nooitgedacht and Tweebosch, firmly into perspective.

And, furthermore, French was not alone. He was well served by excellent subordinates, the men who led his flying columns and chased down the bitter-einders: "On the 22nd September French sent Roberts the names of officers who had done well at the head of columns, or in command of groups. Of the eighteen listed by French, few ended their careers below the rank of Lieutenant-General, and two—Allenby and Haig—became Field Marshals."[101]

When French took command of operations in the Cape in June 1901[102] he was fortunate to have the services of yet more outstanding column commanders, the best of which was probably Lieutenant-Colonel Harry Scobell.* His columns travelled light: no wagons were used and his mules carried just three days' rations for a six-day hunt.[103] By good intelligence, hard riding and dogged determination, Scobell's column hunted down Commandant Lotter's commando and destroyed it in the battle of Groenkloof on the 5th September 1901. Lotter had been regarded as one of the best of the Boer commanders but simply could not shake the relentless pursuit of Scobell's 9th Lancers and Cape Mounted Riflemen.[104] The commando's hiding place was betrayed by a local Afrikaner loyalist, and so confident was Lotter in his position that only a few guards had been posted.[105] Scobell's attack achieved complete surprise and Lotter's heavily outnumbered men quickly surrendered—fourteen were killed and 126 captured. Far from the bitter-einders being considered gallant heroes by the locals, the people of Graaff-Reinet decorated their town with bunting and cheered Scobell's men as they marched in their captives.[106]

French set Scobell after Fouché's commando in November 1901. In concert with Lord Lovat's Scouts, Scobell rode Fouché ragged, forcing the commando to splinter into smaller raiding parties.[107] Scobell's column then worked with that of Lieutenant-Colonel Munro's to hunt down these scattered bands in the

---

* Later Major-General Sir Henry Jenner Scobell KCVO, CB (2 January 1859–1 February 1912)

area around Barkly East. Both British flying columns were about 620 strong, all mounted and with just a few guns. While they certainly outnumbered Fouché's 500-strong commando, the advantage was far from overwhelming and numbers counted for little in operations to root out the widely strewn bitter-einders. This was not a set-piece battle; it was ongoing and highly dangerous small-unit work, patrolling, following up intelligence reports and chasing shadows. Scobell's success was achieved in dozens of small skirmishes with a few prisoners taken here and a few there.

So when the conflict is viewed a little more dispassionately, it is difficult to agree with claims that there were no great imperial generals or that the Boers were blessed with an abundance of such. The introduction of magazine rifles, machine guns, barbed wire and trenches had wholly revolutionized warfare, shifting the advantage massively in favour of troops defending prepared positions—a situation which would not change until the invention of the tank some fifteen years later. In the conventional war, the republicans were able to take advantage of this reality, not because their commanders were better than their imperial counterparts, but simply because they were the ones who needed to be ejected from territory they had captured. On the occasions when the boot was on the other foot it is notable just how unsuccessful Boer attacks on British entrenchments were.

It is also often forgotten that the guerrilla war did not just simply end, and—though it makes for a handy and oft-used excuse—the bitter-einders were by no means forced to give up because of the "suffering of their women and children in the concentration camps". Indeed, so rapidly had the conditions in the camps improved that any such concern for their families was over those *not* in the camps, but rather for those who remained with the commandos on the veldt.[108]

None other than über-bitter-einder de Wet argued in favour of continuing the war because "morale was still reasonably good, largely because the commandos' womenfolk were either safely in the concentration camps, or could fend for themselves on the veldt".[109] Instead, and as other more realistic Boer generals were prepared to admit, the uncomfortable truth was that thousands of guerrillas were being captured month in, month out as their commandos were hunted down and crushed, one by one, by aggressive, hard-riding and well-led imperial columns.

All in all, Louis Creswicke's assessment of de Wet would seem a more balanced appraisal of the bitter-einder commanders than Pakenham's purple prose: "Though he can scarcely be described as a great general, he may be called a bold and cunning Guerrilla chief; a man whose powerful and dominating personality is endowed with both the magnetism and the passion of a leader. He displays withal a sense of soldierly chivalry, and has striven to contend against the treacherous and cruel instincts of his rude followers. He was present at Paardeberg and thought up the plan to allow the escape of General Cronjé but this was not acted upon. He was in command at the engagement of Sanna's Post (31 March 1900). During the guerrilla phase, he managed to evade the many troops engaged in sweeps against him. He was elected Chief Commandant of the Free State forces. In 1914 he joined the rebel cause and was captured on the farm Waterbury near Vryburg in the OFS. This was the first time he had ever been captured."

And that's the critical difference: the so-called great Boer generals rose to prominence, above all, by virtue of not being caught rather than by what they achieved, a most unusual way to define a successful commander. Remaining at large at the head of a guerrilla band is dangerous and arduous, but still a far simpler task than that of defeating such a force. Indeed, winning a guerrilla war is probably the toughest task that can be asked of any conventional army; it is infinitely more difficult than being the guerrillas. Success is judged by entirely different standards in asymmetric war. For a guerrilla leader to be classed as successful, he merely has to avoid capture and blow up the odd railway culvert. If you can also pull off the occasional coup against supply lines, rear echelon troops or an isolated outpost, you are considered one of the greats. For a leader in the conventional army opposing him, it is a completely different story.

Yet the much-maligned imperial forces in South Africa are one of few armies in history ever to have won such a campaign, comprehensively and overwhelmingly winning a guerrilla war in under eighteen months. Indeed, even those with access to vast resources—like the Americans in Vietnam—or those prepared to resort to horrific brutality—like the Germans in Yugoslavia or the Soviets in Afghanistan—have failed. That is not to say that de la Rey, de Wet and Botha did not cause havoc out of all proportion to their numbers and resources, but then so did the likes of Ned Kelly, Geronimo and Yasser Arafat: not quite the same as being a great general. It is worth noting that, during the First World War, when the boot was firmly on the other foot, Smuts and his South African forces proved no more adept against the German guerrilla-style resistance they encountered in East Africa than the British had against that of the bitter-einders.*

---

* for a fascinating account of this much overlooked campaign, read *Tip & Run* by Edward Paice

Exotically-named 'aeronauts' were sent up in such balloons to direct artillery fire by field telephone.

Searchlights were commonly used to flash signals to and from the besieged towns in the early stages of the war.

"They leisurely descend into spruits, roll across, and wheel up stiff, long climbs, like flies climbing a wall"—imperial forces were also quick to make use of new-fangled traction engines.

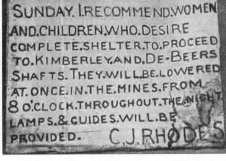

This train is equipped with one of the signalling lamps developed the remarkable Captain Percy Scott RN.

Cecil Rhodes offers the townspeople of Kimberley the chance to shelter in the De Beers mines to escape the Boer shelling.

Imperial pontoon bridge unit. Caught completely by surprise, the British army of 1899 was in no state to fight a major war, and only had eighty yards' worth of such bridges.

"Slogging over Africa"—dauntless, but long-suffering imperial infantry cross a similar pontoon bridge and push on.

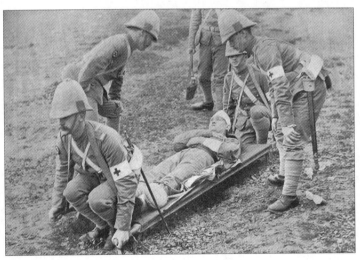

Though imperial troops benefited greatly from the latest medical advances, almost twice as many died of disease than from enemy action—something often overlooked in the stampede to blame the British for all the civilian deaths of the conflict.

Despite the modern-day myths, professional nurses were recruited from all over the Empire to serve in the concentration camp hospitals.

Concentration camp medical staff were well paid and helped train large numbers of Afrikaans girls as nurses.

A happy, healthy and very well-dressed group of camp residents.

Not quite so happy, but equally well-dressed and healthy camp residents pose for the camera. Hundreds of such photos are ignored by most latter-day histories of the conflict, presumably as they do not support the popular notion that the camps were all unspeakable hellholes.

Though often dismissed today as a white elephant, Kitchener's great chains of blockhouses helped to hem in the remaining bands of bitter-einders. Thousands were being hunted down and captured every month by imperial flying columns.

CHAPTER TWELVE

The superhuman Boer

"The sleet of bullets, slanting down the hill, swept our fellows down by scores. But
there was never any faltering. They had been told to take the hill. Two hundred and fifty
stopped on the way through no fault of theirs. The rest went on and took it."
—a Rimington Tiger describing the Tommies assaulting Boer positions, 1899[1]

"The British soldiers have not the individuality or resources of our men,
but for indomitable courage, uncomplaining fortitude
and implicit obedience, they are beyond criticism."
—Captain Slocum, US Army, quoted in Pemberton's *Battles of the Boer War*

"There was one [train attack] however, upon the northern line near Naboomspruit which
cost the lives of Lt. Best and eight Gordon Highlanders, while ten were wounded. The
party of Gordons continued to resist after the smash, and were killed or wounded to a
man. The painful incident is brightened by such an example of military virtue, and by the
naïve reply of the last survivor, who on being questioned why he continued to fight until
he was shot down, answered with fine simplicity, 'Because I am a Gordon Highlander.'"[2]

"These Yeomen are useless. After being some months in the field, they learn a bit; but
by the time they are any use, they have probably been captured two or three times;
presenting the Boers, on each occasion, with a horse, rifle
and 150 rounds of ammunition per man."[3]
—Colonel (later Field Marshal) Allenby, bemoaning British part-timers

During the Battle of Belmont, a sergeant of the 3rd Grenadier Guards
"was hit by no less than nine separate bullets, besides having his bayonet carried away
off his rifle by another shot, making a total of ten hits. He continued till the end of the
action with his company in the front of the attack, where on inspection it was found
he had only actually five wounds, but besides some damage to his clothing had both
pouches hit and all his cartridges exploded. He did not go to hospital till the next day,
when he felt a little bruised and stiff".[4]

"Why the Boers keep on, beats me. Those about here are as sick of it as we are, and, in
many cases, very hard up. A nice old gentleman of 69 came in to surrender yesterday (a
very cold and wet day) with bare feet, having neither boots nor socks left."
—Colonel Allenby's diary entry[5]

"he is a courageous, willing, and faithful warrior, and that it is to his fidelity and
patriotism that the British army may attribute its success."
—General Ben Viljoen opines on the much-maligned British Tommy

"The usual story. Ten English killed, forty wounded,
and one Burgher with a scratch on the little finger!"
—a Bethal resident mocks the state-approved lies
peddled by the Transvaal propaganda machine[6]

I was in a bar in a small town in South Africa a few years ago. On hearing my
accent, a drunken young chap staggered over to me, insisting on telling me
a joke. It was a re-hash of that old one about a general marching along with
1,000 men, and they spot one of the enemy (in this reincarnation, a Boer) on
top of a hill. The Boer shouts down at the general to send up his toughest
man. Then, when he has killed him, he shouts for the general to send ten
of his toughest men, and so on. This laborious process continued until the
general sent 500 men against this superhuman, and one survivor crawled
back down the hill, saying: "General, it's a trap, there are two of them." The
funny thing is that, over the years, I've heard the joke told in various ways,
but the general was always from the army that *lost* the war, be he Italian,
Argentinian or Iraqi. So, leaving aside the salient fact that the British *won* the
war, I knew what was coming and managed to laugh politely. The drunken
comedian then sagely told me that "This joke tells you everything about the
Boer War". I asked why that was and he assured me that "You outnumbered
us, like a hundred to one, but we still beat you".

Were these only the inane ramblings of one drunk then it would not be so
bad, but—to a greater or lesser degree—and leaving aside the obvious fact
that the Boers did *not* beat the British, this remains a widely held view of the
war: that the Boers were such amazing warriors they vanquished the might
of the British Empire or, to those who realize they did not achieve that at all,
it was only by flooding South Africa with millions of men that the British
somehow managed to beat this race of Titans. Indeed, I've heard the British

advantage described as being anything from a hundred to a thousand to one over the years—incremental according to how many Klippies and Cokes the speaker has shoved down his neck.

Various supposedly humorous emails fly about, spreading and entrenching the myth—an example of which is:

> *Gedurende die Boere Oorlog bevind 'n boer en sy seun hulle in die loopgraaf.*
> *Die seun vra: "Pa hoeveel manne is ons?"*
> *Pa sê: "50."*
> *Seun vra: "Hoeveel is die Engelse?"*
> *Pa sê: "So 10,000."*
> *Daar is 'n ruk lank stilte.*
> *Seun sug: "Beteken dit ons gaan vandag weer fokken LAAT klaarmaak?"*

loosely translated as:

> During the Boer War a farmer and his son find themselves in a trench.
> The boy asks: "Dad, how many men are we?"
> Dad says: "50."
> Son asks: "How many are the British?"
> Dad says: "10,000."
> There is a moment's silence.
> Son sighs: "Does this mean we're going to finish fucking LATE again today?"

No doubt all this nonsense serves various purposes: not only does it help perpetuate the 'all British generals are idiots' fancy so endearing to the British Left, but it also supports the superhuman Boer fable so cheerfully accepted in South Africa. Of course, and just like such myths of the First World War, there has to be an excuse for the British emerging on the winning side, and in the popular view of the Boer War the oft-recycled claim that the Boers were massively outnumbered admirably serves this purpose. But were the Boers really so much better than the Brits? Were the Tommies really so hopeless? Is the massively outnumbered excuse valid?

~

The legend of the superhuman Boer did not come about by accident. As Bill Nasson put it, carefully building this fable of martial brilliance became a crucial building-block of a nationalist Afrikaner history: "a myth of national origin"[7] if you will. Few Afrikaans books on the war emerged until the 1930s, but thereafter they started coming thick and fast, all seeking to portray the national character as "wiry, valiant and persevering … it was equally vital to commemorate superhuman bravado, exemplified by the gritty epic of *bittereinder* resistance and the seemingly clairvoyant genius of the younger Boer generalship … the courage and determination of the diehard Boer fighters revealed those character traits supposedly typical of the Afrikaner".[8]

During the war itself, the Boer propaganda machine put the later work of Dr Goebbels to shame. Their casualties were almost always reported as being one or two men and really must be taken with a pinch of salt. Official war news reports found in Bloemfontein after its capture[9] made for amusing reading. Cronjé's surrender at Paardeberg was not mentioned whatsoever, whereas one witness recorded: "out of curiosity I began counting the numbers of British killed that were chronicled after each reported engagement. Very soon I counted no fewer than 190,000—far more men than we had at that time in the whole of South Africa".[10] Unfortunately, as there are rarely any other reliable figures, these insane claims are still bandied about. The republican propaganda machine also carefully cultivated the image of the British Tommies as being cowardly, claiming that at Durban, "a harrowing picture was drawn of the British officers flogging their reluctant and weeping men ashore, who in a few days were to become food for the Boer Mausers".

The battle of Driefontein was fought on the 10th May 1900 and saw the Boers routed from the field, fleeing in what General Christiaan de Wet described as a panic and leaving over a hundred of their comrades dead on the field. To Kruger's propagandists, however, Driefontein was a great victory, and the official war reports spun tales of "many thousands" of dead khakis. Getting carried away, the reports even claimed that the British, "as a last resort, turned their cannon on to their own infantry to make them advance, only to be shot down by our burghers in front".[11]

In January 1900, the Cape Dutch language newspaper, *Ons Land*, added propaganda fuel to the flames: "In the fight at Modder River, at Kimberley, we beat them [the British] at every point; their dead and wounded lay for days on the battlefield. The English themselves acknowledge that they lost more than 3,000 men. We know that it is more. At Colenso, Tugela, we completely crushed them. There they lost 5,070 killed and wounded. Truly God fights our battles for us in this unrighteous war."[12] Needless to say, this was just a little off the mark: as we know, the British won at Modder River and lost 72 men killed. Colenso was indeed a defeat for the British—the writer managed to get something right—but they only lost 143 men killed (with around 750 wounded), rather than the 5,070 he jubilantly squawked about.

Similarly, the last issue of the *Standard and Diggers' News* to be printed before imperial troops captured Johannesburg enthusiastically reported a glorious republican victory just two days earlier. In reality, imperial troops broke through the last Boer positions defending Johannesburg and the burghers holding the key position of Doornkop broke and ran: a telegram to Louis Botha described this rout thus: "*De lafaards die de positie bij Doornkop moesten behouden, vluchten van daar zonder bijna een schoot te schieten.*" (The cowards who were supposed to defend Doornkop fled practically without any shots being fired.)[13] According to the *Standard and Diggers' News*, however, the British army was utterly routed and thousands of their dead and wounded littered the battlefield: "Utter defeat of the enemy and many cannon captured. The enemy left over seven thousand dead and wounded on the field. The burghers fought with great bravery, and lost only two killed and seven wounded. The enemy attacked in great numbers and with two hundred cannon."[14]

And it was not just Kruger's propaganda machine, post-war Afrikaner Nationalists and apartheid-era social engineers who were keen to peddle the notion of the superhuman Boer. The Victorians loved the concept of the 'plucky loser' and it was common for colonial foes to be talked up and congratulated on putting up a good scrap. First appearing in 1890, Kipling's *Fuzzy-Wuzzy* was an ode to the fighting prowess of the Dervishes, but— among others—also paid homage to the Zulus, the Pathans, the Burmese and the Boers "who knocked us silly at a mile".* This tribute to the formidable enemies of Empire was hugely popular. Writing in *Fortnightly*, Francis Adams stated that "no single ballad has had such a furore of success".[15] The British army also had a valid reason for talking up their foes: it helped explain away defeats and made victory all the more impressive. In an even

---

* Kipling was obviously referring to the first Boer War here

more Machiavellian twist, Leo Amery's history of the war was written in such a way that "the story of the war could be made the best instrument for preaching Army Reform" and from a stand point that "unflinching frankness of criticism was needed in the public interest". It should also be remembered that it was Amery who orchestrated the press campaign to remove Sir Redvers Buller from the Aldershot command in October 1901. Sir George White complained that Amery ascribed "successes to accidents or to glaring failures on the part of the enemy rather than to allow any credit to those senior officers to whom blame is meted out with no grudging hand when opportunity offers". Major-General Sir Frederick Maurice, who wrote the War Office's official history, pointed out that Amery's account overlooked the fact that the British army had initially been numerically inferior to a well-armed and -organized enemy and sought to "throw the whole blame on our 'ignorant generals' and our 'stupid soldiers'".[16] Though perhaps influenced more by youthful exuberance than plots to prompt army reform, a young Winston Churchill reckoned that "the individual Boer, mounted, in a suitable country, is worth four or five regular soldiers" and the raiding units raised in the Second World War were famously named 'commandos', a name proudly retained by the Royal Marines to this day.

The success of the legend is such that it has long since passed into common knowledge. As well as the aforementioned jokes, there is, for example, a 'quote' which floats about the internet, though which seems to have no basis in historical reality: "Give me 20 divisions of American soldiers and I will breach Europe. Give me 15 consisting of Englishmen, and I will advance to the borders of Berlin. Give me two divisions of those marvellous fighting Boers and I will remove Germany from the face of the earth." This is attributed to Field Marshal Montgomery, though I have never been able to find any evidence that he actually ever said anything of the sort. The fact that about two divisions' worth of 'those marvellous fighting Boers' were unable to conquer a sparsely defended Natal in 1899 would make it unlikely that as astute a soldier as Montgomery would have made such a claim.

The website for the Clarens tourist route (in the eastern Free State) proudly, yet mindlessly, does its bit to spread the myth: "By December 1899 the Boers had beaten the British in three battles—at Stormberg, Magersfontein and Spionkop. This was followed by success at Colenso. The Boers had also successfully besieged Ladysmith, Kimberley and Mafikeng." It is unclear why this website claims Colenso came after Spion Kop (which was not fought until January in any case), or quite what was 'successful' about the Boer sieges of Ladysmith, Kimberley or Mafeking—all of which ended in defeat for the republicans. An even more remarkable tourist resource is a map of the Natal Midlands produced by South African company, Map Studio.[17] Colenso battlefield is flagged with an information (*sic*, disinformation) box which delightedly squeals: "1,100 British soldiers died yet just 8 Boer lives were lost!" Needless to say, my emails to them to correct this utterly inaccurate fallacy have gone unanswered, so this absolute poppycock has been lapped up by thousands of tourists and day-trippers over the years.

With tedious predictability, Pakenham's account of the war is also full of comments which keep the legend of the superhuman Boer alive and kicking. His index describes, for example, the battle of Elandsriverpoort* as being where "Smuts cuts up 17th Lancers at".[18] Pretty damning at first glance, until you read on to find that only 'C' Squadron of the 17th was there†—the 130 Lancers were thus outnumbered by about two to one. Barely able to contain himself, Pakenham declares the action was "brief, bloody and decisive— as near a massacre as anything that spring" before assuring his readers the Boers were "De la Rey's veterans, their battle skills honed and polished", while the Lancers were "relative amateurs".[19] To further hammer home the fib, Pakenham gives the impression that the Lancers surrendered "when the confused butchery was over—twenty-nine killed and forty-one wounded on the British side‡, compared to one dead and six wounded among the Boers— the victors took stock of their captures".

Though, and like with any action, there is a degree of confusion caused by conflicting reports, the reality is rather different: on the 17th September 1901 a portion of Smuts's commando approached the camp of 'C' Squadron of the Lancers under the guise of captured khaki and opened fire. Nevertheless, the Lancers reacted quickly, and the Boer attack was effectively held off.[20]

---

* The battle took place near the town of Tarkastad in what is today the Eastern Cape. It is also known as Modderfontein after the nearby farm—not be confused with the Modderfontein where Smuts's men butchered hundreds of native villagers. Pakenham adds to the confusion by referring to the account as both the battle of Elands River and Elandsriverpoort. Once more, this should not be confused with the siege of Elands River.

† This can be only be a genuine misunderstanding of matters military, or a deliberate attempt to talk up Smuts's feat; with Pakenham, both options are equally plausible.

‡ It is sometimes said that the 17th Lancers suffered more losses at Modderfontein than they did during their part in the Charge of the Light Brigade – this is not true: 147 men of the 17th Lancers took part in that epic of the Crimean War – only 38 answered the roll call afterwards.

Midway through the battle, another party of bitter-einders, also wearing khaki and carrying Lee-Metfords, approached from the direction of where 'A' Squadron, 17th Lancers was camped. The men of 'C' Squadron naturally assumed these were friends riding to their relief and allowed them to enter their positions.[21] From then on the fighting was confused and savage, but the Lancers gave no impression of being 'relative amateurs'—Smuts himself later said "how gallantly those boys fought against us, many being killed because they knew not how to surrender."[22] Pakenham's quoted casualty figures are also disputed by other accounts, which state that the bitter-einders suffered thirty killed and wounded in the action.[23]

Pakenham also neglects to mention that the Lancers never raised a white flag; Smuts's men had no time to 'take stock' of anything—the battle was still raging as they pillaged the camp—and Smuts's burghers bolted as soon as 'A' Squadron was spotted approaching (this time for real). It was this flight that signalled that the "confused butchery was over". As the commanding officer of the Lancers wrote, "Our men held the position to the last, and not a man surrendered. Out of 130 men, 29 were killed and 41 wounded. The other men were still fighting when the next squadron came to their support and the enemy made off. All the officers were either killed or wounded. Such nice fellows too."[24]

The report by Lord Kitchener—not a man noted for giving undo praise—was similarly fulsome: "taken at a great disadvantage, our men offered a most gallant resistance, and worthily maintained the traditions of their regiment … the Boers … also suffered heavily before the approach of another squadron of the 17th Lancers compelled them to break off the engagement."[25] So, though they were certainly badly mauled, the outnumbered and treacherously deceived Lancers of 'C' Squadron fought with outrageous bravery and the survivors were still doing so when Smuts withdrew with the approach of 'A' Squadron. This is not the normal definition of a massacre; indeed, Smuts certainly had not thought of it as such: though his men made off with horses, ammunition and such, he said they "had paid dearly for it".[26]

However, the most bizarre aspect of Pakenham's version is the lunatic claim that Smuts's "new race of giants broke out of the Bamboo Mountains and rode in triumph into the open plain".[27] This is pure fantasy, even by Pakenham's alarming standards. While undoubtedly bouyed by their victory, the reality is that, desperate to get away from the relieving squadrons of Lancers, Smuts's fleeing Boers tried to enter Maraisburg, but were driven off by the local part-timers of the town guard. The following days saw Smuts fleeing in the face of various British columns and his attempts to enter Adelaide and Seymour, and to cross the Great Fish River at Carlisle Bridge, were all beaten off by local forces.[28] Harried every step of the way by the 'relative amateurs' of the 17th Lancers and other columns, Smuts was in helter-skelter flight. A flying column caught Smuts at Oud Murazie on the 27th September, capturing several of his men before the rest fled; the prisoners were court-martialled and shot for wearing British khaki.[29] On the 3rd October a troop of Lancers caught up with one of his pickets and crushed it. On the 6th, Smuts was so hard pressed that he had to split his force, his deputy, van der Venter, striking out toward Somerset East with half the men, while Smuts pushed on with the rest toward the Graaff-Reinet railway.[30] Haemorrhaging horses and men all the while, Smuts escaped: though he did manage to defeat a small force of local part timers and make off on their horses,[31] it is difficult to see anything remotely triumphant about these weeks of non-stop flight.

As we have already seen, as well as this rather peculiar account of Elandsriverpoort, the 'definitive account' of the war simply ignores a string of actions which do not support the myth of the superhuman Boer. The siege of Elands River, the battle of Cannon Kop, de la Rey's rout at Wildfontein and the defence of Kuruman, for example, are either completely overlooked or given scant attention at best. None of this is to suggest that the Boers did not put up a good fight and provide a stern test for the imperial troops throughout the war. Indeed, it was openly admitted that the conflict taught the British no end of a lesson, with bouts of inquiries, commissions and soul-searching when victory was finally achieved. But how much of this was due to the fighting qualities of the Boers, and how much was to do with it being the first modern guerrilla war the British had fought? And was the lesson not to underestimate the Boers? Or not to underestimate anyone armed with magazine rifles and machine guns and who fought by their own rules, out of uniform and with the backing of a sizeable section of the civilian population? Would a guerrilla war fought in 1900 against similarly armed French-speaking rebels in Quebec or Irish separatists have been any easier? Churchill's claim about a Boer being worth four or five regular soldiers contains a grain of truth, though the critical part of his statement is the caveat of the Boer in question being "mounted, in a suitable country". Rather than their valour, discipline or skill, it was the mobility their horses provided that initially provided the Boers with such a significant advantage over the foot-slogging British infantry; but this was quickly replicated by the imperial forces, with large numbers of mounted infantry units being formed. So is there any reason to claim that a mounted Boer was any better than an imperial mounted infantryman? And when the Boers weren't mounted and weren't in terrain of their liking, were they really any better than the Tommies?

⁊

It is often forgotten that, despite the carefully cultivated post-war image, the Boers were by no means a homogeneous bunch of bearded, biltong-eating, bible-toting backveldt outdoorsmen who could shoot a farthing at a 1,000 yards. Of course, those who were indeed tough farmers or grizzled frontiersmen made for naturally formidable—if decidedly individualistic—warriors, men who were perfectly at home in the saddle, hard, resourceful and crack-shots with their Mausers, their martial skills honed by the years of endless native wars. But many others in the republican ranks were tender-footed townsmen, more at home behind a desk or shop-counter than in the field. Deneys Reitz described his comrades in the Pretoria Commando as "mostly young fellows from the Civil Service and the legal offices and shops in the town. Few of them had ever seen war, or undergone military training".[32] This also excludes the substantial bywoner or white-trash element.

As we will see later, not only were the republicans not all the backveldt Boers of legend, many were not even Afrikaners in the first place. There is no reason to assume that these thousands of cosmopolitan urbanites, or the recently arrived Dutch and Irish idealists, would suddenly be transformed into superhuman soldiers by some form of osmosis. Indeed, as all burghers were liable for commando service, there was very little screening of unsuitables or undesirables: while a British colonial unit like the Imperial Light Horse accepted just ten per cent of 5,000 applicants,[33] the commandos could not afford to be anything like as picky. As General Ben Viljoen recalled, "immediately martial law is promulgated the entire Boer adult male population is amenable for military service. In the ranks of a commando one finds men of every profession, from the advocate and doctor to the blacksmith and plumber."[34] So unless one believes that, simply by living in the republics, people were transformed into a master race, one has to accept that plenty of burghers were cowardly, reluctant, short-sighted, asthmatic, flat-footed and generally unsuited to military life—as with any nation.

Within the ranks of the republicans, those commandos primarily made up of men who weren't 'real' Boers were looked down upon. Those mainly made up of backveldt Boers or formed from picked paramilitary personnel, like the infamous ZARPs, could reasonably be considered something of an elite. Deneys Reitz talks highly of those commandos made up of "real old-fashioned Free State Boers".[35] In contrast, those drawn from townsmen or recently arrived Hollanders or Germans attracted scorn from their comrades. When the Hollander Corps was destroyed at Elandslaagte, General Joubert's only comment was: "You Hollanders were probably drunk again."[36] The German Corps was also smashed in the same action, and Joubert and Kruger refused permission for either to be re-formed, the reason given that these European mercenaries, dreamers and idealists had proved to be unskilled at the Boer way of war. One general said that there was an "ineradicable prejudice against the Dutch and German Corps".[37]

As has been mentioned, the republicans often proved formidable in defence, but this is hardly surprising. Firing a magazine rifle at advancing troops from hidden positions and trenches was arguably the easiest facet of warfare of the age, certainly far easier than assaulting such a position. While the field craft and individual marksmanship of many of the federals—especially the backveldt Boers—was impressive, they also proved to be very one-dimensional: adept in holding entrenched positions (as long as their flanks were secure), time and time again, they rarely matched the Tommies' gallantry or skill in attack. A Boer night assault on British positions at Lancaster Hill near Vryheid on the 11th December 1900, for example, quickly settled down to a lengthy exchange of general long-range fire. Despite initially taking the defenders by surprise, the federals showed no inclination to press home their advantage and—on encountering barbed wire and machine-gun fire—were loath to make any close assaults. The death of just one burgher, a C. G. Gunter, in their attempt on the Maxim gun was enough to give his comrades second thoughts. Gunter's death, "though one of only two confirmed Boer fatalities in the entire battle, severely shook the Boers and resulted in a marked reluctance to press home their attacks".[38]

There were exceptions, of course: some of the republicans who assaulted

Wagon Hill did so with great bravery and determination, for example. But even there, this was overshadowed by the fact that many of their comrades did not bother to join in, or did so reluctantly,[39] which certainly contributed to the attack failing and led to animosity between the various commandos. The American scout, Major Burnham,* was a veteran of the Plains Indian Wars and both Matabele wars. He served the Empire in the Boer War and recorded his first-hand experiences of the failings of the Boer system of war: "The Boer was never willing to sacrifice his personal property for the common good, neither would he instantly and implicitly obey the orders of his commanders. He was a shining example of the ultra-individualistic idea, which is both a fault and a virtue. In the early days of the war it was almost impossible for the Boer commander to extract obedience from his men. Every project of any importance had to be talked over and argued about at length that the moment for its successful execution often passed."[40]

Curiously, even the ill-disciplined individualism of the Boers is often held up as being some sort of an advantage over the 'unthinking automatons' of the British army, but the harsh reality is that successful armies are not built from individuals who do as they please, when they please, or those who are disinclined to expose themselves to undue danger. Deneys Reitz told of the chaotic set-up within the commandos: "Each commando was divided into two or more field cornetcies, and these again were sub-divided into corporalships. A field-cornetcy was supposed to contain 150 to 200 men, and a corporalship nominally consisted of 25, but there was no fixed rule about this, and a popular field-cornet or corporal might have twice as many men as an unpopular one, for a burgher could elect which officer he wished to serve under."[41] General Viljoen recalled the bizarre fashion in which officers were selected and promoted: "From these ranks the officers are chosen, and a man who one day is but an ordinary soldier might be the next promoted to the rank of field-cornet or commandant, and might possibly in a few days attain the position of a general."[42]

Despite the myth, this undisciplined free-for-all was far from effective. Time after time, the independent-minded burghers took it upon themselves

---

* Frederick Russell Burnham DSO (1861–1947) grew up in the American West and was a self-taught tracker and Indian fighter in the Apache Wars. Burnham arrived in Africa seeking adventure and, fighting for the imperial cause, served in several colonial campaigns. Lord Roberts summoned him to serve as his chief of scouts in the Boer War and his passion for field craft would later inspire Baden-Powell to establish the Boy Scouts

to abandon outlying positions or refused to join assaults. Others simply disappeared when it suited them and pickets went to sleep or wandered off. Reitz recalled camp life as "a pleasant experience. There were no drills or parades and, except for night picket and an occasional fatigue party to the railway depot to fetch supplies, there were no military duties. Our commando received many fresh drafts ... but discipline was slack, and there was a continual stream of burghers going home on self-granted leave, so that we never knew from day to day what strength we mustered".[43]

Viljoen's reminiscences dispel the highly popular belief that the federal armies were blessed with far better junior officers than Sandhurst could produce: "The Boer officers can be divided into two classes—the brave and the cowardly. The brave officer fights whenever he gets the chance, whereas his chicken-hearted brother always waits for orders and makes elaborate plans to escape fighting. It is quite easy in the Boer Army to succeed in the course adopted by the latter class, and it is not infrequently occurred that the Boers preferred this class of officer to his more reckless comrade, for they argued— 'we like to serve under him because he will keep us out of danger'. And just as the officers could be divided, so could the men."[44]

With troops who came and went as they liked, or disappeared whenever a dangerous mission was whispered about, and junior officers who made 'elaborate plans' to avoid combat, it proved impossible for the republican generals to coordinate their attacks: commanders could never be sure how many of their men would deign to turn up, a state of affairs that would quite simply have been unthinkable in the British army. As we saw earlier, out of 700 Boers tasked for a last-ditch assault on Mafeking, for example, only 240 bothered showing up.[45]

Orders were ignored when looting opportunities presented themselves and, by the time of the guerrilla war, many of the so-called commandos were little more than lawless gangs of bandits.[46] Discipline and obedience of orders is considered essential by militaries all over the world, and none has rushed to copy the chaotic rabble that epitomized the republican forces during the conflict.

Contrary to the legend of the sturdy, unflappable burgher, this almost complete lack of discipline was an issue throughout the war. As we have seen, at Talana Hill, hundreds of republicans simply ran away as soon as the Royal Artillery opened up on them. At Colenso the Boers refused to occupy outlying positions, and their lack of discipline meant that Botha's trap was prematurely sprung. The same thing had happened at Modder River, and at Spion Kop many of the republicans decided they had had enough and started trekking off midway through the battle. Indeed, even when they were not in the face of the enemy, there was still a chance that panic might spread through the undisciplined federal forces: "One night before they came to the positions they took up, at Polfontein, about eight o'clock in the evening, the Boers were being harangued by the predikant. He was in the middle of his sermon when a stampede of horses took place. The noise of the horses' feet sounded as if a charge of cavalry was coming on, the burghers raised a shout 'heir kom de Engelsh'. Clergyman and congregation fled helter skelter to their wagons. Some could not find their rifles, others under the wagons, calling on the name of the Lord to deliver them from the enemy. One man, he told me, whom I know well, and a great warrior in his own estimation, clinging on to the wagon wheel, could not hold his rifle he was in such a shivering funk, calling for some whisky to steady his nerves. A young fellow he saw with an iron pot on his head, another instead of putting the cartridge into the magazine of his rifle was trying to push it down the muzzle."[47]

This abject Boer terror of British cavalry was a feature throughout the conflict; indeed, this dread afflicted even their hard core. We saw how de la Rey's column abandoned their guns and were routed when charged at Wildfontein and how de Wet's men fled from half a dozen troopers during his absurd invasion of the Cape. In another remarkable charge just twenty men of the 5th Dragoon Guards surprised and routed a commando of four hundred.[48] In an even more astounding incident a mix-up in orders saw Lieutenant Grant of the 12th Lancers conduct a solo charge against a laager of bitter-einders. Despite being charged by just a single horseman, the Boers broke in confusion and panic. Grant shot three, killing two and wounding the third; three others surrendered and in the chaos their comrades were so spooked that they began shooting at each another in panic. When the bitter-einders finally regained their composure and realized they had been set upon by just one Lancer, they took Grant prisoner and locked him in a farmhouse. Later that night, however, something else scared the republicans and they fled, leaving Grant asleep in the house.[49]

While nothing quite matched the fear the federals had of being caught in the open by British cavalry, their terror of the Tommies' glinting bayonets came a close second. Republican troops rarely hung around to engage in mêlée with assaulting imperial troops and generally took to their heels when the cold steel got too close for comfort. Indeed, the use of lances, sabres and bayonets was considered barbaric by the Boers,[50] a remarkable claim from men who casually shot hundreds of blacks and coloureds in cold blood, not to mention wounded Tommies. Of course, none of this is to suggest that there were no incidents where imperial troops panicked, displayed cowardice or disobeyed orders, but the popular notion of the republicans being some sort of invincible superhumans rapidly collapses before any sort of scrutiny. The simple fact is that the republicans had good units and bad units—exactly like the imperial armies.

Ah, say the groupies, but the Boers were so massively outnumbered that you cannot possibly compare the two. It was, as we are always told, a case of David versus Goliath and there was simply no way the plucky republicans could vanquish the massed imperial armies.*

So let's take a look at just how massively outnumbered the Boers supposedly were. As we have seen, in the opening weeks of the war, it was actually the federals who enjoyed a significant numerical superiority over the British, not the other way round. Not that this reality is ever admitted or even bothers some writers on the subject: Johannes Meintjes, in his introduction to *With Bobs and Kruger* assures us that "By the middle of 1899 President Kruger and the Transvaal made world headlines when they rejected Britain's ultimatum. And by October, it was war: a handful of Boers against the might of the British Empire".[51] Leaving aside the schoolboy howler about who issued the ultimatum, Meintjes wastes no time in reminding us that there was only ever just a "handful of Boers". Seemingly obsessed with this phrase, in another account he talks of "a handful of Boers come to grips with a British army which eventually numbered nearly half a million men".[52] All very damning stuff and fairly typical of most latter-day accounts of the war.

The reality is very different. Incredible as it may sound, the war departments in Pretoria and Bloemfontein (and the federal officers at the front) had no means of knowing the exact strength of their forces in the field. There were no

---

*   so why start a war?

official lists in either capital and none of the commandos had even a nominal roll, let alone conducted roll-calls, so working out how big the 'handful' was takes a bit of effort,[53] which is perhaps why it's easier to tell everyone it was just a 'handful'. However, working on the numbers of captives, confirmed dead and the number of bitter-einders who surrendered at the end of the war, both Walker's[54] and the National Army Museum's histories of the war come up with a very similar figure. The latter gives the total as 87,365, broken down as follows: "the Transvaal raised 26,871 men initially, to which 14,779 were added later, while the Free State raised 21,345, to which 6,264 were added. Both states had a small regular force manning artillery, 800 men in the Transvaal, manning twelve fortress guns, thirteen obsolete mountain guns and twenty-one Maxim 'pom-poms' (quick-firing 1-pounders), and 375 men in the Free State, manning nineteen field guns, four mountain guns and three Maxims ... in addition 13,300 'rebels' from the colonies of Natal and the Cape joined the Commandos, as did 800 foreigners. There was also a Foreign Corps of 2,120, including 500 Irish, 320 Dutch, 200 Germans, 100 Scandinavians, 75 Italians, 50 French, 50 Americans and 25 Russians. The Boer forces eventually totalled 87,365."[55]

While their apologists are always quick to point out that this many Boers were never in the field at any one time, they also overlook four important factors. Firstly, during the guerrilla war, the very fact that the bitter-einders weren't all in the field at once, and turned from guerrilla to farmer and back to guerrilla again as it suited them, in many ways made them much harder to fight. Several months after surrendering, for example, a group of burghers could pop up again behind imperial lines, cause a bit of trouble and then return to civilian life again. This amorphous feature made it extremely difficult to track them down and destroy them.

Secondly, this figure only reflects those who were confirmed by the British as being active combatants. Those who served at some stage, but who had quietly slipped back to their farms by the time of the surrender would not be included. There really is no way of ever knowing how many hundreds or thousands fit into this category.

Thirdly, the enormous number of black camp followers who marched with the Boers is never included. These men performed all manner of rear-echelon military tasks which freed up the vast majority of Boers to act as mounted infantry. While the numbers of signallers, engineers, pioneers and service corps personnel are all considered when adding up the number of imperial troops who served in southern Africa, the thousands of blacks who performed similar tasks for the Boers is generally overlooked. Obviously, the British also made use of Africans as wagon drivers, labourers and the like, but the republicans took this to another level, with many Boers taking their African 'boy' on commando with them: "All behind-the-line services on commando were carried out by black people, who constructed fortifications, herded horses and cattle, drove wagons and performed labour duties in military camps. Many burghers were accompanied by one (or more) of their servants who acted as an agterryer (after-rider), performing such tasks as supervising his employer's horse, loading his rifles while in combat, and in exigent circumstances fighting alongside him."[56] And yet these tens of thousands of what were essentially rear-echelon troops are never considered when assessing the size of the Boer forces. In contrast, the 8,500 doctors and hospital staff of the British Army Medical Corps[57] who were serving in South Africa in 1902, for example, are always included in the imperial total.* Also included are the thousands of Royal Engineers in the theatre which, in December 1900, included a telegraph battalion, two bridging units and three balloon sections.[58]

The fourth factor was the impact of the simmering discontent in parts of the Cape Colony and, later, the potential for rebellion in the conquered republics. The threat—rather than the actions—of tens of thousands of potential rebels still has to be considered when assessing numbers for the simple reason that it forced the imperial high command to 'waste' their manpower in scattered garrisons and on lines of communication, protecting bridges and railways far from the front line. Of course, these static troops and town guards also played a role against raiding bitter-einders so the impact of this intangible threat is not easy to quantify. Though we have to allow for a degree of self-interest in his statement, Kitchener claimed that these garrisons and lines-of-communication units took up so much manpower that only eleven per cent of the troops he had at his disposal was available for offensive operations against the bitter-einders.[59]

So how many troops did the British have available? One figure you often hear bandied about is that it took half a million British troops to beat the Boers.

---

* The Army Medical Corps was formed in 1898 after the Army Medical Service had proved to be unsatisfactory. In 1900 the AMC's commitment to South Africa already included 850 doctors.

Not only is this figure inaccurate, but those who toss it about demonstrate a complete lack of understanding of military matters. It is perfectly true to say that 448,435 imperial personnel served in the Boer War,[60] but utterly untrue to suggest that the British ever had anything like that number in South Africa *at the same time*: there was an ongoing cycling of units and personnel. In contrast, during the war, the 87,365 confirmed republicans did not 'switch out' after a tour of duty. They might have been shot, captured, decided to give up the fight or be lying low for a while, but the big difference is that they did not leave the theatre when replaced by another batch; it was this constant switch-out of units over two and a half years that artificially inflates the imperial total. Claiming that the British army fielded an army nearly half a million strong in South Africa is as stupid and inaccurate as saying that Britain has kept an army of 100,000 in Afghanistan in the modern era—something like that number may end up having served there over the course of the conflict,[*] but there have only ever been 10,000–12,000 Brits in the theatre at any one time. Similarly, though some 60,000 Australians served in the Vietnam War, their peak commitment was just 7,672: no one would ever claim that Australia fielded a 60,000-strong army in Vietnam.

It must also be remembered that this 448,435 (which, for the benefit of those who struggle with maths, is 51,565 shy of half a million) included all the police units from Natal, the Bechuanaland Protectorate, the Cape and Rhodesia, as well as the 8,511 officers and men of the South African Constabulary which was formed after the conquest of the two republics. Also included are the thousands of part-timers who served in the town guards, district mounted troops[†] and various other auxiliary units raised across southern Africa.[61]

Indeed, the very suggestion that Great Britain could send an army 'half a million' strong to South Africa is ridiculous. Though it suits Boerphiles to pretend that the British army in 1899 was some gargantuan Behemoth, it was actually tiny by the standards of the day, certainly when compared to her continental rivals. The British Empire was not held by military might; in 1870 all British troops had been removed from Canada and Australasia, leaving the defence of these colonies totally in the hands of locally raised forces.[62]

---

[*] as of 2009, the BBC reported the total number who had served there was 71,560

[†] These units were formed in some 125 locations. By mid-1901, around 6,000 South Africans were serving in the town guards and district mounted troops of the Cape Colony. These part-timers were called upon as needed, to defend their settlements from raiding bitter-einders. They served in khaki, were issued Lee-Enfields and, if killed in action, were buried with full military honours.

Other than India, the British army was only expected to provide garrisons in small, strategic spots, usually coaling stations, such as Mauritius, Hong Kong and Singapore. This withdrawal of British troops from some colonies in 1870 provided a reduction of British troops serving overseas (excluding India) from 49,650 to 23,941 and prompted an overall reduction in the size of the British army.[63] So the British army was actually shrinking at the height of the imperial period.

The 1893 *Army Handbook* gives a theoretical figure for the standing British army of just 227,300 men,[64] of whom 148,500 were infantrymen and 19,500 cavalrymen.* While the Royal Artillery accounted for some of the remainder, many thousands of others were in non-teeth arms: engineers, pioneers, signallers, balloon companies, railway and transport companies, medical and veterinary units and so forth. One hundred and eight thousand soldiers were based in the United Kingdom, 68,000 in India and the rest scattered across the Empire in garrisons, the largest of which were in Malta (7,500) and Gibraltar (5,000).[65] Ignoring this salient fact, Breytenbach's apartheid-regime-approved, pro-Kruger work muddies the waters by ludicrously claiming the British had 1,053,865 soldiers under arms, a large majority of whom would be available for service in South Africa, apparently.[66] Departing even further from reality, Breytenbach goes on to explain that these million-plus soldiers did not even include those in Uganda, British East Africa, British Central Africa and Somaliland. This is the sort of fantastical nonsense which is regurgitated to explain away the republican defeat.

Moving on from Breytenbach's lunatic rantings and back to reality, the seventy-one infantry battalions which the British army retained in the motherland were theoretically kept at eighty per cent of fighting strength (801 all ranks), meaning that they would have to be filled out with reserves before any deployment.[67] In practice, this was not as simple as it sounds. During a War Office exercise into the deployment of the UK-based forces abroad (without weakening the colonial garrisons), it was found that eighteen battalions needed 180 men to be brought up to full strength, eighteen needed 300 men and thirty-five needed four hundred and eighty.[68] In 1899 the rest

---

* With the calling-out of reserves and militia, the British army could be expanded to 337,300. Fifty-two battalions (1,032 men per battalion) were stationed in India, thirteen in the Med / tropics and five in Egypt. This larger figure should be compared to the three-million-strong army that Germany could mobilize, France's four million and the mind-boggling ten million which could readily be fielded by the Russian army.

of the British army was scattered about the world in penny packets, geared toward fighting small, colonial police actions rather than large conventional battles. It was by no means ready to deploy hundreds of thousands of men to South Africa, or anywhere else, especially with a global Empire to worry about.[69]

As we know, when tensions rose through the 1890s, a report by British army intelligence stated that, in the event of war with the Boer republics, the Empire would need to deploy a force of 200,000 men to secure victory in South Africa.[70] To put this enormous number into perspective, on the 10th September 1899, just one month before the Boer attack, there were only 9,940 regulars[71] scattered across South Africa. So if—as it is currently fashionable to claim—the British were planning some sort of invasion of the Boer republics, they were doing so with less than five per cent of the troops that their own planners said they needed.

As late as the 4th February, almost four months after the Boer invasions, imperial strength was still nowhere near this 200,000 figure and indeed was only marginally greater the total Boer forces available: "the effective strength of fighting men in Cape Colony, exclusive of the seven militia battalions and the garrisons of Mafeking and Kimberley, was 51,900". In Natal, it was "34,830, of whom 9,780 were in Ladysmith".[72] This was immediately prior to the period when Roberts smashed the Boer armies during their Black Month.

It should also be recalled that both Roberts on the western front and Buller in Natal were facing an enemy occupying well-dug-in defensive positions. As mentioned earlier, the odds military planners work on for a successful infantry assault are three to one. The American army today expounds that an urban assault requires odds of five to one to achieve success, and to breach well-sited entrenchments this can be increased to something like six or even ten to one, depending on the quality of the fortifications, terrain and the like. The oft-squawked claim that the British enjoyed overwhelming odds during this phase of the war simply ignores this reality. Indeed, Pakenham does not even wait until that point to start perpetuating this myth, claiming that "French vastly outnumbered Kock" at Elandslaagte,[73] before going on to cite figures which show that French had a three-to-one advantage. Indeed, as large numbers of his force were gunners and cavalrymen (the latter were held in reserve and only unleashed when the battle was won), French enjoyed odds of slightly above one and a half to one in terms of his infantry who would have to storm the positions occupied by Kock's defenders. By Pakenham's own admission, the republicans occupied a "natural strongpoint" and the Tommies would be advancing across very open land: "there was no wood, there were no walls; in fact, there was no cover except the stones and ant-hills strewn across the rolling veld". By any standards, French's force was hardly overwhelming for the task; indeed, it was only really the bare minimum that military planners reckon on for such a job.

౞

Imperial forces certainly continued to pour into South Africa as the war went on: "By the beginning of April 1900, eleven infantry divisions, including the VIIIth (not all landed), were under Lord Roberts' command. Of these, four were in Natal."[74] Another account reports that the pre-war garrison "was augmented by 55,000 on the arrival of the First Army Corps. Late in December came the Fifth Division of about 11,000, under Sir Charles Warren, followed by the Sixth Division of 10,000 men. The Seventh and Eighth Divisions of 10,000 men respectively were shortly to increase the forces at the disposal of Lord Roberts, together with some 2,000 additional Cavalry, 10,000 Yeomanry, 9000 Volunteers, seven battalions Militia, drafts for regiments at the front amounted to 10,000 and about 20,000 local forces. The Naval Brigade was composed of about 1,000; so that in all, roughly established, we were on the eve of putting 184,000 men into the field."[75] This number was beginning to approach the limit of imperial troops that would serve in South Africa at any one time.* In April 1901, for example, Kitchener was "forced to lose many thousands of his veteran Yeomanry, Australians and Canadians, whose terms of service were at an end. The volunteer companies of the infantry returned also to England, and so did nine militia battalions, whose place was taken, by an equal number of new-comers".[76] This cycling-out of troops meant that veteran units were always being replaced by new, green ones.

Though imperial forces in southern African peaked at around 230,000 for a brief period,[77] for the vast majority of the guerrilla war, Kitchener had a total

---

* Brian Gardner, in his history of the siege of Mafeking, claims that, at the time of relief of that town in May 1900 there were only 107,726 regular British troops in theatre.

of between 195,000 and 200,000 men[78] under his command.* This figure included about 140,000 regulars, with the rest being locally raised militia units, police and the part-timers of the Yeomanry regiments. About a tenth of Kitchener's army—20,000 men—was unavailable at any given time due to sickness or leave.[79] Worse still, such was the massive commitment to protecting his lines of communications and garrisoning towns for fear of rebellion that, as we saw in chapter eight, only about 22,000 troops were available for the flying columns and, of these, only 13,000 were in combat units.[80]

By way of comparison, 20,779 bitter-einders turned themselves in at the surrender in May 1902.[81] As the imperials accounted for 29,952 Boers (killed, wounded and, overwhelming, taken prisoner) between the 1st January 1901 and the final surrender, this means—as we saw in chapter eight—there were at least 50,371 Boers still fighting (though certainly not all in the field at the time, obviously) on the 1st January 1901.[82] Suddenly the odds no longer look so outrageously overwhelming as is always claimed, nor are they in any way exceptional for such warfare.

To put these figures into some sort of perspective, in another guerrilla war of the period, American Brigadier-General Nelson Miles was put in charge of hunting down Geronimo and his followers in April 1886. Miles commanded 5,000 soldiers, 500 Apache scouts, 100 Navajo scouts and thousands of civilian militia. This was the force deemed necessary to find and destroy Geronimo and his twenty-four warriors. Fifty years after the Boer War, British and imperial troops were embroiled in another guerrilla war, this time in Malaya. Despite the advent of air support, radios and armoured vehicles in the intervening years, it still took well over 200,000 troops, police and home guard volunteers† to find, contain and defeat some 5,000 communist terrorists.[83] Similarly, over the thirty years of 'The Troubles' in Ulster, a total of 300,000 members of security forces served in the province, containing an estimated total of just 10,000 IRA terrorists. Likewise, in the Greek Civil War of 1946–9, 225,000 government troops—with British and American assistance—were required to defeat around 30,000 communist rebels, whereas the Algerian insurgency of 1954–62 saw an estimated 50,000 rebels triumph over French colonial forces over 400,000 strong.

---

* Kitchener was under constant pressure from penny-pinching London bureaucrats to cut even this

† made up of about 30,000 British and other imperial troops, 40,000 police, 44,000 special constables and enormous numbers of home-guard units

The simple reality of guerrilla warfare / counter-terrorism is that large numbers of conventional troops, police and paramilitaries are needed. The Boer War was by no means unique in this regard. In military circles the theoretical ratio of counter-insurgency forces to guerrillas needed to defeat a terrorist campaign is ten to one.[84] Indeed, this is the figure still used by military planners today; as recently as 2007, the US Department of Defense produced a document entitled *Handbook on Counter Insurgency* which quotes this as the rule-of-thumb ratio for such operations.[85]

According to the accepted military theory, huge numbers of these troops or police will form garrisons and may never even see a guerrilla during their deployment. Their role is to deny ground to the terrorists and to provide reassurance to the civilian population. Others will pass their deployment escorting supply convoys and such like, while only between ten and twenty per cent will be available for offensive operations, spending their tour of duty searching for the proverbial needle in the haystack, actively rooting out an elusive enemy and breaking up his bands. It is simply nonsense to consider the odds in such a conflict in the same way as one does in a conventional war, let alone a conventional battle.

As we have seen, for much of the guerrilla war Kitchener had nothing like a ten-to-one advantage; in early 1901 it was more like four to one. Interestingly, as commandos were broken up and captured and the bands of bitter-einders were slowly but surely destroyed in unrelenting small-unit actions, the odds improved to almost exactly ten to one by the time of victory. Despite Kitchener's supposed overwhelming numbers, he was only able to scrape together 9,000 mounted men to scour the western Transvaal, looking for an estimated 3,000 bitter-einders. With just 9,000 men spread out in small columns and searching an area the size of Wales,[86] and in terrain even more rugged, it is little wonder the Boers were able to slip through the net so easily. In another operation, on the border of Swaziland, it was calculated that 60,000 men were needed to form an adequate cordon in such broken country; finding this number was simply impossible and thus the bitter-einders were easily able to slip through the yawning gaps in the imperial lines.[87]

Equally, there were simply not enough men to garrison all the towns. The

Transvaal town of Ermelo, for example, was initially not garrisoned, leaving loyalists and even non-fanatical republicans in a very awkward position; many of the latter "declared that they would gladly surrender could the British undertake to garrison and hold the place, but otherwise they dared not do so, as the enemy would be certain to wreak their vengeance".[88]

While the numbers involved in the strategic picture are interesting, what really mattered was the numbers on a tactical level: it was of little consequence how many troops were in South Africa as a whole if you commanded a hundred men and were suddenly attacked by 500 bitter-einders. The guerrilla war was the 'war of the sieve': as fewer Boers remained in the fight the harder they became to find and bring to battle. And as long as they stayed hidden and managed to shoot a policeman, murder some Africans or blow up a railway line now and again, the conflict dragged on. The sheer numbers of imperial troops in South Africa meant that the guerrillas could not win, but they could keep on indulging in pinprick attacks as long as a few dozen of them remained at large, in the forlorn hope that the British would somehow decide simply to pack up and go home. The will-o'-the-wisp nature of the bitter-einders— combined with the support they received from some sections of the civilian population—meant that they could often avoid combat whenever they were at a disadvantage, and endeavour only ever to attack when they enjoyed favourable odds. This was the theory, at any rate.

Though there were large numbers of imperial troops in the theatre, they could not be everywhere at once. The only way to hunt for the needles in the haystack was by deploying flying columns of cavalry and mounted infantry to scour the veldt, following up intelligence reports and engaging in vast sweeps. These columns were generally in the region of 600–1,500 strong, so if they bumped into a commando, or were surprised by one, they rarely enjoyed any significant advantage in terms of numbers. Of course, the idea was that when one was tracked down, two or more flying columns would unite and together tackle a commando, but it did not always work out like this. Indeed, all the so-called humiliations suffered by the British in the guerrilla war— Nooitgedacht, Tweebosch, Bakenlaagte and Blood River Poort—were all achieved by Boer forces that outnumbered their opponents. This is not of course to say there was anything wrong with the Boers fighting like this: this is how an insurgency is fought and it made perfect sense for the bitter-einders to avoid larger imperial units like the plague, and only strike when they could assemble such superior numbers as to be confident of victory. Despite the bitching of the Tommies at the time, this was by no means cowardly: it was completely pragmatic, just as pragmatic, for example, as Buller ensuring he outnumbered Botha at Tugela Heights. But either way, the perception that the bitter-einders were always vastly outnumbered on a tactical level is incorrect. And even still, the majority of their attacks were driven off, whatever numerical advantage they enjoyed.

❧

From the very start of the war, problems of supply had been as serious as a shortage of numbers for the republics: hemmed in on all sides by British territory, and that of her ally, Portugal, there was no way that Kruger could expect to replenish his war machine from overseas once the balloon went up. Even had Kruger's fantasies come true and he had gained the support of one of the other Great Powers, the Royal Navy's undisputed command of the seas meant that no nation would have helped substantially in any case. For Kruger's gang to simply ignore this reality and assume that all would work out for the best was sheer insanity.

As we have seen, the Transvaal had established a nascent arms industry in the run-up to the war, but with the loss of their towns, even this could no longer support those who wanted to carry on the fight; those who claim the loss of cities was inconsequential to the Boers overlook this point. Other than small bullet-making cottage industries on farms, the bitter-einders soon had no way of replenishing their ammunition or explosives other than stealing from imperial troops. Some bitter-einders claimed that bullets were actually relatively easy to obtain and could be picked up in the wake of British columns as the Tommies carelessly dropped or discarded them.[89] While this proved enough to sustain small bands of guerrillas, it was hardly the sort of solid logistical plan required for embarking on a war against Great Britain in 1899.

Though they were in a far better position to make good their supply shortage, the British were initially taken off guard and were far from being well supplied either. Of course, this was nothing compared to the dire straits in which the republicans quickly found themselves, but the imperial forces also suffered shortages of matériel throughout the conflict. The army was by no means ready to fight a major war in 1899, with Sir Henry Brackenbury,* director-general of ordnance, issuing a dire warning that Britain was "attempting to maintain the largest Empire the world has ever seen with armament and reserves that would be insufficient for a third class military power". As early as November 1899—just one month into the war—the British had only eight weeks' supply of .303 ammunition left and the reserves of artillery shells would be exhausted even before that. Imperial firms were capable of producing only two and a half million rounds a week when the demand exceeded three million. In some months the director of army contracts was purchasing supplies which had previously been considered sufficient for twenty years. In several cases the arms-manufacturing companies were still two years behind completion of orders by May 1901.[90] Uniforms were quickly reduced to tattered rags[91] and an unattended pair of decent boots might well be stolen by a desperate comrade. Winter clothing and warm coats were described as "a luxury which at that time could not be bought for love or money".[92]

The supply of decent horses proved to be an unsolvable problem for the British throughout the war. European-bred horses suffered on the "thin, reedy, bitter grass" in the dry seasons and suffered from horse-sickness at the lower altitudes and during wet months.[93] Endless, gruelling sweeps took a terrible toll and the wastage of horses in imperial service was appalling. The resulting shortage was a significant handicap during the guerrilla war, with even the flying columns struggling to find sufficient steeds to mount all their men. Obviously, this meant that such a column was reduced to moving at the pace of an infantryman, giving it little or no chance to catch mounted bitter-einders. Even illustrious cavalry regiments were unable to find and care for enough horses for all their troopers: Colonel Allenby's diary of the guerrilla war recorded, "I have lost 70 horses in two days"[94] and, later, "I've lost 32 horses in nine days, only two of which were lost in action. The rest died from exhaustion and short food."[95] In 1901 monthly reports showed that the 5th Dragoon Guards boasted only 340 horses for 373 men. The 13th Hussars was better served with 578 horses for 544 men, but even with this number of remounts and spares, much of the regiment was reduced to following their comrades on foot after a fortnight's hard campaigning.[96]

In March 1902, after Methuen's defeat at Tweebosch, the self-loathing young radical Lloyd George delightedly wrote that the "English here are like

---

* General Sir Henry Brackenbury, GCB, KCSI (1837–1914)

things with their tails cut off".[97] He like took great joy in the oft-made claims that the British army was unworthy of a great power and that it lurched from one catastrophe to another, utterly outfought by the plucky Boers. It's an appealing notion to those who want to believe it, but it completely ignores the reality that, despite all manner of disadvantages, the British fought and won a guerrilla war 6,000 miles from their home base. By contrast, the French had to rent shipping from Britain in order to invade Madagascar in 1895, the Germans were unable to contribute even a battalion to the international peacekeeping operation on Crete in 1897, and the United States experienced extreme logistic difficulties in invading Cuba, just ninety miles from the American coast, in 1898.[98]

The war certainly stretched the British army to the very limit: by March 1900, for example, only one regular infantry battalion remained in the UK, leaving the volunteer force as the only additional defence against possible invasion. Maligned by the leftist press at home and ravaged by sickness, the hard-pressed and poorly supplied Tommies and Jocks nevertheless persevered, winning the conventional campaign within a few months, before going on to defeat the Boer guerilla forces in the hardest sort of war—and without anything like the overwhelming odds of the modern mythology.

CHAPTER THIRTEEN

Hidebound by tradition

"They are trying to render the officer less distinctive; all medal ribbons to be taken off,
Sam Browne belts under the jacket, buttons dulled, also scabbards. Infantry officers'
swords are to be taken away and they are to carry carbines … All the pipeclay has been
taken off the men's belts and haversacks are being stained with Condy's fluid."
—diary entry of the 21st November 1899[1]

"I consider that the British infantry bore the brunt of the fighting of the War, especially in
its earlier stages. Where the cavalryman failed to break through our lines the infantryman
stepped in and paved the way for him. We found we could always better
stand an attack from cavalry than from infantry."
—Ben Viljoen describes how formidable were the Tommies in attack[2]

"When the King's Royals went into action their Regimental dog accompanied them as
usual. He has never been out of the firing line, and has never had a scratch."
—war correspondent Donald McDonald reporting on the action of Wagon Hill[3]

"Let us admit it fairly, as a business people should,
We have had no end of a lesson; it will do us no end of good,
Not on a single issue, or in one direction or twain,
But conclusively, comprehensively, and several times and again."
—Rudyard Kipling's assessment of the Boer War

"For 'eaven's sake, sir, dismount. Your 'andle bar's drawing fire."
—a Tommy admonishing a correspondent whose shiny bicycle was reflecting the sun[4]

"All well. Four hours bombardment. One dog killed. BADEN-POWELL."
—message from beleaguered Mafeking, October 1899[5]

One history of the war splendidly declares, "The British Army at the time was the opposite of the Boers. Hidebound as it was by tradition, conservatism, and outdated techniques, its recent reputation was based almost without exception on victories won by vastly superior firepower over half-armed natives."[6]

Another historian, J. F. C. Fuller, claimed that British generals displayed a "Brown Bess" or "Peninsular" mentality of "shoulder to shoulder formations, of volleys in rigid lines and of wall-like bayonet assaults".[7] In one form or another, these are commonly held views of the war: many will even assure you that the British marched forward shoulder-to-shoulder wearing scarlet jackets and white cross-belts, only to get scythed down by Mauser bullets. It is no doubt appealing to some to believe that the British army of the day was hopelessly old-fashioned, obsessed with tradition, wedded to archaic tactics and harboured a deep suspicion of technology and progress. Though this is all frightfully amusing, is there really any truth in it?

Despite a few wild claims from some quarters* and several artists' impressions of various battles, the British army had completed the transition from red coats to khaki (via a very short-lived flirtation with grey) long before the Boer War: indeed, khaki had been introduced for service in Africa as early as 1882. The battle of Ginnis, fought in the Egyptian Sudan in 1885,[8] is accepted to be the last time British troops fought in their famous red coats† and even then the troops had been ordered to switch out of their issue khaki uniforms and back into red as a psychological ploy to overawe their opponent.

In many other ways, British infantry equipment was thoroughly modern: the imperial infantryman was armed with either the Lee-Metford or the virtually identical Lee-Enfield. Replacing the single-shot, large-calibre Martini-Henry, the Lee-Metford was a revolutionary .303 magazine rifle which was introduced in 1888 and had already proved its worth in the Matabele Wars and in the Sudan.

At the start of the Boer War there were initial problems with the sighting-in, meaning accurate fire at long range was compromised. When this was rectified, however, it was basically equal to the German Mauser that many

---

* including, somewhat alarmingly, battlefield guides I encountered on tours of both Elandslaagte and Spion Kop

† There is one tiny caveat to this: during the Sudan campaign of the late 1890s, the gunners of a battery of British Maxims attached to the Egyptian army preferred to wear their scarlet home-service uniforms to the standard service-issue khaki.

Boers carried.* From 1895, the Lee-Metford started being slowly replaced by the Lee-Enfield which was itself essentially a re-barrelled Lee-Metford. Rugged, reliable, accurate and hard-hitting, the Lee-Enfield is arguably one of the best infantry weapons ever made: seventeen million were produced and it is still in service in several countries. In various marks and variants, the Lee-Enfield served as the standard British army infantry rifle until the 1960s. Re-barrelled to 7.62mm as the L42 sniper rifle, it was only finally withdrawn from British service in the 1980s.

Far from being loath to adopt new-fangled weaponry, the British army had long since embraced machine guns and most units arrived in South Africa equipped with the fearsome Maxim gun.† Like the Lee-Metford, the Maxim had proved highly effective in the Matabele wars and the Sudan campaign. Indeed, such was the importance given to machine guns that many were stripped from fortresses in Great Britain to bolster the firepower of units deploying to South Africa.[9]

The British were less well served in terms of artillery, with the standard Armstrong 15-pounder field piece proving to be outclassed by the more modern Boer guns. But is this evidence of the British being 'hidebound by tradition'? Such claims ignore the fact that an army cannot simply replace its weapons whenever a new invention comes along. Weapon systems—be they rifles, field guns or battleships—take years to develop and introduce. They cannot be replaced every year and, in the case of the British 15-pounder, this was a modification of the 12-pounders which had only entered service with the Royal Artillery in 1883: the invention of the new smokeless propellant, cordite, permitted a heavier shell to be fired and the 12-pounders were machined to accept this.[10] It was undoubtedly a cheap-and-nasty attempt to lengthen the service life of the 12-pounder and recognized as such by officers at the time, but there was no way the Treasury would fork out to replace hundreds of field guns after just a few years' service. None of this has anything to do with tradition: it is rather a simple question of timing and economics; all weapon systems have a shelf life and have to give many years of service to justify their purchase and introduction. To use a more modern

---

* While the Mauser round was ballisticly superior, the Enfield's / Metford's magazine held twice as many rounds. Both were extremely rugged, dependable rifles.

† The famous Vickers gun, introduced in 1912, was an improved version of the Maxim gun and was used by the British army through both World Wars. It was only finally taken out of British service in the 1960s.

example, when the Chieftain tank was introduced to the British army in 1966, it was considered a world-leading design. During nearly thirty years of service, however, other better designs were adopted by other armies, and by the time the last Chieftains were finally withdrawn from service in 1995, it was a very dated example indeed. When its replacement, the Challenger, was first adopted, it too was considered one of the best tanks in the world, and so the cycle began again. The fact that the Cold War British army did not adopt a better tank sooner was nothing to do with being 'hidebound by tradition', but the simple fact that—except when actually embroiled in a major war—no nation can afford to change out major weapon systems every year or two whenever something slightly better comes onto the market.

In contrast, the Boers republics had re-armed during the 1890s and had thus acquired some of the very latest field pieces available at the time: the 1896/7 model Creusot 75mm QF in Boer service was the most technically advanced gun in South Africa.[11] What is often forgotten is that the Boers also had a lot of older pieces and indeed had a complete mismatch of guns in service: by October 1901, the British had captured no less than twenty-one different types[12]—a logistician's nightmare. Another common charge levelled at the Royal Artillery is that tradition led them to lay their guns out in the open in neat rows, whereas the shrewder Boers hid theirs in well-camouflaged dugouts. At first glance the republican method seems far superior, but this is to ignore the fact that the Boers were often defending positions, while the gunners of the Royal Artillery generally found themselves supporting infantry attacks against such. Indirect fire was very much in its infancy, and as the 15-pounder was a relatively short-range, direct-fire, line-of-sight weapon, the only way to bring it into action was to move it into position, deploy and commence firing. As it was not possible to mask this action—how could one hide teams of horses and limbers?—then having the guns set up in a straight line was no more or less ridiculous than having them set up in a wiggly line. The chances of there being a convenient linear obstacle at a suitable range which would offer a degree of cover to the gunners was slim, and their protection came mainly from setting up just outside effective rifle range and quickly suppressing any Boer guns. This they did time and again. When Colonel Long mistakenly deployed his guns too far forward at Colenso the results were predictable. But the very fact that his error became so infamous is indication enough that it was very much the exception. The leading expert on artillery in the Boer War, the late Major Darrell Hall, summed up the Royal Artillery: "In most cases the British guns were inferior, but they were used boldly and discipline was very good."[13]

Undoubtedly, it would have been advantageous had it been possible to fit the 15-pounders with bullet-proof gun-shields, but the absence of these had nothing to do with tradition, despite what ill-informed critics suggest.[14] Gun-shields only became practical with the introduction of the revolutionary 'French 75', first adopted by the French army in early 1898* and which was to prove itself in the Boxer Rebellion of 1900. Though later marques of the British 15-pounder were fitted with a rudimentary axle-spade system[15] which went some way to controlling its recoil, it—like all other field guns prior to the French 75—still lurched backward after each shot, thus making a gun-shield utterly impractical.[16] The French 75, however, was equipped with a hydro-pneumatic recoil mechanism which meant the gun remained stationary after firing. More importantly, this also radically improved rates of fire as the gun did not need to be repositioned and aimed after every shot. In the years that followed the introduction of the French 75 the armies of the world all rushed to obtain quick-firers of their own: between 1901 and 1905 Great Britain,† Russia, Denmark, Sweden, Norway, Portugal, the Netherlands and the USA all adopted very similar guns.[17]

Other than swapping out their entire arsenal of field guns the year before the war began and replacing them with the as-yet-unproven French 75 (clearly completely impossible), it is difficult to know what the Royal Artillery could have done differently. It is worth noting that no Boer artillery pieces were equipped with gun-shields:‡ the lack of gun-shields thus had nothing to do with tradition and everything to do with the laws of physics. There was no insane desire to expose British gunners to fire for the sake of it and, indeed, when the roles were reversed and the guns of the imperial forces were holding defensive positions, they were also positioned in dug-outs or sand-bagged emplacements.[18]

---

*   officially known as the Canon de 75 modèle 1897, this ground-breaking field piece remained in service into the Second World War

†   The British army replaced the 15-pounder with the 18-pounder, an 83.8mm piece capable of firing over twenty rounds a minute. These proved to be magnificent weapons and served throughout the First World War.

‡   both sides fitted shields to pom-poms and machine guns which, unlike true artillery pieces, had no issues with recoil

In stark contrast, the Boer artillery generally proved unable or unwilling to leave their defensive positions to offer close support to assaults on British positions.[19] At Wagon Hill, for example, republican guns supported their infantry with long-range fire from their emplacements,[20] but none were moved forward to offer close support to their assaults, or to help fight off the inevitable counter-attacks. Ultimately, all the Boer attacks were driven off. The British, on the other hand, were far more dashing with their artillery, even in a defensive action like Wagon Hill: the Royal Artillery had no hesitation in bringing their guns out of their shelters to where they could actually influence the action and wasted no time in moving their guns forward to flay the assaulting federals. Major Abdy, commanding the 53rd Battery, brought his 15-pounders forward through the river while the republican attacks were underway: "there, directly in front of them, at 2,200 yards range, was the slope of Caesar's Camp crowded with Boers dotted about in fancied security. In a moment, the wicked shrapnel was bursting over them at its deadliest range."[21] Ten minutes later Major Blewitt led the 21st Battery out to engage the assaulting Boers on the western end of the plateau.[22] Abdy's battery came under long-range fire from a Long Tom and a howitzer, but—contrary to the popular myth—the major had made skilful use of the available cover and his casualties were "trifling". One who no doubt considered his wounds to be rather more than trifling was Sergeant Boseley "whose left arm and leg were carried away by a shell and who was taken off the field waving his remaining arm and adjuring his section to 'buck up'".[23] The bold deployment of the 53rd Battery in particular "produced immediate and valuable effect upon the situation on the summit ... when [the attacking Boers] felt Abdy's shrapnel and saw their supports dispersing behind them from the same cause, they began to waver, and Carnegie, seizing the opportunity, instantly ordered his company to advance with fixed bayonets. The Boers did not await the charge. Chasing them from the crest, the Gordons reoccupied the advanced sangars".[24] After three hours, and their mission completed, the 53rd calmly withdrew into cover.

There was little evidence of similar aggression or dash from the republican artillery during the war. Though their field craft and camouflage were excellent, and there is no doubting the individual skill of the Boer gunners, they proved loath to expose themselves to danger. Republican artillery tactics were also poor. Boer guns "were usually deployed individually. They were seldom organised in batteries and, more often than not, they were simply used as long range rifles. There was little co-ordination between guns, and this made the concentration of fire on specific targets very nearly impossible".[25]

Though saddled with an out-classed field piece, there was little sign of the gunners being hidebound by tradition in South Africa. Two Royal Navy cruisers, HMS *Terrible* and HMS *Powerful*, arrived in the Cape within forty-eight hours of the Boer invasion. By good fortune, Captain Percy Scott, commanding the HMS *Terrible*, was considered the Royal Navy's leading gunnery expert with a genius for improvisation.[26] Scott recognized that the British garrison was outnumbered and outgunned: "we had insufficient troops to resist the Boer invasion, our base was 6,000 miles from the scene of operations, and we had no artillery to cope with the enemy's, either in power or range ... we had on board [the HMS *Terrible*] long-range 12-pounder guns, specially supplied for use against torpedo boats. They were superior in range to any field artillery that either we or the Boers had ... it occurred to me that there would be no difficulty in mounting these guns on wheels for service on shore. I purchased a pair of Cape waggon wheels and axle-trees, and made a sketch embodying my rough ideas. Mr Johns, our excellent carpenter, remained up all night with some of his shipwrights and blacksmiths hard at work, and in 24 hours we had this little gun ready. To make sure that everything was right, we fired a few rounds, and the mounting behaved very well."[27]

These improvised 12-pounders—plus a pair of heavier 4.7-inch naval guns also fitted on mountings designed by the indefatigable Captain Scott—were soon in action. On the 25th October the naval commander-in-chief at Simon's Town received a telegram from Sir George White, commander of imperial forces in Natal. White urgently requested a naval brigade with long-range artillery and Scott's improvised naval guns were thus rushed to Ladysmith. They arrived in the midst of battle and immediately went into action, silencing the Boer artillery.

This engagement took place on the 30th October. It had taken just six days to adapt the 4.7-inch naval guns for land use, build the mountings, transport them 1,000 miles and engage the enemy.[28] Hidebound by tradition indeed.

Showing similar ingenuity, the defenders of Mafeking constructed a 5-inch howitzer out of a length of steel pipe. This home-made gun was initially unsuccessful, but later joined the defences of the town and was named

'The Wolf' in honour of the nickname the natives had bestowed on Baden-Powell.[29] It was an ugly-looking thing but could fling an 18-pound shell out to 4,000 yards.[30] Even more successful was a field piece constructed during the siege of Kimberley. Recognizing that the garrison's puny guns were hopelessly mismatched by those of the Boers, some de Beers engineers, led by the American George Labram, offered to design and build a heavier piece. None of the engineers had any experience of such things, there was no special plant or machinery available and the only plans Labram's team had were some descriptions found in a stray copy of an engineering journal. Nevertheless, the gun was designed, quickly built and brought into action against the Boers just twenty-four days later. Named in honour of Rhodes, the 'Long Cecil' threw a 28-pound shell out to 7,000 yards.[31] It was in action throughout the remainder of the siege, firing 225 shells in all. Of course, some will dismiss this remarkable weapon as having been built by civilian engineers rather than the British army, but that is to miss the point that the supposedly conservative British army proved ready to embrace such a Heath-Robinson field piece.

There was also no hesitation to adopt new guns in rather more conventional ways. After being on the receiving end of them from the Boers, dozens of Vickers-Maxim 1-pound 'pom-pom' guns were quickly purchased and rushed into service in South Africa.[32] These pom-poms were considered something of a wonder weapon at the time, and were much liked by the British troops and much disliked by the Boers on the receiving end of them.[33]

So what of infantry tactics? Ignoring the hundreds of examples where it did not happen, critics invariably focus on the two occasions where British infantry were caught in close order and thus suffered heavily. There is nothing to excuse Hart's Irish Brigade being caught in this formation at Colenso, but it is well worth remembering that the other British battalions in that action advanced in open order. The Irish Brigade suffered because of Hart's unforgiveable blunder, not British army doctrine—indeed, the 1896 edition of *Infantry Drill* advocated adopting extended formations when within half a mile of the enemy.[34] The other example usually cited is Wauchope's Highland Brigade at Magersfontein, but they were unfortunate to be caught in the transition from advancing under cover of darkness (where adopting close order made sense to retain control of the men) before they could deploy into open order. It is certainly true that Wauchope could have—and should have—shaken his men into looser formations sooner—indeed, he was being urged to do so by some of his officers—but it was still a question of timing, rather than a determination to carry out the actual assault in close order, which was never Wauchope's intention.

At the first battle of the war, Talana Hill, the British infantry advanced with spacing of as much as ten yards between men, while in the other early battles, such as Elandslaagte, Belmont, Graspan* and Modder River, the tactics of the British infantry proved equally successful, with troops advancing in looser formations and in rushes under covering fire. Just a few weeks into the war, British attacking lines would often see spacing of up to 20 yards between men, while at Diamond Hill, this was increased to 30 yards.[35] Far from supporting the ludicrous notion that the Tommies typically marched forward shoulder to shoulder, General Ben Viljoen described how the British infantry really attacked, assaulting "in scattered formation … much less visible to our marksmen. When advancing to the attack the British foot soldiers were wont to crawl along on their faces, seeking cover whenever that was available; thus advancing, and especially when they were supported by artillery, their men proved very difficult to repulse".[36] Many of those units mobilized from India were veterans of the North West Frontier, adept at fire-and-manoeuvre, and proved too much for the defending republican forces. In fact, as historians such as Edward Spiers, Tim Moreman and, most recently, Stephen Miller, have all pointed out, those regiments which had served during the great rising on the North West Frontier in 1897 were already painfully aware of the destructive effects of assaulting an enemy armed with modern breech loaders,[37] which rather torpedoes the tedious claims that the British army of the period had only ever fought half-armed natives. The infantry tactics employed by Hart, and the mistake made by Wauchope, were not the norm: they are the two glaring exceptions in over two and a half years of war.

There is also no evidence that British commanders were slow to adapt their infantry tactics, with changes being made early in the war. In Natal, Buller fine-tuned his tactics after his initial failures: the battle of Tugela Heights saw troops of the Natal Field Force move in short rushes, using available cover

---

* At Graspan, the small Royal Navy Brigade did not extend their formation as much as the infantry and, though victorious, suffered accordingly.

and with the support of creeping barrages which continued to hammer the Boer trenches until the attacking infantry were just fifteen yards from them.[38] As we have seen, it has been claimed that it was Buller who first evolved "the tactics of truly modern war".[39] Also as witnessed earlier, Roberts issued a series of 'Notes for Guidance in South African Warfare' in January 1900. These were primarily concerned with infantry tactics and all built on the lessons of the war to date.[40] Actually Roberts's notes were more of a refresher than anything especially ground-breaking, as the British army had, in any event, been moving to a more flexible approach throughout the 1890s. Vastly increased defensive firepower and the advent of smokeless powder had long been recognized as prompting a sea change in the tactics needed in an infantry assault. This has led one historian to state that Roberts's notes were a "textbook summary of the advanced tactical ideas of the previous three decades".[41] It is also instructive that German army observers criticized Roberts for tending to avoid frontal assauts, reporting that "Lord Roberts's system throughout the whole campaign was to manoeuvre rather than to fight", before going on to lambast him for trying to avoid heavy losses. Roberts countered, "I manoeuvred in order to be able to fight the Boers on my own and not their terms," noting that the Boers would have been delighted to have faced frontal British attacks in prepared positions as at Magersfontein.[42]

As part of this determination to reduce heavy losses, and from the very outset of the war, officers had started to discard their Sam Browne belts and began carrying rifles to make them less distinctive to Boer sharpshooters.[43] Brass buttons were removed or covered, white kit was stained and unit flashes made as small as possible.[44] Royal Marines landing in Durban dyed their white tropical uniforms with coffee before they were rushed up the line to help stem the Boer invasion.[45] Elsewhere on the Natal front one war correspondent described the pragmatic approach taken by British infantry units from the very first engagements: "I noted also that the British officer had wisely transmogrified himself so that it was impossible for the Boers' selected marksmen any longer to distinguish by outward appearances, even a battalion commander from an ordinary 'Tommy'. Numbers of the officers also carried rifles—swords and Sam Browne belts being now a thing of the past."[46]

౽

If any of the various arms of the British army could be expected to be hidebound by tradition, it would surely be the cavalry. But there is little evidence of this. When the Royal Scots Greys (2nd Dragoons) arrived in South Africa, their first move was to dye their famous grey horses less distinctive browns and greens,[47] which must have made for a rather incongruous sight. The Lancer regiments had begun the war armed with their traditional weapons, as indeed had the front-rank men of other, sabre-armed, cavalry regiments. After a few months, however, this cold steel was largely substituted in favour of rifles or carbines.[48] The switch became official in October 1900, with Kitchener's order adding: "The rifle will henceforth be considered the cavalry soldier's principal weapon."[49] When the colonel of the 5th Lancers complained, he was informed his men could either keep their lances and remain in camp, or abandon the weapon and stay in action.* Compare this pragmatism to the fact that the French army began the First World War with twelve regiments of *cuirassiers*, sword-armed horsemen who rode into battle wearing metal breast plates and plumed helmets like knights of old.

As often mentioned, the British also moved rapidly to form additional mounted infantry companies and regiments, units that blurred the age-old distinctions between cavalry and infantry. The concept of mounted infantry was not exactly new in the British army: as early as 1888, battalions had begun training men in this role, with each battalion expected to be able to deploy one company as mounted infantry.[50] More remarkable still was that, with the guerrilla war signalling a reduction in the importance of artillery, gunners were formed into units of the Royal Artillery mounted rifles and proved highly effective. That these various hybrid units were embraced, and then massively expanded during the Boer War, suggests practicality and realism rather than stick-in-the-mud obsession with tradition.

For an army accused of being conservative, there was also no hesitation in raising a large number of irregular corps;[51] by 1901, there were over thirty such units,[52] the vast majority raised locally from South African loyalists. And for an army accused of using outdated techniques, there was also little hesitation

---

* One should not instantly dismiss the colonel as a stick-in-the-mud reactionary, as he may well have had a point—several other officers, including Sir John French, observed that the Boers held a deep dread of lances, and their removal from service seems to have been well received by the bitter-einders.

in raising special units like Rimington's Tigers and the Bushveldt Carbineers to fulfil tasks alien to regular British troops. This dabbling with what might be termed 'special forces' was actually nothing new and had previously been tried in the Sudanese campaigns, where picked men were selected from other units to form four elite Camel Corps regiments.[53]

In an earlier example, the famous Corps of Guides of the British Indian army was founded as early as 1846. It was unique in being a mixed infantry–cavalry unit and quickly gained the stature of a *corps d'elite* on the North West Frontier. The Guides received better pay than other units, thus allowing recruiters to pick and choose only the very best applicants. An even earlier example is the elite Rogers' Rangers, a 600-strong light infantry unit raised from North American loyalists to support the British army in the French and Indian Wars of the mid-1700s.[54] The Rangers excelled at reconnaissance and special operations behind the lines, and were greatly valued by the British high command. The name of this formidable and unconventional unit lives on in the US Army Ranger units.

The Boer War equivalent of the Rangers was arguably Rimington's Scouts, or 'Tigers' as they were commonly known. Formed by Major Rimington, a regular British army officer, the Tigers were made up of picked local frontiersmen and hunters with good knowledge of both the terrain and local language.[55] Working independently in small groups, Rimington's Tigers— and a similar, but smaller unit, the Natal Guides—acted as the eyes and ears of British commanders, quickly earning reputations akin to that of the Long Range Desert Group of Second World War fame.

Another elite unit raised during the war was the Bushveldt Carbineers.* A small, multi-national unit—despite claims that they were an Australian unit, only forty per cent were Aussies—of mounted infantry, the Bushveldt Carbineers (BVC) has been described as one of the pioneers of modern counter-insurgency (COIN) tactics. Recruits who could ride and shoot were sought "For Special Service in Northern Districts of Transvaal"[56] and a number of English-speaking residents of the region—including Lieutenant Neel, a doctor from Spelonken and Lieutenant Kelly, a merchant from Pietersburg—joined the regiment.[57] Displaced refugees from the region also joined, bringing with them invaluable local knowledge, as well as a rather less helpful desire for revenge. In an unconventional move, the BVC also actively

---

* renamed the Pietersburg Light Horse on 1 December 1901

recruited 'joiners' from Boer internment camps, with ultimately over a tenth of the regiment made up of such. It was a precursor to the tactics of the Selous Scouts in the Rhodesian bush war seventy-odd years later where 'turned terrorists' were brought into the ranks to improve intelligence-gathering and deceive the enemy.[58] The BVC was effective, hard-hitting and highly controversial: when a Boer train-wrecking gang was caught but refused to confess where on the railway line they had laid their mine, they were loaded onto a trolley and rolled down the line until they detonated their own device. The BVC would become infamous for the execution of prisoners ordered by Lieutenant Harry 'Breaker' Morant,* events which ultimately led to his own execution on the 27th February 1902.

Even conventional imperial units were, if anything, even more inclined to engage in aggressive SAS-style raiding actions than were the republicans. We have seen examples of the active defence of Ladysmith, Mafeking, Elands River and Wepener in terms of the British penchant of launching daring night raids on Boer guns; in contrast and despite their reputation for cunning lightning attacks, the federal besiegers made no such raids against British gun positions during any of their lengthy sieges. While the republicans were content to remain essentially passive during sieges, it was the imperial troops who retained the initative.

Though it was certainly a time of transition and change—and mistakes were undoubtedly made—there is little in the tactics or equipment adopted by the British army that suggests they were stuck in the past and still fighting the Crimean War. Claims that there was a "Peninsular" mentality of "shoulder to shoulder formations, of volleys in rigid lines and of wall-like bayonet assaults" are quite simply ludicrous, as General Viljoen's reminiscences substantiate. Indeed, after complimenting the British infantry on their tactics and use of cover, the general goes on to confess that the Boers were the ones who had issues with leaders stuck in the past: "In this campaign it was noticeable that during the last stages of the struggle the younger officers replaced the older ones. Many of these latter got tired of the War and surrendered to the British, others were removed from their commandos as being too old-

---

* Lieutenant Harry Harbord Morant (1864–1902) was an Englishman who immigrated to Queensland in 1883. A somewhat enigmatic character, Morant made a name for himself as a horseman, poet and womanizer. When the Boers invaded Natal, he volunteered for service in South Africa with the 2nd Contingent, South Australian Mounted Rifles. His actions while later serving in the BVC remain controversial to this day—to some he is cult hero who was fighting the Boers their own way, to others, he is a cold-blooded murderer. As usual, the truth is probably somewhere in between.

fashioned in their methods and incapable of adapting themselves to the altered circumstances."[59]

In many other ways the Boer War can be considered the first modern war fought by Great Britain. Imperial forces made widespread use of railways, the telegraph, field telephones, steam traction engines, armoured trains, electric searchlights, blockhouses, wire entanglements, entrenchments and so forth.[60] The British sent 'aeronauts' up in tethered hot air balloons for reconnaissance, and even to direct artillery fire. A contemporary witness recorded one such aeronaut performing fire control from his balloon by means of a field telephone: "all interest was now centred on a strange object which was seen rising near the river. This was the war balloon … the scaly, brown-coloured monster … for two hours the balloon floats high in the air, almost as high as Spion Kop, and Capt. Phillips, RE, the daring aeronaut, is scanning the Boer position from his swaying basket in mid-air, and describing what he sees to the earth below by telephone."[61]

While its impact diminished with the fluidity of the guerrilla war, the field telephone was a significant advance and was used to good effect in defensive actions and sieges.[62] One observer admiringly described the professionalism of the British signallers and their advanced equipment: "your respect for the grimy-looking gentlemen in khaki enormously increases when you find that, so far from being a mere 'absent minded beggar', one is an expert in signalling, and another is a telegraphist, and another accomplished in the knowledge and practice of ballooning. However fast, the telegraph wire is still well to the front. Just outside my tent was a two-wheeled cart. On it was a big roller from which the wire had been unrolled as we proceeded. It is dropped along the veldt quite casually, but there are no accidents. Your horse trips on it sometimes, but neither he nor the wire is any the worse. And then follow the Royal Engineers with poles, and very soon the line is quite an orthodox affair properly mounted on black and white poles like a barber's sign. Meanwhile on the same telegraph cart at the end of the wire there is a small machine which keeps buzzing its all-important messages in a pertinacious and garrulous way."[63] More advanced still was the deployment of 'Marconi wireless telegraphy' at De Aar.[64]

Despite these advances, the runner and the galloper remained very much in use throughout the war, but the carrier pigeon was given a modern twist during the siege of Ladysmith and used to carry photographic copies of military maps to the relief column.[65] Other forms of communications included heliograph and flashing coded messages by searchlight. Indeed, the defenders of Mafeking made their own searchlight: "Sergeant Moffat, in charge of the Signallers, with the aid of a Mr Walker, the agent for the South African Acetylene Gas Company, had constructed a searchlight out of two biscuit-tins pressed into a cone and an acetylene burner; it vastly impressed the Boers when trained towards, if not on, them at night."[66]

The ubiquitous Captain Percy Scott RN devised a method of signalling by Morse code with a searchlight and Venetian blind shutter, the forerunner of the Aldis lamp. The contraption was mounted on a railway truck and sent up to the Tugela front where it was aimed at clouds at night to bounce signals to the garrison.[67] Though these probably all sound rather quaint, the use of the telegraph and such was a massive step forward and permitted coordination of units over large areas. The home-made searchlight at Mafeking was just one example of the ingenuity shown. As well as the construction of the 'Wolf' and 'Long Cecil', home-made mines were constructed during the sieges and shells were manufactured in railway workshops and even in the Mafeking soda-syphon factory.[68] Home-made grenades were also made by the defenders of Mafeking. Sergeant Page, champion bait-thrower of Port Elizabeth, delivered his grenades by casting them onto the Boer positions using his fishing rod.[69]

Though the ox-wagon and the train were overwhelmingly the main means of supply, Buller's Natal Field Force soon boasted half a dozen traction engines. These revolutionary machines greatly impressed all who saw them: "they require few attendants, don't gibe, and can each easily haul twelve tons. Yesterday and today these puffing Billies have been running to-and-fro transporting stores from the railway siding to the respective brigade camps, one of which, Hart's, is two miles away. They leisurely descend into spruits, roll across, and wheel up stiff, long climbs, like flies climbing a wall … On the flat, dry veldt the streamers strip along at a brisk eight miles an hour."[70]

For the time the British army was also well served by cutting-edge medical facilities. The medical corps embraced the most up-to-date medical thinking of the age: surgical equipment was sterilized and great care taken to avoid the introduction of germs.[71] Though there was still little understanding of inoculation and bacteriology, general anaesthesia (using chloroform) was standard for all operations; the army even embraced portable field X-ray machines.[72] While a generation or two previously, even a relatively minor wound might see a soldier die as a result, medical advances had a profound impact. In operations to relieve the siege of Kimberley, for example, only two per cent of wounded soldiers would later die of their injuries,[73] a statistic unheard-of in earlier wars. The introduction of the personal field dressing just prior to the war was one of the major factors in this transformation. Carried by every solider, it consisted of a sterile gauze pad stitched to a bandage and covered with water-proofing that could later be removed to allow a wound to dry.[74]

Karl Landsteiner's breakthrough research into the different blood types only began in 1900/1 and it was not until 1907 that the first successful blood transfusion occurred.[*] Throughout the Boer War, British doctors instead transfused saline in the case of blood loss, but this was only effective in less severe cases. X-rays had only been discovered in 1895, but X-ray machines were already in British army service during the Sudan campaign of 1898, and at least nine such machines were sent to South Africa during the Boer War.[75] These machines proved invaluable in finding bullets and shell splinters inside wounded personnel. Almost as remarkable was the Princess Christian hospital train which "was manned by the 20th Bearer Company and the 20th Field Hospital Corps and staffed by 13 civilian doctors. On arrival at Durban it was fitted up in the railway workshops, and began running in Natal on March 17, 1900. It is built on the corridor system, and contains wards, a surgery, compartments for nurses and invalid officers, linen and kitchen store closets, a dining-room and a perfectly appointed kitchen".[76] Though all these medical advances meant that wounded soldiers received far better treatment than in previous campaigns, the Boer War remains noteworthy for being the last conflict in which more British troops died of disease[†] than in battle— twice as many in fact. This stark reality is forgotten in the mindless stampede to blame the British for all the deaths in the concentration camps.[77]

৯

---

[*] the Rhesus factor was not discovered until 1937, meaning that, until then, blood transfusions were still rather hit or miss

[†] there was even an outbreak of bubonic plague in Cape Town in 1901

So, all in all, it is very difficult to take the charge that the British army was hidebound by tradition in any way seriously. Of course, there were age-old customs like regimental mascots, bagpipes, kilts and the like, but these are recognized by most as a positive influence, fostering a formidable *esprit de corps*. There were definitely shortcomings in the British army: as early as March 1900, Allenby, a free-thinking officer who was grudgingly sympathetic to the Boers, bitched to a staff officer that a properly trained general staff was needed, and that an overhaul in the promotion system was required.[78] He moaned about the mistakes of his superiors and claimed he had "no use for these modern Major-Generals".[79] As Allenby ended the war a full colonel and went on to become a field marshal, he can hardly claim that the army did not recognize and promote talent.

In truth, and despite its *raison d'être* being to fight small colonial wars and police actions, the British army had embraced staff officers as early as the Crimean War; Allenby himself attended staff college at Camberley[80] in 1896/7, though it was not until 1905 that a true general staff was established. Even then, unlike the vast continental armies, the British army was too small to support separate staff and command career streams. Officers would typically alternate between staff and command. The duties of this newly organized general staff were shared among a director for military operations, a director of staff duties and a director of military training. The adjutant-general's staff (as opposed to the general staff) was given overall responsibility for the soldier's welfare and reporting to them were various other directors in charge of recruitment, medical services and the like.[81] In 1908 the various yeomanry and militia regiments were reorganized into the Territorial Force, which was renamed the Territorial Army after the First World War.[82] After lessons learned in the Boer War, the structure of the infantry battalion was changed* and marksmanship became the obsession of the British infantry, as the Germans were to learn to their cost in the opening battles of the First World War.

But despite this post-war overhaul and however valid some of Allenby's complaints were, the Boer War myths of solid lines of scarlet-clad men marching forward shoulder to shoulder are laughable and quite simply untrue. Indeed, the enthusiasm of the British army to learn from the Boer

---

* The system of eight companies, each made up of two half-companies, was revised to one of four companies, each made up of four platoons.

War rather refutes any allegation of stifling conservatism. As Kipling said, there were plenty of lessons to be taken from the war, but that can be said of any war that has ever been fought. Even the short, sharp and highly successful Falklands War prompted the British army to introduce new boots and other equipment, and for future Royal Navy ship design to heavily favour point-defence weapons and fire-fighting systems—but no one ever claims that the British sent men in poor footwear and inadequate ships to the South Atlantic because of being hidebound by tradition.

All in all, the British army of the Boer War was very much a twentieth-century force. There were shortcomings, but by and large it embraced modern weapons (some of which remained in service for generations to come) with alacrity, and on all but the rarest occasion employed modern tactics. Despite the leftist fantasy of an über-conservative, fuddy-duddy officer class, technology and progress were by no means shunned: indeed, if anything, the readiness to adopt and utilize new equipment, tactics and units was quite remarkable.

CHAPTER FOURTEEN

Who was fighting the white man's war?

"The Dutch are not beaten. What is beaten is Krugerism,
a corrupt and evil government, no more Dutch in essence than English."
—Cecil Rhodes, 1900

"What is the true and original root of Dutch aversion to British rule? It is the abiding fear
and hatred of the movement that seeks to place the native on a level with the white man
… the Kaffir is to be declared the brother of the European, to be constituted
his legal equal, to be armed with political rights."
—Winston Churchill, 1900

"Among the marvellous escapes recorded, and these were not a few, was one of a negro
who was shot through the brain by a bullet. The projectile passed through one temple
and lodged into the other, yet the man still survived, and showed a decided intention to
recover … The invulnerability of the nigger cranium has its advantages."
—Louis Creswicke in Volume 3 of *South Africa and the Transvaal War*

"a 'colour-blind' franchise operated in the Cape whereby any adult male, irrespective
of the colour of his skin, was entitled to register as a voter provided he could pass a
simple literacy test and either owned property to the value of £75 or possessed an annual
income exceeding £50. The franchise was looked upon by members of the black elite
as the corner-stone of their liberties and opportunities in Cape society."
—Peter Warwick in *Black People and the South African War, 1899–1902*

"A war in South Africa would be one of the most serious wars that could possibly be
waged. It would be in the nature of a civil war. It would be a long war, a bitter war,
and a costly war, and it would leave behind it the embers of a strife which,
I believe, generations would hardly be long enough to extinguish."
—Joe Chamberlain, speaking in 1896

Most contemporary accounts of the Boer War state that it was a 'white man's war' and most modern histories of the conflict fall over themselves to 'reveal' the shocking truth that it was actually no such thing. While it would be farcical to claim that the war only impacted the whites in South Africa (which was not what the phrase 'white man's war' meant in the first place), this new, politically correct, view is equally flawed. Perhaps, unsurprisingly, those who challenge to concept of the 'white man's war' are driven more by the politics of the 'new' South Africa and the current obsession with rewriting colonial history than any evidence, facts, statistics or knowledge of the standard practices of the day. Of course, no one would deny that the war directly and indirectly affected much of the black population of southern Africa, or that many thousands of blacks performed essential roles as labourers, wagon drivers and scouts. Many more—like our friend with the 'invulnerable cranium'—were wounded or killed in the various sieges or raids; others starved as a direct result of the conflict and many thousands died of disease in refugee camps. How many of these poor devils would have succumbed to disease whether they were in the camps or not is always overlooked by squawking critics: no one accuses the UN, Oxfam or Bob Geldof of killing those who die in modern-day refugee camps.

Limited numbers of Africans also served in combat roles on both sides, with endless accusations and counter-accusations of such. The most notable example of this was during the siege of Mafeking, though the outrage that followed Baden-Powell's decision to arm the natives glaringly illustrates that this was considered very much the exception, not the rule; General Cronjé even wrote, imploring him to "disarm your blacks and thereby act the part of a white man in a white man's war".[1] It is also well known that other imperial commanders began to issue rifles to some African runners and scouts in response to the horrific manner in which the Boers treated those unfortunate enough to fall into their hands,[2] though arming scouts for the purposes of self-defence is hardly the same as deploying large numbers of Africans in a combat role.

As the guerrilla war dragged on, the British used increasing numbers of armed Africans to man blockhouses. By the end of the conflict, it was reckoned that the British were supported by around 10,000 such armed blacks.[3] Though this may sound a lot, it actually represented only around five per cent of the imperial forces in South Africa at the time. One should not, therefore, allow these anomalies and the tragic civilian deaths to cloud the reality that, by and large, both sides overwhelmingly fought the war using white troops. This was almost unique in the colonial period where Great Britain usually waged her campaigns by deploying a small hard-core of British troops, backed by a large number of locally raised forces. For example, at the battle of Atbara during the 1898 Sudan campaign, General Kitchener commanded three brigades of Sudanese and Egyptian troops, but only one of British.[4] Two years earlier, at Abu Hamed, General Hunter commanded no British infantry at all.[5] Even at Omdurman—one of the most famous battles of the colonial period—Kitchener's army comprised just 8,000 British troops, while his Egyptian and Sudanese regiments added a whopping 17,000 to his bayonet strength; that is, uniformed non-white imperial troops outnumbered British troops by more than double in the deciding battle of the campaign. As well as all the locally recruited wagoneers, muleteers, camel drivers, labourers, cooks and bottle-washers, the imperial order of battle contained ten Egyptian and six Sudanese infantry battalions,* as well as four Egyptian field artillery batteries, a horse artillery battery and a Maxim machine-gun battery. In terms of the number of non-white combat units, no order of battle in the Boer War looked anything like this.

The Sudan campaign was how colonial wars were usually fought, and the Boer War was indeed a glaring exception. Both Matabele wars of the 1890s saw large numbers of Africans serving in combat roles on the side of the Rhodesian–imperial forces. When Dr Jameson's columns invaded Matabeleland in 1893, the Rhodesians only fielded around 750 white troops. The balance of the invasion force was made up of about 500 warriors recruited from the Mashona and groups of dissident Matabele, plus the 1,000 warriors supplied by King Khama of the Bechuana. The most famous of all colonial wars—the Zulu War of 1879—followed the same pattern. The British bolstered their own comparatively paltry numbers of redcoats by raising units of native allies such as the Natal Native Contingent and the Natal Native Horse. Indeed, even at Isandlwana—every Brit-basher's favourite colonial defeat—hundreds of black imperial soldiers were slaughtered,[6] with several companies of the NNC wiped out.

And it was not just the British who fought their colonial wars in this fashion: it was the standard of the day, with the French, Portuguese, Belgians

---

* 1st–5th, 7th, 8th, 15th, 17th and 18th Egyptian Infantry and the 9th–14th Sudanese Infantry

and Germans all relying heavily on locally raised units throughout the period. The garrison of German East Africa, for example, was not made up of German army units, but rather *Schutztruppe Feldkompanies*, each formed from six German officers and NCOs, and 160 African NCOs and soldiers. At the outbreak of the First World War, fourteen such *feldkompanies* formed the garrison and throughout the war in East Africa, 14,498 askari fought for Germany, alongside just 3,595 white Germans.[7] Initially, Britain deployed a force of around 8,000 fighting troops against the German forces, of which just one battalion, the 2nd Battalion Loyal North Lancs, was British, with the rest being Indian.[8]

In stark contrast, the Boer War was quite simply fought differently. Even during extreme situations, like the siege of Wepener, so determined were the British to fight a 'white man's war', that they turned down offers of assistance from black allies, restraining the Basuto, despite their position being surrounded and under great threat: "if there was a force eager to attack them, it was the Basutos, and these were only held back from rushing into the fray by the personal influence of Sir Godfrey Lagden and his British colleagues who can never sufficiently be applauded for the skill and diplomacy with which they managed to keep, by invisible moral coercion, a fiery horde from rushing over the borders and possibly massacring the Free Staters as came in their way."[9]

Chamberlain referred to this policy in a speech in the House of Commons on the 28th August 1901: "Throughout this war, we have given instructions that natives should not be employed as belligerents. We have undoubtedly made a great and immediate sacrifice in doing that. We might have had, if we had lifted one little finger, 20,000 Basuto horsemen on the flanks of the Boers, and we might have had a large force of Swazis and Kaffirs in Cape Colony and elsewhere." And this cannot simply be dismissed as empty rhetoric: when New Zealand offered to send mixed-race units to South Africa, these were respectfully declined. The Malay States offered 300 guides and Nigeria a similar number of Hausas, but their offers were also turned down on racial grounds. Kitchener requested the deployment of African troops, like the Sudanese he had commanded during his campaign there, men whom he felt would "forget their stomachs and go for the enemy".[10] His request was firmly rejected by the War Office, and the Commander in Chief was reminded that he was fighting a white man's war.

As long as the war went on, the offers of support continued to roll in: "The British High Command received continual offers of assistance from African leaders, offers which could have, at a stroke, unleashed 60,000 Basutos to sweep down from their mountain fastness onto the Free State or—worse still—100,000 Zulus to storm into the Transvaal and take terrible revenge against their traditional foe. All such offers were politely declined."[11] More remarkable still, and though the tiny* British army was absolutely stretched to the limit throughout the war, all offers of non-white troops† from the magnificent, 150,000-strong Indian army were courteously refused. Instead contributions of white contingents as small as "150 mounted infantry and a machine gun from New Zealand" and "a 200-strong contingent of mounted infantry drawn from the white planter community in Ceylon"[12] were jubilantly accepted and trumpeted in the press.

And it's not as though deploying the splendid regiments of the Indian army overseas was without precedent: indeed, it was almost unheard of for Britain *not* to deploy units of the Indian army in a colonial war. Leo Amery described this oddity in theatrical terms: "A British war in which the Indian army, European and native, plays no part is almost like the play of Hamlet with the Prince of Denmark left out."[13] Amery was absolutely correct: British Indian troops served in the Boxer Rebellion, which was fought at the same time as the Boer War, while elsewhere during the late Victorian period, Indian units served the imperial cause in Burma, Afghanistan and Turkmenistan. When the Great War began just a few years after the Boer War, Indian troops would serve gallantly in a wide variety of campaigns, including the Western Front, Mesopotamia, Gallipoli and East Africa. In 1868 Indian troops had been deployed to Africa, serving in the British punitive raid on Abyssinia. Indeed, Indian units—complete with forty-four elephants to carry the artillery[14]—made up half of General Napier's forces at Magdala, with the 3rd Bombay Light Cavalry, 23rd Punjab Regiment, 27th Bombay Native Infantry and various corps and batteries of Indian sappers and gunners serving with distinction.

In contrast, the markedly different attitude displayed by the British during the Boer War led Indian troops to describe it as a "Sahib's War".[15] Despite the

---

* in comparison to her European rivals

† When British regiments stationed in India were sent to South Africa, there was uproar in the Boer ranks, with many ill-educated rumourmongers unable to understand that these troops were not Indian.

revisionist rantings of the PC brigade, the reality is that there was a definite British determination to fight the Boer War as a 'white man's war' and by so doing denied themselves the services of these excellent troops—essentially fighting with one arm tied behind their backs.

Another interesting comparison can be made with American-Philippine War, which, as we know, was fought virtually concurrently with the Boer War. The American forces which served in the Philippines included three Negro regiments.* The 25th Infantry Regiment was the first to arrive, disembarking in Manila on the 31st July 1899. As they were assembling on the quayside, they were heckled by some white troops who demanded to know what the 'coons' were doing there. A few members of the 25th informed the redneck loudmouths that they had come to "take up the white man's burden". The 25th was soon followed by the 24th Infantry and 10th Cavalry.[16] The deployment of these non-white troops caused plenty of discord within the American forces, with some white officers worrying that the black American troops would not be eager to fight their non-white Filipino 'brothers': "I doubt whether half-disciplined Negroes, under the command of Negro officers, if brought face-to-face with their colored Filipino cousins could be made to fire upon them or fight them. If the Negro understands the Filipinos are fighting for liberty and independence, ten chances to one they would take side with them."[17] These regular black regiments were soon joined by locally raised non-white units. As the war went on, and American regiments were withdrawn to serve in China to quell the Boxer rebellion, "MacArthur moved to expand greatly the native constabulary and field forces. These groups ... would be used to supplement American troops, to guide US forces in remote areas, to gather intelligence, and to serve as police in various areas ... having native forces carry some of the burden of policing, scouting and fighting eased the burden on American forces".[18]

All but the most determined historical revisionist would have to accept that colonial wars were fought largely with non-white native troops and that the Boer War was waged very differently from Britain's other colonial conflicts. Unlike famous actions such as Omdurman, Magdala, Isandlwana and Atbara, there were no major battles in the Boer War where non-white regiments

---

* the American army was racially segregated until as recently as the Korean War

formed a significant entry in the imperial order of battle,* with the possible exception of Baden-Powell's aforementioned and highly controversial 'Black Watch' at Mafeking. As the conflict descended into guerrilla war, there was an increasing, though still relatively small-scale, use of non-white troops in combat units; the Border Scouts, for example, was raised from coloureds in the Uppington area.[19] There were also other, more irregular, units which made use of non-white troops: Bergh's Scouts, for example, had so many that it gained the nickname '*kafferkommando*'.[20] Some of the part-time town guards in parts of the Cape also relied on non-white troops: in Garies, for example, there were only ninety whites in the 471-strong town guard.[21] So while the war certainly impacted South African non-whites to a large degree, and black and coloured imperial fighting troops unquestionably played a role, it was an infinitely lesser one than in all other colonial conflicts. The simple fact is that the Boer War was regarded as being 'different' from other colonial wars. Both the British and the Boers were well aware of the political niceties of southern Africa, and neither had any great desire to arm, or in any way prompt an uprising from, large numbers of the Africans who greatly outnumbered them even at that time. Indeed, some historians consider the battle of Holkrans—where, just before the end of the war, a Zulu impi mounted a retaliatory attack against a party of bitter-einders—as a crucial turning point: it was the first time during the war that blacks had attacked the Boers in a major action. As eminent historian Ken Gillings wrote: "When Gen. Louis Botha was told of the disaster, he felt that it was pointless to continue the struggle when even the black population was turning against them. It is for this reason that this incident, arguably, can be described as one of the most decisive actions of the Anglo-Boer War." The bitter-einders were outraged by the attack and a monument erected at the site even describes the Boer dead as having been "murdered" in the action. Holkrans changed everything, threatening to expand what had been previously been fought, by and large, as a 'white man's war' into a war that neither side wanted, one that would involve hundreds of thousands—even millions—of South African blacks and could have potentially resulted in untold bloodshed. It is indeed instructive that the bitter-einders surrendered soon after Holkrans.

Sending a large British army to Africa—rather than the usual expeditionary

---

* The battle of Holkrans, fought between a Boer commando and a Zulu impi on 6th May 1902, can be discounted as, though their help was no doubt appreciated, the Zulu warriors were certainly not under imperial command.

force, bolstered by vast numbers of local troops—was unique for the period. Equally unusual was the raising of tens of thousands of troops from within the white settler community of South Africa and the dispatch of white troops from other colonies. It may not be a term that sits nicely with modern sensibilities, but based on the standards of the day, and in comparison to all other contemporary colonial conflicts, it is indeed perfectly reasonable to think of the Boer War as a 'white man's war'.

ঌ

Although this term 'white man's war' is often challenged, the title 'Anglo-Boer War' rarely is. The myth of the war being fought between 'Boers and Brits'—or even, as some South Africans prefer to claim, between Great Britain and South Africa—is alive and well. In truth, it was far more complex than this and, as Frank Welsh rightly states, "Nor, again, was it a war between two colonies and two republics. A worrying number of Cape Dutch joined or assisted the Commandos, while a majority of the urban Transvaalers fled to Natal and the Cape."[22] These Transvaal refugees formed famous uitlander regiments like the Imperial Light Horse and Imperial Light Infantry, and were by no means all English-speakers. Equally, Natal provided enthusiastic imperial troops out of all proportion to the paltry size of its white population: even very early in the war, the Bishop of Natal reckoned that a third of white adult males were under arms.[23]

Even though South Africa did not officially exist as a nation until 1910, the Boer War could more accurately be described as the South African Civil War. Ben Viljoen of the Johannesburg Commando described the Imperial Light Horse as "a corps principally composed of Johannesburgers, who were politically and racially our bitter enemies".[24] This was no exaggeration: many of the most aggressive and effective imperial units were raised from South African loyalists to whom it was a bitterly personal conflict. To the veteran Tommies, it was just another war; they had no reason to hate the Boers any more than they had to hate the Afghans, Boxers, Aros or Fuzzie-Wuzzies. To the South African loyalists, however, it was a "war to the knife"[25]—they had suffered at the hands of Kruger's regime, they had been burned out of house and home by the invading Boers; to them the conflict was a fight for their very way of life. Like the dashing troopers of the Imperial Light Horse, the various units raised from Natalians were also renowned for their fighting spirit and desire to wreak revenge on the invaders, quickly earning a reputation of being keen "to fight the Boers on every conceivable occasion".[26]

When a patrol of the Cape Police was ambushed near Hoopstad on the 24th October 1900, the Boers behaved very differently toward their fellow 'South Africans' than to the Britons of the Imperial Yeomanry who rode to reinforce the police. The allegedly pious bitter-einders would not permit the colonials to bury their dead, but extended the courtesy to the Yeomanry. When the town of Jacobsdal (near Kimberley) was attacked early in the morning the following day, the garrison was made up of men from the locally raised Cape Town Highlanders.* In a hard-fought defence, the Highlanders lost fourteen killed and sixteen wounded, some of whom were shot by disloyal townsfolk who had allowed Boers to slip into their houses during the night. The garrison of just sixty was reinforced by other 'South Africans' in the form of a small party of Cape Police and other Cape Town Highlanders—perhaps fifty in number—which was enough to drive off the 300-strong attacking force. The punishment for the treacherous townsfolk was for their houses to be burned down, with large stores of ammunition uncovered in three of the dwellings.

It was a war that split families and caused recrimination for generations, with the allegiance of many districts and towns divided between loyalists and republicans. While several villages on the borders of the Cape Colony instantly switched their allegiance to the Boer invaders, driving loyalists out at gunpoint, others remained steadfastly faithful to the Empire. When an imperial cavalry force, made up mainly of Canadians and Queenslanders, reached the town of Douglas, "nothing was to be seen but Union Jacks and red ensigns … never was there a more enthusiastic demonstration". Alas, the cavalry had no choice but to evacuate the town as it was not strong enough to hold it. The townspeople were thus moved to the safety of British-held Belmont.[27]

Instead of 'Boers and Brits', one should more accurately consider the belligerents as 'republicans and loyalists', though of course it suited post-war, Afrikaans-dominated governments to paint the enemy as the British, rather than include thousands of their own people. In this sense, the Boer War is

---

* The Cape Town Highlanders was formed in 1885 as volunteer regiment. These part-time soldiers were mobilized for service in the Boer War, primarily employed on garrison duties and defending the Cape Town–Kimberley railway. The regiment still exists today as a reserve mechanized infantry unit of the South African army.

similar to the American War of Independence, a conflict that was in truth a civil war,[28] but which was similarly reinvented for political reasons and rebranded as having being fought between the British and the Americans; this despite the fact that large numbers of American loyalists fought for the Crown, and many actions were fought purely between rival groups of Americans. Though attention tends to focus on Piet de Wet and those thousands of Afrikaans 'traitors' who switched allegiance from the commandos to the National Scouts and Orange River Colony Volunteers, this is to ignore the many thousands of other Afrikaners who fought for the imperial cause. The South African Light Horse, for example, was formed in the Cape at the start of the war and was "composed mainly of South Africans—including not a few loyal Afrikanders. The Stellenbosch Mounted Infantry, which had not been called out because the district was regarded as disloyal in sentiment, joined it en masse—but with a free sprinkling of other colonials, Texan cowboys and British yeomen".[29] Others joined British units in ones and twos, serving as guides and scouts. As Colonel Allenby recorded: "Where there is one Boer now, there were 100 then; and their spirit is much tamer. My three guides were fighting me in those days. They are such good, charming fellows."[30] Captain Miller of the Gordon Highlanders wrote home to say, "The Boers are funny fellows. We caught one the other day who immediately offered to be a guide, and took part the day after in a night march, and brought in one of his pals, as pleased as Punch—and this is a common thing. Immediately they are caught they are all anxious (I have seen few exceptions) to serve against their own people."[31] Indeed, so many of the able-bodied male inmates at Winburg concentration camp volunteered to join Bergh's Scouts that this put a strain on the running of the camp. The Winburg superintendent even complained to the military authorities about this, but received little sympathy.

As we have seen, surrendered 'joiners' comprised some ten per cent of the strength of the Bushveldt Carbineers. Remarkably, this, the most controversial unit raised in the war, had been founded at the suggestion of a group of local Pietersburg businessmen who were eager for a mounted corps to operate in their district and defend them against raids from the bitter-einders. A Mr Levy, a storekeeper at Pienaar's River, donated £500 toward the unit. Mr M. Kelly, a Pietersburg merchant, and Dr Neel of Matapan, Spelonken, each donated £100, with others contributing smaller amounts.[32] Another irregular imperial unit raised in South Africa, Kitchener's Fighting Scouts, was commanded by the famous Afrikaans hunter, Johannes Colenbrander,[33] while the Burgher Police were recruited from loyalist Afrikaners under English officers[34] and, unsurprisingly, the 1,000-strong Cape Mounted Police contained many Afrikaners.[35] Interestingly, Brabant's Horse, a unit which Pakenham claimed to be "mostly Afrikaners"[36] was actually composed "chiefly of Eastern Province farmers"[37] and a glance through the nominal roll shows just a sprinkling of Afrikaans names, along with a remarkable twenty-eight Andersons, which must have made roll-call interesting.

General Ben Viljoen devotes an entire chapter of his *My Reminiscences of the Anglo-Boer War*[38] to 'Trapping Pro-British Boers' in the guerrilla campaign. What he described as 'treachery' he admitted was "rampant, and many burghers were riding to and fro to the enemy".[39] He goes on to describe how the war tore communities apart, as some families, wanting nothing more to do with it, desperately tried to side with the British. Viljoen claimed he "often came across cases where fathers fought against their own sons, and brother against brother".[40] Those who had no interest in continuing the guerrilla war were terrorized and hounded by the bitter-einders, with the common punishment for holding such views being confiscation of all one's possessions,[41] which was also quite handy in justifying looting. With matchless impudence, Viljoen even berates the British for accepting the services of anti-Kruger volunteers to fight against their own people,[42] cheerfully ignoring the fact that the Boers had earlier *forced* English-speaking Transvaalers to fight against the British army.

It is impossible to know how many Afrikaners ultimately fought for the imperial cause. Inter-marrying makes it difficult to define who was an Afrikaner and who was not. Few Afrikaners were keen to advertise their imperial service after the war, but there are many Afrikaans names in the lists of those who served with various town guards and the district mounted troops raised in various locations. The small Barkly West town guard, for example, included five du Toits, a Marais, two Nels, three Steyns, three Strausses and a van Niekerk.[43] Potchefstroom's part-time defenders included two Bekkers, a Potgieter, a Schoeman, two Sternbergs and a van Niekerk,[44] while the Tarkastad town guard included two de Klerks, a de Villiers, four Kloppers, a Muller, a Nel, two Schmidts, two Schroders, three Swartzes and two Venters.[45] The Zeerust town guard was placed under the command of Heinrich Dietrich, a German immigrant who had become a burgher of the

Transvaal long before the war, but who supported the British over Kruger. His small unit included a Marais, two Potgieters, a Pretorius, a Scheepers, two Slabberts, two Taljaars, a Theunissen, two van der Lindes, a van der Spuy and a Wilsenach.[46] The tiny Hay district mounted troop included a Badenhorst, a Groenewald, a Joubert, a Scherman, a van der Merwe, a van der Westhayzen, a van Heerden and a van Zyl.[47] And these are by no means the exception: other town guard and district mounted troop lists show names like Buitendag, Cronjé, Lombard, Konig, Oosterlaak, Rensberg, Rudolf, van Wijk, Erasmus, Baaitjes, Beguidenhout, Bezuidenhout, Brandt, Coetzee, Conradie, de Vos, du Preez, Joubert, Kock, Jansen, Meintjes, Pieterse, Plaaitjes, Theron, van de Burgh and van Heerden.

Some will whine that some of these are not 'real Boers' (whatever that means) or—more reasonably—claim that intermarrying meant that those with Dutch, German or Huguenot names were not necessarily Afrikaans *per se*. (Conversely, a clutch of British names such as Smith and MacDonald had also become common Afrikaans surnames; one only needs study the cross-section of names on any concentration camp memorial.) But what is known is that 52,414 white South Africans[48] fought on the imperial side, something rarely mentioned. Though much is made of those rebels who joined Smuts's raid into the Cape, less attention is paid to the imperial units raised in the conquered republics. As well as those raised later in the war from 'joiners', whole new colonial regiments were formed from white residents: the Rand Rifles, for example, was formed in late 1900, and the Johannesburg Mounted Rifles in January 1901.[49] The supposedly exotic nature of recruits in the Johannesburg Mounted Rifles—JMR—quickly earned the regiment the nickname 'Jews: Mostly Russian' from the Tommies.

಄

The list of South African-raised regiments who fought for the imperial cause is long and illustrious, and many are honoured in a memorial at the War Museum in Johannesburg. There were only four permanent regular southern African paramilitary units before the war: the British South Africa Police from Rhodesia, the Cape Mounted Rifles, the Cape Police and the Natal Police. In addition, there were a couple of dozen units listed as 'permanent volunteer forces', which included some of the most famous names in South African martial history: the Cape Town Highlanders, the Duke of Edinburgh's Own Volunteer Rifles, the Durban Light Infantry and the Natal Carbineers.[50]

A large number of other South African units were formed (and some disbanded) during the war. South Africans fought for the Empire in units with names as splendidly diverse as the Railway Pioneer Regiment, Thorneycroft's Mounted Infantry, the East Griqualand Mounted Rifle Volunteers, Kitchener's Horse, the Namaqualand Border Scouts, the Cape Colony Cyclists Corps, the Western Province Mounted Rifles[51] and the somewhat less than glamorously titled Corps of Cattle Rangers.

Though they receive more attention than the contribution of South African units, the numbers sent by Australia,* New Zealand and Canada were far smaller. Australian contingents totalled around 16,000, while those of New Zealand and Canada numbered about 6,000 apiece.[52] Though relatively diminutive, these colonial units were of a very high quality and their mounted infantry units were some of the best imperial regiments of the conflict. Other, smaller, contributions of combat troops came from the settler communities of Ceylon and India, though these were strictly whites-only.

And if the imperial forces were far from being made up of just 'Brits', the republicans forces were more cosmopolitan still. Kruger's attack on the British Empire served as a rallying call for malcontents, romantics, mercenaries, idealists, ne'er-do-wells, troublemakers and sundry riff-raff from all over the globe. It is thought that, in addition to the 13,300 rebels from Natal and the Cape who fought for the Boers, 800 foreigners served in the commandos, and another 2,120 in the 'Foreign Corps'. This latter formation included 500 Irish, 320 Dutch, 200 Germans, a hundred Scandinavians, seventy-five Italians, fifty French, fifty Americans and twenty-five Russians.[53] Irish nationalists were drawn to Kruger's crusade like flies to faeces, and not just those already based in southern Africa. As early as 1896, the Royal Irish Constabulary and the Metropolitan Police's Special Irish Branch[†] reported that a stream of nationalist agitators was leaving for the Transvaal. A leading firebrand, John McBride, was one especially bellicose and unpleasant such fellow. Described as a "short, red-headed, vehement whirlwind", McBride "launched into a no-hold-barred battle to win the local Irish over to militant republicanism".[54] As we have seen, it was not only the civilian Irish community of South

---

* these units were sent by the individual colonies which later formed Australia

† the unit was later renamed Special Branch as its responsibilities expanded

Africa that was targeted in this campaign, but attempts were also made to prompt Irish regiments to mutiny. Career troublemaker MacBride* was later described as "boozy, slovenly and abusive", and was immortalized by a fellow revolutionary in the poem *Easter 1916* as "a drunken vainglorious lout".[55]

❧

Just as many Afrikaners fought for the British, a significant number of English-speaking South Africans chose to fight for the Boers: Conan-Doyle described the 'urban Boers' as men who were "smartened and perhaps a little enervated by prosperity and civilisation, men of business and professional men, more alert and quicker than their rustic comrades. These men spoke English rather than Dutch, and indeed there were many men of English descent among them". In fact, the men who handled Joubert's secret communications were both English.[56] Though the reasons for their decision are not recorded, plenty of such English-speaking Boers were renegades and extremists. We have already met the treacherous Jack Hindon, ex-British army deserter turned train-wrecker *extraordinaire* who fought for the Boers against his own countrymen. James Bain was a similarly loathsome individual; also a former British soldier who served in Kruger's secret service before the war, he would fight for the Boers in the Irish Brigade. Bain was a traitor, radical socialist and troublemaker who flirted with Marxism and had links to various European revolutionaries, communists and anarchists.[57] When he was captured the British treated him with undeserved leniency, exiling him to St Helena instead of stringing him up. He went on to become a thorn in the side of the post-war regime, organizing trade unions and mass strikes.

And such cases were far from unusual. Boer shelling of Mafeking was directed by a deserter called Trooper E. J. Hay, formerly of the Protectorate regiment. Once he had thrown his lot in with the republicans, Hay was in a desperate position. As one townsman remarked, "I shouldn't care to be Hay after the war as there is £50 on his head, and the Boers are hard up."[58] Hay would later take part in the unsuccessful attack on the town toward the end of the siege, briefly strutting about with his former colonel's sword on his belt.[59] Another remarkable 'British Boer' served at the siege of Ladysmith, though

---

* Robert McBride, who claims to be related to John McBride, continued the family tradition, joining terrorist group Umkhonto we Sizwe and blowing up the crowded Magoo's Bar in Durban in 1986. For his efforts he was later appointed chief of the Metro Police for the East Rand in 2003.

was cut from a rather different cloth than Hay. Spencer Drake had lived in the Transvaal for many years, and though descended from Sir Francis Drake and well known to Lord Randolph Churchill, he threw his lot in with the federals.[60] General Cronjé even used a British Boer called Everitt to request the unconditional surrender of the town: he rode into Mafeking waving four white handkerchiefs tied together and was treated to lunch by Baden-Powell before being sent on his way.

Our friend Captain Miller described a series of failed Boer assaults in early 1901: "they simultaneously attacked all down the line, but in every case were beaten off ... They were desperate men ... some seemed absolutely indifferent to life. I suppose all they have to live for is gone. The leader in one case was a Glasgow man—and many of those who attacked our regimental outposts were Scotch and English."[61] It is small wonder such renegades were desperate men— they had thrown their lot in with Kruger against their own kind, and now faced the hangman's noose. The padre of the Guards Brigade came across another group of 'Boers' largely from the Home Countries: "in the little town jail I saw nine prisoners of war, only two of whom were genuine Boers. Some were Scotch, some were English, some were Hollanders; and one a fiery Irishman, who expressed so fervent a wish to be free, to revel in further fightings against us, that it was deemed desirable to adorn his wrists with a pair of handcuffs."[62] Many other Boers were European by birth* and journeyed to the Transvaal to join the crusade. In addition to those Hollanders based in South Africa at the outbreak of the war who volunteered to take part in the Boer invasion, a fair number of their Netherlands-based compatriots travelled to Pretoria via Lourcenço Marques to enlist in Kruger's army.[63] A small group of military engineers and artillery experts, including Lieutenants Boldingh and Keulemans and two sergeants, was even released from the Dutch army for service with the Boers.[64] In his book, *Brothers in Arms*, about Hollanders fighting for the Boers, Chris Schoeman falls over himself to convince his readers that, despite being paid to fight for a foreign power, somehow they were not mercenaries, because "These men received little remuneration from the Boer republics". Perhaps a mercenary is one who fights for another country

---

* A common trait: even as late as the 1960s and '70s, many Afrikaners were recent European immigrants, South African prime minister and the 'Architect of Apartheid', Dr Hendrik Verwoerd, being a notable example. Born in Holland, he was schooled in Bulawayo, Rhodesia, even winning a Beit Scholarship before continuing his studies in Nazi Germany. He was assassinated in 1966 by another immigrant, an unhinged parliamentary messenger, Dimitri Tsafendas. (The blood-stained carpet was only removed from the House of Assembly in 2004.)

for *a lot* of money rather than just for money? But either way, Schoeman inadvertently contradicts himself only one page later, stating that there was tension between Lieutenant Boldingh and locally recruited officers because he was earning twice what they were: 14/- a day instead of the 7/- for the locals.[65] So by any standard—even Mr Schoeman's made-up one—these men were mercenaries. And whether one approves or disapproves of such things, the simple fact is that mercenaries were far from unusual in the federal armies. Many were German or French, with one such German soldier of fortune making the rather improbable boast that he had served with the British army in the charge of the Light Brigade almost fifty years earlier. A group of French and German dogs of war served under one Baron von Weiss,[66] but were badly cut up and captured during the failed attack on Mafeking. This all proved very embarrassing when it transpired that Baron von Weiss was actually on leave from the German army at the time and shamelessly requested he be released so he could return to his unit.[67]

Other Boers were from all manner of exotic locations. Possibly the finest republican unit of the war was Danie Theron's scouts, a *corps d'elite* only some eighty strong, which quickly developed a formidable reputation as the eyes and ears of the republicans. Interestingly, however, "Many were not Boers: at various times the unit was said to contain men from Holland, France, Germany, Russia, Ireland, Bulgaria, Greece and Algeria".[68]

Though there were those who travelled thousands of miles to volunteer for Kruger's cause (or at least make money from it), some locals weren't quite so eager, with many Cape Afrikaners press-ganged into service as we saw in chapter five. And it was not only Afrikaners who were forced to fight for a cause they did not support. In the aftermath of the fight at Wagon Hill, some British Tommies and Boers met while searching the battlefield for wounded and dead comrades: "One of these Dutchmen signalled to the captain to come to one side, and he did so, 'I'm not a Dutchman,' said the enemy, 'I'm English, and there are hundreds like myself in the Boer lines—English, Scotch, Irish and German. We had to take the field, or we should have been shot. But they don't trust us. They would have none of us in this assault, but we were to have come up and garrisoned the hill when they had taken it. We shall be glad when the British are in Pretoria.'"[69] Indeed, there were so many English-speaking Boers (both volunteers and pressed men) among the besiegers of Ladysmith that one could often hear songs being sung round the campfires in English. After the successful British raid against the artillery on Gun Hill, a new English-language ditty was quickly adopted by the republicans, mocking the supposedly 'elite' Boer gunners and parodying the song *While London Sleeps*: "While Long Tom sleeps, and all his guards are sleeping, Fifty Tommies climbed the hill and blew him in a heap."[70]

Though against any civilized rules of war, the forcible recruiting of loyalists was widespread: "Republican conscription was equally wide reaching ... Even sons of British parentage were not allowed to cross the border and so escape this, in many a case, hateful obligation ... one of the sons of my Methodist farmer friend had been thus employed at Magersfontein, but had now seized the first opportunity of taking the oath and returning home."[71] One can imagine that if any these English-speaking Boers surrendered, they could expect to suffer terribly at the hands of the bitter-einders if they were unfortunate enough to be recaptured. Similarly, most of those few Natal Afrikaners who threw their lot in with the invading republicans had to flee when the Boers retreated after finding themselves in an "awkward position". One retreating Boer remembered "women in tears, with their children and infants in arms, cast reproachful glances at us for being the cause of their misery".[72] The same witness claimed that the local black population took their revenge on these Natal Boers, swooping down on their farms to loot and plunder.

It was a complicated and confused war in every way. It is bizarre enough that Irish loyalists and republicans faced one another on the battlefields of Natal, but an even more unusual encounter was recorded by Albert Hilder of the Royal Canadian Dragoons. One of the Boers they captured turned out to be a Canadian, born and brought up in Toronto. When asked why he was fighting his own countrymen, he declared that it was a matter of choice: he didn't like the British or Canadian methods.[73] It is not easy to define why some chose the sides they did: Kruger's invasions appealed to all manner of people for all manner of different reasons, rather than being a simple case of Boer versus Brit. Dozens of wars-by-proxy were being fought: to some it was the march of commercial progress against a corrupt, medieval theocracy. To others it was a chance to bring down the British Empire. To many of the republicans it was simply a war of loot and pillage, or to profit at the expense of African farmers or herders. To others it was a chance to build a new type of empire in Africa. Though their Marxist daydreams may not have sat comfortably with the later apartheid regime, extremist socialists like James Bain saw the Transvaal as a "wholesome rural world, which was trying to stave off the power of brutal capitalism". To hare-brained men like Bain, the Boer War was an idealistic clash between the rural world and the urban one.[74]

Many of those who sympathized with the republican cause, like Olive Schreiner, were so blinded by their irrational hatred of the British Empire that they instantly decided that Kruger's clique were the goodies, only then bothering to start "searching for a position that could reconcile her empathy with the Boers with her understanding of the racial injustice faced by the indigenous peoples".[75] Then, just like now, there were those who would support literally anyone against the British, no matter how corrupt, warlike, racist and undemocratic they were. Other left-wingers were equally happy to tie themselves in knots to back anyone who attacked the British Empire. When Keir Hardie was asked to explain his support for Kruger's crooked gang, he wrote: "As Socialists, our sympathies are bound to be with the Boers. Their Republican form of government bespeaks freedom, and is hateful to tyrants, whilst their methods of production for use are much nearer our ideal than any form of exploitation for profit."[76] Given that Kruger reigned over a corrupt, undemocratic nation with a blatantly racist constitution, at least this insane outburst shows there are none so blind as those who will not see. Olive Schreiner, Keir Hardie and James Bain would be delighted to know that this irrational mindset is still alive and well today.

CHAPTER FIFTEEN

A hopeless cause?

"Afrikanderdom has awakened to a sense of earnestness which we have not observed since the heroic war of liberty in 1881. From the Limpopo, as far as Capetown, the second Majuba has given birth to a new inspiration and a new movement amongst our people in South Africa … The flaccid and cowardly imperialism that had already begun to dilute and weaken our national blood, gradually turned aside before the new current that permeated our people … Now or never the foundation of a wide-embracing nationalism must be laid … The partition wall has disappeared … never has the necessity for a policy of a colonial and republican union been greater; now the psychological moment has arrived; now our people have awakened all over South Africa; a new glow illumines our hearts; let us lay the foundation-stone of a real United South Africa on the soil of a pure and all-comprehensive national sentiment."
—Afrikaner Bond mouthpiece, *Ons Land*, trumpets the defeat of the Jameson Raid and calls for the building of Afrikaans-led united South Africa

"With or without preliminary Boer successes, I cannot credit that any large number of Cape Colonists will raise the standard of revolt. Undoubtedly the South Afrikander Bond has, intentionally or not, openly or covertly, been neither more nor less than a gigantic conspiracy against British rule, British speech, and equality of rights. But the plotters lack the courage to give forcible effect to their sectional prejudices; consequently, there will be no general insurrection attempted in the Colony."
—writing days after Kruger launched his invasion, war correspondent Bennet Burleigh accurately opines that the Cape Afrikaners will not rise in revolt[1]

"Mr H. Steyn, the ex-president's brother, was arrested for not answering to a sentry's challenge and was sent to the Cape on parole. On the way he expressed himself freely to his fellow-travellers, condemning the Boer sieges and destruction of railways and bridges as mistakes. He said the intention was to invade the Cape, but the British were too quick for his countrymen."[2]
—F. T. Stevens in *Complete History of the South African War, in 1899–1902*

When Kruger launched his invasions in October 1899 the German foreign minister, Count von Bülow, confidently reported, "The vast majority of German military experts believe that the South African war will end with a complete defeat for the English. Nobody here believes that the English will ever reach Pretoria."[3] The count and various esteemed German military advisers might have thought a republican victory was inevitable at the time, but this is far from the view now commonly held. Instead, Kruger's crusade is generally thought of as a last desperate gamble, a forlorn hope, doomed to failure from the very beginning.

Of course, it is a question that can never really be answered, but let's take a moment to consider it anyway: could the Boers have won? Was theirs a hopeless cause from the start, or did they miss their chance?

Before one can even attempt to address these questions, one needs to understand the aims of the republicans to examine whether they were attainable or not. As we have seen, many modern writers prefer to dismiss all the evidence to the contrary, and to claim that Kruger's objectives were very modest; most seek to convince their readers, or perhaps themselves, that Kruger's war was "expressly of a limited nature", and not one of conquest,[4] that the war was rather started to preserve the "sovereignty of the state" or that the Boers were "fighting for their independence". The problem with such attempts to exonerate the republicans of all blame is the mass of evidence to the contrary. Even Professor Scholtz has to grudgingly admit that such blasé statements of innocence are contradicted by historical reality. Despite his claims that the war was categorically *not* one of conquest, the professor confesses that the republicans acted as "permanent governors and not temporary sojourners" in the land they captured and that they forced the British subjects who lived therein to join their armies. He also concedes that there were plans to provoke a massive uprising in the Cape Colony which would see it declaring unilateral independence from Britain and forming a "third Boer republic".[5] But let's be charitable for a moment, and accept the claims that the aim of poor old misunderstood Kruger was only ever simply to retain the sovereignty and independence of the Boer republics: could this laudable and reasonable objective have been achieved? And how? The answer is most certainly yes, and without any effort at all or a single shot being fired. Until Kruger and Steyn embarked on their assaults on British territory, the sovereignty of their republics was never in doubt in the first place, so the simplest way to have preserved it would have been to desist from attacking the pre-eminent Great Power of the age.

As we have seen, the British had absolutely no gripe whatsoever with the Orange Free State, so until Steyn nonsensically signed an offensive pact with Kruger's Transvaal, and then joined his invasion of British territory, the Free State had no reason at all to fear for its sovereignty. As for the Transvaal, its independence was slightly limited by the British retention of 'suzerainty' but this had so little practical impact as to be almost irrelevant. Theoretically, this suzerainty allowed Great Britain a say in the foreign affairs of the Transvaal but had not stopped Kruger from expanding his borders, nor his agents from seeking alliances with European powers, gaining the services of their military advisers and buying massive amounts of armaments from them.

The British were certainly pressing for electoral change in the Transvaal, but this is completely different from threatening their sovereignty; it is highly unlikely that they would have gone to war to secure this—and even when Kruger's invasions of British territory led to the annexation of the Transvaal, it was given self-rule within a few years. As we have seen, any comparison between the numbers of troops sent to defend British territories in southern Africa in 1899 and what the British military calculated it would need to conquer the Boer republics shows that an offensive war was simply not a realistic proposition. As well as the obvious lack of military planning for an invasion of the Transvaal, the British government would never have secured popular support for such a venture. Unlike the Transvaal, Great Britain was a functioning democracy with a free press and, even when British territory was invaded by the Boers, there were still those in politics and the media who sympathized with Kruger's plucky underdogs. Given that significant numbers of Britons felt this way even after a Boer invasion ignited the war, one can only imagine what the reaction of France, Germany and Russia would have been to an unprovoked British invasion of the Transvaal.

Nor should it be forgotten that lobbying for a fair franchise is completely different from threatening the independence of a nation. As General Joubert rightly stated, all that Kruger needed to do to avoid war was to adopt a five-year franchise.[6] It really was as simple as that: the introduction of a fairer franchise system would have involved no loss of sovereignty or independence. The world pressed for electoral reform in South Africa throughout the apartheid-era, but no one suggested that this was a threat to the nation's independence. The situation in the late 1890s was very similar: a large number of people who, by the accepted standards of the day, should have had the vote, didn't. These people, quite understandably, appealed to Britain to get involved and apply pressure to rectify what was patently a grossly unfair situation. Of course, it suits Boerphiles to postulate that the war was all about the Transvaal's independence, as such a smokescreen effortlessly paints the British government as the baddies while ignoring the reality of the situation. Enfranchising tens of thousands of tax-paying uitlanders who had lived in the ZAR for years would no doubt have ended Kruger's rule, but it would no more have ended the independence of the Transvaal than democratic elections ended the independence of South Africa in 1994.

Any government elected after the extension of the franchise to include large numbers of uitlanders would undoubtedly have made radical changes in the Transvaal, and the country would never have been quite the same again. But given that—in comparison with the British territories of South Africa—Kruger's Transvaal was a corrupt, racist, poorly run and utterly undemocratic kleptocracy, this would have been no bad thing. A more democratic Transvaal might well have gone on to gravitate toward the British Empire, but again, why would this have been a problem? And if it was the desire of the majority of the expanded electorate for this to happen, then so be it: that's the whole point of a democracy. It should never be forgotten that the Afrikaners only made up about half of the whites in the Transvaal, and that whites in turn made up a only small minority of the total population of that country; the fact that a small clique drawn a minority group would no longer be running the nation in no way means that the independence of the Transvaal would have ended. Kruger's propaganda machine and his current groupies seek to equate 'independence' with 'continued power for a small unrepresentative gang', but this is entirely irrational. Indeed, it would be like saying that the leaders of the United States would have been entitled to deny the vote to all but those of English extraction, on the spurious basis that the Pilgrim Fathers and the settlers of Jamestown were from England. The Transvaal, like the United States, was a nation founded by immigrants* and for one particular small group of such immigrants to demand the right to rule over all the others indefinitely was, and is, completely indefensible. So by any reasonable

---

* it is largely ignored today that, in anthropological terms, even the black tribes of the Transvaal were fairly recent arrivals on the scene

standard, or accepted use of the word, the independence of the Transvaal was never under threat: only the continuation of Kruger's corrupt regime was.

෨

So we have to accept that Kruger's aim in starting the war was nothing to do with independence, but rather a base desire to stay in power and for his 'chosen people' to continue to dominate the Transvaal. The fact that the British were the dominant power in southern Africa, and that a large section of the uitlanders were Britons who would always look to London to champion their cause, complicated his position immeasurably. The only way to square the circle was either to allow the uitlanders a fair franchise and hope beyond hope that they would vote for him, or replace Great Britain as the pre-eminent power in the sub-continent. Kruger was a cunning enough fellow to know that the uitlanders would never vote for him, but, to hang on to power a bit longer, he probably considered agreeing to Milner's demands at Bloemfontein, before dragging out the process of implementation, coupled with his old trick of simply rigging elections. That he did not risk this is perhaps because he had met his match in Milner and knew quite plainly that he would not have got away with it. So to preserve his hold on the levers of power, Kruger was left with little choice but to replace Great Britain as the major power in the region—something he, and his ilk, had long dreamed of.

As we have seen, the republican invasion plans were by no means the limited incursions as painted by some today, but were envisaged as delivering a knockout blow that would see the British driven from South Africa, relinquishing their position and allowing Kruger unfettered rule of an empire stretching "from the Zambesi to the Cape", which was the stated aim of the Afrikaner Bond.

Even if Steyn and Kruger had been content with the aims that they shared with Count Sternberg, this would have seen the Kimberley diamond fields annexed by the Orange Free State,[7] and the whole of Natal added to the ever-expanding Transvaal,[8] leaving a shattered and humiliated Great Britain with a vastly reduced presence in the region.

෨

As we know, the Boer invasions of Natal and the Cape Colony ultimately failed but could they have succeeded? Firstly, as witnessed earlier, the whole strategy of the Boer attack was fundamentally flawed. Natal was staunchly pro-British and thus never going to rise in support of a republican incursion. The Cape, on the other hand, was home to enormous numbers of Afrikaners and a far more likely recruiting ground.

Despite this, the republican army directed its main effort at Natal—and the capture of Durban—while largely ignoring the Cape Colony for the first month of the war. It was this failing more than any other that cost Kruger his chance of a South African empire. Even had Durban somehow fallen to the invaders, imperial reinforcements could have landed at a dozen other ports; it would have been a major inconvenience for the imperial cause, but not a knockout blow. In contrast, if Natal had been screened by forces dug in along the mountainous border, and 40,000 aggressively led Boer commandos had been unleashed into the Cape Colony, it is possible that this would have sparked a general uprising from the many Kruger sympathizers and Bondsmen there. From a conventional military point of view, this arguably would have given the republicans their best chance of victory. The result might have been the much-longed-for establishment of a 'third republic' in the Cape, with British South African territory reduced to just a naval base on the Cape Peninsular and in Natal. But even this best-case-scenario is at odds with Kruger's stated desire to capture Natal and, specifically, Durban.

However successful the Cape uprising might have proved, the republicans would still have struggled to seize imperial-held towns: when we look at their abysmal record in capturing defended positions—Ladysmith, Mafeking, Kimberley and even Kuruman and Wepener—there is no reason to believe that they could have swept into the likes of Cape Town, Port Elizabeth or East London unless massive numbers of the townspeople were in open insurrection.

Taking staunchly loyal Durban was a virtual impossibility: the British need only have landed just a few thousand troops, and imperial command of the sea would have ensured that the city could not have been starved into submission; the big guns of the Royal Navy's battleships and cruisers would have been devastating in defence of the town or firing in support of landings. Consider that just one of the Royal Navy's nine Majestic-class battleships—

each mounting four 12-inch guns,* twelve 6-inch guns and a further twenty-eight 12- and 3-pounder guns—comprised more firepower than all the artillery of both republics combined.

Alternatively, what if the Boers—with their chosen strategy of directing their main effort at Natal—had managed to win a Majuba-style victory?† Some writers have suggested that this was the republican plan all along, and that they believed the deliverance of a crushing defeat would be enough to prompt a British surrender. The problem with this theory is that the republicans never showed the necessary enthusiasm to force any of their sieges to a conclusion and these were their best chance of dealing a hammer blow to imperial prestige. If, however, they had shown a bit more grit and somehow forced the surrender of Ladysmith, for example, would the unthinkable capture of 12,000 imperial troops have sent the British scurrying to the negotiating table? Unlikely. Salisbury was cut from a very different cloth than the spineless Gladstone who threw in the towel so readily in the first Boer War; indeed, Gladstone was negotiating even before Majuba. We can never know for sure, but based on public reaction to the imperial defeats of Black Week, it is likely that a major Majuba-style defeat would actually have further galvanized the British public behind the war.

So how could the republicans have won? One alternative sometimes bandied about is that the Boers should have played to their supposed strengths and fought a guerrilla war from the outset, rather than trying to take the British army on in a conventional campaign. We have seen plenty of evidence in the run-up to war that the Transvaal Secret Service tinkered with sparking insurgency campaigns in neighbouring British territories,[9] but unless accompanied by an invasion it is unlikely these would have amounted to anything more than minor, if irksome, uprisings. The problem with this strategy is that, while sponsoring a terrorist campaign in a neighbouring country is a useful way to unsettle it and divert attention, it is very difficult to gain control of a neighbouring territory by such means unless there is a

---

* the revolutionary 12-inch Mk VIII could fling an 850lb shell—i.e. nine times the weight of a Long Tom shell—out to 10,000 yards

† it should be noted that Majuba was actually a skirmish; its impact has been blown out of all proportion to the numbers involved

sizeable chunk of the population therein who are 'on sides'. This was arguably the situation in the Cape Colony, and with additional gun-smuggling and propaganda, it is just about conceivable that extremist Bondsmen in some areas might have been persuaded to rise up against the British and fight for a 'third republic' without Kruger having to get directly involved. The chances were mighty slim, however; even when the republicans provided the catalyst of a conventional invasion, precious few Cape Afrikaners rose up and threw in their lot with Kruger and it is likely that any small-scale rebellion or guerrilla campaign would have been contained by local paramilitary forces. If British agents had discovered who was behind the scheme, HM government would have had a cast-iron *casus belli* against the republican states—though the reader will recall that it had overlooked the Transvaal's pre-war aggression in Rhodesia and Bechuanaland.[10]

Alternately, the republicans could have played for time: many in the Afrikaner Bond anticipated embarking on their invasion only when Britain was otherwise engaged in another conflict.[11] During the Boer War, and despite their enormous commitment to South Africa, Britain still managed to send 12,000 troops to China to help put down the Boxer Rebellion, as well as fighting and winning the War of the Golden Stool* and the Anglo-Aro War, and all while maintaining their far-flung garrisons and refusing to send non-white troops to fight the Boers. It is obvious, therefore, that for the distraction of another conflict to have proved decisive, Great Britain would have had to have been embroiled in a very major war with one of the other Great Powers, not something that happened terribly often and not something that would occur again for another fifteen years. Obviously, if the Boers had invaded at the same time that France made a play for Egypt or Russia had moved against India, for example, this would have had an enormous impact on the war in South Africa. Yet despite the best efforts of the Transvaal diplomatic corps, no Great Power could be persuaded to join the party.

Interestingly, and as we know, another member of the Bond told Michael Farrelly that they would have preferred to have had another twenty years to prepare for war,[12] which would have seen the Boer War pretty much coincide with the First World War. Could the republics have triumphed militarily if they had somehow managed to pull the wool over Milner's eyes, placated the

---

* despite its foul name, this conflict was actually named after a throne and was fought in present-day Ghana

growing resentment of the uitlanders, hung on for fifteen years and invaded the Cape and Natal in 1914 rather than 1899?

Kruger died in 1904 and Joubert in 1900, but many of the other Boer big-hitters were young in 1899 and would still have been around in 1914, and so, if anything, the loss of the pedantic Joubert would have been advantageous to any invasion plans. The delay would also have allowed the Transvaal to complete the purchase of vast numbers of modern artillery pieces—a programme cut short by war breaking out in 1899—and to continue spreading sedition and dissent in the Cape. It is impossible to know what sort of garrison such a hypothetical invasion would have faced, but only four battalions were actually deployed in the Cape in 1914.

Elsewhere at that time, the British army was certainly heavily committed to France—two divisions were held back in defence of the United Kingdom, but the British Expeditionary Force sent over the channel in 1914 still boasted four infantry divisions and a cavalry division, larger than the army corps that was mobilized to South Africa in late 1899 and representing most of Britain's deployable regular army. Over the course of the Great War the British expanded their army massively though, and as well as the many dozens of divisions deployed on the Western Front, were able to commit hundreds of thousands of imperial troops to side-shows like Gallipoli (490,000 imperial troops served in the eight-month campaign), Mesopotamia (350,000 imperial troops served there over the course of the war) and Macedonia (there were seven British divisions in theatre in 1917), so sending a significant expeditionary force to South Africa would not have been impossible later in the war, though perhaps unrealistic in 1914.

It should also be recalled that the Great War was not being fought as a 'white man's war'—Indian troops served with distinction in many theatres and the British utilized large numbers of African troops in German East Africa—so it is perfectly conceivable that they would have mobilized black South Africans following a 1914 Boer invasion. And had the republicans managed to hang on until 1914 to launch their invasions—which, given the increasingly volatile nature of uitlander protests, seems unlikely—obviously their chances of success or failure would have been strongly linked to that of their German allies. As the Germans lost, there is no reason to suppose that—even had the initial invasions of Natal and the Cape been successful—an Afrikaans empire could have lasted any longer than the Great War did. One must also consider that the First World War saw enormous industrialization of warfare and, by 1916, there would have been no way an Afrikaans empire could have even begun to compete in such a conflict. They would simply have had no answer to imperial tanks, armoured cars, aircraft and massed heavy artillery.

~

As it was, the only way Kruger could have won in 1899/1900 was through a lack of British political resolve, or if a more determined thrust into the Cape Colony had seen the Afrikaners rise *en masse* and declare for the Afrikaner Bond, which was never likely to happen and, as we have seen, many even fought against the invasion. Even had the Boers somehow managed to snatch both Cape Town and Durban (bearing in mind they failed to capture a single significant town throughout the war), Kruger might have been able to force some sort of a peace on the British, but militarily, there would have been little to stop imperial forces re-invading with an unopposed amphibious assault (South Africa's sea board is far too long to be protected). Alternatively, Portugal might have been coerced into permitting an expeditionary force to transit their colony of Mozambique (properly, Portuguese East Africa) to access Rhodesia or attack the Transvaal. In light of this, it is difficult to see how Kruger really could have expected his invasions to have succeeded, other than perhaps by his lunatic faith in Divine intervention. They were launched for the most dubious and base of reasons and essentially doomed to failure from the start, completely relying on the off-chance that the British would back down after a tactical defeat or another of the Great Powers would wade in on the side of the republicans.

The guerrilla war was similarly futile and, short of the British government suddenly deciding to throw in the towel, could never have achieved anything. As long as bitter-einders continued to be rounded up in their hundreds month on month, London was never going to simply abandon the large loyalist population of southern Africa. Indeed, the continuing antics of the bitter-einders served only to prolong the misery of their own people. They fought for the least pleasant of reasons, using the least pleasant of methods and for a hopelessly unwinnable cause.

As we have seen, some Boers who continued the fight into the guerrilla phase of the war were forced so to do for risk of their farms being torched by their more extreme brethren. Others were fooled into continuing the struggle by charismatic leaders or by the endless anti-British propaganda spewed from the pulpit. One can feel varying degrees of sympathy in all such cases, but when one strips away all the apartheid-era propaganda and other such nonsense, many of the hard-core bitter-einders were little better than murderers, renegades and bandits. Even those who could be labelled idealists were fighting for the continuance of rule by a miniscule minority, and against any sort of progress, democracy and the nascent moves toward racial equality found in British territory. None are in any way deserving of their reputation as gallant freedom fighters.

Afterword

"Given a fair field, man to man, Tommy is more than a match for the Boer,
even at the latter's own game. And the Boer now knows that for a fact."
—Bennet Burleigh sums up the respective forces after a few weeks of the war

"If you had tried to keep on friendly terms with us there would have been no war. But
you want to drive us out of South Africa. Think of a great Afrikander Republic—all South
Africa speaking Dutch—a United States under your President and your Flag, sovereign
and international." Their eyes glittered. "That's what we want," said one.
"Yaw, yaw," said the others, "and that's what we're going to have."
—Winston Churchill describes a conversation with some of his captors

"It is not business to allow lazy black men (even though they be brothers and neutrals) to
sit and pick their teeth outside their kraals whilst tired white men are breaking their hearts
trying to do heavy labour in short time. It is more the duty of a Christian soldier
to teach the dusky neutral the dignity of labour, and to keep him under guard,
to prevent his going away to talk about it."
—Captain E. D. Swinton DSO, RE on the importance of digging in,
and of getting other people to do it for you

"I do not think the Colonial Office ever expected the Boers to fight at the point they did—
and to the extent there was an element of bluff in the policy. But looked at in the light
of subsequent events one doubts whether Kruger ever intended to agree substantially
and honestly with the English demands. The enormous armament of the Transvaal
and its complete preparation for war seem to show that fighting
has been resolved upon for a long time past."
—Sir James Rose-Innes on the realities of the war, 6th November 1899

"The guerrilla fights the war of the flea, and his military enemy suffers the dog's
disadvantages: too much to defend; too small, ubiquitous,
and agile an enemy to come to grips with"
—Robert Taber in *War of the Flea: The Classic Study of Guerrilla Warfare*

So there we have it: a glimpse into the other side of the Boer War. No claims are made that this work is exhaustive or that it shows both sides of the coin: that was never the intention. If, however, it provokes some to challenge the commonly held view of the war, then I—unlike Paul Kruger—have achieved what I set out to do. That said, I encourage anyone who has found this book interesting or thought-provoking, or who has felt his blood boil at every page, to read more deeply into the subject; there are many different viewpoints and few 'right' and 'wrong' answers. I would especially encourage readers to seek out contemporary books, diaries and personal accounts of the men who served in and around the war, rather than blindly trust to those written by leftist academics several decades after the event or—worse—by the state-sponsored, bitter, Brit-hating, revisionist historians of the apartheid era.

The Boer War, like any war, will always prompt strong reactions from both sides even more than a century later, but that should not allow one to be blinded to the realities of the conflict. Once the anti-British propaganda is stripped away, it is plain that the Boers were not the innocent victims of the piece as so commonly portrayed. Kruger's Secret Service agents were fighting a war by proxy against British power in South Africa well before the Jameson Raid; episodes like the 'Bogus Conspiracy' should leave no one in any doubt as to Kruger's cunning and determination to provoke and justify a conflict with the British Empire.

The overall objective of the invasions is clear: Kruger and his clique wished to replace Great Britain as the dominant power in southern Africa. The only confusion was over just how much of British South Africa they would settle for: northern Natal, a route to the sea, or the whole colony? All of Bechuanaland and Griqualand West, or perhaps just the Kimberley diamond fields? How much of the Cape Colony would the British have been permitted to retain? It defies belief how some historians tie themselves in knots to explain away all the evidence to the contrary and claim that all the poor, blameless Boers wanted was their independence. The republican Boer regimes must be unique in having started a war by invading and annexing neighbouring territories, renaming captured towns, looting, murdering, pillaging and burning and yet still somehow managing to emerge as the innocent party in a war they blatantly started.

At no time did the republicans face 'half a million' British troops and nor were the Boers the gallant, superhuman warriors that their apologists like to pretend—sometimes they fought well, sometimes they fought badly. Ultimately, they were defeated militarily. Many of their senior officers proved hopelessly out of their depth and relied on the Almighty, rather than strategy and tactics, to win the war for them. And despite post-war propaganda efforts, even the younger, more dynamic leaders like de la Rey, de Wet and Smuts were on the wrong end of defeats more often than not.

Apartheid-era revisionist history has done a good job of painting the Afrikaners as a 'united *volk*' standing up to the might of the British Empire, but this was far from the case: the majority of Afrikaners wanted nothing to do with Kruger's insane invasion and even many of those who initially joined his crusade threw in the towel as soon as they could. Many thousands of other Afrikaners fought gallantly for the imperial cause, just as many of the so-called Boers were from Dublin, Glasgow, Liverpool, Boston, Moscow and Vienna.

As in all wars, atrocities occurred, but they were much more often perpetrated by the republicans rather than by imperial forces: there is no reason to continually focus on the failings and mistakes of the British and to ignore the Boer penchant for mass murder, castration, looting and pillage. Kruger's regime was not one deserving of our respect or sympathy: even by the standards of the day, it was corrupt, racist, aggressively expansionist, anti-Semitic and tacitly tolerant of slavery. If Kruger's Transvaal had somehow managed to replace Great Britain as the dominant power in southern Africa in 1899, this would have had an entirely negative effect on the sub-continent, as was demonstrated when men of a similar ilk eventually gained power in 1948.

I have no doubt that the painful truths set out in this book will not appeal to all, but so be it. Numerous writers spit out books with the sole intention of painting the British Empire in the blackest possible light, and without anyone turning a hair, so it seems only reasonable to present the other side of the argument. If I have done this and encouraged some to take a deeper and more objective interest in the Boer War, then it has been worthwhile.

Notes

Introduction
1. The *Daily Telegraph*, 26 June 2010
2. Scholtz, *Why the Boers Lost the War*, p. 1
3. Ibid, p. 6
4. Scholtz, p. 150
5. Pakenham, *The Boer War*, p. 573
6. Ibid, p. 45
7. Scholtz, p. 6
8. Nasson, *The War for South Africa*, p. 25

Chapter 1
1. Fitzpatrick, *The Transvaal from Within*, p. xiii
2. Ibid, p. xiv
3. Cook, *Rights and Wrongs of the Transvaal War*, p. 25
4. Welsh, *A History of South Africa*, p. 238
5. Creswicke, *South Africa and the Transvaal War*, Vol. 1, p. 1
6. Garrett, *The Story of an African Crisis*, p. 8
7. Ibid, p. 8
8. Ibid, p. 8
9. Botha *From Boer to Boer and Englishman*, p. 15
10. Welsh, p. 225
11. Walker, *A History of Southern Africa*, p. 314
12. Chilvers, *The Yellow Man Looks On*, p. 44
13. Walker, p. 312
14. Tingay & Johnson, *Transvaal Epic*, p. 76
15. Walker, p. 316
16. Welsh, p. 226
17. Thompson, *A History of South Africa*, p. 102
18. Ibid, p. 103
19. Gordon, *The Growth in Boer Opposition to Kruger, 1890–1895*, p. 8
20. Haggard, *A History of the Transvaal*, p. 18
21. Fisher, *The Transvaal and the Boers: A Brief History*, p. 46
22. Ibid, p. 46
23. Haggard, p. 18
24. Jeal, *Explorers of the Nile*, p. 82
25. Fisher, p. 35
26. Ibid, p. 36
27. Thompson, p. 104
28. Creswicke, Vol. I, ch. 2
29. Thompson, p. 103
30. Welsh, p. 237
31. Roberts, *Kimberley, Turbulent City*, p. 29
32. Thompson, p. 106
33. Botha, p. 14
34. Thompson, p. 106
35. Ibid, p. 129
36. Carter, *A Narrative of the Boer War*, p. 23
37. Heale, *Of Bullets and Boys*, p. 2
38. Haggard, p. 19
39. Carter, p. 20
40. Ibid, p. 21
41. Welsh, p. 254
42. Haggard, p. 23
43. Welsh, p. 254
44. Haggard, p. 22
45. Gibson, *The Story of the Imperial Light Horse*, p. 14
46. Fisher, p. 50
47. Welsh, p. 257
48. Fisher, p. 50
49. Haggard, p. 16
50. Creswicke, Vol. I, p. 30
51. Fisher, p. 50
52. Haggard, p. 28
53. Fisher, p. 52
54. Carter, p. 29
55. *Ibid*, p. 45
56. Haggard, p. 30
57. Ibid, p. 22
58. Carter, p. 49
59. Welsh, p. 269
60. Carter, p. 83
61. Ibid, p. 80
62. Ibid, p. 138
63. Ibid, p. 141
64. Ibid, p. 206
65. Roberts, *History of the English-Speaking Peoples*, Vol. IX, p. 265
66. Featherstone, *Victorian Colonial Warfare*, p. 64
67. Carter, p. 27
68. Welsh, p. 270
69. Fisher, p. 73
70. Creswicke, Vol. I, p. 103
71. Mason, *The Birth of a Dilemma: The Conquest and Settlement of Rhodesia*, p. 110
72. Theal, *History of South Africa from 1873–1884*, p. 133
73. Ibid, p. 146
74. Ibid, p. 147
75. Ibid, p. 148

76. Ibid, p. 150
77. Walker, p. 396
78. Theal, p. 152
79. Walker, p. 396
80. Theal, p. 153
81. Farrelly, *The Settlement After the War*, p. 68
82. Theal, p. 155
83. Ibid, p. 155
84. Ibid, p. 156
85. Walker, p. 403
86. Ibid, p. 399
87. Theal, p. 159
88. Ibid, p. 149
89. Ibid, p. 161
90. Ibid, p. 165
91. Ibid, p. 175
92. Ibid, p. 171
93. Ibid, p. 19
94. Ibid, p. 20
95. Walker, p. 402
96. Theal, p. 27
97. Encyclopaedia Britannica, 1911 edition, Swaziland entry
98. Haggard, p. 96
99. Encyclopaedia Britannica, 1911 edition, Swaziland entry
100. Nutting, *Scramble for Africa,* p. 287
101. Fitzpatrick, p. 45
102. Farrelly, p. 68
103. Encyclopaedia Britannica, 1911, p. 522
104. Scoble & Abercrombie, *The Rise and Fall of Krugerism*, p. 111
105. Ibid, p. 112
106. South African Military History Society, *Military History Journal*, Vol. 8 No. 5
107. Sternberg & Henderson, *My Experiences of the Boer War*, p. 78
108. Farrelly, p. 64
109. Botha, p. 18
110. Gordon, *The Growth in Boer Opposition to Kruger*, 1890–1895, p. 13
111. Wheatcroft, *The Randlords*, p. 5
112. Fitzpatrick, p. 310
113. Ibid, p. 307
114. Gordon, p. 8
115. Fitzpatrick, pp. 305-11
116. Gordon, p. 13
117. Ibid, p. 14
118. Fitzpatrick, p. 308
119. Biggar, *The Boer War: Its Causes and Its Interest to Canadians*, p. 28
120. Botha, p. 9

121. Walker, p. 412
122. Gibb, *The History of the British South Africa Police*, p. 91
123. Porter, *The Origins of the South African War, 1899–1902*, p. 72
124. Pakenham, p. 21
125. Conan-Doyle, *The Great Boer War*, p. 27
126. Colvin, *The Life of Jameson*, Vol. II, p. 12
127. Guardian, 18 November 2010
128. Conan-Doyle, p. 32
129. Garrett, p. 63
130. Bower, *Secret History of the Jameson Raid and the South African Crisis*, pp. 60-1
131. Ibid, p. 47
132. Pakenham, p. 21
133. Scholtz, p. 1
134. Meredith, *Diamonds, Gold and War*, p. 319
135. Walker, p. 442
136. Pakenham, p. xxii
137. Conan-Doyle, p. 35
138. Buttery & Cooper-Key, *Why Kruger Made War*, p. 35
139. Fitzpatrick, p. viii
140. Botha, p. 23
141. Ibid, p. 22
142. Ibid, p. 23
143. Fitzpatrick, p. ix
144. Welsh, p. 130
145. Yakan, *Almanac of African Peoples and Nations*, p. 689
146. Farrelly, p. 176
147. Scholtz, p. 6
148. Nathan, *Paul Kruger: His Life and Times*, p. 452

Chapter 2
1. Porter, p. 409
2. Ibid, p. 29
3. Ibid, p. 28
4. Hobson, *The War in South Africa, Its Causes and Effects*, p. 197
5. Lowry, p. 34
6. Bower, p. 47
7. Lowry, p. 42
8. Scholtz, p. 151
9. Lowry, p. 38
10. Stephens, *Fuelling the Empire: South Africa's Gold and the Road to War*, p. 263
11. Ibid, p. 259
12. Walker, p. 497
13. Porter, p. 408
14. Colvin, Vol. II, p. 259

15. Lewsen, *Selections of the Correspondence of J. X. Merriman, 1905–1924*, p. 161
16. Lowry, p. 44
17. Stephens, p. 262
18. Lowry, p.38
19. Ibid p. 45
20. Scholtz, p. 151
21. Farrelly, p. 66

Chapter 3
1. Cohen & Major, *History in Quotations*, p. 693
2. Lowry, p. 209
3. Abercrombie, *The Secret History of South Africa*, p. 240
4. Heyer, *A Brief History of the Transvaal Secret Service System*, p. 16
5. Ibid, p. 15
6. Hyslop, *The Notorious Syndicalist*, p. 113
7. *Star* (NZ), Issue 6695, 'The Transvaal Secret Service Stirring Up The Natives', 17 January 1900, p. 1
8. Heyer, p. 20
9. Lowry, p. 209
10. Meintjies, *President Paul Kruger*, p. 206
11. Lane, *The War Diary of Burgher Jack Lane*, 1899–1900, p. xxxiii
12. Porter, p. 71
13. Cook, *The Rights and Wrongs of the Transvaal War*, p. 92
14. *Times*, 25 May 1900
15. Cook, p. 93
16. Ibid, p. 93
17. Meintjies, *President Paul Kruger*, p. 218
18. Sternberg & Henderson, p. 69
19. Farrelly, p. 86
20. Cook, p. 94
21. Stevens, *Complete History of the South African War, in 1899–1902*, p. 19
22. Farrelly, p. 76
23. Ibid, p. 92
24. Fitzpatrick, p. xv
25. Walker, p. 390
26. Vershoyle, F., Vindex, *Cecil Rhodes: His Political Life and Speeches, 1881–1900*, p. 533
27. Farwell, *The Great Boer War*, p. 30
28. Roberts, *Salisbury, Victorian Titan*, p. 719
29. Porter, p. 52
30. Ibid, p. 53
31. Ibid, p. 97
32. Ibid, p. 101
33. Ibid, p. 96
34. Ibid, p. 98
35. Ibid, p. 137
36. Ibid, p. 104
37. Davenport, *The Afrikaner Bond: The History of a South African Political Party, 1880–1911*, p. 206–7
38. Ibid, p. 48
39. Meintjies, *President Paul Kruger*, p. 216
40. Walker, p. 388
41. Farrelly, p. 85
42. Thomas, *Origin of the Anglo-Boer War Revealed: The Conspiracy of the 19th Century Unmasked*, p. 51
43. Davenport, p. 47
44. Scoble & Abercrombie, p. 283
45. Farrelly, p. 269
46. Hancock & van der Poel, *Selections from the Smuts Papers*, Vol. IV, p. 321
47. The *New Zealand Tablet*, 25 October 1900
48. Farrelly, p. 96
49. Ibid, p. 78
50. Currey, *Vinnicombe's Trek*, p. 137
51. Stevens, p. 12
52. Ibid, p. 18
53. Farrelly, p. 89
54. Davenport, p. 65
55. Ibid, p. 66
56. Ibid, p. 88
57. Ibid, p. 89
58. Fitzpatrick, p. xvii
59. Cook, p. 94
60. Ibid, p. 95
61. Sternberg & Henderson, p. 73
62. Botha, p. 26
63. Wilson, *The International Impact of the Boer War*, p. 13
64. Ibid, p. 16
65. Farrelly, p. 168
66. War Office, *Military Notes of the Dutch Republics of South Africa*, p. 27
67. Farrelly, p. 285
68. Walker, p. 471
69. Fitzpatrick, p. 233
70. Walker, p. 472
71. Marlowe, *Milner: Apostle of Empire*, p. 47
72. Headlam, *The Milner Papers*, Vol. I, p. 226
73. Farrelly, p. 175
74. Ibid, p. 176
75. Ibid, p. 177
76. Ibid, p. 179
77. Welsh p. 323

78. Colvin, p. 186
79. Ibid, p. 187
80. Burleigh, *The Natal Campaign*, p. 9
81. Welsh p. 325
82. Porter, p. 130
83. Welsh p. 326
84. Ibid, p. 322
85. Farrelly, p. 183
86. Ibid, p. 178

Chapter 4
1. Scoble & Abercrombie, p. 126
2. Roberts, p. 722
3. Farwell, p. 33
4. Baynes, *My Diocese During the War*, p. x
5. Roberts, p. 717
6. Sternberg & Henderson, pp. 11-12
7. Scoble & Abercrombie, p. 17
8. Abercrombie, p. 74
9. Ibid, p. 93
10. Scoble & Abercrombie, p. 166
11. Lee, *To the Bitter End*, p. 127
12. Scoble & Abercrombie, p. 133
13. Ibid, p. 159
14. Ibid, p. 166
15. Walker, p. 476
16. Walker, p. 483
17. Stephens, p. 298
18. Fitzpatrick, p. 261
19. Walker, p. 477
20. Farrelly, p. 180
21. Meintjies, *President Paul Kruger*, p. 222
22. Farrelly, p. 173
23. Walker, p. 478
24. Cook, p. 120
25. Walker, p. 479
26. Cook, p. 120
27. Hyslop, p. 139
28. Farrelly, p. 182
29. Ibid, p. 183
30. Walker, p. 479
31. Cook, p. 123
32. Amery, Vol. 1, p. 301
33. Ibid, p. 302
34. Walker, p. 480
35. Ibid, p. 480
36. Meintjies, *President Paul Kruger*, p. 225
37. Gardner, *Mafeking: A Victorian Legend*, p. 16
38. Walker, p. 480
39. Pakenham, p. 66
40. Cook, p. 138
41. Porter, p. 225
42. Kruger, *The Memoirs of Paul Kruger*, p. 306
43. Cook, p. 139
44. Pakenham, p. 67
45. Headlam, p. 424
46. Walker, p. 480
47. Cook, p. 141
48. Pakenham, p. 68
49. Amery, Vol. 2, p. 120
50. Nasson, p. 37
51. Thomas, p. 80
52. Gibson, p. 18
53. Naville, *The Transvaal Question from a Foreign Point of View*, p. 36
54. Pakenham, p. 76
55. War Office, p. 14
56. Frere, *Letters from an Uitlander*, p. 21
57. Ibid, p. 20
58. Warwick, *Black People and the South African War, 1899–1902*, p. 58
59. Ibid, p. 55
60. Ibid, p. 65
61. Walker, p. 482
62. Ibid, p. 480
63. Nathan, p. 441
64. Walker, p. 478
65. Ibid, p. 481
66. Symons, *Buller's Campaign*, p. 111
67. Ibid, p. 112
68. Ibid, p. 115
69. Ibid, p. 113
70. Amery, Vol. 2, p. 120
71. Conan-Doyle, p. 60
72. Ibid, p. 61
73. Gibson, p17
74. Ibid, p18
75. Ibid, p15
76. Pakenham, p. 71
77. Thomas, p. 82
78. Ibid, p. 83
79. The *Sydney Morning Herald*, Saturday, 20 July 1899
80. Cook, p. 146
81. Ibid, p. 147
82. Roberts, p. 724
83. C.9415, p. 43
84. Cook, p. 150
85. Amery, Vol. 1, p. 300
86. Cook, p. 173
87. Ibid, p. 174
88. Cd. 369, p. 4
89. Cd. 547, p. 9
90. The *Times*, 28 October 1899

91. Cook, p. 175
92. Amery, Vol. 1, p. 302
93. The *Age*, 8 August 1899, and many others
94. Currey, p. 134
95. Amery, Vol. 1, p. 303
96. Cook, p. 177
97. The *Cape Times*, 24 August, 1899
98. Pakenham, p. 86
99. Walker, p. 481
100. Pakenham, p. 82
101. Ibid, p. 87
102. Cook, p. 179
103. C.9521, p. 45
104. C.9521, p. 46
105. Cook, p. 183
106. Ibid, p. 182
107. Farrelly, p. 216
108. Cook, p. 183
109. Cd.369, p. 6
110. Cook, p. 300
111. Pakenham, p. 86
112. Scoble & Abercrombie, p. 251
113. Cd.369, p. 2
114. Cd.369, p. 6
115. Cook, p. 191
116. Ibid, p. 198
117. C.9521, p. 64
118. Cook, p. 206
119. Ibid, p. 202
120. Cd.369, p. 6
121. Cook, p. 216
122. Farrelly, p. 214
123. The *Daily News*, 3 October 1899
124. Farrelly, p. 213
125. Roberts, p. 734
126. C.9530, p. 16
127. The *Daily News*, 27 September 1899
128. Ibid, 23 September 1899
129. Cd.369, p. 5
130. Cd.9530, p. 18
131. Abercrombie, p. 137
132. Pakenham, p. 104
133. Buttery & Cooper-Key, p. 16
134. Cook, p. 241
135. Stott, *The Boer Invasion of Natal*, p. 19
136. Stevens, p. 25
137. Stott, p. 30
138. Stevens, p. 26
139. Farrelly, p. 228
140. Brooke-Norris, *The Story of the Rand Club*, p. 65
141. Warwick, p. 127
142. Stott, p. 30
143. Warwick, p. 129
144. Walker, p. 486
145. Lane, p. 1
146. Ibid, p. 9
147. Cook, p. 241
148. Davitt, *The Boer Fight For Freedom*, p. 46
149. Amery, Vol. 2, p. 121
150. Walker, p. 484
151. C.9530, p. 47
152. C.9530, No.53
153. Farrelly, p. 222
154. Stott, p. 34
155. Burleigh, *The Natal Campaign*, p. 119
156. Sternberg & Henderson, p. 92
157. Cd.43, p. 139
158. Cd.43, p. 191
159. Farrelly, p. 227
160. Sternberg & Henderson, p. 88
161. Ibid, p. 86
162. Ibid, p. 93
163. Viljoen, *My Reminiscences of the Anglo-Boer War*, p. 273
164. Amery, Vol. 3, p. 68
165. Ibid, p. 69
166. Farrelly, p. 215
167. Amery, Vol. 3, p. 69
168. Scholtz, p. 87
169. Ibid, p. 133
170. Ibid, p. 86
171. Amery, Vol. 3, p. 69
172. Gibson, p. 16
173. Nasson, p. 36
174. Pakenham, p. 104
175. Abercrombie, p. 137
176. Commando, p. 15
177. Kotzé, *Memoirs and Reminiscences*, p. 32
178. Nasson, p. 36
179. Conan-Doyle, *The War in South Africa, Its Cause and Conduct*, ch. 11
180. Scholtz, p. 18
181. Ibid, p. 18
182. Ibid, p. 19
183. Stott, p. 219
184. Scholtz, p. 22
185. Porter, p. 392
186. Ibid, p. 371
187. Stott, p. 32
188. Porter p. 375
189. Stephens, p. 264
190. Cook, p. 231
191. Farrelly, p. 173
192. Creswicke, Vol. 3, p. 15

193. Amery, Vol. 2, p. 380
194. Sternberg & Henderson, p. 21
195. Roberts, p. 732
196. Ibid, p. 732

Chapter 5
1. Welsh, p. 270
2. Botha, *From Boer to Boer and Englishman*, p. 27
3. Hyslop, p. 138
4. Scholtz, p. 7
5. Nasson, p. 90
6. Pakenham, p. 77
7. Ibid, p. 76
8. Ibid, p. 77
9. Chalmers, p. 58
10. War Office, p. 52
11. Ibid, p. 52
12. Ibid, p. 29
13. Churchill, *My Early Life*, p. 228
14. War Office, p. 50
15. Ibid, p. 51
16. Ibid, p. 38
17. Ibid, p. 73
18. Ibid, p. 82
19. Ibid, p. 83
20. *Soldiers of the Queen*, issue 123, December 2005
21. Pakenham, p. 95
22. Baynes, p. 6
23. Pakenham, p. 99
24. Ibid, p. 107
25. Ibid, p. 97
26. Ibid, p. 111
27. Carver, *The National Army Museum Book of the Boer War*, p. 13
28. Farrelly, p. 225
29. Frere, p. 18
30. Churchill, p. 226
31. War Office, p. 15
32. Walker, p. 482
33. Headlam, p. 41
34. Lowry, p. 121
35. Nathan, p. 441
36. Cook, p. 297
37. Thomas, p. 64
38. Creswicke, Vol. 2, p. 85
39. Amery, Vol. 2, p. 294
40. Creswicke, Vol. 3, p. 50
41. Ibid, Vol. 3, p. 78
42. Pakenham, p. 105
43. War Office, p. 52
44. Scholtz, p. 7
45. Pakenham, p. 106
46. Scoble & Abercrombie, p. 246
47. Currey, p. 133
48. Ibid, p. 139
49. Farrelly, p. 263
50. Creswicke, Vol. 1, p. 188
51. Burleigh, p. 1
52. Ibid, p. 2
53. Burne, *The Naval Brigade in Natal*, p. 105
54. Burleigh, p. 4
55. Burne, p. 105
56. Sternberg & Henderson, p. 25
57. Ibid, p. 54
58. Ibid, p. 56
59. Farrelly, p. 266
60. Reitz, p. 15
61. Ibid, p. 16
62. Lane, p. 6
63. Ibid, p. 3
64. Stalker, *The Natal Carbineers: The History of the Regiment from its Foundation, 15th January, 1855, to 30th June, 1911*
65. Cook, p. 296
66. Farrelly, p. 59
67. Churchill, p. 250
68. Farrelly, p. 61
69. Nathan, p. 447
70. Ibid, p. 449

Chapter 6
1. Gardner, p. 50
2. Churchill, p. 229
3. Gardner, p. 63
4. Colville, *The Work of the Ninth Division*, p. 10
5. Roberts, A., *Salisbury, Victorian Titan*, p. 743
6. Nasson, p. 64
7. Ibid, p. 66
8. Ibid, p. 109
9. Ibid, p. 65
10. Pakenham, p. 168
11. Breytenbach, *Geskiedenis van die Tweede Vryheidsoorlog 1899–1902*, Vol. 1, ch. 15
12. Pakenham, p. 168
13. Scholtz, p. 18
14. Nasson, p. 108
15. Stalker, ch. 9
16. Pakenham, p. 168
17. Gibson, p. 144
18. Stott, p. 215
19. Warwick, p. 82

20. Ibid, p. 85
21. Lane, p. 49
22. Ibid, p. 52
23. Amery, Vol. 2, p. 123
24. Scholtz, p. 19
25. Macnab, *The French Colonel: Villebois-Mareuil and the Boers, 1899–1900*, p. 90
26. Ibid, p. 81
27. Mahan, *The Story of the War in South Africa*, p. 9
28. Amery, Vol. 2, p. 122
29. Stalker, ch. 9
30. Kruger, R., *Goodbye Dolly Gray: The Sory of the Boer War*, p. 74
31. Gibson, p. 42
32. Burleigh, p. 9
33. Torlage & Watt, *A Guide to the Anglo-Boer War Sites of KwaZulu-Natal*, p. 5
34. *Ibid*, p. 5
35. Stott, p. 39
36. Conan-Doyle, p. 82
37. Nasson, p. 199
38. Conan-Doyle, p. 84
39. Stott, p. 40
40. Ibid, p. 41
41. Selby, *The Boer War: A Study in Cowardice and Courage*, p. 58
42. Carver, p. 15
43. Kruger, R., p. 78
44. Conan-Doyle, p. 88
45. Stott, p. 54
46. Conan-Doyle, p. 89
47. Selby, p. 54
48. Torlage & Watt, p. 14
49. Reitz, p. 28
50. Selby, p. 55
51. Ibid, p. 56
52. Conan-Doyle, p. 91
53. Selby, p. 56
54. Conan-Doyle, p. 92
55. Reitz, p. 29
56. Conan-Doyle, p. 93
57. Selby, p. 57
58. Gibson, p. 29
59. Selby, p. 58
60. Kruger, R., p. 81
61. Carver, p. 16
62. Conan-Doyle, p. 97
63. Ibid, p. 98
64. Selby, p. 59
65. Carver, p. 16
66. Hall, *The Hall Handbook of the Anglo-Boer War*, p. 125
67. Conan-Doyle, p. 99
68. Selby, p. 60
69. Gibson, p. 31
70. Burleigh, p. 20
71. Selby, p. 64
72. Gibson, p. 34
73. Selby, p. 65
74. Lee, p. 86
75. Burleigh, p. 21
76. Sternberg & Henderson, p. 65
77. Nasson, p. 105
78. Viljoen, p. 18
79. Ibid, p. 25
80. Pakenham, p. 169
81. Gibson, p. 42
82. Selby, p. 66
83. Maurice & Grant *et al*, *The Official History of the War in South Africa 1899–1902*, Vol. 1, p. 45
84. Reitz, p. 32
85. Gibson, p. 43
86. Griffith, *Thank God We Kept the Flag Flying: The Siege and Relief of Ladysmith, 1899–1900*, p. 66
87. Nasson, p. 131
88. Pakenham, p. 147
89. Lee, p. 88
90. Maurice & Grant *et al*, Vol. 2, p. 532
91. Chalmers, p. 60
92. Gibson, p. 43
93. Creswicke, Vol. 2, p. 142
94. Carver, p. 19
95. Selby, p. 70
96. Reitz, p. 40
97. Burleigh, p. 29
98. Selby, p. 74
99. Reitz, p. 43
100. Conan-Doyle, p. 113
101. Ibid, p. 110
102. Gibson, p. 47
103. Selby, p. 74
104. Conan-Doyle, p. 123
105. Selby, p. 75
106. Gibson, p. 49
107. de Wet, *Three Years' War*, p. 23
108. Judd, *The Boer War*, p. 53
109. Gibson, p. 48
110. Kruger, R., p. 96
111. Carver, p. 20
112. Gibson, p. 46
113. Reitz, p. 44
114. Sharp, *The Siege of Ladysmith*, p. 44
115. Conan-Doyle, p. 213

116. Chalmers, p. 58
117. Amery, Vol. 2, p. 312
118. Conan-Doyle, p. 219
119. Amery, Vol. 2, p. 313
120. Conan-Doyle, p. 220
121. Gardner, p. 93
122. Baden-Powell, p. 216
123. Ibid, p. 217
124. Amery, Vol. 2, p. 271
125. Gardner, p. 94
126. Amery, Vol. 2, p. 266
127. Baden-Powell, p. 228
128. Amery, Vol. 2, p. 268
129. Baden-Powell, p. 233
130. Gardner, p. 71
131. Amery, Vol. 2, p. 272
132. Conan-Doyle, p. 129
133. Baden-Powell, p. 223
134. Ibid, p. 234
135. Gardner, p. 50
136. Ibid, p. 60
137. Amery, Vol. 2, p. 269
138. Ashcoft, *Victoria Cross Heroes*, p. 116
139. Gardner, p. 59
140. Baden-Powell, p. 226
141. Ibid, p. 262
142. Ibid, p. 273
143. Ibid, p. 277
144. Ibid, p. 237
145. Ibid, p. 240
146. Amery, Vol. 2, p. 269
147. Baden-Powell, p. 241
148. Gardner, p. 71
149. Amery, Vol. 2, p. 269
150. Gibbs, Vol. 1, p. 225
151. Ashcroft, p. 117
152. Gibbs, *The History of the BSAP*, Vol. 1, p. 225
153. Ibid, p. 226
154. Gardner, p. 75
155. Baden-Powell, p. 242
156. Ibid, p. 243
157. Amery, Vol. 2, p. 270
158. Gibbs, Vol. 1, p. 228
159. Lane, p. 5
160. Judd, p. 55
161. Pakenham, p. 118
162. Roberts, B., p. 29
163. Ibid, p. 27
164. Ibid, p. 32
165. Botha, p. 15
166. Roberts, B, p. 312
167. Ibid, p. 308
168. Amery, Vol. 2, p. 276
169. Ibid, Vol. 2, p. 276
170. Kruger, R., p. 165
171. Maurice & Grant *et al*, Vol. 3, p. 3
172. Amery, Vol. 2, p. 297
173. Maurice & Grant *et al*, Vol. 3, p. 3
174. Creswicke, Vol. 3, p. 26
175. Maurice & Grant *et al*, Vol. 3, p. 2
176. Amery, Vol. 2, p. 279
177. Ibid, p. 280
178. Ibid, p. 292
179. Ibid, p. 294
180. Nasson, p. 126
181. Warwick, p. 130
182. Ibid, p. 119
183. Nasson, *Abraham Esau's War: A Black South African War in the Cape, 1899–1902*, p. 117
184. Kruger, R., p. 99
185. Ibid, p. 101
186. Amery, Vol. 2, p. 298
187. Pakenham, p. 188
188. Slogging Over Africa, p. 66
189. Kruger, R., p. 110
190. Selby, p. 85
191. Kruger, R., p. 111
192. Barthrop, *Slogging Over Africa, The Boer Wars 1815–1902*, p. 66
193. Phillips, *A Tiger on Horseback: The Experiences of a Trooper and Officer of Rimington's Guides—The Tigers During the Anglo-Boer War 1899–1902*, p. 21
194. Conan-Doyle, p. 133
195. Pakenham, p. 188
196. Nasson, p. 136
197. Colville, p. 4
198. Selby, p. 86
199. Phillips p. 24
200. Selby, p. 87
201. Kruger, R., p. 113
202. Selby, p. 88
203. Lane, p. 19
204. Selby, p. 88
205. Amery, Vol. 2, p. 342
206. Conan-Doyle, p. 141
207. Pilcher, *Some Lessons from the Boer War, 1899–1902*, p. 17
208. Phillips, p. 29
209. Judd, p. 60
210. Phillips, p. 39
211. Carver, p. 26
212. Colville, p. 6
213. Carver, p. 26

214. Colville, p. 12
215. Carver, p. 26
216. Selby, p. 94
217. Conan-Doyle, p. 144
218. Selby, p. 94
219. Conan-Doyle, p. 146
220. Selby, p. 95
221. Lane, p. 27
222. Phillips, p. 42
223. Selby, p. 95
224. Amery, Vol. 2, p. 358
225. Ibid, Vol. 2, p. 384
226. Lane, p. 29
227. Nasson, p. 138
228. Carver, p. 27
229. Colville, p. 17
230. Selby, p. 93
231. Nasson, p. 126
232. Sternberg & Henderson, p. viii

Chapter 7
1.   Colville, *The Work of the Ninth Division*, p. 16
2.   Hall, *The Hall Handbook of the Anglo-Boer War*, p. 127
3.   Selby, *The Boer War: A Study in Cowardice and Courage*, p. 79
4.   Ibid, p. 96
5.   Colville, p. 14
6.   Carver, p. 32
7.   Ibid, p. 34
8.   Colville, p. 15
9.   Maurice & Grant, *The Official History of the War in South Africa, 1899–1902*, Vol. 2, p. 1
10. Sternberg & Henderson, p. 114
11. Lane, p. 68
12. Ibid, p. 88
13. Maurice & Grant, Vol. 2, p. 2
14. Carver, p. 42
15. Ibid, p. 41
16. Bourquin & Torlage *The Battle of Colenso*, p. 12
17. Selby, p. 106
18. Bourquin & Torlage, p. 24
19. Ibid, p. 19
20. Maurice & Grant, Vol. 1, p. 360
21. Ibid, p. 361
22. Bourquin & Torlage, p. 31
23. Burleigh, p. 125
24. Ibid, p. 119
25. Carver, p. 49
26. Sternberg & Henderson, p. 70

27. Reitz, p. 60
28. Lane, p. 52
29. Jones. S., *From Boer War to World War, Tactical Reform of the British Army, 1902–1914*, p. 60
30. Carver, p. 50
31. Amery, Vol. 2, p. 388
32. Maurice & Grant, Vol. 1, p. 309
33. Amery, Vol. 2, p. 389
34. Gibson, p. 69
35. Griffith, p. 151
36. Gibson, p. 70
37. Amery, Vol. 3, p. 169
38. Maurice & Grant, Vol. 2, p. 547
39. Sharp, *The Siege of Ladysmith*, p. 31
40. Amery, Vol. 3, p. 172
41. Pakenham, p. 271
42. Reitz, p. 59
43. Maurice & Grant Vol. 2, p. 549
44. Conan-Doyle, p. 238
45. Maurice & Grant, Vol. 1, p. 281
46. Holmes, *The Little Field Marshal: A Life of Sir John French*, p. 74
47. Maurice & Grant, Vol. 1, p. 281
48. Holmes, p. 74
49. Maurice & Grant, Vol. 1, p. 282
50. Holmes, p. 78
51. Stirling, *Our Regiments in South Africa*, p. 119
52. Holmes, p. 79
53. Ibid, p. 80
54. Selby, p. 135
55. Ibid, p. 137
56. Ibid, p. 140
57. Maurice & Grant, Vol. 2, p. 569
58. Maurice & Grant, Vol. 4, p. 700
59. Carver, p. 67
60. Sharp, p. 67
61. Carver, p. 76
62. Roberts, p. 752
63. Knox, *Buller's Campaign with the Natal Field Force of 1900*, p. 55
64. Selby, p. 124
65. Maurice & Grant, Vol. 2, p. 399
66. Selby, p. 127
67. Maurice & Grant, Vol. 2, p. 416
68. Maurice & Grant, Vol. 1, p. 433
69. Ibid, p. 435
70. Holmes, p. 82
71. Maurice & Grant, Vol. 1, p. 437
72. Holmes, p. 85
73. Maurice & Grant, Vol. 1, p. 443
74. Ibid, p. 445

75. Ibid, p. 448
76. Ibid, p. 443
77. Holmes, p. 87
78. Selby, p. 167
79. Holmes, p. 89
80. Maurice & Grant, Vol. 2, p. 17
81. Ibid, p. 23
82. Sternberg & Henderson, p. 159
83. Holmes, p. 90
84. Ibid, p. 91
85. Selby, p. 173
86. Maurice & Grant, Vol. 3, p. 394
87. Carver, p. 95
88. Lane, p. 98
89. Selby, p. 174
90. Holmes, p. 93
91. Selby, p. 175
92. Maurice & Grant, Vol. 2, p. 79
93. Holmes, p. 95
94. Colville, p. 42
95. Selby, p. 185
96. Ibid, p. 181
97. Maurice & Grant, Vol. 2, p. 242
98. Pilcher, *Some Lessons from the Boer War, 1899–1902*, p. 100
99. Maurice & Grant, Vol. 2, p. 425
100. Gillings, *The Battle of the Thukela Heights*, p. 4
101. Maurice & Grant, Vol. 2, p. 432
102. Ibid, p. 429
103. Ibid, p. 432
104. Ibid, p. 435
105. Knox, p. 84
106. Ibid, p. 85
107. Amery, Vol. 2, p. 450
108. Gillings, p. 11
109. Knox, p. 86
110. Ibid, p. 88
111. Gillings, p. 13
112. Maurice & Grant, Vol. 2, p. 461
113. Gillings, p. 20
114. Knox, p. 97
115. Gillings, p. 25
116. Knox, p. 103
117. Ibid, p. 104
118. Ibid, p. 108
119. Gillings, p. 38
120. Ibid, p. 44
121. Reitz, p. 88
122. Carver, p. 125
123. Gillings, p. 32
124. Selby, p. 187
125. Holmes, p. 97
126. Ibid, p. 98
127. Selby, p. 187
128. Maurice & Grant Vol. 2, p. 201
129. Selby, p. 188
130. Maurice & Grant, Vol. 2, p. 209
131. Ibid, p. 210
132. Ibid, p. 211
133. Ibid, p. 229
134. Selby, p. 188
135. St Leger, *Boer War Sketches: With the Mounted Infantry at War*, p. 246
136. Carver, p. 130
137. Maurice & Grant, Vol. 2, p. 32

Chapter 8

1. Knox, p. 108
2. *The Sword of the Prophet*, p. 3
3. Martin, *The Concentration Camps: 1900–1902: Facts, Figure and Fables*, p. 8
4. Diary of Captain George Clarke, entry for 13 June 1900
5. Pakenham, p. 487
6. Donovan, *A Terrible Glory: Custer and The Little Bighorn*, p. 174
7. Maurice & Grant, Vol. 2, p. 263
8. St Leger, p. 117
9. Lowry, p. 204
10. Carver, p. 145
11. Maurice & Grant, Vol. 2, p. 243
12. Ibid, p. 248
13. Ibid, p. 258
14. Selby, p. 196
15. Holmes, p. 102
16. Maurice & Grant, Vol. 2, p. 299
17. Carver, p. 147
18. Maurice & Grant, Vol. 2, p. 314
19. Ibid, p. 316
20. Pakenham, p. 395
21. Maurice & Grant, Vol. 3, p. 40
22. Nasson, p. 191
23. Maurice & Grant, Vol. 3, p. 31
24. Ibid, p. 27
25. Ibid, p. 538
26. Ibid, p. 41
27. Ibid, p. 49
28. Amery, Vol. 4, p. 105
29. Diary of Private J. W. Milne, Gordon Highlanders, entry for 5 May 1900
30. Amery, Vol. 4, p. 118
31. Lowry, E. P., *With the Guards' Brigade During the Boer War: On Campaign from Bloemfontein to Koomati Poort and Back*, p. 71

32. Maurice & Grant, Vol. 3, p. 62
33. Ibid, p. 63
34. Amery, Vol. 4, p. 129
35. Churchill, *Ian Hamilton's March*, p. 527
36. Carver, p. 147
37. Ibid, p. 153
38. Ibid, p. 154
39. Ibid, p. 152
40. Maurice & Grant, Vol. 3, p. 183
41. Diary of Private J. W. Milne, Gordon Highlanders, entry for 2 May 1900
42. Carver, p. 160
43. Morris, *A Canadian Mounted Rifleman at War, 1899–1902*, p. 33
44. Nasson, p. 199
45. Selby, p. 200
46. Nasson, p. 201
47. Selby, p. 201
48. Carver, p. 162
49. Warwick, 1899-1902, p. 131
50. Holmes, p. 107
51. Carver, p. 163
52. Diary of RSM Ernest J. Sullivan (Regimental No. 4430), Worcestershire Regiment
53. Holmes, p. 108
54. The *South African Military History Society*, Vol. 11, No. 6, December 2000
55. Lee, p. 124
56. Selby, p. 207
57. Conan-Doyle, p. 481
58. Lee, p. 171
59. Carver, p. 202
60. Ibid, p. 204
61. Amery, Vol. 2, p. 274
62. Ibid, p. 274
63. Carver, p. 169
64. Unger, *With 'Bobs' and Kruger*, p. 256
65. The *South African Military History Society*, Vol. 11, No. 6, December 2000
66. Unger, p. 269
67. Ibid, p. 254
68. Ibid, p. 262
69. Martin, p. 3
70. War Office, p. 44
71. Warwick, p. 121
72. Maurice & Grant, Vol. 4, p. 468
73. Warwick, p. 122
74. Nasson, *Abraham Esau's War*, p. 112
75. Botha, p. 29
76. Nasson, *Abraham Esau's War*, p. 120
77. Ibid, p. 112
78. Wilson, *After Pretoria: The Guerrilla War*, p. 11
79. Lee, p. 137
80. Nasson, p. 211
81. Schoeman, *Brothers in Arms: Hollanders in the Anglo-Boer War*, p. 62
82. The *South African Military History Society*, Vol. 12, No. 1, June 2001
83. Amery, Vol. 5, p. 199
84. Ibid, p 199
85. Wilson, p. 70
86. Ibid, p. 71
87. Ibid, p. 72
88. Ibid, p. 43
89. Conan-Doyle p. 633
90. Carver, p. 213
91. Stevens, p. 389
92. Wilson, p. 72
93. Ibid, p. 20
94. Creswicke, p. 32
95. Ibid, p. 33
96. Wilson, p. 20
97. Ibid, p. 20
98. Nasson, p. 223
99. Conan-Doyle, p. 648
100. Warwick, p. 101
101. Nasson, *Abraham Esau's War*, p. 103
102. Pakenham, p. 573
103. Nasson, *Abraham Esau's War*, p. 106
104. Burleigh, p. 62
105. Nasson, *Abraham Esau's War*, p. 103
106. Ibid, p. 102
107. Ibid, p. 101
108. Carver, p. 211
109. Nasson, *Abraham Esau's War*, p. 122
110. Ibid, p. 128
111. Ibid, p. 131
112. Ibid, p. 132
113. Ibid, p. 107
114. Warwick, p. 121
115. Jooste, *Innocent Blood*, p. 152
116. Wilson, p. 76
117. Ibid, p. 78
118. Ibid, p. 80
119. Conan-Doyle, p. 655
120. Jooste, p. 152
121. Pakenham, p. 573
122. Conan-Doyle, p. 655
123. Holmes, p. 113
124. Maurice & Grant, Vol. 4, p. 704
125. Lowry, E. P., p. 61
126. Maurice & Grant, Vol. 4, p. 705
127. Carr, *Pioneer's Path: Story of a Career on the Witwatersrand*, p. 125

128. Ibid, p. 119
129. Ibid, p. 121
130. Ibid, p. 125
131. Botha, p. 31
132. Martin, p. 3
133. Currey, p. 163
134. Conan-Doyle, p. 645
135. Botha, p. 34
136. Stevens, p. 363
137. Ibid, p. 364
138. Conan-Doyle, p. 593
139. Wilson, p. 10
140. SAMHS newsletter no.329, Natal
     Branch, November 2002
141. The *Bathurst Free Press and Mining
     Journal*, 7 September 1901
142. Conan-Doyle, p. 626
143. Carver, p. 243
144. Wilson, p. 34
145. Milne, *Anecdotes of the Anglo-Boer War*,
     p. 74
146. Wilson, p. 28
147. Carver, p. 237
148. Conan-Doyle, p. 651
149. Holmes, p. 115
150. Witton, *Bushveldt Carbineers*, p. 48
151. Carver, p. 184
152. Ibid, p. 188
153. Lowry, E. P., p. 59
154. Lane, p. xxiv
155. Diary of Captain George Clarke, Royal
     Artillery, entry for 27 August, 1900
156. Nasson, *Abraham Esau's War*, p. 118
157. Nasson, p. 242
158. Carver, p. 238
159. Jooste, p. 71
160. Maurice & Grant, Vol. 4, p. 454
161. Ibid, p. 69
162. Carver, p. 211
163. Maurice & Grant, Vol. 4, p. 470
164. Carver, p. 241
165. Diary of Captain E. C. F. Wodehouse,
     2nd Batt. Worcestershire Regt., entry
     for 29 March 1902
166. Maurice & Grant, Vol. 4, p. 705
167. Lee, p. 172
168. The *South African Military History Society*,
     Vol. 11, No. 6, December 2000
169. Lee, p. 172
170. Diary of RSM Ernest J. Sullivan
     (Regimental No. 4430), Worcestershire
     Regiment
171. Wilson, p. 9

172. Pakenham, p. 563
173. Pakenham, p. 491
174. Conan-Doyle, p. 740
175. Warwick, p. 164
176. Unger, p. 271
177. Conan-Doyle, p. 648

Chapter 9
1. Nasson, p. 210
2. Ibid, p. 243
3. Morris, p. 83
4. Lowry, E. P., p. 59
5. Stott, p. 122
6. Ibid, p. 40
7. Currey, p. 143
8. Meintjies, *The Commandant General*,
    p. 174
9. Ibid, p. 175
10. Stott, p. 111
11. Amery, Vol. 2, p. 301
12. Stott, p. 215
13. Ibid, p. 109
14. Creswicke, Vol. 2, p. 131
15. Burleigh, p. 62
16. Baynes, p. 86
17. Ibid, p. 92
18. Ibid, p. 118
19. Amery, Vol. 2, p. 300
20. Gibson, p. 144
21. Stott, p. 165
22. Ibid, p. 211
23. Unger, p. 336
24. Stott, p. 114
25. Ibid, p. 121
26. Conan-Doyle, p. 218
27. Hobhouse, *The Brunt of the War and
    Where it Fell*, p. 9
28. The *Daily Chronicle*, 31 May 1900
29. Unger, p. 269
30. Martin, p. 4
31. Amery, Vol. 2, p. 294
32. Conan-Doyle, p. 204
33. Amery, Vol. 3, p. 118
34. Roberts, p. 767
35. Beckett, *Modern Insurgencies and
    Counter-Insurgencies*, p. 25
36. Silbey, *A War of Frontier and Empire: The
    Philippine-American War, 1899–1902*,
    p. 157
37. Ibid, p. 196
38. Miller, *Benevolent Assimilation*, p. 220
39. Silbey, p. 194
40. Miller, p. 238

41. Ibid, p. 88
42. Silbey, p. 148
43. Theal, *History of South Africa Since 1795*, Vol. 8, p. 242
44. Ibid, p. 246
45. Ibid, p. 253
46. Ibid, p. 255
47. Ibid, p. 264
48. Ibid, p. 278
49. Ibid, p. 285
50. Ibid, p. 286
51. Ibid, p. 294
52. Theal, p. 298
53. Ibid, p. 489
54. Martin, p. 8
55. Carver, ch. 6, various letters
56. Martin, p. 2
57. Ibid, p. 3
58. Lee, p. 173
59. Martin, p. 2
60. Wilson, p. 19
61. Diary of RSM Ernest J. Sullivan (Regimental No. 4430), Worcestershire Regiment
62. Morris, p. 55
63. Ibid, p. 22
64. Carr, p. 110
65. Ibid, p. 106
66. Ibid, p. 122
67. Ibid, p. 127
68. St Leger, p. 226
69. Ibid, p. 227
70. Ibid, p. 265
71. Unger, p. 251
72. Morris, p. 31
73. Lowry, E. P., p. 73
74. Ibid, p. 59
75. Diary of Capt. George Clarke, Royal Artillery, 17 September 1900
76. Lowry, E. P., p. 51
77. Nasson, *Abraham Esau's War*, p. 112
78. Wilson, p. 77
79. Ibid, p. 76
80. Nasson, *Abraham Esau's War*, p. 101
81. Ibid, p. 105
82. Ibid, p. 105
83. Burne, *With the Naval Brigade in Natal*, p. 39
84. Stott, p. 139
85. Ibid, p. 182
86. Sibbald, *The War Correspondents: The Boer War*, p. 142
87. Creswicke, Vol. 3, p. 10

88. Amery, Vol. 2, p. 274
89. Beckett, p. 42
90. Hastings, *Catastrophe, Europe Goes to War, 1914*, p. 537
91. Ibid, p. 38
92. Ibid, p. 30
93. Ibid, p. 27
94. Ibid, p. 26
95. Jooste, p. 192
96. Ibid, p. 202
97. Creswicke, Vol. 3, p. 75
98. Beckett, I. F. W., *The South African War and the Late Victorian Army*
99. Stevens, p. 377
100. Witton p. 59
101. Ibid, p. 59
102. Stott, p. 211
103. Nasson, p. 268
104. St Leger, p. 274
105. Burne, p. 101
106. Ibid, p. 103

Chapter 10

1.   Walker, p. 498
2.   Pakenham, p. 569
3.   Ibid, p. 570
4.   Nasson, p. 245
5.   van Heyningen, *The Concentration Camps of the Anglo-Boer War*, p. 268
6.   Barthrop, *Slogging Over Africa*, back cover
7.   Miller, p. 243
8.   Ibid, p. 232
9.   Roberts, p. 803
10. Miller, p. 9
11. Pretorius, *Scorched Earth*, p. 42
12. Conan-Doyle, p. 506
13. Unger, p. 326
14. The *Brisbane Courier*, Monday, 18 June 1900
15. Martin, p. 53
16. The *Nelson Evening Mail*, 20 June 1900
17. The *Advertiser* (Adelaide), Thursday, 30 August 1900
18. The *Examiner*, Friday, 24 August 1900
19. Amery, Vol. 4, p. 457
20. The *Marlborough Express*, Wednesday, 5 September 1900
21. The *Brisbane Courier*, Wednesday, 5 September 1900
22. The *Bruce Herald*, Tuesday, 4 September 1900
23. The *Examiner*, Monday, 18 June 1900

24. van Heyningen, p. 46
25. Ibid, p. 48
26. Ibid, p. 53
27. Hobhouse, p. 34
28. Martin, p. 3
29. Ibid, p. 9
30. Ibid, p. 1
31. Roberts, p. 805
32. Martin, p. 8
33. Maurice & Grant, Vol. 4, p. 660
34. Ibid, p. 661
35. Devitt, *The Concentration Camps in South Africa*, p. 19
36. Burne, p. 108
37. van Heyningen, p. 252
38. Devitt, p. 25
39. Warwick, p. 46
40. Ibid, p. 146
41. Ibid, p. 147
42. Ibid, p. 155
43. Ibid, p. 157
44. Martin, p. 7
45. Ibid, p. 5
46. Martin, Vol. 5, p. 66
47. Nasson, p. 289
48. Martin, p. 58
49. Milne, p. 28
50. Martin, p. 60
51. van Heyningen, p. 253
52. Milne, p. 27
53. Martin, p. 58
54. Lane, p. xxiv
55. Roberts, p. 804
56. 'A Tool For Modernisation? The Boer Concentration Camps of the South African War, 1900–1902', *South African Journal of Science*, Vol. 106, No. 5–6, Pretoria, May/June 2010
57. Patterson, *Life in Victorian Britain*, p. 53
58. Ibid, p. 56
59. Ibid, p. 55
60. Ibid, p. 59
61. Martin, p. 36
62. Devitt, p. 29
63. Theal, *History of South Africa since 1795*, Vol 8, p. 491
64. Roberts, B., p. 225
65. Martin, p. 38
66. Devitt, p. 37
67. Wise, *The Blackest Streets: The Life and Death of a Victorian Slum*, p. 8
68. van Heyningen, p. 41
69. Ibid, p. 40
70. Wise, p. 9
71. Martin p. 37
72. Ibid, p. 36
73. James, *Lord Roberts*, p. 315
74. Martin p. 26
75. Ibid p. 34
76. Silbey, p. 201
77. Jeal, *Stanley: The Impossible Life of Africa's Greatest Explorer*, p. 47
78. Hastings, p. 513
79. Martin, p. 30
80. van Heyningen, p. 16
81. Ibid, p. 17
82. Lane, p. 50
83. Ibid, p. 51
84. Stott, p. 163
85. Ibid, p. 211
86. Martin, p. 41
87. 'A Tool For Modernisation? The Boer Concentration Camps of the South African War, 1900–1902'
88. van Heyningen, p. 210
89. Milne, p. 27
90. 'A Tool For Modernisation? The Boer Concentration Camps of the South African War, 1900–1902'
91. van Heyningen, p. 211
92. Sibbald, p. 227
93. Ibid, p. 229
94. Martin p. 77
95. van Heyningen, p. 21
96. Martin, p. 79
97. Ibid, p. 80
98. 'A Tool For Modernisation? The Boer Concentration Camps of the South African War, 1900–1902'
99. van Heyningen, p. 214
100. Lee, p. 175
101. van Heyningen, p. 128
102. Ibid, p. 146
103. Ibid, p. 211
104. Martin, p. 81
105. Ibid p. 82
106. Warwick, p. 148
107. Milne, p. 28
108. van Heyningen, p. 18
109. Lee, p. 185
110. Roberts, p. 803
111. de Villiers, *White Tribe Dreaming: Apartheid's Bitter Roots as Witnessed by Eight Generations of an Afrikaner Family*, p. 238
112. 'A Tool For Modernisation? The Boer

Concentration Camps of the South
African War, 1900–1902'
113. Martin, p. 15
114. Ibid, p. 17
115. Hobhouse, p. 159
116. Allenby, p. 46
117. Martin, p. 55
118. Lee, p. 185
119. Martin, p. 31
120. Ibid, p. 34
121. Roberts, p. 804
122. 'A Tool For Modernisation? The Boer
concentration camps of the South
African War, 1900-1902'
123. Ibid
124. van Heyningen, p. 253
125. Martin, p. 61
126. van Heyningen, p. 254
127. 'A Tool For Modernisation? The Boer
concentration camps of the South
African War, 1900-1902'
128. Martin, p. 65
129. Ibid, p. 59
130. van Heyningen, p. 265
131. Ibid, p. 264
132. Ibid, p. 267
133. Martin, p. 51
134. Ibid, p. 65
135. Roberts, p. 805
136. Martin p. 19
137. Headlam, Vol. 2, p. 298
138. Roberts, p. 805
139. The Number of the South African
War (1899–1902) Concentration Camp
Dead: Standard Stories, Superior
Stories and a Forgotten Proto-
Nationalist Research Investigation, 3.10
140. Ibid, 3.7
141. Ibid, 3.16
142. van Heyningen, p. 234
143. Ibid, p. 235
144. The Number of the South African
War (1899–1902) Concentration Camp
Dead: Standard Stories, Superior
Stories and a Forgotten Proto-
Nationalist Research Investigation, 3.19
145. Ibid, 5.2
146. van Heyningen, p. 316
147. Walker, p. 498
148. Roberts, p. 805
149. Abercrombie, p. 239
150. van Heyningen, p. 19
151. Roberts, p. 805
152. Martin, p. 18
153. Walker, p. 498

Chapter 11
1. Maurice & Grant, Vol. 4, p. 135
2. Pearse, *Four Months Besieged: The Story of
Ladysmith*, p. 148
3. Pakenham, p. 457
4. Nasson, p. 109
5. Ibid, p. 129
6. Ibid, p. 121
7. Ibid, p. 129
8. Ibid, p. 123
9. Viljoen, p. 272
10. McFadden, *The Battle of Elandslaagte: 21
October 1899*, p. 15
11. Jeal, *Baden-Powell*, p. 237
12. Lane, p. 64
13. Gardner, *Mafeking: A Victorian Legend*,
p. 88
14. Ibid, p. 166
15. Ibid, p. 181
16. Ibid, p. 186
17. Reitz, p. 43
18. Viljoen, p. 30
19. Burne, p. 105
20. Pakenham, p. 574
21. Burne, p. 65
22. Pakenham, p. 456
23. The *South African Military History Society
Journal*, Vol. 11, No. 3/4, October 1999
24. Pakenham, p. 457
25. Maurice & Grant, Vol. 1
26. Pakenham, p. 207-241
27. Ibid, p. 395
28. Nasson. p. 189
29. Amery, Vol. 4, p. 57
30. Pakenham, p. 395
31. Amery, Vol. 4, p. 56
32. Maurice & Grant, Vol. 2, p. 316
33. Ibid, p. 314
34. Creswicke, Vol. 5, p. 54
35. Ibid, p. 54
36. Ibid, p. 58
37. Ibid, p. 58
38. Kruger, *Goodbye Dolly Gray*, p. 281
39. Creswicke, Vol. 5, p. 63
40. Amery, Vol. 4, p. 66
41. Amery, Vol. 5, p. 13
42. Conan-Doyle, p. 635
43. Amery, Vol. 5, p. 288
44. Conan-Doyle, p. 636
45. Ibid, p. 637

46. Maurice & Grant, Vol. 4, p. 61
47. Ibid, p. 63
48. Ibid, p. 90
49. Stevens, p. 390
50. Ibid, p. 392
51. Maurice & Grant, Vol. 4, p. 85
52. Ibid, p. 88
53. Stevens, p. 395
54. Maurice & Grant, Vol. 4, p. 90
55. The *South African Military History Society Journal*, Vol. 2 No. 1, June 1971
56. Pakenham, p. 531
57. Maurice & Grant, Vol. 4, p. 310
58. Ibid, p. 305
59. Ibid, p. 314
60. Pakenham, p. 536
61. Maurice & Grant, Vol. 4, p. 313
62. Conan-Doyle, p. 608
63. The *South African Military History Society Journal*, Vol. 2, No. 1, June 1971
64. Ibid
65. Pakenham, p. 532
66. The *South African Military History Society Journal*, Vol. 2, No. 1, June 1971
67. Pakenham, p. 532
68. The *South African Military History Society Journal*, Vol. 2, No. 1, June 1971
69. Maurice & Grant, Vol. 4, p. 220
70. Ibid, p. 221
71. *South African Military History Society Journal*, Vol. 8, No. 1, June 1989
72. Maurice & Grant, Vol. 4, p. 222
73. Pakenham, p. 470
74. Nasson, p. 217
75. Pakenham, p. 479
76. 1410 *Ibid*, p. 480
77. Maurice & Grant, Vol. 4, p. 4
78. Ibid, p. 6
79. Pakenham, p. 556
80. Maurice & Grant, Vol. 3, p. 358
81. Odgers, *Army Australia: An Illustrated History*, p. 41
82. www.marico.co.za/elandsriver/
83. Conan-Doyle, p. 596
84. Maurice & Grant, Vol. 4, p. 131
85. Ibid, p. 133
86. Walker, p. 497
87. Maurice & Grant, Vol. 4, p. 134
88. Ibid, p. 135
89. Conan-Doyle, p. 611
90. Creswicke, Vol. 7, p. 34
91. Maurice & Grant, Vol. 4, p. 135
92. Conan-Doyle, p. 612
93. Ibid, p. 613
94. Ibid, p. 613
95. Jones & Jones, *A Gazetteer of the Second Anglo-Boer War 1899–1902*, p. 245
96. Conan-Doyle, p. 613
97. Sibbald, p. 220
98. Conan-Doyle, p. 609
99. Ibid, p. 610
100. Ibid, p. 609
101. Holmes, p. 115
102. Ibid, p. 112
103. Pakenham, p. 527
104. The *South African Military History Society Journal*, Vol. 1 No. 5
105. Jooste, p. 71
106. Ibid, p. 72
107. Maurice & Grant, Vol. 4, p. 368
108. Pakenham, p. 566
109. Ibid, p. 567

Chapter 12
1. Phillips, *A Tiger on Horseback: The Experiences of a Trooper and Officer of Rimington's Guides—The Tigers During the Anglo-Boer War 1899–1902*, p. 23
2. Conan-Doyle, p. 633
3. Gardner, *Allenby*, p. 50
4. Lowry, E. P., p. 42
5. Gardner, *Allenby*, p. 46
6. Currey, p. 149
7. Nasson, p. 285
8. Ibid, p. 287
9. St Leger, p. 267
10. Ibid, p. 268
11. Ibid, p. 269
12. Ibid, p. 271
13. http://www.knra.co.za/history_articles/boer-position_TB.htm
14. St Leger, p. 269
15. Knowles, *A Kipling Primer*
16. Beckett, I. F. W.
17. KwaZulu-Natal: Pietermaritzburg, Midlands & Drakensberg map, 2nd ed., Map Studio
18. Pakenham, p. 645
19. Ibid, p. 524
20. Maurice & Grant, Vol. 3, p. 275
21. Ibid, p. 276
22. Correspondance with the curator of the The Queen's Royal Lancers & Nottinghamshire Yeomanry Museum
23. Jones & Jones, p. 151; Maurice & Grant, Vol. 3, p. 275

24. The *South African Military History Society Journal*, Vol. 13, No. 1, June 2004
25. Stirling, p. 454
26. Ibid
27. Pakenham, p. 525
28. Maurice & Grant, Vol. 3, p. 277
29. Wilson, p. 94
30. Maurice & Grant, Vol. 3, p. 278
31. Wilson, p. 94
32. Reitz, p. 20
33. Gibson, p18
34. Viljoen, p. 275
35. Reitz, p. 42
36. Schoeman, p. 31
37. Ibid, p. 32
38. The *South African Military History Journal* Vol. 10, No. 4, December 1996
39. Carver, p. 67
40. Burnham, *Scouting on Two Continents*, p. 277
41. Reitz, p. 21
42. Viljoen, p. 275
43. Reitz, p. 46
44. Viljoen, p. 276
45. Carver, p. 152
46. Maurice & Grant, Vol. 4, p. 468
47. Lane, p. 5
48. Stirling, p. 412
49. Wilson, p. 80
50. Selby, p. 65
51. Unger, p. vi
52. Meintjies, *President Paul Kruger*, p. 239
53. Hillegas, *With the Boer Forces*, ch. 12
54. Walker, p. 488
55. Carver, p. 14
56. Warwick, p. 11
57. Carver, p. 263
58. Stirling, p. 513
59. Carver, p. 202
60. Maurice & Grant, Vol. 4, p. 674
61. WO126/145 to WO126/163
62. The *Army Handbook of the British Empire, 1893*, p. 9
63. Ibid, p. 57
64. Ibid, p. 15
65. Carver, p. 13
66. Breytenbach, *Geskiedenis van die Tweede Vryheidsoorlog 1899–1902*, Vol. 1, ch. 1
67. *The Army Handbook of the British Empire, 1893*, p. 104
68. Ibid, p. 110
69. Symons, p. 105
70. Gardner, p. 48
71. Hall, p. 79
72. Carver, p. 54
73. Pakenham, p. 135
74. Maurice & Grant, Vol. 3, p. 35
75. Creswicke, Vol. 3, p. 15
76. Conan-Doyle p. 624
77. Warner, *Kitchener: The Man Behind the Legend*, p,123
78. Ibid, p,131
79. Lee, p. 137
80. Carver, p. 202
81. Maurice & Grant, Vol. 4, p. 705
82. Ibid, p. 705
83. Warner, p,124
84. Brown, Coté Jr., Lynn-Jones & Miller, *Offense, Defense and War*, p. 360
85. 1528 U.S. Army / Department of Defense, *Counterinsurgency Handbook*, pp. 1-13
86. Wilson, p. 13
87. Ibid, p. 26
88. Ibid, p. 28
89. Lee, p. 137
90. Beckett
91. Gardner, *Allenby*, p. 39
92. St Leger, p. 206
93. Beckett
94. Gardner, *Allenby*, p. 50
95. Ibid, p. 45
96. Wilson, p. 13
97. Gooch, *The Boer War: Direction, Experience and Image*, p. 1
98. Beckett, I. F. W.

Chapter 13

1. Lee, p. 88
2. Viljoen, p. 272
3. McDonald, *How We Kept the Flag Flying*, p. 168
4. Ross, p. 58
5. Ibid, p. 67
6. Ibid, p. 17
7. Fuller, *The Conduct of War, 1789–1961*, pp. 139-40
8. *Soldiers of the Queen*, Issue 11
9. Symons, p. 111
10. The *South African Military History Society Journal*, Vol. 2, No. 1, June 1971
11. Ibid, No. 5, June 1973
12. Ibid, No. 2, December 1971
13. Ibid, No. 3, June 1972
14. Barthrop, p. 52
15. Hall, *Halt! Action Front! With Colonel*

Long at Colenso, p. 10

16.   Gudmundsson, *On Artillery*, p. 8
17.   Ibid, p. 7
18.   Sharp, p. 40
19.   The *South African Military History Society Journal*, Vol. 2, No. 2, December 1971
20.   McDonald, p. 156
21.   Amery, Vol. 3, p. 189
22.   Maurice & Grant, Vol. 1, p. 562
23.   Amery, Vol. 3, 190
24.   Maurice & Grant, Vol. 1, p. 563
25.   The *South African Military History Society Journal*, Vol. 2, No. 2, December 1971
26.   Sharp, p. 3
27.   Ibid, p. 5
28.   Ibid, p. 6
29.   Gardner, p. 131
30.   The *South African Military History Society Journal*, Vol. 2, No. 3, June 1972
31.   Ibid
32.   Holmes, p. 82
33.   Gardner, *Allenby*, p. 36
34.   Jones, S., p. 77
35.   Ibid, p. 78
36.   Viljoen, p. 272
37.   Beckett, I. F. W.
38.   Jones, S., p. 149
39.   Beckett, I. F. W.
40.   Maurice & Grant, Vol. 1, p. 445
41.   Beckett, I. F. W.
42.   Jones, S., p. 60
43.   Barthrop, p. 66
44.   Kruger, R., p. 111
45.   Lee, p. 85
46.   Burleigh p. 55
47.   Stevens, p. 378
48.   Wilson, p. 79
49.   Jones, S., p. 174
50.   Hall, p. 37
51.   Amery, Vol. 2, p. 289
52.   Amery, Vol. 5, p. 84
53.   Asher, *Khartoum, The Ultimate Imperial Adventure*, p. 187
54.   Beckett, p. 2
55.   Amery, Vol. 2, p. 136
56.   photo of Bushveldt Carbineer recruitment poster on www.bushveldtcarbineers.com.au
57.   Wotton, p. 49
58.   Moorcraft & McLaughlin, *The Rhodesian War: A Military History*, p. 44
59.   Viljoen, p. 276
60.   Beckett, I. F. W.

61.   Knox, p. 71
62.   Selby, p. 137
63.   Baynes, p. 165
64.   Stevens, p. 378
65.   Sharp, p. 32
66.   Gardner, p. 63
67.   Sharp, p. 32
68.   Gardner, p. 131
69.   Ibid, p. 150
70.   Burleigh, p. 119
71.   Lee, p. 68
72.   Beckett, I. F. W.
73.   Lee, p. 69
74.   Ibid, p. 71
75.   Ibid, p. 78
76.   Wilson, p. 71
77.   Beckett, I. F. W.
78.   Gardner, *Allenby*, p. 33
79.   Ibid, p. 51
80.   Ibid, p. 14
81.   Mallinson, *The Making of the British Army*, p. 274
82.   Ibid, p. 275

Chapter 14

1.   Pakenham, p. 398
2.   Warwick, p. 101
3.   Carver, p. 252
4.   Featherstone, *Omdurman, 1898*, p. 48
5.   Ibid, p. 40
6.   David, *Zulu*, p. 148
7.   Paice, p. 404
8.   Ibid, p. 406
9.   Creswicke, Vol. 5, p. 60
10.   Lowry, p. 189
11.   Farrelly, p. 34
12.   Lowry, p. 189
13.   Amery, Vol. 3, p. 44–45
14.   Marsden, *The Barefoot Emperor*, p. 288
15.   Lowry, p. 158
16.   Silbey, p. 107
17.   Ibid, p. 111
18.   Ibid, p. 165
19.   Hall, p. 86
20.   van Heyningen p. 245
21.   Pretorius, *A to Z of the Anglo-Boer War*, pp. 457–8
22.   Welsh, p. 321
23.   Baynes, p. 79
24.   Viljoen, p. 15
25.   Colvin, Vol. 2, p. 12
26.   Burleigh, p. 46
27.   Creswicke, Vol. 3, p. 66

28. Beckett, p. 3
29. Amery, Vol. 3, p. 94
30. Gardner, *Allenby*, p. 53
31. Miller, M. *A Captain of the Gordons*, p. 127
32. Witton p. 49
33. Amery, Vol. 5, p. 131
34. Wilson, p. 109
35. Amery, Vol. 2, p. 110
36. Pakenham, p. 395
37. Amery, Vol. 2, p. 289
38. Viljoen, ch. 38
39. Ibid, p. 208
40. Ibid, p. 209
41. Ibid, p. 213
42. Ibid, p. 209
43. WO 100/280
44. WO 100/284
45. WO 100/285
46. WO 100/286
47. WO 100/281
48. Carver, p. 252
49. Hall, p. 87
50. Ibid, p. 84
51. Ibid, p. 86
52. Carver, p. 252
53. Ibid, p. 14
54. Hyslop, p. 137
55. Ibid, p. 149
56. Meintjies, p. 181
57. Hyslop, p. 4
58. Gardner, p. 152
59. Ibid, p. 185
60. Ibid, p. 105
61. Miller, M. p. 78
62. Lowry, E.P., p. 59
63. Schoeman, p. 6
64. Ibid, p. 69
65. Ibid, p. 70
66. Ibid, p. 181
67. Ibid, p. 189
68. Lee, p. 127
69. McDonald, p. 167
70. Currey, p. 151
71. Lowry, E.P., p. 27
72. Viljoen, p. 31
73. Morris, p. 34
74. Hyslop, p. 93
75. Ibid, p. 92
76. Ibid, p. 93

Chapter 15
1. Burleigh, p. 2
2. Stevens, p. 379
3. Mallinson, p. 269
4. Scholtz, p. 132
5. Ibid, p. 133
6. Pakenham, p. 104
7. Viljoen, p. 86
8. Ibid, p. 88
9. Heyer, *A Brief History of the Transvaal Secret Service System*, p. 15
10. Ibid, p. 20
11. Farrelly, p. 178
12. Ibid, p. 96

Appendix I
Constant changes to the voting rules in the Transvaal

1. Old Grond-Wet: The possession of property or residence for one year qualified for the franchise for white males.
2. 1882: In spite of the President's statement to the Royal Commission that no difference would be made between newcomers of suitable age and the old burghers as regards the franchise, it was raised to five years' residence. The proof accepted for this residency period was the Veldkornets' books—and very bad proof, too, in some instances.
3. 1890: This law was very cleverly drawn up to escape undue attention. It provided that 'all persons naturalized previous to the law come in under the old privileges—that the right of vote for a Second Raad now created would be given; but it was necessary to be eligible for ten years for election to the Second Raad before one could aspire to the higher privilege of voting for the First Volksraad'. This made the term of probation fourteen years.
4. 1891–93: Minor alterations were made in the law; but it was not substantially altered, being deemed a sufficient barrier to non-Afrikaners. A serious condition, however, was put in in 1893, it being necessary to get the assent by vote of the First Volksraad before one could become a full burgher.
5. Law 3 of 1894: This was the finishing touch. It provided that the would-be burgher, after serving fourteen years' apprenticeship, and being at least forty years of age, would only be entitled to register a vote for the First Volksraad provided a majority of the burghers in his ward signified their assent in writing to his obtaining it. In addition, the law disfranchised

all children born of *uitlanders* in the country, the law being retrospective in this particular.

Appendix II
Imperial Divisional Commanders, October 1899–June 1901

I	Methuen
II	Clery, Lyttelton, Clery
III	Gatacre, Chermside
IV	White (Ladysmith Garrison), Lyttelton
V	Warren, Hildyard
VI	Kelly-Kenny
VII	Tucker
VIII	Rundle
IX	Colvile
X	Hunter
XI	Pole-Carew
Cavalry Division	French
Colonial Division	Brabant

Appendix III
Imperial Brigade Commanders, October 1899–June 1901

1st (Guards)	Colville, Pole-Carew, Jones
2nd	Hildyard, E. Hamilton
3rd (Highland)	Wauchope, MacDonald
4th (Light)	Lyttelton, Norcott, Cooper
5th (Irish)	Hart
6th (Fusilier)	Barton
7th	I. Hamilton, W. Kitchener
8th	Howard
9th	Featherstonehaugh, Pole-Carew, C. Douglas
10th	Talbot-Coke
11th (Lancashire)	Woodgate, Wynne, W. Kitchener, Wynne
12th	Clements
13th	C. Knox
14th	Chermside, Maxwell
15th	Wavell
16th	B. Campbell
17th	Boyes
18th	Stephenson
19th	Smith-Dorrien
20th	Paget
21st	B. Hamilton
22nd	Allen
23rd	W. Knox

Appendix IV
Locally raised Imperial South African units

Ashburner's Light Horse

Baca Contingent
Bechuanaland Rifle Volunteers
Beddy's Scouts
   Bergh's Scouts
Bethune's Mounted Infantry
Border Horse
Border Mounted Rifles
Border Scouts
Brabant's Horse
Brett's Scouts
British South Africa Police
   Burgher Camps Department
Bush Veldt Carbineers / Pietersburg Light
   Horse
Bushmanland Borderers

Camperdown and District Rifle Association
Canadian Scouts
Cape Colonial Ordnance Department
Cape Colony Cyclists' Corps
Cape Colony Volunteers
Cape Garrison Artillery
Cape Government Railways
Cape Medical Staff Corps
Cape Mounted Rifles
Cape Police
Cape Town Highlanders
Clanwilliam Convoy Guard
Colonial Light Horse
Colonial Scouts
Commander in Chief's Body Guard
Corps of Cattle Rangers
Criminal Investigation Department
Cullinan's Horse

Damant's Horse
Dennison's Scouts
Diamond Fields Artillery
Diamond Fields Horse
District Mounted Rifles
Driscoll's Scouts
Duke of Edinburgh's Own Volunteer Rifles
Dundee Rifle Association
Durban Light Infantry

East Griqualand Field Force
East Griqualand Mounted Rifles
East Griqualand Mounted Volunteers
Eastern Province Horse

Farmer's Guard
Field Intelligence Department
Fingo Levies
Fraserburg Scouts
French's Scouts
Frontier Light Horse
Frontier Mounted Rifles

Geoghegan's Scouts
Glen Gray Native Levy
Gorringe's Flying Column
Grahamstown Volunteers

Hannay's Scouts
Heidelberg Volunteers and Scouts
Herbert Mounted Rifles
Herschel Native Police
Highlands Rifle Association
Humansdorp Garrison Colonial Defence
   Force

Imperial Bearer Corps
Imperial Hospital Corps
Imperial Light Horse
Imperial Light Infantry
Imperial Military Railways
Imperial Yeomanry Scouts

Johannesburg Mounted Rifles
Johannesburg Police

Kaffrarian Rifles
Karkloop Rifle Association
Kimberley Mounted Corps
Kimberley Regiment
Kitchener's Fighting Scouts
Kitchener's Horse
Komga Mounted Infantry
Kuruman Defence Force
Kuruman Scouts

Lidgetton Rifle Association
Loch's Horse
Lydenburg Mounted Police

Mafeking Cadet Corps
Mafeking Railway Volunteers
Malmesbury Defence Force
Malmesbury Police Force 3
Malton District Rifle Association
Marshall's Horse
Matatiele European Reserve
Melmoth Rifle Association
Menne's Scouts
Midland Mounted Rifles
Montmorency's Scouts
Morley's Scouts
Mount Coke Contingent
Murray's Horse
Namaqualand Border Scouts
Natal Carbineers
Natal Field Artillery
Natal Government Railways
Natal Government Railways Bridge Guards
Natal Guides
Natal Mounted Infantry
Natal Mounted Rifles
Natal Naval Volunteers
Natal Royal Rifles
Natal Volunteer Ambulance Corps
Natal Volunteer Hotchkiss Detachment
Natal Volunteer Indian Ambulance Corps
Natal Volunteer Medical Corps
Natal Volunteer Staff
Natal Volunteer Transport Service
Natal Volunteer Veterinary Corps
National Scouts
Native Labour Corps
Nesbitt's Horse
New England Mounted Rifles
New Hanover Rifle Association
Nottingham Road Rifle Association

O'kiep Volunteers and Town Guard
   Orange River Colony Volunteers
Orange River Scouts
Orpen's Light Horse
Oudtshoorn Volunteer Rifles

Port Alfred Imperial Mounted Police

Prince Alfred's Guard Mounted Infantry
Prince Alfred's Volunteer Guard
Prince of Wales' Light Horse
Protectorate Regiment
Provisional Mounted Police
Provisional Transvaal Constabulary

Queenstown Rifle Volunteers

Railway Pioneer Regiment
Rand Rifles
Rhodesia Regiment
Rhodesian Volunteers
Roberts' Horse
Ross Machine Gun Battery
Rundles Scouts

Scott's Railway Guards
Scottish Horse
Settle's Scouts
South African Constabulary
South African Light Horse
St Helena Volunteer Sharpshooters
Standerton Mounted Police
Steinaecker's Horse
Struben's Scouts
Swellendam Railway Guard

Thorneycroft's Mounted Infantry
Town Guard and District Mounted Troops
Tucker's Scouts

Umlass Road Rifle Association
Umvoti Mounted Rifles
Umzimkulu Reserves
Upper Tugela Rifle Association
Utrecht Mounted Police
Vallentin's Heidelberg Volunteers
Victoria West District Mounted Police
Victoria West District Scouts
Vryburg Scouts
Warhburg Rifle Association
Warren's Mounted Infantry
Warren's Scouts
Warwick's Scouts
Western Light Horse
Western Province Mounted Rifles
Weston Rifle Association
Wilgefontein Rifle Association

Note: This list excludes Town Guards

Selected Bibliography

Abercrombie, H.R., *The Secret History of South Africa*, Central News Agency, Johannesburg, 1951

Amery, Louis, *The Times History of the War in South Africa*, Vols. 1–7, Sampson Low, Marston & Co. Ltd., London, 1900–02

Ashcroft, Michael, *Victoria Cross Heroes*, Headline, London, 2007

Asher, Michael, *Khartoum, The Ultimate Imperial Adventure*, Penguin, London, 2006

Aston, P. E., *The Raid on the Transvaal by Dr Jameson,* Dean & Son, London, 1897

Barthrop, Michael, *Slogging Over Africa, The Boer Wars 1815–1902*, & Co., London, 2002

Baynes, Arthur Hamilton, *My Diocese During the War*, George Bell & Sons, London, 1900

Beckett, Ian, *Modern Insurgencies and Counter-Insurgencies*, Routledge, London, 2001

Beckett, I. F. W., *The South African War and the Late Victorian Army*, Army History Unit, Canberra ACT, 2000

Biggar, Emerson Bristol, *The Boer War: Its Causes and Its Interest to Canadians*, Biggar, Samuel & Co., Toronto, 1899

Blake, Robert, *A History of Rhodesia*, Eyre Methuen, London, 1977

Bleszynski, Nick, *Shoot Straight You Bastards!*, Random House, Sydney, 2002

Botha, Paul, *From Boer to Boer and Englishman*, Hugh Rees, London, 1900

Bourquin, S. B., & Torlage, Gilbert, *The Battle of Colenso*, reprint by Ravan Press, Johannesburg 1999

Bower, Sir Graham, *Secret History of the Jameson Raid and the South African Crisis*, Van Riebeeck Society, Cape Town, 2002

Breytenbach, J. H., *Geskiedenis van die Tweede Vryheidsoorlog 1899–1902*, Vol. 1, Government Printer, Pretoria, 1966

Brooke-Norris, S., *The Story of the Rand Club*, Purnell, Cape Town, 1976

Brown, Michael E., Coté Jr., Owen R., Lynn-Jones, Sean M., Miller, Steven E. (eds.), *Offense, Defense and War*, The MIT Press, Cambridge MA, 2004

Bulpin, T. V., *Storm over the Transvaal*, Howard Timmins, Cape Town, 1955

Bulpin, T. V., *To the Banks of the Zambesi*, Books of Africa, Cape Town, 1968

Burne, C. R. N., *With the Naval Brigade in Natal*, reprint by Leonaur, London, 2008

Burleigh, Bennet, *The Natal Campaign*, reprint by General Books LLC, 2009

Burnham, F. R., *Scouting on Two Continents*, William Heinemann Ltd, London, 1926

Buttery, John A. & Cooper-Key, Aston M., *Why Kruger Made War*, William Heinemann Ltd, London, 1900

Carr, William S., *Pioneer's Path: Story of a Career on the Witwatersrand*, Juta & Co, Cape Town, 1953

Cartwright, A. P., *Gold Paved the Way*, MacMillan, London, 1967

Carver, Field Marshal Lord, *The National Army Museum Book of the Boer War*, Sidgwick & Jackson in association with the National Army Museum, London, 1999

Chalmers, Alan, *Bombardment of Ladysmith Anticipated: The Diary of a Siege*, Covos Day, Johannesburg, 2000

Chilvers, Hedley A., *The Story of De Beers*, Cassell & Co. Ltd., London, 1939

Chilvers, Hedley A., *The Yellow Man Looks On*, Cassell & Co. Ltd., London, 1933

Chisholm, Ruari, *Ladysmith*, Jonathan Ball, Johannesburg, 1979

Churchill, Sir Winston, *A History of the English-Speaking Peoples,* Vol. 4, Cassell & Co. Ltd., London, 1958

Churchill, Sir Winston, *My Early Life*, Odhams, London, 1947

Churchill, W.S., *Ian Hamilton's March*, Longmans, Green, London, 1900

Churchill, Sir Winston, *The Boer War*, Pimlico, London, 2002

Coetzer, Owen, *The Road to Infamy*, William Waterman, Johannesburg, 1996

Cohen, Louis, *Reminiscences of Johannesburg & London*, Holden, London, 1924

Cohen, Louis, *Reminiscences of Kimberley*, Bennett & Co., London, 1900

Cohen, M. & Major, John, *History in Quotations*, Weidenfeld & Nicolson, London, 2008

Colville, Major-General Sir H. E., *The Work of the Ninth Division*, reprint by Naval & Military Press in association with the National Army Museum, London, 2010

Colvin, Ian, *Cecil John Rhodes*, Dodo Press, London, 2008

Colvin, Ian, *The Life of Jameson*, Vols. 1 & 2, Edward Arnold & Co., London, 1922

Conan-Doyle, Sir Arthur, *The Great Boer War*, Smith Elder & Co., London, 1900

Conan-Doyle, Sir Arthur, *The War in South Africa, Its Cause and Conduct*, Smith Elder & Co., London, 1902

Cook, Edward, *Rights and Wrongs of the Transvaal War*, Edward Arnold, London, 1901

Creswicke, Louis, *South Africa and the Transvaal War*, Vols. 1–8, Caxton, London, 1903

Crisp, Robert, *The Outlanders*, Peter Davies, London, 1964
Crwys-Williams, Jennifer, *South African Despatches*, Ashanti, Johannesburg, 1989
Currey, R. N., *Vinnicombe's Trek: Son of Natal: Stepson of Transvaal 1854–1932: A Family Chronicle of the Time of the Zulu and Boer Wars*, University of Natal Press, Pietermaritzburg, 1989

Davenport, T. R. H., *The Afrikaner Bond: The History of a South African Political Party, 1880–1911*, Oxford University Press, Cape Town, 1966
David, Saul, *Zulu*, Penguin, London, 2005
Davitt, Michael, *The Boer Fight for Freedom*, Funk & Wagnalls, New York, 1902
Devitt, Napier, *The Concentration Camps in South Africa During the Anglo-Boer War of 1899-1902*, Shuter & Shooter, Pietermaritzburg, 1941
de Villiers, Marq, *White Tribe Dreaming: Apartheid's Bitter Roots as Witnessed by Eight Generations of an Afrikaner Family*, Viking Penguin, New York, 1988
de Wet, Christiaan Rudolf, *Three Years' War*, Charles Scribner's Sons, New York, 1902
Donaldson, Ken, *South African Who's Who 1910*, Who's Who Publishing Co., Johannesburg, 1910
du Toit, S. J., *Rhodesia*, Books of Rhodesia, Bulawayo, 1977
Duminy, A. H., *Fitzpatrick Selected Papers*, McGraw-Hill, Johannesburg, 1976
Durbach, Renée, *Kipling's South Africa*, Chameleon, Cape Town, 1988

Emden, Paul, *Randlords*, Hodder & Stoughton, London, 1935

Farrelly, M. J., *The Settlement After the War in South Africa*, MacMillan & Co., London, 1900
Farwell, Byron, *The Great Boer War*, Pen & Sword, Barnsley, 2009
Featherstone, Donald, *Victorian Colonial Warfare: Africa 1842–1902*, Blandford, London, 1993
Featherstone, Donald, *Omdurman, 1898: Kitchener's Victory in the Sudan*, Osprey, London, 1993
Fisher, William E. G., *The Transvaal and the Boers; A Brief History*, Negro Universities Press, New York, 1896
Fitzpatrick, Sir Percy, *South African Memories*, Cassell & Co., London, 1979
Fitzpatrick, Sir Percy, *The Transvaal from Within*, William Heinemann Ltd., London, 1900
Frere, Bartle Compton Arthur, *Letters from an Uitlander, 1899–1902*, John Murray, London, 1903
Fuller, J. F. C., *The Conduct of War, 1789–1961*, Eyre & Spottiswoode, London, 1979
Fuller, Sir T. E., *Cecil Rhodes*, Longmans Green & Co., London, 1910

Gale, W. D., *One Man's Vision*, Hutchinson & Co., London, 1935
Gale, W. D., *The Heritage of Rhodes*, Oxford University Press, London, 1950
Gardner, Brian, *Allenby*, Cassell & Co., London, 1965
Gardner, Brian, *Mafeking: A Victorian Legend*, Cassell & Co., London, 1966
Garrett, F. Edmund, *The Story of an African Crisis, Being the Truth about the Jameson Raid and Johannesburg Revolt of 1896, Told with the Assistance of the Leading Actors in the Drama*, Archibald Constable, London, 1897
Geen, M. W., 'The Making of the Union of South Africa*, Longmans Green & Co., London, 1946
Gibbs, Peter, *Death of the Last Republic*, Frederick Muller, London, 1957
Gibson, G. F., *The Story of the Imperial Light Horse*, G. D. & Co., Johannesburg, 1937
Gibbs, Peter, *The History of the BSAP*, Vols. 1 & 2, British South Africa Police, Salisbury, 1972
Gillings, Ken, *The Battle of the Thukela Heights*, Ravan Press, Johannesburg, 1999
Gooch, John (ed.), *The Boer War: Direction, Experience and Image*, Routledge, Abingdon & New York, 2000
Gordon, C. T., *The Growth of Boer Opposition to Kruger,1890–1895*, Cape Town University Press, Cape Town, 1970
Graumann, Sir Harry, *Rand Riches*, Juta & Co., Johannesburg, 1936
Grey, Albert, *Hubert Hervey, Student and Imperialist: A Memoir*, Edward Arnold, London, 1899
Griffith, Kenneth, *Thank God We Kept the Flag Flying: The Siege and Relief of Ladysmith, 1899–1900*, Hutchison, London, 1974
Gross, Felix, *Rhodes of Africa*, Cassell & Co., London, 1956
Gudmundsson, Bruce, *On Artillery*, Praeger, West Port CT, 1993

Haggard, Henry Rider, *The Last Boer War*, Kegan Paul, Trench, Trübner & Co. Ltd., London, 1899
Hall, Darrell, *Halt! Action Front! With Colonel Long at Colenso*, Covos Day, Johannesburg, 1999
Hall, Darrell, *The Hall Handbook of the Anglo-Boer War*, University of Natal Press, Pietermaritzburg, 1999
Hamley, Richard, *The Regiment*, Covos Day, Johannesburg, 2000
Hancock, W. K. (ed.), & van der Poel, Jean (ed.), *Selections from the Smuts Papers*, Vol. 4, Cambridge University Press, Cape Town, 2007
Headlam, Cecil, *The Milner Papers*, Vol. I, Cassell & Co., London, 1931

Heyer, A. E., *A Brief History of the Transvaal Secret Service System: From its Inception to the Present Time, its Objects, its Agents, the Disposal of its Funds*, Wm. Taylor, Cape Town, 1900
Hillegas, Howard C., *With the Boer Forces*, reprint by BiblioBazaar, 2008
Hind, R. J., *Harry Labouchère and the Empire*, The Athlone Press, London, 1972
Hobhouse, Emily, *The Brunt of the War and Where it Fell*, Methuen & Co., London 1902
Hobson, J. A., *The War in South Africa, Its Causes and Effects*, James Nisbet & Co., London, 1900
Hole, Hugh M., *The Jameson Raid*, Philip Alan, London, 1930
Holmes, Richard, *The Little Field Marshal: A Life of Sir John French*, Weidenfeld & Nicolson, London, 1981
Hutchinson, G. T., *Frank Rhodes*, BiblioBazaaar, London, 2010
Hyslop, Jonathan, *The Notorious Syndicalist: J. T. Bain: A Scottish Rebel in Colonial South Africa*, Jacana Media, Johannesburg, 2004

James, David, *Lord Roberts*, Hollis & Carter, London, 1954
James, Lawrence, *The Rise and Fall of the British Empire*, Abacus, London, 1995
Jeal, Tim, *Baden-Powell: Founder of the Boy Scouts*, Pimlico, London, 1989
Jeal, Tim, *Explorers of the Nile: The Triumph and Tragedy of a Great Victorian Adventure*, Faber & Faber, London, 2012
Jeal, Tim, *Stanley: The Impossible Life of Africa's Greatest Explorer*, Yale University Press, New Haven CT, 2007
Jenkins, Roy, *Gladstone: A Biography*, MacMillan, London, 1995
Jerrold, Walter, *Lord Roberts of Kandahar VC: The Life-Story of a Great Soldier*, S. W. Partridge & Co., London, 1900
Johnson, Frank, *Great Days: The Autobiography of an Empire Pioneer*, G. Bell & Sons, London, 1940
Jones, Huw M. & Jones, Meurig G. M., *A Gazetteer of the Second Anglo-Boer War 1899–1902*, The Military Press, Milton Keynes, 1999
Jooste, Graham, *Innocent Blood: Executions During the Anglo-Boer War*, Spearhead, Cape Town, 2002
Judd, Denis, *The Boer War*, Granada Publishing, London, 1977

Knight, Ian, *Marching to the Drums: Eyewitness Accounts of War from the Kabul Massacre to the Siege of Mafikeng*, Greenhill, London, 1999
Knowles, F. L., *A Kipling Primer*, Brown & Co., Boston, 1899
Knox, Ernest Blake, *Buller's Campaign with the Natal Field Force of 1900*, R. B. Johnson, London, 1902
Kotzé, Sir John Gilbert, *Memoirs and Reminiscences*, Maskew Miller, Cape Town, 1934
Kruger, Paul, *The Memoirs of Paul Kruger: Four Times President of the South African Republic*, George A. Morang & Co. Ltd., Toronto, 1900
Kruger, Rayne, *Goodbye Dolly Gray: The Sory of the Boer War*, Cassell & Co., London, 1959

Lane, William, *The War Diary of Burgher Jack Lane, 1899–1900*, Van Riebeeck Society, Cape Town, 2001
Le Sueur, Gordon, *Cecil Rhodes: The Man and His Work*, John Murray, London, 1913
Lee, Emanoel, *To the Bitter End Photographic History of the Boer War, 1899–1902*, Penguin, London, 1986
Lewsen, Phyllis, *Selections of the Correspondence of J. X. Merriman*, various volumes, Van Riebeeck Society, Cape Town, 1960
Leyds, William, *The Transvaal Surrounded*, T. Fisher Unwin, London, 1919
Lines, G. W., *The Ladysmith Siege*, Naval & Military Press, Uckfield, 2003
Longford, Elizabeth, *Jameson's Raid: Prelude to the Boer War*, Jonathan Ball, Johannesburg, 1960
Lowry, Donal, *The South African War Reappraised*, Manchester University Press, Manchester, 2000
Lowry, Edward P. *With the Guards' Brigade During the Boer War: On Campaign from Bloemfontein to Koomati Poort and Back*, Leonaur, London, 2009

Macnab, Roy Martin, *The French Colonel: Villebois-Mareuil and the Boers, 1899–1900*, Oxford University Press, Cape Town, 1975
Magnus, Philip, *Gladstone: A Biography*, John Murray, London, 1954
Mahan, Captain A. T., *The Story of the War in South Africa, 1899–1900*, Sampson Low, Marston & Co., London, 1900
Mallinson, Allan, *The Making of the British Army: From the English Civil War to the War On Terror*, Bantam Press, London, 2009
Marais, J. S., *The Fall of Kruger's Republic*, Clarendon Press, Oxford, 1961
Marlowe, John, *Milner: Apostle of Empire: A Life of Alfred George, The Right Honourable Viscount Milner of St James's and Cape Town, KG, GCB, GCMG, 1854–1925*, Hamish Hamilton Ltd., London, 1976

Marsden, Philip, *The Barefoot Emperor: An Ethiopian Tragedy*, Harper Perennial, London, 2008
Martin, Colonel Arthur Clive, *The Concentration Camps: 1900–1902: Facts, Figure and Fables*, Howard Timmins, Cape Town, 1957
Mason, Philip, *The Birth of a Dilemma: The Conquest and Settlement of Rhodesia*, Oxford University Press for The Institute of Race Relations, London, 1958
Maurice, Major-General Sir Frederick & Grant, Captain Maurice Harold *et al*, *The Official History of the War in South Africa 1899–1902*, Vols. 1–4, reprint by Naval & Military Press, London, 2004
May, H. J., *Music of the Guns*, Hutchinson, Johannesburg, 1970
Maylam, Paul, *The Cult of Rhodes*, David Philip, Cape Town, 2005
McCord, J. J., *South African Struggle*, J. H. De Bussy, Pretoria, 1952
McDonald, Donald, *How We Kept The Flag Flying: The Story of the Siege of Ladysmith*, Ward, Lock & Co, London, 1900
McNab, Roy, *The French Colone: Villebois-Mareuil and the Boers, 1899–1900*, Oxford University Press, 1975
McFadden, Pam, *The Battle of Elandslaagte: 21 October 1899*, Ravan Press, Johannesburg, 1999
Meintjies, Johannes, *The Commandant General*, Tafelberg-Uitgewers, Cape Town, 1971
Meintjies, Johannes, *President Paul Kruger*, Purnell Book Services Ltd, London, 1974
Meredith, Martin, *Diamonds, Gold and War: The Making of South Africa*, Simon & Schuster, London, 2007
Miller, Margaret, *A Captain of the Gordons*, Sampson Low, Marston & Co. London, 1909
Miller, Stuart Creighton, *Benevolent Assimilation: The American Conquest of the Philippines, 1899–1903*, Yale University Press, New Haven CT, 1982
Millin, Sarah G. *Rhodes*, Chato & Windus, London, 1933
Milne, Rob, *Anecdotes of the Anglo-Boer War*, Covos Day, Johannesburg, 2000
Morris, A. G., *A Canadian Mounted Rifleman at War, 1899–1902*, Van Riebeeck Society, Cape Town, 2000
Morris, Donald, *The Washing of the Spears: The Rise and Fall of the Zulu Nation*, Pimlico, London, 1994

Nasson, Bill, *The War for South Africa*, Tafelberg, Cape Town, 2010
Nasson, Bill, *Abraham Esau's War: A Black South African War in the Cape, 1899–1902*, Cambridge University Press, Cambridge, 1991
Naville, Edouard, The Transvaal Question from a Foreign Point of View, William Blackwood, Edinburgh, 1900
Nathan, Manfred, *Paul Kruger: His Life and Times*, Knox, Durban, 1946
Nevinson, W. H., 'Ladysmith (Diary of the Siege), Indypublish, 2007
Norris-Newman, Charles, *In Zululand with the British Army*, Leonaur, London, 2006
Nutting, Anthony, *Scramble for Africa: The Great Trek to the Boer War*, Constable, London, 1970

Odgers, George, *Army Australia: An Illustrated History*, Child & Ass., 1988

Pakenham, Thomas, *The Boer War*, Futura Publications, London, 1982
Pakenham, Thomas, *The Scramble for Africa*, Abacus, London, 1992
Paterson, Michael, *Life in Victorian Britain*, Robinson, London, 2008
Paice, Edward, *Tip & Run: The Untold Tragedy of the Great War in Africa*, Weidenfeld & Nicolson, London, 2007
Pearse, Henry H. S., *Four Months Besieged: The Story of Ladysmith*, MacMillan & Co, London, 1900
Pemberton, Baring, *Battles of the Boer War*, Pan, London, 1969
Phillips, L. March, *A Tiger on Horseback: The Experiences of a Trooper and Officer of Rimington's Guides—The Tigers During the Anglo-Boer War 1899–1902*, Leonaur, London, 2006
Pilcher, Colonel Thomas, *Some Lessons from the Boer War, 1899–1902*, Isbister & Co. Ltd., London, 1903
Porter, A. N., *The Origins of the South African War: Joseph Chamberlain and the Diplomacy of Imperialism*, David Philip, Cape Town, 1980
Pretorius, Fransjohan, *Scorched Earth*, Human & Rousseau, Cape Town, 2001
Pretorius, Fransjohan, *A to Z of the Anglo-Boer War*, Scarecrow Press, Maryland, 2010
Proctor, John, *Boers and Little Englanders: The Story of the Conventions*, George Allen, London, 1897

Raal, Sarah, *Met die Boere in die Veld*, Nasionale Pers Bpk., Cape Town, 1936
Radziwill, Princess Catherine, *Cecil Rhodes: Man and Empire-Maker*, Cassell & Co, London, 1918
Ransford, Oliver, *The Battle of Majuba Hill*, John Murray, London, 1967
Reitz, Deneys, *Commando*, Faber & Faber, London, 1929
Roberts, Andrew, *Salisbury, Victorian Titan*, Phoenix, London, 2000

Roberts, Brian, *Kimberley, Turbulent City*, David Philip, Cape Town, 1976
Rose, E. B., *The Truth about The Transvaal*, Simpkin, Marshall, Hamilton, Kent, London, 1900
Ross, Edward, *Diary of the Siege of Mafeking*, Van Riebeeck Society, Cape Town, 1980
Rouillard, Nancy, *Matabele Thompson*, Faber & Faber, London, 1936
Russell, Douglas, *Winston Churchill: Soldier: The Military Life of a Gentleman at War*, Brassey's, London, 2005

Sauer, Hans, *Ex Africa*, Geoffrey Bles, London, 1937
Schoeman, Chris, *Brothers in Arms: Hollanders in the Anglo-Boer War*, Random House Struik, Cape Town, 2012
Scholtz, Leopold, *Why the Boers Lost the War*, Palgrave Macmillan, Basingstoke, 2005
Scoble, John & Abercrombie, Hugo Romilly, *The Rise and Fall of Krugerism*, Frederick A. Stokes Co., New York, 1900
Selby, John Millin, *The Boer War: A Study in Cowardice and Courage*, reprint by Barker, Doraville GA, 1969
Sharp, Gerald, *The Siege of Ladysmith*, Purnell & Sons, Cape Town, 1976
Shaw, Gerald, *The Garrett Papers*, Van Riebeeck Society, Cape Town, 1984
Sibbald, Raymond, *The War Correspondents: The Boer War*, Jonathan Ball, Johannesburg 1993
Silbey, David, *A War of Frontier and Empire: The Philippine-American War, 1899–1902*, Hill & Wang, New York, 2008
Smuts, J. C., *Jan Christiaan Smuts*, Cassell & Co, London, 1952
St Leger, Captain Stratford, *Boer War Sketches: With the Mounted Infantry at War*, Galago, Alberton, 1986
Stalker, Rev John (ed.), The Natal Carbineers: The History of the Regiment from its Foundation, 15th January, 1855, to 30th June, 1911, P. Davis & Sons, Pietermaritzburg, 1912
Stead, William Thomas, *Joseph Chamberlain, Conspirator or Statesman?: An Examination of the Evidence as to His Complicity in the Jameson Conspiracy, Together with the Newly Published Letters of the Hawkesley Dossier*, 'Review of Reviews' Office, London, 1900
Steevens, George, *From Cape Town to Ladysmith*, William Blackwood & Sons, London, 1900
Sternberg, A. G., & Henderson, G. F., *My Experiences of the Boer War*, Longmans, Green, London & New York, 1901
Stevens, F.T., *Complete History of the South African War, in 1899–1902*, W. Nicholson & Sons, London, 1902
Stephens, John, *Fuelling the Empire: South Africa's Gold and the Road to War*, John Wiley & Sons Ltd., Chichester, 2003
Stirling, John, *Our Regiments in South Africa*, William Blackwood & Sons, Edinburgh, 1903
Stott, Clement H., *The Boer Invasion of Natal*, S. W. Partridge & Co., London, 1900
Swaisland, Cecille, *A Lincolnshire Volunteer*, University of Hull, Hull, 2000
Symons, Julian, *Buller's Campaign*, House of Stratus, Cornwall, 2001

Tamarkin, Mordechai, *Cecil Rhodes and the Cape Afrikaners: The Imperial Colossus and the Colonial Parish Pump*, Jonathan Ball, Johannesburg, 1996
Taylor J. B., *Memoirs of a Randlord*, Stonewall Books, Cape Town, 2003
Theal, George McCall, *History of South Africa 1873–1884*, Vols. 1 & 2, George Allen & Unwin Ltd., London, 1919
Theal, George McCall, *History of South Africa Since 1795*, Vols. 1–5, George Allen & Unwin Ltd., London, 1920
Theal, George McCall, *History of South Africa Before 1795*, Vols. 1–3, George Allen & Unwin Ltd., London, 1910
Thomas, C. H., *Origin of the Anglo-Boer War Revealed: The Conspiracy of the 19th Century Unmasked*, reprint by BiblioBazaar, London, 2008
Thorgold, Algar, *'The Life of Henry Labouchère*, Constable, London, 1913
Tingay, Paul & Johnson, Jill, *Transvaal Epic*, Khenty Press, Howick, 1978
Torlage, Gilbert & Watt, Steve, A Guide to the Anglo-Boer War Sites of KwaZulu-Natal, Ravan Press, Johannesburg, 1999
Trollope, Anthony, *South Africa*, Vol. 2, Nonsuch Publishing, Stroud, 2005
Twain, Mark, *More Tramps Abroad*, Chatto & Windus, London, 1898

Unger, Frederic William, *With 'Bobs' and Kruger*, reprint by Struik, Cape Town, 1977

van Heyningen, Dr Elizabeth, *The Concentration Camps of the Anglo-Boer War*, Jacana Media, Johannesburg, 2013
van Wyk, Peter, *Burnham, King of Scouts: Baden-Powell's Secret Mentor*, Trafford, Victoria, 2006
Vershoyle, F., Vindex, *Cecil Rhodes: His Political Life and Speeches, 1881–1900*, Chapman & Hall Ltd., London, 1900
Viljoen, Gen Ben, *My Reminiscences of the Anglo-Boer War*, Dodo Press reprint, Gloucester, 2010

Walker, Eric, *Lord De Villiers and His Times*, Constable, London, 1925
Walker, Eric, *A History of Southern Africa*, Longmans, Green & Co. Ltd., London, 1959
War Office, Intelligence Division, *Military Notes of the Dutch Republics of South Africa*, facsimile reprint by Boer War Books, York, 1983
Warhurst, P. R, *Anglo-Portuguese Relations in South Central Africa, 1890–1900*, Longmans Green & Co. Ltd., London, 1962
Warner, Philip, *Kitchener: The Man Behind the Legend*, Cassell reprint, London, 2006
Warwick, Peter, *Black People and the South African War, 1899–1902*, Cambridge University Press, Cape Town, 1983
Watt, Steve, *The Siege of Ladysmith*, Ravan Press, Johannesburg, 1999
Welsh, Frank, *A History of South Africa*, Harper Collins, London, 1998
Wheatcroft, Geoffrey, *The RandLords: The Men Who Made South Africa*, Weidenfeld & Nicolson, London, 1993
Wills, W. A, *The Downfall of Lobengula*: *The Cause, History, and Effect of the Matabeli War*, Books of Rhodesia, Bulawayo, 1971
Wilmot, A., *The History of South Africa*, Kegan Paul, Trench, Trubner & Co., Cape Town, 1901
Wilson, Herbert Wrigley, *After Pretoria: The Guerrilla War*, General Books LLC reprint, Memphis TN, 2012
Wilson, Keith, *The International Impact of the Boer War*, Acumen, Chesham, 2001
Wise, Sarah, *The Blackest Streets: The Life and Death of a Victorian Slum*, Vintage, London, 2008
Witton, George, *Bushveldt Carbineers*, Leonaur, London, 2007
Wright, I I. M., *Sir James Rose Innes, Selected Correspondence*, Van Riebeeck Society, Cape Town, 1972
Wrigley-Wilson, Herbert, *After Pretoria: The Guerrilla War*, General Books LLC reprint, Memphis TN, 2012

Yakan, Mohamad, *Almanac of African Peoples and Nations*, Transaction, London, 1999

Blue Books

Cd.43 (1900) Further correspondence relating to affairs in South Africa
C.8159 (1896) Papers relating to the commandeering of British subjects in the South African Republic in 1894
C.9345 (1899) Papers relating to the complaints of British subjects in the South African Republic
C.9415 (1899) Further correspondence relating to proposed political reforms in the South African Republic
C.9521 (1899) Further correspondence relating to political affairs in the South African Republic
C.9530 (1899) Further correspondence relating to political affairs in the South African Republic
Cd.369 (1900) Correspondence relating to the recent political situation in South Africa
Cd.528 (1901) Papers relating to negotiations between Commandant Louis Botha and Lord Kitchener
Cd.547 (1901) Further correspondence relating to affairs in South Africa

Periodicals and other

Cape Times archives
Of Bullets and Boys
Ladysmith Historical Society, *Diary of the Siege of Ladysmith*, Nos. 1–7
Royal Artillery Journal various
Soldiers of the Queen various editions
The Number of the South African War (1899–1902) Concentration Camp Dead: Standard Stories, Superior Stories and a Forgotten Proto-Nationalist Research Investigation
Ladysmith's 20 VCs, Charles Aikenhead
'A Tool For Modernisation? The Boer Concentration Camps of the South African War, 1900–1902', *South African Journal of Science*, Vol. 106, No. 5–6, Pretoria, May/June 2010
South African Military History Society Journals
The Rhodesian Society, *Rhodesiana* magazine various
The Times of London online archives

Index

Chris Ash grew up in the Shetland Isles and studied at Aberdeen University. After a brief and undistinguished dalliance with the British Army (Lovat Scouts and Gordon Highlanders), he drove his Land Rover to South Africa and decided to stay. Since then, he has worked in oil and mineral exploration all over Africa and the Middle East. His interest in South African history was sparked by watching *Zulu* and *Breaker Morant* as a child, ameliorated by countless drunken arguments over the years. He is a regular speaker on the remarkable life of Dr Leander Starr Jameson, the subject of his first book, *The If Man*. Away from work and history, Ash enjoys cricket, rugby, upsetting the politically-correct, J&B and messing about in Landies. He is married to the long-suffering Stefanie and commutes between Johannesburg and Abidjan.